Literary Movements *for Students*

National Advisory Board

Jennifer Hood: Young Adult/Reference Librarian, Cumberland Public Library, Cumberland, Rhode Island. Certified teacher, Rhode Island. Member of the New England Library Association, Rhode Island Library Association, and the Rhode Island Educational Media Association.

Christopher Maloney: Head Reference Librarian, Ocean City Free Public Library, Ocean City, New Jersey. Member of the American Library Association and the New Jersey Library Association. Board member of the South Jersey Library Cooperative.

Kathleen Preston: Head of Reference, New City Library, New City, New York. Member of the American Library Association. Received B.A. and M.L.S. from University of Albany.

Patricia Sarles: Library Media Specialist, Canarsie High School, Brooklyn, New York. Expert Guide in Biography/Memoir for the website *About.com* (http://biography.about.com). Author of short stories and book reviews. Received B.A., M.A. (anthropology), and M.L.S. from Rutgers University.

Heidi Stohs: Instructor in Language Arts, grades 10-12, Solomon High School, Solomon, Kansas. Received B.S. from Kansas State University; M.A. from Fort Hays State University.

Barbara Wencl: Library Media Specialist, Como Park Senior High School, St. Paul, Minnesota. Teacher of secondary social studies and history, St. Paul, Minnesota. Received B.S. and M.Ed. from University of Minnesota; received media certification from University of Wisconsin. Educator and media specialist with over 30 years experience.

Literary Movements *for Students*

Presenting Analysis, Context, and Criticism on Literary Movements

Volume 2

David Galens, Project Editor

Detroit • New York • San Diego • San Francisco • Cleveland • New Haven, Conn. • Waterville, Maine • London • Munich

Literary Movements for Students, Volume 2

Project Editor
David Galens

Editorial
Anne Marie Hacht, Madeline S. Harris, Ira Mark Milne, Pam Revitzer, Kathy Sauer, Timothy J. Sisler, Jennifer Smith, Daniel Toronto, Carol Ullmann

Research
Sarah Genik

Permissions
Debra Freitas, Lori Hines

Manufacturing
Stacy Melson

Imaging and Multimedia
Lezlie Light, Kelly A. Quin, Luke Rademacher

Product Design
Pamela A. E. Galbreath, Michael Logusz

For more information, contact
The Gale Group, Inc.
27500 Drake Rd.
Farmington Hills, MI 48331-3535
Or you can visit our Internet site at
http://www.gale.com

LIBRARY OF CONGRESS CATALOGING-IN-PUBLICATION DATA

Literary movements for students : presenting analysis, context, and criticism on commonly studied literary movements / David Galens, project editor.
v. cm.
Includes bibliographical references and indexes.
ISBN 0-7876-6517-7 (set : hardcover) -- ISBN 0-7876-6518-5 (v. 1 : hardcover) -- ISBN 0-7876-6519-3 (v. 2 : hardcover)
1. Literary movements--History. 2. Literary movements--Bio-bibliography. 3. Literature--History and criticism.
I. Galens, David.

PN597 .L58 2002
809'.91--dc21 2002010928

Printed in the United States of America
10 9 8 7 6 5 4 3 2

Table of Contents

Novels That Include the Names of French Soups

I. A. Richards, the well-known literary critic, once said, "A book is a machine to think with." In making this observation, Richards underscored the reciprocal relationship between reader and text and the fact that words don't just sit there full of meaning waiting to be discovered, but rather gain their meaning by the breadth and quality of knowledge readers bring to them. *Literary Movements for Students* provides readers with this knowledge by describing various literatures in their historical and cultural contexts, by providing representative examples of the best-known movements, and by encouraging students to explore those movements more deeply.

"Literary Movements" is really a misnomer, for often the texts described under this heading were considered neither literary nor part of a discernible movement when they were written. Labels are often attached to certain writers or texts by critics and literary historians for efficiency's sake and with the benefit of hindsight, often decades, sometimes centuries, after a text has been written. Part of identifying a movement is arguing for what features define the writing associated with it, and then locating those features in specific texts. This necessarily means that the description of movements is not objective, but colored by a critic or literary historian's own particular agendas, whether or not he or she is aware of such agendas. That said, there still needs to be some kind of organizing principle for studying texts, or else there would be no basis for discussion, no way of developing knowledge about them, of understanding how a poem or a novel or a play fits into its time or what it shares in common with other texts. Academia organizes itself, for better *and* worse, in disciplines, and the discipline of literature organizes itself in periods, which themselves are associated with movements. This kind of packaging enables closer scrutiny of the object studied, which paradoxically results in a more comprehensive understanding of the material. By organizing texts and writers in terms of literary movements, this series aims to provide readers with a foot in the door, a way to think about well-known texts and tools with which to think about them. It's important to remember, however, that it is just one way, not the only way, to study literature.

The word "literary" gained its current meaning as a term used to denote a quality of poems, plays, and fiction in the eighteenth century, when writing itself proliferated, and professional literary critics emerged to police it by giving names to this or that kind of writing. An adjectival form of "literature," "literary" was used to exclude other types of writing such as philosophy and history. Today it has an even narrower connotation, serving to mark literature that is "serious" and "cerebral," as opposed to "popular" such as the romance novel or the suspense thriller. One recent example of both the merits and pitfalls of associating one's work with the term is novelist Jonathan Franzen's now well-known spat with talk show host Oprah Winfrey in 2001. Franzen declined to have his novel, *The Corrections*, be named Winfrey's book of the month selection for her book club, which would have virtually guaranteed it financial success, claiming that Winfrey's endorsement ruined his reputation in "high art" circles. Franzen eventually retracted his comment, but the damage had already been done. In this instance, Franzen was protecting his image as a producer of *literary*, as opposed to popular, novels. Franzen is not, however, a member of any literary movement if we understand "movement" to signify organized activities by a group of people with a stated objective, though his writing might be included under Realism.

Some literary movements did begin with a clear intention, organized activities, and a set of principles—surrealism, for example. French poet Guillame Apollinaire coined the term "surrealism," and André Breton, another French poet, spelled out the principles in the *Manifesto of Surrealism*. Other movements, such as twentieth-century Expressionism, elements of which are evident in art and theater of the nineteenth century, are more nebulous, harder to pin down in terms of features or history. There are no Expressionist manifestos, and some critics claim that no such animal as Expressionism even exists. Often, the term given to a literary movement becomes a point of contention for critics whose view of literary history differs from establishment norms. Postcolonialism is a good case in point. Some want to limit the term to signify texts produced in former British colonies after the fall of the British Empire. Others argue that almost all literature (including American) is, in theory, postcolonial, because in the end history is a series of wars and occupations, of one culture displacing another. Movements are not static, but dynamic, evolving from the fray of competing interests and historical developments. An entry on Postcolonialism written ten years from today will no doubt look radically different than the one you read here. It might include novels by writers from some of the former Soviet republics, or perhaps poems from an author of a state yet to be formed, whose people are now battling for independence. Ultimately, it is the shape of the movement itself that is important to grasp, and the context of how, when, and why a particular literature came into being. *Literary Movements for Students* gives you that "how," "when," and "why."

Say, for example, that you've just seen a production of Samuel Beckett's *Waiting for Godot* and were so impressed that you bought and read the book. You've heard Beckett's name associated with Absurdism, but don't really know what that is. If you look up Absurdism in *Literary Movements for Students*, you will find an overview of the movement, including its history, its prominent features, its primary practitioners, and how it is embodied not only in literature and Beckett's work, but in other media and disciplines such as film, painting, and philosophy. You might also find Beckett under Existentialism. *Literary Movement for Students* isn't reductive, but rather expansive in its treatment of movements, charting the crevices and crannies as much as the road most traveled. Movements are provisional by their very nature, contingent on institutional and historical forces, so you'll find a degree of crossover here, with writers and texts sometime listed under more than one movement. That's a good thing.

In the preface to his study historicizing the human sciences, *The Order of Things*, Michel Foucault notes the hilarity of a passage from a story by Jorge Luis Borges in which Borges describes a Chinese encyclopedia's taxonomy of animals. Some of the categories include "belonging to the emperor," "fabulous," "embalmed," "frenzied," and "that from a long way off look like flies." One can also imagine a system of describing literature based on a principle other than literary movements. Such a system might include categories like "books over thirty-four pages," "poems with wine stains," "plays involving a butter dish, a butler, and two pencils," and "novels that include names of French soups." While teaching a course based on texts from one of these categories might well prove engaging, (I'd certainly like to try), one would have a difficult time justifying it to a curriculum review committee. The fact is, literature illustrates, and often instigates, social trends, and history speaks through writers, whether they want it to or not. As of today, critics have yet to make a case for novels that include the names of French soups to be considered a major literary movement. But you might want to check back in ten years, just in case.

Chris Semansky
Chemeketa Community College
Salem, Oregon

Introduction

Purpose of the Book

The purpose of *Literary Movements for Students* (*LMfS*) is to provide readers with a guide to understanding, enjoying, and studying literary movements by giving them easy access to information about a given literary movement. Part of Gale's "For Students" literature line, *LMfS* is specifically designed to meet the curricular needs of high school and undergraduate college students and their teachers, as well as the interests of general readers and researchers considering specific literary movements.

The information covered in each entry includes an introduction to the literary movement; discussion of certain representative authors and works associated with the movement; analysis of the movement's predominant themes; and an explanation of related literary techniques.

In addition to this material, which helps the readers to analyze the movement itself, students are also provided with important information on its literary and historical background. This includes a historical context essay, a sidebar comparing the time or place the movement occurred to modern Western culture, a critical essay, and previously published criticism on the movement (if available). A unique feature of *LMfS* is a specially commissioned critical essay on each literary movement, targeted toward the student reader.

To further aid the student in studying and enjoying each literary movement, information on media adaptations is provided (if available), as well as reading suggestions for works of fiction and nonfiction on similar themes and topics. Classroom aids include ideas for research papers, study questions, and lists of critical sources that provide additional material on each movement.

Selection Criteria

The titles for both volumes of *LMfS* were selected by surveying numerous sources on teaching literature and analyzing course curricula for various school districts. Some of the sources surveyed included: literature anthologies; *Reading Lists for College-Bound Students: The Books Most Recommended by America's Top Colleges*; and Arthur Applebee's 1993 study *Literature in the Secondary School: Studies of Curriculum and Instruction in the United States*.

Input was also solicited from our advisory board, as well as educators from various areas. From these discussions, it was determined that the first volume should deal with earlier movements that took place approximately before the twentieth century, while the second volume should deal primarily with the more modern movements of the twentieth century and beyond. Because of the interest in expanding the canon of literature, an emphasis was also placed on discussing works by international, multicultural, and women authors. Our advisory board members—educational professionals—helped pare down the list for each volume. As always, the editor welcomes suggestions for movements to be included in possible future volumes.

How Each Entry Is Organized

Each entry, or chapter, in *LMfS* focuses on one literary movement. Each entry heading lists the full name of the movement and the approximate year of the movement's origin. The following elements are contained in each entry:

- **Introduction:** a brief overview of the movement, which provides information about its first appearance, its literary standing, any controversies surrounding it, and related themes.
- **Representative Authors:** this section includes basic facts about several authors associated with the movement, focusing on their relationship to the movement, including specific works written by the authors that might be typical of the movement.
- **Representative Works:** a description of specific works that have been identified as typical or representative of the movement.
- **Themes:** an overview of the major topics, themes, and issues related to the movement. Each theme discussed appears under a separate subhead and is easily accessed through the boldface entries in the Subject/Theme Index.
- **Style:** this section addresses important style elements of the movement, such as setting, point of view, and narration, as well as important literary devices used, such as imagery, foreshadowing, symbolism. Literary terms are explained within the entry but can also be found in the Glossary.
- **Movement Variations:** this section briefly discusses variations of the movement, including variations in geography (i.e., different countries), history (i.e., periodic revivals of the movement), philosophy, and art.
- **Historical Context:** this section outlines the social, political, and cultural climate *in which the movement took place.* This section may include descriptions of related historical events, pertinent aspects of daily life in the culture, and the artistic and literary sensibilities of the time in which the movement took place. Each section is broken down with helpful subheads.
- **Critical Overview:** this section provides background on the critical reputation of the movement, including any public controversies surrounding the movement. For older movements, this section includes a history of how the movement was first received and how perceptions of it may have changed over the years; for more recent movements, direct quotes from early reviews may also be included.
- **Criticism:** an essay commissioned for *LMfS* that specifically deals with the movement and is written specifically for the student audience, as well as one or more pieces of previously published criticism on the movement (if available).
- **Sources:** an alphabetical list of critical material used in compiling the entry, with full bibliographical information.
- **Further Reading:** an alphabetical list of other critical sources which may prove useful for the student. It includes full bibliographical information and a brief annotation.

In addition, each entry contains the following highlighted sections, set apart from the main text as sidebars:

- **Media Adaptations:** if available, a list of important film and television adaptations related to the movement, including source information. The list may also include such variations as audio recordings, musical adaptations, and stage adaptations.
- **Topics for Further Study:** a list of potential study questions or research topics dealing with the movement. This section includes questions related to other disciplines the student may be studying, such as American history, world history, science, math, government, business, geography, economics, psychology, etc.
- **Compare and Contrast:** an "at-a-glance" comparison of the cultural and historical differences between the time and culture of the movement and late twentieth-century or early twenty-first-century Western culture. This box includes pertinent parallels between the major scientific, political, and cultural movements of the time or place in which the literary movement took place and modern Western culture.
- **What Do I Study Next?:** a list of works that might complement the featured literary movement or serve as a contrast to it. This includes works by the same representative authors and others, works of fiction and nonfiction, and works from various genres, cultures, and eras.

Other Features

LMfS includes "Novels That Include the Names of French Soups," a foreword by Chris Semansky, an educator and author who specializes in poetic works. This essay examines how literary movements come about in societies and how people study such movements. The essay also discusses how *Literary Movements for Students* can help teachers show students how to enrich their own reading/viewing experiences.

A Cumulative Author/Title Index lists the representative authors and representative works covered in each volume of *LMfS*.

A Cumulative Nationality/Ethnicity Index breaks down the representative authors and the authors of representative works covered in each volume of *LMfS* by nationality and ethnicity.

A Subject/Theme Index, specific to each volume, provides easy reference for users who may be studying a particular subject or theme rather than a single work or movement. Significant subjects from events to broad themes are included, and the entries pointing to the specific theme discussions in each entry are indicated in **boldface**.

Each entry may include illustrations, including photos of the representative authors, stills from stage productions, and stills from film adaptations.

Citing Literary Movements for Students

When writing papers, students who quote directly from any volume of *Literary Movements for Students* may use the following general forms. These examples are based on MLA style; teachers may request that students adhere to a different style, so the following examples may be adapted as needed.

When citing text from *LMfS* that is not attributed to a particular author (e.g., the Themes, Style, Historical Context sections, etc.), the following format should be used in the bibliography section:

The Bildungsroman. *Literary Movements for Students*. Ed. David Galens. Vol. 1. Farmington Hills, MI: The Gale Group, 2003.

When quoting the specially commissioned essay from *LMfS* (usually the first piece under the "Criticism" subhead), the following format should be used:

Kerschen, Lois. Critical Essay on the Bildungsroman. *Literary Movements for Students*. Ed. David Galens. Vol. 1. Farmington Hills, MI: The Gale Group, 2003.

When quoting a journal or newspaper essay that is reprinted in a volume of *LMfS*, the following form may be used:

Carpenter, Charles A. "'Victims of Duty'? The Critics, Absurdity, and *The Homecoming*." *Modern Drama* Vol. 25, No. 4 (December 1982), 489–95; excerpted and reprinted in *Literary Movements for Students*, Vol. 2, ed. David Galens (Farmington Hills, MI: The Gale Group, 2003), pp.

When quoting material reprinted from a book that appears in a volume of *LMfS*, the following form may be used:

Perry, Margaret. "The Major Novels." *Silence to the Drums: A Survey of the Literature of the Harlem Renaissance*. Greenwood Press, 1976, pp. 61–88; excerpted and reprinted in *Literary Movements for Students*, Vol. 2, ed. David Galens (Farmington Hills, MI: The Gale Group, 2003), pp.

We Welcome Your Suggestions

The editor of *Literary Movements for Students* welcomes your comments and ideas. Readers who wish to suggest movements to appear in future volumes, or who have other suggestions, are cordially invited to contact the editor. You may contact the editor via E-mail at: **ForStudentsEditors@gale.com.** Or write to the editor at:

Editor, Literary Movements for Students
The Gale Group
27500 Drake Rd.
Farmington Hills, MI 48331-3535

Literary Chronology

c. 750 B.C.?: Homer, author representative of Classicism, flourishes about this time.

c. 750 B.C.: *Iliad*, written by Homer and representative of Classicism, is created.

c. 534 B.C.: Thespis, author representative of Greek Drama, flourishes about this time.

c. 530 B.C.: Epicharmus, author representative of Greek Drama, is born.

c. 525 B.C.: Aeschylus, author representative of Greek Drama, is born.

c. 496 B.C.: Sophocles, author representative of Greek Drama, is born.

c. 485 B.C.: Euripides, author representative of Greek Drama and Classicism, is born.

472 B.C.: *Prometheus Bound*, written by Aeschylus and representative of Greek Drama, is produced.

458 B.C.: *Oresteia*, written by Aeschylus and representative of Greek Drama, is produced.

c. 456 B.C.: Aeschylus, author representative of Greek Drama, dies.

c. 450 B.C.: Aristophanes, author representative of Greek Drama, is born.

c. 450 B.C.: Crates, author representative of Greek Drama, flourishes about this time.

c. 445 B.C.: Eupolis, author representative of Greek Drama, flourishes about this time.

441 B.C.: *Antigone*, written by Sophocles and representative of Greek Drama, is produced.

c. 440 B.C.: Epicharmus, author representative of Greek Drama, dies.

431 B.C.: *Medea*, written by Euripides and representative of Classicism and Greek Drama, is produced.

c. 430 B.C.: Sophron, author representative of Greek Drama, flourishes about this time.

427 B.C.: *Oedipus the King*, written by Sophocles and representative of Greek Drama, is produced.

c. 420 B.C.: Cratinus, author representative of Greek Drama, dies.

c. 420 B.C.: Phrynichus, author representative of Greek Drama, flourishes about this time.

c. 414 B.C.: *Birds*, written by Aristophanes and representative of Greek Drama, is produced.

c. 411 B.C.: Eupolis, author representative of Greek Drama, dies.

411 B.C.: *Lysistrata*, written by Aristophanes and representative of Greek Drama, is produced.

c. 406 B.C.: Euripides, author representative of Greek Drama and Classicism, dies.

c. 406 B.C.: Sophocles, author representative of Greek Drama, dies.

c. 405 B.C.: *Bacchae*, written by Euripides and representative of Greek Drama, is produced posthumously.

405 B.C.: *Frogs*, written by Aristophanes and representative of Greek Drama, is produced.

c. 401 B.C.: *Oedipus at Colonus*, written by Sophocles and representative of Greek Drama, is produced.

c. 385 B.C.: Aristophanes, author representative of Greek Drama, dies.

c. 342 B.C.: Menander, author representative of Greek Drama, is born.

317 B.C.: *Dyscolus*, written by Menander and representative of Greek Drama, is produced.

c. 292 B.C.: Menander, author representative of Greek Drama, dies.

70 B.C.: Vergil, author representative of Classicism, is born.

19 B.C.: Vergil, author representative of Classicism, dies.

c. 19 B.C.: *Aeneid*, written by Vergil and representative of Classicism, is published.

1217: Giovanni Bonaventure, author representative of the Medieval Mystics, is born.

1259: *The Soul's Journey into God*, written by Bonaventure and representative of the Medieval Mystics, is published.

c. 1260: Meister Eckhart, author representative of the Medieval Mystics, is born.

1274: Giovanni Bonaventure, author representative of the Medieval Mystics, dies.

1293: John Ruusbroec, author representative of the Medieval Mystics, is born.

1295: Henry Suso, author representative of the Medieval Mystics, is born.

1300: Richard Rolle, author representative of the Medieval Mystics, is born.

1300: Johannes Tauler, author representative of the Medieval Mystics, is born.

c. 1300–c. 1327: Meister Eckhart's Sermons, written by Meister Eckhart and representative of the Medieval Mystics, is published.

1304: Francesco Petrarch, author representative of Humanism, is born.

c. 1327: Meister Eckhart, author representative of the Medieval Mystics, dies.

c. 1334: *The Exemplar*, written by Henry Suso and representative of the Medieval Mystics, is published.

1335: *The Spiritual Espousals*, written by John Ruusbroec and representative of the Medieval Mystics, is published.

c. 1340: *The Fire of Love*, written by Richard Rolle and representative of the Medieval Mystics, is published.

1342: Julian of Norwich, author representative of the Medieval Mystics, is born.

1347: Catherine of Siena, author representative of the Medieval Mystics, is born.

1349: Richard Rolle, author representative of the Medieval Mystics, dies.

c. 1350: *Familiar Letters*, written by Francesco Petrarch and representative of Humanism, is published.

c. 1350: *Theologia Germanica*, written by an unknown author and representative of the Medieval Mystics, is published.

c. 1350–c. 1400: *The Cloud of Unknowing*, written by an unknown author and representative of the Medieval Mystics, is published.

1361: Johannes Tauler, author representative of the Medieval Mystics, dies.

1366: Henry Suso, author representative of the Medieval Mystics, dies.

c. 1373: *Revelations of Divine Love*, written by Julian of Norwich and representative of the Medieval Mystics, is published.

1374: Francesco Petrarch, author representative of Humanism, dies.

1380: Catherine of Siena, author representative of the Medieval Mystics, dies.

1381: John Ruusbroec, author representative of the Medieval Mystics, dies.

1405: Lorenzo Valla, author representative of Humanism, is born.

c. 1416: Julian of Norwich, author representative of the Medieval Mystics, dies.

1433: Marsilio Ficino, author representative of Humanism, is born.

1444: *Book of Elegances, or Elegances of the Latin Language*, written by Lorenzo Valla and representative of Humanism, is published.

1447: Catherine of Genoa, author representative of the Medieval Mystics, is born.

1452: Girolamo Savonarola, author representative of Humanism, is born.

1457: Lorenzo Valla, author representative of Humanism, dies.

1463: Giovanni Pico della Mirandola, author representative of Humanism, is born.

c. 1466: Desiderius Erasmus, author representative of Humanism and Renaissance Literature, is born.

1469: Niccolò Machiavelli, author representative of Renaissance Literature, is born.

1478: Baldassare Castiglione, author representative of Humanism, is born.

c. 1478: Sir Thomas More, author representative of Humanism and Renaissance Literature, is born.

1494: Giovanni Pico della Mirandola, author representative of Humanism, dies.

c. 1494: François Rabelais, author representative of Renaissance Literature, is born.

1496: *Oration on the Dignity of Man*, written by Giovanni Pico della Mirandola and representative of Humanism, is published posthumously.

1498: Girolamo Savonarola, author representative of Humanism, dies.

1499: Marsilio Ficino, author representative of Humanism, dies.

1500: *Adages*, written by Desiderius Erasmus and representative of Humanism, is published.

1510: Catherine of Genoa, author representative of the Medieval Mystics, dies.

1511: *The Praise of Folly*, written by Desiderius Erasmus and representative of Renaissance Literature, is published.

1516: *Utopia*, written by Sir Thomas More and representative of Humanism and Renaissance Literature, is published.

c. 1522: *The Spiritual Dialogue*, written by friends of Catherine of Genoa on the basis of Catherine's teachings and representative of the Medieval Mystics, is published.

1527: Niccolò Machiavelli, author representative of Renaissance Literature, dies about this time.

1528: *Book of the Courtier*, written by Baldassare Castiglione and representative of Humanism, is published.

1529: Baldassare Castiglione, author representative of Humanism, dies.

1532: *The Prince*, written by Niccolò Machiavelli and representative of Renaissance Literature, is published.

1533: Michel de Montaigne, author representative of Renaissance Literature, is born.

1535: Sir Thomas More, author representative of Humanism and Renaissance Literature, dies.

1536: Desiderius Erasmus, author representative of Humanism and Renaissance Literature, dies.

1547: Miguel de Cervantes Saavedra, author representative of Renaissance Literature, is born about this time.

1553: François Rabelais, author representative of Renaissance Literature, dies.

1558: Thomas Kyd, author representative of Elizabethan Drama, is born.

1559: George Chapman, author representative of Elizabethan Drama, is born.

1564: Christopher Marlowe, author representative of Elizabethan Drama and Renaissance Literature, is born.

1564: William Shakespeare, author representative of Elizabethan Drama and Renaissance Literature, is born.

c. 1572: Thomas Dekker, author representative of Elizabethan Drama, is born.

1572: Ben Jonson, author representative of Elizabethan Drama, is born.

c. 1573: Thomas Heywood, author representative of Elizabethan Drama, is born.

1580: *The Essays*, written by Michel de Montaigne and representative of Renaissance Literature, is published.

1586: *The Spanish Tragedy*, written by Thomas Kyd and representative of Elizabethan Drama, is published.

c. 1587: *Tamburlaine the Great*, written by Christopher Marlowe and representative of Elizabethan Drama, is published.

1592: Michel de Montaigne, author representative of Renaissance Literature, dies.

1592: *The Jew of Malta*, written by Christopher Marlowe and representative of Elizabethan Drama, is published.

1593: Christopher Marlowe, author representative of Elizabethan Drama and Renaissance Literature, dies.

1594: Thomas Kyd, author representative of Elizabethan Drama, dies.

1598: *Everyman in His Humour*, written by Ben Johnson and representative of Elizabethan Drama, is published.

1600: *Hamlet*, written by William Shakespeare and representative of Elizabethan Drama and Renaissance Literature, is published.

1600: *The Shoemaker's Holiday*, written by Thomas Dekker and representative of Elizabethan Drama, is published.

1603: *A Woman Killed with Kindness*, written by Thomas Heywood and representative of Elizabethan Drama, is published.

1605–1615: *Don Quixote*, written by Miguel de Cervantes Saavedra and representative of Renaissance Literature, is published.

1616: William Shakespeare, author representative of Elizabethan Drama and Renaissance Literature, dies.

1616: Miguel de Cervantes Saavedra, author representative of Renaissance Literature, dies.

1631: John Dryden, author representative of Neoclassicism, is born.

1632: Thomas Dekker, author representative of Elizabethan Drama, dies.

1634: George Chapman, author representative of Elizabethan Drama, dies.

1637: Ben Jonson, author representative of Elizabethan Drama, dies.

1639: Jean Racine, author representative of Classicism, is born.

1641: Thomas Heywood, author representative of Elizabethan Drama, dies.

1660: Daniel Defoe, author representative of Neoclassicism, is born.

1667: *Andromaque*, written by Jean Racine and representative of Classicism, is published.

1668: *Of Dramatick Poesie: An Essay*, written by John Dryden and representative of Neoclassicism, is published.

1694: Voltaire, author representative of the Enlightenment, is born.

1699: Jean Racine, author representative of Classicism, dies.

1700: John Dryden, author representative of Neoclassicism, dies.

1709: Samuel Johnson, author representative of Neoclassicism, is born.

1711: David Hume, author representative of the Enlightenment, is born.

1712: Jean-Jacques Rousseau, author representative of the Enlightenment, is born.

1712: *The Rape of the Lock*, written by Alexander Pope and representative of Neoclassicism, is published.

1713: Denis Diderot, author representative of the Enlightenment, is born.

1717: Horace Walpole, author representative of Gothic Literature, is born.

1719: *Robinson Crusoe*, written by Daniel Defoe and representative of Neoclassicism, is published.

1727: *Gulliver's Travels*, written by Jonathan Swift and representative of Neoclassicism, is published.

1731: Daniel Defoe, author representative of Neoclassicism, dies.

1733: Christoph Martin Wieland, author representative of the Bildungsroman, is born.

1738: *London*, written by Samuel Johnson and representative of Neoclassicism, is published.

1749: Johann Wolfgang von Goethe, author representative of Classicism and the Bildungsroman, is born.

1751–1765: *Encyclopédie*, written by Denis Diderot and representative of the Enlightenment, is published.

1757: William Blake, author representative of Romanticism, is born.

1759: *Candide*, written by Voltaire and representative of the Enlightenment, is published.

1760: William Beckford, author representative of Gothic Literature, is born.

1762: *Émile*, written by Jean-Jacques Rousseau and representative of the Enlightenment, is published.

1762: *The Social Contract*, written by Jean-Jacques Rousseau and representative of the Enlightenment, is published.

1764: Ann Radcliffe, author representative of Gothic Literature, is born.

1764: *The Castle of Otranto*, written by Horace Walpole and representative of Gothic Literature, is published.

1770: William Wordsworth, author representative of Romanticism, is born.

1771: Charles Brockden Brown, author representative of Gothic Literature, is born.

1772: Samuel Taylor Coleridge, author representative of Romanticism, is born.

1775: Matthew Gregory Lewis, author representative of Gothic Literature, is born.

1775: Jane Austen, author representative of Romanticism, is born.

1776: David Hume, author representative of the Enlightenment, dies.

1776: *Declaration of Independence*, written by Thomas Jefferson and others and representative of the Enlightenment, is published.

1778: Jean-Jacques Rousseau, author representative of the Enlightenment, dies.

1778: Voltaire, author representative of the Enlightenment, dies.

1780: Charles Robert Maturin, author representative of Gothic Literature, is born.

1784: Denis Diderot, author representative of the Enlightenment, dies.

1784: Samuel Johnson, author representative of Neoclassicism, dies.

1786: *Vathek*, written by William Beckford and representative of Gothic Literature, is published.

1788: George Gordon, Lord Byron, author representative of Romanticism, is born.

1790–1832: *Faust*, written by Johann Wolfgang von Goethe and representative of Classicism, is published.

1792: Percy Bysshe Shelley, author representative of Romanticism, is born.

1794: *The Mysteries of Udolpho*, written by Ann Radcliffe and representative of Gothic Literature, is published.

1794: *Songs of Innocence and of Experience*, written by William Blake and representative of Romanticism, is published.

1795: John Keats, author representative of Romanticism, is born.

1795: *Wilhelm Meister's Apprenticeship*, written by Johann Wolfgang von Goethe and representative of the Bildungsroman, is published.

1795: *The Monk*, written by Matthew Gregory Lewis and representative of Gothic Literature, is published.

1797: Mary Wollstonecraft Shelley, author representative of Gothic Literature, Romanticism, and Science Fiction and Fantasy Literature, is born.

1797: Horace Walpole, author representative of Gothic Literature, dies.

1798: *Wieland*, written by Charles Brockden Brown and representative of Gothic Literature, is published.

1799: Honoré de Balzac, author representative of Realism, is born.

1803: Ralph Waldo Emerson, author representative of Transcendentalism, is born.

1809: Edgar Allan Poe, author representative of Gothic Literature, is born.

1810: Charles Brockden Brown, author representative of Gothic Literature, dies.

1810: Margaret Fuller, author representative of Transcendentalism, is born.

1812: Charles Dickens, author representative of Realism and the Bildungsroman, is born.

1812–1818: *Childe Harold's Pilgrimage*, written by George Gordon, Lord Byron and representative of Romanticism, is published.

1813: Christoph Martin Wieland, author representative of the Bildungsroman, dies.

1813: Søren Kierkegaard, author representative of Existentialism, is born.

1813: *Pride and Prejudice*, written by Jane Austen and representative of Romanticism, is published.

1817: Jane Austen, author representative of Romanticism, dies.

1817: Henry David Thoreau, author representative of Transcendentalism, is born.

1818: *Frankenstein*, written by Mary Wollstonecraft Shelley and representative of Romanticism, Gothic Literature, and Science Fiction and Fantasy Literature, is published.

1818: Matthew Gregory Lewis, author representative of Gothic Literature, dies.

1819: "To Autumn," written by John Keats and representative of Romanticism, is published.

1819: George Eliot, author representative of Realism, is born.

1819: Walt Whitman, author representative of Transcendentalism, is born.

1820: *Melmoth the Wanderer*, written by Charles Robert Maturin and representative of Gothic Literature, is published.

1820: *Prometheus Unbound*, written by Percy Bysshe Shelley and representative of Romanticism, is published.

1821: Fyodor Dostoevsky, author representative of Existentialism and Realism, is born.

1821: Gustave Flaubert, author representative of Realism, is born.

1821: John Keats, author representative of Romanticism, dies.

1821: Charles Baudelaire, author representative of Symbolism, is born.

1822: Percy Bysshe Shelley, author representative of Romanticism, dies.

1823: Ann Radcliffe, author representative of Gothic Literature, dies.

1824: Charles Robert Maturin, author representative of Gothic Literature, dies.

1824: George Gordon, Lord Byron, author representative of Romanticism, dies.

1827: William Blake, author representative of Romanticism, dies.

1828: Leo Tolstoy, author representative of Realism, is born.

1828: Jules Verne, author representative of Science Fiction and Fantasy Literature, is born.

1832: Johann Wolfgang von Goethe, author representative of Classicism and the Bildungsroman, dies.

1834: "The Fall of the House of Usher," written by Edgar Allan Poe and representative of Gothic Literature, is published.

1834: Samuel Taylor Coleridge, author representative of Romanticism, dies.

1835: Mark Twain, author representative of the Bildungsroman, is born.

1836: *Nature*, written by Ralph Waldo Emerson and representative of Transcendentalism, is published.

1837: William Dean Howells, author representative of Realism, is born.

1840: Émile Zola, author representative of Naturalism and Realism, is born.

1842: Stéphane Mallarmé, author representative of Symbolism, is born.

1842–1855: *The Human Comedy*, written by Honoré de Balzac and representative of Realism, is published.

1844: William Beckford, author representative of Gothic Literature, dies.

1844: Paul Verlaine, author representative of Symbolism, is born.

1845: *Woman in the Nineteenth Century*, written by Margaret Fuller and representative of Transcendentalism, is published.

1847: *Jane Eyre*, written by Charlotte Brontë and representative of the Bildungsroman, is published.

1848: Joris-Karl Huysmans, author representative of Symbolism, is born.

1849: August Strindberg, author representative of Expressionism, is born.

1849: Edgar Allan Poe, author representative of Gothic Literature, dies.

1849–1850: *David Copperfield*, written by Charles Dickens and representative of Realism, is published.

1850: Honoré de Balzac, author representative of Realism, dies.

1850: Guy de Maupassant, author representative of Realism, is born.

1850: William Wordsworth, author representative of Romanticism, dies.

1850: Margaret Fuller, author representative of Transcendentalism, dies.

1851: Mary Wollstonecraft Shelley, author representative of Romanticism, Gothic Literature, and Science Fiction and Fantasy Literature, dies.

1852: *The Blithedale Romance*, written by Nathaniel Hawthorne and representative of Transcendentalism, is published.

1854: Arthur Rimbaud, author representative of Symbolism, is born.

1854: *Walden*, written by Henry David Thoreau and representative of Transcendentalism, is published.

1855: Søren Kierkegaard, author representative of Existentialism, dies.

1855: *Leaves of Grass*, written by Walt Whitman and representative of Transcendentalism, is published.

1856: H. Rider Haggard, author representative of Colonialism, is born.

1857: Joseph Conrad, author representative of Colonialism, is born.

1857: *Madame Bovary*, written by Gustave Flaubert and representative of Realism, is published.

1857: *Flowers of Evil*, written by Charles Baudelaire and representative of Symbolism, is published.

1861: *Great Expectations*, written by Charles Dickens and representative of the Bildungsroman, is published.

1862: Maurice Maeterlinck, author representative of Symbolism, is born.

1862: Henry David Thoreau, author representative of Transcendentalism, dies.

1864: Frank Wedekind, author representative of Expressionism, is born.

1865: Rudyard Kipling, author representative of Colonialism, is born.

1866: H. G. Wells, author representative of Science Fiction and Fantasy Literature, is born.

1866: *Crime and Punishment*, written by Fyodor Dostoevsky and representative of Realism, is published.

1867: Charles Baudelaire, author representative of Symbolism, dies.

1868: W. E. B. Du Bois, author representative of the Harlem Renaissance, is born.

1870: Charles Dickens, author representative of Realism and the Bildungsroman, dies.

1870: Frank Norris, author representative of Naturalism, is born.

1870: *Twenty Thousand Leagues under the Sea*, written by Jules Verne and representative of Science Fiction and Fantasy Literature, is published.

1871: James Weldon Johnson, author representative of the Harlem Renaissance, is born.

1871: Stephen Crane, author representative of Naturalism, is born.

1871: Theodore Dreiser, author representative of Naturalism, is born.

1871–1872: *Middlemarch*, written by George Eliot and representative of Realism, is published.

1874: Amy Lowell, author representative of Imagism, is born.

1874: *Songs without Words*, written by Paul Verlaine and representative of Symbolism, is published.

1875: Thomas Mann, author representative of the Bildungsroman, is born.

1875–1877: *Anna Karenina*, written by Leo Tostoy and representative of Realism, is published.

1876: *The Afternoon of a Faun*, written by Stéphane Mallarmé and representative of Symbolism, is published.

1878: Georg Kaiser, author representative of Expressionism, is born.

1879: E. M. Forster, author representative of Colonialism, is born.

1880: "Ball of Fat," written by Guy de Maupassant and representative of Realism, is published.

1880: George Eliot, author representative of Realism, dies.

1880: Gustave Flaubert, author representative of Realism, dies.

1880: Aleksandr Blok, author representative of Symbolism, is born.

1880: *The Brothers Karamazov*, written by Fyodor Dostoevsky and representative of Existentialism, is published.

1881: Fyodor Dostoevsky, author representative of Existentialism and Realism, dies.

1882: James Joyce, author representative of Modernism and the Bildungsroman, is born.

1882: Jessie Redmon Fauset, author representative of the Harlem Renaissance, is born.

1882: Virginia Woolf, author representative of Modernism, is born.

1882: Ralph Waldo Emerson, author representative of Transcendentalism, dies.

1883: Franz Kafka, author representative of Existentialism and Expressionism, is born.

1883: Eugene O'Neill, author representative of Expressionism, is born.

1883: *The Story of an African Farm*, written by Olive Schreiner and representative of Colonialism, is published.

1884: *Against the Grain*, written by Joris Huysmans and representative of Symbolism, is published.

1885: Isak Dinesen, author representative of Colonialism, is born.

1885: F. S. Flint, author representative of Imagism, is born.

1885: Ezra Pound, author representative of Imagism and Modernism, is born.

1885: *The Adventures of Huckleberry Finn*, written by Mark Twain and representative of the Bildungsroman, is published.

1885: *Germinal*, written by Émile Zola and representative of Realism, is published.

1886: Alain Locke, author representative of the Harlem Renaissance, is born.

1886: Hilda Doolittle, author representative of Imagism, is born.

1886: John Gould Fletcher, author representative of Imagism, is born.

1886: *Illuminations*, written by Arthur Rimbaud and representative of Symbolism, is published.

1887: *She*, written by H. Rider Haggard and representative of Colonialism, is published.

1887: Georg Trakl, author representative of Expressionism, is born.

1888: T. S. Eliot, author representative of Modernism, is born.

1889: Claude McKay, author representative of the Harlem Renaissance, is born.

1890: *A Hazard of New Fortunes*, written by William Dean Howells and representative of Realism, is published.

1891: Zora Neale Hurston, author representative of the Harlem Renaissance, is born.

1891: Nella Larsen, author representative of the Harlem Renaissance, is born.

1891: Arthur Rimbaud, author representative of Symbolism, dies.

1891: *Spring's Awakening*, written by Frank Wedekind and representative of Expressionism, is published.

1892: Richard Aldington, author representative of Imagism, is born.

1892: J. R. R. Tolkien, author representative of Science Fiction and Fantasy Literature, is born.

1892: Walt Whitman, author representative of Transcendentalism, dies.

1893: Guy de Maupassant, author representative of Realism, dies.

1893: *Pelleas and Melisande*, written by Maurice Maeterlinck and representative of Symbolism, is published.

1894: Jean Toomer, author representative of the Harlem Renaissance, is born.

1894: Aldous Huxley, author representative of Science Fiction and Fantasy Literature, is born.

1895: Paul Eluard, author representative of Surrealism, is born.

1895: *Jude the Obscure*, written by Thomas Hardy and representative of the Bildungsroman, is published.

1895: *The Red Badge of Courage*, written by Stephen Crane and representative of Naturalism, is published.

1895: *The Time Machine: An Invention*, written by H. G. Wells and representative of Science Fiction and Fantasy Literature, is published.

1896: André Breton, author representative of Surrealism, is born.

1896: Paul Verlaine, author representative of Symbolism, dies.

1897: William Faulkner, author representative of Modernism, is born.

1897: Louis Aragon, author representative of Surrealism, is born.

1897: Phillipe Soupault, author representative of Surrealism, is born.

1898: C. S. Lewis, author representative of Science Fiction and Fantasy Literature, is born.

1898: Stéphane Mallarmé, author representative of Symbolism, dies.

1899: "The White Man's Burden," written by Rudyard Kipling and representative of Colonialism, is published.

1899: Miguel Ángel Asturias, author representative of Magic Realism, is born.

1899: Jorge Luis Borges, author representative of Magic Realism, is born.

1899: *McTeague: A Story of San Francisco*, written by Frank and representative of Naturalism, is published.

1899–1900: *Heart of Darkness*, written by Joseph Conrad and representative of Colonialism, is published.

1900: Stephen Crane, author representative of Naturalism, dies.

1900: Robert Desnos, author representative of Surrealism, is born.

1900: *Lord Jim*, written by Joseph Conrad and representative of Colonialism, is published.

1900: *Sister Carrie*, written by Theodore Dreiser and representative of Naturalism, is published.

1901: *A Dream Play*, written by August Strindberg and representative of Expressionism, is published.

1901: *Kim*, written by Rudyard Kipling and representative of Colonialism, is published.

1902: Langston Hughes, author representative of the Harlem Renaissance, is born.

1902: Frank Norris, author representative of Naturalism, dies.

1902: Émile Zola, author representative of Naturalism and Realism, dies.

1902: *The Immoralist*, written by André Gide and representative of Existentialism, is published.

1903: Countee Cullen, author representative of the Harlem Renaissance, is born.

1903: *The Call of the Wild*, written by Jack London and representative of Naturalism, is published.

1904: Alejo Carpentier, author representative of Magic Realism, is born.

1905: Jean-Paul Sartre, author representative of Existentialism, is born.

1905: Jules Verne, author representative of Science Fiction and Fantasy Literature, dies.

1906: Samuel Beckett, author representative of Absurdism, is born.

1907: Robert Heinlein, author representative of Science Fiction and Fantasy Literature, is born.

1907: Joris-Karl Huysmans, author representative of Symbolism, dies.

1908: Arthur Adamov, author representative of Absurdism, is born.

1908: Simone de Beauvoir, author representative of Existentialism, is born.

1910: Jean Genet, author representative of Absurdism, is born.

1910: Mark Twain, author representative of the Bildungsroman, dies.

1910: Leo Tolstoy, author representative of Realism, dies.

1911: "The Woman at the Store," written by Katherine Mansfield and representative of Colonialism, is published.

1912: Eugène Ionesco, author representative of Absurdism, is born.

1912: August Strindberg, author representative of Expressionism, dies.

1913: Albert Camus, author representative of Existentialism, is born.

1913: *Sons and Lovers*, written by D. H. Lawrence and representative of the Bildungsroman, is published.

1913: *Poems*, written by Georg Trakl and representative of Expressionism, is published.

1914: William Burroughs, author representative of the Beat Movement, is born.

1914: Georg Trakl, author representative of Expressionism, dies.

1914: *Sword Blades and Poppy Seed*, written by Amy Lowell and representative of Imagism, is published.

1915: *Of Human Bondage*, written by Somerset Maugham and representative of the Bildungsroman, is published.

1915: *The Metamorphosis*, written by Franz Kafka and representative of Expressionism, is published.

1915: *Cathay*, written by Ezra Pound and representative of Imagism, is published.

1916: *A Portrait of the Artist as a Young Man*, written by James Joyce and representative of the Bildungsroman, is published.

1916: *Goblins and Pagodas*, written by John Gould Fletcher and representative of Imagism, is published.

1916: *Sea Garden*, written by Hilda Doolittle and representative of Imagism, is published.

1917: *The Citizens of Calais*, written by Georg Kaiser and representative of Expressionism, is published.

1917–1969: *The Cantos*, written by Ezra Pound and representative of Modernism, is published.

1918: Frank Wedekind, author representative of Expressionism, dies.

1918: *The Twelve*, written by Aleksandr Blok and representative of Symbolism, is published.

1919: *Images of War*, written by Richard Aldington and representative of Imagism, is published.

1919: *The Magnetic Fields*, written by André Breton and Philippe Soupault and representative of Surrealism, is published.

1920: William Dean Howells, author representative of Realism, dies.

1920: Isaac Asimov, author representative of Science Fiction and Fantasy Literature, is born.

1920: Ray Bradbury, author representative of Science Fiction and Fantasy Literature, is born.

1920: *The Emperor Jones*, written by Eugene O'Neill and representative of Expressionism, is published.

1920: *Otherworld: Cadences*, written by F. S. Flint and representative of Imagism, is published.

1921: Aleksandr Blok, author representative of Symbolism, dies.

1922: "The Waste Land," written by T. S. Eliot and representative of Modernism, is published.

1922: Jack Kerouac, author representative of the Beat Movement, is born.

1922: Kurt Vonnegut Jr., author representative of Postmodernism and Science Fiction and Fantasy Literature, is born.

1922: *Ulysses*, written by James Joyce and representative of Modernism, is published.

1923: *Cane*, written by Jean Toomer and representative of Harlem Renaissance, is published.

1923: *Harmonium*, written by Wallace Stevens and representative of Modernism, is published.

1924: Joseph Conrad, author representative of Colonialism, dies.

1924: Franz Kafka, author representative of Existentialism and Expressionism, dies.

1924: *Manifesto of Surrealism*, written by André Breton and representative of Surrealism, is published.

1925: H. Rider Haggard, author representative of Colonialism, dies.

1925: Amy Lowell, author representative of Imagism, dies.

1925: Frantz Fanon, author representative of Postcolonialism, is born.

1925: *A Passage to India*, written by E. M. Forster and representative of Colonialism, is published.

1925: *The Trial*, written by Franz Kafka and representative of Existentialism, is published posthumously.

1925: *Color*, written by Countee Cullen and representative of Harlem Renaissance, is published.

1925: *The New Negro: An Interpretation*, written by Alain Locke and representative of Harlem Renaissance, is published.

1925: *An American Tragedy*, written by Theodore Dreiser and representative of Naturalism, is published.

1926: Neal Cassady, author representative of the Beat Movement, is born.

1926: Allen Ginsberg, author representative of the Beat Movement, is born.

1926: Michel Foucault, author representative of Postmodernism, is born.

1926: *The Sun Also Rises*, written by Ernest Hemingway and representative of Existentialism, is published.

1926: *The Weary Blues*, written by Langston Hughes and representative of Harlem Renaissance, is published.

1926: *Capital of Sorrow*, written by Paul Eluard and representative of Surrealism, is published.

1926: *Paris Peasant*, written by Louis Aragon and representative of Surrealism, is published.

1927: *God's Trombones: Seven Negro Sermons in Verse*, written by James Weldon Johnson and representative of Harlem Renaissance, is published.

1927: *To the Lighthouse*, written by Virginia Woolf and representative of Modernism, is published.

1927: *Liberty or Love!*, written by Robert Desnos and representative of Surrealism, is published.

1928: Edward Albee, author representative of Absurdism, is born.

1928: Carlos Fuentes, author representative of Magic Realism, is born.

1928: Gabriel García Márquez, author representative of Magic Realism, is born.

1928: *Home to Harlem*, written by Claude McKay and representative of Harlem Renaissance, is published.

1928: *Quicksand*, written by Nella Larsen and representative of Harlem Renaissance, is published.

1929: *A Farewell to Arms*, written by Ernest Hemingway and representative of Modernism, is published.

1929: *The Sound and the Fury*, written by William Faulkner and representative of Modernism, is published.

1930: Harold Pinter, author representative of Absurdism, is born.

1930: Gregory Corso, author representative of the Beat Movement, is born.

1930: Derek Walcott, author representative of Postcolonialism, is born.

1930: Jacques Derrida, author representative of Postmodernism, is born.

1931: Donald Barthelme, author representative of Postmodernism, is born.

1931: Toni Morrison, author representative of Postmodernism, is born.

1932: Fernando Arrabal, author representative of Absurdism, is born.

1932: *Brave New World*, written by Aldous Huxley and representative of Science Fiction and Fantasy Literature, is published.

1934: Fredric Jameson, author representative of Postmodernism, is born.

1934: *Call It Sleep*, written by Henry Roth and representative of Modernism, is published.

1936: Václav Havel, author representative of Absurdism, is born.

1936: Rudyard Kipling, author representative of Colonialism, dies.

1937: *Out of Africa*, written by Isak Dinesen and representative of Colonialism, is published in English.

1937: *Their Eyes Were Watching God*, written by Zora Neale Hurston and representative of Harlem Renaissance, is published.

1937: *The Hobbit*, written by J. R. R. Tolkien and representative of Science Fiction and Fantasy Literature, is published.

1938: James Weldon Johnson, author representative of the Harlem Renaissance, dies.

1938: Ishmael Reed, author representative of Postmodernism, is born.

1938: *Nausea*, written by Jean-Paul Sartre and representative of Existentialism, is published.

1940: J. M. Coetzee, author representative of Postcolonialism, is born.

1941: James Joyce, author representative of Modernism and the Bildungsroman, dies.

1941: Virginia Woolf, author representative of Modernism, dies.

1941: Julia Kristeva, author representative of Postmodernism, is born.

1942: Isabel Allende, author representative of Magic Realism, is born.

1942: Gayatri Chakravorty Spivak, author representative of Postcolonialism, is born.

1943: Michael Ondaatje, author representative of Postcolonialism, is born.

1943: Terry Eagleton, author representative of Postmodernism, is born.

1943: *The Little Prince*, written by Antoine de Saint-Exupery and representative of Existentialism, is published.

1944: *Fictions*, written by Jorge Luis Borges and representative of Magic Realism, is published.

1945: Georg Kaiser, author representative of Expressionism, dies.

1945: Theodore Dreiser, author representative of Naturalism, dies.

1945: Robert Desnos, author representative of Surrealism, dies.

1946: Countee Cullen, author representative of the Harlem Renaissance, dies.

1946: H. G. Wells, author representative of Science Fiction and Fantasy Literature, dies.

1946: *The Stranger*, written by Albert Camus and representative of Existentialism, is published.

1947: Salman Rushdie, author representative of Postcolonialism, is born.

1947: *The Maids*, written by Jean Genet and representative of Absurdism, is published.

1947: *No Exit*, written by Jean-Paul Sartre and representative of Existentialism, is published in English.

1948: Claude McKay, author representative of the Harlem Renaissance, dies.

1949: Jamaica Kincaid, author representative of Postcolonialism, is born.

1949: Maurice Maeterlinck, author representative of Symbolism, dies.

1949: *The Kingdom of This World*, written by Alejo Carpentier and representative of Magic Realism, is published.

1949: *Men of Maize*, written by Miguel Ángel Asturias and representative of Magic Realism, is published.

1950: John Gould Fletcher, author representative of Imagism, dies.

1950: *The Bald Soprano*, written by Eugène Ionesco and representative of Absurdism, is published.

1950: *I, Robot*, written by Isaac Asimov and representative of Science Fiction and Fantasy Literature, is published.

1950: *The Martian Chronicles*, written by Ray Bradbury and representative of Science Fiction and Fantasy Literature, is published.

1950–1956: "The Chronicles of Narnia," written by C. S. Lewis and representative of Science Fiction and Fantasy Literature, are published.

1951: Laura Esquivel, author representative of Magic Realism, is born.

1952: Paul Eluard, author representative of Surrealism, dies.

1952: *The Chairs*, written by Eugène Ionesco and representative of Absurdism, is published.

1953: Eugene O'Neill, author representative of Expressionism, dies.

1953: *Waiting for Godot*, written by Samuel Beckett and representative of Absurdism and Existentialism, is published.

1953: *Invisible Man*, written by Ralph Ellison and representative of the Bildungsroman, is published.

1954: Alain Locke, author representative of the Harlem Renaissance, dies.

1954: *The Mandarins*, written by Simone de Beauvoir and representative of Existentialism, is published.

1955: Thomas Mann, author representative of the Bildungsroman, dies.

1955: *Ping-Pong*, written by Arthur Adamov and representative of Absurdism, is published.

1956: "Howl," written by Allen Ginsberg and representative of the Beat Movement, is published.

1957: Li-Young Lee, author representative of Postcolonialism, is born.

1957: *Endgame*, written by Samuel Beckett and representative of Absurdism, is published.

1957: *On the Road*, written by Jack Kerouac and representative of the Beat Movement, is published.

1958: "BOMB,"written by Gregory Corso and representative of the Beat Movement, is published.

1958: *A Coney Island of the Mind*, written by Lawrence Ferlinghetti and representative of the Beat Movement, is published.

1958: *The Dharma Bums*, written by Jack Kerouac and representative of the Beat Movement, is published.

1958: *Things Fall Apart*, written by Chinua Achebe and representative of Postcolonialism, is published.

1959: *The Zoo Story*, written by Edward Albee and representative of Absurdism, is published.

1959: *Naked Lunch*, written by William Burroughs and representative of the Beat Movement, is published.

1960: Albert Camus, author representative of Existentialism, dies.

1960: Zora Neale Hurston, author representative of the Harlem Renaissance, dies.

1960: F. S. Flint, author representative of Imagism, dies.

1961: Jessie Redmon Fauset, author representative of the Harlem Renaissance, dies.

1961: Hilda Doolittle, author representative of Imagism, dies.

1961: Frantz Fanon, author representative of Postcolonialism, dies.

1961: *The American Dream*, written by Edward Albee and representative of Absurdism, is published.

1961: *Stranger in a Strange Land*, written by Robert Heinlein and representative of Science Fiction and Fantasy Literature, is published.

1962: Isak Dinesen, author representative of Colonialism, dies.

1962: Richard Aldington, author representative of Imagism, dies.

1962: William Faulkner, author representative of Modernism, dies.

1962: *Aura*, written by Carlos Fuentes and representative of Magic Realism, is published.

1963: W. E. B. Du Bois, author representative of the Harlem Renaissance, dies.

1963: Aldous Huxley, author representative of Science Fiction and Fantasy Literature, dies.

1963: C. S. Lewis, author representative of Science Fiction and Fantasy Literature, dies.

1963: *The Bell Jar*, written by Sylvia Plath and representative of the Bildungsroman, is published.

1963: *Cat's Cradle*, written by Kurt Vonnegut Jr. and representative of Postmodernism, is published.

1963: *Conjure: Selected Poems, 1963–1970*, written by Ishmael Reed and representative of Postmodernism, is published.

1964: Nella Larsen, author representative of the Harlem Renaissance, dies.

1964: *The Garden Party*, written by Václav Havel and representative of Absurdism, is published.

1965: T. S. Eliot, author representative of Modernism, dies.

1965: *The Homecoming*, written by Harold Pinter and representative of Absurdism, is published.

1966: André Breton, author representative of Surrealism, dies.

1967: Langston Hughes, author representative of the Harlem Renaissance, dies.

1967: Jean Toomer, author representative of the Harlem Renaissance, dies.

1967: *One Hundred Years of Solitude*, written by Gabriel García Márquez and representative of Magic Realism, is published.

1967: *Of Grammatology*, written by Jacques Derrida and representative of Postmodernism, is published.

1968: Neal Cassady, author representative of the Beat Movement, dies.

1969: Jack Kerouac, author representative of the Beat Movement, dies.

1969: *Slaughterhouse Five*, written by Kurt Vonnegut Jr. and representative of Science Fiction and Fantasy Literature, is published.

1970: Arthur Adamov, author representative of Absurdism, dies.

1970: E. M. Forster, author representative of Colonialism, dies.

1972: Ezra Pound, author representative of Imagism and Modernism, dies.

1973: J. R. R. Tolkien, author representative of Science Fiction and Fantasy Literature, dies.

1974: Miguel Ángel Asturias, author representative of Magic Realism, dies.

1977: *Ceremony*, written by Leslie Marmon Silko and representative of Postcolonialism, is published.

1980: Jean-Paul Sartre, author representative of Existentialism, dies.

1980: Alejo Carpentier, author representative of Magic Realism, dies.

1980: *Desire in Language: A Semiotic Approach to Literature and Art*, written by Julia Kristeva and representative of Postmodernism, is published.

1981: *Midnight's Children*, written by Salman Rushdie and representative of Postcolonialism, is published.

1982: Louis Aragon, author representative of Surrealism, dies.

1982: *The House of the Spirits*, written by Isabel Allende and representative of Magic Realism and Postcolonialism, is published.

1983: "Postmodernism and Consumer Society," written by Frederic Jameson and representative of Postmodernism, is published.

1983: *Overnight to Many Distant Cities*, written by Donald Barthelme and representative of Postmodernism, is published.

1984: Michel Foucault, author representative of Postmodernism, dies.

1985: *Love in the Time of Cholera*, written by Gabriel García Márquez and representative of Magic Realism, is published.

1986: Jean Genet, author representative of Absurdism, dies.

1986: Simone de Beauvoir, author representative of Existentialism, dies.

1986: Jorge Luis Borges, author representative of Magic Realism, dies.

1986: *Decolonizing the Mind*, written by Ngugi wa Thiong'o and representative of Postcolonialism, is published.

1986: *Rose*, written by Li-Young Lee and representative of Postcolonialism, is published.

1987: *Beloved*, written by Toni Morrison and representative of Postmodernism, is published.

1988: Robert Heinlein, author representative of Science Fiction and Fantasy Literature, dies.

1988: *A Small Place*, written by Jamaica Kincaid and representative of Postcolonialism, is published.

1989: Samuel Beckett, author representative of Absurdism, dies.

1989: Donald Barthelme, author representative of Postmodernism, dies.

1990: Phillipe Soupault, author representative of Surrealism, dies.

1990: *Outside History: Selected Poems, 1980–1990*, written by Eavan Boland and representative of Postcolonialism, is published.

1992: Isaac Asimov, author representative of Science Fiction and Fantasy Literature, dies.

1992: *The English Patient*, written by Michael Ondaatje and representative of Postcolonialism, is published.

1994: Eugène Ionesco, author representative of Absurdism, dies.

1994: *Breath, Eyes, Memory*, written by Edwidge Danticat and representative of Postcolonialism, is published.

1997: William Burroughs, author representative of the Beat Movement, dies.

1997: Allen Ginsberg, author representative of the Beat Movement, dies.

1999: *Disgrace*, written by J. M. Coetzee and representative of Postcolonialism, is published.

2001: Gregory Corso, author representative of the Beat Movement, dies.

Acknowledgments

The editors wish to thank the copyright holders of the excerpted criticism included in this volume and the permissions managers of many book and magazine publishing companies for assisting us in securing reproduction rights. We are also grateful to the staffs of the Detroit Public Library, the Library of Congress, the University of Detroit Mercy Library, Wayne State University Purdy/Kresge Library Complex, and the University of Michigan Libraries for making their resources available to us. Following is a list of the copyright holders who have granted us permission to reproduce material in this volume of ***Literary Movements for Students (LMfS)***. Every effort has been made to trace copyright, but if omissions have been made, please let us know.

COPYRIGHTED MATERIALS IN LMfS, *VOLUMES 1 and 2, WERE REPRODUCED FROM THE FOLLOWING PERIODICALS:*

Forum for Modern Language Studies, v. XXIX, January, 1993 for "Magic Realism: A Typology," by William Spindler. © Forum for Modern Language Studies 1993. All rights reserved. Reproduced by permission of Oxford University Press and the author.—***Harvard Theological Review***, v. 84, April, 1991. Copyright © 1991 by the President and Fellows of Harvard College. Reproduced by permission.—***The Journal of Men's Studies***, v. 3, May, 1995. © 1995 by the Men's Studies Press. All rights reserved. Reproduced by permission.—Charles A. Carpenter, "'Victims of Duty'? The Critics, Absurdity, and 'The Homecoming'," in ***Modern Drama***, Vol. XXV, December, 1982, pp. 489–95. © 1982 University of Toronto, Graduate Centre for Study of Drama. Reproduced by permission.—***Yale French Studies***, May, 1964 for "The Significance of Surrealism" by Henri Peyre; May, 1967 for "New Critics and Old Myths" by Serge Doubrovsky; May 1967 for "The Classicism of the Classics," by Jean Hytier. Copyright © 1964, 1967. Reproduced by permission of the publisher and the respective authors.

COPYRIGHTED MATERIALS IN LMfS, *VOLUMES 1 and 2, WERE REPRODUCED FROM THE FOLLOWING BOOKS:*

Arnott, Peter D. From ***Public and Performance in the Greek Theatre***. Routledge, 1989. © 1989 Peter D. Arnott. All rights reserved. Reproduced by permission.—Byerly, Alison. From ***Realism, Representation, and the Arts in Nineteenth-Century Literature***. Cambridge University Press, 1997. © Alison Byerly 1997. Reproduced by permission.—Chenieux-Gendron, Jacqueline. From "Prohibition and Meaning," in ***Surrealism***. Translated by Vivian Folkenflik. Columbia University Press, 1990. Copyright © 1990 Columbia University Press. All rights reserved. Reproduced by permission.—Clements, Patricia. From ***Baudelaire & The English Tradition***. Princeton University Press, 1985. Copyright © 1985 by Princeton University Press. Reproduced by permission.—Cooper, David E. From ***Existentialism: A Reconstruction***. Basil Blackwell, 1990. Copyright © David E. Cooper 1990. All rights reserved. Reproduced by permission.—Doody, Margaret Anne. From "Sensuousness in the Poetry of Eighteenth-Century Women Poets," in ***Women's Poetry in the Enlightenment: The Making of a Canon, 1730-1820***. Edited by Isobel Armstrong and Virginia Blain. Macmillan Press Ltd., 1999. © Macmillan Press Ltd. 1999. All rights reserved. Reproduced by permission.—Hall, Jr., Vernon. From ***Renaissance Literary Criticism: A Study of Its Social Content***. Columbia University Press, 1945. Copyright, 1945, by Columbia University Press. Reprinted by permission.—Hunter, G. K. From "The Beginnings of Elizabethan Drama: Revolution and Continuity," in ***Renaissance Drama: Renaissance Drama and Cultural Change***. Edited by Mary Beth Rose. Northwestern University Press, 1986. Copyright © 1986 by Northwestern University Press. All rights reserved. Reproduced by permission.—Koster, Donald N. From ***Transcendentalism in America***. Twayne Publishers, 1975. Copyright © 1975 by G. K. Hall & Co. All rights reserved. Reproduced by permission.—Krupat, Arnold. From "Postcolonialism, Ideology, and Native American Literature," in ***Postcolonial Theory and the United States: Race, Ethnicity, and Literature***. Edited by Amritjit Singh and Peter Schmidt. University Press of Mississippi, 2000. Copyright © 2000 by University Press of Mississippi. All rights reserved. Reproduced by permission.—Loomba, Ania. From ***Colonialism/Postcolonialism***. Routledge, 1998. © 1998 Ania Loomba. All rights reserved. Reproduced by permission.—Loomis, Roger Sherman. From "A Defense of Naturalism," in ***Documents of Modern Literary Realism***. Edited by George J. Becker. Princeton University Press, 1963. Copyright © 1963 by Princeton University Press. All rights reserved. Reproduced by permission.—MacAndrew, Elizabeth. From ***The Gothic Tradition in Fiction***. Columbia University Press, 1979. Copyright © 1979 Columbia University Press. All rights reserved. Reproduced by permission.—Martindale, Joanna. From "Introduction," in ***English Humanism: Wyatt to Cowley***. Croom Helm, 1985. © 1985 Joanna Martindale. Reproduced by permission.—Martines, Lauro. From "The Italian Renaissance," in ***The Meaning of the Renaissance and Reformation***. Edited by Richard L. DeMolen. Houghton Mifflin Company, 1974. Copyright © 1974 by Houghton Mifflin Company. All rights reserved. Reproduced by permission.—McCaffery, Larry. From "Introduction," in ***Postmodern Fiction: A Bio-Bibliographical Guide***. Edited by Larry McCaffery. Greenwood Press, 1986. Copyright © 1986 by Larry McCaffery. All rights reserved. Reproduced by permission.—Parrinder, Patrick. From "Science Fiction: Metaphor, Myth or Prophecy," in ***Science Fiction, Critical Frontiers***. Edited by Karen Sayer and John Moore. Macmillan Press Ltd., 2000. © Patrick Parrinder 2000. All rights reserved. Reproduced by permission of the author.—Perkins, David. From ***A History of Modern Poetry: From the 1890s to the High Modernist Mode***. The Belknap Press, 1976. Copyright © 1976 by the President and Fellows of Harvard College. All rights reserved. Reproduced by permission.—Perry, Margaret. From ***Silence to the Drums: A Survey of the Literature of the Harlem Renaissance***. Greenwood Press, 1976. Copyright © 1976 by Margaret Perry. All rights reserved. Reproduced by permission.—Ritchie, J. M. From ***German Expressionist Drama***. Twayne Publishers, 1976. Copyright © 1976 by G. K. Hall & Co. All rights reserved. Reproduced by permission.—Roberts, Adam. From ***Science Fiction***. Routledge, 2000. © 2000 Adam Roberts. All rights reserved. Reproduced by permission.—Sheppard, Richard. From "The Problematics of European Modernism," in ***Theorizing Modernism: Essays in Critical Theory***. Edited by Steve Giles. Routledge, 1993. © 1993 by Richard Sheppard. All rights reserved. Reproduced by permission.—Sitter, John. From "About Wit: 'Locke, Addison, Prior, and the Order of Things'," in ***Rhetorics of Order: Ordering Rhetorics in English Neoclassical Literature***. Edited by J. Douglas Canfield and J. Paul Hunter. University of Delaware Press, 1989. © 1989 by Associated University Presses, Inc. All rights reserved. Reproduced by permission.—Smith, Molly. From ***Breaking Boundaries: Politics and Play in the Drama of Shakespeare and his Contemporaries***. Ashgate Publishing Ltd., 1998. © Molly Smith, 1998. All rights reserved. Reproduced by permission.—Swales, Martin. From ***Irony and the Novel: Reflections on the German Bildungsroman***, at inaugural lecture, University College London, February 9, 1978. Reproduced by permission.—Tanner, Tony. From ***The Reign of Wonder: Naiveté and Reality in American Literature***. Cambridge University Press, 1965. © Cambridge University Press 1965. Reproduced by permission.—Wellek, Rene. From ***Discriminations: Further Concepts of Criticism***. Yale University Press, 1970. Copyright © 1970 by Yale University. All rights reserved. Reproduced by permission.—Windeatt, Barry. From "Introduction," in ***English Mystics of the Middle***

Ages. Cambridge University Press, 1994. © Cambridge University Press 1994. Reproduced by permission.—Wolfson, Susan J. From "The Language of Interpretation in Romantic Poetry: 'A Strong Working of the Mind'," in ***Romanticism and Language***. Cornell University Press, 1984. Copyright © 1984 by Cornell University. All rights reserved. Reproduced by permission.

PHOTOGRAPHS AND ILLUSTRATIONS APPEARING IN LMfS, *VOLUME 1 and 2, WERE RECEIVED FROM THE FOLLOWING SOURCES:*

16th century printing shop showing engravers and hand-operated printing presses, Illustration. © Hilton-Deutsch Collection/Corbis. Reproduced by permission.—Albee, Edward, photograph. © Jerry Bauer. Reproduced by permission.—Allende, Isabel, photograph. Archive Photos. Reproduced by permission.—Anatomical chart created by Leonardo da Vinci, illustration. Corbis Corporation. Reproduced by permission.—Ancient Greek actors wearing masks and dressing as old men, "In Camei," written on image, copper engraving from antique cameo. © Bettmann/Corbis. Reproduced by permission.—Aragon, Louis, photograph. The Library of Congress.—Asimov, Isaac, photograph. AP/Wide World Photos. Reproduced by permission.—Asturias, Miguel Angel, 1967, photograph. Archive Photos, Inc. Reproduced by permission.—Autographed photograph of surrealist poets (left to right) Andre Breton, Paul Eluard, Tristan Tzara, and Benjamin Peret. Corbis Corporation. Reproduced by permission.—Barge arriving at Greenwich Palace along the Thames, during reign of Charles I, photograph. Hulton/Archive. Reproduced by permission.—Barthelme, Donald, photograph by Jerry Bauer. © Jerry Bauer. Reproduced by permission.—Blake, William, illustrator. From an illustration in ***William Blake at the Huntington***, by Robert N. Essick. Harry N. Abrams Inc., Publishers, and The Henry E. Huntington Library and Art Gallery, 1994. Copyright © 1994 The Henry E. Huntington Library and Art Gallery.—Book illustration from 1887 edition of ***The Rime of the Ancient Mariner***, written by Samuel Taylor Coleridge, 19th Century Art. © Corbis. Reproduced by permission.—Burroughs, William S., sitting during filming of movie with same title as his Beat Movement book, ***Naked Lunch***, photograph. The Kobal Collection. Reproduced by permission. —Byron, Lord George Gordon, illustration. The Bettmann Archive. Reproduced by permission.—Carpentier, Alejo, photograph. © Jerry Bauer. Reproduced by permission.—Clemens, Samuel, photograph. AP/Wide World Photos. Reproduced by permission.—Clift, Montgomery and Shelley Winters in the film "A Place in the Sun," 1951, photograph. The Kobal Collection. Reproduced by permission.—Corrected proof for "The Waste Land" from "T. S. Eliot's 'The Waste Land': A Facsimile and Transcript of the Original," edited by Valerie Eliot.—Cover of ***The Red Badge of Courage***, by Stephen Crane. Bantam Books, 1983. Reproduced by permission of Bantam Books, a division of Random House, Inc.—Dali, Salvador, surrealist painter, painting for New York, Chicago, and Paris exhibitions, Riviera, France, photograph. © Bettmann/Corbis. Reproduced by permission.—de Beauvoir, Simone, photograph. AP/Wide World Photos. Reproduced by permission.—Debussy, Claude, photograph. Archive Photos, Inc. Reproduced by permission.—Defoe, Daniel, photograph. Archive Photos, Inc. Reproduced by permission.—Detail from "The Congo," painting by Fritz Klingelhofer. From a cover of ***The Heart of Darkness***, by Joseph Conrad. J. M. Dent, 1996. Reproduced by permission of Christie's Images, London.—Detail showing Plato and Aristotle from "The School of Athens," painting by Raphael, ca. 16th century art. © Ted Spiegel/Corbis. Reproduced by permission.—Doolittle, Hilda, 1949, photograph. AP/Wide World Photos. Reproduced by permission.—Dostoevski, Fyodor Mikhailovich, photograph. The Library of Congress.—"The Dreadful Plague in London, 1665," engraving. Hulton Archive/Getty Images. Reproduced by permission.—East Harlem street, photograph. Corbis Corporation. Reproduced by permission.—Emerson, Ralph Waldo, photograph. UPI/Corbis-Bettmann. Reproduced by permission.—Emperor Napoleon I, painting. Musee de Versailles. Reproduced by permission.—Erasmus, Desiderius, painting.—Exterior view of Lafayette Theatre in Harlem, 7th Avenue between 131st and 132nd Streets, photograph. Corbis. Reproduced by permission.—Fletcher, John Gould, photograph. AP/Wide World Photos. Reproduced by permission.—Frederic W. Pailthorpe illustrator. From ***Great Expectations***, by Charles Dickens. Dodd, Mead & Company, 1942.—French soldier falling after being shot in no-man's-land near Verdun, c. 1916, photograph. © Hulton-Deutsch Collection/Corbis. Reproduced by permission.—Frontispiece containing beginning text from an edition of "Endymion," poem written by John Keats. © Archivo Iconografico, S.A./Corbis. Reproduced by permission.—Fuller, Margaret, painting by John

Plumbe. The Library of Congress.—Gaslight Poetry Cafe, New York, New York, photograph. © Bettmann/Corbis. Reproduced by permission.—Ginsberg, Allen, reads poetry to a crowd after New York Supreme Court decision allowed poets to give uncensored readings in public parks, Washington Square Park, New York, New York, photograph. AP/Wide World Photos. Reproduced by permission.—Globe Theatre (exterior view showing windows, banners, crowds in front), illustration. © The Folger Shakespeare Library. Reproduced by permission of the Folger Shakespeare Library.—Globe Theatre, view of Southwark on the Thames River in the 16th century, illustration by Wenceslaus Hollar (1647). © The Folger Shakespeare Library. Reproduced by permission of the Folger Shakespeare Library.—Goethe, Johann Wolfgang von, photograph. Archive Photos. Reproduced by permission.—Gutenberg Printed Bible on Display, photograph. © Bettmann/Corbis. Reproduced by permission.—Haggard, H. R., photograph. The Library of Congress.—Hassett, Marilyn, in the film "The Bell Jar," by Sylvia Plath, photograph. The Kobal Collection. Reproduced by permission.—Havel, Vaclav, photograph. AP/Wide World Photos. Reproduced by permission.—Hollywood's idea of human cloning, as seen in the 1931 movie "Frankenstein," photograph. Corbis-Bettmann. Reproduced by permission.—Hughes, Langston, photograph by Nickolas Muray. Archive Photos. Reproduced by permission.—Hume, David, portrait engraving. © Corbis. Reproduced by permission.—"The Hunter (Catalan Landscape)," 1923–1924, oil on canvas, painting by Joan Miro. The Museum of Modern Art, New York. © 1999 The Museum of Modern Art, New York. © Artists Rights Society (ARS), New York/ADAGP, Paris. Reproduced by permission of The Museum of Modern Art, New York, and Artists Rights Society, Inc.—Hurston, Zora Neale, photograph. AP/Wide World Photos. Reproduced by permission.—Huston, Anjelica, and Donal Donnelly in the film "The Dead," 1987, photograph. The Kobal Collection. Reproduced by permission.—An illustration of "The Temptation of Ambrosio," from Matthew Gregory Lewis, ***The Monk***, photograph.—Image of "Utopia" from the March 1518 edition printed in ***Basel*** by John Froben, woodcut by Ambrosius Holbein (brother of Hans Holbein the Younger). W.W. Norton & Company, Inc. Reproduced by permission.—Jesus Christ presenting St. Catherine of Siena with crown while God and angels observe from above, painting by Pier Francesco Bissolo. © Hulton Getty/Liaison Agency. Reproduced by permission.—Johnson, Samuel, engraving. Archive Photos, Inc. Reproduced by permission.—Jonson, Ben, portrait, on frontispiece to 1616 edition of his works, 17th century art. Hulton/Archive. Reproduced by permission.—Kafka, Franz, photograph. AP/Wide World Photos. Reproduced by permission.—Kerouac, Jack, photograph. © Jerry Bauer. Reproduced by permission.—Kipling, Rudyard, photograph. Archive Photos, Inc. Reproduced by permission.—Lithgow, John, as Don Quixote, riding with Bob Hoskins (on donkey), as Sancho Panza, in a scene from the television movie "Don Quixote," photograph. AP/Wide World Photos. Reproduced by permission.—London, Jack, photograph. The Library of Congress.—Maeterlinck, Maurice, photograph. AP/Wide World Photos. Reproduced by permission.—Maupassant, Guy de, photograph.—"Mayan Women," painting by Roberto Montenegro. © Archivo Iconografico, S.A./ Corbis. Reproduced by permission.—McKellen, Ian, as Gandalf the White, wearing wizard hat, scene from the film version of J. R. R. Tolkien's novel ***The Lord of the Rings: The Fellowship of the Ring***, directed by Peter Jackson, photograph. The Kobal Collection. Reproduced by permission.—Men standing next to gun carriages loaded with defenses during time of Paris Commune, insurrectionary government formed at the end of the Franco-Prussian War, probably Paris, France, photograph. © Hilton-Deutsch Collection/Corbis. Reproduced by permission.—Moreau, Gustave, "The Apparition." c. 1874–1876. Oil on canvas. Musee Gustave Moreau, Paris. The Art Archive/Dagli Orti.—Muckross House, Killarney, Ireland, photograph. © Dave G. Houser/Corbis. Reproduced by permission.—"Non White Shop" sign above door, 1973, Johannesburg, South Africa, photograph. AP/Wide World Photos, Inc. Reproduced by permission.—Palin, Nicki. From a cover of ***The Iliad***. Retold by Barbara Leonie Picard. Oxford, 1992. Copyright © Oxford University Press 1960. All rights reserved. Reproduced by permission of Oxford University Press.—People surrounding throne seat, manuscript illustration, text image, 14th Century, medieval Italian, photograph. © Historical Picture Archive/Corbis. Reproduced by permission.—Poe, Edgar Allan, photograph. Corbis-Bettmann. Reproduced by permission.—Poet's Corner, Westminster Abbey, London, England, UK, photograph. © Bettmann/Corbis. Reproduced by permission.—Pound, Ezra, photograph. Archive Photos. Reproduced by permission.—Procession of flagellants wearing conical hats, carrying statue of Virgin Mary, painting. © Archivo Iconografico,

S.A./Corbis. Reproduced by permission.—Queen Victoria, 1897, photograph. Archive Photos, Inc./ Popperfoto. Reproduced by permission.—Racine, Jean, lithograph. The Library of Congress.—Robeson, Paul, as Brutus Jones, throwing his hands up, surrounded by ghosts, scene from the 1933 film "The Emperor Jones," photograph. © Underwood & Underwood/Corbis. Reproduced by permission.—Rousseau, Jean Jacques, photograph. AP/ Wide World Photos. Reproduced by permission.—Ruins of ancient Greek theater, Taormina, Sicily, Italy, photograph. © Michael Maslan Historic Photographs/Corbis. Reproduced by permission.—Ruins of orchestra of Greek Theater and arena of Roman Amphitheater, Cyrene, Libya, photograph. © Roger Wood/Corbis. Reproduced by permission.—Ruins of the Parthenon, atop the Acropolis, Athens, Greece, photograph by Susan D. Rock. Rock. Reproduced by permission.—Rushdie, Salman, holding ***Satanic Verses***, photograph. AP/ Wide World Photos. Reproduced by permission.—Russian peasants, photograph. Corbis-Bettmann. Reproduced by permission.—Said, Edward, Professor, photograph. UPI/Corbis Bettmann. Reproduced by permission.—Scene from the film "2001: A Space Odyssey," photograph. The Kobal Collection. Reproduced by permission.—Scene from the Science Fiction and Fantasy film "Brazil," directed by Terry Gilliam, photograph. The Kobal Collection. Reproduced by permission.—Scene from the theatrical production of "Waiting for Godot," play written by Samuel Beckett, at Lyric Theatre, Hammersmith, London, England, UK, photograph. © Robbie Jack/Corbis. Reproduced by permission.—Sculpture of a Greek Theater Mask, Castle of St. Peter, Bodrum, Turkey, photograph. © Chris Hellier/Corbis. Reproduced by permission.—"Self-Portrait with Black Clay Vase and Spread Fingers," painting by Egon Schiele. Archivo Iconografico, S.A./Corbis. Reproduced by permission.—Shelley, Mary Wollstonecraft, illustration. Corbis-Bettmann. Reproduced by permission.—Statue of Daniel O'Connell, O'Connell Street, Dublin, Ireland, photograph. © David Reed/Corbis. Reproduced by permission.—Strindberg, August, painting by Richard Bergh. The Bettman Archive. Reproduced by permission.—Title page from ***The Plays of Christopher Marlowe***, photograph. © Archivo Iconografico, S.A./ Corbis. Reproduced by permission.—Title page of "Encyclopedia," 1751, Editor, Diderot, Denis, photograph. The Library of Congress.—Vergil, drawing. Archive Photos, Inc. Reproduced by permission.—Verne, Jules, 1904, photograph.—Voltaire, French author, holding literary and scientific discussion, illustration. © Bettmann/Corbis. Reproduced by permission.—Vonnegut, Kurt, New York City, 1979, photograph. AP/Wide World Photos. Reproduced by permission.—W.C. Fields, with unknown children and woman, Freddie Bartholomew and Elsa Lanchester, photograph. The Kobal Collection. Reproduced by permission.—Walden Pond, view from Henry David Thoreau's hut, Lincoln, Massachusetts, photograph. © Bettmann/Corbis. Reproduced by permission.—Wedekind, Frank, photograph. Hulton-Deutsch Collection/Corbis-Bettmann. Reproduced by permission.—Whitman, Walt. From a cover of ***Song of Myself: Walt Whitman***. Shambhala, 1993. Cover art courtesy of the Yale Collection of American Literature, Beinecke Library; Yale University. Reproduced by permission of Shambhala Publications, Inc.—Williams, William Carlos, photograph. Archive Photos, Inc. Reproduced by permission.—Winfrey, Oprah with Kimberly Elise and Thandie Newton in scene from "Beloved," photograph. Fotos International/Archive Photos. Reproduced by permission.—Woodcut print of "A Dance of Death," from "Liber Chronicarum," compiled by Hartmann Schedel, photograph. © Historical Picture Archive/Corbis. Reproduced by Corbis Corporation.—Woolf, Virginia, photograph. © Hulton-Deutsch Collection/Corbis. Reproduced by permission.—Young girl standing by a power loom, photograph. National Archives and Records Administration.—Zola, Emile, photograph. AP/Wide World Photos. Reproduced by permission.

Contributors

Diane Andrews Henningfeld: Andrews Henningfeld is a professor of English literature and composition who has written extensively for educational and academic publishers. Entry on Gothic Literature. Original essay on Gothic Literature.

Bryan Aubrey: Aubrey holds a Ph.D. in English and has published many articles on mystical literature. Entry on the Medieval Mystics. Original essay on the Medieval Mystics.

Greg Barnhisel: Barnhisel directs the Writing Center at the University of Southern California in Los Angeles. Entry on Modernism. Original essay on Modernism.

Liz Brent: Brent has a Ph.D. in American culture and works as a freelance writer. Entries on Realism and Symbolism. Original essays on Realism and Symbolism.

Jennifer Bussey: Bussey holds a master's degree in interdisciplinary studies and a bachelor's degree in English literature. She is an independent writer specializing in literature. Entries on the Enlightenment and Naturalism. Original essays on the Enlightenment and Naturalism.

Suzanne Dewsbury: Dewsbury is a writer and instructor of English and American Studies. Entry on Absurdism. Original essay on Absurdism.

Carole Hamilton: Hamilton is an English teacher at Cary Academy in North Carolina. Entry on Humanism. Original essay on Humanism.

Joyce Hart: Hart has degrees in English literature with a minor in Asian studies and focuses her writing on literary topics. Entry on Imagism. Original essay on Imagism.

Pamela Steed Hill: Hill is the author of a poetry collection, has published widely in literary journals, and is an editor for a university publications department. Entry on the Beat Movement. Original essay on the Beat Movement.

Beth Kattelman: Kattelman holds a Ph.D. in theatre from Ohio State University. Entry on Elizabethan Drama. Original essay on Elizabethan Drama.

David Kelly: Kelly is a professor of literature and creative writing at Oakton Community College and College of Lake County and has written for numerous scholarly publications. Entry on Existentialism. Original essay on Existentialism.

Lois Kerschen: Kerschen is a freelance writer and the director of a charitable foundation for children. Entry on the Bildungsroman. Original essay on the Bildungsroman.

Judi Ketteler: Ketteler has taught literature and composition. Entry on Transcendentalism. Original essay on Transcendentalism.

Rena Korb: Korb has a master's degree in English literature and creative writing and has written for a wide variety of educational publishers. Entry on Greek Drama. Original essay on Greek Drama.

Laura Kryhoski: Kryhoski is currently employed as a freelance writer. Entries on Classicism and Neoclassicism. Original essays on Classicism and Neoclassicism.

Carl Mowery: Mowery holds a Ph.D. in composition and literature from Southern Illinois University. Entry on Postmodernism. Original essay on Postmodernism.

Doreen Piano: Piano is a Ph.D. candidate in English at Bowling Green University in Ohio. Entry on Magic Realism. Original essay on Magic Realism.

Ryan D. Poquette: Poquette has a bachelor's degree in English and specializes in writing about literature. Entries on Renaissance Literature, Science Fiction and Fantasy Literature, and Surrealism. Original essays on Renaissance Literature, Science Fiction and Fantasy Literature, and Surrealism.

Susan Sanderson: Sanderson holds a Master of Fine Arts degree in fiction writing and is an independent writer. Entry on the Harlem Renaissance. Original essay on the Harlem Renaissance.

Chris Semansky: Semansky holds a Ph.D. in English from the State University of New York at Stony Brook, and he is an instructor of literature and writing whose essays, poems, stories, and reviews appear in publications such as *College English, Mississippi Review, New York Tribune, The Oregonian,* and *American Letters & Commentary.* His books include *Death, But at a Good Price,* (1991) and *Blindsided* (1998). Entries on Expressionism and Postcolonialism. Original essays on Expressionism and Postcolonialism.

Shaun Strohmer: Strohmer holds a Ph.D. in English from the University of Michigan and is an independent scholar, freelance writer, and editor. Entry on Colonialism. Original essay on Colonialism.

Kelly Winters: Winters is a freelance writer. Entry on Romanticism. Original essay on Romanticism.

Absurdism

Movement Origin

c. 1950

Absurdism, and its more specific companion term Theatre of the Absurd, refers to the works of a group of Western European and American dramatists writing and producing plays in the 1950s and early 1960s. The term "Theatre of the Absurd" was coined by critic Martin Esslin, who identified common features of a new style of drama that seemed to ignore theatrical conventions and thwart audience expectations. Characterized by a departure from realistic characters and situations, the plays offer no clear notion of the time or place in which the action occurs. Characters are often nameless and seem interchangeable. Events are completely outside the realm of rational motivation and may have a nightmarish quality commonly associated with Surrealism (a post-World War I movement that features dream sequences and images from the unconscious, often sexual in nature). At other times, both dialogue and incidents may appear to the audience as completely nonsensical, even farcical. However, beneath the surface the works explore themes of loneliness and isolation, of the failure of individuals to connect with others in any meaningful way, and of the senselessness and absurdity of life and death.

The writers most commonly associated with Absurdism are Samuel Beckett, Eugène Ionesco, Jean Genet, Arthur Adamov, Harold Pinter, and Edward Albee, as well as a number of lesser-known dramatists. The avant-garde nature of absurdist writing contributed in part to its short life as a literary movement. Features of the plays that seemed

completely new and mystifying to audiences in the 1950s when absurdist works first appeared, soon became not only understandable, but even commonplace and predictable. With the exception of Ionesco, most playwrights abandoned the absurdist style after the 1960s; however, many of the individual plays are now considered classics of European and American drama.

Representative Authors

Arthur Adamov (1908–1970)

Arthur Adamov was born August 23, 1908, in Kislovodsk, Russia, to Sourene and Helene Bagatourov Adamov, wealthy Armenians who were in the oil business. The family moved to Paris when Adamov was twelve, and he was educated in Switzerland and Germany. Although he wrote poetry, essays, and an autobiography, Adamov is most famous as a playwright. In the early part of his writing career, he was associated with Surrealism and Absurdism. His plays, written in French, focused on the loneliness and isolation of all humans, on the limited ability of individuals to make meaningful connections with others, and on the inevitable and meaningless nature of death. His most famous play from this period of his life is *Le ping-pong* (1955; translated as *Ping-Pong* in 1959). After the mid-1950s, Adamov rejected Absurdism and began writing plays that were more realistic, more optimistic, and more concerned with individuals in social and political contexts. As he revealed in his autobiographical writings, he was plagued by guilt and neuroses all his life. He drank heavily and towards the end of his life his mental and physical health failed to the point where he could no longer work. He died March 16, 1970, from an overdose of barbiturates.

Edward Albee (1928–)

Edward Albee was born on March 12, 1928, in Virginia, to unknown parents who gave him up for adoption shortly after his birth. His adoptive father was Reed Albee, who owned part of the Keith-Albee theater circuit, and his adoptive mother was the former Frances Cotter. Albee was raised in a wealthy home in Larchmont, New York, with his parents and his grandmother. He made frequent trips to the city to attend the theater during his childhood, and his parents often hosted a variety of theater people in their home. Albee attended Trinity College in Hartford, Connecticut, in 1946-47, but did not earn a degree. He wrote poetry in the early part of his career, but with little success. He turned to drama and in 1958 published his one-act play *The Zoo Story*, which premiered the following year in Berlin and shortly thereafter in New York. In 1959, Albee wrote *The Sandbox* and in 1961, *The American Dream*, both of which opened in New York during 1960-61. Although Albee has written many more plays, these first three are the ones critics generally associate with the Theatre of the Absurd. All three are spare, single-act dramas featuring few characters and are concerned with the isolation of the individual and the artificial nature of American values. Albee's dramas have received numerous awards, among them three Pulitzer Prizes: in 1967 for *A Delicate Balance*, in 1975 for *Seascape*, and in 1994 for *Three Tall Women*.

Fernando Arrabal (1932–)

Fernando Arrabal was born in Melilla, Morocco, on August 11, 1932, to Fernando and Carmen Teran Arrabal Ruiz. As a child, Arrabal lived in Spain in the early days of the reign of Francisco Franco, the fascist dictator. He was educated at the University of Madrid, and in 1958 he married a professor, Luce Moreau; the couple had two children. In 1967, Arrabal was imprisoned in Spain for his political views. His release was accomplished through the efforts of P.E.N., an international organization of writers. Although Arrabal's work was strongly influenced by Surrealism and Absurdism, the designation with which he preferred to describe his drama was "Theatre of Panic." His work has a nightmarish quality involving insanity, brutal violence, and sadistic sexuality. He is noted for creating gentle, child-like characters who are paradoxically responsible for the most unspeakable acts of brutality and degradation.

Samuel Beckett (1906–1989)

Nobel Prize winner Samuel Beckett was born in Foxrock, Dublin, Ireland, on April 13, 1906, to William Frank Beckett, a surveyor, and Mary Jones Roe Beckett, a nurse. He attended a Protestant public school and earned a bachelor of arts degree from Trinity College in 1927 and a masters of arts degree in 1931. Although Beckett taught for a short time, he hated the teaching profession and soon resigned his position. He began traveling in Europe and eventually settled in Paris in 1937. Beckett did most of his writing in French; his work included poetry, critical essays, and novels. However, he is perhaps most famous for his dramas, particularly his masterpiece *Waiting for Godot* (1954), consid-

Edward Albee

ered by many critics the defining work of Absurdism. The two-act play presents two men who engage in apparently pointless conversation while waiting by the side of the road for Godot, who fails to appear on two successive evenings. It is a play in which virtually nothing happens. The same could be said of Beckett's 1957 play *Endgame*, considered by some critics an even bleaker view of human existence than *Waiting for Godot*. Beckett continued to write plays, novels, and other prose works into his eighties; he died in Paris on December 22, 1989, of respiratory failure.

Jean Genet (1910–1986)

Jean Genet was born in Paris on December 19, 1910, to an unknown father and a mother who immediately abandoned him. His early years were spent in an orphanage, and he was later turned over to a foster family, who accused him of stealing from them. He spent some time in a reformatory for adolescents from which he escaped; he then joined the French Foreign Legion, from which he deserted. He wandered around Europe for the next twenty years, supporting himself through thievery and prostitution. Genet began writing in prison, where he was serving a life sentence. His supporters in the literary world were eventually able to secure a presidential pardon in 1948, after which Genet devoted himself to his writing, to the arts, and to political activism. He was an admirer of the Black Panther Party and soon became a cult figure, in part because of Jean-Paul Sartre's essay which characterized Genet as a saint and a martyr. Genet's first writing consisted of poetry, novels, and a fictionalized autobiography. In 1947, while still in prison, he wrote his first play, *The Maids* (1947), and after his release he continued writing dramas, many of which became major productions. His most productive and successful period as a playwright was the late 1950s and early 1960s. Beginning in 1970 Genet lived in the Middle East among the members of the Palestinian Liberation Organization (PLO), whose cause he supported. He died in Paris on April 15, 1986, from throat cancer, and his memoirs offering an account of his years with the PLO were published later that year.

Václav Havel (1936–)

Václav Havel, playwright, political dissident, and current president of the Czech Republic, was born in Prague on October 5, 1936, to Václav M. and Bozena Vavreckova Havel. He was educated at a technical school and at Prague's Academy of Art and served in the Czech Army in 1957-59. Throughout the 1960s, Havel worked with theater groups in Czechoslovakia, serving in various capacities from stagehand to playwright-in-residence. He gained success with his early plays, *The Garden Party* and *The Memorandum*, both of which deal with the dehumanizing effects of government bureaucracy. When the former Soviet Union invaded Czechoslovakia in 1968, Havel was imprisoned and his plays were banned. But his international reputation grew as his works were successfully staged outside Czechoslovakia. Within his own country, he became well known as a spokesman for human rights. With the collapse of the Soviet Union in 1989, Havel saw his plays return to the Czech stage; he was elected president of Czechoslovakia (now the Czech Republic) that same year, an office he continued to hold as of 2002.

Eugène Ionesco (1912–1994)

Eugène Ionesco was born in Slatina, Romania, on November 26, 1912. His parents were Eugène, a lawyer, and Marie-Therese Icard Ionesco. He became a French citizen and spent most of his life in Paris. Ionesco was a painter and a playwright; a number of his plays are associated with the Theater of the Absurd, among them *The Bald Soprano* (1950), *The Lesson* (1951), and *Rhinocéros* (1959). Ionesco used black humor to criticize social and political institutions, insisting that the only possible response to an absurd world is laughter. Nonetheless, he claimed he was not an Absurdist, and he preferred the term "Theatre of Derision" to Theatre of the Absurd. One of his favorite targets for derision, especially in his early plays, was language itself, which he considered ineffective in helping individuals communicate and even dangerous and harmful when used to manipulate. Ionesco's work enjoyed great success in the 1950s and 1960s, but his later plays were not as well received. He turned away from drama and began to concentrate on his painting and on publishing his nonfiction. Ionesco died March 28, 1994, in Paris.

Harold Pinter (1930–)

Harold Pinter was born October 10, 1930 in a working-class neighborhood in Hackney, London, England, to Hyman and Frances Pinter. His otherwise happy childhood was marred by the nightly terror of the London air raids during World War II. He attended the Hackney Downs Grammar School where he excelled in acting, writing, and sports. In 1948 he began studying at the Royal Academy of Dramatic Art, and over the next several years he worked as an actor with a variety of repertory companies. In 1957, his first play, *The Room*, was produced in Bristol, England; it was followed by *The Birthday Party* (1958), *The Dumbwaiter* (1959), and numerous other plays, radio and television dramas, and screenplays. Pinter is considered one of the most important playwrights of the post-World War II generation, and his plays have enjoyed success with both audiences and critics.

Representative Works

The American Dream

A long one-act play by Edward Albee, *The American Dream* (1961) targets the artificial values of family life and features plot events that are not only absurd, but grotesque. The main characters are Daddy, who is weak and ineffectual, and Mommy, who is domineering and cruel. All relationships in the play are governed by material considerations. When the couple adopts a baby, or their "bumble of joy" as they call him, they are actually buying him. Mommy and Daddy gradually destroy the baby as they discover he is less than perfect, depriving him of eyes, hands, tongue, sexual organs—every possible means of communicating with others. When the baby dies, the couple frets over the loss of their investment, regretting that he's already been paid for. Albee also uses humor in *The American Dream* to attack the phony language and stage clichés of sentimental theatrical productions. For example, Mommy, describing the cause of Grandma's death, says "It was an offstage rumble, and you know what that means." The play, along with Albee's other early one-act plays (*Zoo Story* and *The Sandbox*), was successful both commercially and critically, although some critics believe all three are too heavily influenced by the work of Ionesco. The three plays were especially well received on American college campuses during the 1960s.

The Bald Soprano

The Bald Soprano, written originally in French (*La cantatrice chauve*) in 1950 and translated into English in 1958, was Eugène Ionesco's first play. It features such absurdist elements as a clock that strikes seventeen and a married couple who fail to recognize each other in a social situation. The Martins are guests at the home of the Smiths. They engage in polite conversation, each feeling they have met before. A series of questions and answers between the two reveals that they live in the same house and are, in fact, husband and wife. Although the dialogue of *The Bald Soprano* has been described as hilariously funny, the play as a whole is considered a tragedy as Ionesco attacks the stilted, artificial quality of language that hinders communication between individuals.

The Chairs

Written in 1952, Eugène Ionesco's *The Chairs* features the breakdown of language as well as one of the playwright's most famous metaphors for absurdity: the multiplication of inanimate objects. As an elderly couple sets up chairs for an invisible audience arriving to hear an important speech, the chairs begin to multiply until they fill the entire stage. Meanwhile, the orator delivering the speech, which the old man has written to convey an important message to the world, is unable to produce anything except guttural sounds. *The Chairs* makes the point that language and communication are illusions; it is one of Ionesco's most highly acclaimed plays.

Endgame

Samuel Beckett's one-act play *Endgame* (1957) is not as famous as *Waiting for Godot*, but is an even darker work dealing with the master/slave relationship. The setting is sparse and claustrophobic, the dialogue is often comic, and the activities of the characters resemble slapstick comedy. Yet overall, the interaction of the principles is characterized by cruelty and bitterness, and the tone of the work, despite its humorous moments, is grim and pessimistic. *Endgame* made its U.S. debut at New York's Cherry Lane Theatre in 1958. The play's reception was mixed; many critics who had praised *Waiting for Godot* were disappointed in the bleak view of humanity Beckett seemed to be presenting in *Endgame*.

The Garden Party

Originally *Zahradni slavnost* (1964), Václav Havel's *The Garden Party* (1969), targets the nature of bureaucracy and its dehumanizing effect on individuals. Havel creates a world where language is not a tool in the service of the individual but rather acts as weapon by which the individual is controlled. The play's main character speaks in clichés and slogans and is unable to accomplish anything within a bureaucratic system that perpetuates itself and defies humans' attempts to intervene in its operation. *The Garden Party* was Havel's first play, and while it was a critical success, it was banned in Czechoslovakia after the Soviet invasion of 1968.

Václav Havel

The Homecoming

Harold Pinter's *The Homecoming*, written in 1965, was the playwright's third full-length drama. The story involves a London working-class family whose eldest son has lived in the United States for several years where he is a professor of philosophy at a university. He returns, along with his wife Ruth, to his father's home, but when he later goes back to the United States, she refuses to accompany him. Instead, she plans to stay behind and care for her husband's father, uncle, and brothers, and to earn her living as a prostitute. The play features several absurdist elements but is also characterized by violence, both emotional and physical, between the family members. *The Homecoming* has generated a great deal of controversy because of the shocking nature of the plot. Critical debate has usually centered on the possible motivation for Ruth's bizarre decision. *The Homecoming* was revived on Broadway in 1991.

The Maids

In Jean Genet's second play, *The Maids*, the writer for the first time explores a world outside the prison, a setting he used in all of his earlier works. The characters are Claire and Solange, maids to an elegant lady who mistreats them. They take turns playacting the roles of mistress and servant whenever the real mistress is away. Fearful that their plot to have their mistress's lover imprisoned is about to be discovered, they determine to poison the lady, but she leaves before they carry out their plan. The two maids lapse into their usual role-playing, and Claire, assuming the part of the mistress, takes the poison and dies in her place. The world represented in the play has been likened to a hall of mirrors, where identities and perceptions are reflected back and forth between characters switching roles between master and servant. Questions of identity and impersonation were further complicated by Genet's insistence that all of the female parts be played by young men. *The Maids* was commissioned and produced by Louis Jouvet in 1947, making it one of the earliest dramas to be associated with the Theatre of the Absurd.

Ping-Pong

Critics consider Arthur Adamov's *Ping-Pong*, originally produced in French in 1955 and translated into English in 1959, the masterpiece of his early absurdist plays, with its emphasis on futility. The play's two characters are young students, Victor and Arthur. Although they are initially studying medicine and art respectively, they become obsessed with every aspect of pinball machines, from the mechanics of their operation to the details of their distribution and maintenance. Reality, including personal relationships, is viewed through possible associations to pinball. At play's end Victor and Arthur appear as old men, close to death, who have wasted their entire lives on their obsession. Although Adamov typically refused to assign a temporal or spatial setting to his early plays, he was more or less forced to do so by the subject matter in this work. Choosing a contemporary pastime like pinball as the centerpiece of the drama necessarily called for a contemporary urban setting. Critics praised *Ping-Pong*, but Adamov himself ultimately rejected it, along with his other absurdist plays. Towards the end of his career, he began writing realist dramas concerned with social and political issues.

Waiting for Godot

The most famous and most critically acclaimed work associated with Absurdism is Samuel Beckett's *Waiting for Godot*, produced in 1953 in Paris as *En Attendant Godot* and translated into English a year later. The setting is sparse, almost vacant, and the characters are two tramps, Vladimir and Estragon, who do little except wait, on two successive nights, for someone who never appears. While waiting they engage in a series of apparently random discussions, some involving philosophy, and a variety of antics—from taking off their shoes to eating a carrot—that seem vaguely reminiscent of a comedy routine or a vaudeville act. They also attempt suicide twice but fail each time. At the end of the play, when Godot has still not appeared, the characters agree to leave, at least according to their limited dialogue, but the stage directions contradict their words by insisting that "they do not move." One of the most important productions of *Waiting for Godot* took place in San Quentin prison in 1957, performed by the members of the San Francisco Actors' Workshop. Several critics have commented on the enthusiastic reception the prisoners gave the play, suggesting that they seemed to instinctively grasp its meaning at the same time audiences apparently more educated and more sophisticated were confused by the play's unconventional nature. Many critics believe *Waiting for Godot* is Beckett's most important work, citing its influence on the Theatre of the Absurd and on contemporary drama in general.

The Zoo Story

Edward Albee wrote his first drama *The Zoo Story* (1959), in three weeks. Uncluttered, even sparse, the play features two characters, working-class Jerry and middle-class Peter, who meet in Central Park. Jerry pours out his life story to Peter, and it is a life characterized by loneliness, alienation, and failure. Peter refuses to connect with Jerry and does not want to hear any more of his tale. Provoking Peter into a fight, Jerry kills himself on a knife he gave to Peter, thus involving him, despite his objections, in another's death if not in his life. Albee employs the diction of small children in *The Zoo Story*, a device he used in many of his later plays. The one-act play won an Obie Award in 1960 and established its author as a promising American playwright.

Themes

Absurdity

Absurdity is the most obvious theme explored in Absurdism. Absurdity characterizes a world that no longer makes sense to its inhabitants, in which rational decisions are impossible and all action is meaningless and futile. Absurdity also describes many situations and events that take place in plays associated with the movement, such as orators who speak in gibberish (*The Chairs*), a clock that strikes seventeen (*The Bald Soprano*), or a rhinoceros that walks across the stage (*Rhinocéros*).

Cruelty and Violence

Beneath the nonsense and slapstick humor of Absurdism lurks an element of cruelty, often revealed in dialogue between characters but occasionally manifested in acts of violence. Pinter's plays are noted for the latter. In *The Room*, a blind man is brutally beaten; in *The Birthday Party*, the celebration becomes an interrogation and eventually an abduction; and in *The Dumb Waiter*, a pair of assassins are involved in an apparently random murder. Similarly, in Ionesco's *The Lesson*, a professor frustrated by his students' inability to understand his meaningless lessons, savagely kills them one after another. The seemingly innocent, child-like characters created by Arrabal engage in unspeakable acts of torture, even murder. On a less physical level is the cruelty hiding behind the apparently humorous dialogue in Beckett's *Endgame*, which features a master/servant relationship in which Hamm dominates Clov. Hamm, in turn, has suffered from the cruelty of his parents when he was a child. His father recounts how the youngster would cry because he was afraid of the dark, and their response, according to the father, was "We let you cry. Then we moved out of earshot, so that we might sleep in peace."

Domination

Several well-known absurdist works feature pairs of characters in which one is the dominator and the other the dominated. Some of these are quite literally master/servant relationships, such as in Genet's *The Maids* or Beckett's *Endgame*. Others reproduce the master/slave relationship within marriage, as in Albee's *The American Dream* where Mommy dominates the spineless Daddy character or within the traditional teacher/student dynamic, as in Ionesco's *The Lesson*.

Futility and Passivity

The futility of all human endeavor characterizes many absurdist works, such as Adamov's *Ping-Pong* in which two promising students abandon their studies and devote their lives to the appreciation of pinball machines. Adamov's earlier play *La Parodie* (1947) shares the idea that individuals are powerless to direct their own lives; it does so by presenting two characters, one who refuses to live and one who embraces life with joy. The fate of both is ultimately exactly the same. Havel's early plays, such as *The Garden Party*, deal with the inability of even the most ambitious individual to make any headway against a self-perpetuating bureaucracy. Beckett's *Waiting for Godot* suggests that human effort is meaningless and leads to nothing in the end. Beckett's characters are so ineffective and doomed to failure that they are unable even to commit suicide successfully despite two attempts.

Media Adaptations

- A video recording of *Waiting for Godot*, featuring Burgess Meredith and Zero Mostel and directed by Alan Schneider, was made for Grove Press Film Division, 1971.
- Eugene Ionesco's *The New Tenant* was filmed for Encyclopedia Britannica Educational Corporation, 1975.
- Jean Genet's *Balcony* is available on videocassette from Mystic Fire, 1998.
- Edward Albee's *Zoo Story* is available on audio CD, Universal Records, 2001.
- *Waiting for Godot*, by Samuel Beckett, is available on audiocassette, featuring a performance by Joe Dinicol for CBC Radio, 2000.
- A website on the Theatre of the Absurd can be found with links to other sites and a chat room at http://vzone.virgin.net/numb.world/rhino.absurd.htm.
- A useful web site on Beckett is "The Samuel Beckett On-Line Resources and Links Page" at http://www.samuel-beckett.net/ which contains numerous reviews and scholarly articles on Beckett's life and work, as well as reviews of books about Beckett.

Their passivity, established by their interminable waiting, is even more famously illustrated by the closing scenes of both first and second acts, in which each stands rooted to his spot on the stage despite having made the decision to leave.

Language

The failure of language to convey meaning is an important theme in the literature of Absurdism. Language is either detached from any interpretation that can be agreed to by all characters, or it is reduced to complete gibberish. A play entitled *The Bald Soprano*, for example, has nothing to do with a soprano, much less a bald one. The standard philosophical discourse is mocked by the nonsensical dialogue in *Godot*; although it is meaningless, it bears a strong resemblance to the structure of the real thing. The language of religious fervor is employed by Adamov in *Ping-Pong*, but the object being venerated is a pinball machine. The characters in Havel's plays speak in clichés and slogans, from which all real meaning has been drained.

Loneliness and Isolation

Many absurdist works illustrate the loneliness and isolation of individuals, resulting from the nature of modern life and, in some cases, from the impossibility of effective communication between humans. Albee's *The Zoo Story* offers a prime example of this theme, featuring a character so eager to make a connection with a complete stranger that he is willing to die in order to do so. If the two men are unable to achieve contact in life, at least the man is able to involve the stranger, however unwillingly, in his death. Ionesco's *The Bald Soprano* explores the same theme with a husband and wife who are so isolated from each other that they fail to recognize their connection in a social setting and have only a vague sense of having met before.

Materialism

Materialism is criticized in Albee's *The American Dream*, where even relationships between family members are subject to the terms of profit and loss statements. A woman marries a man she does not love simply because he is wealthy, and they buy a baby to complete their family. The baby dies, leaving them to mourn their financial loss rather than their emotional loss. Adamov's characters in *Ping-Pong* devote their lives to the worship of a thing, which some critics consider a critique of capitalism and materialism.

Style

Character

Absurdism often abandons traditional character development to offer figures who have no clear identity or distinguishing features. They may even be interchangeable, as are the supporting characters in *Waiting for Godot* who appear as master and servant in the first act and trade places when they return for the second act. Role playing causes confusion among the characters in Genet's *The Maids* where the audience initially thinks the figure onstage is the lady of the house being served by her maid Claire, but then realizes that Claire is impersonating the mistress and the other maid, Solange, is impersonating Claire. These exchanges continue throughout the play which deprives the audience of any stable sense of character identity.

Denouement

In conventional literature or drama, the denouement serves to tie up the loose ends of the narrative, resolving both primary and secondary plot conflicts and complications. Since so little happens in most absurdist works, the denouement has little to resolve. Thus endings tend to be repetitious, such as the nearly identical ending of both acts of *Waiting for Godot*. Such repetitive actions reinforce the idea that human effort is futile, which serves as a prominent theme of Absurdism. In Ionesco's *The Lesson*, which features the murder of a student by a professor, the audience learns that it is the fortieth such murder that day. Since the ending of the play consists of yet another student arriving for yet another lesson, the audience has every reason to believe the newly arrived student will meet the same fate.

Dialogue

Since the ability of language to convey meaning is called into question by Absurdism, dialogue is of special importance in absurdist works. Artificial language, empty of meaning, consisting of slogans and clichés, is a hallmark of the movement. Many of the texts contain dialogue that appears to be meaningless but that mimics the style of educated or sophisticated speech. Often there is a marked contradiction between speech and action, as in *Godot* when the characters claim they are leaving but actually stay.

Plot

Absurdism at its most extreme abandons conventional notions of plot almost entirely. Beckett's *Waiting for Godot* has been described as a play in which nothing happens. Its opening line is "Nothing to be done," and the characters proceed to do just that—nothing. Although the characters do engage in various actions, none of those actions is connected in any meaningful way, nor do the actions develop into any sort of narrative or logical sequence of events.

Setting

The use of setting is one of the most unconventional stylistic features of Absurdism. Typically, an absurdist play will be set in no recognizable time or place. Stage settings tend to be sparse, with lots of vacant space conveying the sense of emptiness associated with characters' lives. The empty chairs of Ionesco's *The Chairs* serves as an example, as does *Waiting for Godot*'s nearly bare stage with a single spindly tree as the only prop. But the setting can also be cramped and confining, such as the claustrophobic single room of Beckett's *Endgame*.

Movement Variations

Philosophy

Absurdism is often linked to Existentialism, the philosophical movement associated with Jean-Paul Sartre and Albert Camus, among others. Although both existentialists and absurdists are concerned with the senselessness of the human condition, the way this concern is expressed differs. The philosophers explored the irrational nature of human existence within the rational and logical framework of conventional philosophical thought. The absurdists, however, abandoned the traditional elements of literature in general and theater in particular—setting, plot, character development—in order to convey a sense of absurdity and illogic in both form and content.

In general, the two movements also differ in the conclusions each seems to draw from the realization that life is meaningless. Many absurdist productions appear to be making a case for the idea that all human effort is futile and action is pointless; others seem to suggest that an absurd existence leaves the individual no choice but to treat it as farce. The existentialists, however, claimed that the realization that life had no transcendental meaning, either derived from faith or from the essence of humanity itself, could (and should) serve as a springboard to action. An individual's life, according to the existentialists, could be made meaningful only through that individual's actions.

Topics for Further Study

- Some critics have referred to situations in absurdist works as "Kafka-esque." Read Franz Kafka's *The Trial* or view the 1962 film adaptation by Orson Welles and determine whether the work fits the category of Absurdism.
- Absurdist works were avant-garde, even shocking, in the 1950s. By the 1980s, however, elements of Absurdism had found their way into music videos, television commercials, and print ads. Find examples of these elements in two or three music videos and/or advertisements and discuss the way the features of Absurdism are being used today.
- The French surrealist filmmaker Luis Buñuel teamed up with surrealist artist Salvador Dali to produce the 1928 film *Un chien andalou* (*An Andalusian Dog*), featuring a scene in which a man drags a pair of pianos filled with dead donkeys across a room. Try to obtain a copy of *An Andalusian Dog* from a public or university library or read about Buñuel's film in *The Branded Eye: Buñuel's Un chien andalou*, by Jenaro Talens, University of Minnesota Press, 1993. How do such surrealistic film scenes compare with Theatre of the Absurd?

Politics and Social Change

Because many absurdist works have no temporal or spatial setting, they are often considered apolitical, that is, they are neither criticizing nor endorsing any country's culture, society, or political system. There are, however, exceptions. Václav Havel's plays, for example, are concerned with the dehumanizing effects of government bureaucracy, particularly within Communist Czechoslovakia. The works apparently hit their target, since the government banned them and imprisoned the playwright. Eugène Ionesco's *Rhinocéros* could also be considered political, since the author claimed that the inspiration for the play was the gradual acceptance of Nazi fascism by an antifascist friend. Based on a 1940 entry in Ionesco's journal, the play opens with a rhinoceros charging past as two friends converse. Although everyone ignores the rhinoceros at first, eventually most of the characters accept its presence, and one by one they even decide to become rhinoceroses themselves. A lone individual is determined to fight the growing herd. Ironically, Ionesco's play varies from the usual plotless, apolitical style of most absurdist dramas to offer a powerful critique of mob mentality and conformity. The individual who decides to fight rather than join the herd is also unusual, since most absurdist characters are anonymous, passive, and ineffectual—certainly not given to heroic actions.

The failure of most absurdist works to call for any meaningful action may also account for the almost total absence of women playwrights involved in the movement. Toby Silverman Zinman, in "Hen in a Foxhouse: The Absurdist Plays of Maria Irene Fornes," suggests that although female dramatists shared the "deep disillusionment" common to most practitioners of Absurdism, most of them were committed to changing the conditions that led to that disillusionment. While they may have employed some of the formal elements associated with Absurdism, they rejected its bleak vision that human effort is futile.

Historical Context

Although the roots of Absurdism can be traced to the beginning of the twentieth century, the movement reached its peak in the years immediately following World War II, a war of catastrophic proportions that saw the armies of fascist Germany overrun most of Europe and the Japanese attack the United States at Pearl Harbor. An estimated 48 million people in Europe were killed and millions more became refugees. Bombs turned cities to rubble. As the Allied Forces liberated the concentration camps at the end of the war, Europeans and Americans were confronted by the enormity of the Holocaust, Germany's final solution for Jews, Gypsies, homosexuals, and political prisoners. Faced with the evidence of evil on such a grand scale, people were often overcome by feelings of pessimism and helplessness. At the same time, the U.S. bombing of Hiroshima and Nagasaki in 1945 introduced the reality of nuclear war and the possibility of a future nuclear disaster that could potentially eliminate all human kind. The change to using nuclear weapons ushered in the Cold War of the 1950s as the United States and the Soviet Union, former allies against Germany, became enemies. The two sides entered into an arms race and began stockpiling nuclear weapons. Thus, the achievement of peace after World War II was clouded by the specter of an even more horrific war to come, and this sense of the future led to feelings of hopelessness and futility.

The continental United States, however, was untouched physically by the war. Returning soldiers were more optimistic than their European counterparts and were anxious to pursue the American Dream. They married in record numbers and began having children, producing the well-known postwar baby boom, lasting from 1946 to 1964. Cities and schools became overcrowded and many urban families, aided by the prosperity of the postwar years, eventually moved to the suburbs.

Women had worked in a variety of jobs during the war, filling in for the men who were fighting overseas and contributing to the war effort by producing weapons and supplies for the troops. The idea of women working in factories was popularized by the poster image of Rosie the Riveter as a capable worker doing her patriotic duty. After the war, however, these same women were encouraged to return to their homes and care for their husbands and children, thereby giving up their places in the job market to the returning soldiers. The nuclear family of husband, stay-at-home wife, and small children living in a single-family home in the suburbs became the 1950s idealization of the American Dream.

In the arts, the social and community concerns of the Depression years and the war years gave way to introspection and individual visions. In some cases, artists began to concentrate on form rather than content. Abstract art—Cubism, Surrealism, Expressionism—with its emphasis on individual expression replaced artistic modes tied to political themes. In Hollywood, the optimistic and patriotic films of the war years were replaced in the late 1940s and early 1950s by *film noir*, a dark, gritty, urban genre that exposed the menacing underside of American life. The Cold War also inspired a host of monster and horror films that served as allegories for potential invasion by a foreign enemy; perhaps the most famous of these was *The Invasion of the Body Snatchers* (1955).

Critical Overview

Some critics trace the roots of Absurdism back to the beginning of the twentieth century, but for most, the movement itself began at mid-century. Ruby Cohn, for instance, makes a claim for 1950—the

Compare & Contrast

- **1950s:** In the midst of the Cold War, Americans are fearful of a nuclear attack by the Soviet Union. Fallout shelters are designed and built, and school children regularly practice "duck and cover" procedures in the event of an air raid.

  Today: After the September 11, 2001, terrorist attacks on New York City and Washington, D.C., many Americans live in fear that terrorists may strike again at any time, anywhere in the country. Security firms offer classes for civilians in how to disarm a potential terrorist on an airplane.

- **1950s:** The Soviet Union and the United States engage in a Cold War as two enemies with nuclear capability, each stockpiling weapons in an attempt to achieve nuclear superiority.

  Today: The Soviet Union has separated into individual countries; the largest of these, Russia, is now an ally of the United States in the space program and in the war against terrorism.

- **1950s:** Soldiers returning from World War II are eager to resume a normal life by marrying and starting families, leading to the postwar baby boom. Prosperity and family life are celebrated in popular culture, particularly television shows like *I Love Lucy*, *Father Knows Best*, and *Leave It to Beaver*, all of which feature stable, nuclear families.

  Today: As women have delayed marriage to concentrate on careers and as the divorce rate skyrockets, television situation comedies are more likely to focus on single life rather than on families consisting of father, mother, and young children. Some examples are *Seinfeld*, *Friends*, and *Will and Grace*.

year Ionesco's *The Bald Soprano* first appeared on the French stage—as the starting point of Theatre of the Absurd. Martin Esslin, who in 1961 identified and labeled the movement, begins with *Waiting for Godot* and many critics follow his lead. Written in 1950 but not staged until 1953, Beckett's most famous drama is also considered by many scholars to be the most representative of the movement. Esslin originally identified three other practitioners of Absurdism: Eugène Ionesco, Jean Genet, and Arthur Adamov, as well as a number of lesser-known playwrights. In later editions of his landmark study, *The Theatre of the Absurd*, Esslin elevated Harold Pinter from minor to major figure and devoted an entire chapter to his plays.

As the scholar who defined the movement, Esslin takes pains to point out that the writers he discusses would not necessarily associate themselves with Absurdism. Many of them, in fact, rejected the label completely; Ionesco preferred Theatre of Derision, and Arrabal chose Theatre of Panic to describe his plays. Esslin acknowledges that of the playwrights he discusses "each has his own personal approach to both subject-matter and form; his own roots, sources, and background." He maintains, however, that at the same time they "in spite of themselves, have a good deal in common." Those common elements are, for Esslin:

> "Pure" theatre; i.e. abstract scenic effects as they are familiar in the circus or revue, in the work of jugglers, acrobats, bullfighters, or mimes
> Clowning, fooling, and mad-scenes
> Verbal nonsense
> The literature of dream and fantasy, which often has a strong allegorical component

There is a certain amount of overlap among these categories, and individual playwrights employ the separate elements in different ways, but all employ them in ways that differ from older theatrical traditions and in ways that made Theatre of the Absurd "shocking and incomprehensible" to its earliest audiences.

That ability to shock theatergoers resulted from the movement's abandonment (or rejection) of traditional plot, character development, setting, dialogue, and denouement. For Esslin, this amounts

A scene from the play Waiting for Godot *written by Samuel Beckett*

to innovation and experimentation and is an indication of an art form's vitality, necessary in a changing world. As he puts it: "Under such conditions no art can survive that complacently falls back on past traditions and standards. Least of all the theatre, which is the most social of the arts and most directly responds to social change." Thus, Esslin views Absurdism as a positive development in the history of the theater.

Where Esslin sees vitality, however, other critics have seen decadence. Avadhesh K. Srivastava in "The Crooked Mirror: Notes on the Theatre of the Absurd," considers Theatre of the Absurd excessively concerned with inward reality "without the stabilizing influence of a moral perspective" and, therefore, decadent. The playwrights identified with the movement, Srivastava claims, have nothing in common with each other except their rejection of traditional theatrical conventions. Their agreement is based on a negative, therefore, "runs counter to the text-book aims of drama. It is neither cathartic nor edificatory; neither suspense nor spectacle." As such, Srivastava suggests that a certain amount of fraud and manipulation is involved. By calling itself theater, Theatre of the Absurd is setting up its audiences to expect something which it then fails to deliver.

Esslin acknowledges that the play that started it all was "scorned as undramatic" originally, but he points to its overwhelming popularity with audiences all over the world and its eventual acceptance by critics, dramatists, and scholars. The same could be said for other plays associated with the Theatre of the Absurd. Although they were initially considered incomprehensible, they soon became familiar and highly acclaimed. While Absurdism itself was short-lived as a movement, its influence, particularly in the realm of popular culture, has continued into the twenty-first century.

Criticism

Suzanne Dewsbury

Dewsbury is a writer and instructor of English and American Studies. In this essay, she examines Absurdism's short life as a formal movement and its long-range effects on Western culture.

Critic Martin Esslin identified the common elements shared by a number of dramatic works of the 1950s and provided the label "Theatre of the Absurd" to those works. At first, audiences found these works incomprehensible; viewers left the theaters not knowing what to make of these plays that defied all the traditional elements of staged drama. The textbook case, Samuel Beckett's *Waiting for Godot*, had no plot, a setting that consisted of only a bare tree, and two characters whose actions resembled slapstick more than theater. It was produced on stage for the first time in 1953, and for the first time in London in 1955 where critics and audiences alike considered it "completely obscure." Nine years later, Esslin reports, *Godot* was revived in London. Although it was generally well received, by this time the work "had one great fault: its meaning and symbolism were a little too obvious." In an age of mass communication, the revolutionary quality of avant-garde art quickly fades. That which shocks the public one minute bores it the next, and this, in part, accounts for the short life-span of Theatre of the Absurd.

Another reason for the movement's demise may be that drama must eventually have a plot. If nothing happens in absurdist productions, there are only so many times a theater audience is willing to attend the staging of nothing. What new observations or insights into nothing are available? Once the point has been made that life is meaningless and all effort is futile, what more can be said? If human endeavor amounts to nothing, if as Esslin puts it, "strenuous effort leads to the same result as passive indolence," then what would be the point of bothering to attend a play or, for that matter, bothering to write one?

Many of the practitioners of Theatre of the Absurd apparently felt the same way since, with few exceptions, they turned to dramas grounded in realist conventions, and to works that offered some possibilities for action. Harold Pinter provides one example. Many of his early works, often associated with Theatre of the Absurd, have been called "comedies of menace," but the source of the menace in question is mysterious and unmotivated. In Pinter's later plays, those written in the 1960s and after, the menace often arises from the desire of certain characters to dominate others. While still complex, these later works are more accessible than those he wrote in the 1950s because they provide recognizable character development and motivation.

Arthur Adamov is another playwright whose works are often divided into two distinct periods, with 1957 as the year of demarcation. Plays written before that date exhibit the characteristics of Surrealism and Absurdism; those written after 1957 are realistic and politically committed. Adamov himself made a formal break with the past and publicly rejected his earlier work that treated the individual as hopeless and helpless in favor of characters with free will.

For all these reasons, Theatre of the Absurd as a formal movement began to dissolve by the early 1960s, but its effects on Western culture, particularly popular culture, endured and are still being felt today. Since the 1960s individual elements of Absurdism have been incorporated with increasing frequency into film, television shows, and music videos.

An early example is Stanley Kubrick's *Dr. Strangelove, or: How I Learned to Stop Worrying and Love the Bomb* (1966), a satiric look at the nuclear arms race. The film's premise is that nuclear weapons have been programmed by both the United States and the Soviet Union in ways that render humans helpless to disarm them. Thus, when an insane American general sets off the signal to

"... Theatre of the Absurd as a formal movement began to dissolve by the early 1960s, but its effects on Western culture, particularly popular culture, endured and are still being felt today."

attack Russia, the U.S. government is powerless to recall the bombers. Russia, meanwhile, has built a doomsday machine that will automatically retaliate with enough force to destroy the world. The only possible purpose of such a device is deterrence, of course, but the Russians have not quite gotten around to telling the world about it—creating an absurd situation that renders human action futile.

The film's dialogue, too, is reminiscent of Absurdism, when Merkin Muffley, the American president, and Dimitri Kissoff, the Soviet premier, discuss the impending end of the world like two petulant children arguing over which of them is more sorry about the situation: "Don't say that you're more sorry, Dimitri, I'm just as capable of being sorry as you are," complains the president. He then has to call Information to get the number for Russia's Air Defense Headquarters in order to provide them with the coordinates to shoot down the B-52s. In yet another absurd situation, when the rogue general has been subdued, the officer who has obtained the code to call off the attack must try to get through to the president on a pay phone. He does not have sufficient change and must call collect; however, the White House refuses to accept the charges. In *Dr. Strangelove* the fate of the world resides in the hands of ineffectual individuals embroiled in absurd situations.

Theatre of the Absurd often employed elements of farce and black humor, and in this sense, the films of Mel Brooks might also be included in its legacy. *The Producers*, originally a film and later a successful Broadway play, treats the horrors of World War II as farce, involving the production of a musical called "Springtime for Hitler." Similarly, Terry Gilliam's *Brazil* (1985) interrupts a brutal torture scene to threaten the victim with an

What Do I Study Next?

- Just as the playwrights of Absurdism rejected existing theatrical traditions, the poet e. e. cummings departed from the norms of traditional poetry with his unconventional use of grammar, syntax, and punctuation. His collection *100 Selected Poems*, published in 1989 by Grove Press, contains such poems as "anyone lived in a pretty how town," "next to of course god america i," and "my sweet old etcetera."
- Some of the most famous images of artist René Magritte, like the green apple or the black bowler hat, are often described as absurdist. Robert Hughes's *The Portable Magritte*, Universe Publishers (2001), provides an illustrated study of Magritte's work.
- Kurt Vonnegut's *Slaughterhouse Five*, Dell Publishing (1969), draws on the author's own experiences as a prisoner of war in the German city of Dresden during the World War II Allied firebombing that killed hundreds of thousands of German civilians. In many ways, the novel shares Absurdism's sense of futility in the wake of mass destruction.
- Many music videos employ the elements of Absurdism, and a number of books are available on music video as a popular art form. Among them are: *Thirty Frames per Second: The Visionary Art of the Music Video* by Steven Reiss, Neil Feineman, and Jeff Ayeroff, Harry N. Abrams, Inc. Publishers (2000); *Rocking Around the Clock: Music Television, Postmodernism, and Consumer Culture* by E. Ann Kaplan, Methuen Drama (1987); and *Dancing in the Distraction Factory: Music Television and Popular Culture* by Andrew Goodwin, University of Minnesota Press (1992).

---

even worse fate, that is, the loss of his credit rating. *Brazil*'s absurdity centers on the meaninglessness of language and the individual's powerlessness against government bureaucracy, much like the plays of Václav Havel. Foolishly optimistic platitudes and double-speak slogans are everywhere in *Brazil*. Individual agencies of the bureaucracy compete rather than cooperate, resulting in the arrest and murder of an innocent citizen.

Although television rarely treats such dark subjects as the Holocaust or government brutality, Matt Groening's long-running animated comedy *The Simpsons* occasionally comes close. Its main character, Homer Simpson, is either ineffectual or farcical, both as a worker and as a family man. Like Beckett's tramps, he spends most of his time doing nothing. When he does act, the results are usually disastrous, suggesting that the consequences of action are even worse than the consequences of passivity. The fact that Homer works with radioactive materials in his job at a nuclear power plant creates the same doomsday scenario as *Dr. Strangelove* with the fate of Springfield in the hands of inept or ineffectual workers in absurd situations.

The Simpsons typically features random visual elements, like toasters that become time machines or animals in unusual contexts that possess attributes not usually associated with their species. Reminiscent of Ionesco's rhinoceros traversing the stage, a huge swordfish lands on the hood of Homer's car as he drives down the street. On another occasion, the family dog is replaced by a killer badger who disembowels Homer. In a segment involving Homer's attempt to become a farmer, an elephant is used as a measuring device to determine the height of the corn crop, in an obvious allusion to the musical *Oklahoma*, however, in this case the elephant is carnivorous. *The Simpsons* recalls Esslin's description of Theatre of the Absurd: "grotesque, frivolous, and irreverent," although the show's more serious fans might argue that the show is never frivolous.

Another television program that evokes the style and themes of Absurdism is the long-running situation comedy *Seinfeld*. The show is set in Manhattan and features four characters: Jerry, George, Elaine, and Kramer, each of whom lives alone. They are less involved in plots than in situations.

In fact, *Seinfeld*'s producers repeatedly described the program as a show about nothing. Little happened to change the characters' lives over the course of several years; much like *Godot*'s tramps, the characters seemed to be hanging out waiting for something to happen to them. The farcical element was provided by Kramer, whose bizarre antics were clownish and slapstick.

The world of popular music adapted many of the features of Absurdism even, or perhaps especially, in the names chosen for groups. In the pop group The Bare-Naked Ladies, there are no ladies, much less bare-naked ones—just as there were no sopranos, much less bald ones, in Ionesco's *The Bald Soprano*. The same might be said for the Violent Femmes and the Dead Milkmen. Absurd names are often assumed by individual artists, such as Jello Biafra, or given to album names, like Primus's *Pork Soda*.

Music videos have long made use of absurdist elements, from the bizarre, seemingly unconnected images of 1980s videos, usually featuring so-called "alternative music," to the more recent efforts of Missy Elliot, where the artist calmly removes her head, or the Crystal Method video in which an inflatable doll turns killer (and the witness explaining the situation to the police is another inflatable doll). Many music videos are very conventional. They consist of mini-narratives, concert footage, or vanity pieces featuring the recording artists in a variety of scenes illustrating conspicuous consumption—expensive clothes, expensive cars, and scantily clad members of the opposite sex. In other videos, bizarre elements, such as props, costumes, and images may be featured, but they are usually loaded with sexual symbolism—making them more a part of the surrealist tradition than the absurdist movement. The videos of Madonna or The Red-Hot Chili Peppers might fit into this category. But in a great many other, more sophisticated music videos, elements of Absurdism abound, but they no longer carry the same meaning, which in Theatre of the Absurd was to point out that there was no meaning. A half-century after the movement's peak, acknowledging life's absurdity seems to be an accepted part of postmodern life. It is no longer particularly disturbing; it just makes for some interesting visual moments. And the popular culture is only too willing to mine the art of the past in order to create those moments.

Source: Suzanne Dewsbury, Critical Essay on Absurdism, in *Literary Movements for Students*, The Gale Group, 2003.

Charles A. Carpenter

In the following essay, Carpenter discusses the nature of absurdity in Pinter's play, concluding that most critics ignore the work's true power in trying to penetrate the meaning of the playwright's absurdist touches.

Pinter's *Homecoming* may be the most enigmatic work of art since the Mona Lisa, an image its main character, Ruth, evokes. At the turning point of the play, Ruth's professor-husband, Teddy, watches intently as she lies on the living-room couch with one of his brothers while the other strokes her hair. His father, Max, claiming he is broadminded, calls her "a woman of quality," "a woman of feeling." Shortly after Ruth frees herself she asks Teddy, out of the blue: "Have your family read your critical works?"

This provokes the smug Ph.D. to a slightly manic assertion: "To see, to be able to *see!* I'm the one who can see. That's why I can write my critical works. Might do you good . . . have a look at them . . . see how certain people can view . . . things . . . how certain people can maintain . . . intellectual equilibrium." His reaction to this intensely disconcerting moment parallels that of Pinter critics who, like Teddy, refuse to let themselves be "lost in it." This is, of course, the natural reaction for people whose public image depends upon maintaining their intellectural equilibrium. But it is hardly the appropriate reaction either for Teddy, who restricts his protestations to eating his pimp—brother Lenny's cheese-roll, or for people genuinely experiencing a Pinter play.

Whatever else this response may involve, it must surely involve letting oneself be "lost in it." The jolt ot one's intellectual equilibrium—what Bert States has dubbed "the shock of nonrecognition" [see his essay "Pinter's *Homecoming* The Shock of Nonrecognition," *Hudson Review*, Autumn 1968]—must be acknowledged as a validly evoked response. The urge for rational illumination that so often follows–the nose-tickle crying for a sneeze—must be regarded as an integral second stage of that evolked response. In experiencing these repeated "Pinteresque" moments, we are put precisely in the dilemma of Camus's "absurd man" described in *The Myth of Sisyphus*. We are confronted with bewilderment, disruption, chaos, what Beckett referred to as "this buzzing confusion." In response, we involuntarily reach out for clarity, understanding, Godot: the little explanation that is not there. We become like Ionesco's

A scene from the absurdist film Brazil, *directed by Terry Gilliam*

Detective in *Victims of Duty*, who lays its underpinning bare: "I don't believe in the absurd. Everything hangs together; everything can be comprehended . . . thanks to the achievements of human thought and science." Camus's hero, the true believer in absurdity, acknowledges this recurring double take as a poignant byproduct of the absurd human condition, and in so doing, Camus says, reveals his "lucidity." Moreover, he becomes capable of reveling in the actual impact of the situation: the rich dark comedy of it, if you will. Sisyphus grows happy with his stone.

At these moments, in life or at a Pinter play, bizarre actions and reactions, churning with apparent meaning but inherently unexplainable, trigger the automatic desire for explanation built into us. An earlier pivotal incident in *The Homecoming* put the idea in the form of a graphic enigma. Before her outright defection, Ruth invites her all-male audience to watch her as she moves her leg, but warns them that even though their minds may stray to the underwear that moves with it, all she is doing is moving her leg. She continues: "My lips move. Why don't you restrict . . . your observations to that? Perhaps the fact that they move is more significant. . .than the words which come through them." What do Ruth's words mean? Be strict phenomenologists! Pay no attention to the inadvertently moving underwear, on which I have taken pains to rivet your attention; consider what I am saying insignificant—though I have made it surge with significance. Her words are of course absurd, since they cancel themselves out logically. But can we resist taking the lure and, on impulse, groping for the significance so deviously implied? Only the dull or jaded could. What we can try to avoid, however, is blurring the moment by detaching ourselves from the play in a face-saving quest for comprehension.

Glance at a more flagrant example. Soon after Ruth meets Lenny in Act I, he abruptly asks her if he can hold her hand. She asks why, and he says, "I'll tell you why." He then spins an involved story about being approached under an arch by a lady whose chauffeur, a friend of the family, had tracked him down. Deciding she was "falling apart with the pox," he spurned her advances, "clumped her one," and stopped short of killing her only because of the inconvenience. "So I just gave her another belt in the nose and a couple of turns of the boot and sort of left it at that." A baffling reason for wanting to hold Ruth's hand! If at this point we care more about recovering our intellectual aplomb than about letting the play carry us along in its inexorable absurd flow, we will wrench ourselves away from its grip on us; assume the pose of the Critic-Detective; and forget that the scene, in spite of its spray of beckoning clues (partly because of them, in fact), will finally defy comprehension, and that the play, by its nature, is chuckling at our knee-jerk response to one of its more transparent brain-teasers. In Camus's terms, the extent to which we avoid the role of public explainer and acknowledge the way the play has "caught" us becomes the genuine measure of our lucidity.

That avoidance and acknowledgement also give us a much better chance to enjoy the play—to relish the delectable, audacious absurdity of such moments. The distinctive power of *The Homecoming* derives largely from the bizarrely disconcerting quality of the things that happen to characters depicted as real people in the real world. Think of what typical first-nighters probably tell their friends about the play: a professor visits his grubby home after several years abroad and brings his wife, about whom he has not even told his family. The repulsive father calls her a whore, and the two repulsive brothers treat her like one. She does not seem to mind, and after a little bargaining accepts a deal to stay on as the family pet. The husband stands by complacently, smirk on his face, and finally leaves. If these spectators get around to elaborating on the play, they probably recall more and more incidents that involve "absurd" actions and a dazzling variety of reactions: Ruth making Lenny "some kind of proposal" soon after she meets him; Max lurching from extreme to extreme in his treatment of Ruth; Joey emerging after two hours of "not going any hog" with Ruth upstairs; Lenny getting the bright idea of putting her "on the game" in a Greek Street flat and Ruth raising the ante extravagantly before accepting; everyone ignoring uncle Sam's traumatic revelation—and prone body—at the end. Untutored spectators are not apt to lose sight of what makes the play so eccentric and electric; as they reflect rather idly on their experience, they are more than likely to keep focusing on those bizarre moments that amused, shocked, fascinated, and above all puzzled them.

But what can trained literary analysts do that "mere" playgoers cannot? Some will warp and deface this perspective; others will develop and refine it. Those who take the latter path may begin simply by noting more or less covert instances of bizarre behavior which have to be perceived to be appreciated: when Teddy chats with Lenny in scene one, for example, he does not mention the existence of Ruth (who has gone for a 1:00 a.m. stroll), and he goes to bed before Ruth returns, in effect leaving her to Lenny. An especially profitable avenue is open for critics with a penchant for close analysis: focus on details that lend themselves readily to facile interpretation, such as Max's stick or Lenny's comment to Teddy that his cigar has gone out, and demonstrate their immunity to interpretation.

Ruth's enigmatic farewell to her husband, "Eddie...Don't become a stranger," is a manageable example. As Bernard Dukore notes, the fact that Ruth calls him Eddie suggests that "Teddy" is meant as a nickname not for Theodore but for Edward—a suggestion which invites comparisons to the similarly cuckolded stuffed shirt named Edward in *A Slight Ache.* But she may also be symbolically withdrawing from him by muffing his name; or she may be knocking the "Theo"—the divinity—out of what is left of him; or she may be hinting he is no longer her teddy bear—or Teddy boy, for that matter. The rest of her statement, "Don't become a stranger," must be easier; the heavy odds are that she means the opposite of what she says. Or, after all, does she still want to keep a line open to her own children, even though she now has a new set? Or is her pleasantry, as a scholar sitting beside me in the British Museum once assured me, the way a London prostitute says, "So long—come again" to her clients? Surely the play's obtrusive "homecoming" metaphor must be hiding in there somewhere. Or does Ruth mean, Teddy, don't make yourself becoming to a stranger! it must be more sensible to grant the incomprehensibility of such conundrums than to flail for "the solution" and thus flout their essential nature. In a play like this, we know—to a certain extent—that we cannot know.

A full-fledged analysis concentrating on the play's bizarre and disconcerting effects, or at least trying not to dissipate them, might well aim to project what Kelly Morris has deftly termed [in her essay "*The Homecoming*," *Tulane Drama Review*, Winter 1966] "the suction of the absurd." As the play progresses, characters and audience alike get caught up in this suction. Take as a central example Lenny's victimization—or manhandling, if you prefer—by Ruth. In Act I she toys frivolously with him, countering his macho moves with audacities that throw him off kilter. From his lightly mocking "You must be connected with my brother in some way. . . . You sort of live with him over there, do you?" and his leering offer to relieve her of her drink, he is reduced by a little seductive bullying to shouting: "What was that supposed to be? Some kind of proposal?" No doubt he is conscious to some degree of having been manipulated, and alert spectators will have observed the Venus' flytrap in

"It seems unfortunate as well as symptomatic that few critics in the past fifteen years have taken an approach that accepts and even relishes the absurdity of Pinter's depicted world."

action, so that both he and the audience have a chance to shake off the disconcerting effect of Ruth's bizarre behavior.

Relief gets harder as the "suction" intensifies in Act II. When Teddy is present, Ruth joins Lenny in ruffling his proud feathers enough to convince him that he had better grab Ruth and flee if he is to avoid being "lost" in the situation. After Lenny prompts him to absurd evasions of a few philosophical basics ("What do you make of all this business of being and not-being?"), Ruth calls attention to the elegant reality of her leg. Then she declares Teddy's adopted land full of rock, sand, space, and insects. Lenny may believe he has gained an ally, or even a potential filly for his stable, since he pretends to leave with Max and Joey but reappears the instant Teddy goes upstairs to pack. In sharp contrast to his first encounter with Ruth, this time he is low-keyed and conciliatory. Again he digresses about a lady, but he gave this one a flowery hat instead of "a short-arm jab to the belly." When Ruth reminisces dreamily about her life as a nude model (I assume) before she went off to America, Lenny seems to read her behavior as confirmation that she is making him "some kind of proposal."

Whether or not Lenny does, when Teddy comes downstairs to take Ruth home, he steps into the most bizarre auction scene in all domestic drama, and it is engineered by Lenny. The jaunty pimp puts on some jazz, asks Ruth for "just one dance" before she goes, receives full compliance, kisses her a few times, hands her over to Joey for a bit of mauling, parts them with a touch of his foot, and pours drinks for all to celebrate the realignment. Though it is Teddy who visibly strains against the pressure of absurdity at this moment, Lenny has actually set himself up for a subtle comic downfall. Ruth's siege of deep-felt nostalgia—not about "working" as any kind of sex object but about posing for photographers at a genteel country estate—was entirely introspective and self-directed. To put it graphically, Lenny may have gathered that she was showing him her underwear when she was really just moving her leg. By the time she responds to his advances, he is deceived into thinking he has her pegged and will endure no more tremors from her behavior. He is thus a prime candidate for a shake-up.

Ruth administers the shake-up in two salvos, turning Lenny's cockiness as a shrewd exploiter of women into the sullen acquiescence of a man conned by one. It would be misleading to represent this as a conscious plot on her part, however; view it rather as the effect of her disturbing actions, whatever their roots. First, she somehow manages to play mother-beloved instead of whore to Joey, the test case client Lenny has arranged. Lenny covers up his anxiety quite well when he learns this, but is clearly jolted by the realization that Ruth may be a mere tease. Joey snorts that he can be happy "without going any hog," but what will the paying customers say? Second, Ruth responds to the idea of paying her way as a prostitute by making exorbitant demands that Lenny thought he could handle but cannot. he had said to the men: "I know these women. Once they get started they ruin your budget." Ruth reduces him to:

> LENNY. We'd supply everything. Everything you need. [Note the qualification—everything you *need*
>
> RUTH. I'd need an awful lot. Otherwise I wouldn't be content.
>
> LENNY. You'd have everything. [Qualification dropped.]

Lenny does not squirm perceptibly during his public humiliation, even when it also becomes clear that Ruth will most probably refuse to "pull her weight" inside the house (no homecoming for Max and Lenny either). But as the final tableau implies, Ruth has effectively thrust him into the background whadow, big bear-enforcer Joey at her side. Whether Lenny becomes a cover-up-at-all-costs stoic or he is rendered catatonic as this barrage of the unmanageable shatters his delusion of firm control, he is certainly caught up in the "suction of the absurd"—no less than Teddy, in fact, and Teddy can at least escape. The audience, caught in the same suction (though with the cushion of aesthetic distance), leaves with heads buzzing: no escape but in the critics' explanations. Why Ruth carries out these strikingly unexpected acts of apparent self-gratification, by the way, is a wide-open question, but her spate of nostalgia for the best moments of the old life may have served vaguely as the impetus. Or perhaps it was simply her way of thanking Teddy for offering her the opportunity to help him with his lectures when they return.

This brief essay does not pretend to be a fully developed interpretive argument about *The Homecoming*. It is meant to exemplify the direction that might be taken by critical analysis which tries to be faithful to the genuine absurd experience of the play as it unfolds. The finely crafted progression of bizarre and disconcerting events might be approached from many other points of view. Mine, for example, completely neglects the two crucial offstage presences, Jessie and MacGregor, and fails to address Sam's important role. Nor does it do justice to one of the most prominent effects on that average first-nighter on whom I stake so much: the raunchy, ugly, gorgeous vulgarity of the piece. "What I mean," Lenny twits Teddy, ". . . you must know lots of professors, head of departments, men like that. They pop over here for a week at the Savoy, they need somewhere they can go to have a nice quiet poke. And of course you'd be in a position to give them inside information. . . . You could be our representative in the States." This excites Max: "Of course. We're talking in international terms! By the time we've finished Pan American'll give us a discount." There. I haven't neglected that.

It seems unfortunate as well as symptomatic that few critics in the past fifteen years have taken an approach that accepts and even relishes the absurdity of Pinter's depicted world. Precious few have resisted the urge to chase the will-o'-the-wisp of a solution to the mind-bending indeterminacies *The Homecoming* in particular exudes. The gradual drift of criticism away from the reality of the play is marked by the actual titles of three early studies: the earliest, "Puzzling Pinter" [Richard Schechner, *Tulane Drama Review*, Winter 1966]; the others, "A Clue to the Pinter Puzzle" [Arthur Ganz, *Educational Theatre Journal*, Vol. 21, 1969]; and "Not So Puzzling Pinter" [Herbert Goldstone, *Theatre Annual*, Vol. 25, 1969]. Ionesco's Detectives have been at work. What they have accomplished often seems dazzling in its perception and profundity. Some of it even seems inevitable when one is immersed in it. But if it violates the inherent nature of the play by trying to defuse its stunningly absurd time bombs, then what it is doing is busily explaining away the chief source of the play's power and of its richly deserved stature.

Source: Charles A. Carpenter, "'Victims of Duty'? The Critics, Absurdity, and *The Homecoming*," in *Modern Drama*, Vol. XXV, No. 4, December 1982, pp. 489–95.

Sources

Albee, Edward, *The American Dream*, Coward, 1961.

Banarjee, R. B., "The Theatre of the Absurd," in *The Literary Criterion*, Vol. 7, No. 1, 1965, pp. 59–62.

Banker, B. K., "The Theatre of the Absurd and Existentialism: An Overview," in *Indian Journal of American Studies*, Vol. 26, No. 2, Summer 1996, pp. 45–49.

Beckett, Samuel, *Endgame*, Grove Press, 1958.

———, *Waiting for Godot*, Grove Press, 1954.

Campbell, Matthew, "Samuel (Barclay) Beckett," in *Dictionary of Literary Biography*, Vol. 233: *British and Irish Dramatists Since World War II*, edited by John Bull, The Gale Group, 2001, pp. 35–49.

Cohn, Ruby, "Introduction: Around the Absurd," in *Around the Absurd: Essays on Modern and Postmodern Drama*, edited by Enoch Brater and Ruby Cohn, University of Michigan Press, 1990, pp. 1–9.

Esslin, Martin, *The Theatre of the Absurd*, Overlook Press, 1969.

MacNicholas, John, "Edward Albee," in *Dictionary of Literary Biography*, Vol. 7: *Twentieth-Century American Dramatists*, edited by John MacNicholas, Gale Research, 1981, pp. 3–23.

McMahon, Joseph H., and Megan Conway, "Jean Genet," in *Dictionary of Literary Biography*, Vol. 72: *French Novelists, 1930–1960*, edited by Catharine Savage Brosman, Gale Research, 1988, pp. 170–86.

Srivastava, Avadhesh K., "The Crooked Mirror: Notes on the Theatre of the Absurd," in *Literary Criterion*, Vol. 11, No. 2, 1974, pp. 58–62.

Zinman, Toby Silverman, "Hen in a Foxhouse: The Absurdist Plays of Maria Irene Fornes," in *Around the Absurd: Essays on Modern and Postmodern Drama*, edited by Enoch Brater and Ruby Cohn, University of Michigan Press, 1990, pp. 203–20.

Further Reading

Banker, B. K., "The Theatre of the Absurd and Existentialism: An Overview," *Journal of American Studies*, Vol. 26, No. 2, Summer 1996, pp. 45–49.

Banker's article discusses the influence of the Existentialist philosophers Jean-Paul Sartre and Albert Camus on Absurdism.

Beckett, Samuel, *Waiting for Godot*, Grove Press, 1954.

Beckett's two-act play about two tramps who wait in vain by the side of the road for Godot to arrive is perhaps the most famous example of Absurdism.

Cohn, Ruby, *Casebook on "Waiting for Godot,"* Grove Press, 1967.

Cohn's book features reviews and interpretations of Beckett's most famous play and offers an assessment of its impact.

Lamont, Rosette C. *Ionesco: A Collection of Critical Essays*, Prentice-Hall, 1973.

Lamont presents a collection of scholarly essays ranging from an interpretation of *The Chairs* to an analysis of the structure of *The Bald Soprano* and *The Lesson.*

Beat Movement

Movement Origin

c. 1944

The roots of the Beat literary movement go back to 1944 when Jack Kerouac, Allen Ginsberg, and William Burroughs met at Columbia University in New York. It was not until the 1950s that these writers and other "Beats" would be recognized as a *movement* and as a *generation* of post-World War II youths whose attitudes and lifestyles were far removed from typical Americana. Kerouac used the term "beat" to describe both the negatives of his world and the positives of his responses to it. On one hand, "beat" implied weariness and disinterest in social or political activity, and on the other it was reminiscent of the Beatitudes of Jesus—declarations of blessedness and happiness uttered during the Sermon on the Mount. While certain measures of blissfulness—often drug-induced—may have applied to followers of the Beat Movement, so would feelings of disillusionment, bitterness, and an overwhelming desire to be free of social constraints.

The work of Beat writers is characterized by experimental styles and subjects, including spontaneous writing without regard for grammar, sexually explicit language, uninhibited discussion of personal experiences, and themes ranging from a rejection of American values and fear of nuclear war to sexual escapades and road trips. Representative works of the movement are Kerouac's novel *On the Road*, Burroughs's novel *Naked Lunch*, and poems such as Ginsberg's "Howl" and Gregory Corso's "BOMB." None of these works appeared on American bookshelves until nearly a decade after Kerouac first used the word "beat" to signify

an outlook on writing and an outlook on life. What had begun as a small cluster of rebellious outcasts in New York City soon grew into a larger group based in San Francisco and eventually spread its influences across the country. Beats appeared everywhere in the 1950s, paving the way for the hippies of the following decade.

Representative Authors

William Burroughs (1914–1997)

William Burroughs was born February 5, 1914, in St. Louis, to well-to-do parents with a family history of successful business ventures. But even as a youth, Burroughs did not fit in with his upper-class, Midwestern background, for he was a bookish boy with homosexual tendencies and a fascination with guns and lawlessness. Burroughs was a top student and eventually earned a degree from Harvard, though he never lost his attraction to crime. In 1943, Burroughs moved to New York to become involved in the city's gangster underworld, which led to his experimentation with heroin and several run-ins with the law. There, Burroughs also met Allen Ginsberg and Jack Kerouac, two members of a small group of social nonconformists at Columbia University who would become major players in the Beat Movement. Also at Columbia, Burroughs met Joan Vollmer, who became his common-law wife, gave birth to their son, and found herself on the wrong end of one of Burroughs's pistols.

Although he was usually surrounded by literary types, Burroughs did not start writing until 1950 when he decided to write a semi-autobiographical story, *Junkie*. Without finishing the first novel, he began another in 1951, this one also somewhat autobiographical, titled *Queer*. By this time, he had moved his family to Mexico to escape drug charges. It was there that he accidentally killed his wife by attempting to shoot a glass off her head, William Tell-style. Later, Burroughs confessed that it was Joan's death that gave him the incentive to pursue writing seriously.

Throughout the 1950s, Burroughs continued to write, but his material was generally considered too obscene for print. Finally, in 1959, his most famous book, *The Naked Lunch*, was published in Paris. Three years later, it was published in the United States as simply *Naked Lunch*. This book brought celebrity to Burroughs, though mostly among the underground, and he went on to write several more books, plays, and film scripts and to receive an American Academy and Institute of Arts and Letters Award in 1975. Although many do not consider him one of the original Beat writers, he is now often called one of the most popular. Both his writing style and lifestyle were undeniably characteristic of the movement, but his work has found an even greater audience in more recent decades. Burroughs died in Lawrence, Kansas, August 2, 1997.

Neal Cassady (1926–1968)

Neal Cassady was born February 8, 1926, in Salt Lake City and grew up in a poor section of Denver with an alcoholic father. Cassady learned quickly how to fight and how to steal, and, perhaps most importantly, how to charm people while he was doing it. After years in and out of reform schools and juvenile prisons, Cassady developed the instincts of a con artist and the rebellion of a free-spirited, fun-loving bum who wanted only to travel, ramble on in stream-of-consciousness conversations, and have sex with whomever seemed the most beneficial partner at the moment. Essentially, it was Cassady's personality that was his major contribution to the Beat Movement. Though his autobiography was published in 1971 followed by some collections of letters, he never produced a single book while the Beat Movement was in full swing.

Cassady wound up in New York in 1946 where, through a friend at Columbia, he met Ginsberg and Kerouac. Ginsberg was promptly captivated by his western ruggedness and cowboy nature, and the two became lovers even while Cassady carried on various affairs with women, whom he claimed to prefer. But, it was his relationship with Kerouac that made Cassady one of the most influential instigators of the Beat Generation. In the late 1940s, the two went on a series of car trips across the United States, and these often harrowing, always riotous adventures became the basis for Kerouac's most famous book, *On the Road*. Kerouac captured Cassady's "voice" in the novel, essentially writing it the way Cassady talked: fast, off the cuff, without any hesitation or self-consciousness. The two travelers eventually parted, but Cassady continued his road adventures, winding up in Mexico in the late 1960s. There, after a night of too much alcohol, Cassady wandered out into the cold and rain and passed out. He slipped into a coma and died the following day, February 4, 1968.

Gregory Corso (1930–2001)

Gregory Corso was born March 26, 1930, in New York City. Of the writers who became famous among the Beats, Corso had one of the most natural poetic talents: he was capable of producing powerful lyric verse in an expressive, yet genuine voice, as well as bawdy, poetic ramblings, typically uninhibited and sexually explicit—hallmarks of Beat writing. Corso published his first volume of poetry, *The Vestal Lady on Brattle and Other Poems*, in 1955 and his second, *Gasoline*, in 1958. Also in 1958, Corso published a broadside of one of his most famous poems, "BOMB," which was a love poem to the atomic weapon, written in the shape of a mushroom cloud. He became immediately popular with fellow Beat writers and with mainstream readers as well, but the popularity he enjoyed in the 1950s and 1960s dwindled over the decades. Still, he continued to write and publish and received the Jean Stein Award for Poetry from the American Academy and Institute of Arts and Letters in 1986. His most recent publication was *Mindfield: New and Selected Poems*, published in 1989 and reprinted in 1998. Corso died from prostate cancer in Minneapolis on January 17, 2001.

Allen Ginsberg (1926–1997)

Allen Ginsberg was born June 3, 1926, in Paterson, New Jersey, and grew up a shy, sensitive boy in a highly chaotic household. His father was a poet, teacher, and Jewish Socialist, and his mother was a radical Communist and unconstrained nudist with symptoms of paranoid schizophrenia. Her bouts with mental illness weighed heavily on the young Ginsberg, as he was often the only one she trusted when the rest of the world was, in her mind, plotting against her. But Ginsberg had another struggle with which to contend—his sexual orientation to boys was another issue he faced.

Ginsberg took his father's advice to study labor law at Columbia. Although he had shown an interest in poetry previously, it was not until he met fellow student Kerouac and nonstudents Burroughs and Cassady that he turned his attention to literary pursuits. His friendship with these three and others among the rebel crowd had other influences as well: drugs, crime, and opportunities to express his homosexuality freely. Ginsberg was eventually suspended from Columbia. By then he was writing poetry profusely though not publishing much. His break came in 1955 when he joined other Beat poets for a public reading in San Francisco and delivered a resounding performance of what became his trademark poem, "Howl." Just as Kerouac's *On the Road* was the symbolic novel of the Beats, "Howl" was—and probably still is—the symbolic poem. Ginsberg's popularity was almost instantaneous after this reading, and his first collection, *Howl and Other Poems*, was published in 1956. Other books followed in a relatively short period, and Ginsberg's fame and infamy grew. Despite an obscenity trial for "Howl," (which was eventually declared not obscene), he found recognition among the prestigious literary mainstream and was awarded a Guggenheim Fellowship in 1963. In 1969, he received a grant from the National Institute of Arts and Letters, and, in 1974, a National Book Award for *Fall of America*. Ginsberg published poetry collections throughout the 1980s and 1990s, most recently *Cosmopolitan Greetings: Poems, 1986–1992* and *Selected Poems 1947–1995*. Ginsberg died of a heart attack while suffering from liver cancer, April 5, 1997, in New York City.

Jack Kerouac

Jack Kerouac (1922–1969)

Jack Kerouac was born March 12, 1922, in Lowell, Massachusetts. His father was a successful printer in Lowell, but by the mid-1920s, the economy of the city began to collapse, and the older Kerouac turned to gambling in hopes of supplementing his income. Young Jack was already interested in creating stories, inspired by radio talk shows, but he was also a star player on his high school football team. When Kerouac was awarded a football scholarship to play at Columbia, his family moved to

New York with him. But at the university, Kerouac fell in with the renegade crowd, including Ginsberg, Burroughs, and Cassady, and he had a fight with his coach who, afterwards, refused to let him play. Eventually, he dropped out of Columbia, bitterly disappointing his family.

As a student, Kerouac had begun writing a novel, and his new friends praised his work. With Ginsberg's promotional help, Kerouac's first book, *The Town and the City*, was published in 1950, gaining him respect as a writer but not bringing him fame. Throughout the 1950s, Kerouac wrote novels that went unpublished for a time, including *Dr. Sax* and *The Subterraneans*, interspersed with his cross-country adventures with Cassady. But, one book that resulted from those travels put him on the map as one of the most—if not the most—significant writer of the Beat Movement: *On the Road*, published in 1957, was an immediate success. It was Kerouac who had coined the term "beat" to reflect both the downtrodden, world-weary attitudes of the post-World War II generation and, at the same time, the optimistic, "beatific" will to live unconstrained by social conventions. His own life certainly reflected these definitions, particularly the former, and he had difficulty tolerating his sudden stardom. He turned to alcohol for consolation and escape but was never able to control the drinking and manage a writing career at the same time. His last somewhat successful novel, *Big Sur*, was published in 1962. His health destroyed by alcohol, Kerouac died of a stomach hemorrhage in St. Petersburg, Florida, October 21, 1969.

Representative Works

"BOMB"

Corso's most famous poem, "BOMB," was originally published as a "broadside," a single large sheet of paper printed on one side, by City Lights Books in 1958. It then appeared in Corso's 1960 collection, *The Happy Birthday of Death*. Arranged in the shape of a mushroom cloud, the poem is Corso's ironic attempt to mitigate the destruction of an atomic war by portraying the bomb-drop as a Christlike second coming. Essentially, the explosion marks the end of human history and the beginning of heavenly eternity. Although the theme is dark and chilling, Corso presents it in typical Beat style with a rush of fragmented images, raw language, and a wry sense of humor. It is primarily the latter attribute that turned off many would-be supporters. With lines such as, "I sing thee Bomb Death's extravagance Death's jubilee / . . . to die by cobra is not to die by bad pork," Corso offended members of the Campaign for Nuclear Disarmament when he read the poem at New College in Oxford in 1958. The crowd heckled him. Some reviewers were kinder, however, expressing appreciation for the extraordinary imagery in "BOMB" and declaring the bizarre humor right on target with the Beat attitude. Critics on either side would have to admit that the poem brought Corso to the front of the Beat literary movement, although his work is probably least remembered.

A Coney Island of the Mind

A Coney Island of the Mind is one of Lawrence Ferlinghetti's most well-received collections of poems, selling over one million copies since its publication in 1958. Popular among the Beats as a publisher and owner of City Lights bookstore in San Francisco, Ferlinghetti solidified his recognition as a poet with this book, in which the poems present a kaleidoscopic view of the world as a place with discontinuous images and a carnival-like absurdity. When Ferlinghetti did public readings from this collection, he was usually accompanied by jazz music in the background, and many of the poems themselves have a spontaneous rhythm and obvious cadence. *Coney Island* found an audience with both Beat and mainstream readers, as well as critics from both sides. Most cite similar reasons: even though the central theme of the collection may be the meaninglessness of life, individual poems still intrigue readers with poignant, definable thoughts.

The Dharma Bums

Published in 1958, Kerouac's novel *The Dharma Bums* is based on his friendship with poet Gary Snyder and a mountain-climbing trip they took to Yosemite in 1955. Snyder, portrayed as Japhy Ryder in the book, is known for both his Beat-style poetry and his serious study of Zen Buddhism. Like Kerouac's *On the Road*, published a year earlier, *The Dharma Bums* recounts the raucous adventure of two friends with rambling details and spontaneous confessions, but its greatest significance is the symbolic search for spiritual enlightenment that the friends' trip represents. While the characters in much of Kerouac's other work go on wild journeys as a means to escape life and to run away from themselves, here Japhy and Ray Smith (Kerouac) set out in search of dharma, or supreme truth, in an effort, essentially, to find themselves. Despite the turnabout in themes, *The Dharma Bums*

William S. Burroughs with some of the props from the film Naked Lunch, *based on his novel*

was well received as an archetype of Beat ideology, heralding a discontent with standard values and the quest to find something more satisfying for the spirit, as well as for the mind and body.

"Howl"

The opening lines of Ginsberg's lengthy poem "Howl," published in *Howl and Other Poems* in 1956, are some of the most recognized in twentieth-century poetry: "I saw the best minds of my generation destroyed by madness, starving / hysterical naked, / dragging themselves through the negro streets at dawn looking for an / angry fix." Dedicated to Carl Solomon, a lifelong friend whom Ginsberg met at the Columbia University Psychiatric Institute in 1948, "Howl" is a three-part, free verse lamentation on the social and personal woes of post-World War II American society. Part I describes the despair felt by many individuals during this unsettling era; Part II identifies social conformity, big government, and materialism as some of the causes for human discontent and restlessness; and Part III is a series of statements directly addressing Solomon, praising true friendship and announcing the poet's feeling of victory over social control of his emotional and sexual identity.

Today, "Howl" is widely considered to be the most important poem to come out of the Beat Movement, with some critics claiming it revolutionized American poetry in general. There were those who felt the same way in the 1950s, but there were also many who would have preferred to see Ginsberg's work burned instead of read. The sexually explicit language, mostly homosexual in nature, shocked readers and critics alike. The San Francisco Police Department was not impressed either, and authorities, declaring the work obscene, promptly arrested its publisher, Ferlinghetti. During the obscenity trial, several well-known and well-respected poets testified in support of Ferlinghetti, Ginsberg, and the freedom of poetry in general, and they eventually succeeded in persuading the judge. "Howl" was declared not obscene, and the notoriety of the trial greatly enhanced its popularity, as well as sales of the book.

Naked Lunch

Burroughs's most widely known novel, *Naked Lunch*, was not published in the United States until 1962 when it was finally declared not obscene following three years of legal trials. A publisher in Paris had accepted it in 1959. While thousands of people can claim they have read the book, few may be able to say they know what it is about, for *Naked Lunch* has no consistent story, no running narrative, no uniform point of view, and no readily recognizable theme. Loosely, it tells the tale of junkie William Lee and a hodgepodge of grotesque characters who flail about in a bleak, sadistic world of drug addiction, sexual depravity, and madness. The subject matter, such as it is, is not what made this book one of the hallmarks of the Beat literary movement. Rather, it is the style, or the origins of its style, that piqued readers' curiosity and brought critical attention—negative as much as positive—to Burroughs's creation.

Naked Lunch is composed of a series of random sketches and rambling notes. Burroughs wrote hundreds of snippets while living in Tangiers, and, with the help of writer friends Kerouac and Ginsberg, among others, he haphazardly assembled the pieces and presented them to a publisher, claiming however the publisher stacked the pages on his desk would be just as suitable a way to publish them as any. As a result, one can actually read *Naked Lunch* front to back, back to front, or any direction coming and going. It was this seeming lack of true literary endeavor as well as talent that irked many reviewers of Burroughs's work. Some claimed it took no intelligence to create the so-called novel and even less to read it. In spite of the harsh, even insulting criticism, *Naked Lunch* became a national best-seller and sealed its author's literary reputation, for better or for worse.

On the Road

Kerouac's novel *On the Road*, published in 1957, has been called the quintessential work of the Beat Movement. Like many of his other works, this book draws on the author's own experiences and relationships, and its characters are derived from real people. In this case, the two central players are Sal Paradise, based on Kerouac himself, and Dean Moriarty, based on his free-spirited, rabble-rousing companion, Cassady. *On the Road* chronicles the cross-country road trips of Paradise and Moriarty, symbolizing their fervent search for values greater than those they consider typically American. What results is perhaps most emblematic of the Beat Generation's feelings of detachment and dissatisfaction. Instead of finding the values they seek, Paradise and Moriarty become saturated in drugs, alcohol, sex, and crime—all leading to disjointedness and a scattering of their lives amidst the chaos. Many Beats considered this book their anthem because they could so strongly identify with the cycle of hope and disappointment that endlessly revolves throughout its pages. General readers tended to find the work amusing, if not enjoyable, and critics tended to be split down the middle. Some praised *On the Road* for giving voice to an entire generation of disenchanted, embittered Americans, and others denounced it as an illiterate, incoherent exercise in self-absorption and self-pity. Like other controversial Beat material, Kerouac's work outlasted the worst criticism and wound up in the annals of prominent American literature. *On the Road* was, and still is, an exceptional work, as much for its style as for its message.

Themes

Disillusionment

At the end of World War II, Americans enjoyed a period of blissful relief and charged-up happiness unlike any realized before. Although an odd mixture of pride and sorrow over the dropping of atomic bombs left many people uneasy about the path to victory, it did not waylay the renewed spirit of optimism and drive for prosperity that swept the country at a feverish pace. The latter part of the 1940s and most of the 1950s have been called times of innocent fun, social quietude, and old-fashioned family values. The end of the war turned Rosie the Riverter into June Cleaver, as most women gave up their wartime jobs to raise the first of the baby boomers while dads worked as the sole breadwinners in the family. But, not everyone welcomed a neatly prescribed life with the perfect spouse, two kids, and a white picket fence around a well-manicured lawn. Some people were disillusioned with postwar complacency and protested social norms that smelled more like social control than simply a style of living. A faction of those people became self-identified members of the Beat Generation.

Disillusionment may be considered the "core" theme of the Beat Movement, for it encompasses the basic reason for the split from mainstream society that the original Beats desired. Although the foundations of the movement may be traced to the four kindred personalities of Kerouac, Burroughs, Corso, and Ginsberg, there is little doubt that countless other Americans were experiencing a shift in feelings in the wake of a war with unsurpassed technological destruction. To have the nation responsible then settle into an era of homeland peace, frivolity, and abundance was too much for some to swallow. People attracted to what would become the Beat lifestyle turned in that direction because of an initial distrust of America's renewed sense of pride and accomplishment, many fearing that a gratified society was a vulnerable one, left open to greater governmental and social control. Rather than be mollified by the quaintness of the average happy family in the average happy neighborhood, the disillusioned Beats struck out against such expected contentment in favor of being intentionally discontented.

Social Nonconformity

If disillusionment is a core theme of the Beat Movement, social nonconformity is another motif that directly resulted from it. Looking solely at the four major originators, one may assume that only criminals and drug addicts were true members of the Beat Generation. But, as tempting as it seems, that assumption is an unfair generalization of the entire group. Surely, most Beats visibly and vocally pronounced themselves social outsiders, but, for some, being different meant wearing a particular style of clothing, listening to jazz music improvisations, using hip language, and showing complete disinterest in social and political concerns. For others, nonconformity did entail a more reckless lifestyle; from heavy use of alcohol and other drugs to theft, homicide, and gangster involvement, many took life to a steep extreme, and some, of course, fell over the edge.

The most common responses of nonconformity shared by both moderate and extremist Beats were a rejection of materialism, scoffing at traditional American values, and complete indifference toward social activism. At the same time, individual expression and personal enlightenment were highly regarded, and the pursuit of self-awareness often translated into free-spirited, spur-of-the-moment adventures across town or across the country. Obviously, some members of the Beat Generation had to maintain steady jobs, but mobility was key to staying clear of social constraints and circumscribed behavior. Perhaps the strongest statement of nonconformity expressed by this generation was to accept and, indeed, celebrate its description as "beat." The term essentially pointed a finger in society's face and said, "Look what you've done to us."

Spontaneity

While spontaneity is more an action than an idea, it has been called the primary virtue and a one-word summary of the Beat Movement. This theme more than any other speaks to the frenzied, intense emotional states that many Beats found both exhilarating and necessary. Moreover, it embodies the tendency not to think twice about hopping into a car and taking off for unknown destinations just for the thrill of adventure and the prospect of discovering something new about oneself and life in general. To be impulsive was not to be cautious. For the Beats, caution was a symptom of social conformity, and living off the cuff was an openly defiant response to such careful, regimented existence.

While living life as an unbridled, impetuous free spirit may seem harmless enough—even attractive, though most citizens would not admit it—

Media Adaptations

- *The Life and Times of Allen Ginsberg*, directed by Jerry Aronson and released in 1994, is a comprehensive, affectionate documentary on the poet's life. It runs eighty-three minutes and includes accounts of Ginsberg's troubled childhood, his fame as a Beat and, later, as a hippie, and as a compassionate, still active, older poet.
- John Antonelli's documentary *Kerouac* was released in 1995. The film begins and ends with Kerouac reading excerpts from *On the Road* and uses an actor to portray some of the scenes from the Beat writer's life. Actual footage of Kerouac includes TV clips, one showing his appearance on the *William F. Buckley Show*, in which he insults Ferlinghetti and declares himself a Catholic.
- In 1997, writer and director Stephen Kay released *The Last Time I Committed Suicide*, a visual adaptation of actual letters written by Cassady and sent to Kerouac. The movie chronicles Cassady's life as an oversexed young man in Denver and features rich, excellent detail of postwar American culture.
- The four-CD set *Howls, Raps and Roars: Recordings from the San Francisco Poetry Renaissance*, produced by Fantasy Records, was released in 1993. It includes fifty-four minutes of Allen Ginsberg reading "Howl," "Footnote to Howl," and "Supermarket in California," among other poems, as well as readings by Kenneth Rexroth, Ferlinghetti, Corso, and others.

spontaneity often manifested itself in dangerous activities for the Beat Generation that not only changed the rapid-fire lives of many, but also ended some. Indiscriminate sexual encounters with numerous partners, often strangers, were common among Beat followers, and these spontaneous acts occasionally led to unwanted pregnancies and sexually transmitted diseases. Physical pleasure also came in liquid form—whether whiskey to drink or heroin to inject, drugs flowed freely among the Beats, and the desire for an immediate rush far outweighed any concern about overdosing or even dying. The abuse of cigarettes and marijuana helped maintain a moderate high in between heavier drug trips, and the continuous search for sensory experiences was considered a justifiable reason for remaining open to spontaneous urges.

Style

The "Cut-Up" Technique

The "cut-up" technique of composing prose originated with Burroughs, and it was a spin-off of his unusual method of putting together his most famous novel, *Naked Lunch*, from snippets of notes he wrote down and then pieced together. His follow-up novels, *The Soft Machine*, *The Ticket That Exploded*, and *Nova Express*, were constructed from chunks of various writings which he had literally cut up and then randomly paired into a new work. In doing so, he came up with such lines as the following: "He rents an amphitheater with marble walls he is a stone painter you can dig can create a frieze while you wait" and "The knife fell—The Clerk in the bunk next to his bled blue silence—Put on a clean shirt and Martin's pants—telling stories and exchanging smiles—dusty motors," both from *Nova Express*. Once Burroughs introduced it, the cut-up style of writing became a hit with the Beats, and others experimented with it in poetry, essays, and even political speeches, just for fun. The typical method is to take a written page, cut it down the middle vertically, then cut each of those two pieces in half horizontally, so that there are four "chunks" of writing. Next, arrange the chunks in different pairs to see what new lines or phrases appear. Burroughs found the results refreshing, even when the pieced-together prose made little or no sense and could not be translated literally. This style protected against what he and other experimental writers considered the confining boundaries of traditional word usage and standard grammar. The cut-up style was as much a rebellion against language control as a quirky creative impulse, and Burroughs claimed rebellion was the more important factor.

Spontaneous Prose

While the cut-up technique may have been the strangest literary form spawned by the Beat Movement, another just as unusual for its time was what Kerouac called "spontaneous prose," and it became the most prominent and recognizable style of the Beats. As the name suggests, this type of writing is not plotted or preconceived in any way. Instead, it consists of a flow of thoughts, written down as it occurs in a continuous stream of images and movement. There is very little regard for punctuation, which threatens to get in the way of the lines' pulsing rhythm. Kerouac compared writing spontaneous prose to a jazz musician blowing on a horn, sometimes with long, drawn-out notes, other times in quick, snappy toots, but always creating rhythm through improvisation. As with proper grammar, a writer's consciousness is seen as a hindrance to spontaneity and should be avoided—that is, writing without consciousness is a must for the Beat writer. Yet another taboo is revision. Once the language has flowed directly from the mind to the paper, the writer should not go back and revise. To do so, of course, is to take the spontaneity out of spontaneous writing, and, for the Beat writer, that means ruining the work.

Contemporary Idiom

The Beat Generation did not invent writing in contemporary idiom, for novelists and poets throughout history often used a colloquial language with which to tell tales and give voice to characters, though often it was interspersed with more formal language from an objective narrator. The Beats, however, took the idiom of their generation to daring new levels with the inclusion of words and subject matter previously considered too immoral or illegal to print. But, Beat writers knew that if one was going to be truly spontaneous, then nothing could be held back. If the mind thought it, the hand should write it, and, obviously, the mind can entertain shocking, illicit, and highly personal material. The use of sexually explicit language, as well as forbidden four-letter words, became the norm in Beat writing, and this characteristic drew most of the negative attention to the movement's poets and novelists. While many critics of the outlandish new writing could overlook, or simply scoff at, odd techniques and their so-called unliterary re-

Topics for Further Study

- In the 1950s, the Beat Movement touted frequent drug use, sexual freedom, disinterest in social and political issues, and disregard for law. How do you think a movement like this would fare at the beginning of the twenty-first century? Why would American society tolerate a new Beat Movement or why would it not?
- Though few in number, all the original members of the Beat Generation were young, white males, yet women and African Americans were certainly affected by and involved in the movement. Do some research to find out more about the lesser-known Beats and write an essay on how their lives were similar to or different from the prominent ones.
- Of the three main artistic facets of the Beat Movement—writing, visual art, and music—the writings were the most controversial and often least welcomed by mainstream Americans. Why do you think this was true? What was it about Beat literature that was so different from Abstract Expressionist art and bebop music?
- Author Gertrude Stein coined the term "Lost Generation" in the 1920s as a label for the intellectuals, poets, artists, and writers who fled to France after World War I. What did Stein mean by this term and how was the Lost Generation different from or similar to the Beat Generation?

sults, most railed against the description of all kinds of sexual encounters in the language of the street. The protests were enough to keep some novels and poems off American bookshelves for years while publishers and authors endured obscenity trials, but, in the end, the use of contemporary idiom, even at its extreme, was deemed legal. By the twenty-first century, it was deemed literature.

Movement Variations

Abstract Expressionism

While Beat writers were having their heyday throughout the 1950s, visual artists were also struggling against social conformity and the restrictions they felt postwar society placed on them with its expectations about art. What arose was a kind of "Beat" painting and sculpture that took the name "Abstract Expressionism," and its techniques and resulting works rocked the art world as much as Beat writing disturbed the literary scene.

A group of painters and sculptors known as the New York School led the Abstract Expressionism revolt by advocating individual emotions and the freedom to present those emotions with as little inhibition as possible. The idea was to make the art of the moment, just as Kerouac's spontaneous prose made literature of the moment. And like the Beat writers, abstract expressionists welcomed confrontation with a complacent society trying to settle into a safe, benign, middle-class life after World War II. There should be no complacency, according to the artists, and they rebelled against the image of the lofty painter standing at his easel overlooking a serene meadow and capturing the pastoral landscape on his canvas. Abstract expressionists often used huge canvases, and many rejected that conventional surface altogether. They used paper-mâché and three-dimensional objects as surfaces, and, in place of common artists' brushes and scrapers, they used spray cans, garden tools, sticks, and a variety of other objects to create their work. Even more outrageous, the abstract expressionists employed whatever material was convenient to incorporate into a piece of art—from broken glass and sand piles to toilet seats and garbage.

One major avant-garde artist of this period, Jackson Pollock, created "drip paintings" by literally holding a can of paint above a surface and letting it drip onto it. Pollock was also known for stepping back from a large canvas with his can in hand, then slinging it so that the paint splashed in wild streaks all over the surface. Robert Rauschenberg created what he called "combines," or artworks that integrated three-dimensional objects such as umbrellas, stuffed toys, and tires with other material. And in 1959, Claes Oldenburg walked through the streets of New York City wearing a paper-mâché elephant mask, his first one-man art show. Later, he collaborated with Coosje van Bruggen, his wife, to design and build huge public artworks of common objects, such as a giant clothespin in Philadelphia, big shuttlecocks strewn across the museum lawn in Kansas City, and a large spoon with a cherry perched on it in Minneapolis.

Music

When Cleveland disk jockey Alan Freed started using the term "rock and roll" in 1951, it was in reference to his radio show, "Moondog House Rock and Roll Party"; the music he was playing was rhythm and blues. By the end of the decade, however, those simple yet volatile words were the signature label for a revolution in music that spawned singers as diverse as Elvis Presley, Bob Dylan, the Bee Gees, and the Goo Goo Dolls, among others. But the Beat Movement promoted another type of music, almost a combination of rhythm and blues and what eventually became the thumping gyrations of rock and roll. It was a style of jazz called "bebop," and its artists were black musicians who played primarily in big-city nightclubs, some becoming famous recording artists such as Miles Davis, John Coltrane, Dizzy Gillespie, and Charlie Parker.

Bebop is a discordant, unmelodious, and syncopated music that arose from its musicians' desire to separate themselves from typical mainstream jazz and the predictable harmonies and rhythms of 1940s swing music. Like Beat writers and visual artists, bebop musicians were fiercely individualistic, and they proved it with wholly improvised solos and nontraditional rhythms that tended to change from performance to performance. Again, it was the freedom to create the music of the moment, and, while it enjoyed a solid audience that grew tremendously throughout the 1950s—particularly in large cities and bohemian pockets of smaller towns—bebop also offended the more traditional music lovers with its dissonant, if not cacophonous, instrumental sounds. But that, of course, suited bebop musicians just fine. As more and more people, both black and white, joined the ranks of bebop fans, the musicians found themselves having to reach even greater levels of musical dissonance just to maintain that rebellious, outsider edge.

Film

The Beat Movement in film encompassed a wide variety of forms: documentaries about the Beat Generation, movies based on the lives of the most prominent Beats, and movies based on their novels. Some films featured appearances by Beats who either played themselves or characters based on their own personalities, while other movies, without a direct Beat connection, had themes, characters, and subjects that showed obvious influence by the movement.

Pull My Daisy, which came out in 1959, is the only film that well-known Beat writers actually created themselves. As could be expected, it was a spontaneously arranged movie, derived from an unfinished play by Kerouac called *The Beat Generation*. The plot concerns Cassady and his wife Carolyn, who are trying to fit in with typical middle-class suburbanites only to have their Beat friends crash a sedate party and ruin the couple's reputation in the neighborhood. Among the actors are Ginsberg and Corso, and Kerouac provides a voice-over although he is never seen on screen.

Kerouac's novel *The Subterraneans*, made into a film and released in 1960, is based on incidents in the lives of Ginsberg, Corso, and Kerouac himself. Considered by Beats and non-Beats alike to be a bad attempt at making a "real" Hollywood movie, *The Subterraneans* was a box office flop, and today it is hardly remembered, even by movie buffs. A more successful Beat film did not appear until 1991 when *Naked Lunch* made it to the big screen, but it is a common misconception that the movie is based on Burroughs's novel. Instead, it is a semi-fantasy based on Burroughs's life during the time in which he was writing the book. The "plot" refers to Burroughs's job as a pest exterminator, and scenes include people snorting or shooting up bug spray, typewriters coming to life as sexually charged insects, and an escape to Tangiers where the main character endures insect-filled nightmares and tries to write a book. The movie *Drugstore Cowboy*, released in 1989, featured an appearance by Burroughs himself who plays—as one may guess—a drug-addicted priest who knows more about the dope scene in Portland than anyone else in town. Both *Drugstore Cowboy* and *Naked Lunch* enjoyed moderate box office success.

Documentaries about the Beat movement include *The Beat Generation* (1959), *The Beatniks* (1960), and *The Beats: An Existential Comedy* (1980). Films with indirect Beat connections include *American Pop* (1981), an animated film in which a rebellious son hears a reading of "Howl" and takes off on an adventure similar to Kerouac's in *On the Road*; *Hairspray* (1988) in which a Beatnik character reads "Howl" in order to frighten away a group of "squares"; and *Wild at Heart* (1990), which is based on a novel by Barry Gifford, who coauthored *Jack's Book*, an oral biography about Kerouac.

Historical Context

The Beat Movement got its start in the late 1940s and began losing momentum by the early 1960s, but the entire decade in between was a bountiful time for Beats. The members of the movement, keenly aware of the realities of the time, were not lulled into the sentimentality commonly associated with the 1950s. There is a distinct irony about the decade that many Americans old enough to remember those years often overlook. The nostalgia that has become synonymous with it—convertibles and road trips, hula-hoops and Elvis, TV and the technology boom, and "I Like Ike" pins on the lapels of happy suburbanites—tends to blur other events of the period that suggest anything but merriment and complacency. The Cold War with the Soviet Union, back yard bomb shelters, "duck and cover" exercises in grade school classrooms, the Communist revolution in Cuba, McCarthyism at home, and increased racial tensions all tell the story of a United States quite different from the wistful, fond memories that some older Americans still hold.

Although the United States and the Soviet Union had been allies in World War II, the death of Joseph Stalin in 1953 resulted in Nikita Khrushchev's rise to power and his eventual strengthening of Soviet political and military control over Eastern Europe. Both the United States and the Soviet Union had nuclear weapons capabilities, and as tensions between the two world powers escalated, so did the buildup of arsenals on both sides. In the United States, personal tensions mounted as well, and some families constructed bomb shelters in their back yards while their children learned how to drop to the classroom floor and cover their heads in the event that bomb sirens sounded during school hours. In an attempt to improve relations, President Eisenhower and Khrushchev were to meet at a summit in Paris in 1959, but two weeks prior to the event, a U.S. spy plane was shot down over Russia. The summit still took place, but the Soviet leader stormed out before it was over, and another planned meeting between Khrushchev and Eisenhower in Moscow was canceled. Meanwhile, closer to home, Fidel Castro led a Communist revolution in Cuba and became that country's ruler in 1959.

The Cold War and the threat of real war was a major impetus behind Eisenhower's decision to launch the largest public works program in U.S. history—the construction of the Interstate Highway System, which would connect the nation coast to coast and provide emergency runways for military aircraft, as well as quicker evacuation routes. The use of major highways for war purposes never materialized, but the possibility of it was indicative of how threatened both the U.S. Government and the American people felt during the 1950s. Worries were not confined to the physical horrors of war, however. They also involved concerns about the Communist takeover of the United States. Nothing short of mass hysteria resulted when Senator Joseph McCarthy of Wisconsin began holding hearings on the alleged Communist infiltration of the U.S. military. McCarthy and his followers also began identifying as Communists people in other government agencies, as well as well-known people in the movie industry and professors at universities. The senator's accusations were groundless; nonetheless, reputations were ruined and esteemed professionals were blacklisted. McCarthy's frenzied heyday ended when Eisenhower, military officials, and members of the media banded together to prove his "Red Scare" fraudulent. Ultimately, the senator was formally censured by Congress.

Many U.S. citizens feared being overcome by a foreign power. Those fears were not nearly as debilitating as problems Americans caused for themselves with racial intolerance and hatred. The 1950s saw the beginnings of one of the most significant movements of the century—the Civil Rights movement—sparked by the Brown v. the Board of Education decision in 1954, which made racial segregation in schools illegal. Blacks began openly defying previous "separatist" rules, including such historical acts as Rosa Parks's refusal to give up her seat to a white man and move to the back of a bus in Montgomery, Alabama, in 1955. This one act initiated a yearlong bus boycott in Montgomery, organized by the Reverend Martin Luther King, Jr. After Eisenhower signed the Civil Rights Act in

Compare & Contrast

- **1940s:** The beginnings of the Cold War between the United States and the Soviet Union create an uneasy current of fear and doubt in an otherwise hopeful and complacent post–World War II United States. The conflict involves massive arms buildup by both nations, including nuclear warheads—the most worrisome aspect of the Cold War.

  Today: The United States and Russia are allies in the war on terrorism, although President George W. Bush's decision to withdraw from the 1972 Anti-Ballistic Missile Treaty, which forbids testing and deployment of a ballistic missile defense system, greatly concerns Russian officials.

- **1940s:** In an effort to flee the crime and "unsavory" elements of the big city, many Americans head to the suburbs. In Long Island, New York, builders erect Levittown, a middle-class suburb with prefabricated housing materials, the first of its kind. Over the next decade, land values increase, sometimes up to 3000 percent, in prime suburban neighborhoods, where population increases by 44 percent.

  Today: Many inner-city areas are little more than dilapidated slums with high crime rates and widespread drug trafficking. Sociologists largely blame the "white flight" of the 1940s and 1950s for the decline of the cities, although there are current efforts to restore many downtowns and historical areas of cities and to draw people of all races and economic levels back there to live.

- **1950s:** The beginning of what many will call the commercialization of the United States comes in the form of fast food and theme parks. Ray Kroc buys out a hamburger franchise from the McDonald brothers and the golden arches are born. Harland Sanders begins his Kentucky Fried Chicken franchise. In California, Disneyland opens, the first theme park in the U.S. "history of leisure," and the Barbie doll is introduced to delighted children and adult collectors alike.

  Today: Fast food chains are the mainstay of many Americans' diets, although the once omnipotent McDonald's has tough competition from other burger restaurants as well as from pizza, taco, and deli sandwich servers. The Disney empire has expanded to include Disney World in Florida and similar theme parks throughout the world. Although the parks in the United States still flourish, EuroDisney has suffered some losses over recent years.

- **1950s:** Homosexual relationships are common among the Beat Generation but condemned by mainstream Americans as well as by the legal system. Labeled as sexual psychopaths under many states' laws, gays and lesbians are classed together with child molesters and rapists. In one instance in 1954, police in Sioux City, Iowa, arrest twenty suspected homosexual men after two children are brutally murdered. Although authorities never claim the men have anything to do with the crime, they are sentenced to a mental institution until "cured."

  Today: Legal recognition of same-sex unions and spousal benefits for long-term domestic partners are important gay-rights issues. While there is some relaxation of social attitudes towards gays and lesbians in current times, the legal system still presents a struggle for gays and lesbians. By the end of the twentieth century, thirty states have explicitly banned same-sex marriages, and, at the national level, the Defense of Marriage Act (1996) restricts the federal definition of marriage to heterosexual couples.

1957, tensions mounted even further, and, in one instance, Governor George Wallace of Arkansas refused to protect black students entering Central High School in Little Rock. Eisenhower was forced to send federal troops to the site. For the rest of the decade and on into the 1960s, issues of racism and civil rights continued to divide the country, often at the expense of human life.

In spite of the obvious causes of fear and doubt that ran rampant throughout the United States during the 1950s, some Americans still lived and many tried to emulate the Ozzie and Harriet life they viewed on their prized new gadget, the television. Along with a fascination with TV came the new rage in dining—frozen TV dinners, often enjoyed directly in front of the box for which they were named. Americans who preferred even faster food began to experience a new chain of hamburgers called McDonald's, and poultry lovers learned that they could grab a quick meal at Kentucky Fried Chicken. The significant form of entertainment to emerge from the decade was rock and roll, and when Sun Records released Elvis Presley's first record in 1954, the music industry was changed permanently. Perhaps the most significant impact of an innovation on the American way of life was one originally considered a preventive military move. The tens of thousands of miles of highway constructed during this period put the country on the move. People drove. They bought stylish new automobiles and took lengthy family vacations across state or across country. Many moved to recently built suburbs and enjoyed the longer drive to work, and still others began shopping and frequenting establishments in places they would once have considered too distant. More than any other American "value," mobility was adopted by the Beat Generation as much as it was by the Ozzies and Harriets across the country. Although their reasons, purposes, and destinations may have been quite different, both groups found themselves happily on the road.

Gaslight Poetry Café, a popular spot for Beat poets

Critical Overview

Criticism of the Beat Movement was initially almost as divided as the Beats themselves were from mainstream American society. While there was little disagreement that the Beat Generation had indeed caused a stir with its literature, art, and music, supporters and detractors argued mostly about the true artistic value of the methods and the results. The prevalent negative critique claimed, simply, that their writings were not literature. Beat writers were attacked for their disregard for proper grammar and their often incoherent, rambling prose that seemed accessible only to its authors. Supporters, however, found the strange styles and shocking subjects refreshing and justified the creative techniques as valid reactions to a humdrum, conservative mainstream. Decades after their fading away—and after the beatniks and hippies of the 1960s, disco freaks of the 1970s, and "me" generation of the 1980s—a more objective criticism emerged.

Recent Beat Movement reviewers have largely put aside the debate over what was real writing talent and what was not in order to concentrate on why the movement began in the first place and what influence it had on its own generation and those that followed. In his 1992 publication of *Understanding the Beats*, author Edward Halsey Foster claims that "writing was for the Beats a means through which the self might be redeemed, or at the very least a place where its redemption might be recorded." Foster went on to rationalize the unorthodox writing style as "a literature through which the individual could flourish beyond all factionalism, all ideologies." This philosophical contention echoes many critics' hindsight summaries of what the Beat Movement was all about. Most now agree that there was merit after all in its writings and other artistic expressions. Perhaps Steven Watson says it best in his response to Kerouac's historical definition of the Beat Generation as those who "espouse mystical detachment and relaxation of social and sexual tensions," a description the Beat icon provided for *Random House Dictionary*.

In *The Birth of the Beat Generation*, published in 1995, Watson says that "As the twentieth century draws to a close, the Beat Generation has outlived that historical moment, surviving notoriety and media blitz to become classic literature for succeeding generations."

Criticism

Pamela Steed Hill

Hill is the author of a poetry collection, has published widely in literary journals, and is an editor for a university publications department. In the following essay, Hill explores how the fractured, volatile lives of the primary Beat writers translated directly into the fractured, volatile works they produced.

The clearest dividing line between reviewers who praise the volumes of poetry, novels, stories, and essays from the Beat Movement and those who do not is the disagreement over what is real literature and what is not. Beat writers themselves did not make the decision easy, and most probably did not care at the time, nor would they care today. Indifference was "where it was at." Yet, like it or not, the originators of the movement became famous, even sporadically wealthy, but they often had problems handling the popularity, as well as the money. To be "normal" was not an option, and their work needed to reflect that. As a result, the writing was unorthodox, controversial, outlandish, and shocking, at least for that time. But were the styles, themes, and subjects wholly premeditated and cheaply contrived or could they be helped, considering the personal lives of the authors? Probably no other so-called "movement" of writers was as directly related to life experiences as the one coined "Beat," and a discussion of the movement is inseparable from a discussion of its authors. Few in number and relatively short in staying power, the Beat Generation produced the only kind of writing its members could have mustered.

There is little disagreement over the small number of main players who could legitimately call themselves Beats. Corso claimed the movement consisted only of Burroughs, Kerouac, Ginsberg, and himself, and that four people did not even make up a "generation." In *The Birth of the Beat Generation*, author Steven Watson says that "By the strictest definition, the Beat Generation consists of only William Burroughs, Allen Ginsberg, Jack Kerouac, Neal Cassady, and Herbert Huncke, with the slightly later addition of Gregory Corso and Peter Orlovsky." Corso may not have appreciated his placement as a "slightly later addition," but Watson's list is still small, no matter how the names are juggled. Moreover, the people behind the names appear to have had life's cards stacked against them from the beginning. Violent childhoods, broken families, bizarre fascinations, and no regard for personal health are the common experiences and common attitudes of the Beats, and their writing was little more than a public explosion of private fireworks. Considering that all survived their beginnings to become internationally known, the volatile foundations of these writers are worth a look.

Without doubt, Burroughs was oddest of them all. Typical, brief biographies neglect to mention that he began investigating methods of forging hard metals for weapons when he was eight years old; that he built homemade bombs as a teenager, one of which blew up in his hands, sending him to the hospital for six months, and another which he tossed through a window of his school principal's house; that, also as a teenager, he ingested a bottle of chloral hydrate and nearly died; that he almost killed a college classmate when he aimed at the fellow's stomach but ended up blowing a hole in his dorm room wall; that he severed the tip of his little finger with a pair of poultry sheers in protest of his first male lover's infidelity. All this by the time he was twenty-five. Burroughs's adulthood in New York and elsewhere is more documented than his childhood and adolescence, but it too rings of the same macabre fascinations and dangerous activities that enveloped his early years. The writing he did as both a youth and as an adult reflects his morbid obsessions and ghoulish practices, as well as his blatant disregard for laws and social mores. How aptly named is the "cut-up" technique for an author whose own mind and body consistently felt the puncturing and rending of a base, depraved, and fractured existence.

Another prominent Beat writer, Corso, also grew up with violence, although initially he was not the one asking for it, as it seems Burroughs was. After his mother abandoned him at the age of six months, Corso was placed in foster homes, living with three sets of parents in ten years. At twelve, he stole a radio from a neighbor and was sentenced to juvenile detention, the first of many run-ins with the law. In detention, the young Corso endured so many beatings that, in desperation, he rammed his hands through a window and was sent to the chil-

What Do I Study Next?

- In 2000, literary historian Thomas Newhouse published *The Beat Generation and the Popular Novel in the United States, 1945–1970.* Newhouse provides history and criticism on popular American novels in chapters covering "The War at Home: The Novel of Juvenile Delinquency," "Hipsters, Beats, and Supermen," "Breaking the Last Taboo: The Gay Novel," and "Which Way Is Up? The Drug Novel."
- Thomas Owens provides a thorough look at the innovative and controversial style of jazz that came alive in the 1940s and 1950s in *Bebop: The Music and Its Players* (1995). Focusing on the roots of bebop and moving into a study of its major players, including Charlie Parker and Dizzy Gillespie, Owens presents a readable, yet studious, account of the music and the techniques of the musicians. Serious jazz lovers will enjoy this work.
- In Michael Leja's 1993 book *Reframing Abstract Expressionism: Subjectivity and Painting in the 1940s*, the author suggests that Abstract Expressionist artists were part of a culture-wide initiative to "re-imagine the self." Incorporating the works and interests of other personalities of the period, Leja compares such artists as Jackson Pollock, Mark Rothko, and Willem de Kooning to contemporary essayists, Hollywood filmmakers, journalists, and popular philosophers.
- In 1997, Yale professor John Lewis Gaddis published *We Now Know: Rethinking Cold War History.* An expert on this period in history, Gaddis argues that there was indeed an international Communist conspiracy, that Castro and Khrushchev were victorious over Kennedy in the Cuban missile crisis, and that, ultimately, the Cold War was inevitable. This is a thought-provoking look at a volatile time in U.S. history.

dren's psychiatric ward at Bellevue hospital. After another stint in a boys' home, he wound up living on the street, where he honed his theft skills. At sixteen, he and two other street kids robbed a finance company of $7,000, and all of them went to prison. Corso was released at age twenty when he headed to New York and met the other members of the Beat Generation.

Ginsberg's childhood was not filled with as much personal violence as was Burroughs's and Corso's, but it was just as torn though in a different direction. Bouts with schizophrenia landed his mother in a sanatorium when Ginsberg was only three years old, and she was in and out of institutions for the rest of her life. Being without his mother for extended periods of time was hard on the boy, but being with her proved even more challenging. When she was home, Naomi Ginsberg went on vocal tirades in support of Communism and insisted on walking around naked. She forced her son to listen to her paranoid fantasies, including her fear that Ginsberg's father was poisoning their food, that she had to cover her ears with kitchen pots to ward off evil, and that there were insects threatening to take over their home. Ginsberg began to console himself with two primary comforts: writing and sexual fantasies. He became consumed with both and often melded the two in his secret diary. His well-publicized work as an adult is proof that he never got over it.

By comparison to his three main cohorts, Kerouac seems to have led an almost normal childhood, but normal is definitely a relative term. At age four, Kerouac endured the death of his nine-year-old brother, and he clung to his Catholic teachings with fanatical adherence, believing in visions of ghosts and statues whose heads could move on their own. A shy loner, Kerouac turned to writing and used the prose process as a means of sexual stimulation. Writing himself into a frenzy, so to speak, remained a habit, if not trademark, throughout his adult writing career. So too did the alcoholism he picked up from his father. Perhaps more so than the others, Kerouac tried to live a valid

> **"The Beats, it seems, are now praised for the very practices that condemned them fifty years ago. A complacent, smug America needed a good shaking, and the Beats provided it. But the question remains: did they provide it through good writing?"**

"literary" life, but there were too many obstacles in the way, many of which he created himself.

These biographical summaries obviously portray the worst of their authors' lives and, admittedly, they lean to the darker side for a purpose. To address Beat writing is to address Beat writers, and, while there are numerous other published Beats, the four mentioned here are considered the core group. There are also numerous other writers of all genres, all decades, all centuries whose lives were surely as violent, despairing, eerie, and dreadful as those described here, so what is the difference? What makes the Beat Movement so intrinsically tied to the similar quirks and experiences of the people involved? First, size. Even if one extends the circle of Beat writers beyond the Columbia group, beyond Greenwich Village, across the country to San Francisco, the number of members is still fewer than that of other well recognized literary movements. Extending the circle, however, is generally artificial, for a discussion of the Beats always returns to the handful of original members. Second, the personalities and resulting behavior of those members play a significant role in shaping the movement, as well as in confining it to a tight space in literary history. Most important, the writers themselves incite the debate on whether the word "literary" should even apply to their works.

Those who fare best in the debate are the poets. Generally given more license to experiment with styles and to ignore rules of syntax and grammar, poets Ginsberg and Corso tended to be criticized more for their subjects than their presentations. Explicit sexual references and anti-American pronouncements overshadowed the often incoherent, rambling lines and forced imagery. The prose writers were measured—and still are—with a different yardstick. Is cutting up pages of someone else's words and randomly splicing them together to create one's own work really "writing?" Even when individuals slice and shuffle their own words, is that literature? Regarding spontaneous writing, does it take real talent to sit at a typewriter and tap out every thought that comes to mind without any regard for plot, cohesion, readability, or an interesting subject? In the 1950s, many people answered no to all these questions. Hindsight, however, has been kinder. Now, critics are tempted to judge the products of the Beats based on nonliterary facets such as cultural restrictions and postwar fears. The Beats, it seems, are now praised for the very practices that condemned them fifty years ago. A complacent, smug America needed a good shaking, and the Beats provided it. The question remains: did they provide it through good writing?

That question will not be answered here or anywhere else. Like any "art" debate, it comes down to personal opinion. Perhaps the more intriguing point to ponder is whether the main writers of the Beat Generation—those who gave it both voice and a name—were only imitating their broken, scattered, "beat" lives with the works they produced. And further, could they have produced anything else? The contention here is no. The Beats wrote what they wrote because they lived how they lived. Rebels produce rebellious work—the more dissenting the lifestyle, the more defiant the writing. It is hard to imagine a Burroughs or a Ginsberg writing like William Faulkner or Robert Frost, or even like Norman Mailer or Gary Snyder, for that matter. While these writers and poets and countless others could surely be called defiant or even shocking by certain audiences, the Beats wore their pain, anger, criminality, and deviance on their sleeves like well-earned badges. They displayed grim personal lives openly through their actions and even more deeply through the words they put on paper.

Source: Pamela Steed Hill, Critical Essay on the Beat Movement, in *Literary Movements for Students*, The Gale Group, 2003.

Stephen Davenport

In the following essay, Davenport explores sexuality and gender within the Beat movement.

On a lovely autumn day in 1987, I walked into the office of an English professor I had taken a course with the year before, one of the most influential and widely quoted literary historians in the country, the first woman to be appointed an editor for either of the major Norton anthologies, in her case *The Norton Anthology of American Literature*, an Americanist who, despite the title of her contentious essay "The Madwoman and Her Languages: Why I Don't Do Feminist Theory," was at that point doing what she had always been doing: important feminist work. Five years later, much of that work—"The Madwoman" and thirteen of her other most important essays—would be collected and published under the title *Feminism and American Literary History*.

On that lovely autumn day, there in her spacious office—she was then the Director of the School of Humanities—I asked her if she would direct my dissertation. "What's it going to be about?" she asked. "Jack Kerouac," I ventured. She looked at me. I looked at me, too. I don't remember much about the short conversation that ensued except that she insisted upon my dissertation not becoming, as she put it, "some big macho trip."

Allen Ginsberg reads poetry in Washington Square Park in New York City

Fast-forward to a less lovely March afternoon in 1994. Though I had a full-time, albeit non-tenure-track, job at a nearby college, I was driving the same piano truck I had been driving since I had begun my Kerouac project, moving the same pianos with the same guys in the same way for the same few extra dollars. Aware that I had been recently divorced, one of those same guys, the only one not to be completing or defending a dissertation or turning one into a book and whining about each or all of those steps, asked me how things were going. I told him I was looking forward to a road trip north to deliver a paper at a conference. "What's it about?" he asked. "It's for AMSA, the American Men's Studies Association, and it's called '"Putting My Queer Shoulder to the Wheel"': The Beat Reinscription of Cultural and Literary Diversity.'" "Hey," he cautioned me, "that sounds politically incorrect on two counts." An alumnus of the same university laboratory high school that has produced more than one Nobel Prize winner and exactly one George Will, Ken seized the opportunity. "First," he said, "you're not gay. And, second, that sounds like a deeply reactionary group." He looked at me. I looked at my hands at ten and two on the wheel.

Autobiographical hors d'oeuvres like the two served above are common enough. They entertain; they instruct. They build community; they serve as confession. In the act of baring ourselves—or getting, as Beat poet Allen Ginsberg would say, "naked"—we simultaneously proclaim our differences and reveal our similarities. If Ginsberg were to walk into an AMSA conference session and repeat his celebrated gesture of disrobing in public and those of us attending the session were to follow suit by unsuiting, we would see simple theme and variation at work. If we chose instead to sit fully clothed in a circle and tell our stories, reveal ourselves for good and bad, in all our ugly beauty, we would be practicing the same "nakedness" that Ginsberg practiced and promoted.

Aside from everything else they might bare about me, the two stories that open this essay—the first about an influential mentor who happens to be a woman, the second about a concerned friend who happens to be a man—suggest an uneasiness about the way in which I position myself in relation not just to the Beat movement that Kerouac and Ginsberg served as figureheads, but also to the men's movement. The larger story that this essay builds is a cautionary tale about the liberation of post-WWII America from the constrictions of what Paul Goodman referred to at the time as "the Organized System." As with any American story about the human desire for self-expression in

> **"Yet, if we want to write a story of cultural liberation in postwar America, culminating in the civil rights movement, the gay rights movement, the women's movement, as well as the men's movement, we would do well to begin with the Beats."**

the face of conformity—or, at its most basic, life in the face of death—the identification of a primary liberator or liberating force is as historically reductive as it is culturally familiar.

Yet, if we want to write a story of cultural liberation in postwar America, culminating in the civil rights movement, the gay rights movement, the women's movement, as well as the men's movement, we would do well to begin with the Beats, who "act[ed] out a critique of the organized system that everybody in some sense agree[d] with." The Beat critique provided, according to John Tytell "the confirmation that America was suffering a collective nervous breakdown in the fifties, and that a new nervous system was a prerequisite to perception." The rewiring of America called for, as it usually does, a redefinition of what it means to be American. The Beats, to their credit, were active agents in that rewiring, no matter how sloppy the job in its early stages. This essay describes the job the Beat movement—arguably, postwar America's first men's movement—did and the bits of rewiring it left undone for later movements.

In the Beat aesthetic, the body and the word are inseparable. Among the "best minds" of Ginsberg's generation, as he announced on that most famous of Beat nights, the October 13, 1955, Six Gallery poetry reading of "Howl," were those "who howled on their knees in the subway and were dragged off the roof waving genitals and manuscripts" (line 35). "'Open form,'" he later said, "meant 'open mind.'" In a short how-to called "Essentials of Spontaneous Prose," Jack Kerouac argued for the same kind of openness, a nakedness he associated with birthing imagery:

> [W]rite outwards swimming in sea of language to peripheral release and exhaustion. . . Never afterthink to "improve" or defray impressions, as, the best writing is always the most painful personal wrungout tossed from cradle warm protective mind . . . always honest, . . . spontaneous, "confessional" interesting, because not "crafted."

In theory, then, "afterthinking" or "crafting" is a life-denying impulse or act. In closing form, we close minds; in discouraging diversity, we encourage dishonesty; in limiting variation, we impoverish theme; in differentiating between genitals and manuscripts or the body and the word, we weaken our creative and procreative capacity. We kill, in other words, the potential in art, in life, in our individual and communal selves when we separate the body and the word or, put differently, the material and the spiritual.

Autobiography and spontaneity, body and word, genitals and manuscripts—all of these elements are central to the Beat aesthetic. One evening in 1955, as Kerouac waited for him, Ginsberg grabbed a pencil and in twenty minutes turned an experience he had shared with Kerouac earlier that day into a now often anthologized poem called "Sunflower Sutra." If the story is true, Ginsberg composed the poem at a rate of more than one word every other second for twelve hundred seconds. Even if the story is only partly true, the final line is a powerful example of the Beat aesthetic:

> We're not our skin of grime, we're not our dread bleak dusty imageless locomotive, we're all golden sunflowers inside, blessed by our own seed & hairy naked accomplishment-bodies growing into mad black formal sunflowers in the sunset, spied on by our eyes under the shadow of the mad locomotive riverbank sunset Frisco hilly tincan evening sitdown visions.

Spontaneously composed autobiographical art as material as it is spiritual. In short, body and word.

Perhaps the strongest, clearest expression of our individual and communal need to keep body and word linked lies in our autobiographical impulse, our drive to reinvent ourselves, our "hairy naked accomplishment-bodies," with each story we tell. As both of the recent Jungian best sellers—Robert Bly's (1990) *Iron John: A Book about Men* and Clarissa Pinkola Estés' (1992) *Women Who Run with the Wolves: Myths and Stories of the Wild Woman Archetype*—demonstrate, the need to tell such stories crosses gender lines. And as the Murphy Brown episode in which a group of men struggle unsuccessfully to keep Murphy from entering their circle and seizing their talking-stick reminds us, men and women will and do cross artificially imposed gender lines regardless of interference.

Twenty-three years ago, the first hardcover textbook devoted to feminist literary criticism, Susan Koppleman Cornillon's (1972) *Images of Women in Fiction: Feminist Perspectives*, was published. A collection of essays, it included one by Florence Howe, who had just finished heading up the Modern Language Association's 1969–1971 Commission on Women and would soon become MLA's president. Making one of feminism's most important arguments—that no account, critical or literary, is ever disinterested—Howe called on autobiography as a starting point: "I begin with autobiography because it is there, in our consciousness about our own lives, that the connection between feminism and literature begins." It is also there—in autobiography—that masculinity and literature connect.

Certainly both of the two major publishing events in Beat history, Ginsberg's (1956) *Howl and Other Poems* and Kerouac's (1957) *On the Road*, stressed just that: that the line between life and literature is autobiography. In foregrounding "our consciousness about our own lives," the Beats walked that line, one that led naturally to what is arguably their primary cultural contribution: their interest in and promotion of diversity. Arguably the best summation of the Beats' cultural critique is the close of Ginsberg's (1956) "America":

> I'd better get right down to the job.
> It's true I don't want to join the Army or turn
> lathes in precision parts factories, I'm nearsighted
> and psychopathic anyway.
> America I'm putting my queer shoulder to the
> wheel.

Fearing a postwar encroachment of homogeneity, these "naked angels," as John Tytell called them, consistently celebrated heterogeneity. They sent out for instance, an early call for multiculturalism, they decried the loss of regional diversity, and they publicly approved of homosexuality long before Stonewall. Everyone's "hairy naked accomplishment-body" needed to be blessed: everyone's story needed to be reinscribed in the "hairy naked accomplishment-body" of America itself if America was to realize its own "golden sunflower" by living up to its promise as the great social experiment of modern times. The "queer shoulder" of Ginsberg's challenge began autobiographically with Ginsberg himself, a homosexual, Jewish, Russian-American child of a Socialist father and a Communist mother, and if he was not really "psychopathic," he certainly did a turn in the Columbian Presbyterian Psychiatric Institute. The less literal "shoulder" Ginsberg wanted admitted to the "wheel" was the Demonized Other, the Unassimilated American. Kerouac's primary idea of the Other was what he called the "fellaheen" (i.e., Mexicans, Native Americans, and African Americans); William Burroughs' list began with petty thieves and drug addicts.

According to Burroughs, the third of the three major Beat figures, America was in fact ready for a sea change:

> Once started, the Beat movement had a momentum of its own and a world-wide impact.... The Beat literary movement came at exactly the right time and said something that millions of people of all nationalities all over the world were waiting to hear. You can't tell anybody anything he doesn't know already. The alienation, the restlessness, the dissatisfaction were already there waiting when Kerouac pointed out the road.
>
> Artists to my mind are the real architects of change.... Art exerts a profound influence on the style of life, the mode, range and direction of perception.... Certainly *On the Road* performed that function in 1957 to an extraordinary extent. There's no doubt that we're living in a freer America as a result of the Beat literary movement, which is an important part of the larger picture of cultural and political change in this country during the last forty years, when a four letter word couldn't appear on the printed page, and minority rights were ridiculous.

Women's rights were also "ridiculous," but they get no mention here. That should come as no surprise, considering Burroughs' very public stance as a misogynist. In an interview published in 1974, Burroughs blames Western dualism on the creation of women: "I think they were a basic mistake and the whole dualistic universe evolved from this error." If women are the result of a key creational error, they are also, as Burroughs adds, at the root of a national problem: "America is a matriarchal, white supremacist country. There seems to be a definite link between matriarchy and white supremacy." For Burroughs, then, woman is the Ultimate Other, both Demonized and Demonizing, for she carries with her into the universe the basic concept of difference and perpetuates it in America with her role in race relations. She is, in other words, the Other who (m)others Others, a perfect queer-shoulder machine.

But what of the Beat movement in general? Were women to be included in the roll call of Others who might conceivably put their "queer" shoulders to the wheel? Were their "hairy naked accomplishment-bodies," their stories, their body and word to be included in the rewiring of America that the Beat critique called for?

The issue of voice is a central one in Joyce Johnson's (1983/1984) *Minor Characters: The Romantic Odyssey of a Woman in the Beat Generation*, winner of the 1984 National Book Critics Circle Award. Kerouac's girlfriend at the time *On the Road* was published and a witness to the public clamor that resulted, Johnson closes *Minor Characters* with the image of herself at "twenty-two, with her hair hanging below her shoulders, all in black like Masha in *The Seagull*—black stockings, black skirt, black sweater." Johnson's happy, pleased to be seated "at the table in the exact center of the universe, that midnight place where so much is converging, the only place ... that's alive." Johnson sees, however, that

> as a female, she is not quite part of this convergence. A fact she ignores, sitting by in her excitement as the voices of the men, always the men, passionately rise and fall and their beer glasses collect and the smoke of their cigarettes rises toward the ceiling and the dead culture is surely being wakened. Merely being here, she tells herself, is enough.

And at that time, it is.

Aware of the marginalization of women in Beat culture, literary historian Michael Davidson argues that

> The Beats offered a new complex set of possible roles for males that, even if they subordinated women, at least offered an alternative to the consumerist ideology of sexuality projected by the *Playboy* magazine stereotype of heterosexuality and to the *Saturday Evening Post* version of the nuclear family.

The Beats, then, offered men a way out of the organized system, and though they were guilty of replicating "square" culture's subordination of women, they offered women a way out, too. For many women, Beat culture was preferable to a life in the suburbs.

Even so, replication of this sort is especially disheartening when it occurs within a subculture that purports to be egalitarian and liberationist by nature. Consider, for instance, the goals of the bohemian occupants of Greenwich Village thirty to forty years earlier:

> 1. The idea of salvation by the child...
> 2. The idea of self-expression...
> 3. The idea of paganism...
> 4. The idea of living for the moment...
> 5. The idea of liberty...
> 6. The idea of female equality...
> 7. The idea of psychological adjustment...
> 8. The idea of changing place...

That the Beats adhered to all but one of these tenets bespeaks their bohemian roots and aspirations; that their "idea of liberty" did not extend equally to women points to their investment in square, or patriarchal, conventions. Looking back at Beat culture in a June 1989 *Village Voice* article, feminist writer and activist Alix Kates Shulman decries the conspicuous absence of the Emma Goldmans and Isadora Duncans of an earlier generation of bohemians: "[B]y the time the Beats were ascendant, the postwar renewal of mandatory domesticity, sexual repression, and gender rigidity had so routed feminism that it lapsed even in bohemia."

During the height of public interest in Beats and beatniks, the place of women in Beat culture was publicized by detractors and exponents alike. In 1959, *Life* attacked Beat males on a number of grounds, one of which was their financial dependence on women. The year before, *Playboy* had also attacked the Beats. If Beat women did all the work at home and in the marketplace to support their men, they also, according to *Playboy*, did all the work in bed: "When the hipster makes it with a girl, he avoids admitting that he likes her. He keeps cool. He asks her to do the work, and his ambition is to think about nothing, zero, strictly from nadaville, while she plays bouncy-bouncy on him." In both versions, the Beat male offends. In the *Life* version, the problem is work; in the *Playboy*, sex. In neither case, the square nor the hip, is the Beat rebel masculine enough.

Even sympathetic accounts like Lawrence Lipton's (1959) *The Holy Barbarians* and Paul Goodman's (1960) *Growing Up Absurd* wondered aloud why women would be interested in a lifestyle that seemed so obviously to subordinate them. Lipton asked, "What are they like, these women of the beat generation pads? Where do they come from, how do they get here? And why?" Goodman suggested that the Beats might be even more exclusionist than their "square" counterparts: "What is in it for the women who accompany the Beats? The characteristic Beat culture, unlike the American standard of living, is essentially for men, indeed for very young men who are 'searching.'"

The typical woman in a Beat narrative, whether a memoir or a novel, lives in the margin of a margin. Consider, for instance, the following description by Joyce Johnson, a woman who, like her famous boyfriend, wanted to be a writer. She knew that margin all too well:

> The whole Beat scene had very little to do with the participation of women as artists themselves. The real communication was going on between the men, and the women were there as onlookers. Their old ladies. You kept your mouth shut, and if you were intelligent and interested in things you might pick up what you could. It was a very masculine aesthetic.

As Beat artists, the men were marginalized figures, their shoulders "queer," their status "other." As "onlookers" of the overlooked, their "old ladies" were doubly marginalized. Neither ladies nor artists in their own right, they were at that point too wild for some, not wild enough for others. The rewiring of America had begun, though, and the Beat convergence of body and word around a "table in the exact center of the universe" was instrumental in bringing "the dead culture" back to life. If the Joyce Johnsons of Beat culture suffered because they were women, they chose to do so because suburbia offered the same job without the benefits.

Like the American social experiment that can boast of many successes, so can the Beat experiment. Burroughs may be right when he claims, "There's no doubt that we're living in a freer America as a result of the Beat literary movement." Beats like Ginsberg and Kerouac certainly redefined both the wheel and the shoulder that would make it turn. But the embodied manuscripts they imagined waving seditiously from rooftops were certainly genitally male, the pen as phallus as pen, that old inky sword ripping a highly masculine signature across the body and mind of America. At their worst as a cultural agent, they suffered a failure of the imagination, reverting to old patterns. As Catharine R. Stimpson so ably puts it: "The Beats often feminized invective to scorn the fag. Such a practice is but one mark of a cultural boundary they could rarely cross: a traditional construction of the female, and of the feminine." The Beat movement was, in many ways, what Nina Baym, my dissertation director, did not want to have to deal with: "some big macho trip."

At their best, the Beats forced a national dialogue about alternative discourse and community, and, in their unofficial credo that "open form" means "open mind," they helped America realize what it already knew: that there's room at the wheel for everyone's word and hairy naked accomplishment-body, everyone's story and shoulder, regardless of whether everyone's genitals can wave like manuscripts from rooftops. Did the Beats realize that at the time? Apparently not, but the failure of feminism in Beat culture is the failure of feminism in 1950s' America. Twentieth-century bohemian enclaves, regardless of the decade, have always depended on what Davidson calls "elaborate pecking orders and cult loyalties", and gender has always, regardless of the enclave, produced margins into which women have had to write themselves.

In the twentieth-century narrative of bohemian involvement in women's rights, the Beats are not well positioned historically. Without the advantage of the feminist networks and forums that had some say in European and American bohemian communities prior to World War II, the Beat project has come to constitute, for many, a movement of men for men. Though it sought to rewire America through confrontational, confessional art and liberationist politics, its shortsightedness left key bits of the job undone.

Given historical reminders like this one, can today's men's movement avoid what my piano-moving buddy Ken Stratton suspects is a reactionary impulse and remember that no account, whether literary or critical, is ever disinterested is ever free of autobiography, is ever anything but the story of someone's Other as it is simultaneously the story of everyone's shoulder positioning itself at the wheel? The men's movement, like the women's movement out of which and against which it has grown, is a set of competing—and, in some cases, hostile—practices (e.g., profeminist, mythopoetic, men's rights). Thus, it is not so much a movement as it is a narrative of competing stories, of hairy naked accomplishment-bodies born in autobiography and lived in consciousness and reinvention. The degree to which the men's movement moves at all depends upon the wheel and how many competing "queer shoulders," how much diversity, it permits and how much we have learned, or unlearned, from past movements.

Source: Stephen Davenport, "Queer Shoulders to the Wheel: Beat Movement as Men's Movement," in *The Journal of Men's Studies*, Vol. 3, No. 4, May 1995, pp. 297–307.

Stephen Prothero

In the following essay, Prothero examines spirituality and religion within the Beat movement.

For the beat generation of the 1940s and 1950s, dissertation time is here. Magazine and newspaper critics have gotten in their jabs. Now scholars are starting to analyze the literature and legacy of the beat writers. In the last few years biographers have lined up to interpret the lives of Jack Kerouac, Allen Ginsberg, and William Burroughs, and publishers have rushed into print a host of beat journals, letters, memoirs, and anthologies. The most recent *Dictionary of Literary Biography* devotes two large volumes to sixty-seven beat writers, including Neal Cassady, Herbert Huncke, Gary Snyder, Gregory Corso, John Clellon Holmes, Lawrence Ferlinghetti, Philip Lamantia, Peter Orlovsky, Michael McClure, and Philip Whalen.

Historical writing on relatively recent subjects tends to get bogged down in issues raised by early critics, and recent scholarship on the beat generation is no exception to this rule. From the pages of *Life* and *Partisan Review*, contemporary scholars have inherited two key interpretive lines that I want to call into question here: first, the tendency to view the beat movement rather narrowly as a literary or cultural impulse; and second, the inclination to judge this impulse negatively, as a *revolt against* rather than a *protest for* something.

Although there was a smattering of early critical acclaim for the beat writers, neither their literature nor their movement fared well with the critics. One reviewer called William Burroughs's *Naked Lunch* "a prolonged scream of hatred and disgust, an effort to keep the reader's nose down in the mud for 250 pages." Kerouac's *On the Road* was said to distinguish itself from true literature by its "poverty of emotional, intellectual, and aesthetic resources, an ineptitude of expression, and an inability to make anything dramatically meaningful". What bothered the critics most about the beats was their negativity. *Life* claimed they were at war with everything sacred in Eisenhower's America—"Mom, Dad, Politics, Marriage, the Savings Bank, Organized Religion, Literary Elegance, Law, the Ivy League Suit and Higher Education, to say nothing of the Automatic Dishwasher, the Cellophane-wrapped Soda Cracker, the Split-Level House and the clean, or peace-provoking H-bomb." The *Nation* dismissed the beats as "nay-sayers"; even *Playboy* called them "nihilists."

This interpretation reached its rhetorical heights in a 1958 *Partisan Review* review of *On the Road* by Norman Podhoretz. While *Life* had compared the beats with communists and anarchists, Podhoretz grouped them with Nazis and Hell's Angels. "The Bohemianism of the 1950s is hostile to civilization; it worships primitivism, instinct, energy, 'blood,'" he wrote. "This is a revolt of the spiritually underprivileged and the crippled of soul." In a follow-up note in the next issue, Podhoretz asked those who wrote in to defend the beat writers, "Where is the 'affirmation of life' in all this? Where is the spontaneity and vitality? It sounds more like an affirmation of death to me."

The beats responded to this critical chorus with one voice. "Beat," Kerouac asserted, stood not for "beat down" but for "beatific." "I want to speak *for* things," he explained. "For the crucifix I speak out, for the Star of Israel I speak out, for the divinest man who ever lived who was German (Bach) I speak out, for sweet Mohammed I speak out, for Buddha I speak out, for Lao-tse and Chuang-tse I speak out." To those who called "Howl," a "howl against civilization," Ginsberg replied that his signature poem was a protest in the original sense of "pro-attestation, that is testimony in favor of Value." He too described his protest in religious terms. "'Howl' is an 'Affirmation' by individual experience of God, sex, drugs, absurdity," he explained. "The poems are religious and I meant them to be."

Apologies of this sort have convinced most scholars of American literature that the beat movement amounted to something rather than nothing. Beat literature is, as a result, edging its way into the American literary canon. But exactly what (and how much) beat poems and novels amount to remains a matter of debate. Few interpreters now ignore entirely the obvious spiritual concerns of the beats' work. But the tendency among literary scholars is to see those concerns as tangential rather than constitutive.

Surprisingly, historians of American religion have demonstrated even less interest in beat spirituality. The beats are conspicuously absent from standard surveys of the field and from recent monographs on American religion in the postwar period. Historians of American religion who have explored beat spirituality have tended to focus almost exclusively on the beats' engagement with Zen and then to dismiss that engagement as haphazard. Thus Carl T. Jackson, echoing Alan Watts's earlier contention that "beat Zen" is "phony zen," contends in a recent article that the beats (with one exception) deviated from some hypostatized "authentic" Zen and therefore fail to qualify as "real" Zen Buddhists. While such judgments may do something to safeguard Zen orthodoxy (whatever that may be), they tend, perhaps unintentionally, to render beat spirituality illegitimate even while informing us about it.

Forty years ago Perry Miller contended that transcendentalism, which had previously been interpreted largely in literary terms, was essentially a "religious demonstration" and as such deserved a prominent place not only in American literature but also in American religious history. This article presents an analogous, if somewhat more modest, argument for the beat movement. My thesis is that the beats were spiritual protesters as well as literary innovators and ought, therefore, to be viewed at least as minor characters in the drama of American religion. If, as Miller argues, transcendentalism represented a religious revolt against "corpse-cold" Unitarian orthodoxy, the beat movement represented a spiritual protest against what the beats perceived as the moribund orthodoxies of 1950s America.

A "New Vision"

The beat movement began with the meeting of Kerouac, Burroughs, and Ginsberg in New York in 1944, coursed its way through the San Francisco poetry renaissance of the 1950s, and spent itself sometime in the early 1960s. It was led by three main figures—a working-class French-Canadian Catholic from Lowell, Massachusetts (Kerouac), a middle-class Russian-American Jew from Paterson, New Jersey (Ginsberg), and an upper-class Anglo-American Protestant from St. Louis (Burroughs)—and included a large supporting cast of novelists, poets, and hangers-on. What united these men (and the vast majority of them were men) was a "new consciousness" or a "new vision."

Like any spiritual innovation, this new vision included a rejection of dominant spiritual norms and established religious institutions. Neither of the two most popular spiritual options of the early postwar period—the new evangelicalism of Billy Graham and the mind cure of Rabbi Joshua Liebman's *Peace of Mind* (1946), Monsignor Fulton J. Sheen's *Peace of Soul* (1949), and the Rev. Norman Vincent Peale's *The Power of Positive Thinking* (1952)—seemed viable to the beats in the light of the long postwar shadow cast by the Holocaust, the bomb, and the cold war. Thus Burroughs, Kerouac, and Ginsberg joined neo-orthodox theologians H. Richard and Reinhold Niebuhr in rejecting any easy return to normalcy and in damning the evangelical and mind-cure revivals as vacuous at best. For this beat trio, neither positive thinking nor evangelical Christianity could make sense of God's apparent exodus from the world. But somehow Oswald Spengler's *The Decline of the West*, a book the beats studied and discussed in the late 1940s, could.

Inspired by Spengler's apocalypticism, the beats announced the death of the tribal god of American materialism and mechanization. ("There is a God / dying in America," Ginsberg proclaimed.) But in keeping with Spengler's cyclical view of history, they prophesied that a new deity was arising from the wreckage. (Ginsberg called it ". . . an inner / anterior image / of divinity / beckoning me out / to pilgrimage.")

In 1938, two years after his graduation from Harvard, William Burroughs wrote a humorous yet foreboding short story entitled "Twilight's Last Gleamings." Loosely based on the sinking of the Titanic, this cynical satire is a dark allegory on the fall of America and the refusal of Americans to accept the inevitability of their own deaths and the demise of their civilization. Burroughs's characters are Neros with urban savvy: con men conning, robbers robbing, preachers preaching as the ship goes down. The moral of this story is well expressed in a later poem by Lawrence Ferlinghetti:

> The end has just begun
> I want to announce it
> Run don't walk
> to the nearest exit.

Along with this preoccupation with America's eschaton, the theme of individual suffering and death looms in beat writing. Unlike Liebman, Sheen, and Peale, who resolved to will into existence a "placid decade," the beats devoted their lives and their literature to understanding and explicating the private hells of those who remained on the margins of postwar prosperity. Burroughs's first four books—*Junkie*, *Queer*, *Naked Lunch*, and *Yage Letters*—document in factualist style the horrors of addiction to "junk" in its many forms (drugs, sex, power). Much of Ginsberg's work, including "Howl" and "Kaddish," explores madness and death. Three of Kerouac's novels—*Maggie Cassady*, *The Subterraneans*, and *Tristessa*—are odes to lost loves; and his *Big Sur* depicts his own alcohol-induced breakdown.

If the beats had stopped here, critics' categorization of their work and thought as morbid or mad might have been accurate. But like the Lutheran preacher who hits her congregation with sin only to smother them with grace, the beats sought to move beyond predictions of social apocalypse and depictions of individual sadness to some transcendental hope. "The Beat Generation is insulted when linked to doom, thoughts of doom, fear of doom, anger of doom," Ginsberg, Corso, and Orlovsky protested in 1959. "It exhibits on every side, and in a bewildering number of facets," John Clellon Holmes added, "a perfect craving to believe... the stirrings of a quest." Thus the beats' *flight from* the churches and synagogues of the suburbs to city streets inhabited by whores and junkies, hobos and jazzmen never ceased to be a *search for* something to believe in, something to go by.

From the perspective of *Religionswissenschaft*, the beats shared much with pilgrims coursing their way to the world's sacred shrines. Like pilgrims to Lourdes or Mecca, the beats were liminal figures who expressed their cultural marginality by living spontaneously, dressing like bums, sharing their property, celebrating nakedness and sexuality, seeking mystical awareness through drugs and meditation, acting like "Zen lunatics" or holy fools, and perhaps above all stressing the chaotic sacrality of human interrelatedness or *communitas* over the pragmatic functionality of social structure. The beats, in short, lived both on the road and on the edge. For them, as for pilgrims, transition was a semipermanent condition. What distinguished the beats from other pilgrims, however, was their lack of a "center out there." The beats shared, in short, not an identifiable geographical goal but an undefined commitment to a spiritual search. They aimed not to arrive but to travel and, in the process, to transform into sacred space every back alley through which they ambled and every tenement in which they lived. Thus the beats appear in their lives and in their novels not only as pilgrims but also as heroes (and authors) of quest tales, wandering (and writing) *bhikkhus* who scour the earth in a never fully satisfied attempt to find a place to rest. This commitment to the spiritual quest is expressed by Burroughs in *Naked Lunch:*

> Since early youth I had been searching for some secret, some key with which I could gain access to basic knowledge, answer some of the fundamental questions. Just what I was looking for, what I meant by basic knowledge or fundamental questions, I found difficult to define. I would follow a trail of clues.

On the trail that Kerouac, Ginsberg, and Burroughs followed after the war, one important clue was provided by Spengler: the suggestion that the solution to their individual crises of faith (and to America's crisis of spirit) might lie outside western culture and civilization, in the Orient and in the "fellaheen" or uprooted of the world.

A Preferential Option for the Fellaheen

Inspired by a populism akin to contemporary Latin American theologians' preferential option for the poor, the beats looked for spiritual insight not to religious elites but to the racially marginal and the socially inferior, "fellah" groups that shared with them an aversion to social structures and established religion. Hipsters and hoboes, criminals and junkies, jazzmen and African-Americans initiated the beats into their alternative worlds, and the beats reciprocated by transforming them into the heroes of their novels and poems.

Shortly after Kerouac, Ginsberg, and Burroughs teamed up in New York in 1944, their circle of acquaintances expanded to include "teaheads from everywhere, hustlers with pimples, queens with pompadours... the unprotected, the unloved, the unkempt, the inept and sick" who hung out at the penny arcades, peep shows, and jazz clubs in the Bowery, Harlem, and Times Square. Kerouac described them in his first novel, *The Town and the City*, like this:

> soldiers, sailors, the panhandlers and drifters, the zoot-suiters, the hoodlums, the young men who washed dishes in cafeterias from coast to coast, the hitch-hikers, the hustlers, the drunks, the battered lonely young Negroes, the twinkling little Chinese, the dark Puerto Ricans, and the varieties of dungareed young Americans in leather jackets who were seamen and mechanics and garagemen everywhere... All the cats and characters, all the spicks and spades, Harlem-drowned, street-drunk and slain, crowded together, streaming back and forth, looking for something, waiting for something, forever moving around.

Recalling Dostoevsky's "underground men," Ginsberg dubbed these characters "subterraneans." Kerouac, assigning them a place a little closer to heaven, christened them "desolation angels."

Of all these fallen angels, the beats were especially enamored of Herbert Huncke, who according to Ginsberg "was to be found in 1945 passing on subways from Harlem to Broadway scoring for drugs, music, incense, lovers, Benzedrine Inhalers, second story furniture, coffee, all night vigils in 42nd Street Horn & Hardart and Bickford Cafeterias, encountering curious & beautiful solitaries of New York dawn." Huncke embodied for the beats both marginality and spirituality.

> In his anonymity & holy Creephood in New York he was the sensitive vehicle for a veritable new consciousness which spread through him to others sensitized by their dislocations from History and thence to entire generations of a nation renewing itself for fear of Apocalyptic Judgement. So in the grand

> Karma of robotic Civilizations it may be that the humblest, most afflicted, most persecuted, most suffering lowly junkie hustling some change in the all-night movie is the initiate of a Glory transcending his Nation's consciousness that will swiftly draw that Nation to its knees in tearful self-forgiveness.

Initiated by Huncke into this "holy Creephood," Ginsberg, Kerouac, and Burroughs now identified with the beat-up and the beat-down. Kerouac dropped out of Columbia, and the same university expelled Ginsberg. Burroughs began what would turn into a life of participant-observation of the netherworlds of gangsters, addicts, and hustlers. Kerouac explored the jazz clubs and marijuana bars of Harlem. Ginsberg investigated the lives of the working class in Paterson, New Jersey. All three men attempted to transform their experiences into literature worthy of Rimbaud or Baudelaire. By venerating Huncke (who according to beat lore was the first to use the term "beat") as a saint, the beats risked transforming their "new vision" into an amoral, nihilistic apocalypticism. What prevented this outcome, at least for Ginsberg and Kerouac, was the arrival in New York in 1947 of Neal Cassady.

The "secret hero" of Ginsberg's "Howl" and the inspiration for the ecstatic Dean Moriarty of Kerouac's *On the Road*, Cassady was born, quite literally, on the road (in a rumble seat in Salt Lake City while his mother and father were making their way to Hollywood). His parents separated when he was six years old, so he was raised by an alcoholic father in western pool halls, freight yards, and flophouses. While a teenager, Cassady supposedly stole over five hundred cars and seduced nearly as many women. He did six stints in reformatories before landing in San Quentin in the late 1950s.

Kerouac and Ginsberg celebrated and romanticized Cassady as a "holy goof." Kerouac, who by 1947 had grown tired of the apocalyptic intellectualism of Burroughs, greeted the lusty Cassady as a "long-lost brother." Contrasting Cassady to Huncke, Kerouac observed that "his 'criminality' was not something that sulked and sneered; it was Western, the west wind, an ode from the Plains, something new, long prophesied, long a-coming (he only stole cars for joy rides)." Ginsberg also embraced Cassady, who soon became his lover, in mythic terms—as "cocksman and Adonis of Denver." Burroughs, however, dissented, dismissing Cassady as a con man. Thus Cassady's arrival precipitated a split of sorts in the nascent beat movement. The pro-Huncke Burroughs persisted in a more absurdist and apocalyptic reading of the "new vision" (beat as beat down) while Ginsberg and Kerouac attempted to incorporate in their new, pro-Cassady consciousness some redemptive force or transcendental hope (beat as beatitude).

"Cassady redeemed the beatific beats' 'new vision' by pointing the way to what would become two major affirmations of Kerouac's and Ginsberg's spirituality: the sacralization of everyday life and the sacramentalization of human relationships."

Cassady redeemed the beatific beats' "new vision" by pointing the way to what would become two major affirmations of Kerouac's and Ginsberg's spirituality: the sacralization of everyday life and the sacramentalization of human relationships. If Dean Moriarty preaches a gospel in *On the Road*, it is that every moment is sacred, especially when shared with friends. And if he incarnates an ethic, it is that since all human beings are of one piece, every person must share in every other person's sorrow just as surely as all people will be delivered to heaven together in the end. Thus Cassady personified for Kerouac and Ginsberg the sacred connections of *communitas*. While Huncke symbolized the misery of lonely individuals suffering and dying in dark Times Square bars, Cassady symbolized the splendor of cosmic companions digging the open road.

Shortly after their initial encounter in 1947, Ginsberg and Cassady bowed down together at the edge of an Oklahoma highway and vowed always to care for one another. Seven years later Ginsberg and Peter Orlovsky agreed to "explore each other until we reached the mystical 'X' together" and promised "that neither of us would go into heaven unless we could get the other one in." Such covenants expressed ritualistically Ginsberg's credo "that we are all one Self with one being, one consciousness." They represented an attempt to routinize the group's *communitas*, to incarnate

Whitman's vision of "fervent comradeship" in a spiritual brotherhood of beatific monks.

Cassady inspired in this way a shift in the beatific beats' writing from the pessimistic, Dreiserian realism that would mark Burroughs's work to a more optimistic, even transcendental realism: literature as "a clear statement of fact about misery... *and* splendor [my emphasis]." Like Burroughs, Ginsberg and Kerouac would continue to depict the suffering of the fellaheen, but unlike him they would insist that such suffering was both revelatory and redemptive. Thus Ginsberg transformed the profanity of working-class life in Paterson into a hierophany:

The alleys, the dye works,
Mill Street in the smoke,
melancholy of the bars,
the sadness of long highways,
negroes climbing around
the rusted iron by the river,
the bathing pool hidden
behind the silk factory
fed by its drainage pipes;
all the pictures we carry in our mind

images of the thirties
depression and class consciousness
transformed above politics
filled with fire
with the appearance of God.

And thus Kerouac insisted that while authors must "accept loss forever," they should nonetheless "believe in the holy contour of life."

Turning East

If the beats followed Spengler's clue in looking to fellaheen like Huncke and Cassady for spiritual insight, they also followed his lead in steering their spiritual quest toward Asia. While other Americans were forging Protestant-Catholic-Jewish alliances during Eisenhower's presidency, the beats were moving toward a far more radical ecumenism. In addition to the Catholicism of Kerouac, the Protestantism of Burroughs, and the Judaism of Ginsberg, the beats studied gnosticism, mysticism, native American lore, Aztec and Mayan mythology, American transcendentalism, Hinduism, and especially Buddhism.

This religious eclecticism was epitomized by Jack Kerouac who, though born a Catholic, practiced Buddhist meditation and once observed the Muslim fast of Ramadan. When asked in an interview to whom he prayed, Kerouac replied, "I pray to my little brother, who died, and to my father, and to Buddha, and to Jesus Christ, and to the Virgin Mary." His pluralism reached still farther in this creedal chorus from *Mexico City Blues:*

I believe in the sweetness
of Jesus
And Buddha—
I believe
In St. Francis
Avaloki
Tesvara,
the Saints
Of First Century
India A D
And Scholars
Santivedan
And Otherwise
Santayanan
Everywhere

Only Ginsberg, a self-styled "Buddhist Jew," approached Kerouac's eclecticism. In a poem entitled "Wichita Vortex Sutra" he invoked a litany of gods:

million-faced Tathagata gone past suffering
Preserver Harekrishna returning in the age of pain
Sacred Heart my Christ acceptable
Allah the Compassionate One
Jaweh Righteous One
all Knowledge-Princes of Earth-man, all
ancient Seraphim of heavenly Desire, Devas, yogis
& holyman I chant to—

Clearly the beats were not wed exclusively to any one religious tradition. One religion, however, did inspire more of them more deeply than any other, namely, Buddhism, especially the Zen and Yogacara formulations of the Mahayana school. Though Burroughs had introduced them through Spengler to Asian thought in 1945, Kerouac and Ginsberg did not begin to study Buddhism in earnest until 1953. In that year a reading of Thoreau's *Walden* inspired Kerouac to learn more about Asian religious traditions. He began his investigation by reading Ashvagosa's biography of Gautama Buddha. Struck by the Buddha's injunction to "Repose Beyond Fate," Kerouac sat down to meditate. He then experienced what he later described as "golden swarms of nothing." Immediately he left to go to San Jose to enlighten Neal Cassady. But Cassady had already found his own prophet in the person of Edgar Cayce, whose strange brew of Christian metaphysics, clairvoyance, reincarnation, and karma had whetted his eclectic appetite. While in San Jose, Kerouac began to study Mahayana Buddhist scriptures, especially the Diamond Sutra, the Perfection of Wisdom Sutra, and the Sutra of the Sixth Patriarch, as they appeared in Dwight Goddard's *A Buddhist Bible.*

Buddhism attracted Kerouac because it seemed to make sense of the central facts of his experience (suffering, impermanence) and to affirm his intuition that life was dreamlike and illusory. Perhaps more importantly, by locating the origin of suffering in desire, the Buddhist sutras seemed to offer a way out. In the summer of 1954 Kerouac wrote to Burroughs, who was now living in Tangier, about his discovery of Buddhism and his vow to remain celibate for a year in an attempt to mitigate his desire and thus his suffering. Burroughs wrote back, urging Kerouac not to use Buddhism as "psychic junk." "A man who uses Buddhism or any other instrument to remove love from his being in order to avoid suffering has committed, in my mind, a sacrilege comparable to castration," he wrote. "Suffering is a chance you have to take by the fact of being alive." Interestingly, Burroughs wrote a letter that same summer to Ginsberg, urging him to "dig" Tibetan Buddhism if he had not yet done so. Burroughs was opposed not to Buddhism itself but to its use in the West as some sort of "final fix."

Ginsberg took Burroughs's advice, and by mid-decade the novels and poems of Kerouac and Ginsberg were filled with references to Buddhism. In one eighteen-month period between 1954 and 1956 Kerouac meditated daily and still found the time to write five books with a decidedly Buddhist bent. Three of these works, *Some of the Dharma* (a thousand-page personal meditation), *Buddha Tells Us* (an American version of the Surangama Sutra), and *Wake Up* (a life of the Buddha) have never been published. A book of Buddhist poems, *Mexico City Blues*, and a beat sutra entitled *The Scripture of the Golden Eternity* appeared in 1959 and 1960 respectively.

In 1955 Ginsberg and Kerouac met Gary Snyder, a mountain poet and Zen initiate, who contributed greatly to their understanding of Buddhism and their commitment to it. Just as Neal Cassady appeared as Dean Moriarty, the hero of *On the Road*, Snyder was immortalized as Japhy Ryder, the thinly veiled protagonist of *Dharma Bums*. Although Kerouac was clearly intrigued by Snyder and by Zen, he devoted a good portion of *Dharma Bums* to arguments between Ray Smith (himself) and Ryder (Snyder) and to criticisms of Zen. Smith, who presents himself not as a Zen Buddhist but as "an old fashioned dreamy hinayana coward of later mahayanism," clashed with Ryder and his Zen on a number of occasions. One of Smith's arguments was that showing compassion (*karuna*) was more important than achieving insight (*prajna*). Smith was especially critical of the violence that sometimes attended uncracked Zen koans. "It's mean," he complained to Ryder, "All those Zen masters throwing young kids in the mud because they can't answer their silly word question." "Compassion," Smith contended, "is the heart of Buddhism." Unlike Ryder who had no use for Christianity. Smith revered not only Avalokitesvara, the bodhisattva of compassion, but also Jesus Christ. "After all," he explained, "a lot of people say he is Maitreya [which] means 'Love' in Sanskrit and that's all Christ talked about was love."

Despite such disputes, Kerouac, Snyder, and Ginsberg agreed on a few crucial points that they shared with Buddhism (especially the Mahayana tradition's Yogacara school). They believed, for example, that life is characterized by suffering (*dukkha*) and impermanence (*anicca*). Yet they also believed that this world, at least as it appears to our senses, is ephemeral and illusory. "Happiness consists in realizing that it is all a great strange dream," Kerouac wrote in *Lonesome Traveler.* And he echoed the sentiment (albeit in decidedly biblical grammar) in *Dharma Bums:* "Believe that the world is an ethereal flower, and ye live."

This shared awareness of what Ginsberg called "the phantom nature of being" was tremendously liberating for the beatific beats. It enabled them both to confront suffering and death as major obstacles in this relative world of appearances and to see their ultimate insignificance from the absolute perspective of heaven or nirvana. It empowered them, moreover, to deny the absolute reality of the material world even as they affirmed enthusiastically our spiritual experiences in it. Out of such paradoxes came the this-worldly joy of statements like "This is it!," "We're already there and always were." "We're all in Heaven now," "The world has a beautiful soul," "The world is drenched in spirit," "everything's all right."

There is a constant tension in beat literature, therefore, between misery and splendor, between an overwhelming sadness and an overcoming joy. "The world is beautiful place / to be born into," Lawrence Ferlinghetti observed, "if you don't mind happiness / not always being / so very much fun / if you don't mind a touch of hell now and then." In the beat cosmos God is both absent and everywhere. Dualisms between sacred and profane, body and soul, matter and spirit, nirvana and samsara do not hold. Thus Ginsberg's celebrated encounter with the poet William Blake in Harlem in 1948 incorporated both a vision of death ("like hearing the doom of the whole universe") and a vision of heaven ("a breakthrough from ordinary habitual quotidian consciousness into consciousness that was really seeing all of heaven in a flower"). And so one of Ginsberg's most profane poems, "Howl," contains his boldest affirmation of the sacred camouflaged in the profane:

> Holy! Holy! Holy! Holy! Holy! Holy! Holy! Holy!
> Holy! Holy! Holy! Holy! Holy! Holy! Holy! Holy!
> Holy! Holy!
> The world is holy! The soul is Holy! The skin is
> holy! The nose is holy! The tongue and cock and
> hand and asshole holy!
> Everything is holy! everybody's holy! everywhere
> is holy! everyday is in eternity! Everyman's an
> angel!

Conclusions

After the beat generation graduated from young adulthood to middle age in the 1960s, beat writers went in different directions. Following an extended stint at the wheel of the bus of Ken Kesey's Merry Pranksters, Cassady collapsed along a railroad track and died of exposure in Mexico in 1968. Kerouac's seemingly endless cycles of exile and return to his mother's home in Lowell ended in 1969 when he died an alcoholic's death of cirrhosis of the liver. Burroughs, perhaps the least likely of beats to make it past middle age, is alive and well and enjoying the acclaim of European critics. Ginsberg too has survived even his transmigration from literary rebel to de facto poet laureate of the United States. In this way beat writers have earned a place in the history of American letters.

What I have argued here is that the beats also deserve a place in American religious history. More than literary innovators or bohemian rebels, the beats were wandering monks and mystical seers. They went on the road—from New York to San Francisco to Mexico City to Tangier—because they could not find God in the churches and synagogues of postwar America. They venerated the poor, the racially marginal and the socially inferior because they saw no spiritual vitality in the celebrated postwar religious revival of mainstream white preachers. And they experimented with drugs, psychoanalysis, bisexuality, jazz, mantra chanting, Zen meditation, and new literary forms in an attempt to conjure the gods within.

Like the transcendentalists who inspired them, the beats were critics of "corpse-cold" orthodoxies; they were champions of spiritual experience over theological formulations who responded to the challenge of religious pluralism by conjuring out of inherited and imported materials a wholly new religious vision. Like Emerson, the beats aimed to make contact with the sacred on the nonverbal, transconceptual level of intuition and feeling, and then to transmit at least a part of what they had experienced into words. Like Thoreau, they insisted on the sanctity of everyday life and the sainthood of the nonconformist. And like George Ripley and his associates at Brook Farm, they aimed to create a spiritual brotherhood based on shared experiences, shared property, shared literature, and an ethic of "continual conscious compassion." With transcendentalists of all stripes, the beats gloried in blurring distinctions between matter and spirit, divinity and humanity, the sacred and the profane.

The beats diverged from their transcendentalist forebears (and toward their neo-orthodox contemporaries), however, in maintaining a more sanguine view of the problems of human existence and the possibility of social progress. In the beat cosmos, society is running toward apocalypse; individuals are doomed to suffer and die, and perhaps to endure addiction or madness along the way. But in the beatitudes according to Kerouac and Ginsberg, those who suffer are blessed, and the sacrament of friendship can redeem a portion of that suffering. In the last analysis, "The bum's as holy as the seraphim!" and everyone—junkies and criminals, beats and squares, Catholics and Buddhists, culture-peoples and fellaheen—is raised up from the dreamworld of our quotidian existences and "buried in heaven together."

On the question of whether this is a compelling spiritual vision, reasonable people can and will disagree. All I argue here is that the vision is in fact spiritual and, as such, warrants the scrutiny of scholars of American religion. Precisely how such scrutiny might alter our understanding of American religion and culture I cannot say. But I suspect greater attention to beat spirituality will open up at least one avenue of revision.

Traditional accounts of American religion and culture in the 1950s have tended toward consensus rather than dissension. Social critics and historians have described early postwar America as a "one-dimensional" society in which "organization men" produced a mass culture consumed by "lonely crowds." Religious historians too have depicted the decade as placid rather than contentious—an age in which a general anxiety was rather effectively relieved by a generic faith in a Judeo-Christian God and the American Way of Life. From this perspective the 1960s appear as something of a historiographic non sequitur. Thus, according to religious historian Sydney Ahlstrom, the sixties represent "a radical turn" in America's religious road, a crossroads between a more consensual Protestant (or Judeo-Christian) America and a more conflictual "Post-Protestant America."

While this article does not directly engage this prevailing thesis, it does support recent scholarly work underscoring continuities rather than discontinuities between the 1950s and 1960s. While the ostensibly radical religious pluralism of the sixties may not seem inevitable to students of beat spirituality, it comes as far less of a surprise. A decade before the death-of-God movement in theology and the eastward turn in religion the beats were announcing the death of the gods of materialism and mechanization and looking to Buddhism for spiritual insight. And nearly two decades before the rise of black and Latin American liberation theologies the beats incorporated the socially down and the racially out in their radically inclusive litany of the saints. To study the beats alongside Graham, Peale, Liebman, and Sheen is to glimpse the existence of countercurrents of spiritual resistance coursing around (if not through) the placid religious mainstream.

Source: Stephen Prothero, "On the Holy Road: The Beat Movement as Spiritual Protest," in *Harvard Theological Review*, Vol. 84, No. 2, April 1991, pp. 205–22.

Sources

Burroughs, William S., *Nova Express*, Grove Press, Inc., 1964, pp. 25, 134.

Corso, Gregory, "Bomb," in *Happy Birthday of Death*, New Directions, 1960.

Foster, Edward Halsey, *Understanding the Beats*, University of South Carolina Press, 1992, p. 197.

Ginsberg, Allen, "Howl," in *Howl and Other Poems*, City Lights, 1956.

Watson, Steven, *Birth of the Beat Generation: Visionaries, Rebels, and Hipsters, 1944–1960*, Pantheon Books, 1995.

Further Reading

Charters, Ann, *Kerouac*, Straight Arrow Books, 1973.

This book is regarded as one of the most honest portrayals of both Kerouac and the Beats in general. Here, Charters thoroughly chronicles the life of the man that some consider "king" of the Beats. In the final section of the book, her description of a visit she made to Kerouac's home in 1966 and the condition in which she found Kerouac himself implies anything but royalty.

Knight, Brenda, *Women of the Beat Generation: The Writers, Artists, and Muses at the Heart of a Revolution*, Conari Press, 1996.

This book profiles forty members of the Beat Generation who are often overlooked—the women of the movement. Although their exploits and accomplishments are not as well publicized as those of their male counterparts, female Beats wrote poetry, took drugs, went on the road, listened to jazz, and lived on the fringe just as the men did. This insightful book includes fascinating biographies, more than fifty rare photos, and excerpts of the original writings of Beat women.

Miles, Barry, *Ginsberg: A Biography*, Simon and Schuster, 1989.

Miles, a friend of Ginsberg, does an excellent job of portraying his subject as both the legendary Beat poet and as an average man in everyday life. This book provides a solid biography of Ginsberg and explores the effect of the Beat Movement on American culture and mind-set and how it anticipated the more radical times of the 1960s.

Morgan, Ted, *Literary Outlaw: The Life and Times of William S. Burroughs*, Henry Holt, 1988.

In this biography of Burroughs, Morgan expertly depicts a subject whom many may consider difficult to write about. The biographer's success derives from the thoroughness of his research that provides details on such subtopics, as a history of Los Alamos, Texas, where Burroughs attended school. *Literary Outlaw* provides a fair and provocative look at a Beat icon whose decadent life makes for fascinating reading.

Existentialism

Movement Origin

c. 1960

Existentialism is a philosophical approach that rejects the idea that the universe offers any clues about how humanity should live. A simplified understanding of this thought system can be found in Jean-Paul Sartre's often-repeated dictum, "Existence precedes essence." What this means is that the identity of any one person—their essence—cannot be found by examining what other people are like, but only in what that particular person has done. Because no one can claim that his or her actions are "caused" by anyone else, existentialist literature focuses on freedom and responsibility.

Existentialism attained the height of its popularity in France during World War II. While the German army occupied the country, the cluster of philosophers and writers who gathered together to discuss and argue their ideas at the cafes of Paris captured the attention of intellectuals around the world. The oppressive political climate under the Nazis and the need for underground resistance to the invading political force provided the ideal background for Existentialism's focus on individual action and responsibility.

Although the French war-era writers are most frequently associated with Existentialism, its roots began much earlier. Existentialism can be seen as humanity's response to the frightening loneliness that prompted Friedrich Nietzsche to pronounce in the 1880s that "God is dead." Civilization's loss of faith in religious and social order created an understanding of personal responsibility. This led to literary works that reflect the existentialist's loneliness, isolation, and fear of the uncaring universe. Fyodor Dostoevsky's novels, written in the 1860s and 1870s, show existential themes, as do twentieth-century works by Franz Kafka, Ernest Hemingway, James Baldwin, and Nathaniel West. The French existentialists were so influential on writers throughout the world that it is almost impossible to find a contemporary book that does not show some influence of their thought.

Representative Authors

Simone de Beauvoir (1908–1986)

Beauvoir was born in Paris on January 9, 1908, and lived there most of her life. She was educated at the Sorbonne, where she met Jean-Paul Sartre in 1929. They began a personal and intellectual relationship that continued the next fifty years. Mostly known for her 1949 book *The Second Sex*, a two-volume examination of the roles of women throughout history, Beauvoir was also a prolific writer of fiction. Her novels, mostly based on events of her own life, provide readers with fictionalized versions of the vibrant intellectual scene in Paris throughout the forties and fifties. They include *She Came to Stay* (1949), based on the romantic complication between herself and Sartre and a young student who lived with them; *The Blood of Others* (1946), about a young man's struggle to remain uninvolved in the political situation around him; and *The Mandarins* (1954), about the dissolution of the Parisian intellectual community after the war. *The Mandarins* won the prestigious Goncourt Prize. Beauvoir also wrote plays and philosophical texts. Her death on April 14, 1986, marked the end of the original generation of existentialists.

Albert Camus (1913–1960)

Albert Camus was one of the most influential figures in the existentialist movement that emerged in Paris in the years before and during the Second World War, although he himself refused to accept the label "existentialist." He was born November 7, 1913, in Mondovi, Algeria, a country in northern Africa that at the time was a colony of France. Soon after France entered in World War I, Camus's father was drafted into the army, and he never returned. Albert Camus and his brother were raised by his mother and grandmother in poverty, in a three-room apartment in the working class section of the city of Algiers.

Camus studied philosophy at University of Algiers. Graduating in 1936, he was unable to work as a teacher because he had tuberculosis. He became affiliated with a leftist theater group and wrote for a newspaper, and moved to Paris just before the start of World War II. In 1942, he published one of the most important and influential novels of his career, *The Stranger*, about a man who, acting out of complex circumstances, kills a man who he does not know. The situation explored in the book, and the protagonist's detached, curious attitude about his own behavior, captured the basic mood of Existentialism, and made Camus an international success. His second most significant novel, *The Plague*, was published in 1947. The novel's depiction of a plague that sweeps across a country was seen as an allegory for the wartime occupation of Nazi forces, and of the struggle of the individual against political oppression.

As his fame grew, Camus distanced himself from the existentialist movement in Paris, rejecting their Marxist political stance in favor of political action free of any party. The intellectual rift between him and Jean-Paul Sartre became well known in France. Camus's literary reputation suffered, as his opponents painted him as a populist who was afraid of offending the bourgeoisie because his main interest was selling books. He stayed active in the theater, writing plays and sometimes directing, and in 1957, at age forty-three, Camus won the Nobel Prize for literature. He died in an automobile accident near Paris on January 4, 1960.

Fyodor Dostoevsky (1821–1881)

Dostoevsky was a Russian novelist whose works examined human existence as a tragedy in which the struggle for rationality was constantly undermined by the universe's inherent senselessness. Born October 30, 1821, in Moscow, he was the son of a surgeon—a cruel and strict man who was murdered by one of his serfs when Dostoevsky was seventeen. In college Dostoevsky studied to be a military engineer, a career path he abandoned after graduation in order to be a writer. His early novels were well received, but they did not anticipate the intellectual achievements he was to later reach.

In his twenties, Dostoevsky began associating with a group of radical socialists, for which he was arrested and sentenced to death. The death sentence was commuted, but the feeling of impending death affected him for the rest of his life. He served for four years of hard labor, followed by four years of military service.

Franz Kafka

In 1864, he published *Notes From the Underground*, a short novel that presented the view that humans valued freedom over all things, even happiness. This emphasis on freedom is what identifies Dostoevsky as an antecedent of the existentialist movement. His next novel, *Crime and Punishment*, remains his most popular work, and it presents the existential situation of a man who killed another man while robbing him, and learns to cope with the moral ramifications of his action. His novels *The Possessed* and *The Idiot* each address the issue of moral behavior in a world where the actions of humanity are not controlled by God. His final novel, *The Brothers Karamazov*, was completed just months before Dostoevsky's death from emphysema complications on January 28, 1881. Its plot concerns four sons who each bear some guilt in the death of their father, mirroring the guilt Dostoevsky himself felt after his father's murder.

Franz Kafka (1883–1924)

Kafka was a uniquely talented writer of short stories and novels. His works often provided a surreal look at the world, touching upon themes of modern life such as alienation, absurdity and the deeply felt dread that often appear in existential literature.

Born in Prague, Bohemia (now Czechoslovakia), on July 3, 1883, Kafka spent his childhood in Prague's Jewish ghetto. He was educated as a lawyer and spent some time in a government job, working on workman's compensation claims. He published several important short stories in his lifetime, including *The Hunger Artist* and *The Metamorphosis*. In spite of his request that the manuscripts of his novels be destroyed after his death, his literary executor saved them and published them. They include *The Trial*, about a man who finds himself accused of a crime, although no one will tell him the charge against him; and *The Castle*, about a similarly indecipherable bureaucracy that keeps the main character from entering the building of the title.

Kafka died of tuberculosis on June 3, 1924, at the age 41. He thought that his literary career had been a failure, when in fact his insights into the fear and confusion caused by modern social life were to make him one of the most influential writers of the twentieth century.

Søren Kierkegaard (1813–1855)

Kierkegaard was born on May 5, 1813, in Copenhagen, Denmark. His father rose from poverty to amass a considerable fortune, retiring early to devote his time to Christian philosophy. At eighteen, Kierkegaard entered the University of Copenhagen to study theology. On his twenty-second birthday, Kierkegaard's life changed when he found out that his father's Christianity was flawed: the older man had once cursed God, and had years earlier impregnated a servant. This drove Kierkegaard from religious studies to a life of hedonistic excess. Another significant event in his life happened when, at twenty-seven, he became engaged to a beautiful heiress, but called the engagement off two days later. The woman went on to marry and lead a happy life, but Kierkegaard continued to obsess over her throughout his writing career.

Kierkegaard's writings are a mixture of fiction, philosophy, letters, journal entries, aphorisms, and parables. He rejected formal philosophical systems of knowledge, maintaining that no one system could ever offer a complete understanding of the world. His first work, *Either/Or*, was an assemblage of short unrelated sketches aimed at convincing readers that life was a series of choices. He went on to produce over twenty books. The most significant of these, such as *Fear and Trembling* and *The Concept of Dread*, explore the terrible aspects of human freedom. The other significant aspect of his philosophy was that it was fervently Christian in nature but strongly opposed to the organized church.

Kierkegaard died in Copenhagen on November 11, 1855. During his lifetime he was mocked in newspapers and vilified in churches, and his writing was not read outside of Denmark until well into the twentieth century. Today his ideas are recognized as the groundwork of existential thought.

Jean-Paul Sartre (1905–1980)

Sartre was the single most important figure of French Existentialism. Born June 21, 1905, in Paris, France, and raised by middle-class Protestants, Sartre made the decision at an early age to be a writer, and to expose the hypocrisy of the comfortable life offered to him by his parents and grandparents. In college he studied philosophy, particularly the branch known as Phenomenology, which concerned itself with the fact that life could be experienced but not really known. Throughout the 1930s, he wrote both fiction and philosophy with equal sincerity, leading, in 1938, to the autobiographical novel *Nausea*, which helped define the uneasy position humanity finds itself in the modern world. A short story collection followed. His reputation as a literary writer established, Sartre distinguished himself as one of the century's most important philosophers with the 1943 publication of *Being and Nothingness*, in which he examined the human situation as the awkward position of existing but being aware of nonexistence.

In the years after World War II, when Existentialism reached the height of its popularity, Sartre remained in the international spotlight as a philosopher, writer, and political activist. He wrote several plays that are still performed today, including *Dirty Hands*, *No Exit*, and *The Flies*, all demonstrating the existentialist motto, coined by Sartre, "To be is to do." In 1964, Sartre was awarded the Nobel Prize for literature, but did not accept it because he did not think that such an establishment should define a writer's achievement. Sartre was a familiar face around Paris and was continuously in the news until his death on April 15, 1980, from a lung ailment.

Representative Works

The Brothers Karamazov

Most of Dostoevsky's works concerned the existentialist struggle between freedom and responsibility, but it was handled with significant grace in his last novel, *The Brothers Karamazov*, first published in 1880. In this book, a son kills his father, while his two brothers, each for his own reasons, feel a sense of guilt over having let the event occur. One chapter in particular, "The Grand Inquisitor," is instrumental in promoting existential themes long before the term "Existentialism" even came into usage. This section, a dream sequence, concerns a debate between an inquisitor who represents the devil, and Christ himself, regarding the question of whether humans are or should be free. This book has long been considered Dostoevsky's most brilliant work, the most thought-provoking novel by one of Russian literature's most philosophical writers.

Fyodor Dostoevsky

The Immoralist

André Gide was a great influence on the French existentialists, particularly his 1902 novel *The Immoralist*. It concerns a scholar from Paris who falls ill while traveling with his new bride in Tunis. He survives, but his illness leaves him with a taste for life that he was lacking before, so that he quits his intellectual work, leaves Paris to live on a farm, and eventually ends up traveling away from civilization, further and further south on the African continent. The quest for authenticity, for escaping the familiar and conventional, is one that the existentialist writers would return to again and again, as their characters came to recognize what they thought to be true was really false. Unlike the protagonists of existentialist books like Camus's *The Stranger*, however, Gide's Michael is constantly thinking over his situation, not just reacting, making him a well-rounded character while other existential heroes come off as being hollow.

The Little Prince

The Little Prince, written and illustrated by the French author Antoine de Saint-Exupery, is often categorized with children's books, perhaps because it has cartoon illustrations or because it rejects the arbitrary rules that adults put on life. It is this last element, however, that qualifies it as a work of existential literature. The story is a fantasy about an airplane pilot who crashes in the Sahara desert, where a little prince who lives on an asteroid with a single flower approaches him. He explains his travels to different asteroids and the people that he has met on each. The book offers a satire of serious adults, including a judge and businessman. Its affirmation of childlike innocence has made it a perennial favorite since it was first published in 1943, but the issues that it raises about the superficiality of social structure and the purity of freedom make it one of the more uplifting examples of existential thought.

The Mandarins

Readers interested in the postwar existentialist movement in Paris find two benefits from Simone de Beauvoir's novel *The Mandarins*. First, it is a book true to the existentialist ethos, with characters that struggle to follow their philosophical beliefs while giving in to the basic romantic entanglements that complicate ideological purity. Just as compelling is that it is a thinly veiled autobiography, recording Beauvoir's own affairs and affiliations during the late forties and early fifties, when the world's greatest thinkers sought out the apartment she kept with Jean-Paul Sartre. Beauvoir brings a feminist sensibility to her characters that the male existentialists show no interest in. This book was the winner of France's highest literary award, the Priz Goncourt. Though it is not one of the most frequently read works of existential literature today, it is considered Beauvoir's finest novel.

Nausea

Nausea was Jean-Paul Sartre's first novel, published in 1938. It is a fictionalized account of the author as a young man, and is generally considered to be one of the most influential books in the French existential movement. The book, written in the form of diary entries, presents the life of a writer, Antoine Roquentin, who finds himself feeling sick about no particular complaint, but rather about life itself. Because of its unique style and theme, *Nausea* excited the passions of some literary critics and philosophers when it was first published, while others found it to be too obscure and self-important. Today, readers are interested in it as much for the movement that it created as for the ideas that were made familiar by later writers in the movement.

No Exit

Jean-Paul Sartre's surreal stage play gave the world the phrase "Hell is other people." The setting is minimal: three characters are confined to one room together, none remembering how they got there, carrying on with social interaction until they realize that their small-talk and amenities are the whole point of being there, that they have been damned to each other's company for eternity. Though the catchphrase already mentioned has become the thing that readers and viewers focus upon, the more important point is why these characters have been condemned to hell: they have all lived with "bad faith," which was Sartre's concept of a life lived insincerely, fearing instead of embracing the universe's lack of meaning. This play was instrumental in bringing the concept of Existentialism to America in the late 1940s, and Sartre's storytelling and language are powerful enough to keep the play interesting for modern audiences, so that it is still produced frequently today.

The Stranger

Albert Camus's 1946 novel *The Stranger* is one of the most widely-read books of the twentieth century. Its plot concerns a young Algerian man, Meursault, who kills a man for no good reason after a minor scuffle, and the court trial that ensues. During the trial, the emphasis is not on whether or not Meursault committed the murder, nor even what his motive might have been, but rather on the type of person he is. The prosecution focuses on external matters, such as how the defendant treated his mother and his girlfriend, making it clear that it is his existence, not just his action, that is on trial.

Meursault represents the quintessential existential hero—aloof and cool. He does not think his actions matter much, and is not afraid to accept the responsibility for anything he has done. Some critics have written this novel off as dated—a clear look at a worldview that has passed like any fad. Others believe that the sense of alienation and absurdity Camus has captured will never pass from style.

The Sun Also Rises

Ernest Hemingway is often considered to have looked at the world with an existential point of view, and that is most obvious in his first novel, *The Sun Also Rises*. Published in 1926, the story concerns a man who has been injured in World War I, who is trying to find meaning to his life by traveling from one destination in Europe to another, always seeking excitement and distraction. Hemingway's distinctive style does not let readers in on the thoughts of his protagonist, Jake Barnes, but his precise descriptions of actions and tightly focused dialog make the feelings of the character known. While later Hemingway novels were to have more tightly structured plots, the disillusionment and freedom in *The Sun Also Rises* made it an ideal vehicle for existential ideals.

The Trial

When Franz Kafka died in 1924, his novel *The Trial* was not finished, but his literary executor put the pieces together to publish it the following year. The story concerns Joseph K., a government bureaucrat who is awakened in his bed one morning and taken off to jail. He is released soon after but is told to report back to court regularly. Throughout the whole experience, no one—not the officers who arrest him, the judge, nor his own lawyer—tells Joseph what crime he is accused of. As with all of Kafka's works, this absurd situation is used to explore deeper philosophical truths about the nature of society and of the individual, showing how the political system can isolate a person from the basic truths that he once took for granted. The book was written long before the French philosophers coined the term "existentialist" in the 1940s, but its themes and style are the same as the ones they were to use. Though Kafka died in obscurity, he is now considered one of the most talented literary figures of the twentieth century.

Waiting for Godot

Written by Irish playwright Samuel Beckett and first produced in Paris in 1953, *Waiting for Godot* has become a mainstay of modern theater. Its absurdist plot concerns two tramps, Vldimir and Estragon, who wait near a barren tree on an empty stretch of road for someone named "Godot," who clearly represents their pointless hopes. The fact that nothing significant happens during the play's two acts helps to make the existential point of the play—the lack of meaning when life is not actively pursued. Beckett's artful use of language makes it easy for readers and viewers to experience the play without becoming bored. Even when the dialog seems to make no sense, and when the characters seem to be bickering with each other pointlessly, there is a deeper meaning to Beckett's structure that offers a running commentary on the state of modern existence.

Themes

Atheism

Existentialism seems to necessarily require that one abandon any belief in God, because the concept of God contradicts the idea of personal responsibility that is at the center of the movement. Jean-Paul Sartre, the most prolific existentialist writer, was a fervent atheist, as were Simone de Beauvoir and Albert Camus. The characters in their novels can be seen as people coping with the loss of the concept of God by trying to determine the proper behavior in His absence.

There is, however, a strong subcategory of existential writers who combine religious feelings with Existentialism. One was Søren Kierkegaard, who solved the question of how to reconcile a belief in God with responsibility of one's own actions in his philosophical works such as *Either/Or*, *Fear and Trembling*, and *The Concept of Dread*. For Kierkegaard, there was no contradiction between freedom and God. In fact, the basis of religious belief was the ability to choose freely to believe. Another religious existentialist was Martin Buber, whose 1923 philosophical work *I and Thou* brought together Jewish, Christian, and humanist beliefs. The book uses personal relationships, such as the ones one forms with other humans ("Thou"), to explain the human relationship to God, who is seen as the ultimate "Thou."

Freedom

Existentialism proceeds from the principle that human behavior is based on nothing except free choice. It rejects those theories that try to find other factors that control behavior, such as economic, social, or psychological systems that exist in order to explain what people do. Existential writers do sometimes recognize such comprehensive worldviews, but they do not accept them as being acceptable explanations or excuses for behavior. Sartre, for instance, was a lifelong supporter of the Marxist theory of class struggle, but he would not accept Marx's theory that certain behaviors were *necessary* for certain classes. Instead, he would

Media Adaptations

- Jean-Paul Sartre and Simone de Beauvoir are featured in the 1979 documentary film *Sartre by Himself*. Released as a motion picture in America in 1983, it is now available from Citidal Video. Urizen Books published a book of the interviews from the film in 1978.
- William Hurt, Raul Julia, and Robert Duvall starred in a 1994 film of *The Plague* by Albert Camus. The cassette is available from LIVE Home Video.
- Marcello Mastroianni, Anna Karina, and Georges Wilson starred in the 1968 film version of *The Stranger*, Camus's most famous novel. The film is in French with English subtitles, and is available on cassette from Paramount Pictures.
- The life of Jean-Paul Sartre is the subject of *Existence is Absurd*, a video presentation that was part of the Maryland Public Television series *From Socrates to Sartre*, narrated by Thelma Z. Lavine and available from Insight Media.
- Kafka's *The Trial* was adapted as a film by playwright Harold Pinter in 1993.
- A six-videocassette course teaching the basics of Existentialism, entitled *No Excuses: Existentialism and the Meaning of Life*, is available from The Teaching Company, of Springfield Virginia. Dr. Robert Solomon conducts the twenty-four lectures in this 2000 series.
- An audiocassette recording of Sartre's play *No Exit* was released in 1973 by the Edwards/Everett Company of Deland, Florida.
- A British Broadcasting Corporation program, *Daughters of Beauvoir*, is available on a 1989 videocassette from Filmmakers Library of New York.
- An audio cassette adaptation of Albert Camus's novel *The Plague* was recorded at Constitution Hall in Washington, D.C., on May 11, 1973, with Alec McCowan narrating. Featuring music by the National Symphony Orchestra, it was released in 1975 by Decca.

explain why members of one class might behave similarly as a choice made by people who were unaware of their freedom to choose.

This sense of freedom sometimes leads the protagonists in existential works to commit actions that are commonly considered "evil," as if to assert to themselves that no universal system of justice will bring punishment down on their heads. Thus, Raskolnikov in Dostoevsky's *Crime and Punishment*, Meursault in Camus's *The Stranger*, and Bigger Thomas in Richard Wright's *Native Son* each commit murders with no remorse. In each of these books, the transgression is not punished by divine justice, such as the ways that other writers might have the criminals fall victim to illness or bad luck, but they are prosecuted by the legal system.

Guilt and Innocence

One of the central concerns of existential thought is that, in the absence of divine or biological rules, people must be responsible for their own actions. This is the price of freedom—with no rules from God or psychological traumas to excuse what one does, the responsibility for each action falls on the individual. Hemingway's characters offer a good example of this. They follow rules of behavior that they establish for themselves, often referred to as the "Hemingway code." While other writers might present characters that are victims of fate, the characters in Hemingway's books and other existential literature are responsible for their own fate. Other examples of this are Sartre's play *Dirty Hands*, which shows its protagonist accepting guilt for murdering an obviously dangerous opponent during wartime, and Beauvoir's *The Blood of Others*, in which a student who is shaken by the inadvertent death of a colleague decides that he must still participate in violent radical political activity.

The presumption of innocence that comes from absolute freedom is inverted in the works of Franz

Kafka, most notably in his novel *The Trial*. Instead of being an existential hero who chooses to make himself guilty, Joseph K. is proclaimed guilty by a dense and illogical legal system, for reasons that he cannot understand. Rather than focusing attention on the free individual, Kafka shows the repressive social order that makes it difficult for the individual to realize that he is, in fact, free to decide his own fate. By making the bureaucracy that condemns Joseph K. such an impersonal and irrational thing, Kafka shows how transparent it is. In this novel, the legal system is frightening, but it is not in control of the individual. The superficial charge of guilt helps readers see how shallow it is to believe in any universal system of guilt or innocence.

Identity and Self

Existentialism, like any philosophical movement, is a search for the right way to understand human identity. Other systems might conceive of identity in relation to something, such as when psychologists find the roots of identity in past experiences or in the effects of chemical balances in the brain, or when Romanticism frames identity in terms of humanity's relationship to nature. In Existentialism, however, there is no point of reference for human identity. A person's identity does not exist in anything except that person's actions. As Sartre explained it, existence precedes essence—there are no rules governing a person's essential identity until after that person exists.

French Existentialism crossed over to America in the early 1950s, at a time that the Civil Rights movement was just beginning to give a voice and identity to black Americans. The two were a natural fit. Blacks who had been treated in American society in accordance with the color of their skin were open to the existential concept that a person creates his or her own identity. One of the preeminent American novelists of the twentieth century, Ralph Ellison, explored existential themes as they applied to the race issue in his 1952 novel *Invisible Man*, about a black man's struggle for self-identity against society's narrow definitions of him.

Alienation

Alienation was considered by many intellectuals throughout the nineteenth and twentieth centuries to increasingly be the condition of civilized humans. It is the feeling of isolation, of not belonging, of standing alone. Since the advent of the Industrial Age, social philosophers like Karl Marx have shown how people are alienated from the work that they do, with the connection severed by the economic system. Psychologists have shown alienation as a rift between the conscious and unconscious aspects of self. Theologians have shown humanity as becoming increasingly alienated from reality as the importance of God has diminished.

Existentialism can be seen as a response to the social phenomenon of alienation. As the feeling of being left out of society grew, so did the existentialist's philosophy that it is natural to be separate from society, because the idea of belonging to society was an illusion all along. It is no coincidence that one of the most prominent novels of the French existentialist movement was Albert Camus's *The Stranger*, which, as its title implies, highlights the idea that its protagonist is outside of the bounds of social order, alienated even from those closest to him. In novels such as *The Deer Park* in 1955, Norman Mailer applied the concept of Existentialism to the particular form of alienation that was felt in post-war America, with fear of the atomic bomb and of Communism. Mailer devised the concept of the "hipster," who reacts to everything with his own wry sense of irony. In fact, the term "existential hero" came to be used to describe characters in books and movies who acted alone, who had no ties to anyone, and who followed the rules of behavior set down by their own understanding of the world.

Style

Persona

Many existential works employ a persona who is a stand-in for the author, with similar life experiences and views. The word persona is a Latin term meaning "mask." Authors in fiction tend to hide behind characters like masks, to get their ideas across in the context of their stories, but this is even more common than usual in existential literature. One can draw strong correlations between characters in Sartre's *Nausea*, for instance, and the people of his early life, and between most of the protagonists in Simone de Beauvoir's novels and her own thoughts. Terry Keefe concluded in his essay "Beauvoir's Memoirs, Diary and Letters" that "in spite of obvious difficulties involved, autobiographical material in Beauvoir's fiction must sometimes be acknowledged to be as telling, or as 'accurate,' as material presented in non-fictional form." The main reason that so many literary works by existential writers feature thinly masked versions of their authors' lives is the genre's strong background in philosophy.

Writers like Sartre and Beauvoir are primarily philosophers, accustomed to pondering themselves and the circumstances of their own lives. The nature of philosophy is to consider the human condition, and to find the individual's place in the world. Existentialism, in particular, rejects the idea that one can understand another person's thoughts in depth. Existential philosophers who have expended most of their energy understanding themselves as unique individuals are naturally inclined to think of the protagonists of their works as masks for themselves.

Mood

Existential literature is often characterized as being grim, depressing, and hopeless. This reputation clings to the movement in spite of the efforts of writers like Jean-Paul Sartre to show it as an optimistic worldview that offers its readers a chance to take control of their own fates. One reason that existentialism is assumed to be bleak is that it consciously tries to change people's minds about their traditional avenues of hope. Those who believe that God will justify the hardship of life after death will find their ideas opposed in existential literature, and those who believe in the ability of science to raise human behavior toward perfection meet the same sort of resistance. Lacking the hope that one can look to these external sources for comfort and salvation, existential thought aligns itself with the sometimes frightening prospect of meaninglessness, directly standing up to the blank void that other philosophies try to fill. The titles of books such as *Fear and Trembling* and *The Concept of Dread* by Søren Kierkegaard, whose works formed the basis of the existentialist movement, give some insight into Existentialism's reputation as a philosophy of despair.

While many works of existential literature do, in fact, tend to emphasize life's pointlessness, it would be too narrow-minded to say that despair is their only message to the world. The inherent pointlessness of life is almost always followed by an encouraging example about how life can be given meaning by the individual. This is most clearly seen in the short stories of Ernest Hemingway. Hemingway's story "A Clean, Well-Lighted Place" has two waiters discussing the bleak existence of an old man who comes to their cafe every night. Readers who focus only on the meaninglessness of the old man's life miss the larger point—that he has somewhere to go that gives him comfort. Similarly, Hemingway's "The Killers" shows a washed-up boxer who waits without hope for two contract killers who are coming to get him, but it is told from the point of view of a young man who is unwilling to sit quietly and accept grim fate.

Structure

Because existential writers do not view their characters as being the results of past events, their works seldom use the linear, chronological plots that most novelists and playwrights use. Ordinary narrative structures are built upon the premise of causality, with one event resulting in the next, following each other in succession to create a cumulative result. While other writers present a psychological web that shows how each character's personality is constructed, characters in existential works are not bound to such rigorous, straightforward interpretation. As a result, existential works tend to float across a sequence of events that do not always appear to be related.

Existentialism tends to support an absurd view of the world, one that ignores commonly-assumed rules of reality. In Franz Kafka's short story *The Metamorphosis*, for instance, a man wakes to find himself transformed into a giant bug—the situation is completely improbable, but it helps the author make a point about the unexamined absurdity of common daily life. Samuel Beckett's play *Waiting for Godot* takes place in an unnamed, barren wilderness, with two people sitting under a tree at a crossroads. The play does not have a plot, just a series of events that happen to occur after one another. The lack of any meaningful causal relationship between the events helps to reinforce the existential idea that life has no inherent meaning or structure.

Humanism

Humanism is the cultural and literary attitude that spread through Europe in the thirteenth and fourteenth centuries as a response to oppressive church doctrine. At the time, the position of clerics was that human beings were weak and immoral. Humanism offered the optimistic view that humanity was rational, and was thus able to understand truth and goodness without the Church's intervention. To some extent, Existentialism is the ultimate form of Humanism, because it takes all responsibility for human happiness and achievement out of the hands of fate and places it in the hands of humanity.

There has been some debate about whether Existentialism is really a humanistic philosophy. Many existentialists would define themselves as humanists, because of their commitment to human

Topics for Further Study

- Describe the plot of a movie that you have seen that you would call "Existential," and explain what you think are the existential elements about it.
- Writers have noted that the American way of life, with its emphasis on personal freedom, is particularly well-suited to existential thought. Write a dialog between Thomas Jefferson, the main author of the U.S. Constitution, and Jean-Paul Sartre, the key figure in Existentialism, with each character explaining his position to the other.
- Research the basic beliefs of Zen Buddhism, and compare them to those of Existentialism, pointing out how they are alike and how they differ.
- Some critics have charged that Americans are too commercial to accept an abstract philosophical concept. Design an advertising campaign to "sell" Existentialism to the general public.
- Look through newspapers and magazines for examples of what the existentialist writers would call "bad faith," and discuss them in class.

responsibility over reliance on outside influences. Detractors, on the other hand, say that the philosophy's emphasis on the nothingness and meaninglessness of the world paint too dismal a picture for humanity. They refuse to believe that the existentialist position that action is necessary but pointless can be considered a positive attitude toward humanity. Jean-Paul Sartre addressed this controversy in his early essay "Existentialism is a Humanism."

Movement Variations

Nihilism

Nihilism is the concept of nothingness or nonexistence. It is generally considered a dark, hopeless philosophical stance, one that recognizes no values and sets no goals for life. The word comes from the Latin phrase *nihil*, meaning "nothing," and was coined by the Russian writer Ivan Turgenev in his 1862 novel *Fathers and Sons*. The concept is related to the philosophy of the ancient Greek skeptics, who rejected the idea of any philosophical certainty, and it has appeared in one form or another throughout the history of Western civilization.

Throughout the first half of the twentieth century, nihilism was most closely associated with Friedrich Nietzsche, the German philosopher who saw it as more than just despair, but as a force of destruction. In his book *The Will To Power*, published in 1901, Nietzsche argued that the meaninglessness presented by nihilism would win acceptance over other systems of thought, and that nihilism would eventually lead to society's collapse.

When Existentialism became popular all over the world in the 1950s and 1960s, Sartre's idea of life as "nothingness" was seen as a nihilistic position. Leaders of the movement such as Sartre and Camus struggled to show Existentialism as a positive force, but their insistence that true existentialists should embrace life despite its emptiness was not quite convincing. The rejection of external values always led back to the idea that existence must be meaningless. Existentialism became almost synonymous with nihilism; leading to a popular caricature of existentialists as grim, dark, empty individuals. Existentialists, on the other hand, thought of themselves as fighting nihilism by giving life meaning in spite of its natural meaninglessness.

Absurdism

The main philosophers of the French existential movement, including Sartre, de Beauvoir and Camus, wrote dramas for the stage in addition to novels and essays. It is fitting, then, that one of Existentialism's lasting legacies has been the Theater of the Absurd. Absurdist dramas followed no direct linear plot line, instead mocking the traditional forms by presenting the unexpected, and by actively defying any attempts to read meaning into the events on stage. There was always a tendency for artists to violate conventions, to make people think by refusing to give them what they are comfortable with, but this tendency increased by leaps and bounds in the early twentieth century, with Dadaism and Surrealism. It was only after Existentialism gained international attention in the 1950s, making the concept of "meaninglessness" a familiar subject among intellectuals, that a school of drama based in absurdity was developed. Samuel Beckett published *Waiting for Godot* in 1953; *The Bald Soprano*, by Eugène Ionesco, was performed in 1956; and Edward Albee's *The Zoo Story* played on Broadway in 1959. These are among the most important and representative works in the Theater of the Absurd.

The term "absurd" was first used to describe literary works by Albert Camus. In 1961, theater critic Martin Esslin's book *Theater of the Absurd* named the movement that was already in full swing. Esslin observed how absurdist drama avoided making statements about the human condition by presenting it in its most raw form. This often led to situations that would be incomprehensible within the common view of reality but which were well suited for the stage. Unlike existential fiction, which focused on the internal struggle for beliefs, drama does not present internal thoughts to the audience at all, and so can focus its energies on the strange instability of the external world. Today, Absurdism is a staple of the theater, with constant revivals of the plays from the fifties and sixties and new plays that, while not purely absurd, incorporate absurdist elements.

Phenomenology

Jean-Paul Sartre, who first put the phrase "Existentialism" into use as a branch of philosophy, based his thought on his studies in the philosophy of phenomenology. The two are very closely linked. Phenomenology is a twentieth-century philosophical movement that examines the relationship between experience and consciousness. The founder of this movement was German philosopher Edward Husserl. In his 1913 text *Ideas: A General Introduction to Pure Phenomenology*, Husserl studied the structures within consciousness that enabled the human mind to conceive of objects outside of itself. Because the mind is able to think of things that do not exist as well as things that do exist, Husserl focused upon the mind's activity, leaving aside the overall question of existence. Husserl called actions such as remembering and perception "meanings," and the act of examining these meanings "phenomenological reduction."

Although Husserl is credited with generating phenomenology, the name that is most often associated with that movement is that of his colleague Martin Heidegger. Heidegger focused attention squarely on the question of being, presenting the experience of life as "Dasein," or "being there," putting emphasis on experience as opposed to abstract concepts. Language was also a strong part of Heidegger's phenomenology because humans would have no way of contemplating existence without it. As Heidegger phrased it, "Only where there is language is there world." His philosophical works gave serious consideration to the philosophical value of poetry.

In college, Sartre studied phenomenology, and his theories about Existentialism grew out of Heidegger's ideas. The relationship between the two philosophies can even be seen in the title of Sartre's major philosophical work, *Being and Nothingness*, which mirrors the title of Heidegger's own 1927 masterwork *Being and Time*. Sartre's Existentialism adapted Heidegger's phenomenology, combining his emphasis on language and experience with Husserl's idea that consciousness is always directed away from itself at objects, and not at the nothingness of the subjective self. Since the 1940s the two philosophies have been so closely related that they are often referred to by the combined term "existential phenomenology."

Historical Context

Antecedents

Philosophies are meant to capture the truth, and so there are likely to be traces of any philosophy at any time throughout history. For example, traces of Existentialism can be found in the life of the Greek philosopher Diogenes, who in the fourth century B.C.E. founded the Cynics, who distrusted civilization's artifice. existential ideas also appear at various times throughout the world's literature, such as when Job in the Old Testament questioned whether his concept of God was truly relevant to his troubles, or when Shakespeare had Hamlet question the purpose of his own existence by asking, "To be, or not to be?"

Compare & Contrast

- **1930s–1940s:** The world falls into its second global conflict in thirty years, and it looks like international war will be the nature of the modern world.

  Today: Conflicts tend to be small, regional affairs. One side might be able to assemble a coalition or a mission of United Nations forces from around the world, but it has never been met with a similar international force.

- **1930s–1940s:** News about events in other countries travels by radio broadcasts, leaving much about other nations to the imagination. After World War II, broadcasters and consumers begin investing heavily in television: from 1945 to 1948 the number of U.S. homes with TVs rises from 5000 to a million, and by 1950, 8 million sets have been sold.

  Today: News about world events travels faster on the Internet than news organizations can prepare it for broadcast.

- **1940s:** World War II ends when America uses atomic bombs, for the first time unleashing a force that could destroy the planet in hours. The postwar years are characterized as "The Atomic Age," as people try to understand this potential for instant destruction.

  Today: The potential for nuclear annihilation has existed for three generations. In all of that time, nuclear arms have not been used in battle.

- **1940s:** Soldiers returning from World War II start a population boom, which leads to a new youth culture. Existentialism's emphasis on the "now" appeals to the youth culture's break with the past.

  Today: Advertisers have long realized the purchasing power of youths, and much of popular culture is aimed at consumers between ages ten and twenty.

- **1940s–1950s:** Europe is the respected focus of Western culture, the center of progressive thinking. In the 1950s, while most of the European countries are struggling to rebuild after World War II destroyed their manufacturing ability, America rises to be an economic superpower.

  Today: America's continuing economic might has given American ideas the kind of worldwide attention that European thinkers once enjoyed.

The first philosopher to touch upon existential themes was the French writer Blaise Pascal, who, in the seventeenth century, rejected the idea that rational humans could explain God. Like the later existentialists, Pascal accepted life as a series of irrational paradoxes.

As a formal philosophy, Existentialism began to take form in the 1800s, with the writings of Danish philosopher Søren Kierkegaard. Kierkegaard thought of life as an impossible choice between two conflicting attitudes: the aesthetic, which is based on immediate experience, or existence, and the ethical, which is based on ideals. He presented the ethical life as false, based upon imaginary concepts, but the aesthetic life was not satisfying either. In fact, for Kierkegaard, the aesthetic life led only to despair, because human consciousness is not satisfied with the sheer, raw experience that might be enough to distract an unconscious being. His writings, particularly his book *Either/Or*, were not essays or treatises. They had a literary style to them, presenting his ideas as character sketches, dialogs, and imaginary correspondences.

Unlike Kierkegaard, the German philosopher Friedrich Nietzsche was an atheist who believed that religious belief was a sign of weakness, which would leave society vulnerable to destruction by those who held no such illusions. Nietzsche's completely unsentimental atheism paved the way for the existential view that life is based on nothingness.

The most immediate antecedent to Existentialism was the twentieth-century philosophy of phenomenology, especially as practiced by the German writer Martin Heidegger. Phenomenology raised questions about how humans could ever know the world that they encounter outside of their own consciousness. As with Existentialism, phenomenology relied heavily on examples from literature for understanding, giving the imagined world nearly as much credibility as the experienced world.

French Existentialism

Although earlier philosophers and writers had ideas upon which this philosophy was based, it was Jean-Paul Sartre who gave it the name Existentialism. In school, Sartre studied the works of German philosophers, wrote his exit exam on Nietzsche, and he studied in his postgraduate years under Edward Husserl, who is widely considered a founder of phenomenology, a philosophy similar to Existentialism. In 1928, at the age of 23, he met Simone de Beauvoir. The two fell in love and spent most of the next fifty years living together on and off, although they never married. In 1938, one of the major texts of existentialist literature, Sartre's novel *Nausea*, was published, giving the world its first sense of the moral despair of the philosophy and the cold, unsentimental intellect of the fiction.

The year after *Nausea* was published, Adolph Hitler gave up any pretense of peace by attacking Poland. France went to war against Germany, and was captured in 1940. While France was occupied by Germany, the new existential movement flourished. The principle figures if the movement were acquaintances in Paris, including Sartre, Beauvoir, and Albert Camus (although Camus would come to resent being called an existentialist when hostilities formed between himself and the others). Their ideas were spread by a magazine that Sartre edited, *Les Times Moderne ("Modern Times")*, and through their plays and novels, which had gained international attention. The war was a perfect backdrop for plays and novels with existential themes, which concerned protagonists who were willing to act politically rather than die passively. The war gave French Existentialism an air of tragic Romanticism, as existential heroes, well aware that nothing they did could change the insanity of the larger social order, still made noble choices, presumably without the false encouragement of sentiment or religion.

After the war ended in 1945, Existentialism became a household word, but the writers who made it famous moved on to other interests. Sartre became increasingly interested in Marxism, and the main circle of French existentialists shunned Camus when he rejected Sartre's political stance. Although Sartre was to identify himself as an existentialist for the rest of his life, his postwar writings never captured the world's imagination as had the radical works produced under the Nazis.

In America, Existentialism reached its height of popularity in the 1950. Since the stock market crash of 1929, the country had suffered desperate times, and the cautious conservatism that had characterized the generations of the Depression and the war gave way to a new youth culture. The disaffected Beat generation, lacking any major political struggle, grappled with meaninglessness, and was ripe for Existentialism's message that the world is absurd and that individuals create their own morality.

Critical Overview

"Existential literature" is a phrase that is seldom used anymore. The description has become, for the most part, irrelevant. One reason that literary works are not labeled existential as much as they used to be is that the movement, which captured the world's imagination during World War II, has faded from public attention since the 1980 death of its most charismatic practitioner, Jean-Paul Sartre. Modes of literature and philosophy that once would have been described as "existential" are now described by different terms. On the positive side, the main reason that the description existential seems so irrelevant is the massive popularity that it had in the 1940s and 1950s. Calling literature existential is almost a way of stating the obvious, since most contemporary literature presumes an existential worldview.

From the start, existential literature was seen as little more than a forum for the existential philosophers to present their ideas. For example, Charles I. Glicksberg, in his 1945 essay "Literary Existentialism," wrote, "Though Existentialist literature, particularly in the field of fiction and drama, does exist, it has thus far contributed nothing by way of innovation in aesthetic form. By and large, it is a literature based upon a philosophy, a Weltanschauung, a method of interpreting the life of man upon earth, his character and destiny." It soon developed that the most important reason for reading the literature produced by the French existentialists was to prove, if only to oneself, that one belonged to their intellectual society. In 1951, James Collins introduced his book *The Existentialists* with an explanation about the relationship

Depiction of London during the Great Plague, which struck in the year 1665

between Existentialism and how one lives. Stating his intention to focus his study on disagreements between members of the existential community, he noted that, in studying the people and not their writings, "the picture that [emerges] is drawn more in terms of methods and problems than of a common fund of doctrinal content." As with Glicksburg, the literature was deemed less important than the ideas and the people who lived those ideas.

The shift in Existentialism's relevance in literature came during the 1960s, and can be seen in the writings of Hazel E. Barnes, one of the movement's most prolific observers. In her 1959 book *The Literature of Possibilities*, Barnes begins her exploration of existential ideas with the bold statement, "About the middle of this century novelists and playwrights stopped making men and women to order for psychologists and began to re-create Man." A few sentences later she attributes that view to Jean-Paul Sartre, but only after she has drawn readers in with that challenging claim. By 1967, in the chapter "Existentialism and Other Rebels" of her book *Existentialist Ethics*, Barnes was defending the philosophy from being lumped with other, similar movements with which it might be confused—Ayn Rand's Objectivism, the Beatnik or Hipster nihilism espoused by Norman Mailer and others, and Oriental philosophies, especially Zen Buddhism. "Like man himself, philosophy is always 'in situation,'" Barnes wrote, continuing that Existentialism "is acutely aware of its own position in the world order of the twentieth century. It can envision its own transcendence." One of Existentialism's strongest supporters, Barnes could already see it dissolving, losing its character to similar philosophies, new and old.

Today, critics frequently point out existential elements in literary works, usually those set in contradictory or self-defeating situations. While used frequently to describe specific elements of literary works, it is seldom used in an attempt to understand an author's worldview. In literature, the word *Existential* refers to a mood, rather than to a specific philosophy.

Criticism

David Kelly

Kelly is a professor of literature and creative writing at Oakton Community College and College of Lake County and has written for numerous scholarly publications. In the following essay, Kelly argues the case for using Sartre's novel Nausea *as the touchstone for gauging existential literature.*

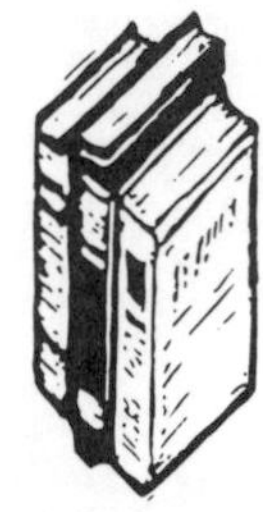

What Do I Study Next?

- American author Walker Percy's 1961 novel *The Moviegoer* tells a poignant and humorous existential story. The plot concerns a young man who tries to find meaning for his life at the movies, with no satisfaction.
- *Dangling Man* (1944) was Nobel laureate Saul Bellow's first novel. It presents a young man in the existential limbo of having been drafted into the army and waiting to be called up.
- *The Plague*, by Albert Camus, examines how people react to an outbreak of bubonic plague in the north African town of Oran, Algeria. The range of human behaviors covered in this novel are as relevant today as they were when it was published in 1947.
- Students often find Jean-Paul Sartre's philosophical writings dense and unintelligible, but the essays in his book *Existentialism and Human Emotions* are chosen to introduce the philosophy to broad audiences.
- *Thus Spake Zarathustra* is philosopher Friedrich Nietzsche's lively, loose-knit allegorical exploration of the relationship between humanity and the world, considered to be the masterpiece of his formidable career. Nietzsche does not directly lecture but instead presents vignettes, mysteries, and riddles, laying the foundation for the existential approach to literature.
- By 1961, when Joseph Heller's absurdist war novel *Catch-22* was published, the existential view of life's meaninglessness had prevailed upon a generation. Set in a bombing squadron during World War II, the book uses humor to raise questions about contradictions that come from order and logic.
- John Barth's sprawling 1956 novel *The Floating Opera* approaches serious existential themes with humor and fantasy. The book hardly holds to a single plot, but its events center around man so extremely disillusioned with the world that he cannot even find a reason for his own suicide.
- One of the central texts of the existential worldview, Søren Kierkegaard's 1843 book *Fear and Trembling* examines the Biblical story of Abraham and Isaac to raise questions about man's place in the world and relation to God. This book is one of the best examples of religious Existentialism, as opposed to the French atheistic existentialism.
- Famed psychotherapist and theologian Rollo May explained the considerable use of Existentialism in understanding the workings of the mind in *The Discovery of Being: Writings in Existential Psychology*, a collection of explanatory essays that was reprinted in 1983.

The concept of "existential literature" is a tricky one. Since Existentialism is a philosophy that means to describe existence, everything that has ever been done or written should rightfully fall within its bounds, since everything exists. Even works meant to illuminate other philosophies could be interpreted by existentialists as the authors' attempts to cope with their existential condition, and might reasonably be categorized as existential. But it is useless to have a category with no distinguishing characteristics to set its members off from everything else: if everything is existential, then there would be no use having the word, because the word "everything" would cover their shared idea well enough.

Another possible way to recognize existential literature would be to limit the phrase to works produced by the members of the French intellectual movement—primarily, Sartre, Beauvoir and Camus—who named this philosophy during the 1940s, and the writers who followed their example. Since these are the writers who willingly associated their works with Existentialism, they would seem to be the ones who are producing the existential literature. Unfortunately, participation in the existential movement alone does little to help define existential literature. The works of Kafka, Dostoevsky, and early Hemingway are all clearly existential in nature, even though their authors never had the philosophy defined for them. What about Hamlet's dilemma, or Abraham's choice to sacrifice Isaac in the book of Genesis? These are clearly existential moments, if not actual examples of existential literature. Closely associating existential literature with the French existential movement also raises the problem of the people who chose to call themselves and their work by that name when it was in vogue. At the peak of Existentialism's popularity in the 1950s, there were hundreds of fans who used the existential concept of *angst* to describe their unhappiness, or mistook medium-sized disappointments for "dread." Their works are not considered truly existential, whether the writers thought they were or not.

Labels are anathema within a philosophy that can be characterized by the catchphrase "existence precedes essence." It would be dishonest to the core beliefs of Existentialism to make any general claims about the essence of existential literature. It is the nature of the philosophy that each piece of literature, especially the literature associated with it, should be experienced before it is defined. More than other literary movements, such as Romanticism or even Modernism, existential literature cannot be identified by checking it against a preexisting list of aspects to see if it fits some sort of profile.

In the absence of any set criteria, there is still a possibility of calling a body of literature "existential" by recognizing what specific works resemble. This open-ended option for identifying things is like the one used by the Supreme Court justice who could not define pornography but felt sure that he would know it when he saw it. Maybe there are not and cannot be rules that identify the varieties of existential literature, but there should at least be some useful standard by which any one work, experienced in and itself, could have the term applied to it in some meaningful way.

The most likely candidate for a work of existential literature that can be used to test other literature against would be Jean-Paul Sartre's 1938 novel *Nausea*. It is not the most accomplished or successful novel of the existential movement, nor even the most fully realized literary work that Sartre himself produced, but this novel has particular characteristics, both in its technique and in its historical situation, that identify it with Existentialism in a way that other works lack.

"Readers can argue which of Sartre's novels or plays was the 'best,' . . . but his first novel, *Nausea*, has a purity that it holds in common with almost all other existential literature that came before it or after."

Nausea was Sartre's first published novel. This means that it was the work that launched the literary career of the man who launched the philosophical movement. At the time, Sartre had published some philosophy, but with *Nausea* he put his philosophy into motion on the page, giving his ideas a reality that talking about them could not achieve. The fact that it was published before he attained a widespread reputation as a literary and philosophical genius almost certainly gave him a freedom that he would have to fight for in later years, when he was aware of the weight a whole world of followers would put on his every word. Later, Sartre was to view the ideas in *Nausea* as "dated," noting that he thought so even at the time of its publication. His philosophy moved on, becoming more involved with questions of political commitment than those of simply existing, such as those shown in his next-most-famous literary achievements, the plays *No Exit* and *Dirty Hands*. Readers can argue which of Sartre's novels or plays was the "best," and even which stage of his evolution was most "authentic," but his first novel, *Nausea*, has a purity that it holds in common with almost all other existential literature that came before it or after.

Stylistically, *Nausea* has the elements that most people have in mind, if only subconsciously, when they speak about existential literature. The story steers clear of a linear plot. Instead, its narrator, Antoine Roquentin, organizes it like a series of journal entries. It is a narrative technique that is common to much existential writing, from Kierkegaard to

Nietzsche to John Hawkes. Just as the point of Sartre's novel, and the cause of Roquentin's nausea, is the contrast between existence and meaning, so too this character's existence is at odds with the faith that readers can traditionally invest in the hidden stream of meaning that holds a plot together. Lacking the desire to sustain a traditional narrative, existential literature works best in short stories, plays (which always take place in the here-and-now), and fragmented novels like *Nausea*, where scene changes appear as random as the situations in life.

Nausea, in fact, dispenses with its faux-diary style without any hesitation. For example, a section called "Sunday" starts on page 40 and continues on to page 57, which would be an extraordinary amount of writing for a diarist, even one as obsessed with his own ideas as Roquentin, to record in a single day. That particular entry is written in the present tense, and it includes four pages of dialog. Clearly, Sartre was not interested in maintaining the illusion that this was anything like a diary: illusion and Existentialism are incompatible. Most works recognized as existential are just as jarring and fragmented, with little attempt to establish a fictional "reality."

Roquentin's story follows his search for meaning, which leads him through familiar channels of live and community, God and Humanism, before leaving his life as empty as it was at the novel's start. The conflict between reality and meaning has Roquentin nauseous at the beginning, and in the end he is just a little short of convincing himself that writing a book about his experiences might help him accept his situation. It is no small achievement for an author to have his protagonist change so slightly over the course of a novel: Sartre achieves this by filling Roquentin's days with minutely observed details. He creates a reality for the reader, one that is just a little too real for Roquentin to bear. Such an intricate rendering of detail is just good fiction writing, existential or otherwise.

One final element that makes this novel exemplary existential fiction is its relationship to the author's life. *Nausea* is generally recognized as a thinly-veiled autobiography. It would be almost impossible to conceive of existential literature that does not have the authenticity of its author's own doubts, fears, and misery as a kind of subtext. Not all philosophies require that their fictional versions be bound to the lives of their authors, but not all philosophies are so intricately tied to the author's sense of authenticity, to the importance of her or his own life. Regardless of whether it was written after Sartre or before, existential literature leaves readers with a strong sense of the teller of the tale. This is why, despite its existential elements, *Hamlet* would not qualify as existential literature: Shakespeare is always indistinguishable in his works. On the other hand, Franz Kafka, who is recognized as a leading existential writer, can tell a richly imagined tale, but his presence is still felt. For instance, Kafka never starved in a circus cage for spectators to watch, as the protagonist does in his story *The Hunger Artist*. Still, no one can doubt that the suffering for art that is the story's central metaphor was indeed Kafka's own suffering.

In his introduction to *Nausea* in the current paperback edition, Hayden Carruth examines the ways in which this novel was certainly not the first or finest work of existential literature, and its protagonist was in no way the first "existentialist man." What makes the book so extraordinary, according to Carruth, is that Sartre's Roquentin is "a man living at an extraordinary metaphysical pitch, at least in the pages of the journal he has left us." This, in the end, might be the thing that makes this the *most* existential work of all. Existentialism is not a philosophy given to sustained fiction, and in this one small book Sartre takes it about as far as it can go. Readers who know Existentialism when they see it are advised to stay away from definitions as much as possible. But, when there is any doubt, they can refer back to this novel, where they will see this particular worldview take form in every word.

Source: David Kelly, Critical Essay on Existentialism, in *Literary Movements for Students*, The Gale Group, 2003.

David E. Cooper

In the following essay, Cooper traces the identification and definition of existentialism and the figures seen as practitioners of the concept.

The Sources of a Name

None of the great existentialist tomes contains the word 'existentialism'. Reports on its origin differ, but it seems to have been coined towards the end of World War II by the French philosopher Gabriel Marcel as a label for the currently emerging ideas of Jean-Paul Sartre and his close friend Simone de Beauvoir. According to the latter, neither of them initially appreciated this baptism.

> During a discussion organized during the summer [of 1945], Sartre had refused to allow Gabriel Marcel to

Jean-Paul Sartre and Simone de Beauvoir

> apply this [word] to him: '... I don't even know what existentialism is'. I shared his irritation ... But our protests were in vain. In the end, we took the epithet ... and used it for our own purposes.

Sartre, in fact, 'took' it rather quickly, for in the autumn of that year he delivered the lecture which became the most widely read of existentialist writings, *Existentialism and Humanism.*

The labcl was soon to be stuck on many other writers. To begin with, it was attached to the two German philosophers of *Existenz*, Martin Heidegger and Karl Jaspers, whose influence upon Sartre had been considerable. Heidegger bridled at this, quickly disowning the title in a piece published in 1947. Jaspers, while unwilling to be identified too closely with Sartre, was sufficiently enamoured of the term to claim that a book of his own, written back in 1919, was 'the earliest writing in the later so-called existentialism'. Then the label was fixed, unsurprisingly, on a number of Sartre's French contemporaries and friends, notably Albert Camus and Maurice Merleau-Ponty, eventually returning like a boomerang upon the neologizing Marcel. None of these readily welcomed the title, either—not so much, as is sometimes suggested, because they were against systems and '-isms' as because no one other than Sartre, in his lecture, had tried to define the word, and this was not a definition under which they could immediately see their own ideas falling. One could hardly expect the Catholic Marcel, for example, to embrace a term which, as defined by Sartre, made the notion of a religious existentialist a virtual self-contradiction.

The next stage was to rake through the remoter philosophical past in search of thinkers deserving of the label, the prime candidates being he two *enfants terribles* of the nineteenth century, Søren Kierkegaard and Friedrich Nietzsche, both of whom were known to have influenced Heidegger, Jaspers and Sartre. This intellectual archaeology was soon to know no bounds, with Pascal, Montaigne, even St Thomas Aquinas and St Augustine, newly excavated as heralds of existentialism. And this labelling game was not confined to the field of philosophy. Novelists reckoned to have concerned themselves with such typically Sartrean themes as anxiety and conflict with others were soon included—Franz Kafka, for example. Nor, as Simone de Beauvoir relates, did the label attach only to people and their thoughts.

> The existentialist label had been attached to all our books ... and to those of our friends ... and also to a certain style of painting and a certain sort of music. Anne-Marie Cazalis had the idea of profiting from the vogue ... she baptized the clique of which she was the centre, and the young people who

"What a person is at any given time, his 'essence', is always a function of what he is on the way to becoming in pursuit of the projects issuing from a reflective concern for his life."

prowled between the *Tabou* and the *Pergola*, as existentialists . . . [They] wore the new 'existentialist' uniform . . . imported from Capri . . . of black sweaters, black shirts, and black pants.

In short, existentialism was not only a philosophy, but as any potted history of our century will point out, it had also become a 'movement' and a 'fashion'.

Although the name 'existentialism' is only of wartime vintage, the special use of the word 'existence' which inspired the name is older. Both Heidegger and Jaspers put it to this use, the latter in fact referring to his writings of the 1920s and 1930s as *Existenzphilosophie*. The two Germans had, in turn, taken up this special use of 'existence' from Kierkegaard who, in Jasper's words, had provided its historically binding meaning'. The story does not end there, since Kierkegaard was apparently only giving a new twist to the word as used by German idealists like Schelling, whom he heard lecturing in the Berlin of 1840—but I shall not pursue the story that far.

What is this special sense of 'existence' from which existentialism derives its name? A full answer would amount to little less than a complete account of existentialism, so for the moment I only indicate an answer. First, 'existence' refers only to the kind of existence enjoyed by human beings. Second, it refers only to those aspects of human being which distinguish it from the being of everything else—'mere' physical objects, for instance. Human beings have digestive systems, but since these are 'merely' physical in nature, they are not a constituent of human *existence*. A cardinal sin, from the existentialist viewpoint, is to conceive of human existence as being akin to the kind of being enjoyed by 'mere' things. The word 'sin' is to be taken with some seriousness here, for it is not just an error to think in this way, but self-deception or 'bad faith'.

Humans differ from non-humans in countless ways, of course. They can laugh, for example. So what are the distinctive traits which the word 'existence' is seeking to highlight? First of all, human existence is said to have a concern for itself. As Kierkegaard puts it, the individual not only exists but is 'infinitely interested in existing'. He is able to reflect on his existence, take a stance towards it, and mould it in accordance with the fruits of his reflection. Or, as Heidegger would say, humans are such that their being is in question for them, an issue for them. Second, to quote Kierkegaard again, 'an existing individual is constantly in the process of becoming.' The same, you might say, is true of objects like acorns or clouds. But the difference is supposed to be this: at any given point in an acorn's career, it is possible to give an exhaustive description of it in terms of the properties—colour, molecular structure, etc.—which belong to it at that moment. But no complete account can be given of a human being without reference to what he is in the process of becoming—without reference, that is, to the projects and intentions which he is on the way to realizing, and in terms of which sense is made of his present condition. As Heidegger puts it, the human being is always 'ahead of himself', always *unterwegs* ('on the way').

The two features of human existence just mentioned lend one sense to that most famous of existentialist dicta, 'existence precedes essence'. What a person is at any given time, his 'essence', is always a function of what he is on the way to becoming in pursuit of the projects issuing from a reflective concern for his life. Unlike the stone, whose essence or nature is 'given', a person's existence, writes Ortega y Gasset, 'consists not in what it is already, but in what it is not yet . . . Existence . . . is the process of realizing . . . the aspiration we are.'

Such characterizations obviously call for elucidation, and existentialism might be thought of as the sustained attempt to provide this, and to explore the implications for people's relationship to the world, each other, and themselves. As they stand, these characterizations are little more than promissory notes. Nor do we progress much further, at this stage, by trawling in some of the further characterizations which many people associate with the existentialist picture of human being. Existence, they will have heard, is a constant *striving*, a perpetual *choice*, it is marked by a radical *freedom* and *responsibility*; and it is always prey to a sense of *angst* which reveals that, for the most part, it is lived *inauthentically* and in *bad faith*. And because the character of a human life is never *given*, existence is *without foundation*; hence it is *abandoned*, or *absurd* even. The reason why recitation of this existentialist lexicon does not, of itself, advance our understanding is that, without exception, these are terms of art. None of them should be taken at face value, and the thinking of Sartre and others is badly misconstrued if they are.

Why do existentialists employ the word 'existence' to express their conception of human being? Partly because of precedent. Kierkegaard so employed the word, and those who more or less shared his insights followed suit. But there is more to it than that. For one thing, Kierkegaard's adoption of the term was not arbitrary. According to a venerable tradition, to hold that a certain thing exists is to hold that certain essences or 'universals' are instantiated, or that certain concepts or definitions are satisfied, by it. The number 2 exists, while the greatest number does not, because in the one case, but not the other, the appropriate essences—such as being between 1 and 3—are instantiated. It was Kierkegaard's contention that, however matters may stand with numbers, this doctrine was mistaken when applied to individual *persons*. A person has a 'concreteness', 'particularity' and 'uniqueness' which make it impossible to equate him with an aggregate of instantiated universals. Søren cannot be 'reduced' to the entity instantiating the following universals . . ., since there is no way of completing the list. Moreover, even if Søren's friends need to have an essence or concept of Søren in mind in order to recognize him, Søren himself does not. He is aware of his existence directly, 'unmediated' by concepts. To know who he is, he does not have to check through a list of definitions to make sure he fits them all. Kierkegaard's constant references to 'the existing individual', 'the existing thinker' and the like, are intended to remind his readers—versed, presumably, in the traditional doctrine or its more recent Hegelian variation—that, with human beings, their existence is peculiarly 'particular', and known to themselves 'immediately'.

A more decisive reason, having to do with the etymology of the word 'exist', helps to explain Heidegger's use of it. In some of his writings he spells the word with a hyphen, 'ex-ist', thereby drawing attention to its derivation from the Greek and Latin words meaning 'to stand out from'. This etymology is fairly apparent in related words like 'ecstacy', for the ecstatic mystic is someone whose soul is liberated from, and so stands outside of, his body. When this origin of 'exist' is borne in mind, it is an apt word for expressing the existentialist thought, mentioned above, that in some sense a person is always already 'beyond' or 'ahead' of whatever properties characterize him at a given time. If, as it is sometimes put, the person is 'in' the future towards which he moves, he stands out from his present. He ex-ists.

An annoying complication is that some existentialists use the word in a more restricted way, applying it only to what others would call *authentic* existence. Although human being is radically unlike that of anything else, people may think and behave as if this were not so, like Sartre's man of bad faith who takes his cowardice or homosexuality to be a fixed and inevitable property, and behaves accordingly. Some of our writers prefer to withhold the term 'existence' in the case of lives marked by chronic bad faith. Kierkegaard distinguishes 'existing essentially' from 'loosely called existing', reserving the former for the life of a person who has 'willed . . . ventured . . . with full consciousness of one's eternal responsibility'. Jaspers is equally demanding: 'I *am* only in the earnestness of choice', and '*Existenz* . . . is present when I am authentic.' I shall not follow this practice of loading the term with an evaluation. 'Existence' will refer to the distinctive being of humans which can then be qualified by words like 'authentic' and 'inauthentic'.

The word 'existentialism' has an additional and very important source. For many philosophers, the word 'existential' is most at home in the expression *existential phenomenology*. There is general agreement that the most significant versions of twentieth-century existentialism are developments, welcome or perverse, from phenomenology, the philosophy elaborated by Edmund Husserl in the early years of the century. Heidegger describes *Being and Time* as a work of phenomenology, while Merleau-Ponty and Sartre use the word in the title or subtitle of their main works. For our immediate purposes, the exact character of phenomenology does not matter. (I discuss it, in some detail, in chapter 3.) But its central feature, crudely expressed, is a focus upon the *meanings* (in a rather special sense) and acts of meaning in virtue of which we refer, and otherwise relate, to the world. What does matter here is that, according to Husserl, this examination could only be properly conducted by first suspending our usual assumptions about the actual existence of things in the world. In a procedure akin to Descartes' methodological doubt, the phenomenologist must suspend belief, or 'put in brackets', any reality beyond consciousness and the 'meanings' in which consciousness trades. The scientist studies colour by examining its physical properties, but the philosopher concerned with the 'meaning' of colour must put aside the assumption of real, physical existence made by the scientist. Otherwise, the phenomenological investigation will be contaminated by irrelevant, contingent data having nothing to do with 'meanings'.

Heidegger, Merleau-Ponty and Sartre are unanimous that this programme of 'pure' phenomenology is impossible. One can neither doubt, nor seriously pretend to doubt, the reality of the world. Even 'to ask oneself whether the world is real,' writes Merleau-Ponty, 'is to fail to understand what one is asking.' Consciousness cannot imagine itself divested of a world, for 'it always finds itself at work *in* the world.' There is no prospect for examining 'meaning' and the 'meaning'-making activities of conscious beings unless these latter are taken to be practically and bodily engaged in the real world. Human being is, in Heidegger's phrase, Being-in-the-world, so that phenomenological understanding must be 'existential', not 'pure'.

Is the word 'existential' ambiguous, then: expressing, on the one hand, a special conception of human being and, on the other, the insistence that the world cannot be 'bracketed'? This would be to overlook an intimate connection between the themes of human existence and existential phenomenology. For Heidegger and those who follow him, it is precisely because the being of humans takes the form of existence that any account of it must presuppose their engagement in the real world. Only if we were creatures of a quite different sort—immaterial souls, say—could we perform even the thought-experiment of divorcing ourselves from the surrounding world. Conversely, the possibility of an existential phenomenology requires that conscious being takes the form of existence. For the 'meaning'-making activities upon which it focuses could only be those of creatures who exist. Instead of treating 'existential' as ambiguous, then, we should approach existentialist philosophy—at least in its paradigmatic forms—along two different, but converging routes.

Existentialists and 'The Existentialist'

I described the rapid spread of the 'existentialist' label after 1945, but how do we determine when the label is appropriate? Who are to count as existentialists? I shall say a little by way of an answer before suggesting that we should not overtax ourselves in search of a precise one.

It is sometimes said that the reason it is hard to draw up an exact list is that existentialism is a mere 'tendency', rather than a coherent philosophy. Now while I do not want to minimize the differences between individual writers, I do hope to demonstrate that there is a coherent, definable philosophy of existentialism—no less, though perhaps no more, homogeneous than logical positivism, say, or pragmatism. The reason it is hard to place certain thinkers is not that the characterization of existentialism must be vague, but because they fit the characterization in some respects and not others. The taxonomist, then, has a weighting problem on his hands.

Existentialism is what esistentialists embrace, and existentialists are people who embrace existentialism. How do we break into this cycle? It is generally agreed that if Heidegger and Sartre are not existentialists, then no one is. A natural policy, therefore, is to apply the name to these two, and then to others according to their kinship with them. This policy is not, however, without problems. For one thing, the thinking of both men underwent large changes. Heidegger's 'turn' (*Kehre*) in the 1930s was in a direction away from the existentialist position of *Being and Time;* and some people find precious little of Sartre's earlier views in his Marxist writings of the 1960s and thereafter. But this is not a serious problem: we can stipulate that by 'Heidegger' and 'Sartre' we mean the authors of certain works only.

A more serious criticism is that the policy exaggerates the affinity between Heidegger and Sartre. It is ludicrous to hold that 'no kinship ever bound the two philosophers . . . that they are radically opposed in every respect', but the days are gone when Heidegger was treated merely as an impenetrable precursor of Sartre. There is now a tendency to read Sartre as a wayward pupil who produced a bowdlerized version of the master's thoughts. Hubert Dreyfus, for instance, thinks that Sartre's revamping of Heidegger was a 'disaster', and that the latter had some justification for calling *Being and Nothingness* *'Dreck'* ('rubbish').

This tendency is as unfortunate, I believe, as the one it succeeded. Rather than devote a separate section to the relation between Heidegger and Sartre, I hope that my discussions of their positions throughout the book will show their affinity. But here are a couple of remarks in advance. First, one should not take Heidegger's own hostile judgement on Sartre too seriously. Only the first few pages of his copy of *Being and Nothingness* were cut open, a little *Dreck* being enough, it seems. By 1946, moreover, when Heidegger wrote his criticism of *Existentialism and Humanism*—not the most dependable expression of Sartre's views, incidentally—he had moved a long way from the ideas which had inspired Sartre. When, a few years after the war, Sartre visited Heidegger in his mountain retreat, his disillusioned verdict was that Heidegger had gone mystical.

More important, the new tendency rests on misunderstandings of Sartre. It treats him as a Cartesian, wedded to Descartes' notion of the *cogito* as the substantial subject of consciousness, and to a dualistic division of reality into the Being-for-itself of consciousness and the Being-in-itself of things. Despite some of Sartre's misleading remarks in these connections, it will emerge, I hope, that:

1 He is as opposed as Heidegger to any Cartesian notion of the *cogito*. ('"Cartesianism" is simply used [by Sartre] as the name of the view that consciousness is always aware of itself,' writes Mary Warnock.

2 'Subjectivity', as Sartre explains, is simply a name for something Heidegger himself insists upon: that 'man is . . . something which propels itself towards a future and is aware that it is doing so.'

3 The For-itself/In-itself distinction is a clumsy reiteration of Heidegger's between the being enjoyed by humans (*Dasein*) and that possessed by things. For neither of them is the distinction, in one crucial sense, dualistic: since they insist that it is impossible to conceive of conscious activity and the world in isolation from one another.

These remarks are contentious and, at this early stage, will not be intelligible to some readers. Their point is to herald the affinity between the two men which warrants the policy of understanding existentialism, initially, by reference to them. But which other philosophers are sufficiently close to these two to belong on the list? There are some whose very style and vocabulary make them prime candidates—Jaspers, Merleau-Ponty, Ortega y Gasset and Simone de Beauvoir. The much neglected Ortega, for example, wrote a couple of essays in 1940, three years before the publication of *Being and Nothingness*, which for several pages could be mistaken for elegant summaries of Sartre's book. There are others who would never pass the stylistic and lexical tests, but whose concerns and conclusions are close to those of the people already mentioned. Marcel, for instance, and the author of existentialism's most lyrical work, Martin Buber. *I and Thou*, which appeared in German in 1923, might compete with Jaspers' *Psychology of World-Views* for the description, 'the earliest writing in the later so-called existentialism'.

Each of these writers subscribes to the two main themes (described above, 'The Sources of a Name') of the distinctive character of human existence and existential phenomenology. (This is so even when they do not indulge in the terms of art of phenomenology and *Existenzphilosophie*.) Each of them emphasizes how, in its being an 'issue' for itself and 'ahead' of itself, human existence is to be contrasted with the being of whatever is 'thing-like'. And each of them insists upon our engagement with a real world as a precondition for understanding those most fundamental of our activities, the making and grasping of 'meanings'. For each of them, the world and human existence are only intelligible in terms of one another. Merleau-Ponty's dictum, 'The world is wholly inside me, and I am wholly outside myself', might have been spoken by any of them.

There is something else these writers share—something, I shall be arguing, which serves to motivate and guide the whole existentialist enterprise. This is the sense that the most serious question with which philosophy has to deal is that of *alienation* in its various forms—alienation from the world, from one's fellows, from oneself. It is to the alienation threatened by a dualism of mind and body and by the scientific image of an objective reality untainted by human concerns, and not to the spectre of scepticism, which philosophy must, before all else, respond. Existentialism itself is just such a response.

Given all this, there is at least one writer who, although he is often included, does not really belong on the list—Albert Camus. *The Myth of Sisyphus* is, to be sure, peppered with some favourite existentialist terms, like 'absurdity', but I have already remarked that, as used by Sartre and others, these are terms of art. What Camus means by 'absurdity' is quite different from Sartre. One reason for excluding Camus is that, unlike the rest of our writers, it is not at all his aim to reduce or overcome a sense of alienation or separateness from the world. In the attitude of Meursault, *The Outsider*, for example, we find a defiant pleasure taken in our alienated condition. Sisyphus, the 'absurd hero', feels a 'silent joy' in living in a world where 'man feels an alien, a stranger . . . his exile . . . without remedy.' Camus wants to invert Merleau-Ponty's dictum into 'The world is wholly outside me, and I am wholly inside myself.' Moreover Camus was, by his own admission or boast, not interested in the weighty philosophical topics which occupied his Parisian friends, Sartre and Merleau-Ponty—the nature of consciousness and perception, the mind-body relation, the problem of 'other minds', and so on. Existentialism, as treated of in this book, is not a mood or a vocabulary, but a relatively systematic philosophy in which topics like these are duly addressed. I shall have rather little to say about those, like Camus, who make a virtue out of being neither a philosopher nor systematic.

A question which has vexed a number of commentators is where to place Kierkegaard and Nietzsche. It was Kierkegaard's use of 'existence' which inspired the very name of existentialism, and his notions of 'dread' and the 'Public' are echoed in Heidegger's discussions of *angst* and the 'they' (*Das Man*) (see chapters 7 and 8). But some of the things said about Camus also apply to Kierkegaard. Despite the endless repetition, he does little to develop his intuitions about existence as 'striving' and 'becoming', and some of those large philosophical topics which failed to disturb Camus scarcely bothered Kierkegaard either. Like Camus, as well, he seems to enjoy the thought that men are aliens in their world. It is only if people do view themselves as 'homeless' that they will then seek that personal relationship with God, which is the pivot of Kierkegaard's concerns.

Nietzsche presents the taxonomist with different problems. Unlike the Dane, he tackles most of the philosophical questions which occupy later existentialist; and in his doctrines of the will to power and perspectivism he is arguing against a dualism of mind and reality. 'We laugh as soon as we encounter the juxtaposition of "man *and* world"'; we are 'sick' of 'the whole pose of "man *against* the world"'. But Nietzsche also makes claims which at least seem to contradict those of later existentialists. For example, he denies that we can act freely. More generally, his *naturalism*, his urge to treat man as *just* one species of 'domestic animal', runs counter, on the surface anyway, to claims about the distinctive character of human existence. But if Nietzsche's name appears less often in this book than it may deserve to, the main reason is that he is too large a figure to be contained within it. If proper attention were given to his views, he would, I fear, take things over. (I speak with some experience, having written a book on Nietzsche that was not originally intended to be that.)

Once reasons for and against including Kierkegaard and Nietzsche on the list are given, it matters little whether they are classified as wayward existentialists or, less anachronistically perhaps, as precursors of existentialism. This might matter more if the book were being done 'by blokes', but as indicated in the preface the aim is, rather, to reconstruct a certain structure of thought. The important thing is not the card-carrying credentials of this or that writer, but his contribution to the development of that structure. It is because I am uncertain or plain ignorant about the contribution of some people often described as existentialism—Berdyaev and Bultmann, for example—that they do not appear. Some of these exclusions may be unjust, but exclusions anyway have to be imposed if the book is not to degenerate into a mere encyclopaedia of existentialist writings.

The main figure in this book, however, is not Heidegger, Sartre nor any of those mentioned above, but The Existentialist. He is not to be identified with any particular author, but nor is he the 'average' existentialist, stripped of whatever opinions distinguish one author from another. A figure who did not take sides on issues which divide these authors would be a pale one indeed. He is, rather, the 'ideal' existentialist, who embodies the best wisdom, in his creator's view, to be gleaned from actual existentialist writers. Put differently, he represents a 'rational reconstruction' of existentialist thought.

This book could be regarded as a journey of thought undertaken by The Existentialist. Its starting point is the issue which, in his opinion, is the largest one to which philosophy should respond—that of *alienation*. As for Hegel and Marx, the issue for him is how alienation is to be 'overcome'. It is in Husserl's phenomenology that he finds the clue to this, though Husserl's 'pure' phenomenology must first be converted into an 'existential' one. The Existentialist is then equipped to provide a systematic account of our Being-in-the-world, which emphasizes both the logical interdependence of mind and world, and the unique character of human existence. This account enables him to 'dissolve' a number of traditional dualisms, like that of mind versus body, which have contributed to people's sense of alienation.

His account, however, throws into relief the depressing possibility of other dimensions of alienation: estrangement from oneself and estrangement from others. He needs, then, to discuss the notion of self, and the relation between this and experience of others. The Existentialist is now able to describe the forms of self-estrangement, such as 'bad faith', which have their basis in relations to others. But to justify his description of our everyday condition as self-estranged, he needs to find evidence that we are capable of a different, 'authentic' existence. He finds this in the experience of *angst*, the 'anticipation' of death, and the sense of absurdity. Whatever else an 'authentic' existence is, it is one of a certain kind of freedom—'existential freedom'. Finally, The Existentialist considers what this authentic life of freedom might imply by way of an ethic to guide our relations with one another.

The Existentialist's journey is one of the most serious a philosopher could make. Not only does it encounter some of the largest and toughest philosophical questions, but it passes through some of the more sombre areas of human enquiry. It is serious, finally, because it is undertaken to 'overcome' threats to human integrity and dignity which all but the self-narcoticized must on occasion experience.

I once heard a distinguished analytic philosopher express the wish that his epitaph should read, 'This man discovered a new sense of the word "If".' (He has since died, but I do not know if his wish was fulfilled.) The Existentialist's ambitions are of a different order, more faithful surely to the original spirit of philosophy.

Some Misconceptions

Existentialism is something everyone has heard of. It belongs among those '-isms', like cubism and surrealism, whose *succès de scandale* make them part of the consciousness of our century. The popular image is, however, full of misconceptions which need to be scotched if understanding of the philosophy examined in this book is not to be prejudiced.

These misconceptions are prevalent among those who have picked up their existentialism from dictionaries, encyclopaedias and popular histories of ideas. Typical is the description of existentialism as 'the metaphysical expression of the spiritual dishevelment of a post-war age'. So, too, is one historian's description of it as 'the assertion that life is more than logic . . . that the subjective and personal must be more highly valued and the objective and intellectualized must be depreciated'. *The Concise Oxford English Dictionary* entry is particularly wayward: 'An anti-intellectual philosophy of life, holding that man is free and responsible, based on the assumption that reality as existence can only be lived, but can never become the object of thought'.

The inaccuracy of these descriptions will become plain in the following chapters, but it will be useful here to indicate some reasons for their currency, and to preview some of their deficiencies. Such descriptions encourage a popular view which might be expressed in something like the following words: 'Existentialism was a philosophy born out of the *angst* of postwar Europe, out of a loss of faith in the ideals of progress, reason and science which had led to Dresden and Auschwitz. If not only God, but reason and objective value are dead, then man is abandoned in an absurd and alien world. The philosophy for man in this "age of distress" must be a subjective, personal one. A person's remaining hope is to return to his "inner self", and to live in whatever ways he feels are true to that self. The hero for this age, the existentialist hero, lives totally free from the constraints of discredited traditions, and commits himself unreservedly to the demands of his inner, authentic being.'

One thing which encourages this kind of view is a failure sufficiently to distinguish existentialist philosophy from the existentialist vogue among black-clad youths prowling between the *Tabou* and the *Pergola*, which Simone de Beauvoir described. Film of the young Juliette Greco singing in the late 1940s gives an idea of the chic appeal which feigned *ennui* and despair apparently had for young Parisians of the time. Few of them, presumably, waded through the six hundred pages of *Being and Nothingness*, and their interpretation of existentialist freedom as a licence to act as unconventionally as possible, *pour épater les bourgeois*, was a complete distortion of Sartre's and de Beauvoir's notion. In fact, they had less affinity with these writers than with the 'hippies' of the 1960s or the 'punks' of the 1970s.

A second factor has been over-reliance on existentialist fiction. This is compounded when Camus's novel, *The Outsider*, is taken as paradigmatic of the genre. Many people, I find, discover the quintessential 'existentialist hero' in Meursault: casually smoking on his mother's coffin, indifferent to God and to marriage, unrepentant at killing an Arab, and unable to find value in anything. In fact, Meursault is no more 'authentic' in Sartre's sense than the bourgeois with his 'respectability' and fake 'sincerity'. Not that the 'message' of Sartre's own novels is always grasped correctly. In *The Age of Reason* the central character, Mathieu, proclaims, 'I recognise no allegiance except to myself . . . All I want is to retain my freedom.' This is his defence of his refusal to marry his pregnant girlfriend. But it is not, as sometimes imagined, Mathieu who is

Sartre's mouthpiece, but his 'respectable' brother, Jacques, who says: 'I should myself have thought that freedom consisted in frankly confronting situations into which one has deliberately entered and accepting one's responsibilities. You have reached the age of reason, my poor Mathieu ... But you try to pretend you are younger than you are'. I shall be discussing various works of existentialist fiction, but this is no substitute for examination of the 'straight' philosophical works.

The most popular of those works is Sartre's lecture *Existentialism and Humanism*, and over-reliance on it is a third source of misconceptions. The lecture was written hurriedly and Sartre soon regretted its publication. For there are passages here which do encourage the view that commitment and moral decision can only be irrational *actes gratuits*, or based upon nothing but inner conviction. It is here, too, that there is much talk of abandonment and despair, but not set in the wider context of Sartre's philosophy which lends proper sense to such notions. Sartre's posthumously published notes, *Cahiers pour une Morale*, give a much more accurate, if far less punchy, expression to his views at the time than the lecture does.

Let us now take some of the misconceptions one by one. It is quite wrong, first, to regard existentialism as the expression of post-war 'dishevelment', despair or malaise. To do so rather obviously confuses existentialism as a philosophy and existentialism as a vogue. All the best-known existentialist works, it should be noted, were written either before the war began or before it ended. To describe existentialism as an expression of an age, moreover, is to suggest that its claims could be only temporarily and locally valid. But if the accounts of the distinctiveness of human existence, of the interdependence of mind and world, of our existential freedom, and so on, are true at all, they are true of human beings at all times and in all places. These accounts, furthermore, stem from reflections on the perennial condition of human beings, and not the particular situation obtaining in post-war Europe. Existentialism, in other words, belongs to philosophy, not to the social sciences.

None of this is to deny that existentialism is historically located. In its mature form, it could not have developed much earlier than it did. The same, though, is true of quantum physics, but it would be absurd to describe that as an 'expression' of a particular age. Existentialism grew, in part, out of Husserl's phenomenology, which in turn was a critical response to nineteenth-century materialism and positivism. So existentialism can certainly be placed in intellectual history: it was not a bolt from the blue. Nor do I want to deny that existentialists have things to say which both help to explain, and are especially pertinent to, modern times. Heidegger, Buber and Marcel all believed that the most salient tendencies of the times, technology and consumerism, are the fall-out from that Cartesian schism between mind and world which turns the latter into a foreign territory, to be conquered and exploited. Existentialism is, in part, directed to the 'overcoming' of that schism.

One reason existentialism gets described as a 'metaphysical expression' of its age is because it is alleged to give voice to an *angst* and despair which, it is said, are peculiarly symptomatic of the twentieth-century condition. It is true that several existentialist writers speak much of these notions, but it is crucial here to recall my warning about their use of words as terms of art. As used by Kierkegaard, 'despair' refers not to a mood of hopeless gloom, but to the position of someone whose life, a contented one perhaps, 'hinges upon a condition outside of itself'. Sartre uses it to refer to the recognition that 'there is no God and no prevenient design, which can adapt the world ... to my will.' As for *angst*, existentialists do not have in mind that fear before a dangerous, uncertain world recorded here by Virginia Woolf:

> The war ... has taken away the outer wall of security. No echo comes back. I have no surroundings ... Those familiar circumvolutions ... which have for so many years given back an echo ... are all wide and wild as the desert now.

Existential *angst* is, rather, a sense of freedom, of a capacity to strike out on one's own in the formation of a scheme of beliefs and values. If *angst* has special significance in modern times, this is not because life has become too 'dishevelled' or 'wide and wild', but because it has become too *comfortable*. Beliefs and values are too easily and readily received from what Kierkegaard called the 'Public', Nietzsche the 'herd', and Heidegger the 'they'. This *angst* is not something to be 'treated'; on the contrary, we need to be called to it, and away from a state of 'tranquillization' induced through bad faith.

The wayward definitions of existentialism quoted [earlier] echo the widespread impression that it is an 'anti-intellectualist' philosophy, which sets itself against reason to the point of preaching irrationalism—or worse: 'Existentialism ... is nothing other than radical nihilism ... the absolute negation of everything, which leaves only a chaotic and meaningless activity.' This is nonsense, but more sober versions of the 'anti-intellectualist' interpretation require some comment.

The first thing to say is that The Existentialist is not an irrationalist in the sense of supporting his claims by appeal to mystical insight, 'gut' feeling, or other non-rational founts of knowledge. He argues, typically, by close description of everyday life, by drawing out people's own implicit understanding of themselves, and by exposing the incoherence of rival claims. He proceeds, that is, as a philosopher, not a seer. Even the gnomic-sounding Buber argues for the presence of the divine 'Thou' in human life by interpreting familiar experiences, and not by appeal to esoteric knowledge.

Second, existentialism does not, in the manner of a Rimbaud or a D. H. Lawrence, exhort us to cultivate wild or 'vital' lives in conscious rejection of the exercise of reason. We are not to think with our hearts or our blood. The only possible exception here might be Kierkegaard. The virtue, it seems, of the 'knight of faith', like Abraham in *Fear and Trembling*, is to obey God's will despite its logical absurdity. The absurdity of faith makes it all the greater. But it is not clear that the pseudonymous 'author' of the book represents Kierkegaard's own settled view, and even the 'author' is equivocal: 'While Abraham arouses my admiration, he also appals me.' Moreover, Kierkegaard is contemptuous of those who would make a virtue of 'absurd belief' in everyday life: it is warranted, if at all, only in very special situations where God issues certain calls to us.

There are, it is true, passages in *Existentialism and Humanism* where Sartre may seem to suggest that rational deliberation is impossible in the area of moral choice, so that the choice is a mere 'invention', an *acte gratuit*. I shall show later how this is a misinterpretation of Sartre.

While The Existentialist is not, in any serious sense, an irrationalist, he is certainly not a 'rationalist' in the philosophical sense that contrasts with 'empiricist'. He does not hold, that is, that the mind is innately equipped with, or predisposed towards, knowledge of certain truths about the world. This is not because he is an 'empiricist', holding that all knowledge is the product of experience. The issue between the two camps is one of several which, for The Existentialist, rest on the false premise that mind and world are logically independent of one another, like a spectator and the show before him. The 'rationalist' differs from the 'empiricist' only in holding that the spectator arrives with a rich intellectual apparatus through which the passing scene gets filtered.

When cultural historians refer to Western rationalism, they intend something broader than 'rationalism' as against 'empiricism'. They mean a tradition which culminates in the Enlightenment and in the positivist conviction that the true repositories of knowledge are the sciences. Existentialism shares no such conviction, and in that respect might be labelled 'romantic'. Its hostility to the pretensions of science, however, is not that of the romantic primitivist, for whom Western science has got things wrong, while African magic or Yin—Yang cosmology has got them right. Rather, the claim of science to provide fundamental understanding of the world rests on misconceptions about understanding, the world, and the relation between the two. The vehicles of the fundamental understanding presupposed by all further knowledge are not the theories and products of science or 'cognition', but practical activities and 'moods'. (Heidegger speaks of 'cognition' reaching 'far too short a way compared with the primordial disclosure belonging to moods'). Before we can 'cognize' the world, we must first encounter it, both understandingly and affectively, as a world of things to be embraced, avoided, used, discarded, and the like. The world described by the scientist has no claim, therefore, to be the one real world. On the contrary, it is parasitic upon the *Lebenswelt*, the 'life-world' in which we move and acquire our primary understanding. Physics may, in its own sphere, possess an 'absolute truth', but that 'makes no difference to that other absolute, which is the world of perception and *praxis*'.

Moreover, the scientific pretension requires that it is possible and necessary for the conquest of real knowledge that the world be stripped of everything which human beings have 'projected' upon it—from colours to meanings, from smells to values. But this is to suppose that mind and world, subject and object, can be treated in logical isolation from one another and separately examined. This dualism, however, is one of those inherited from Descartes which most stand in need of dissolution. For not only is it incoherent, but it is also partly responsible for the sense of the world as alien, as a place of 'unimaginable otherness', accessible if at all only to the man in the laboratory, *au fait* with event-horizons, closed space-times and other postulates of contemporary physics.

One might, I suppose, characterize The Existentialist's insistence on the 'humanness' of the world as a denial of its 'objectivity'. But it would be quite wrong to conclude that existentialism is therefore a 'subjectivist' philosophy, though the term is often applied. For The Existentialist, the question of whether descriptions of the world are objective or subjective is a bad one. They are not objective, if this means being of a kind which a scrupulously detached spectator would provide, for a spectator completely disengaged from the world could have no conception of it at all. But nor are they subjective, if this means that they are glosses smeared over, and therefore occluding, the world as it is in itself. This idea presupposes, no less than the 'objectivist' one does, that there could, at least for God, be a direct, unhindered view of reality 'with its skin off' (as Heidegger puts it).

Nor, of course, is existentialism a form of 'subjective idealism', according to which so-called external things are really contents of the mind or constructs of the imagination. This view contradicts the main tenet of existential phenomenology, that no sense can be made of mind except as engaged, through embodied activity, in a world which cannot, therefore, be contained 'inside' it.

This same point about mind having to be 'out there' in the world as praxis should scotch the strangely entrenched idea that existentialism is 'subjectivist' in being a philosophy primarily concerned with the 'subject', in roughly the Cartesian sense of a mental substance or self underlying consciousness. Robert Solomon, for example, describes existentialism, in France at least, as 'undeniably Cartesian', and the 'culmination' of what he calls 'the transcendental pretence', which includes belief in 'the remarkable inner richness and expanse of the self'. This is the reverse of the truth, for one of the most salient aspects of existentialism, Gallic versions included, is the onslaught on Cartesian notions of self or subject, and on the dualisms which they inspire. For Nietzsche, the self is a 'fiction', invented by people who required something inside others to blame, and inside themselves to go on to an afterlife. Heidegger writes that a person is 'never anything like a substantive inner sphere', while Marcel regards the 'pure subjectivism' of Descartes' *cogito* as among 'the most serious errors of which any metaphysics has been guilty'. Sartre, we saw, refers to the 'subjectivity' which is a 'principle' of existentialism, but makes clear that this is not what belongs to the Cartesian subject: it merely indicates that 'man is a project which possesses a subjective [that is, self-aware] life, instead of being a kind of moss . . . or a cauliflower.' His animosity towards the Cartesian self is plain enough: it is a 'bloodthirsty idol which devours all one's projects', and the 'subjectivity' it possesses is 'magical'. For, just as magical thought invests objects with spirits, like fetishes and jujus, so philosophers like Descartes have 'reified' our mental acts by locating them in a fictitious 'subjectivity-object' that they call 'self' or 'ego'.

I could continue considering further senses in which existentialism is not a subjectivist philosophy, but let me mention only one more. The Existentialist certainly does not embrace a subjectivist theory of truth, if by that is meant the view propounded by Protagoras in Plato's *Theaetetus*, to the effect that each man is the measure of truth, that truth can only be *for me, for you*, or whomever. While he cannot accept a definition of truth as correspondence with a reality independent of all human conceptions of it, The Existentialist is perfectly able to accept that beliefs can be objectively true in the sense of being warranted by criteria on which there is tried and tested public agreement.

People may have been misled here by Kierkegaard's notorious statement that 'truth is subjectivity [and] to seek objectivity is to be in error.' Kierkegaard's meaning, though, cannot be Protagoras', since he immediately adds that 'subjective truth' is 'an objective uncertainty held fast in . . . the most passionate inwardness'—which implies, of course, that there *can* be an objective truth of the matter. He is, in fact, trying to make two points, neither of them Protagorean, in connection with a comparison he makes between a Christian who lends merely intellectual assent to his religion, and a heathen with his passionate, lived faith. The former's belief has greater objective truth, but the latter is more 'in the truth'. This is, first, because the heathen, although his God is not the true one, better appreciates God's essential nature: for God is not a Being to whom, if that nature is grasped, a person can remain emotionally indifferent. Second, the heathen's faith is a truer, more authentic expression of human existence than the cool theology of the Christian. This is because 'essential existing', as against 'loosely-called existing', demands passion and commitment. Whatever one thinks of these points, and Kierkegaard's paradoxical way of making them, they are not subjectivist ones in the sense under discussion.

Finally, it is worth recording one aspect of existentialist thinking which might, at a pinch, be described as subjective. An important existentialist thesis is that 'moods' and emotions can be vehicles of understanding. Now there is a tendency among our writers to focus on the more personal and solitary 'moods', those farthest away from the grief or delight which people display in unison at funerals or football matches. I have in mind, for example, the sense of guilt which, for Jaspers, is indicative of the 'unpeaceful', 'antinomial' nature of *Existenz;* or the 'fidelity' a person may feel towards a dead friend which, for Marcel, indicates the presence of a God who is the source of fidelity. These sombre moods might be described as 'subjective' by way of contrast to the 'social' ones we display alongside others. Existentialists concentrate upon these because they are, arguably, the most distinctively human; the ones, therefore, which are liable to be most disclosive of the character of human existence. Those television nature programmes which specialize, in the 'naked ape' tradition, in telling us how we imitate the beasts and they imitate us, would find it hard to discover analogues in the feline or marsupial worlds to Jaspers' guilt or Marcel's fidelity. It is important to note, though, that if we do describe these 'moods' as 'subjective', there are other senses in which they are certainly *not* subjective. They are not, for example, irretrievably 'private' and incommunicable. Nor are they 'merely' subjective, in the sense of having no significant connection with how reality is. On the contrary, they are supposed to be feelings to which, as William James puts it, things are *known*.

This completes my preliminary survey of some misconceptions about existentialism and of some reasons behind them. The book as a whole will, I hope, confirm that these are indeed misconceptions. We are now ready for The Existentialist to begin the journey whose route I outlined earlier.

Source: David E. Cooper, "Preliminaries," in *Existentialism*, Basil Blackwell, 1990, pp. 1–19.

Sources

Barnes, Hazel E., *Existential Ethics*, Alfred A. Knopf, 1967, p. 121.

———, *The Literature of Possibility*, University of Nebraska Press, 1959, p. 9.

Carruth, Hayden, Introduction, in *Nausea*, New Directions, 1964, p. x.

Collins, James, Preface, in *The Existentialists: A Critical Study*, Henry Regnery Co., 1952, p. xiii.

Glicksberg, Charles I., "Literary Existentialism," in *Existentialist Literature and Aesthetics*, edited by William L. McBride, Garland Publinshing, 1997, pp. 2–39.

Keefe, Terry, "Beauvoir's Memoirs, Diary and Letters," in *Autobiography and the Existential Self*, edited by Terry Keefe and Edmund Smyth, St. Martin's Press, 1995, p. 78.

Further Reading

Baker, Richard E., *The Dynamics of the Absurd in the Existentialist Novel*, Peter Lang Publishing, Inc., 1993.
By its nature, absurdity avoids rational understanding. In this study, Baker uses examples from key existentialist novels to illustrate the philosophical basis for the absurdist attitude.

Beauvoir, Simone de, *Adieux: A Farewell to Sartre*, Pantheon Books, 1984.
Beauvoir gives her impressions of the last ten years of Sartre's life (1970–1980), followed by a lengthy transcript of a conversation that went on between them in 1974.

Bielmeier, Michael G., *Shakespeare, Kierkegaard, and Existential Tragedy*, Edward Mellen Press, 2000.
Starting with the references that Kierkegaard made to Shakespeare's plays, Bielmeier offers a full existential reading of the tragedies.

Borowitz, Eugene, *A Layman's Introduction to Religious Existentialism*, Westminster Press, 1965.
The passionate atheism of the French existentialists is often noted, but there is a powerful school that combines existential thought and religious experience. Borowitz's overview introduces many philosophers and writers who are usually not mentioned in general discussions of the philosophy.

Husserl, Edmund, "The Paris Lectures," in *Phenomenology and Existentialism*, edited by Robert C. Solomon, Littlefield Adams Quality Paperbacks, 1980, pp. 43-57.
Sartre attended these lectures, given at the Sorbonne in 1929, and they greatly influenced his development of a philosophy of Existentialism that was separate from the Phenomenology of Husserl and Husserl's successor, Heidegger.

Sartre, Jean-Paul, "An Explication of *The Stranger*," in *Camus: A Collection of Critical Essays*, edited by Germaine Brée, Prentice-Hall, 1962, pp. 108–21.
Originally published in 1955, Sartre's explication has frequent references to Camus's *The Myth of Sisyphus*, finding the novel to be one of the greatest of French literature.

Solomon, Robert C., *Introducing the Existentialists*, Hackett Publishing Company, 1981.
Solomon brings the subject of Existentialism to life for readers by presenting imagined interviews with Sartre, Heidegger, and Camus. The result is more focused and less abstract than actual interviews with these authors, serving well as an introduction to their thoughts.

Expressionism

Movement Origin

c. 1900

Expressionism arose in Europe in the late nineteenth and early twentieth centuries as a response to bourgeois complacency and the increasing mechanization and urbanization of society. At its height between 1910 and 1925, just before and just after World War I, expressionist writers distorted objective features of the sensory world using symbolism and dream-like elements in their works illustrating the alienating and often emotionally overwhelmed sensibilities. Painters such as Vincent van Gogh, Paul Gauguin, and Edvard Munch helped to lay the foundation for Expressionism in their use of distorted figures and vibrant color schemes to depict raw and powerfully emotional states of mind. Munch's *The Scream* (1894), for example, a lithograph depicting a figure with a contorted face screaming in horror, epitomized the tone of much expressionist art. In literature, German philosopher Friedrich Nietzsche emphasized cultivating individual willpower and transcending conventional notions of reasoning and morality. His *Thus Spake Zarathustra* (1885), a philosophic prose poem about the "New Man," had a profound influence on expressionist thought. In France, symbolist poets such as Arthur Rimbaud and Charles Baudelaire wrote visionary poems exploring dark and ecstatic emotional landscapes.

In Germany in the twentieth century, poets such as Georg Trakl and Gottfried Benn practiced what became known as Expressionism by abandoning meter, narrative, and conventional syntax, instead organizing their poems around symbolic imagery. In fiction, Franz Kafka embodied expressionist themes and styles in stories such as *The Metamorphosis* (1915), which tells of a traveling salesman who wakes to find himself transformed into a giant insect. Expressionist dramatists include Georg Kaiser, Frank Wedekind, Ernst Toller, and August Strindberg, often referred to as the "Father of Expressionism." Some critics claim Strindberg's play *To Damascus* (1902) is the first true expressionist drama; others argue that it is Reinhard Johannes Sorge's *The Beggar*, performed in 1917; and still others claim it is Oskar Kokoschka's *Murderer, the Women's Hope*, written in 1907. The discrepancy underscores the question as to whether or not a coherent literary movement called Expressionism with a common set of features ever really existed, or whether it is more of an attitude towards art and society. In the early 1930s, the Nazi regime, which considered the movement decadent, banned its practitioners from publishing their work or producing their plays.

Representative Authors

Franz Kafka (1883–1924)

Born on July 3, 1883, in Prague, Bohemia (now Czechoslovakia), Franz Kafka was an introverted, sickly, and shy boy who struggled to meet the expectations of a demanding father. After receiving a law degree in 1906, Kafka began writing in earnest, publishing his stories in the literary magazine of his good friend, Max Brod. Kafka died of tuberculosis on June 3, 1924, in Austria. While alive, Kafka directed Brod to burn all of his manuscripts. Brod ignored Kafka's wish and, over the next few decades, edited and published all of his unfinished stories.

Like many of the expressionists, Kafka was influenced by Nietzsche and Strindberg. His writings, primarily novels and stories, depict an absurdist view of the world, which he describes in paradoxically lucid terms. In the use of symbols and types, his stories often resemble parables. Like Gregor Samsa, the protagonist of *The Metamorphosis*, Kafka's characters often find themselves in the midst of an incomprehensible world, consumed with guilt and alienated from those they love. *The Trial*, for example, a novel unfinished at the time of Kafka's death, concerns a bank clerk who is arrested but never told the charges. He attempts to negotiate a Byzantine legal system to find the answer, but never does, and is finally killed "like a dog." Today, the term "Kafkaesque" is used as an adjective suggesting something possessing a complex, inscrutable, or bizarre quality.

Georg Kaiser (1878–1945)

Widely acknowledged as the leader of the expressionist movement in theater, Georg Kaiser was born November 25, 1878, in Magdeburg, Germany. Kaiser's father, an insurance agent, was frequently away on business, and his mother, who schooled her six children at home, raised Kaiser. Like many of the characters in his plays, Kaiser was a traveller, venturing to Argentina for a time and throughout Europe. As business did not temperamentally suit him, he had difficulty making a living. However, his family financed his travels, until 1908, when he married the wealthy Margarethe Habenicht. In plays such as *The Citizens of Calais* (1917) and *From Morn to Midnight* (1917), Kaiser juxtaposed fantasy and reality, used rapidly shifting scenes, and gave his characters generic names to underscore their symbolic and universal significance. Kaiser's plays typically feature a questing protagonist who searches everywhere for meaning but finds none. These characters often commit suicide. Kaiser's famous trilogy of plays—*Coral* (1917), *Gas I* (1918), and *Gas 2* (1920)—are as relevant today as they were eighty years ago in their indictment of mindless and mechanized labor and the selfishness of big business.

Kaiser's influence on the development of European drama cannot be understated. Along with Strindberg and Toller, he changed the direction of twentieth-century drama by opening it up to other dramatic possibilities. Critics consider Kaiser and Bertolt Brecht, who also used expressionist techniques, the two leading German playwrights of the twentieth century. Kaiser's plays were banned when the Nazis came to power in 1933. At the beginning of World War II, the writer fled to Switzerland, where he died of an embolism on June 4, 1945.

Eugene O'Neill (1883–1953)

Born in New York City on October 16, 1883, Eugene O'Neill spent the first years of his life traveling around the country with his family while his father performed. Family dysfunction became a staple theme of his plays, and is a recurring theme of expressionist theatre. O'Neill read Strindberg and Wedekind while recuperating from tuberculosis in 1912, and began writing plays incorporating expressionist techniques and style. Not only was O'Neill the first American to write expressionist

August Strindberg

plays, but he was also the first American playwright to receive international acclaim for his work. *Beyond the Horizon* (1920), O'Neill's first full-length play, received the Pulitzer Prize, and in 1936 the literary community showed its approval by awarding O'Neill the Nobel Prize in Literature. He is the first American playwright to have won the award. Literary historians point to his 1920 play, *The Emperor Jones* as an example of American expressionist theater, as well as *The Great God Brown* (1926). In these plays, O'Neill uses ghosts, music, lighting, and stage sets to externalize the inner life of his characters. Other O'Neill plays include *Desire under the Elms* (1924), *The Iceman Cometh* (1939), and *Long Day's Journey Into Night* (1939-41). After a long illness, O'Neill died of pneumonia on November 27, 1953, in Boston, Massachussetts.

August Strindberg (1849–1912)

Often referred to by literary historians as the "Father of Expressionism," (Johan) August Strindberg was born January 22, 1849, in Stockholm, Sweden. His father, though well intentioned, was a strict disciplinarian whose expectations the writer labored under and rebelled against. Strindberg's lifelong difficulty with women both frustrated him and fueled his creative energies. Strindberg was opposed to the idea of a liberated woman, yet he was also attracted to women who refused to be limited to the role of mother and wife. This conflict contributed to three divorces and a string of failed romances. A novelist and essayist as well as a playwright, Strindberg had his first play produced when he was 21. However, for much of his life he struggled financially, working as a librarian, newsletter editor, tutor, and journalist. His controversial ideas often landed him in trouble, and in 1884 he was tried—yet acquitted—for blasphemy for stories he wrote that belittled women and criticized conventional religious practices. Towards the end of his life, Strindberg achieved critical as well as financial success, and his plays were performed throughout Europe. In 1912, he was awarded the "anti-Nobel Prize" in recognition for the way in which his writing challenged conventions and authority. He died in May of that year from stomach cancer.

Strindberg's early plays, written in a naturalistic vein, address historical matters using realistic dialogue as the primary means of communication. He developed his expressionist style, which he referred to as "dreamplay," in his later work. In plays such as *The Road to Damascus* (1898–1904), *The Dream Play* (1901), and *The Ghost Sonata* (1907), Strindberg uses "types" instead of fully developed characters, and incorporates visual elements and music into the action to symbolize humanity's unconscious desires. In his dream sequences, Strindberg frequently represents humanity's misery and search for meaning and redemption.

Georg Trakl (1887–1914)

Georg Trakl was born February 3, 1887, in Salzburg, Austria, into the middle-class Austrian family of an artistic but emotionally unstable mother. Trakl developed emotional problems as an adolescent. His reading of gloomy writers such as Dostoevsky, Nietzsche, Arthur Rimbaud, Verlaine, and Baudelaire only added to his despair, as did his liberal use of various opiates. Trakl wrote frequently but only began to publish regularly after he met Ludwig von Ficker, editor of the journal *Der Brenner*, who nurtured Trakl's talent and provided him with a vehicle for his poetry. Trakl's emotional health deteriorated during World War I, when, as a dispensing chemist, he had to care for a large number of wounded men. Seeing the obscene wounds of soldiers and witnessing their unrelenting pain compounded Trakl's own misery, and he was hospitalized for depression. In Krakow, Poland, on November 3, 1914, Trakl overdosed on cocaine.

Trakl's poems use symbolic imagery and have a dream-like structure to them. He frequently strings together images that on the surface appear unrelated, but on a deeper level are tonally coherent. In this way, his poems are close to musical compositions in their structure. Although they are frequently about decay, death, and despair, Trakl's poems such as "All Souls," "A Romance to Night," "Mankind," and "Trumpets" often embody a kind of spiritual longing, characteristic of much expressionist verse. American poet Robert Bly helped to renew interest in Trakl's poetry during the 1970s by translating his work and linking it with "deep image" poetry.

Frank Wedekind (1864–1918)

Born Benjamin Franklin Wedekind in Hanover, Germany, on July 24, 1864, Wedekind became one of the first playwrights in Germany to experiment with expressionist techniques. The son of a doctor and an actress, Wedekind studied law before dropping out of school to lead a bohemian life. Wedekind makes his contempt of middle-class society evident in his plays, which attack hypocrisy and repressive sexual mores. In plays such as *Pandora's Box* (1904) and *Spring's Awakening* (1906), Wedekind graphically depicts themes of sexual repression in an effort to force audiences to change their behavior. He is perhaps best known for *Lulu* (1905), in which the protagonist, a femme fatale with a monstrous sexuality, is murdered by Jack the Ripper, a serial killer who terrorized London's streets at the end of the nineteenth century. Wedekind's didactic approach to theater includes using heavily stylized dialogue, bizarre characters and plots, and a loosely knit episodic structure to jar audiences out of their complacency. Bertolt Brecht praised his work and followed Wedekind's example in his own plays. Wedekind died of pneumonia in Munich, Germany, on March 9, 1918.

Frank Wedekind

Representative Works

Spring's Awakening

Wedekind's *Spring's Awakening*, published in 1891 but not performed until 1906, explores the theme of adolescent sexuality in a distinctly modern and expressionistic manner. In nineteen episodic scenes, Wedekind presents the stories of a few teenagers as they struggle through sexual maturity because of the ignorance of their teachers and parents who themselves are sexually repressed. Wedekind's Expressionism is evident in his use of heavily stylized dialogue, which mixes lyrical and cutting irony with prosaic speech to create a seriocomic tone. He also has a character return from the dead, something that could not happen in naturalistic theater. A satirical indictment of the hypocrisy and prudery of middle-class German society, Wedekind's play was heavily censored, though it was also one of the playwright's most successful works.

The Citizens of Calais

The Citizens of Calais catapulted Kaiser into the literary limelight virtually overnight in 1917. Opening just as World War I was coming to a close, the play spoke to the sense of sheer exhaustion felt by the German populace and carried the message of conciliation. For his plot, Kaiser drew on a famous incident that allegedly occurred in 1347 during the Hundred Years' War between England and France. Faced with the destruction of Calais, Eustache, a wealthy merchant, sacrifices himself by committing suicide in an attempt to convince others of the significance of free will and the need for courage. The play is important to expressionist thought for its depiction of the "neuer Mensch" (new man), a modern human being who salvages meaning from the world through taking responsibility for his actions and setting an example for others. Many of Kaiser's plays include a Christlike protagonist who fits this "New Man" profile, and who would lead society into a new age of brotherhood through example.

The Dream Play

Strindberg's 1901 *The Dream Play* foreshadows many expressionist techniques and themes in its presentation of the unconscious. The plot concerns the daughter of an Indian god who adopts human form and discovers, through encounters with symbolic characters, the meaninglessness of human existence. With the obvious exception that the protagonist is female, the action parallels the story of Christ's life. The play itself—presented in sixteen scenes that flash backward and forward in time—takes the form of a dream with symbols such as a growing castle, a chrysanthemum, and a shawl signifying aspects of the dreamer's life such as the imprisoned or struggling soul, and the accumulation of human pain. The characters are also symbolic. Victoria, for example, represents the ideal, yet unattainable, woman. The play has become a staple of European theater and is still performed today.

The Emperor Jones

Eugene O'Neill wrote and staged *The Emperor Jones* in 1920. It was the first American play to utilize expressionist techniques, and the most successful of O'Neill's early work. By using lights, sound, and sets, as well as actors' gestures, symbolically, O'Neill shows the audience his protagonist's psyche. As Brutus Jones, a black American who is tricked into becoming emperor of an island in the West Indies, runs through the jungle chased by rebellious natives, he has a series of encounters that symbolize not only events from his personal history but from his racial heritage as well. In this way, Jones is more of a type representing all black men. The play ran for 204 performances and gave the playwright confidence to continue experimenting with expressionist techniques. Such experiments include the use of masks in *The Great God Brown*, with spoken thoughts in *Strange Interlude* (1928) and *Dynamo* (1929), and with a chorus in *Lazarus Laughed* (1928).

The Metamorphosis

Kafka published *The Metamorphosis* in 1915; it is arguably the best known of his stories and novels and the most anthologized. The plot revolves around Gregor Samsa, a salesman who wakes up to discover he has turned into a giant insect. Samsa is locked in his room and ignored by his family until he dies. Critics point to Kafka's heavy use of symbolism in the story, a primary feature of Expressionism, and some read Samsa's transformation as representative of Kafka's own feeling of inadequacy in relation to his overbearing father. Stylistically and thematically, the story speaks to the experience of many expressionist artists and writers, who sought to find ways to express their sense of alienation from society and family and their quest to find meaning in a meaningless world.

Poems

Trakl's *Poems*, published in 1913, is the only volume he published during his life. In the introduction to *Autumn Sonata: Selected Poems of Georg Trakl*, Carolyn Forche calls Trakl "the first poet of German Expressionism," and notes that Trakl, like fellow expressionists Karl Kraus, Kokoschka, and Egon Schiele, was intensely alienated from the order of German industrial society. Trakl's poems embody this alienation: they are fragments, nightmarish images of a world choked with chaos, and of a tenuous and battered self attempting to function in that world. The logic connecting the images is associative, rather than linear. These lines are from *A Romance to Night*:

> The murderer laughs until he grows pale in the
> wine,
> Horror of death consumes the afflicted.
> Naked and wounded, a nun prays
> Before the Savior's agony on the cross.

Critics debate Trakl's status as a Christian poet, but they are paying more attention to his work than any other German expressionist poet. Studies such as Francis Michael Sharp's *The Poet's Madness: A Reading of Georg Trakl* (1981), Richard Detsch's *Georg Trakl's Poetry: Toward a Union of Opposites* (1983), and a number of new translations of his poems attest to his growing influence on contemporary poetry and his importance to understanding Expressionism poetry.

Themes

Regeneration

The defining event of the expressionist movement is World War I. After the war, much expressionist writing portrayed the attempt to forge a new future for Germany. Writing from this time champions the birth of the "new man," the "new vision," and the "new society." Toller's play *The Transformation* typifies one strain of early postwar expressionist drama, as it shows how one man's spiritual renewal is linked to his country's regeneration. Written as a *stationendrama*, *The Transformation* follows the central character's spiritual progress through a series of episodes, connected only through the character's experience. The protagonist, Friedrich, a young Jewish sculptor, transforms himself from an alienated and wandering artist into a friend of the proletariat who finally finds a cause to believe in and die for. At the end of the play, Friedrich implores the masses to create a society based upon compassion and justice, and to throw off the yoke of capitalist oppression.

Human Condition

Expressionist literature is defined by protagonists and speakers who passionately seek meaning in their lives. They often discover that the life they have been living is a sham, and through a sign or circumstance, or dint of sheer will, attempt to change their lot. Kaiser's dramas, for example, feature protagonists who struggle to make difficult choices in recapturing a sense of authenticity. His play *The Burghers of Calais*, for example, details the action of a central character that kills himself so that fellow townspeople might survive. Another Kaiser play, *From Morn till Midnight* (1917), also concerns a protagonist who seeks regeneration through martyrdom. In much expressionist literature, it is the journey, rather than the goal, which is most important.

Sexuality

Part of the expressionist drive to represent truth involved tackling what expressionists saw as the hypocrisy of society's attitude towards sex and sexuality. Strindberg, Reinhard, and especially Wedekind all explicitly addressed the ways in which society sapped humanity's life force by either ignoring or repressing the sexual drive. More than any other expressionist, Wedekind, who derived many of his ideas from Strindberg and Nietzsche, attacked bourgeois morality in his dramas. In *Spring's Awakening*, he represents institutions such as the German school system as agents of deceit and mindless evil in their attempts to keep students ignorant of their own sexuality. His "Lulu" plays glorify sexuality, as his main character asserts her desire to live passionately. Perhaps no other expressionist writer embraces Nietzsche's call for humanity to embrace life and energy in all of its animalism.

Media Adaptations

- The 2000 film *Pollock*, starring Ed Harris, is a portrait of artist Jackson Pollock, a leader of the abstract expressionist painters popular during the 1940s and 1950s. The film is based on the biography *Jackson Pollock: An American Saga* by Steven Naifeh and Gregory White Smith.
- Mai Zetterling's 1981 documentary *Stockholm* presents a portrait of the Swedish city, its people, and their leaders. The film also includes a historical introduction to the works of Strindberg.
- Actor Paul Robeson starred in the 1933 film adaptation of Eugene O'Neill's play *The Emperor Jones*.
- The Norwegian Film Institute distributes director Unni Straume's film, *Dreamplay*, an adaptation of Strindberg's *The Dream Play*.

Alienation

Before World War I, the alienation portrayed in expressionist literature was often related to the family and society in more general, some might say adolescent, ways. After the war, alienation was more directly related to the state. For example, Kafka's protagonists, such as Gregor Samsa, are ostracized by their families because they do not conform to familial expectations. Most expressionist writers came from middle-class families who embodied the very hypocrisy they sought to expose in their writing. Later dramatists such as Kaiser and Toller wrote about the alienation experienced by workers. Kaiser's *Gas* trilogy graphically depicts the injustice of Wilhelmian capitalism towards the working class, underscoring the inherent corruptness of a system in which owners are pitted against employees, who have no claim to the things they produce. Director Fritz Lang adapted the trilogy into his popular 1927 film, *Metropolis*, underscoring the inhumanity of a society that lets technology grow unchecked.

Topics for Further Study

- After studying the expressionist paintings of Vincent van Gogh, Paul Gauguin, Edvard Munch, Ernst Ludwig Kirchner, Paul Klee, and Wassily Kandinsky, compose a poster in the expressionist style for Strindberg's *The Dream Play* or O'Neill's *The Emperor Jones*. Present the poster to your class and describe its expressionist features.
- With at least three other classmates, brainstorm a list of images for the following emotions and ideas: fear of death, journey of the soul, betrayal of a friend, unrequited love, rebelling against authority. What differences do you notice between your images and those of your classmates? Write a short essay accounting for these differences.
- Research German expressionist director Fritz Lang's movies *M* and *Metropolis*, and present your research to the class. Then show one of the movies and hold a discussion of whether or not Expressionism is successful as an approach for film.
- Edvard Munch's lithograph *The Scream* is often cited as being one of the earliest and most representative of expressionist paintings. It is also one of the most heavily marketed images of the twentieth century. Write a short essay explaining why this is so.
- Read *Citizens of Calais* by Georg Kaiser, poems from Georg Trakl's collection *Poems*, and Kafka's story *The Hunger Artist*, and then compose a list of what is similar about all of these works.

Style

Abstraction

For expressionists, abstraction is the distillation of reality into its essence. Expressionists are not interested in presenting the world as human beings might see it or apprehend it through any of the senses, but rather as they emotionally and psychologically experience it. In drama, abstraction means that a play is conceptual rather than concrete, and it means that plots and characters are frequently symbolic and allegorical. For instance, a character might simply be called "Father," as in Strindberg's play *The Father*, or "Cashier," rather than, say, Mrs. Jones, as in a realistic play. The idea is to show the universality of human experience rather than its particularity. In poetry, writers such as Trakl attempt to represent the psychological depth and texture of the human experience through a series of fragmented and disjointed symbolic images, rather than relying on narrative or a speaker with a coherent identity.

Monologue

Monologues are speeches by a single person, and they are especially prevalent in expressionist theater. Partly, this is due to the didactic nature of much expressionist theater, and partly it is because Expressionism often champions the individual and his vision of the world. When characters speak to themselves, which they often do in expressionist plays, the monologues are called soliloquies. Strindberg, Kaiser, and Toller all made extensive use of monologues and soliloquies in their plays.

Genre

Many expressionists had the idea that art could not be separated into categories such as plays, poetry, or fiction. Instead, they experimented with mixing genres. Plays often contained dance, music, and sets that resembled art galleries, and characters would periodically launch into verse. Expressionists such as Wassily Kandinsky, a painter, poet, and dramatist, practiced this form of "total art" in productions such as *The Yellow Sound*, in which he uses color, music, and characters with names such as "Five Giants," "Indistinct Creatures," and "People in Tights" to abstractly represent the human condition.

Movement Variations

Abstract Expressionism

With its roots in the expressionist movement of the early part of the century, abstract expressionism, also known as the "New York school," was developed in New York City and Eastern Long Island in the mid-1940s. Jackson Pollock, Willem de Kooning, Robert Motherwell, Philip Guston, and others focused on the materiality of painting, often using oversized canvases, incorporating accidents that occurred during composition into the painting, and experimenting with color and space to express the painter's vision. One of the most controversial of the group, Pollock, would lay down huge canvasses, and then drip, throw, and splash paint on it, often using sticks and trowels instead of brushes. The resulting "painting," sometimes a mixture of paint, sand, and glass, embodied the artist's own turbulent creative processes. Because abstract expressionist art was nonrepresentational and because the subject of many of the compositions was the making of the work itself, a large part of the public did not take it seriously at first. However, critics such as Harold Rosenberg and Clement Greenberg, who coined the term "Action Painting," worked hard to popularize it. Robert Coates was the first to use the term "abstract expressionism," in the *New Yorker* in 1936.

Film

Expressionist techniques were used extensively in film in the 1920s, as German directors such as F. W. Murnau, G. W. Pabst, and Robert Wiene adapted techniques from art and theater for the wide screen. The first truly expressionist film is Wiene's *The Cabinet of Dr. Caligari* (1919), which used exaggerated camera angles, painted scenery, and the lighting of individual actors to create a nightmarish atmosphere. Film historians also consider *The Cabinet of Dr. Caligari* to be the first horror film. In the 1940s, directors such as Billy Wilder, Michael Curtiz, and Otto Preminger used the bizarre perspectives and lighting techniques of expressionist film to create what some critics claim is a distinctly American style: film noir. Films such as Wilder's *Double Indemnity* (1944) and Fritz Lang's *The Big Heat* (1953) feature cynical, disillusioned male protagonists stuck battling an existential crisis while searching for the answer to some inscrutable or ill-defined problem, usually concerning a dangerously sexy woman. Many of the noir screenplays from the 1940s are derived from the hard-boiled detective novels of writers such as James M. Cain, Raymond Chandler, and Dashiell Hammett. Film noir is filmed in black-and-white and characterized by gritty urban settings, witty banter, flashbacks, and voice-overs. They do not end happily.

Early Twentieth-Century Painting

Expressionist painting, like literary Expressionism, sought to depict emotional and psychological intensity and, like its literary cousin, formed a response to Realism. One group of expressionists was the Fauves (i.e., wild beasts), represented best by Frenchmen Henri Matisse and Georges Rouault. Like many expressionists, these two were inspired by the painterly innovations of van Gogh and Gauguin, particularly their liberal use of bold colors and distorted shapes to signify raw emotion. Matisse arranged line and color to express the essence of subjects, and is known more for what he leaves out of his paintings than what he puts in. Rouault used violent brush strokes in his portraits of noble figures like Christ to reveal his own inner passion. In Dresden, Germany, a group of artists calling themselves "The Bridge" (Die Brücke) practiced a darker style of Expressionism. They drew inspiration from van Gogh and Gauguin as well, but also from Munch, the Norwegian painter famous for his 1894 lithograph, *The Scream*. Painters including Ludwig Kirchner, Emil Nolde, and Kokoschka put brush to canvas to explore a passionate, yet often angst-ridden view of the world and themselves. They often painted street scenes of Berlin, emphasizing the hostile, alienating quality of modern urban life. In Munich, "The Blue Rider" (Der Blaue Reiter), a group of artists headed by the Russian, Kandinsky, practiced an even more abstract style of Expressionism. Kandinsky and fellow "rider" Franz Marc abandoned all pretenses toward objectivity, composing pictures purely of line and color, with no resemblance to the physical world. Marc's color symbolism and Kandinsky's geometric abstraction were attempts to embody the spiritual dimension of humanity, itself an unseen entity.

Historical Context

Pre-World War I Germany

Expressionism blossomed in Germany in the early part of the twentieth century during the reign of William II. Germany was a relatively prosperous country under Wilhelm, with an established middle class, and it is the very complacency of this middle class, its order, efficiency, and obsession with social conventions, against which many writers and artists rebelled. In particular, expressionists saw hypocrisy in German society's repressive and repressed attitudes towards sex and the simultaneous popularity of prostitution. In *Literary Life in German Expressionism and the Berlin Circles*, literary historian Roy Allen notes, "The flourishing of prostitution in the Wilhelminian era, as the expressionist viewed it, most sharply gave the lie to

Compare & Contrast

- **1910–1920:** Largely as a result of the introduction of new weapons such as tanks, poison gas, and airplanes, more than ten million people die in World War I, creating an atmosphere of pervasive disillusionment and despair.

  Today: Technological advances make it easier for countries and individuals to develop nuclear and biological weapons, increasing the potential for worldwide catastrophe.

- **1910–1920:** In Russia, the Bolsheviks, led by Vladimir Lenin, seize power and proclaim Russia a Soviet Federated Socialist Republic.

  Today: Having largely abandoned communism, Russia makes steps towards a full-fledged democracy and market economy.

- **1910–1920:** Expressionist literature, drama, and art dominate the avant-garde in Europe, shocking audiences and viewers in its departure from Realism.

  Today: The capacity of art and literature to shock is largely gone, and no one movement or approach dominates. Instead of shock, readers and viewers often feel boredom in response to artists' and writers' experimentations.

---

the effectiveness of the Wilhelminian approach to morality, particularly to sexual conduct." Wedekind's plays underscore this hypocrisy. In *Spring's Awakening*, for example, he singles out German schools for their part in keeping children ignorant about their own bodies and sexuality. Sigmund Freud's theories on infantile sexuality and the unconscious during this time had a profound effect on expressionist thinking. In 1900, Freud published *The Interpretation of Dreams*, followed in 1901 by *The Psychopathology of Everyday Life*, and in 1905 by *Three Essays on the Theory of Sexuality*. For expressionists, the sexual instinct provided humanity with its drive and creative force. A society that stifles that drive by either ignoring it or demonizing it, produces citizens who could never wholly be themselves.

However, most expressionists during this time were not political activists, at least not in any substantial way. Instead of taking to the streets, as revolutionaries were doing in Russia, they met in coffee houses and cafes in Berlin and Munich and published their work in journals they often started themselves, after established presses rejected their writing. Herwarth Walden of *Der Sturm* and Franz Pfemfert of *Die Aktion* were two editors who left big publishing houses to start their own magazines dedicated to expressionist writings. Allen characterizes those who were part of the cafe circle of writers and artists as a historical type: "In many respects, the expressionists in these circles exhibit features commonly associated with the bohemian artist as he has appeared in societies dominated by the middle class in the last approximate century and a half."

War Years and After

For many Germans, the start of World War I was a surprise. Some were quickly politicized and voiced their opposition to the war, some fled to Switzerland, and others joined the military and died in battle. Many journals ceased publishing altogether, as military authorities began censoring them for antiwar sentiment. The publication of new journals was banned, without the permission of military authorities. Antiwar or anti-establishment plays were also routinely banned, but at least one director and theater manager, Max Reinhardt, circumvented public censorship by producing "invitation only" plays. After the war, while Germans struggled for direction and purpose, many expressionists joined the Communist Party and fought for the Revolution. They poured back into the cafes, with a new sense of urgency, their art now wedded to a political ideal. Kaiser, Toller, and Carl Sternheim produced plays espousing pacifism and universal brotherhood, while various political factions fought for control of the government. Toller's play *The Transformation*, produced in 1919, captures the spirit of postwar enthusiasm for new beginnings, as does *A Man's Struggles*, written while Toller was imprisoned during the last two years of the war. The former features Friedrich, an example of expressionist drama's "New Man"—a Christlike figure with none of the baggage of being God—who undergoes a series of nightmarish trials and tribulations only to overcome them in the end and lead the masses into a new and glorious future.

Critical Overview

Critics and literary historians do not agree on what constitutes literary Expressionism, or even if it was a movement. For example, in R. S. Furness's book *Expressionism*, he acknowledges the attempts others have made to trace the origin of the movement back to the eighteenth century's *Sturm and Drang*, but claims, "It can also be argued that Expressionism is simply the name given to that form which modernism took in Germany." Roy Allen calls the problem faced by literary historians in trying to define literary Expressionism a "bugbear." Other critics and literary historians are more confident in their assessment. Ernst Toller, who is considered one of the leading postwar expressionist playwrights, writes of the movement, as embodied in drama: "Expressionism wanted to be a product of the time and react to it. And that much it certainly succeeded in doing." Mark Ritter points out, in "The Unfinished Legacy of Early Expressionist Poetry," that early literary Expressionism is particularly difficult to pin down and agrees with Allen that perhaps, "One does much better to conceive of early Expressionism as a number of loosely connected circles, primarily in Berlin." In *German Expressionist Drama*, by Literary historian Renate Benson, it is argued that Expressionism originally emerged in the fine arts, initiated by the Paris exhibition of Fauvist painters, and that literary Expressionism followed. Benson laments the fact that the Nazis banned expressionist drama when Hitler came to power, writing, "It is a tragic irony . . . that young German audiences after 1945 only became acquainted with Expressionism through the works of foreign writers . . . who themselves had been so powerfully influenced by German Expressionists."

What Do I Study Next?

- Siegfried Kracauer's study of early German film (1910–1940), *From Caligari to Hitler*, provides insight into Expressionism's influence on German cinema.
- Giles MacDonogh's 2001 biography, *The Last Kaiser: The Life of Wilhelm II*, tackles three important issues in the ruler's life: his personality, his relationship with his parents, and his role in the outbreak of World War I. Wilhelm II ruled Germany during the peak of Expressionism.
- Bernard S. Myers's book *The German Expressionists: A Generation in Revolt* (1957) surveys expressionist painters and painting in the 1920s and 1930s.
- Roy Pascal's study *From Naturalism to Expressionism: German Literature and Society*, published in 1973, traces the roots of Expressionism to the late nineteenth century, examining its relationship to Naturalism and Realism.
- In 1986, Christopher Waller published *Expressionist Poetry and Its Critics*, a study of how writers such as Rainer Maria Rilke, Thomas Mann, and Robert Musil would critically approach representative expressionist poets.
- Ulrich Weisstein's essay "German Literary Expressionism: An Anatomy," in the May 1981 issue of *German Quarterly*, explores how difficult it is to find common features for works that are often lumped under the category "German Literary Expressionism."

Criticism

Chris Semansky

Semansky holds a Ph.D. in English from the State University of New York at Stony Brook, and he is an instructor of literature and writing whose essays, poems, stories, and reviews appear in publications such as College English, Mississippi Review, New York Tribune, The Oregonian, *and* American Letters & Commentary. *His books include* Death, But at a Good Price *(1991) and* Blindsided *(1998). In this essay, Semansky explores the idea of Expressionism as a literary movement.*

Critics struggle over whether or not there ever was a coherent expressionist movement, or if it is merely a label of convenience for literary historians seeking to characterize a wide range of writing practices in Western Europe in the early twentieth century. What *can* be said is that Expressionism was both part of a larger set of practices and attitudes that come under the umbrella of Modernism, and that it was a response to realistic modes of representation.

Egon Schiele's expressionist style Self-Portrait with Black Clay Vase and Spread Fingers

Modernism, as it applies to literature, is a term broadly used to denote certain features of form, style, and subject matter in writing in the early decades of the twentieth century. Thinkers influential to modernist literature include Friedrich Nietzsche, Sigmund Freud, Albert Einstein, and Karl Marx, all of who challenged status quo ideas about the nature of humanity, morality, society, and writing itself. World War I furthered the adoption of Modernism, as writers such as James Joyce, Ezra Pound, Virginia Woolf, and T. S. Eliot experimented with stream of consciousness, fragmentation, and other nonlinear modes of narration to represent a world whose foundations had been shaken to its roots. Expressionism undoubtedly was a part of Modernism, but was it a movement?

In his study of Expressionism in Berlin, Roy Allen defines the idea of a "literary movement" as "the concerted activities of an organized group or group of individuals work[ing] or tend[ing] towards some goal in behalf of . . . literature." Allen historicizes Expressionism by focusing on those writers who regularly met in cafes in Berlin and published one another's work. However helpful this definition might be for the historian interested in the details of small communities of writers with plans to change the order of things, it is of little use to the student trying to grasp the larger context from which Expressionism springs. Understanding the mind of the writer, as well as stylistic features and themes of what is commonly referred to as Expressionism, provides a more helpful introduction to the phenomenon.

Most critics, historians, and literature handbooks note Expressionism's response to Realism as a mode of representation. In literature, Realism refers to a historical period and a particular approach to writing. As practiced by novelists in the nineteenth century, Realism referred to descriptive writing that was plausible and that represented the ordinary in familiar ways. It attempted to reproduce the world as it was seen. Readers could believe what they read because their own experience confirmed that such stories could, in fact, happen. Instead of some far-flung romantic plot about exotic people in distant places, the realist writer focused on the everyday, describing the mundane and the local. Realists used language as a mirror held up to the world, and were interested in portraying the "thingness" of life. The more "realist" the description, the more it matched the experience of the reader. Wilhelm Raabe, for example, a German Realist writer, described the everyday life of Berliners in his 1857 novel.

"The scream, then, a response to the sudden recognition that the self is at root alone and without intrinsic meaning, is the defining image of Expressionism."

Expressionists responded to Realistic writing and art not only because it embodied what for them was a life-denying way of being in the world, but because they believed that the Realists, in attempting to portray truth, in fact were perverting it. The society that Realists portrayed in all of its middle-class frumpiness and injustices was the same one that expressionists believed was sapping their very lifeblood. Austrian author Hermann Bahr sums up the expressionist attitude best in his 1916 study, *Expressionismus*: "Man screams from the depths of his soul, the whole age becomes one single, piercing shriek. Art screams too, into the deep darkness, screams for help, for the spirit. That is expressionism." The scream, then, a response to the sudden recognition that the self is at root alone and without intrinsic meaning, is the defining image of Expressionism. In this way, expressionist writers anticipated the Existentialists who came to dominate the literary establishment after World War II.

By its nature, a scream distorts the face, denaturalizes it. A quick look at Munch's 1894 lithograph by the same name will attest to this. This is what the expressionists desired—to show the horror of everyday life, not its ordinariness. Poets such as Georg Heym and Jakob van Hoddis displayed this horror in their apocalyptic visions. The latter's poem, *End of the World* provides one early example of expressionist verse:

> The bourgeois' hat flies off his pointed head,
> the air reechoes with a screaming sound.
> Tilers plunge from roofs and hit the ground,
> and seas are rising round the coast (you read).
> The storm is here, crushed dams no longer hold,
> the savage seas come inland with a hop.
> The greater part of a people have a cold.
> Off bridges everywhere the railroads drop.

Juxtaposing mundane statements such as "The greater part of people have a cold" with sensational images of trains dropping from bridges is a feature of much expressionist poetry, as is associative logic in general, but these features do not cut across all expressionist verse. Another side of literary Expressionism is its revolutionary strivings. Apart from all the doom and gloom, many writers, especially after World War I, worked for social change. Expressionist chronicler Walter H. Sokel points out the difficulty of this endeavor in his study *The Writer in Extremis*: "German Expressionism sought to be two things in one: a revolution of poetic form and vision, and a reformation of human life. These two aims were hardly compatible." Sokel notes that by eschewing Realism as the stylistic base of their idealism, expressionist writers were not able to wed their desires for social change with their penchant for artistic experimentation. In other words, by limiting the accessibility of their work to the initiated and the educated, they also limited their potential influence. Some, like Franz Werfel, a Czech, and Hanns Johst adapted. Sokel writes of this group:

> What all of them gained was success in personal terms, a mass audience, the triumph of personal integration and power in the world. What they lost was success in aesthetic terms—the permanence and long-range effectiveness of their works.

In an essay for Victor Miesel's *Voices of German Expressionism*, Gottfried Benn, a leading expressionist writer, goes as far as to call Expressionism "a new form of historical existence" that was European at root, not German. Benn notes that between the years 1910–25 in Europe, "There was hardly another style except an anti-naturalistic style." Ulrich Weisstein, in exploring whether Expressionism is a style or a view of the world, points out that the word "Expressionism" was first used by French painter Julien-Auguste Hervé in 1901 to distinguish the work of Matisse and other painters from their impressionist predecessors, but did not find general acceptance until 1911 when art critics began to use it more liberally to describe Fauvist paintings. It was not until 1915 or so that the term was even used in reference to literature. Underscoring Expressionism's broader philosophical claims, Weisstein writes:

> Luckily . . . [Expressionism's] socio-political aspect can be subsumed under the term Activism. If, excluding this aspect, one defines the term broadly enough to include man's attitude toward himself, his fellow beings and the world at large, one can defend the use of Weltanschauung [i.e., worldview] in the sense of a sharp rejection of previously embraced views on the part of an entire generation.

Considered in this light, Expressionism could be seen as a generational conflict born out of younger artists' disgust with the inadequacies—aesthetic, political, and social—of the previous generation. Combined with the desire not to reproduce the world, but to capture its essence in all of its chaos and rage, the expressionist literary movement was not limited to Germany. Rather, it spread across Europe and the United States, where writers held similar attitudes and were engaged in like literary enterprises. This is more true for poetry and fiction, less so for drama.

Source: Chris Semansky, Critical Essay on Expressionism, in *Literary Movements for Students*, The Gale Group, 2003.

J. M. Ritchie

In the following introduction excerpt, Ritchie provides an overview of formal elements in and original sources of German Expressionism.

I. Formal Features of Expressionist Drama

However disparate the views on Expressionism may be, it is generally true that an Expressionist play will tend to be different from a Neo-Romantic or Naturalistic play, no matter how extensive their common roots. Perhaps the most striking formal feature of Expressionist drama is abstraction. Essentially this means that the Expressionist dramatist is not concerned with projecting an illusion of reality on the stage; instead he gives something abstracted from reality, that is, either something taken from the real world but reduced to the bare minimum, or something totally abstracted from reality in the sense that the norms of time and place and individuation have been completely abandoned. Hence in Expressionism there is constant stress on giving the essence—the heart of the matter—deeper images instead of "mere" surface appearances. Not surprisingly, actions and plots are also pared down to the important outlines and only crucial situations are presented, while all "unnecessary" detail is eliminated. This same tendency is noticeable in the treatment of the dramatic figures, which show no characteristic features of particular individuals but tend to embody principles which the author holds to be important. As such, they bear no names and instead are often simply designated as Father, Mother, Husband, or Wife. Other dramatic figures can similarly represent states of mind, social positions, official functions, etc.; hence they are introduced merely as Cashier, Officer, and the like. The intention is clearly to move away from the specific and the conditioned to a more general sphere of reference and significance.

Abstraction of this kind is, needless to say, by no means restricted to Expressionist drama; indeed, it is a feature of Expressionist art in general. All in all, this is in line with the Expressionists' reaction against the materialistic philosophy of the Naturalists, who tended to show the force of milieu, race, class, and social circumstance as factors conditioning the character of the individual. The Expressionists were not interested in character in this sense and did not attempt to create dramatic characters in their plays. Character for them meant a limitation of scope. They were more concerned with the soul, that which is common to all men. Instead of creating an impression of real people in real situations, the Expressionist dramatists will therefore strive with religious longing for something beyond the merely material, for eternal and transcendental values.

While this is the essential nature of Expressionistic abstraction, the rejection of the principle of mimesis was given various explanations. Kasimir Edschmid, for example, said in a speech on literary Expressionism: "The world is there. It would be senseless to repeat it." But whatever the reasons offered, time and place were ignored by the Expressionist dramatist so that he could feel free to create his own subjective universe. The dream, with its associations apparently lacking in cause or logic, was substituted for normal reality. For this practice there was a model to hand in Strindberg, though there had been forerunners within the German dramatic tradition, among whom Kleist attracted most attention. Thus, from Sorge's *Der Bettler* (The

Beggar) to Kaiser's *Gas II*, one constantly encounters dream-like sequences and figures.

After the dream, the most outstanding formal element in the Expressionist drama is the monologue. This is perhaps not surprising considering its function as the main vehicle for expressing the subjective developments within the soul of the lyrical-dramatic protagonists. The use of the monologue demonstrates yet another contrast with the Naturalists, who had argued that in real life people were supposed to converse and not soliloquize. No sooner had the monologue been banished, however, than it made its way back into the drama with even greater force than before, not least through the monologue dramas of Neo-Romantic dramatists like Hofmannsthal. The revival of the monologue was propitious for the Expressionist dramatist, who did not see life in terms of communication and sociability. Even his very explosions of longing for brotherhood and *Gemeinschaft* express an awareness of the fundamental isolation of man. Thus, egocentricity and solipsism become another hallmark of his works, expressed in formal terms by the long soliloquies of the one central figure, about whom all the other figures cluster like satellites around a major planet. The protagonist expresses *himself* alone; he does not speak for others, however much he may apostrophize mankind in general.

"After the dream, the most outstanding formal element in the Expressionist drama is the monologue. This is perhaps not surprising considering its function as the main vehicle for expressing the subjective developments within the soul of the lyrical–dramatic protagonists."

This solipsistic character of the Expressionist drama explains another feature, namely the scream. The Expressionist dramatist is not concerned to show normal life lived at a normal level or tempo. Instead, he strives for the exceptional and extreme situation, in which the protagonist simply explodes. In this way, once again he breaks through the restricting bonds of normalcy and is beside or beyond himself. At its best this means arriving at a state of ecstasy, which is the aim of the fundamental religious striving of the Expressionists. Ecstasy means experiencing the Divine immediately and absolutely, and not merely attempting to grasp it logically or rationally. At the same time, rhetorical and ecstatic monologues are not merely an expression of the thoughts and feelings of the isolated protagonists; they have a powerful effect on each member of the audience who is there to be stirred up out of his bourgeois mediocrity by powerful utterance. Clearly, such monologues can be as unwieldy as similar speeches in a Baroque drama by Andreas Gryphius or Daniel Caspar von Lohenstein; but the effect, once the improbability is accepted, can be equally overwhelming.

It must be admitted, however, that a potential source of weakness in Expressionist drama is the almost exclusive focus on one central protagonist, while all the other figures in the drama are reduced to mere reflections of his central position. However, it is possible to overstress the dangers of the single-perspective play. The same kind of technique was, after all, employed by Kafka in his fixed-perspective narratives to very powerful effect. At its best, as for example in Kaiser's *Von morgens bis mitternachts* (From Morn till Midnight), the solipsistic drama could be extremely successful in the way all other characters in the play mirror and reflect the problems of the cashier. Less successful is a more lyrical drama like Sorge's *The Beggar*, where even the hero's mother, father, and girlfriend seem to have been introduced simply in order to illuminate significant aspects of the young hero's soul.

As far as the actual structure of an Expressionist drama is concerned, dynamism has been singled out as the one significantly new element. By this is meant not only the forceful nature of the language employed, but also the principle whereby the protagonist is shown following a certain path through life. Hence, the drama becomes a *Stationendrama*, following the ancient religious model of the stations of the cross. This means, in effect, a sequence of scenes which follow rapidly one upon the other, often with no obvious link between them. Here again there were models in the German dramatic canon, notably in the theater of Storm and

Paul Robeson as Brutus Jones from the film The Emperor Jones, *written by Eugene O'Neill*

Stress, though nearer to hand were the examples of Strindberg and Wedekind. Essentially, the dynamic, episodic structure mirrored the inner turmoil and awareness of chaos in the soul of the central figure, who, following the religious model, often goes through a total transformation. Such a *Wandlung* (the title of one of Toller's plays) is most clearly apparent in the case of Kaiser's cashier who is a mere machine-man in a bank and is electrically switched on by the touch of an exotic Italian lady. Through her his transformation becomes possible; he becomes aware of "life" and tries to realize his full potential as a human being. So from being a robot he is awakened to the possibility of human existence and sets off on his quest for fulfillment, being totally transformed from one second to the next. The religious parallels to his *Aufbruch* (new start) and his pilgrimage are made symbolically clear throughout.

Even on the printed page, one major difference between an Expressionist drama and its predecessors is immediately obvious by reason of the frequent alternation between verse and prose. Here again the Expressionist sees no reason to be arbitrarily limited to the single register of natural speech and is prepared to be unnatural and poetic;

not that the verse is generally poetic in the normal melodic sense: instead, the Expressionistic dramatist preferred free verse which he could move into and out of quite easily, depending on the level of speech in the particular moment of the action. In verse he was able to leave the rational, logical world behind and penetrate to the deeper levels to express the stirrings of the soul. Here the poetic utterance conforms to the ecstatic state and the elevated manner. That here the Expressionist was yet again laying himself wide open to attack from hostile critics is readily apparent. Such attacks were not slow to come and have never stopped. Yet such pathos was not a simple sign of artistic impotence; on the contrary, it was a deliberately chosen style of the large gesture and the grand manner. The scream could end in stammering incoherence; pathos could result in Baroque-like effusion; but at its best the drama could be deeply stirring in its combination of rational control and surging emotion. Here once again extreme opposites seem to be the mark of the Expressionist style, which could be extremely dense, concentrated, compressed on the one hand, while on the other this shortness, sharpness, and eruptive spontaneity could overflow into seemingly endless monologues.

It is generally easy to identify the Expressionist style on the page not merely by the alternation of verse and prose but also by the proliferation of exclamation marks, dashes, and question marks, sometimes in clusters, while even the longest speech generally breaks down into shorter units, characterized by missing articles, eliminated particles, and condensed verbal forms in order to create the lapidary style of *Ballung*. Yet while such a style is, or can be, extremely aggressive and disturbing, another feature needs to be mentioned, namely its hymnic quality. Here Sorge's *The Beggar* and Hasenclever's *Der Sohn* (The Son) offer excellent examples of the manner in which the dramatists can soar higher and higher in tone, in the manner of a musical crescendo.

And yet it must not be thought that the Expressionist always operates at such a high level; indeed, it could be argued that the most striking weapon in the Expressionist armory was the ready exploitation of the grotesque, a technique deliberately designed to effect a break from a high level of tension and plunge down to the banal. The possibilities of the grotesque had been amply demonstrated by Wedekind in *Frühlings Erwachen* (Spring's Awakening) and elsewhere, and the Expressionist playwrights were not slow to follow his example. Hence, in the excitement of the Six Day Race in *From Morn till Midnight* the cashier sees five people squeezed together like five heads on one pair of shoulders till a bowler hat falls from one head onto the bosom of a lady in the audience below, to be imprinted on her bosom forever after. The bowler hat is followed by the middle man of the five, who plunges to his doom below as Kaiser puts it, like someone just "dropping" in! Such a use of the grotesque can be screamingly funny, but also screamingly terrifying. The mark of the grotesque is the distortion and exaggeration of the normal, the exploitation of caricature and distortion for effect.

II. The Roots of Expressionist Drama

One question that has exercised the minds of critics is how far back one has to go to find the sources of that modernism in form and content associated with the theater of Expressionism. Medieval mystery plays have often been mentioned in this context, not merely because so many Expressionist plays share the religious striving of such early forms of theatrical production, but also because one of the features of Expressionism seems to have been a highly intellectual longing for a return to simpler forms. Hence, such obvious delight in *tableaux* as the "gothic" setting of Kaiser's *Die Bürger von Calais* (The Burghers of Calais) reveals, while the striking conclusion to Kaiser's play not only deliberately stresses the religious parallels to a secular situation, but also abandons language completely for a mode of expression relying on the visual impact of light, grouping, and gesture. Similarly, the whole play tends to follow a medieval "revue" pattern, in which sequences of scenes, or pictures, take the place of continuity of plot. Constantly referred to in connection with Expressionistic plays is the term *Stationendrama*. Hence, although an Expressionist play may appear on the surface to be very modernistic, modeled for example on Strindberg's *To Damascus*, the idea suggested is the far older one of the quest, involving the equally religious possibility of a revelation or transformation in the course of this path through life. Little wonder, then, that Expressionistic plays often adopted the form of the *Läuterungsdrama*, i.e., the play of purification in which an Everyman figure experiences an illumination and changes his life from one moment to the next. A feature of the Naturalistic play was the depiction of man as a creature of many conditioning factors. Man was a product of his environment, his class, race, and creed; his life ran along certain fixed tracks from which he could not deviate. The Expressionist dramatist, on the other hand, demonstrates that man is always free to choose and change. His are plays of "becoming," like Barlach's *Der blaue Boll* (Blue Boll). This character has been forced into a certain role in society, but, as the play demonstrates, he is a man and not a machine or an animal, and in the epic form of seven stations, or *tableaux*, he makes his "decision." Many Expressionistic plays are therefore also *Entscheidungsdramen*, plays in which a crucial decision for the course of a whole life is made. Very often, as in *Blue Boll*, the decision is a fundamental one involving the "Erneuerung des Menschen," the regeneration of man, a phrase which once again stresses the religious nature of so many Expressionistic works. Not surprisingly, plays of this kind tend toward universal themes and cosmic dimensions, which may mean that the characters are diminished, in one sense, as beings of flesh and blood and expanded, in another, to become representative figures for some aspect of the human dilemma.

But it would be wrong to seek the roots of Expressionist drama exclusively in the religious drama of the Middle Ages. Much more to the point is the general tendency to go back beyond the comparatively recent tradition of nineteenth-century drama to absolute simplicity combined with universal significance. This, Nietzsche had demonstrated, was to be found in the classics, not however, in the Apollonian world of beauty and light, but in the Dionysian sphere of darkness and ritual. Hence, from Kokoschka's *Mörder Hoffnung der Frauen* (Murderer Hope of Womankind) onward, there is an increasing emphasis on myth. The process of condensation and compression becomes a paring down to the quintessential. The result is an economy going beyond the extreme simplicity of Greek classical drama and a concentration on all the hymnic, rhetorical potential of language. But it must be admitted that this process of reduction and concentration, combined with ritual incantations and myth-making, has some unfortunate results. However exciting it may be, Kokoschka's playlet on the myth of the purification of man who, in his struggle with woman, dies to be reborn, is so compressed that the meaning is largely obscured. In a myth-seeking play like Unruh's *Ein Geschlecht* (One Family), which was much praised in its own time, practically every permutation in the relationship between a mother and her children is projected through highly charged language—love, hate, incest, possible fratricide and matricide—while the action, which is not bound to any particular age or country, takes place before a mountain cemetery high above the wars in the valley. The results of such mythologizing can often be ludicrous, as for example in the mother's dying words which sound like an echo from Kleist, whose *Penthesilea* was indeed one of the sources of Unruh's inspiration: "Here, here and there too, plunge all your steel shafts deep into my blood! I'll melt them down till nothing remains to hurt my children."

An example of the fruitful use of classical simplicity is Goering's war play *Seeschlacht* (Naval Encounter). Unruh's play is marked by shouts, screams, and exclamations, and Goering's play too is a *Schreidrama* or "scream play," another label often attached to Expressionist drama. But the striking feature of *Naval Encounter* is the tight discipline and the controlled, hard, highly stylized language. The quick switches from short, sharp stichomythic utterances of classical brevity to long monologues of considerable eloquence are a feature of the new Expressionist style which revels in the conjunction of extremes—ice-cold with feverheat, compression with expansiveness, logicality with ecstasy, stasis with dynamicism. Characteristically, too, there is little or no plot—merely the situation of men moving toward their inevitable fate, in this case sailors in a gun turret going into battle, and hence to their death. There is no realistic detail: the stylization is now complete, the compression to abstract form extreme, the process of depersonalization total. The whole work with its Socratic dialogue has the style and rigor of a classical tragedy with its constant suggestion of forces outside man controlling his destiny. Yet the final outcome is not determined by fatalism but by the individual who stands out against the forces that threaten to control him and mankind. Man's duty to man is thus the chief criterion. Hasenclever, too, adopted the classical style in his antiwar play *Antigone;* his play *Menschen* (Humanity) is an even better example of the dangers of hovering between classical simplicity and a passion-play structure.

However, Expressionist dramatists were not generally accused of excessive formalism (though, as has been seen, the tendency toward classical concentration and condensation laid them open to this charge): they were more likely to be accused of formlessness. On the whole, this charge is probably unfair and brought about by the Expressionistic predilection for the open forms of drama associated with the German Storm and Stress. These open forms, in fact, as used by the previously underestimated Klinger and J. M. R. Lenz, whose works included balladesque and filmic scene sequences, gradually came to be appreciated in the period which began just before World War I and ended just after it. Indeed, Lenz in particular emerged as a model for the twentieth century. An even more important influence than Lenz was Georg Büchner, also an exponent of the open form, whose most important drama was produced successfully for the first time about this period. The impact of his *Woyzeck* can be seen particularly in the Alban Berg opera *Wozzeck*, which it inspired.

Source: J. M. Ritchie, "Introduction," in *German Expressionist Drama*, Twayne Publishers, 1976, pp.15–39.

Sources

Allen, Roy, *Literary Life in German Expressionism and the Berlin Circles*, UMI Research Press, 1983.

Bahr, Hermann, *Expressionismus*, 1916.

Benn, Gottfried, "The Confession of an Expressionist," in *Voices of German Expressionism*, edited by Victor Miesel, Prentice-Hall Inc., 1970.

Benson, Renate, *German Expressionist Drama: Ernst Toller and Georg Kaiser*, Macmillan Press, 1984.

Forche, Carolyn, Introduction, in *Autumn Sonata: Selected Poems of Georg Trakl*, Asphodel Press, 1998.

Furness, R. S., *Expressionism*, Methuen, 1973.

Ritter, Mark, "The Unfinished Legacy of Early Expressionist Poetry: Benn, Heym, Van Hoddis and Lichtenstein," in *Passion and Rebellion: The Expressionist Heritage*, edited by Stephen Eric Bronner and Douglas Kellner, J. F. Bergin, 1983, pp. 151–65.

Sokel, Walter H., *The Writer in Extremis: Expressionism in Twentieth-Century German Literature*, Stanford University Press, 1959.

Toller, Ernst, "Post-War German Drama," in the *Nation*, Vol. CXXVII, No. 3305, November 7, 1928, pp. 488–89.

Weisstein, Ulrich, *Expressionism as an International Literary Phenomenon*, Didier, 1973.

Further Reading

Bridgwater, Patrick, *Poet of Expressionist Berlin: The Life and Work of Georg Heym*, Libris, 1991.

Bridgwater provides an accessible and entertaining biography of one of the leading poets of the expressionist movement.

Brod, Max, *Franz Kafka: A Biography*, Da Capo, 1995.

Brod was a friend of Kafka's, and his biography is an insider's look at Kafka's life. This is an accessible, very sensitive, and thorough biography written on Kafka.

Dove, Richard, *He Was a German: A Biography of Ernst Toller*, Libris, 1990.

Toller was a socialist and leading expressionist dramatist. Dove provides an entertaining biography of his life and art.

Johnson, Walter, *August Strindberg*, Twayne, 1976.

Johnson's work on Strindberg's life and plays is an excellent place to begin study of this expressionist writer.

Styan, John, *Modern Drama in Theory and Practice: Expressionism and Epic Theater*, Cambridge, 1981.

Styan considers expressionist theater as embodying a "rigorous anti-realism" in its representation of the world. Styan argues that Expressionism is most coherent in theater as opposed to poetry or fiction.

Webb, Daniel Benjamin, *The Demise of the "New Man": An Analysis of Ten Plays from Late German Expressionism*, Verlag Alfred Kummerle, 1973.

Webb's study traces the depiction of the "New Man" in expressionist plays from the 1920s and 1930s, concluding that playwrights became disillusioned with the ideal of such an entity and began writing about his downfall.

Willet, John, *Expressionism*, Weidenfeld and Nicolson, 1970.

Willet considers the expressionist movement in relation to historical, political, and social developments.

Harlem Renaissance

Movement Origin

c. 1917

The Harlem Renaissance was a period between World War I and the Great Depression when black artists and writers flourished in the United States. Critics and historians have assigned varying dates to the movement's beginning and end, but most tend to agree that by 1917 there were signs of increased cultural activity among black artists in the Harlem section of New York City and that by the mid-1930s the movement had lost much of its original vigor. While Harlem was the definite epicenter of black culture during this period, and home to more blacks than any other urban area in the nation in the years after World War I, other cities, such as Chicago, Washington, D.C., and Philadelphia, also fostered similar but smaller communities of black artists.

The movement came about for a number of reasons. Between 1890 and 1920, the near collapse of the southern agricultural economy, coupled with a labor shortage in the north, prompted about two million blacks to migrate to northern cities in search of work. In addition, World War I had left an entire generation of African Americans asking why, when they had fought and many had died for their country, they were still afforded second-class status. By the end of the war, many northern American cities, such as Harlem, had large numbers of African Americans emboldened by new experiences and better paychecks, energized by the possibility of change. A number of black intellectuals, such as W. E. B. Du Bois and Alain Locke, were making it clear that the time had come for white

America to take notice of the achievements of African-American artists and thinkers. The idea that whites might come to accept blacks if they were exposed to their artistic endeavors became a popular one.

To this end, magazines such as the *Crisis*, published by the National Association for the Advancement of Colored People, and *Opportunity* featured the prose and poetry of Harlem Renaissance stars Langston Hughes, Countee Cullen, Claude McKay, Nella Larsen, and Zora Neale Hurston. Major New York-based publishing houses began to search for new black voices and print their poems, short stories, and novels. White intellectual society embraced these writers and supported—financially and through social contacts—their efforts to educate Americans about their race, culture, and heritage through their art. Ultimately, however, the financial backing began to run dry in the early 1930s with the collapse of the New York stock market and the ensuing worldwide economic depression. The Renaissance had run its course.

Representative Authors

Countee Cullen (1903–1946)

Born May 30, 1903, in Louisville, Kentucky (although a few accounts claim Baltimore or New York City), Countee Cullen is believed to have been reared by his paternal grandmother, who died when he was fifteen. He was then adopted by the Reverend Frederick Cullen, later the head of the Harlem chapter of the National Association for the Advancement of Colored People, and introduced to the lively intellectual and cultural life of New York. He received an undergraduate degree from New York University and a master's degree from Harvard University.

Cullen, a writer of both poetry and prose, believed that art should be where whites and blacks find common ground. In 1925, his most well-known work, *Color*, was published to nearly universal praise. In the 1930s, he turned to teaching and eventually began producing his plays. Cullen received numerous awards for his work, including a Guggenheim fellowship in 1928. He died of uremic poisoning January 9, 1946, in New York City.

W. E. B. Du Bois (1868–1963)

William Edgar Burghardt Du Bois, or, as he is more commonly known, W. E. B. Du Bois, was born in Great Barrington, Massachusetts, February 23, 1868. Trained as a sociologist, Du Bois received his bachelor's, master's, and doctoral degrees from Harvard University. He condemned racism in America and was one of the founders of the National Association for the Advancement of Colored People (NAACP). He wrote numerous books on race issues and worked as a university professor.

In addition to his support of young writers during the Harlem Renaissance, Du Bois's 1903 sociological examination of African Americans, *The Souls of Black Folk*, helped create the atmosphere in which many of the Renaissance writers and artists could flourish. He coined the phrase "talented tenth" to denote the group of highly educated, culturally adept, and politically astute blacks who would lead the rest of the race into better lives. By the early 1930s, Du Bois became disillusioned about life in America, and his political beliefs forced him to resign from his NAACP position. His politics led to membership in the Socialist Party, and he experienced confrontations with the U.S. government on several occasions. After joining the Communist Party in 1960, Du Bois moved to Ghana, where he died on August 27, 1963.

Jessie Redmon Fauset (1882–1961)

Jessie Redmon Fauset was born in Snow Hill, New Jersey, April 27, 1884, the daughter of a minister. She was the first black woman to graduate from Cornell University, received a master's degree from the University of Pennsylvania, and studied at the Sorbonne in Paris. In addition to writing novels, poetry, short stories, and essays, Fauset taught French in the Washington, D.C., schools and worked as the literary editor for the *Crisis*. It was in this last capacity that she encouraged many of the more well-known writers of the Harlem Renaissance.

While her reputation as an editor of other writers' works has tended to outshine her reputation as a fiction writer, many critics consider the novel *Plum Bun* Fauset's strongest work. In it, she tells the story of a young black girl who could pass for white but ultimately claims her racial identity and pride. She wrote three other novels, with mixed reviews, but most readers of that period's writings believe that Fauset's strengths lay in nonfiction. Fauset died of heart disease April 30, 1961, in Philadelphia.

Langston Hughes (1902–1967)

James Langston Hughes, or just Langston Hughes as he was commonly known, was a writer

Zora Neale Hurston

of poetry, short stories, novels, plays, song lyrics, and essays. His frank portrayals of the black community around him often provoked sharp comments from African-American literary critics. Hughes's retort, that he was simply depicting life as he saw it, did not impress the critics who believed that he should present black life in the best possible light to help improve the plight of African Americans.

Hughes was born in Joplin, Missouri, on February 1, 1902 to a father who was a rancher, a businessman, and a lawyer, and a mother who worked as a teacher. Hughes's background was varied and colorful: by the time his first poetry book, *The Weary Blues*, came out in 1926, he had spent time as a cook, waiter, truck farmer, college student, nightclub doorman in Paris, and sailor, and he had lived in numerous American cities and foreign countries. He died on May 22, 1967, in New York City of congestive heart failure.

Zora Neale Hurston (1891–1960)

Zora Neale Hurston was the daughter of a preacher and a seamstress and was born January 7, 1891, in Eatonville, Florida. Hurston quit school at age thirteen to care for her brother's children but later attended a Baltimore high school, thanks to a generous patron. Her undergraduate and graduate studies in anthropology at Barnard College and Columbia University influenced her novels, plays, and two published collections of African-American folklore.

Hurston fought against a common impression that the poverty often associated with black American culture made it less valuable. She continually encouraged blacks, especially those of the educated middle class, to recognize their rural cultural heritage. Many criticized her writing as bawdy and her most famous work, the novel *Their Eyes Were Watching God*, as simplistic and reactionary. Other readers, ultimately the majority, praised the book as offering positive self-affirmation for African Americans.

Hurston also worked as a maid, a staff writer for Paramount Studios, a librarian at the Library of Congress, and a theater professor, and she received Guggenheim fellowships in 1936 and 1939. On January 28, 1960, she died in Fort Pierce, Florida.

James Weldon Johnson (1871–1938)

While James Weldon Johnson did produce literature during the Harlem Renaissance period, he is noted for his civic leadership and support of young black writers. Born on June 17, 1871, in Jacksonville, Florida, Weldon became at various times a poet, novelist, editor, lawyer, journalist, educator, civil rights leader, songwriter, translator, and diplomat. He received undergraduate and graduate degrees from Atlanta University and did graduate work in creative literature at Columbia University.

Johnson's work as a newspaper owner attracted the attention of such black luminaries as W. E. B. Du Bois. Johnson's only novel, *The Autobiography of an Ex-Coloured Man*, is remembered for its realism, and his groundbreaking study of black music, *The Book of American Negro Spirituals*, educated many Americans about the fact that black music encompassed more than minstrel shows and paved the way for his depiction of black sermons as poetry in *God's Trombones*. During the 1920s, Weldon served as the head of the NAACP and edited a critically acclaimed collection of verse entitled *The Book of American Negro Poetry*. He died following a car accident in Wiscasset, Maine, on June 26, 1938.

Nella Larsen (1891–1964)

Nella Larsen was born in Chicago, Illinois on April 13, 1891; her father was black West Indian and her mother was Danish. This mixed heritage became the foundation for her novels *Quicksand* and *Passing*, in which the heroines struggle with the challenges of being neither black nor white. Many critics have said that *Quicksand*, winner of a Harmon Foundation Prize in 1928, was one of the period's strongest novels. Her education included time at Fisk University in Nashville, the University of Copenhagen, as well as librarian and nursing schools in New York. In 1930, Larsen was the first African-American woman to receive a Guggenheim fellowship.

A series of incidents, including a mistaken charge of plagiarism and her divorce from physicist husband Elmer S. Imes, caused Larsen to leave literary society and spend the final twenty years of her life working as nurse in Manhattan hospitals. She died March 30, 1964, in New York City of heart failure.

Alain Locke (1886–1954)

Alain Le Roy Locke, born September 13, 1886, in Philadelphia, was the son of two schoolteachers. He received a doctorate from Harvard in 1918, after studying philosophy at Oxford University, where he was a Rhodes Scholar. He also studied at universities in Paris and Berlin. Some critics credit Locke with bringing about the Harlem Renaissance in earnest with the 1926 publication of *The New Negro: An Interpretation*, his compilation of the best early-twentieth-century African-American literature.

Locke believed that the best chance for blacks to become accepted in America lay in exposing white communities to the work of black writers and artists. He also encouraged black artists to look to their history and culture for inspiration. In addition to serving as the chair of the Howard University philosophy department for more than forty years, Locke published and edited other books on African-American music, history, and poetry. He died in New York City on June 9, 1954, after a long illness.

Claude McKay (1889–1948)

Claude McKay (born Festus Claudius McKay) was born September 15, 1889, to a farming couple in the British West Indies—what is now Jamaica. McKay reveled in reading British poetry and learning about European philosophy while in school. After he began to write his own poetry, however, one of his teachers encouraged him to stop imitating the English style and develop his own voice—a suggestion he embraced.

In 1912, he left Jamaica to enroll at the Tuskegee Institute in Alabama, thanks to a monetary award for his book of poetry, *Songs of Jamaica*. He made his way to New York City by working as a laborer. McKay's poetry became more militant as he experienced racism and began publishing in the *Liberator*, a magazine run by a well-known American communist, Max Eastman. In 1928, after traveling around the world for a number of years, including trips to the Soviet Union, McKay published his provocative and controversial first novel, *Home to Harlem*. During the 1920s, McKay also participated in Communist Party activities in the United States. He died of heart failure in Chicago on May 22, 1948.

Jean Toomer (1894–1967)

Born in Washington, D.C., on December 26, 1894 into a racially mixed family, Jean Toomer spent his early years living in primarily white, well-to-do neighborhoods. When he was a teenager, the family suffered a financial setback and began living as an average black family, sending Jean to an all-black high school. He attended a number of universities but decided on being a writer during his year at the City College of New York. For one year, between 1921 and 1922, Toomer worked as the principal of a rural black school in Georgia, an experience that gave him a chance to investigate his black roots.

Toomer wrote some of the most experimental and progressive literature of the early twentieth century. His first novel, *Cane*, published in 1923, is a fiction piece, combining both poetry and prose, and is considered a masterpiece of *avant-garde* writing (writing that is considered at the forefront for the period or somewhat experimental). He also published plays, and numerous journals printed his essays and short stories. Toomer died in Doylestown, Pennsylvania on March 30, 1967.

Representative Works

Cane

Jean Toomer's *Cane* is a three-part novel comprising both poems and short stories. Published in 1923, the work was hailed as a revolutionary exploration of black city and rural life in early twentieth century America.

Toomer's experimentation with style, structure, and language reflects the influence of the numerous *avant-garde* writers and artists (those

Langston Hughes

whose work is considered groundbreaking or somewhat experimental) he met while living in the Greenwich Village section of New York City. The book received much praise from the critics for its efforts to break from typical realism and for its exciting use of language but garnered little popular success. While Toomer went on to write essays and plays, *Cane* was his only published book.

Color

In 1925, Countee Cullen published his first collection of poems, *Color*, to high praise. Cullen's work, including the poetry in *Color*, was known for its beauty and lyricism, despite featuring incidents of racism. Alain Locke referred to Cullen as "a genius" in his review in *Opportunity*, published not long after the release of Cullen's collection, comparing Cullen with the poets A. E. Houseman and Edna St. Vincent Millay.

Both black and white readers eagerly awaited Cullen's first book; in fact, his poetry, especially that found in his first collection, was so popular that many blacks of the day knew Cullen's verses by heart. The best-known poem from this collection is "Heritage," in which Cullen considers the meaning of Africa to himself and African Americans. The collection won a Harmon Foundation award in 1925.

God's Trombones: Seven Negro Sermons in Verse

James Weldon Johnson's *God's Trombones: Seven Negro Sermons in Verse* was published in 1927. This collection of poetry established Johnson as one of the literary stars of the period and reflected the style and rhythm of the preaching that the author heard in African-American churches. Countee Cullen, reviewing the collection in *The Bookman*, called Johnson's work "magnificent." Many critics have noted that Johnson does not use dialect in this poetry collection, and generally the response to the poet's decision is favorable.

Home to Harlem

Claude McKay's novel *Home to Harlem* was published in 1928, the first in a series of three novels that many critics see as a trilogy of black life in America. The story centers on the relationship between two black men, Jake and Ray. Jake is an AWOL soldier, intent on returning to Harlem and the good times he remembers there. Ray is his opposite—a highly educated man who has completely lost touch with his culture. Through their conversations and actions, McKay shows two ways of responding to the racial prejudice in America during the 1920s. Ray experiences intellectual angst and leaves the United States for Europe, while Jake remains in Harlem, happy with his life and friends but intent on maintaining his pride.

Home to Harlem was the first bestselling book by a black writer in the United States. The novel was such a commercial success that it was reprinted five times in two months. Many readers were attracted by the book's racy image of jazz-age Harlem; McKay writes of prostitutes, nightclubs, and boozy parties. However, many critics —especially those black critics who believed that positive representations of African Americans would help rid the nation of its racial problems—condemned McKay's novel for its bawdy images of black life in Harlem.

The New Negro: An Interpretation

Many historians and critics of the Harlem Renaissance credit the 1925 publication of Alain Locke's anthology, *The New Negro: An Interpretation*, with encouraging the explosion of energy among black artists and writers in the 1920s and 1930s. The collection includes poetry and prose from such Renaissance stars as Langston Hughes, Countee Cullen, Zora Neale Hurston, and Claude McKay. The high quality of the anthology's work attracted the attention of literary critics of the day and alerted the public to the talents of a previously unknown group of writers. The book also served to alert black writers that they were not alone by exposing them to other writers' efforts and by promoting an atmosphere of inspiration.

The anthology received excellent reviews, including positive comments from W. E. B. Du Bois. Locke felt strongly that a group of African-American artists and writers could bridge the gap between white and black communities, and the publication of the *The New Negro* was an effort to start that process.

Quicksand

Nella Larsen wrote two novels addressing the issue of light-skinned blacks living as whites, *Quicksand* and *Passing*, but *Quicksand*, published in 1928, was the first and more well received. In *Quicksand*, Larsen tells the story of a woman of mixed ancestry, much like herself, who feels comfortable in neither black nor white society.

Critics were impressed with the rich psychological background Larsen gave her characters in the novel, as well as with the novel's use of symbolism. In addition, many readers were happy that a black writer, while still tackling sensitive issues of race and culture, had chosen to place most of the story in a relatively genteel setting, as opposed to many other novels that depicted impoverished black society. With the publication of *Quicksand*, many intellectuals involved in the Harlem Renaissance took positive notice of Larsen, including W. E. B. Du Bois and Alain Locke, and predicted her continued success as an author. The novel won the Harmon Foundation's bronze medal in 1928.

Their Eyes Were Watching God

Critics consider *Their Eyes Were Watching God* Zora Neale Hurston's best fictional work. The 1937 novel (late in the period but still considered a Harlem Renaissance work) is informed by the extensive work Hurston did collecting black folktales throughout the 1920s and 1930s. It tells the story of a black woman struggling to assert her identity—both as an African American and as a woman—in the southern United States around 1900.

The critical reception of *Their Eyes Were Watching God* was mixed; some readers praised its accurate portrayal of small-town black life, while others, such as Richard Wright, accused Hurston of pursuing racial stereotyping to please white audiences. Overall, the novel was under-appreciated when it was first published and viewed as an escapist piece of fiction. It gained considerable respect in the last half of the twentieth century as a feminist tale of empowerment and fulfillment.

The Weary Blues

The Weary Blues, Langston Hughes's first published collection of poetry, released in 1926, contains both traditional lyric poems written on classical subjects and poems about being black in America in the early twentieth century. Some of the strongest verses, in fact, reflect Hughes's love for blues and jazz music by imitating the cadences of popular tunes heard in Harlem nightclubs and on the streets.

Though a few of the poems in this collection were written when Hughes was a teenager, most critics still saw in the volume a special energy and vigor; indeed, many of these poems remain the author's most well known and well loved pieces, such as "The Negro Speaks of Rivers." Many black critics, however, were uncomfortable with his less traditional rhyming schemes and, concerned that Hughes was furthering the negative image of African Americans, disliked his portrayals of unsophisticated blacks and their day-to-day lives. They referred to him as a "racial artist," or an artist who relies too heavily on his identity as an African American. Other critics praised his successful integration of musical styles into his poetry and language, especially in the title piece, "The Weary Blues," which captures the tone of a piano player performing in a nightclub. Hughes's experimental style was both respected and condemned by various readers and critics.

Themes

As many critics have noted, the literature from the Harlem Renaissance displayed a wide variety of themes and topics; in fact, some have blamed this lack of cohesion for its supposed failure to maintain its momentum much past the early 1930s. However, there were a handful of themes and issues that commonly appeared in many of the writers' works.

Race and Passing

The issue of skin color is of critical importance in most of the novels, stories, and poetry of the Harlem Renaissance. For example, a quick examination

Media Adaptations

- In 1984, Francis Ford Coppola directed *The Cotton Club*, a movie starring Richard Gere, Diane Lane, and Gregory Hines, about the famous jazz nightclub in Harlem during the 1920s and 1930s. The film was distributed by Orion Pictures Corporation.
- In 1937, Claude McKay's novel *Banjo* was made into the film *Big Fella*, distributed by British Lion Film Corporation.
- The Langston Hughes short story "Cora Unashamed" was made into a television film of the same name in 2000, distributed by the Public Broadcasting Service.
- *Rhapsodies in Black: Music and Words from the Harlem Renaissance* is a boxed set with four CDs featuring various artists of the period reading and performing their works and music. Langston Hughes, for example, reads his poem "The Negro Speaks of Rivers" and Duke Ellington performs "The Cotton Club Stomp." In addition, some contemporary artists participate in the recording: rapper Ice-T reads Claude McKay's poem "If We Must Die." The set was released in 2000 by Wea/Rhino.
- Langston Hughes's first collection of poetry, *The Weary Blues*, is celebrated on a CD of the same name, featuring Hughes reciting his poetry and the legendary jazz musician Charles Mingus performing music that recreates the atmosphere of a Harlem blues club. The CD was originally released in 1958 and is available on the Uni/Verve label.

of the titles included in Cullen's first collection of poetry, *Color*, indicates that he is very conscious of his race and its defining connotations in America: "To a Brown Girl" and "Black Magdalens" are two of the titles in the collection. In another one of the collection's poems, "The Shroud of Color," Cullen writes of his race and of the experience of being a second-class citizen because of his skin color:

> Lord, being dark, forwilled to that despair
> My color shrouds me in, I am as dirt
> Beneath my brother's heel.

In addition, many of the period's authors refer to a phenomenon known as "passing"—a light-skinned black person living as a white person. In Larsen's *Passing*, the heroine faces tragedy when her white husband becomes aware of her African-American background. In another of Larsen's books, *Quicksand*, the mixed-race heroine struggles to find a place in society where she can feel comfortable and welcome. She feels restricted when she attempts to settle in black society but experiences dissatisfaction and discontent while passing as a white woman.

African Heritage

Many of the period's authors highlighted their African heritage. Some viewed Africa in a romantic light and as an ancient place of origin and therefore a prime source of artistic insight. For example, Hughes, in his poem "The Negro Speaks of Rivers," refers to the thousands of years of African experience inside him when he writes:

> I bathed in the Euphrates when dawns were young.
> I built my hut near the Congo and it lulled me to
> sleep

One of Cullen's best-known poems, "Heritage," celebrates the rich cultural legacy being discovered by many of the Renaissance artists. In the poem, he ponders the meaning of Africa to himself and to other American blacks.

In his anthology, *The New Negro: An Interpretation*, Locke encourages young black artists and writers to look for inspiration in their own African heritage—as separate from the dominant white American-European heritage. The book closes with an essay by Du Bois suggesting that American blacks reach out to blacks in Africa and around the world, initiating a Pan-African movement. In fact, *The New Negro* and other books published during the Renaissance were decorated with African-inspired motifs and designs.

Conflicting Images of Blacks

One of the most difficult issues writers dealt with during the Renaissance was how to portray African-American life. On one hand, many writers and intellectuals had a keen desire to illustrate black society only in the most positive fashion, writing stories filled with middle-class, educated characters working to become successful in a white-dominated America. Others believed that white perceptions of black society should not matter and that all sides of the African-American experience should be exposed and celebrated in the literature. Adding to this dichotomy was the concern that the more sensationalist or primitive images of blacks in literature were the ones that sold—especially to white readers.

Many black intellectuals condemned, for example, the first and only issue of the literary magazine *Fire!!*, published by Walter Thurman. The issue contained stories and poetry by some of Harlem's most famous young writers, but much of what they were writing about did not fit the positive image of the race that black thinkers such as Du Bois and Benjamin Brawley considered appropriate. In fact, after reading the issue, which included pieces about prostitution, homosexuality, hatred of whites, and conflicts between lower-class black men and women, Brawley allegedly burned his copy. Hughes responded to the idea that black writers should be circumspect in what they produce in his 1926 article "The Negro Artist and the Racial Mountain," proclaiming, "If white people are pleased we are glad. If they are not, it doesn't matter. . . . If colored people are pleased we are glad. If they are not, their displeasure doesn't matter, either."

One writer who was often condemned by members of the black intelligentsia for portraying blacks in a negative fashion was McKay. His novel *Home to Harlem* upset many who believed that his story, set amid the nightclubs and speakeasies of Harlem, catered to the image many whites had of blacks as primitive savages who, even when dressed in fine clothes, were ready to succumb to their baser urges at a moment's notice. Some black critics also charged Hurston with writing stories that were unnecessarily bawdy and crude, but she argued that her work accurately reflected the folktales she collected in black rural areas.

Style

Dialect and Colloquialisms

There was no consensus on the use of black or rural dialect in the work of Harlem Renaissance writers; some authors used it liberally while others shunned it entirely. Hurston used dialect in *Their Eyes Were Watching God* to reflect the atmosphere and tone of the language she heard when collecting folktales. For this, Richard Wright later condemned the novel and claimed that she was painting a negative and stereotypical image of blacks for white readers.

Johnson used dialect verse and misspellings in some of his poetry but decided to discard these techniques when writing his collection of rural sermons turned into verse, *God's Trombones*, considered to be, far and away, his best work. He is reported to have said that dialect restricted what he wanted to do in *God's Trombones*. The sermons maintain the rhythm and pacing of speech he admired in black preachers but are delivered in a more sophisticated manner. For example, the poem-sermon entitled "The Creation" is written in standard English but maintains the cadence of powerful oratory:

> Then God himself stepped down—
> And the sun was on his right hand,
> And the moon was on his left;
> The stars were clustered about his head,
> And the earth was under his feet . . . .

Music

Many of the Renaissance poets experimented with using the cadences of popular music in their work, but none was as well known for this technique as Hughes. He used blues and jazz beats in much of his poetry, recreating the sounds and music he heard in the clubs and on the streets of Harlem. Hughes's poetry not only incorporates the rhythms of familiar music but also covers topics common to many blues songs: economic hardship, failed romance, loneliness, and sexual desire. In the poem "The Weary Blues," Hughes writes of a piano player performing at a club and uses the technique of repetition, a familiar technique in many blues songs.

Urban and Rural Settings

Because many of the Harlem Renaissance writers moved to the cities from rural areas, both settings became critical components of their work. For example, Toomer's book of poetry, stories, and a play, *Cane*, includes a section devoted entirely to

Topics for Further Study

- Many of the period's prominent writers studied at Columbia University in New York City. Research the histories of Columbia University and other American universities during the first twenty years of the twentieth century. What were the policies of various institutions in terms of admitting black students? What were the choices for blacks who wished to attend college during the 1920s and earlier in the century? Present your findings in an essay.
- Churches played a key role in the lives of many Harlemites. In addition to holding Sunday services, some churches, such as the Abyssinian Baptist Church, organized community centers, helped feed the poor, and operated homes for the elderly. Investigate the growth of churches in Harlem during the 1920s and 1930s and how many developed into influential and powerful organizations.
- Many critics note that, while the Harlem Renaissance ended during the early 1930s, African-American writers did not stop producing work. Research the important black writers of the 1940s and 1950s, such as Richard Wright, James Baldwin, and Ralph Ellison. Acquaint yourself with themes these writers dealt with, their styles, and so on. Discuss in a short essay any similarities or differences you see between this literature and the literature of the Harlem Renaissance.
- Some historians and critics have argued that the present time is another "renaissance" for black artists, entertainers, and writers, similar in a number of ways to the Harlem Renaissance. Consider the two periods and create a chart showing the similarities and differences between the two as regards politics, social institutions, major cities involved in the arts, and the artistic achievements themselves.

characters in a rural Georgian setting, with images of trees and sugar cane. In the second section, the action takes place in Washington, D.C., and is filled with images of streets, nightclubs, houses, and theaters. Hurston set most of her stories in rural towns, in accordance with her lifelong effort to collect black rural folktales.

The move between rural and urban is also critical to many Renaissance novels. In McKay's *Home to Harlem*, the primary locale of the story is Harlem. But each of the novel's protagonists comes from someplace else: Jake is assumed to be originally from the rural South, and Ray is Haitian. Larsen's novel *Quicksand* follows a mixed race woman who travels from her job at a black southern college to various large cities around the world in search of a place she can truly call home. She ultimately ends up living in rural Alabama, feeling suffocated.

Movement Variations

Visual Arts during the Harlem Renaissance

Visual arts made a strong statement during the Harlem Renaissance, creating images based on newly developed consciousness about heritage and culture. For example, in her article on Harlem Renaissance art and artists in *Print*, Michele Y. Washington notes that black artists' interest in Egypt as part of Africa and their heritage contributed to many of the motifs in the Art Deco style becoming widespread during the 1920s and 1930s.

Aaron Douglas, one of the period's leading artists, used images of African masks and sculpture in his geometric, Art Deco-style drawings. He served as an apprentice to Winold Reiss, the German artist whose geometric and angular drawings were featured on the original cover of Alain Locke's *The New Negro*. Douglas became the premier illustrator for the period's magazines and books and also created large murals on the walls of various Harlem nightclubs.

Many of the leading Renaissance artists had formal art training but used vibrant and energetic African images to break away from the more traditional forms of European art. Like Douglas, many of these artists collaborated with black writers to decorate the covers and insides of their published poetry collections, novels, and magazines.

The Renaissance in Other American Cities

While the energy of the explosion of African-American literature, music, art, and politics was focused primarily in Harlem, other cities also experienced their own versions of the Harlem Renaissance during the 1920s and 1930s. Artists and writers located in cities such as Chicago, Philadelphia, Detroit, and Washington, D.C., were producing valuable and exciting work.

Locke, for example, maintained his contact with Howard University in Washington, D.C., as the chair of its philosophy department for more than forty years. A number of writers got their start in the nation's capital, including Toomer and Rudolph Fisher, and Hughes often spent time there. Chicago was not only a hotbed of musical energy during the 1920s and 1930s, but writers such as Frank Marshall Davis wrote while living there. And, though he wrote just after the period of the Renaissance, Richard Wright used his own Chicago experiences liberally in his work.

Music during the Harlem Renaissance

Music saturated Harlem during the 1920s and 1930s, whether at the numerous Protestant churches, where age-old and new spirituals comforted the congregations, or at the neighborhood's hundreds of speakeasies, nightclubs, and theaters, where jazz and blues tunes pushed dancers well into the early morning hours.

Of all the styles of music in Harlem, the district is probably best known for its jazz. Black bandleaders such as Louis Armstrong, Fletcher Henderson, and Duke Ellington made jazz the neighborhood's (and the nation's) most popular musical style in the 1920s and 1930s, even though many people—including numerous black intellectuals—found its rhythms too harsh and bawdy. But the rage for jazz would not die, and patrons crowded Harlem's countless clubs nearly every night to hear the dynamism and spontaneity that were the hallmarks of jazz.

In 1926, the Savoy Ballroom opened, and its reasonable cover charges encouraged people of all races and economic levels to spend the evening dancing and listening to the best jazz in the world. While many well-known musicians performed there, the Savoy was also a place where unknowns could see if they had the talent to compete. Jazz and blues singers Bessie Smith and Ella Fitzgerald got their starts at the Savoy.

Historical Context

The Great Migration

The Great Migration involved huge numbers of African Americans moving from the rural southern United States to northern industrial cities during the first few decades of the twentieth century in search of better jobs. This shift in population helped foster the cultural richness that became known as the Harlem Renaissance.

For most of the nineteenth century, the southern United States, like most of the rest of the country, was primarily an agricultural society. By the end of the nineteenth century and the beginning of the twentieth century, the northern economy began to shift to a more industrial base. The southern economy became stagnated and provided a strong impetus for black (and white) farm workers to consider moving north, where the jobs were. Southern blacks considered a move to the north as a step toward economic independence and a better life in a region of the country where they believed they might be treated more fairly.

In addition to the worsening southern economy, blacks were attracted to the north by the fact that during World War I, the United States began limiting the number of immigrants allowed in the country. This created a labor shortage in the north just at a time when the factories were expected to increase production to fulfill orders in support of the war effort. Companies that had rejected the idea of hiring blacks were forced to recruit them actively, even sending labor agents into the South to find workers and offer training in areas such as shipbuilding. Soon, family members were returning to their southern homes from New York, Detroit, Chicago, and other urban centers, telling stories of better jobs and higher salaries. Between 1916 and 1919, about half a million blacks moved to the north; roughly one million blacks made the trip in the 1920s. Between 1910 and 1920, New York City's African-American population jumped 50 percent.

The New Negro

"New Negro" was the term white Americans had used to refer to a newly enslaved African. However, during the first few decades of the twentieth century, the phrase denoted an African American who was politically astute, well educated, and proud of his cultural heritage—the very opposite of a docile slave. Booker T. Washington's view of a New Negro was outlined in his 1900 book, *A New*

Compare & Contrast

- **1920s–1930s:** Harlem is well known for its entertainment venues, including the Savoy Ballroom, the Cotton Club, and the Apollo Theater. National acts regularly play at these stages, including Louis Armstrong, Fats Waller, and Lionel Hampton.

  Today: After closing in the 1970s because African-American acts had access to better-paying venues, the Apollo is now a national historic landmark owned by a nonprofit organization that books such international stars as Luther Vandross, B. B. King, hip-hop artists, and unknown musical hopefuls seeking national exposure.

- **1920s–1930s:** Claude McKay publishes his novel *Home to Harlem*, the first bestselling book in the United States written by an African American. Major New York publishing houses search for the next black writer who will satisfy the reading public's sudden interest in African-American voices.

  Today: Popular black authors are no longer a novelty. Works by Maya Angelou, Toni Morrison, and Henry Louis Gates Jr. regularly appear on the national lists of bestselling books.

- **1920s–1930s:** Lynchings and racially motivated murders of blacks are not unusual. In 1920, an estimated thirty-three blacks are lynched; in 1930, an estimated twenty-four blacks die from lynchings.

  Today: According to national hate crime statistics collected by the Federal Bureau of Investigation, three racially motivated murders of African Americans and 462 racially motivated aggravated assaults against African Americans occurred in the year 2000.

Negro for a New Century and encompassed education, self-improvement, and self-respect.

During the Harlem Renaissance, Locke used the term in the title of his anthology of African-American poetry and prose, *The New Negro: An Interpretation*. Locke believed that African-American writers and artists should participate in the leadership of their people and should be involved in showing white America a new vision of blacks as productive and creative forces to be reckoned with. The New Negro, in Locke's estimation, should be an African American who asserted himself or herself economically, politically, and culturally. In his role as the disseminator of the New Negro philosophy, Locke organized a series of traveling African-American art exhibits and helped launch a national black theater movement.

Red Summer of 1919

In the years immediately following World War I, relations between blacks and whites were strained. White war veterans returning to northern cities felt threatened by the increased population of blacks and their stronger economic position—at least when compared to the prewar years. Many blacks returned from the war wondering why, after fighting for their country and receiving commendations for their bravery from the French, they were still treated as second-class citizens at home. Southerners sensed a heightened level of self-confidence among the blacks visiting their families from their jobs in northern cities. Economic pressures hit the general American population after the war when the government lifted price controls and unemployment and inflation rates jumped.

During the summer and early fall of 1919, twenty-five race riots erupted across the nation in Chicago; Charleston, South Carolina; Omaha, Nebraska; Washington, D.C., and other cities. In the space of six weeks, seventy-six lynchings were reported; a dozen of the lynchings were perpetrated on black men still wearing their service uniforms.

Johnson coined the term "Red Summer" while investigating these incidents for the National Association for the Advancement of Colored People. Racial tensions were exacerbated by the nation's postwar fear of the newly formed Bolshevik, or "red," regime in Russia. Many efforts by blacks to improve their economic and political status were met with white suspicions that they were as "radical" as the Russian Bolsheviks.

Life in Harlem during the 1920s and 1930s

Harlem, a neighborhood in New York City, became the preeminent black urban enclave in the United States early in the twentieth century, when thousands of blacks migrated primarily from southern and rural regions. Previously, the area had been a wealthy white neighborhood, but economic hard times and skyrocketing real estate values at the start of the twentieth century created a situation in which clever entrepreneurs began leasing vacant rooms in white-owned buildings to black newcomers to the city. Harlem's black population in 1914 was about fifty thousand; by 1930 it had grown to two hundred thousand.

The neighborhood also attracted black intellectuals, artists, and others interested in participating in Harlem's increasingly vibrant cultural environment. Black political organizations, such as the National Association for the Advancement of Colored People and the National Urban League, established offices in Harlem, as did major black newspapers such as *The Messenger* and *The New York Age.* Marcus Garvey, leader of the "back-to-Africa " movement, set up his Universal Negro Improvement Association in Harlem. Garvey and others energized Harlemites with their messages of black pride and self-sufficiency.

Harlem also became an entertainment capital early in the century. Musical performers moved to Harlem, drawn by the atmosphere and the hundreds of nightclubs and other venues where the jazz sound was wildly popular. Performers Duke Ellington, Louis Armstrong, Fats Waller, and others played to appreciative crowds at nightspots like Smalls's Inn and the Savoy Ballroom. But not only locals patronized the free-spirited nightclubs that began to give Harlem a wild reputation; whites from other parts of New York City "discovered" Harlem and made it the place to be on a Saturday night. Ironically, some of the nightclubs were off-limits to blacks, including the famous Cotton Club, until 1928 catering to a wealthy white clientele intent on experiencing the "exotic" Harlem atmosphere.

Critical Overview

The criticism on the Harlem Renaissance movement tends to focus on its impact on black literature and on the African-American community. In fact, many critics, while acknowledging that the current energy in black literature and music does have its foundations at least partly in the Harlem Renaissance, hold that the movement came up short in terms of staying power. Andrea Stuart, writing in *New Statesman*, questions whether the Harlem Renaissance has had any lasting impact on the lives of ordinary black Americans. "The legacy of the Harlem Renaissance remains a profoundly romantic one for the black bourgeoisie," Stuart comments. But, "on the streets, where the great majority of black culture is made, its echoes are only faintly heard," she claims.

Amritjit Singh notes in his book *The Novels of the Harlem Renaissance: Twelve Black Writers* that the artists involved in the Harlem Renaissance failed to develop a "black American school of literature" for a variety of reasons. The most critical reason, he argues, is that the artists themselves "reflect the spirit of the times in their refusal to join causes or movements" and were interested less in the societal problems of blacks than in their own individual problems. Margaret Perry, in her book *The Harlem Renaissance: An Annotated Bibliography and Commentary*, generally agrees with this concept, noting that the writers of this period "failed to use their blackness to fullness and with total honesty in order to create that unique genre of American literature one called black or Afro-American."

While acknowledging the shortcomings of the Harlem Renaissance as noted by numerous current critics as well as by the era's participants, George E. Kent believes that the movement has still provided American literature with some very "fundamental" accomplishments. He argues in *Black World* that "the short story in the hands of [Jean] Toomer, Eric Waldron, and Langston Hughes became a much more flexible form," and that, while no Harlem Renaissance author created a truly new form of the novel, these writers did provide stories that "occasionally stopped just short of greatness." Kent also praises the playwrighting of the period, though it received little Broadway exposure.

Other readers of the period's literature have noted its influences. Kenneth R. Janken addresses the deep affection black intelligentsia had for

The Lafayette Theatre in Harlem

French culture during the early part of the twentieth century and how this both contributed to the movement and prevented them from seeing the limitations of the French social model. He comments in *The Historian* that, while the Harlem Renaissance certainly was indebted to French intellectuals for much of its philosophy about racial equality and recognition of an African diaspora, it viewed the position of blacks in French society through rose-colored glasses. Harlem Renaissance writers "could not thoroughly critique the French colonial system . . . that continued to exploit the majority of Africans," Janken notes.

Many critics have depicted the Harlem Renaissance as a period of great hope and optimism, but Daylanne K. English disagrees. In *Critical Inquiry*, he argues that, upon closer examination, the opposite is true. "The Renaissance writers were, in fact, preoccupied by the possibility and the picturing of various modern, and only sometimes racially specific, wastelands," notes the author.

Nathan Huggins, in his well-respected 1971 book *Harlem Renaissance*, questions the exclusiveness of the movement to the nation's black population and posits that black and white Americans "have been so long and so intimately a part of one another's experience that, will it or not, they cannot be understood independently." He argues that the creation of Harlem "as a place of exotic culture" was as essential to whites as it was to blacks. Locke's declaration of the New Negro reflected America's continuing fascination with remaking oneself and was, in truth, "a public relations promotion," Huggins asserts. African Americans had to be presented in a better light, in a way the majority of whites could accept and blacks themselves could internalize. "Even the best of the poems of the Harlem Renaissance carried the burden of self-consciousness of oppression and black limitation," he notes.

Aderemi Bamikunle also examines how whites affected the work of Harlem Renaissance writers. He asserts that the white connection with black writing has a long history, going back to the mid-1800s, when white abolitionists found and published black authors who would write "according to a particular genre," specifically, the slave narrative. Bamikunle points to the comments many black writers made during the Harlem Renaissance about the struggle to appeal to both a black and a white audience. "For blacks who felt a strong obligation towards the black race there was bound to be conflict between that obligation and the constraints of writing within a white culture," he argues.

The Harlem Renaissance was not an exclusively male event, and some critics have chosen to highlight black women's roles in the achievements of the period. While Cheryl Wall, writing in *Women, the Arts, and the 1920s in Paris and New York*, admits that no female black writer working during the 1920s and 1930s came close to the talent and skill exhibited by many of the era's leading male writers, she adds that black women "were doubly oppressed, as blacks and as women, and they were highly aware of the degrading stereotypes commonly applied to them." For this reason, she believes, black women poets often wrote more restrained poetry and prose than their male counterparts.

Criticism

Susan Sanderson

Sanderson holds a master of fine arts degree in fiction writing and is an independent writer. In this essay, Sanderson looks at how the Harlem Renaissance writers succeeded in creating a literature of pioneering.

"Though their work could not undo hundreds of years of racism and second-class status, the writers of the Harlem Renaissance did succeed in giving a voice to a generation of black pioneers."

The literature of the Harlem Renaissance was produced by a generation of writers steeped in ideas illuminated most clearly by Howard University philosophy professor and intellectual Alain Locke. Locke first referred to the concept of the New Negro in an article in the March 1925 issue of *Survey Graphic*, a special issue of the journal entitled *Harlem: Mecca of the New Negro*.

In one of the issue's articles, which he expanded later that year into the introduction for his anthology of the best African-American writing, *The New Negro: An Interpretation*, Locke defines the New Negro as one who has thrown off the age-worn stereotypes of the subservient and docile black. For generations of white Americans, he notes, blacks have been "something to be argued about, condemned or defended, to be 'kept down,' or 'in his place,' or 'helped up,' ... harassed or patronized, a social bogey or a social burden." In place of the "Old Negro" comes the New Negro, "vibrant with a new psychology" reflecting that "a new spirit is awake in the masses." Locke expected this new and talented group of African-American artists—many whose work appeared in *Survey Graphic* and later in his anthology—to recreate and improve the image of the race through their art, in hopes that blacks would finally become appreciated by white society.

This was a tall order for barely more than a handful of people. The economic and social conditions of most black Americans at the turn of the century and after World War I were somewhere between deplorable and less-than-adequate. Though their work could not undo hundreds of years of racism and second-class status, the writers of the Harlem Renaissance did succeed in giving a voice

What Do I Study Next?

- W. E. B. Du Bois was one of the black intellectuals involved in launching and encouraging the Harlem Renaissance. David L. Lewis's Pulitzer Prize–winning biography of Du Bois, *W. E. B. Du Bois: Biography of a Race, 1868–1919* (1994), provides readers with a highly detailed narrative of the great thinker and founder of the National Association for the Advancement of Colored People (NAACP) in the years preceding the Harlem Renaissance.
- Black visual artists experienced an explosion in ideas and energy during the 1920s and 1930s similar to that experienced by writers. *Rhapsodies in Black: Art of the Harlem Renaissance* (1997) covers the accomplishments of African-American painters, sculptors, photographers, actors, and singers working during the period. The book, edited by Richard J. Powell and David A. Bailey, includes 150 color plates and 100 black-and-white drawings.
- Starting in 1910, the NAACP published *The Crisis*, a popular magazine that was responsible for giving the up-and-coming writers of the Harlem Renaissance the exposure and experience they needed to develop their talents. *The Crisis Reader: Stories, Poetry, and Essays from the NAACP's "Crisis" Magazine* (1999), edited by Sondra Kathryn Wilson, is a collection of writings drawn from the publication primarily during the 1920s.
- Marcus Garvey and his Universal Negro Improvement Association championed the rights of black Americans but believed that blacks would never achieve equality in a white-dominated country such as the United States. This controversial leader, whose philosophies launched the "back to Africa" movement in the early years of the century and affected the thinking of many black intellectuals and others during the Harlem Renaissance, is examined in the biography *Marcus Garvey* (1987), edited by Mary Lawler and Nathan Huggins.
- George S. Schuyler was a black writer who lived during the Harlem Renaissance and took great pleasure in satirizing and lampooning many of its leaders, artists, and philosophies. Those who read his work in the 1920s and 1930s found him to be harsh and sometimes unfair but always interesting and readable. Critics writing during the 1960s and 1970s were less enthusiastic and condemned him as a reactionary conservative. Schuyler's 1931 novel about a black man who decides to use a formula that will make him white, *Black No More*, caused a sensation. It was reprinted in 1999.

---

to a generation of black pioneers: blacks who followed a grand American tradition by leaving impoverished and difficult conditions for the promise of a better life. Their migratory route was within the United States, primarily from the rural south to the industrial north, and they created strong and vibrant cities and neighborhoods built on their dreams.

In fact, Houston A. Baker, Jr., in his book *Modernism and the Harlem Renaissance*, argues that Locke's anthology is similar to "the valued documents from which we grasp iconic images and pictorial myths of a colonial or frontier America." Locke succeeded, according to Baker, in writing "our first *national* book, offering . . . the sounds, songs, images, and signs of a nation."

Most American students can recite from memory the stories of immigrants leaving their homelands and coming to the United States in hopes of finding something more—whether the story is about the Pilgrims fleeing religious persecution or others leaving a homeland inflamed with war or devastated by famine or poverty. Even after sailing across oceans, those immigrants participated in the nation's strong tradition of internal migration to move to the western United States, the next state, or the next town when opportunity presented itself.

But African Americans at the turn of the century were, for the most part, the children and grandchildren of a people forcibly brought to America rather than offered the opportunity to migrate. That opportunity has always been, in a sense, one of the defining characteristics of being American; as a people, we have always counted on being able to pick up and start over in another place. Only after the official end to slavery in the United States were African Americans able to participate in this very American activity.

The Great Migration, roughly from the 1890s through the first half of the twentieth century, saw literally millions of blacks moving from their southern homes to northern urban centers in search of decent jobs and a life free from fear. Between 1885 and 1905, there were more lynchings in the nation than there were legal executions. In many parts of the South, tenant farming and sharecropping—systems in which the farmers often found themselves in perpetual debt to the landowners—had depleted the soil's fertility and kept the price of cotton low through the beginning of the twentieth century. Working at other jobs, after their crops had failed, left blacks frustrated at their low wages and limited opportunities. Black men's voting rights were often denied through poll taxes and literacy tests. Like other Americans before them, blacks began a migration that changed the face of the nation. For example, New York City's African-American population jumped 50 percent between 1910 and 1920.

Of course, the north was no paradise. Very often, blacks received low wages and were treated just as poorly as they had been back home. When World War I finished, and white soldiers returned to their northern cities wanting jobs, blacks were often the first employees fired.

The fact remained, however, that blacks in huge numbers had taken a step to redefine themselves by choosing where they would live and how they would live. They were at the same time participating in another great American tradition: that of re-envisioning oneself and one's people through stories. Locke's proclamation of the New Negro was a clear indication of this, and his publication of black poetry, fiction, and essays in his anthology was the literal retelling of those stories.

Nathan I. Huggins, writing in his book *Harlem Renaissance*, notes that white Americans have forever desired to cast themselves as new and improved, primarily to separate themselves from their Old World origins. This separation, of course, has always been paired with a corresponding desire to associate oneself with the Old World by taking pride in the cast-off ancestral country. The changes in black society at the beginning of the twentieth century and the development of the Harlem Renaissance, according to Huggins, afforded blacks a similar opportunity to take part in this "intense and national sport" by declaring that the New Negro had been born and was ready to acknowledge his ties to, and appreciation of, ancestral Africa.

The writers of this era were creating the literature of pioneers, people of a new land, and in doing so writers worked to develop the stories that would tell the rest of the world (and white America) what defined them, what made them proud, and what troubled them. Countee Cullen's poem "Heritage," included in Locke's special *Survey Graphic* issue, is a love song to ancestral Africa, for example, but tempered with a sense of regret and caution. He desires to be swept up in the continent's heat and passion but realizes that as someone who is "civilized," he must tell himself to "Quench my pride and cool my blood." Zora Neale Hurston stays closer to home in her subject matter but still recalls the land of her forebears (the rural South, from where so many blacks had migrated) in her novel *Their Eyes Were Watching God*. Hurston follows Janie, a black woman living in rural Florida, and her lifelong search for fulfillment and identity as a woman.

Claude McKay, through his poems and his fictional characters, often wrote about the plight of African Americans in an angry and defiant fashion. Also included in the special *Survey Graphic*, McKay's poem *White Houses*, challenges the racist attitudes and practices of whites against blacks. He opens the poem noticing that "your door is shut against my tightened face," and he is "sharp as steel with discontent" in the next line. But by the end of the poem, McKay warns himself to avoid becoming involved in "the potent poison" of the white man's hate. In his novel *Home to Harlem*, McKay casts two opposites as protagonists: Ray, who, like McKay, is a well-educated black but uncomfortable with Harlem's festive atmosphere and struggling to fit into either white or black society; and Jake, a black man who leads an untroubled life filled with party-going. Eventually, it becomes apparent that Ray's association with whites, specifically through his bourgeois education, has damaged his identity as a black man, and he flees the new world of Harlem for the Old World of Europe.

A question remains, however, if one looks upon these writers as the voices of migrants and pioneers. Pioneers are usually pictured as a hopeful lot; indeed, much of Locke's language in describing the New Negro in the *Survey Graphic* special issue is optimistic: he uses words such as "genius," "vibrant," and "metamorphosis," and comments that these young writers "have all swung above the horizon." But Daylanne K. English raises a good point in her *Critical Inquiry*, when she argues that "Renaissance writers were, in fact, preoccupied by the possibility and the picturing of various modern, and only sometimes racially specific, wastelands." Indeed, looking at the work of McKay and others, the energetic and optimistic pioneers of the Harlem Renaissance may have realized that, despite Locke's belief that art would mend racial fences, some tough times lay ahead. Their words, according to English, seem to testify to "a clear and widespread sense of urgency, even of anxiety and despair." This combination of hope and anxiety about the future, in fact, is apparent in Langston Hughes's "The Dream Keeper":

Bring me all of your dreams
You dreamers.
Bring me all of your
Heart melodies.
That I may wrap them
In a blue cloud-cloth
Away from the too rough fingers
Of the world.

Indeed, the voice sounded by the writers of the Harlem Renaissance offered a sense of both hopefulness and caution to those who would listen. Black writers would continue to work and produce fine results—Richard Wright and Ralph Ellison in the 1940s and 1950s, Maya Angelou and Alice Walker in the century's latter years—but Locke's hope that the best and the brightest of the black pioneers could wash away the sins of a nation never came about.

Source: Susan Sanderson, Critical Essay on the Harlem Renaissance, in *Literary Movements for Students*, The Gale Group, 2003.

Margaret Perry

In the following essay, Perry profiles novels and novelists of the Harlem Renaissance.

There were no novels by Harlem Renaissance writers of major importance in general American literature during the 1920s. All of the black writers were in the massive shadow of literary luminaries such as Hemingway, Fitzgerald, and Sinclair Lewis. There were novels of major and minor importance, however, among black writers; every principal writer produced at least one novel during the years 1924–1932. The release of artistic expression gathered momentum beginning in 1924 when *The Crisis* and *Opportunity* announced creative writing contests and Jessie Fauset and Walter White published their first novels. In 1927, for instance, the black literary output was an unchecked flow of poetry and prose that wound in and around periodicals and publishing houses on the eastern literary scene. Rudolph Fisher had six short stories which appeared throughout the year, Cullen edited a collection of poetry by Negroes, *Caroling Dusk*, and two of his own books of poetry, *Copper Sun* and *The Ballad of the Brown Girl* appeared. Hughes's second book, *Fine Clothes to the Jew*, gave the black press an outlet for denouncing a movement that could not now be stopped. On the other hand, the publication of James Weldon Johnson's *God's Trombones* drew praise from the critics even though he anticipated a chorus of rebuke from them because he consciously avoided dialect. One may safely assert that in the year 1927 dialect was declared dead. (One important exception, of course, was the work of Sterling Brown.)

The prevailing notion of the fiction of the Harlem Renaissance writers during the 1920s was that it exaggerated the more offensive qualities of low-life in the black ghetto—drink, sex, gambling, violence, and exotic behavior. The truth is that the literature spanning the period of the Harlem Renaissance, roughly from 1923 through 1932, focused on *every* aspect of black life. The portrayal of low-life was part of the trend toward freeing readers from seeing the black person as a problem; it was also an attempt to portray blackness with a candor that the newer writers felt had been lacking in the literature of the past. In fiction, several angles of black life were explored in order to emphasize the harsh injustice of prejudice, the basic human worth of the black race, the bourgeois life of blacks, the irrepressible spontaneity and vitality of the race, and the search for a common heritage, so that, in the words of Countee Cullen, blacks would not have to sing:

What is last year's snow to me,
Last year's anything? The tree
Budding yearly must forget
How its past arose or set—

. . .

One three centuries removed
From the scenes his fathers loved,

Spicy grove, cinnamon tree,
What is Africa to me?

The overall controlling symbol of blackness formed the basis for the major themes explored in the fiction and poetry of the Harlem Renaissance writers. In various plot modes and poetic outpourings, the themes of passing, miscegenation, the "tragic mulatto," the Negro's struggle for self-assertion, violence (mostly white), forms of prejudice (white against black, black against black), and the vitality of the Negro were recurrent in the works of these young writers. Some of the works were in the form of propaganda; some offerings bordered on or succumbed to the cult of exoticism; still other works presented a realistic portrayal of Negro life. The novel, of course, was the perfect vehicle for exploring all of the concerns which the Negro writer wished to portray and explicate.

The mediocre novels written by Negroes (e.g., Herman Dreer, Mary Etta Spencer) who preceded the Harlem Renaissance novelists were not immediately replaced by examples of high art. After all, the oral tradition was still the most potent influence on the black artist. The unique need felt by some to propagandize through fiction also hindered other writers from recognizing and employing the better tools of fiction. The body of Harlem Renaissance novels, therefore, is unevenly chiseled, but the primary aim of all Negro novelists, regardless of their style or thematic preoccupation, was to act as truthful interpreters of the black race for the reading public. No longer would there be the fiction of distortion, created by writers who lacked knowledge of the black world or who actually believed in the existing black stereotypes. The Negro novelist of the past, Chesnutt and Dunbar included, had sometimes succumbed to the same easy habits of the white writers in portraying the Negro in caricature. A conscious attempt was made during the 1920s and early 1930s to rid readers of the idea that the black character was a little less than human or so pious and patient in the face of oppression that he achieved an otherworldly sanctification that strained credibility. The one character that the Harlem Renaissance writers seemed unable (or, perhaps, unwilling) to purge from their postbellum literary heritage was the "tragic mulatto." Of course, it can be argued, without straining too greatly, that this type was a real part of the everyday world the Negro writer of the 1920s knew.

To grasp the intent of the various writers and to understand how they attempted to articulate their concerns through artistic expression, individual novels must be examined. The working out of themes and the crystallization of black life and culture were abundant in the novels of the following writers: Rudolph Fisher, Claude McKay, Nella Larsen, James Weldon Johnson, Countee Cullen, and Langston Hughes, whose works will be discussed in this chapter. The novels of Wallace Thurman, Jessie Fauset, Walter White, W. E. B. DuBois, Arna Bontemps, and George Schuyler will be discussed in the next chapter.

"The prevailing notion of the fiction of the Harlem Renaissance writers during the 1920s was that it exaggerated the more offensive qualities of low-life in the black ghetto. The truth is that the literature spanning the period of the Harlem Renaissance focused on *every* aspect of black life."

Rudolph Fisher was a literary craftsman who understood and practiced such arts of fiction as control over plot, characterization, tone, and language, and who had a natural poise in exposition. Fisher was as at ease writing novels as he was writing short stories, although the short stories are of greater artistic quality. Fisher is one of those writers about whom one would like to speculate, "If only he had lived longer"; even so, his accomplishments by 1934 (he died in December of that year) were far from negligible. His first novel, *The Walls of Jericho*, for instance, contains one of the most amusing yet cynical scenes (the Merritt-Cramp conversation) in modern literature. He was the first black writer to have a creditable and absorbing mystery published in America (*The Conjure-man Dies*). As a stylist, Fisher had no peer among the nonexperimental Harlem Renaissance writers. This skill, however, led to his most notable weakness—a clever adroitness that makes his satire somewhat strained in some instances, and, related to this, a feather-light style that sometimes blurs his dramatic impact.

A scene on the streets of East Harlem

The Walls of Jericho (1928) is a study in black realistic fiction, for Fisher follows closely the dictum of Henry James in giving his novel an "air of reality" (as opposed to representing life) through his concern with mimesis rather than theme and form. (This is stated merely for contrast, not in terms of exclusion; Fisher was certainly concerned, as a stylist, with form, and as a man caught up in the spirit of the Harlem Renaissance, he was not oblivious to the importance of theme and motif.) An early commentator on the Harlem Renaissance wrote about Fisher:

> [His] realism does not go searching after exotic places, but walks the streets of Harlem with its lowly. His interest dwells upon transplanted southern country folk who, having reached the city, have not yet had bound upon their natures the *aes triplex* of city sophistication. They are simple, funloving folk, sometimes religious, more usually superstitious, leaning ardently toward the good but not too zealously to be sometimes led astray by bewildering temptations.

There is a plot and subplot in *The Walls of Jericho*, where all strata of Negro society in New York City are represented—the uneducated lower classes (but not the poverty-stricken), the gamblers, the middle class, and the so-called upper class. The hero, Ralph Merrit, a lawyer by profession, can be counted among the few in this last category. He is, in the words of the common Negro, a "dickty," and he receives little support or sympathy at the opening of the book where it is revealed that he has bought a house in a white neighborhood just bordering on Harlem. Despite this move, the extremely pale (but kinky-haired) Merrit has none of the pretentions often present in Negroes of his class, even though it is assumed that he does by the characters Fisher presents in contrast to him—Shine (Joshua Jones), and Jinx and Bubber (Fisher's black Damon and Pythias). As a matter of fact, Merrit's reason for moving into the white neighborhood is not obvious. As he explains:

> All of you know where I stand on things racial—I'm downright rabid. And even though . . . I'd enjoy this house, if they let me alone, purely as an individual, just the same I'm entering it as a Negro. I hate fays. Always have. Always will. Chief joy in life is making them uncomfortable. And if this doesn't do it—I'll quit the bar.

Side by side with the story of Merrit is the romance between Shine and the Negro maid, Linda. She works for Miss Cramp, a bigoted neighbor of Merrit, who sees herself as an enlightened benefactor of the downtrodden and misguided. Miss Cramp takes on causes the way sticky tape picks up lint, and her interest is as short-lived as lint-covered adhesive is useful. Her arrogant notions of racial superiority are mitigated only by her evident obtuseness and sheer ignorance. Such a restricted, narrow mind is beyond repair, as her name implies: she stands as a symbol of the blind, bigoted do-gooder who clutters the world with unproductive activities and confused motives. She is also unfortunately a victim of Fisher's penchant for caricature; the light touch he applies to Miss Cramp lessens the magnitude of what she really symbolizes. Still, it is possible that her name will become as meaningful to the literate reader as the name Babbitt, thereby enriching the descriptive language of America.

The work companions, Shine, Jinx, and Bubber, provide the book with comic characters and also furnish the reader with an insight into staple personalities in black society—persons who are (or, perhaps, were) rarely seen outside of Harlem (at least, in their true character) and therefore remain a mystery to the white world. To citizens of Harlem, the prototypes of Jinx and Bubber were in evidence daily. They add as much to an air of reality as do the places described in the various scenes. Both men conform analogically to the black joker hero and, in a more tenuous fashion, to the trickster hero.

Thematically, Fisher was concerned with the idea of black unity and the discovery of self. He uses the Bible story of Joshua to reinforce his concern for the black man's search for his true nature that will permit him to disengage himself from the deceptions of the past. Every man is Joshua, facing a seemingly impenetrable wall:

> No man knows himself till he comes to an impasse; to some strange set of conditions that reveals to him his ignorance of the workings of his spirit; to some disrupting impact that shatters the wall of self-illusion. This, I believe, is the greatest spiritual battle of a man's life, the battle with his own idea of himself.

It is such knowledge that draws divergent segments of the black population—the Ralph Merrits and the Joshua Joneses—into a unity that can do battle with the white enemy inside the walls of Jericho.

Fisher's second book, *The Conjure-man Dies* (1932), is the first black detective novel published in the United States. The book was an important addition to the literature of the Harlem Renaissance because it exhibited again Fisher's abiding interest in his race and the formulation of ties with the African homeland. Fisher believed that Harlem was a natural setting for the mystery novel:

> Darkness and mystery go together, don't they? The children of the night—and I say this in all seriousness—are children of mystery. The very setting is mystery—outsiders know nothing of Harlem life as it really is . . . what goes on behind the scenes and beneath the dark skins of Harlem folk—fiction has not found much of that yet. And much of it is perfectly in tune with the best of mystery tradition—variety, color, mysticism, superstition, malice and violence.

The semicomic Jinx and Bubber appear in this book also. They liven the action and the conversation, contributing some touches of comic relief to the peculiar, mysterious atmosphere. They were Fisher's favorite characters, "who," as he said, "having shared several adventures with me before, have become very real to me."

Fisher was also fascinated by the technique of constructing a mystery novel—the mingling of fact and fiction, and the opportunity to commence what was to have become, had Fisher lived, a corpus of detective novels known as the Dart-Archer series. In discussing *The Conjure-man Dies*, Fisher stated: "An archer, of course, is a bowman, one who shoots an arrow. Dart is another word for arrow. Dr. Archer and Detective Dart, therefore, stand in the relationship of a bowman and his arrow; the vision of the former gives direction and aim to the action of the latter." The book also gave Fisher a grand chance not only to vivify Harlem as a place of clubs and cabarets but to portray it as the home of the ordinary black folk who supply most of its color and movement.

When Claude McKay died in 1948, it was noted that "it was a request of Mr. McKay that his funeral service be held in Harlem, where he spent so much of his active life." McKay spent the years between 1922 and 1934 out of the United States, but the memory of Harlem and all that it meant to him, both symbolically and sensually, never faded from his mind, even when he had lost some of his younger fervor for its haunts.

McKay was damned as a novelist by DuBois and others (even James Weldon Johnson did not like *Home to Harlem*) who felt that McKay exploited the theme of Negro primitivism and leaned too heavily on the effects of exotic descriptions of lowlife. The formless aspect of his narratives was also disconcerting. This was so even though he included, for example, a subtitle, "A story without a plot," on the title page of the novel *Banjo*. The formlessness, therefore, was clearly intentional.

One of McKay's assets was his unambivalent attitude toward race: he was a black man and he was proud of it. He wasn't interested in assimilation, although he had a forceful streak of the European aesthete in him which he neither exalted nor damned. He once wrote: "Whatever may be the criticism implied in my writing of Western civilization I do not regard myself as a stranger but as a child of it, even though I may have become so by the comparatively recent process of grafting. I am as conscious of my new-world birthright as of my African origin, being aware of the one and its significance in my development as much as I feel the other emotionally." This dualistic sentiment did not mean that he was not conscious of the problem his color presented. One must not forget McKay's own admission that "my main psychological problem . . . was the problem of color. Color-consciousness was the fundamental of my restlessness." McKay was satisfied with his own understanding of himself and his dual heritage; what saddened and often exasperated him was the lack of understanding he found among whites who could not envision how a man as civilized as McKay could refuse to accept the European, Anglo-Saxon value system. This dualism, a problem not to be solved by a simple statement incorporating the idea that the black race had a respectable past, one different from whites but equal to it in terms of the values that were transmitted from one generation to the next, was simply one more result of the white man's refusal to legitimize black experience. As McKay saw it, then, the problem really wasn't his alone; the white person had to share the responsibility for placing McKay, and others like him, in two worlds. And when one exists in two worlds, one can hardly be completely loyal to either of them. McKay understood this, but many of his critics, he surmised, did not.

A spiritual and intellectual cleavage existed as well between McKay and the black bourgeois writers of the Harlem Renaissance. McKay was keenly aware of the inner struggles of the younger black writers. Thus, he portrays his concern about every aspect of blackness, the black soul, and the "new Negro" through Ray, who becomes his spokesman in both of his vagabond novels. These same concerns are also a part of his autobiography, *A Long Way from Home* (1937).

When *Home to Harlem* appeared in 1928, McKay was accused of being too greatly influenced by Van Vechten's *Nigger Heaven*. McKay defended himself against this unsubstantiated charge when his book first appeared; later, in his autobiography, he explained:

> Many persons imagine that I wrote *Home to Harlem* because Carl Van Vechten wrote *Nigger Heaven*. But the pattern of the book was written under the title of "Home to Harlem " in 1925. When Max Eastman read it he said, "It is worth a thousand dollars." Under the same title it was entered in the story contest of the Negro magazine *Opportunity*. But it did not excite the judges. *Nigger Heaven* was published in the fall of 1926. I never saw the book until the late spring of 1927, when my agent . . . sent me a copy. And by that time I had nearly completed *Home to Harlem*.

This explanation ought to be accepted not only because it seems convincing but also because both novels are each so different that the question of Van Vechten's influence becomes academic.

Home to Harlem is a vagabond novel, full of color, noise, and vitality, rounded out by a touch of intellectualism and social criticism. The story is loosely structured around the search by Jake, the primary character, for the "tantalizing brown" whom he enjoys on his first night in that home of homes for the black man, Harlem. Jake is home from the war—the white man's war—an *AWOL* with a taste for English-made suits, an uncomplicated sensualist who lives each day to its fullest. He is the archetypal primitive who will never succumb to the restraints of Puritan American civilization. At the end of the novel, he finds his girl (who, by the way, left him the $50 during that first joyful night) and discovers her name which, quite appropriately, is Felice ("Joy"). While the movement from beginning to end is episodic and disjointed, the novel is successful in: (1) its portrayal of life in Harlem's cabarets, rent parties, pool rooms, and other dives of the more lowly; (2) its exposure of the mentality and weaknesses of bourgeois life; (3) its exploration of the problems of the Negro intellectual (i.e., a person overly cultivated in norms alien to his origins and, therefore, an unhappy disaffected individual); and (4) its examination of the nature and place of sex in the black world.

It is an antithetical world which McKay paints, a world rendered in disjointed sentences, slang, and elliptical Negro phrases that ring with authenticity. There may be a little exaggeration, but McKay's contrast of a world within a world requires some overstatement. The antithesis is also internal, for his aim in presenting characters like Ray and Jake is not to juxtapose opposing elements of society but, more important, to give two sides of the contradictory nature of man: sensual man vs. sensible man.

This kind of probing is an important element in McKay's novel *Banjo* (1929). Ray is also a key character in this book, and Jake is replaced by his counterpart, the Banjo of the title. The book is peopled with men and women who inhabit the fringes of "respectable" society. They live around the waterfront in Marseilles where their existence is a combination of the grim, the grimy, and the happy-go-lucky. The most important segments of the book deal with Ray's tirades against the black American for his aping of whites and discursive conversations that explain McKay's sentiments about the Harlem Renaissance. Here, for instance, is Ray talking to a Martiniquan student:

> 'In the modern race of life we're merely beginners. If this renaissance we're talking about is going to be more than a sporadic and scabby thing, we'll have to get down to our racial roots to create it.'
>
> 'I believe in a racial renaissance,' said the student, 'but not in going back to savagery.'
>
> 'Getting down to our native roots and building up from our own people,' said Ray, 'is not savagery. It is culture.'
>
> 'I can't see that,' said the student.
>
> 'You are like many Negro intellectuals who are belly-aching about race,' said Ray. 'What's wrong with you all is your education. You get a white man's education and learn to despise your own people...
>
> 'You're a lost crowd, you educated Negroes, and you will find yourself in the roots of your own people.'

From such episodes, something can be learned about McKay as Ray's attitudes waver from bitterness to tenderness to moral confusion. At the book's end Ray retains some of his ambivalence, although he makes a positive choice to remain, at least for a time, in the sensual world. His decision, then, is made with an air of one who is still experimenting with notions of how to live one's life.

McKay's last novel, *Banana Bottom* (1933), is not within the basic time or thematic scope of this book and will not be discussed. In one critic's view it "is the first classic of West Indian prose." The West Indian tone and mood prevail in McKay's collection of short stories, too, although the Harlem stories have greater artistic strength. *Gingertown* (1932) contains twelve examples of McKay's short fiction. The Harlem tales, in particular, give an intimate and vivid portrait of Renaissance Harlem. For example, "Brownskin Blues," a story of another Mary Lou (Thurman's), is about a woman whose black skin leads to tragedy. "Mattie and Her Sweetman" portrays the life of an older woman who is supporting a young man. In both of these stories, crude as they are, McKay exhibits control over his characterizations and the setting. "High Ball" is another of his successful tales, in terms of theme and characterization; the protagonist, Nation, is sympathetically and realistically portrayed (see Chapter 7 for further discussion of this story). In this story McKay explores a virulent form of race prejudice and expresses one aspect of the black man's struggle for self-assertion. Curiously, the West Indian tales are the weakest in the book, but they are written with such a lyrical nostalgia that the stories have a unique, seductive quality.

McKay's importance in the Harlem Renaissance is undisputed, even though he was physically absent from the United States during its height. His almost obsessive concern with the nature of contradiction in the black man's character compelled him to write fiction and poetry which embrace many of the earmarks of Harlem Renaissance literature.

McKay, like Cullen, was unable to fulfill his potential, although the body of McKay's work is not unimpressive. What seems to be lacking in his work is a certain breadth which he might have displayed if he had continued in the direction in which he started when he wrote *Banana Bottom*. In it he seems to have turned to another level of expression, the orthodox novel, but he ceased producing significant artistic literature at this point in his life. Stephen H. Bronz assesses McKay in this perceptive summation of his role in the Harlem Renaissance:

> Because McKay was not fully a member of any one group, and because of his radical education and outspoken personality, he set the outer limits of the Harlem Renaissance. No other important Negro writer in the 'twenties protested so fiercely and single-mindedly against prejudice as did McKay in his sonnets of 1919. And no other important Renaissance figure disregarded possible effects on the Negro public image so fearlessly as did McKay in his prose fiction. From his Jamaican days to his strange conversion to Catholicism, McKay forever spoke his mind, sometimes brilliantly, sometimes clumsily, but always forthrightly. In so doing he did much to make the Harlem Renaissance more than a polite attempt to show whites that Negroes, too, could be cultured.

Robert Bone places Nella Larsen, along with Jessie Fauset, W. E. B. DuBois, and Walter White, in the class of "The Rear Guard," that is, "novelists [who] still wished to orient Negro art toward white opinion. They wished to apprise educated whites of the existence of respectable Negroes, and to call their attention—now politely, now indignantly—to facts of racial injustice.

Nella Larsen was a descendant of two widely different racial and cultural backgrounds: her father was a West Indian Negro and her mother was Danish. Larsen's own origins and the subsequent unfulfilled life she led as the wife of an adulterer (whom she finally divorced) provided her with the material for her life's work. Certainly she followed the admonition to young writers to "write what you know about" in her first novel, *Quicksand*. The theme of the tragic mulatto is merged with what Bone describes as the basic metaphor of the novel which is "contained in its title [and] supported throughout by concrete images of suffocation, asphyxiation, and claustrophobia." The story of Helga Crane, daughter of a black man and a Danish woman whom he deserted, is obviously patterned on Larsen's early life. Supported by a sympathetic uncle after her mother's death, Helga grows up with all the bourgeois inclinations of the black middle class. Deep within her, however, is a desire to repudiate the ethic of the bourgeoisie. "The woman as bitch," resting latent within Helga, causes her final doom as she settles into the "quicksand" of a mediocre domesticity. The downward, symbolically circular path to this suffocating pit (her marriage and the South) moves via a series of sharply etched episodes that reveal Larsen's skill at characterization. She shows that she is well aware of the "craft of fiction"; there is vividness, truth (especially in her revelations of a woman's inner life), and an ability to create scenes of encounters among people even though she fails to be entirely convincing in her ending. However, even Percy Lubbock, in *The Craft of Fiction*, notes that an author may lack some part of the craft and still succeed.

Clearly, the plot is subordinate to the characterizations. Helga Crane moves from the stultifying atmosphere of a southern Negro college to New York, via a brief stay in Chicago where she is scorned by her sympathetic white uncle's new wife. Thus, rejected with finality by the American branch of her family, Helga settles in Harlem where she finds temporary contentment. Helga's life is a series of only evanescent fulfillments, for she is plagued with a restlessness that has deeper causes than Miss Larsen bothers to penetrate. It is in Harlem that Helga cultivates and develops her "black" soul. Her embracing of this blackness is emotionally incomplete at this juncture, however. At the beginning of her life in Harlem she reflects:

> Everything was there [in Harlem], vice and goodness, sadness and gayety, ignorance and wisdom, ugliness and beauty, poverty and richness. And it seemed to her that somehow of goodness, gayety, wisdom, and beauty always there was a little more than of vice, sadness, ignorance, and ugliness. It was only riches that did not quite transcend poverty. 'But,' said Helga Crane, 'what of that? Money isn't everything. It isn't even the half of everything. And here we have so much else—and by ourselves. It's only outside of Harlem among those others that money really counts for everything.'

This passage foreshadows a reverse in Helga's attitude; for when she moves from the black world into the white one of her rich relatives in Denmark she momentarily relinquishes the moral superiority of her black universe:

> She liked it, this new life. For a time it blotted from her mind all else... To Helga Crane it was the realization of a dream that she had dreamed persistently ever since she was old enough to remember such vague things as day-dreams and longings. Always she had wanted, not money, but the things which money could give, leisure, attention, beautiful surroundings. Things. Things.

Helga Crane, a nervous and somewhat complex character, is one of the more interesting creations found in the Harlem Renaissance novels. For one thing, she is one female of the bourgeois who displays a desire to be sexually fulfilled. In her decision to reject the physical and social comforts of the white (or, as Harlem Renaissance writers termed it, Nordic) world for the warmth and vitality of the black one, Helga fits the Renaissance's persistent pattern. By fitting into this mold and accepting her blackness, Helga begins to understand what motivated her father's desertion:

> For the first time Helga Crane felt sympathy rather than contempt and hatred for that father, who so often and so angrily she had blamed for his desertion of her mother. She understood, now, his rejection, his repudiation, of the formal calm her mother had represented. She understood his yearning, his intolerable need for the inexhaustible humor and the incessant hope of his own kind, his need for those things, not material, indigenous to all Negro environments.

At this point Helga finds release from false values and commences the backward journey into her true black self. She selects religion to carry her back into the bosom of blackness. The portrait of Helga from this point to the end becomes blurred and confusing. After her "conversion," she turns to Pleasant Green, a greasy, sweaty, mediocre preacher; despite the Oedipal implication of the search for a father, this major move is unconvincing. One explanation for the confused motivation near the end of the book may be that she tired of writing in the midst of describing Helga's Copenhagen experiences. Suddenly, it seems, Helga gives up living and accepts an existence that will limp along in a wearisome, depressing manner.

The reader is left with an inkling that Larsen decided to make Helga forget that part of her past that made her fight for the things she wanted. The author, in an attempt to rescue herself artistically from the book's weak ending, inserts a scene which may provide a clue to what she intended. Helga requests a reading of Anatole France's "The Procurator of Judea." Just as Pilate let himself forget the momentous event of his condemnation of Christ, so Helga, it appears, in requesting to hear this ironic tale, seems to be telling the reader that she is simply going to forget the past. Larsen's skillful use of this device, however, does not compensate for the unsatisfactory religious motivation Helga is given for becoming Mrs. Pleasant Green in the first place.

Nella Larsen's second novel, *Passing* (1929), is written in that hasty, seminonchalant style that put her a notch above some of her black peers of this period in terms of simple narrative technique. Therefore, even though the narrative moves smoothly in *Passing*, the story itself is inconsequential. The ending is melodramatic and, again (surely a Larsen weakness), unconvincing. One is not sure whether Larsen intends the reader to view Clare Kendry's death as suicide (intentional? accidental?) or murder (intentional? accidental?). It is entirely possible that she wanted this confusion to persist forever in the reader's mind, but this certainly does not give the book any artistic complexity that might intrigue the imagination.

One important feature of Larsen's work that is clearly evident here, as it is in *Quicksand*, is her awareness of female sexuality. The latent desire for sexual fulfillment that Helga satisfies with her marriage to the gross preacher is akin to Clare's attraction to her friend's husband. In both cases, the black man either symbolizes or brings sexual gratification, thereby reinforcing the Renaissance view that it is the black, and not the white, race that is fertile, vital, full-bodied, and rich in humaneness.

Miss Larsen never fulfilled the promise of her early successes, and she disappeared from the literary scene after an unpleasant exposure and accusation concerning plagiarism.

A date, or time itself, perhaps, is meaningless within itself; that added element, amplification, is needed to give significance to a date. *The Autobiography of an Ex-Coloured Man* is a case in point: this single novel by James Weldon Johnson was published under a pseudonym in 1912. Its inclusion in a study of the Harlem Renaissance, however, is relevant because of its plot and treatment of racial prejudice in a mode that parallels other novels of this period. Moreover, its reissue in 1927 demonstrates that Johnson's contemporaries also saw the novel as akin to the Harlem Renaissance literature. This book forcefully upholds the notion that Johnson can be promoted as being a precursor of the Harlem Renaissance. The 1927 edition contained an introduction by Johnson's good friend, Carl Van Vechten.

Despite its deceptive title, this book remains one of the most accomplished pieces of lengthy fiction written by a Negro during the first four decades of the twentieth century. It is a dispassionate picture of what it was like to grow up nearly white in the racist society of the early part of this century. The prejudice against blacks was blatantly illogical and so rampant that no excuses were needed. The protagonist of Johnson's novel, knowing the truth of "label a mulatto white and the world's view of him adopts the label," finally succumbs to the advantages of uncomplicated day-to-day living as a "passer." Even so, at the novel's end, he states: "I cannot repress the thought that, after all, I have chosen the lesser part, that I have sold my birthright for a mess of pottage."

The melancholy of Johnson's protagonist, as well as his cowardice, are not romantic poses. In this novel Johnson implants a psychological motif which appears again and again in the literature of the Harlem Renaissance, namely, the belief that the Negro who abandons his people also forsakes a richness that cannot be replaced by the superficial freedom which passing into the white world accords. This motif appeared, for example, in nearly all of the works of Jessie Fauset, Walter White, Claude McKay, and Nella Larsen and was certainly implied in Rudolph Fisher's work and in Countee Cullen's one novel.

The Autobiography of an Ex-Coloured Man is a mingling of realism and irony. The realism is of the simplest kind: Johnson portrays in rich, convincing detail several strata of Negro life in the South and the East. The irony is perhaps unintentional: the whole narrative is, first, one of understatement and, second, one in which the hero's life changes direction radically after one episode—the loss of money for college—which the author intimates as being the "irony of fate." Irony operates rather successfully, too, when we realize that the hero's decision to pass, after his seemingly objective review of both sides, fails to give him the happiness he had expected. Dispassionate objectivity may lead to nowhere, the author seems to say.

Briefly, the novel follows the life of an unnamed light-skinned protagonist who, upon leaving the South at an early, undisclosed age, is reared in genteel, middle-class comfort in Connecticut. He does not discover the fact or meaning of being a Negro until he is ten, when an embarrassing classroom situation forces this fact upon his sensitive nature. Even then, his life is relatively calm, and he successfully completes his adolescence, aloof from most of his classmates but not entirely isolated. The hero, musically talented, proceeds southward to enter Atlanta University. His money is stolen during his first day there; but rather than explain his unhappy circumstances to the university administrators, he gives up college life and commences his life of wandering and his search for self. The conflict that wars within begins to emerge at this point: he wishes to become the best sort of Negro, to present to the world the Negro's musical heritage, and, the easier wish to satisfy, to gratify himself as just another man in the world, to enjoy the normal, even routine joys experienced by the middle- or upper-middle-class white American. As the title of the book suggests, the "hero" finally chooses the last goal. The story follows his wanderings from work in a cigar factory, to piano playing in a club, to travels in Europe with his rich employer, and to the United States again where he collects Negro folk songs. But he now abandons his race, not simply for love of a white woman but also because of the contradictions of his nature. On the one hand, as he says, "I have been only a privileged spectator of their [Negroes] inner life," and on the other, "I am possessed by a strange longing for my mother's people."

As evidenced by the society Johnson describes as well as the duality of the protagonist's nature, the novel can be said to be within that tradition of duality dominant in American fiction. The tradition is clear in the protagonist's inner contradictions and the struggles of good and evil within him, demonstrated in his circumstances, his actions, and, most dramatically, his inner turmoil which makes him realize that he has sold his birthright "for a mess of pottage." This intermingling of black and white taints the hero's moral character much as his physical being was tainted in the belief of American society that such an offspring, the product of racial intermingling, was a corrupted version of the human species. Through the act of passing, the protagonist assumes the role of one who has failed once again to demonstrate personal integrity. There is a continual relinquishing of values portrayed through the actions of the protagonist; for instance, the acquiescence to the easier way out of a dilemma (not going to college), or his lack of shame when confronted with a lapse in his moral character (the chasing and tormenting of a black boy from his school). And, of course, his "passing" is his greatest act of moral cowardice.

There is a quality of the *bildungsroman* in Johnson's work, although the forays into black propaganda and the hero's remaining air of perennial questioning of his chosen path in life weaken the impression that Johnson perceived the book on this level. Indeed, in his autobiography he is curiously reticent about discussing his book in a literary sense and seems more concerned with emphasizing that *The Autobiography of an Ex-Coloured Man* was fiction rather than the story of his life.

Although the writers of the Harlem Renaissance were not oblivious to the influence of the black man's religion in shaping his character, they rarely used religious settings for their novels. The prominent exception, Countee Cullen, is not surprising, inasmuch as he was the adopted son of a minister. Cullen's single novel, *One Way to Heaven*, was published during the waning days of the Harlem Renaissance (1932), but it bears the marks of a Renaissance novel. It is, in Cullen's words, a "two toned picture" which explores the lives of the upper and lower strata of Negro life in Harlem during the 1920s.

Cullen wrote to his good friend, Harold Jackman, and talked of Flaubert: "I would give years of my life to learn to write like that [re *Madame Bovary*] . . . I suppose Flaubert devoted his entire life to mastering words and studying human emotions. Art such as his takes a lifetime to develop." Cullen, though never a Flaubert, achieved a polish in language and an emotional depth in *One Way to Heaven* that clearly can be traced to his admiration of the great masters. It is one of the better novels of the Harlem Renaissance period.

The novel's two stories are frequently interwoven, but it is still primarily a novel with two different stories, one in contrast with the other because two different realms of Harlem life are explored. Indeed, some readers may consider this narrative mode the major weakness of the novel. To be fair to Cullen, between the significance of the title and the focusing upon Sam Lucas at the beginning and the ending, it seems that the Sam-Mattie love story is the primary one.

The opening scene is laid in a church where an evangelist is speaking during a "watch meeting" night. Sam Lucas, a one-armed con man, enters with the intention of performing his faked act of conversion. It is the eve of a new year, with the evangelist out to catch wayward souls and Sam Lucas out to get the most out of his highly practiced art. He strides to the altar and presents his razor and cards as symbols of his conversion. A young lady in the audience, moved by his action, submits to the "spirit" and is truly converted. Thus, their relationship starts on a compromised basis because of his deceit and her subsequent naïveté in believing that religion, which has brought them together, will shape their future life together. They marry, although Sam encounters difficulties unknown to him before in the wooing and winning of Mattie. This is evident in the following scene, which also serves to illustrate the sacred and profane aspects that form a leitmotif in the novel:

> They walked along in a silence which was mainly fear of themselves, fear of the fierce desires at the roots of their beings. . . Sam had forgotten the services of the church as soon and as lightly as he had stepped across its threshold out into the sharp January sun. All that he was concerned with now was the woman at his side. . . He wished he knew how to tackle her; for he felt that she was like some new and strange being, unlike the other women he had known. Those others had been like himself, creatures of action and not of speech. . . He knew when a flippant word meant 'Leave me be.' But this girl . . . She seemed near at hand, as close as if they were linked together by a strip of flesh, yet inaccessible, as if getting religion and joining church had suddenly grown walls about her and shut her away from the world. Her eyes smiled at him, but their message was . . . 'Speak to me' and 'Tell me things.' The palm of his hand was moist with panic.

After marrying, Sam has a hard time keeping up the deception about his new-found religion. He cheats on Mattie, moves out to be with his woman, but returns to Mattie in the end when he is suffering from pneumonia. Just before he dies, he pretends to believe again and Mattie is happy. Cullen suggests that Sam's last act of deception secures his salvation because it is sacrificial.

Mattie is employed as a maid for the Harlem socialite Constancia Brandon, a witty, pretentious, and extravagant woman who mocks as she is mocked. The sycophants who hang about her salon are much more savagely portrayed because they are unaware of the fragility and senselessness of the putative Negro "society." Constancia is well aware of the cracks in the Negro psyche, but she possesses, in addition to intelligence (she is a Radcliffe graduate), common sense and a love for those Negro strengths and unique qualities that enrich life. (The truth or falsity of this premise is not the point, either in this novel or in any of the others that promote the idea of black vitality.) At one point, Constancia states:

> I often think the Negro is God Almighty's one mistake, but as I look about me at white people, I am forced to say so are we all. It isn't being colored that annoys me. I could go white if I wanted to, but I am too much of a hedonist; I enjoy life too much, and enjoyment isn't across the line. Money is there, and privilege, and the sort of power which comes with numbers; but as for enjoyment, they don't know what it is.

As viewed through Constancia, then, blacks are implied to be basically superior to whites in terms of warmth, compassion, humaneness, and ability to enjoy life despite social restrictions and persecution. It is obvious, also, that Cullen admired his Constancia: she outshines Mattie and Sam so outrageously that the reader is left wishing that Cullen had written two books instead of one.

The desire to portray all strata of Harlem social classes weakens the book because the characterizations never achieve full dimensions. The failure to present Harlem in depth is a pity, for one is struck by Cullen's facility with language in his descriptive or narrative passages. His dialogue is natural, too, even though it seems forced in some of the scenes with Constancia. On a deeper level, Cullen demonstrates an awareness of the uses of symbol and metaphor, and he displays a feeling for the sort of literary complexity absent in some of the other Harlem Renaissance novels.

The symbols of the razor and cards, pervasive throughout the book, are manifestations of the evil that Sam professes to have abandoned. The salvation theme is also developed through the symbols of cards and razor and concurrently through the use of dark and light imagery and colors. For instance, red has the dual symbolism of salvation and sin (e.g., the "blood of the Lamb" and red lips). In the case of the red kimona that Sam offers Mattie, the color reflects the shame Mattie shares in joining with Sam, the overt sinner. White functions in the traditional mode to symbolize purity, but black is employed to epitomize beauty instead of dark deeds and foul acts.

Like the razor, Sam, too, is an instrument: he is an instrument of salvation. Heaven has sent Sam to Mattie and she reclaims him for this divine abode. Sam is an instrument of salvation because his final act is presented ultimately as an act of sacrifice rather than of pure chicanery. Without Sam's ruse Mattie would be doomed; she would be barred from the salvation she earnestly seeks.

If there is a single metaphor for Cullen's book it lies in the title: one way to get into heaven is through a type of personal salvation that results from well-meaning deception. Mattie is fooled by the pretense, the "trickster" act of Sam, but Sam, in a roundabout, theological sense, is possibly saved as well. He pretends to hear music and to see bright lights in order to convince Mattie that he has had a vision. Before he dies, "he could feel Mattie's hand tremble on his forehead. Aunt Mandy stood transfixed and mute. He knew that for them he was forever saved." Thus, with careful attention to the details of Sam's vision, Cullen brings to an orderly conclusion the chaos of troubled souls. The fact that Cullen begins and concludes his work with the lives of Sam and Mattie is evidence that they were meant to be the primary focus of Cullen's story. Therefore, Cullen should have concentrated on it. The novel would have been strengthened by greater attention to these confused, common folk, especially since it is their story that supplies the novel with its thematic title.

It was another poet, the most enduring and well-known survivor of the Harlem Renaissance, who wrote perhaps the most appealing and least controversial novel during the waning of the Renaissance. It was during his student days (in his mid-twenties, however) at Lincoln University that Langston Hughes started writing his first novel, *Not Without Laughter* (1930). Although the book was favorably reviewed, Hughes later expressed disappointment with his character portrayals. Here he was perhaps not the best judge, for his characterizations are one of the strengths of this frankly nostalgic novel. Despite weaknesses in the structure and an obvious simplicity in Hughes's interpretation of the lives he describes, the book was warmly applauded by some reviewers whose opinions are worth quoting:

> It is written with understanding, tolerance and beauty, it lays special claim to the attention of those who love life and its mirroring in fiction.
>
> It is significant because even where it fails, it fails beautifully, and where it succeeds—namely, in its intimate characterizations and in its local color and charm—it succeeds where almost all others have failed.
>
> Its strength lies in this simplicity, in its author's unflinching honesty, and in his ability to make the reader feel very deeply the problems of his characters.

Even Martha Gruening, in her article berating the writers of the Harlem Renaissance, gives tribute to Hughes:

> [It] is not only uniquely moving and lovely among Negro novels but among books written about America. It is affirmative in a sense in which no other book by an American Negro is, for it is the story of a Negro happily identified with his own group, who because of his identification tells what is essentially, despite the handicaps of poverty and prejudice, the story of a happy childhood.

Hughes explains what he was attempting to do in *Not Without Laughter* in his autobiography:

> I wanted to write about a typical Negro family in the Middle West, about people like those I had known in Kansas. But I thought I had been a typical Negro boy... We [his family] were poor—but different. For purposes of the novel, however, I created around myself what seemed to me a family more typical of Negro life in Kansas than my own had been.

Reality through nostalgia was a primary concern, then; and to treat the novel as one with a complex theme and motive is to do the book an injustice.

The story centers on the life of Sandy as he grows up in a small town in Kansas (Stanton). His mother, Annjee, is married to a no-account, good-looking mulatto named Jimboy. Annjee's mother, Aunt Hager, a version of the mammy prototype, says of him: "Who ever heard of a nigger named Jimboy, anyhow? Next place, I ain't never seen a yaller dude yet that meant a dark woman no good—an' Annjee is dark!"

Sandy has two aunts, Tempy and Harriett. Tempy has risen in the world and has all the shallow veneer of the "nouveau bourgeois." In reality, she is unsure of herself, although she makes it clear how she is to be treated and, in receiving this phony respect, remains isolated from her warm-hearted, unpretentious family. Tempy and others in her "class" know how tenuous their role is, for they "were all people of standing in the darker world—doctors, school-teachers, a dentist, a lawyer, a hair-dresser. . . One's family as a topic of conversation, however, was not popular in high circles, for too many of Stanton's dark society folks had sprung from humble family trees and low black bottoms."

Sandy's other aunt, Harriett, epitomizes the uninhibited, sensuous, generous woman—the sort of person, as Hughes says, who never "soiled" her mind by too much thinking. She hates the stultifying atmosphere of her home because Aunt Hager is obsessed by religion and its sometime by-product, sin. Harriett displays toward her mother an impatience that erupts in venomous verbal spats. At one point she tells Aunt Hager:

> I don't want to be respectable if I have to be stuck up and dicty like Tempy is... She's colored and I'm colored and I haven't seen her since before Easter... It's not being black that matters with her, though, it's being poor, and that's what we are, you and me and Annjee, working for white folks and washing clothes and going in back doors, and taking tips and insults. I'm tired of it, mama, I want to have a good time once in a while.

Later, she shouts this shocking statement to her mother: "Your old Jesus is white, I guess, that's why! He's white and stiff and don't like niggers!"

In the end it is Harriett (by this time a night club singer) who intercedes in Sandy's behalf to aid him in the first steps towards achieving both his and Aunt Hager's dream of completing his schooling. Sandy's mother is not enthusiastic about education for the boy; work that pays enough to keep one alive is all that she considers necessary. But Harriett, even though rejecting Aunt Hager's way of life for herself, reminds Annjee, "Why, Aunt Hager'd turn over in her grave if she heard you talking so calmly about Sandy leaving school—the way she wanted to make something out of this kid."

The fictional canvas is rich in characterization and in its portrayal of a racial milieu little known at that time in our social history. The style of Hughes's prose is unrestrained and casual, tinged at times with an air of nostalgia and naïveté. The book is weakened by its episodic structure and by its incomplete, faltering characterization of the protagonist, Sandy. The novel sometimes seems to be more a novel about Aunt Hager, for she overwhelms the imagination and is presented in full dimension. Still, Hughes dissected "the ways of black folk" with a skill that he, and others, underestimated. In choosing the mode of the realistic novel, in fusing it with the ambiance of the black folk tradition, Hughes wrote a book that is as charming as it is honest.

Source: Margaret Perry, "The Major Novels," in *Silence to the Drums: A Survey of the Literature of the Harlem Renaissance*, Greenwood Press, 1976, pp. 61–88.

Sources

Baker, Houston A., Jr., *Modernism and the Harlem Renaissance*, University of Chicago Press, 1987, p. 85.

Bamikunle, Aderemi, "The Harlem Renaissance and White Critical Tradition," in *CLA Journal*, Vol. 29, No. 1, September 1985, pp. 33–51.

Cullen, Countee, "And the Walls Came Tumblin' Down," in the *Bookman*, Vol. LXVI, No. 2, October 1927, pp. 221–22.

English, Daylanne K., "Selecting the Harlem Renaissance," in *Critical Inquiry*, Vol. 25, No. 4, Summer 1999, pp. 807–15.

Huggins, Nathan I., *Harlem Renaissance*, Oxford University Press, 1971, pp.10–11.

Hughes, Langston, "The Dream Keeper," in *Survey Graphic*, Vol. 6, No. 6, March 1925, p. 664.

Janken, Kenneth R., "African American and Francophone Black Intellectuals during the Harlem Renaissance," in the *Historian*, Vol. 60, No. 3, Spring 1998, pp. 487ff.

Kent, George E., "The Fork in the Road: Patterns of the Harlem Renaissance," in *Black Word*, Vol. 21, No. 8, June 1972, pp. 13–24, 76–80.

Locke, Alain, "*Color*—A Review," in *Opportunity*, Vol. 4, No. 37, January 1926, pp. 14–15.

———, "Enter the New Negro," in *Survey Graphic*, Vol. 6, No. 6, March 1925, pp. 631–34.

———, "Youth Speaks," in *Survey Graphic*, Vol. 6, No. 6, March 1925, pp. 659–60.

McKay, Claude, "White Houses," in *Survey Graphic*, Vol. 6, No. 6, March 1925, p. 662.

Perry, Margaret, *The Harlem Renaissance: An Annotated Bibliography and Commentary*, Garland Publishing, Inc., 1982, pp. xxxv–xxxvi.

Singh, Amritjit, "'When the Negro Was in Vogue': The Harlem Renaissance and Black America," in *The Novels of the Harlem Renaissance: Twelve Black Writers, 1923–1933*, Pennsylvania State University Press, 1976, pp. 1–39.

Stuart, Andrea, "The Harlem Renaissance in the Twenties Produced a Wealth of Black Talent. But What Was Its Legacy and Who Did It Really Benefit?" in the *New Statesman*, Vol. 10, No. 459, June 27, 1997, pp. 40–41.

Wall, Cheryl A., "Poets and Versifiers, Singers and Signifiers: Women of the Harlem Renaissance," in *Women, the Arts, and the 1920s in Paris and New York*, edited by Kenneth W. Wheeler and Virginia Lee Lussier, Transaction Books, 1982, pp. 74–98.

Washington, Michele Y., "Souls on Fire: The Artists of the Black Renaissance in the 1920s and '30s Defined a New Cultural Identity Reflecting Their African Roots," in *Print*, Vol. 52, No. 3, May–June 1998.

Further Reading

Bontemps, Arna, *The Harlem Renaissance Remembered*, Dodd, Mead, 1972.

This is a collection of essays by a writer and thinker who participated in the Harlem Renaissance. The second chapter provides a useful overview of the period.

Hughes, Langston, *The Big Sea*, Hill and Wang, 1993.

Hughes's autobiography was originally published in 1940. This is a reprint of his memories of his life as a poet in Harlem and as a cook and waiter in various Paris nightclubs during the 1920s.

Lewis, David L., *When Harlem Was in Vogue*, Alfred A. Knopf, 1981.

This book is a social history of Harlem in the 1920s, focusing on the literature and music produced during the era.

———, ed., *The Portable Harlem Renaissance Reader*, Penguin USA, 1995.

This collection includes essays, memoirs, drama, poetry, and fictional pieces from forty-five of the major and minor writers of the Harlem Renaissance.

Wintz, Cary D., *Black Culture and the Harlem Renaissance*, Rice University Press, 1988.

Wintz's book is an exploration of the Harlem Renaissance phenomenon in the context of black social and intellectual history in the United States, and it connects the Renaissance writers with the literary community as a whole.

Imagism

Movement Origin

c. 1909

Imagism flourished in Britain and in the United States for a brief period that is generally considered to be somewhere between 1909 and 1917. As part of the modernist movement, away from the sentimentality and moralizing tone of nineteenth-century Victorian poetry, imagist poets looked to many sources to help them create a new poetic expression.

For contemporary influences, the imagists studied the French symbolists, who were experimenting with free verse (*vers libre*), a verse form that used a cadence that mimicked natural speech rather than the accustomed rhythm of metrical feet, or lines. Rules of rhyming were also considered nonessential. The ancient form of Japanese haiku poetry influenced the imagists to focus on one simple image. Greek and Roman classical poetry inspired some of the imagists to strive for a high quality of writing that would endure.

T. E. Hulme is credited with creating the philosophy that would give birth to the Imagism movement. Although he wrote very little, his ideas inspired Ezra Pound to organize the new movement. Pound's "In a Station of the Metro" is often given as one of the purest of his imagist poems. Amy Lowell took over the leadership role of the imagists when Pound moved on to other modernist modes. Her most anthologized poems include "Lilacs" and "Patterns."

Other important imagist poets include Hilda Doolittle, whose poem "Sea Poppies" reflects the Japanese influence on her writing, and her "Oread"

is often referred to as the most perfect imagist poem; Richard Aldington, who was one of the first poets to be recognized as an imagist, and whose collection *Images of War* is considered to contain some of the most intense depictions of World War I; F. S. Flint, who dedicated his last collection of imagist poems, *Otherworld: Cadences* to Aldington; and John Gould Fletcher, whose collection *Goblins and Pagodas* is his most representative work under the influence of Imagism.

Representative Authors

Richard Aldington (1892–1962)

Richard Aldington was born on July 8, 1892, in Portsmouth, Hampshire, England, to Jesse May and Albert Edward Aldington. He attended University College in London but did not complete his degree, due to the loss of family funds.

In 1912, Aldington met Ezra Pound and Hilda Doolittle, and from this meeting, the Imagism movement began. In the same year, Aldington published his first imagist poems in *Poetry*.

The following year, Aldington traveled to Paris and Italy with Doolittle and on October 18, 1913, they were married. Shortly after, Aldington became the editor of the imagist publication *Egoist*, a position he would hold until 1917. His poems appeared in *Des Imagistes* (1914) as well as the second imagist anthology, *Some Imagist Poets* (1915). He completed his first book, *Images (1910–1915),* also in 1915.

Aldington enlisted in the army in 1916. His most reflective responses to this experience are included in his collection of poems *Images of War* (1919) and his novel, *Death of a Hero* (1929). During the remainder of his writing career, Aldington would publish a wide variety of books, which included biographies, translations, novels, and short stories. In 1941, he published his memoirs, *Life for Life's Sake*.

Aldington was awarded the James Tait Black Memorial Prize for his *The Duke* (1943). He also received the Prix de Gratitude Mistralienne for his *Introduction to Mistral* (1956). He died on July 27, 1962, in Lere, France.

Hilda Doolittle (1886–1961)

Hilda Doolittle (she published under the monogram H. D.) was born in Bethlehem, Pennsylvania, on September 10, 1886, to Helen (Wolle) and Charles Doolittle. She attended Bryn Mawr College for one year.

When she was twenty-five years old, Doolittle went abroad, during which time she renewed her relationship with Ezra Pound, through whom she met Aldington. Pound encouraged Doolittle's writing and sent her poems to the magazine *Poetry*, identifying them with the monogram "H. D.," a signature that Doolittle would embrace.

After the dissolution of her marriage to Aldington, Doolittle became pregnant from a brief love affair with another man and gave birth to a daughter in 1919. She named her Perdita. After her daughter's birth, Doolittle became seriously ill and was nursed back to health by Annie Winifred Ellerman, a writer who went by the name Bryher and who would become Doolittle's companion throughout the remaining years of her life. It was Bryher who arranged for Doolittle to be psychoanalyzed by Sigmund Freud during 1933 and 1934. Doolittle's "Tribute to Freud" refers to this period.

Doolittle's first collections of poems include, *Sea Garden* (1916), *Hymen* (1921), and *Heliodora and Other Poems* (1924). In 1927, she published a complete play in verse, *Hippolytus Temporizes*, her attempt to approximate her favorite Greek dramatist/poets. One of her most often quoted imagist poems is "Oread."

In 1960, Doolittle was the first woman to receive the Award of Merit Medal for poetry from the American Academy of Arts and Letters. On September 27, 1961, Doolittle died of a heart attack in Zurich, Switzerland. Her body was buried in her family's cemetery plot in Bethlehem, Pennsylvania.

John Gould Fletcher (1886–1950)

John Gould Fletcher was born in Little Rock, Arkansas, on January 3, 1886. He was the son of John Gould (a banker and broker) and Adolphine (Kraus) Fletcher. He attended Harvard University, but he left without obtaining a degree.

Having inherited his father's estate early in life, Fletcher did not have to worry about finding employment. Instead, he devoted himself to the study of literature. He eventually traveled to England, where he met Ezra Pound and the other imagist poets.

Shortly after meeting Pound, Fletcher became alienated from him due to Pound's criticism of his poetry. At the same time, Amy Lowell took an interest in Fletcher's work, encouraging him and helping him to find publishers. In exchange, Fletcher introduced Lowell to his theory of the free verse of French poets. According to Glenn Hughes, in his *Imagism and the Imagists*, "Lowell was greatly impressed by both the theory and its results," and she began to use Fletcher's ideas in her own poetry. After learning that Fletcher could not find an English publisher for his *Irradiations: Sand and Spray* (1915), Lowell took Fletcher's manuscript and found a publisher in the States, where it was well received.

Fletcher would go on to produce many more collections. *Goblins and Pagodas* (1916) reflects his return to the United States, during which time he revisited his childhood home and then Boston, where he became enthralled with Japanese art and produced his *Japanese Prints* (1918). The latter work was his attempt to write poems likened to Japanese haiku, a form that influenced many of the imagist poets. After his *Breakers and Granite* (1921), in which he takes a fresh look at the United States after many years of living in Europe, critics classify Fletcher's work as post-imagist. He would go on to win the Pulitzer for his *Selected Poems* (1938).

On May 10, 1950, Fletcher drowned himself in a pool near his childhood home.

F. S. Flint (1885–1960)

Frank Stuart Flint was born on December 19, 1885, in Islington, England. His family was poor, and by the age of thirteen he had to drop out of school and go to work. A few years later, he was able to afford night classes, during which he gained an interest in the French poets and the use of free verse, which would influence his writing.

Flint made the acquaintance of T. E. Hulme, a poet and philosopher, and together they planted the theoretic seeds for the movement that would eventually be called Imagism.

Flint's first collection of poems, *In the Net of the Stars* (1909), did not embody the full characteristics of the imagist poets, but they did reflect more realistic images and were written in a more natural, contemporary voice than those of his contemporaries. Flint's poetry went through a drastic change over the years, as reflected in his next collection, *Cadences* (1915), which included only imagist poetry. His most ambitious collection was *Otherworld: Cadences* (1920), his last collection of poems. Ford Maddox Ford states (in J. B. Harmer's *Victory in Limbo, Imagism 1908–1917*) that of the imagist poets, only Doolittle and Flint "have the really exquisite sense of words . . . and insight that justify a writer in assuming the rather proud title of imagist." Flint died on February 28, 1960, in Berkshire, England.

Amy Lowell (1874–1925)

Amy Lowell was born in Brookline, Massachusetts, on February 9, 1874, to Katherine (Bigelow), an accomplished musician and linguist, and Augustus Lowell, a businessman and horticulturist. From both sides of her family, Lowell enjoyed the benefits of the leisurely life of a Boston aristocrat. Not known for her academic accomplishments during her private school education, she nonetheless continued a pursuit of knowledge through self-education after graduating from high school in 1891.

In 1910, when she was thirty-four years old, Lowell had four of her sonnets published in the *Atlantic Monthly*. In 1912, she funded the publication of her first volume of poetry, *A Dome of Many-Coloured Glass*, which some critics felt relied too heavily on the nineteenth-century romantic tradition, an unpopular form at that time.

During this same year, Lowell met Ada Dwyer Russell, an actress with whom she would share the rest of her life. The poem "A Decade" focuses on Lowell and Russell's relationship, written to celebrate their tenth anniversary together.

During the summer of 1913, after having read Doolittle's poems in the magazine *Poetry*, Lowell went to London to meet Doolittle in person. It was through her association with Doolittle and the other imagist poets that Lowell transformed her own poetry, changing her tight nineteenth-century format to one in favor of technical experimentation and innovation. She eventually became a major sponsor for the imagist movement. Lowell's interests in the movement would eventually clash with Ezra Pound, then considered the leader of the imagists, and Pound would leave. Afterward, Pound began referring to Imagism as "Amygism."

Some of Lowell's more popular collections of poetry include *Sword Blades and Poppy Seed* (1914), *Men, Woman and Ghosts* (1916), *Can Grande's Castle* (1918), *Legends* (1921), *Fir-Flower Tablets* (1921), and *A Critical Fable* (1922). After Lowell's death from a stroke on May 12, 1925, Russell edited several of Lowell's unpublished poems and collected them under *What's O'Clock*. The collection won the Pulitzer Prize for poetry that year.

Ezra Pound

Ezra Pound (1885–1972)

Ezra Pound was born on October 30, 1885, in Hailey, Idaho, to Isabel (Weston) and Homer Loomis Pound, a mine inspector. After receiving a master's degree from the University of Pennsylvania, he left the United States and traveled throughout Europe.

After meeting with Hulme, considered the strongest philosophical influence on the imagist movement, Pound modernized his poetic style. One of Pound's first publications in London, *Personae* (1909) caused a critical sensation. His next publication, *Exultations*, published in the same year, marked what Glenn Hughes, writing in his *Imagism and the Imagists*, called the beginning of "the modern vogue of erudite poetry."

Although Pound is credited with creating, supporting, and educating the imagist poets, he moved quickly through this period and on to other modern forms of poetry. While forming the imagists, Pound wrote "In a Station of the Metro," a poem he considered to embrace the tenets of the movement. Pound's collection *Ripostes* (1912) represents the beginning of his involvement with imagist poetry. Pound created the first anthology of imagist poetry, *Des Imagistes* (1914).

Pound would go on to win the Dial Award for distinguished service to American letters, the Bollingen Library of Congress Award (1949), and the Academy of American Poets fellowship (1963). He died in Venice, Italy, on November 1, 1972.

Representative Works

Cathay

Ezra Pound, although a prominent definer and great promoter of Imagism was not a great practitioner of poetry with an imagist bent. The closest he came to incorporating purely imagist tenets in his poetry was a collection called *Cathay* (1915), which includes poems translated from the eighth-century Chinese poet Li Po (also referred to as Rihaku). By working with these translations, Pound displays the interest and the influence that classical Japanese and Chinese poetry had upon the imagist.

Critics agree that this collection is one of Pound's finest, at least of his earlier publications. The collection significantly marks not only Pound's connection to Imagism but also the beginning of the Western world's appreciation of Asian poetry. Not fully understanding the Chinese language, Pound worked with previously translated poems completed by Ernest Fenollosa. Being unfamiliar with the language gave Pound the freedom of arranging words and creating rhythms and sounds according to his own understanding and knowledge of poetry rather than being heavily influenced by the original intent of the poet.

The wording of Pound's interpretations is clear and direct. Each line presents a spare image, and the emotions are expressed in understatement. These are hallmark descriptions of Imagism. Pound would go on to study Chinese more seriously after completing these poems. He later incorporated what he had learned about this ideographic language into some of his subsequent poems. Studying the Chinese characters, or ideograms—abstract pictures used to convey meaning rather than individual letters in an alphabet—inspired Pound to create new poetic forms.

Goblins and Pagodas

John Gould Fletcher published his *Goblins and Pagodas* in 1916, after a visit back to his childhood home in Little Rock, Arkansas, and then to Boston, where he had previously attended school. His *Goblins and Pagodas* collection is divided into two parts: "The Ghosts of an Old House," in which he writes several poems that reflect on the large home in which he lived in Arkansas, as well as on family members who influenced his development during those early years. The second part of his collection is called "The Symphonies," which, according to Hughes, "represents an ambitious attempt to arrange the intellectual and emotional life of an artist in eleven separate movements, each movement being dominated by a color-harmony." In other words, Fletcher created poems that intertwined poetry, music, and art in an attempt to use the aesthetics of each form to express his understanding of his emotions.

The poems in the first section, reminiscences of Fletcher's youth, are, according to Hughes, "not a great performance," although Hughes does later recant this position by stating that taking the first section as a whole, rather than evaluating the poems individually, produces a more powerful "mosaic."

It is the second section of this collection that most critics believe to be Fletcher's most clearly influenced by the imagist mode. Hughes describes this section of poems as reflecting "beauty and mastery of form, and several are consistently excellent." These poems are longer and more complicated than the ones in the first section, and Fletcher works with concepts for which there was little precedent. In these poems, one way in which he is able to combine poetry, music, and art is by giving colors different emotional values. Some of his attempts lean toward the conventionally accepted, such as using blue to express sadness; but other emotional values that he conveys are completely his own, as in his relating the color orange as the color of war. Of the poems in this section, "Green Symphony" and "Blue Symphony" are the most often anthologized.

Images of War

One of the strongest influences in Richard Aldington's life was his time spent in World War I. The experience made him bitter and cynical. His *Images of War* (1919) is a collection of poems that he wrote both during the war and afterward. He spent fifteen months on the front lines of this brutal combat, and from that came what some critics refer to as some of the most beautiful war poems ever written. The beauty comes from the poems' intensity and Aldington's ability to make the reader feel as if he or she were undergoing the same emotions that Aldington was suffering from.

The poems transport the reader to the trenches and allow them the privilege of hearing Aldington's thoughts on life and death, love and pain, fear and loneliness. Ironically, the poems that Aldington wrote during the war are less cynical than the ones that he wrote several years later. The space of time that occurred between the end of the war and Aldington's writing the later poems allowed him to reflect more on the overall picture of war: the reasons behind war and the consequences of such action. While entrenched in the war, Aldington thought of survival. These poems are very personal accounts of emotional intensity. Once he is removed from the action, however, and suffers from the emotional impact of having survived as well as objectively analyzing why nations would ever employ such drastic means, his poetry becomes bitterer. This collection marks the end of Aldington's purest use of Imagism. From this point on, his writing took on other aspects and influences.

Otherworld: Cadences

F. S. Flint published his last collection of poems under the title *Otherworld: Cadences* in 1920. Most of the poems in this collection center on the effects of war, and thus he dedicates this volume to his fellow imagist poet Aldington, whose own writing was greatly influenced by the experience of World War I.

Not all of the poems in this collection are written with a specific reference to World War I. Some poems stress a more personal war, such as in the title piece, "Otherworld." In this poem, Flint reflects on the battle that he encounters on a daily basis, having to wake up to a world that demands that much of his attention be focused on material details. In contrast, he would much rather sit in his garden and meditate on the beauty of the world, the love of his family, and the goodness of his compatriots. Hughes writes of this poem: "The poem continues, and pictures the deadening routine of the day and the return of the worker at night to his home, weak and disheartened."

Hughes states that some of the poetry in this collection is "soft poetry. It is much softer than most poems written by the imagists. But it is absolutely human." Hughes concludes that even though Flint also writes poems with more of an edge, he is unlike his fellow imagist poets in that he "finds it impossible to conceal his tenderness."

Flint published two collections of poems with similar titles: both had the word *cadence* in them. Cadence was very important to Flint, believing, as he did, that cadence was one of the most important

Hilda Doolittle

marks of imagist poetry. In the preface to *Otherworld: Cadence*, Flint proposes that unrhymed cadence truly marks the difference between traditional and modern poetry.

Sea Garden

Hilda Doolittle's first collection of twenty-eight imagist poems, *Sea Garden* (1916), has been referred to, by J. B. Harmer in his *Victory in Limbo: Imagism 1908–1917*, as representative of one of two of "the chief memorial[s] of the Imagiste group." The poems in Doolittle's first collection are the most influenced by the imagist movement, and according to Harmer, after publication of this book, Doolittle "began to retreat" into more traditional poetic form. Thus, this collection marks both her entry into the movement as well as her exit.

Susan Stanford Friedman, writing in the *Dictionary of Literary Biography,* Vol. 45: *American Poets, 1880–1945*, compares many of the poems in this collection to Georgia O'Keeffe's flower paintings, stating that like O'Keeffe, "H. D.'s flowers indirectly suggest an intense eroticism, whose power comes precisely from its elusive, nonhuman expression." Friedman also states that it is through these poems that Doolittle expresses traits of her personality, such as her "pride in her difference, and her separation from the conventional."

This pride is best witnessed in the poem "Sheltered Garden," in which Doolittle writes that she is tired of the pampered, neat garden and longs to find a fruit tree upon which the fruit is allowed to stay on the branch to naturally whither and die.

Rachel Blau DuPlessis, writing in *H. D.: The Career of that Struggle*, mentions that in Doolittle's poems about flowers, she rebels against convention by depicting the flowers in harsh environments, praising them for their wounds: "These flowers of the sea gardens are of a harsh surprising beauty, slashed, torn, dashed yet still triumphant and powerful." Such is the case with the poem "Sea Rose," in which Doolittle does not praise the flower for its delicacy but rather for its ability to stand against the winds. She repeats this theme in her poem "Sea Poppies," in which she describes the roots of the flower as being caught among the rocks and broken shells and praises it for its endurance.

Sword Blades and Poppy Seed

Amy Lowell spent several years in London, meeting imagist poets and eventually taking over the promotion, education, and organization of this movement. When she returned to the United States in 1914, she published her own collection of imagist poetry, *Sword Blades and Poppy Seed.* The poems in this collection reflect all the theories and philosophies that had been espoused by the imagists, as well as by the French symbolist poets who had greatly influenced the Imagism movement. It is in the preface of this collection that Lowell discusses her interpretation of free verse and what she refers to as polyphonic prose, two concepts that were used by some poets in the imagist movement.

Although Lowell was to become a popular poet, she was often criticized for her lack of originality. In this first collection of hers, the influences of Pound, Doolittle, and Fletcher are very apparent. Lowell was mostly known and praised for her business sense, especially in promoting the movement and finding ways to have the other poets published. However, it is her ability to use polyphonic prose, one of the major aspects of this collection, that impressed many of the other poets. Aldington, in fact, was so impressed with Lowell's ability to use this technique that he wrote an essay in which he recommended that all young poets study this collection of Lowell's.

Polyphonic prose is a type of free verse that uses alliteration (repetition of consonant sounds), assonance (repetition of vowel sounds), as well as other poetic devices to create a poem that is appears like prose, but that reads or sounds like poetry. Although Lowell did not invent polyphonic prose, she is given credit for popularizing it, and it is in this collection that she best displays her ability to use this form.

Themes

War

Several of the imagist poets used war as a theme of their poems and sometimes of their entire collections. One of the most dominant uses of this theme is Aldington's *Images of War*, in which the poet relates his personal experiences in the trenches of World War I. This collection also includes poems that he wrote after the war, poems in which he uses a cynical tone to mark his disgust of societies that allow war to occur in the first place. The poem "The Lover," which appeared in this volume, is one of the most prominent poems in this collection. It brings together an interesting mix of his fears as well as the sexual desires that he experienced during the war.

Pound's *Cathay* is also based on the theme of war. Although Pound wrote these poems from translations of Li Po, an eighth-century poet from China, the original poems focused on war, a timely concern of Pound's, as the effects of World War I were influencing his thoughts.

Male poets were not the only ones who were affected by the war. Many of Doolittle's poems in her collection *Sea Garden* engage images of pain, suffering, and desolation. Some critics relate these images to the ravages of war felt by the entire population, including those who were left at home. Doolittle was married to Aldington at the time he served on the front lines and thus felt the full impact not only of her personal fears and sense of loss but also of Aldington's suffering. Many of the poems in Flint's *Otherworld: Cadences* also portray the devastation of World War I. In fact, he dedicated this work to his fellow poet Aldington because he was well aware of the effect that the war was having on his friend.

Sense of Place

Flint, who lived all of his life in or near London, has many times been referred to as the poet of London. He grew up in the streets of this city and knew the sounds and smells and colors so well that they permeated his poetry. His love of the city was not always an easy one, however, as espoused in some of his writings, such as his poem "Courage," in which he awakens every day and hopes for the strength to face the city one more time without whining. On a lighter note is his "To a Young Lady Who Moved Shyly among Men of Reputed Worth," written quickly at a dinner party in London. The original version of this poem did not meet the tenets of Imagism, so Flint rewrote it and titled it "London." In this form, it has become one of Flint's most admired poems.

John Gould Fletcher returned to his childhood home in Little Rock, Arkansas, and there he wrote poems that would be collected in the book *Ghosts and Pagodas*. He would eventually return to Europe and then come back to the United States again. During his second return, he would travel across the continent and look at his homeland with refreshed eyes. The result would be his *Breakers and Granite* (1921), a sort of salutation to America. This collection demonstrates Fletcher's experiments with free verse and polyphonic prose, demonstrating the imagist influence on his work. The poems describe such diverse images as the Grand Canyon, the farmlands in New England, the small towns along the Mississippi River, southern culture, and life on Indian reservations.

Media Adaptations

- *Ezra Pound Reads* is an audio tape that contains Pound reading several of his "Cantos," as well as his poems "The Gypsy" and "The Exile's Letter." The tape is available from Harper Audio.
- There are several interesting websites that contain biographical information, as well as some of the poems, of imagist poets. These include: http://www.americanpoems.com with poems by Doolittle; http://www.english.uiuc.edu/maps/poets/m_r/pound/bio.htm with an explanation of some of Pound's works; http://www.poets.org with some of Pound's poems; http://www.english.uiuc.edu/maps/poets/g_l/amylowell/life.htm with background information on Amy Lowell.

Nature

Doolittle's *Sea Garden* is filled with images of nature: flowers, bushes, oceans, beaches, and more. Doolittle used nature in this collection to reflect on a variety of emotions, her sense of isolation, and suffering. Fletcher also employed nature in his poetry, beginning with his first collection *Irradiations*, in which he often refers to gardens, forests, and rain. Under the influence of Japanese haiku, which often portrays scenes from nature, Fletcher's poem "Blue Symphony" intertwines colors and images of trees in mists of blue to suggest seasonal changes.

Lowell also reflected on nature in her experiments with polyphonic prose, such as in her "Patterns," in which she envisions herself walking through a garden, as well as in "The Overgrown Pasture." In her poem "November," she describes many different types of bushes and trees as they are affected by the cold of the approaching winter.

One of Flint's earliest poems, "The Swan," has been referred to as a poem that carefully follows the imagist practice of conciseness and suggestiveness. The poem consists of several short lines, written in very concrete terms as it describes the movements of a swan through dark waters. The poem is filled with the colors found in nature, painting a very precise image in words. The image of the swan gives way at the end to a symbol of the poet's sorrow.

Greek Poets

Both Aldington and Doolittle were passionate in their studies of Greek literature and mythology. They both looked to the classical poets to find a model of excellence for their writing. Doolittle was perhaps most inspired by Greek poets, often alluding to Sappho in her works. Her poetry in which this theme is most prominent has readily been referred to as her most original.

There is only one poem of Sappho's that has been retained throughout history in its completed state. The rest of Sappho's poetry exists only in fragment. It is upon these fragments that Doolittle built some of her more fascinating poetry. Doolittle has been credited, by Greek scholars such as Henry Rushton Fairclough (as quoted in Hughes's book), for becoming so completely "suffused with the Greek spirit that only the use of the vernacular will often remind the cultivated reader that he is not reading a Greek poet." Fairclough particularly refers to Doolittle's poem "Hymen" as exemplifying her ability to write under the influence of Greek poetry.

Lesbianism

The theme of lesbianism is portrayed in many of Lowell's poems. She does not name them as such, but her poems depict the love she felt for women, in particular, one woman. In her poem "Decade," she celebrates the tenth anniversary of her relationship with her live-in companion, Ada Dwyer Russell. In her poems "A Lady" and "The Blue Scarf," she alludes to her love of an unnamed woman.

Style

Polyphonic Prose

Amy Lowell was the imagist poet who was most heavily influenced by the practice of polyphonic prose, a term coined by Fletcher (who also enjoyed using this technique), but a practice that Lowell learned from the French poet Paul Fort (1872–1960). Lowell interpreted this form to be similar to free verse but only freer. She called it the most elastic form of poetic expression, as it used all the poetic "voices" such as meter, cadence, rhyme, alliteration, and assonance. When writing in this form, the poem is printed out in prose form, but the sound of the writing reflects the modes of poetry.

Lowell described this technique in an essay she wrote, "A Consideration of Modern Poetry," for the *North American Review* (January 1917). She employed this technique for the first time in her collection *Sword Blades and Poppy Seed* (1914), to which Aldington wrote an article in the *Egoist* commending the collection and suggesting that all young poets should read Lowell's poems to learn the technique. Aldington writes (as quoted in Hughes's book), "I am not a bit ashamed to confess that I have myself imitated Miss Lowell in this, and produced a couple of works in the same style."

Although Lowell's poetry was often criticized for lack of depth, many critics praised her for her use of language, especially her proficiency in using polyphonic prose.

Free Verse

Pound was responsible for creating six tenets of what he believed would help poets understand what Imagism was all about and how it differed from other forms of poetry. Of these six, one of the main tenets was free verse, which, according to the manifesto, would best express the individuality of the poet. The exact wording of this tenet is quoted in David Perkins's book, *A History of Modern Poetry:*

Topics for Further Study

- The controversy over what constitutes a poem remains unsolved. Research the topic of free verse (or *vers libre*). Consider including a historical perspective, the differences in various definitions and proposed applications of this style, as well as aspects of the controversy of the prose poem.
- Both Amy Lowell and Hilda Doolittle were involved in lesbian relationships. Study their poetry and compare how they handled these issues in their writing. You might also want to read some of their prose to give you a fuller background on this issue. For a more complex paper, you could include information on the social implications of lesbianism during the time frame of their relationships. You might also want to read some thoughts on the subject by Gertrude Stein and Virginia Woolf, two other writers around the same time period who also dealt with issues stemming from homosexuality.
- The Greek poet Sappho greatly influenced Hilda Doolittle's writing. Develop as concise a biography as possible about Sappho from the limited information available. Research her poetry to discover how Doolittle's writing reflects upon it; then, using examples from both women, compare specific poems.
- Japanese haiku was a major influence on imagist poetry. Read some of the poetry of Matsuo Basho, then try to write some of your own haiku. Include up to five of your haiku in a paper that explores Basho's life and works.
- F. S. Flint wrote very moving war poetry. Research other poets or other writers of prose who spoke of their war experiences. You may want to choose a different writer for each major war, such as World War II, the Korean War, the War in Vietnam, or even a war from ancient times. Compare their experiences.
- Imagism marked the beginning of the modernist movement in literature and in other art forms. How did Modernism affect other arts such as painting, sculpture, architecture, and music? What were the drastic changes from the romantic or Victorian age to Modernism? Or you might want to switch perspectives and show how Modernism and the postmodern world of art stand in contrast.

From the 1890s to the High Modernist Mode: "We believe that the individuality of a poet may often be better expressed in free-verse than in conventional forms. In poetry, a new cadence means a new idea." Free verse was one manner of escaping the need to rhyme. Pound thought that by releasing poets from this need to rhyme, he would create an atmosphere in which they could better focus on the image.

Pound was not original in this idea, as various forms of free verse had been used in classical Greek literature, in Old English literature (such as *Beowulf*), as well as in French, American, and German poetry. However, Pound and the other imagist poets took the meaning of free verse to new ground. They believed that rhythm expressed emotion, and the imagists understood, according to Perkins, that "for every emotional state there is the one particular rhythm that expresses it." Therefore, limiting rhythm to the fixed stanzas, meters, and other rhythmic standards of conventional poetry disallowed a full rendering of those emotions. In other words, the individuality of the poet's emotions would be thwarted by following traditional rules, and thus the overall effect of the poem would become inauthentic or insincere. Thus, the imagists were encouraged to let go of the old standards and open up their emotions to the freer flow of words that was allowed in the use of free verse. Of the imagist poets, the Americans, more so than their fellow British cohorts, readily took advantage of free verse. The traditional rules of poetry had been created in Europe and therefore had a European character. Through the use of free verse, the American imagists felt that they could compose more individualistic poetry that spoke in an American voice.

There was controversy around this form, as many critics had trouble distinguishing the differences between so-called free verse and actual prose. So the question arose: What makes a poem a poem? Poetry, most critics argued, required form. Aldington defined his use of free verse as poetry in this way: "The prose-poem is poetic content expressed in prose form" (quoted from Hughes). Whereas Fletcher took a more visual and more general approach in attempting to express his understanding of the difference between prose and poetry, believing that all well-written literature could be referred to as poetry, so that it did not matter if poems were written according to very traditional rules or in free verse. In Hughes's book, Fletcher is quoted saying: "The difference between poetry and prose is . . . a difference between a general roundness and a general squareness of outline."

Common and Precise Language

Another tenet in the imagist manifesto dealt with the specific use of language. Imagist poets were told to use the language of common speech, more like the language one would hear in conversation rather than the formal or decorative language often used in traditional poetry. Imagists were also told to be spare in their use of words, to practice using only the words that were needed to describe an image. They should be concrete in their language, to stay away from abstraction.

Image

Pound's definition of what an image was in terms of imagist poetry is rather vague. He stressed that the language should be precise and concentrated in expressing this image, but he never quite defined what the image of the imagist movement was. One of the tenets of the imagist manifesto was the freedom of the poet to choose any subject that he or she wanted. So image was not related to subject matter. However, it is stated that one of the main purposes of poetry is "To present an image" (quoted from Hughes). This image should not be an abstraction. If an abstraction, such as an emotion, is to be expressed, indeed, it should be told, through an image.

Aldington, as stated by Hughes, tried to be a little more specific in his definition of an image by stating that poets should try to create "clear, quick rendering[s] of particulars without commentary." William Carlos Williams, who wrote an occasional imagist poem, may have defined the image best. Ideas are best expressed through things, Williams believed, and there was no better way to express things that contained ideas than through images. The imagists' intent to focus on one image led them to embrace the poetry of Japan, especially haiku, which presented single images in each of its poems.

Japanese Haiku

Japanese haiku is an ancient form of poetry, originating almost seven hundred years ago. Haiku is a very precise poetic form, consisting typically of seventeen syllables in three lines. The Japanese language, which is syllabic rather than based on individual letters of an alphabet, is better suited to this form than is the English language. Therefore, even though the imagist poets became enamored of this form, they technically never wrote an authentic haiku. However, haiku greatly influenced their work. Matsuo Basho (1644–1694) is one of Japan's best-known haiku poets. His most famous poem of this type is a good example:

> An old pond . . .
> A frog jumps in—
> The sound of water.

In comparison is Doolittle's "Oread" (also taken from Harmer's book), which demonstrates the imagist attempt to practice haiku by writing simply and focusing on one image:

> Whirl up, sea—
> whirl your pointed pines,
> splash your great pines
> on our rocks,
> hurl your green over us,
> cover us with your pools of fir.

Movement Variations

Of the six major imagist poets, four of them (Lowell, Doolittle, Pound, and Fletcher) were born in the United States, and all four, upon deciding to dedicate their lives to writing, and more specifically to poetry, traveled throughout Europe. There was a void, as far as poetry is concerned, in America at that time, and those who had a passion for creating poetry felt that they needed to go abroad to find out more about it. The American poetry that did exist in the early part of the twentieth century, according to Pound, was mediocre. As quoted in Perkins, Pound states: "Only the mediocrity of a given time can drive intelligent men of that time to 'break with tradition.'" Thus, the American poets, tired and frustrated by the conventional poets of the previous century, traveled to Europe and helped to open the gates of the modernist period, influencing it with their own credo of Imagism.

Interestingly, once these American poets became involved in creating the imagist movement, some of them (mostly Lowell and Fletcher) tended to veer in different directions from their British contemporaries in their attempts to give the language of their poetry a more American slant.

Historical Context

Modernism

The transition from the Romanticism and Victorianism into Modernism was one of the major shifts in the history of poetry, and some critics credit the imagists with beginning this great change. The romantics were marked by their idealism and embellished language, while the imagists proclaimed that they were realists who would write in a simple vernacular. The romantics were behind the times, the imagists believed. The older poetic form appealed to audiences that were usually made up of the upper social classes. The modernists wanted to communicate with the masses.

"Imagism has been described as the grammar school of modern poetry," writes Perkins. The imagist poets were responsible for creating some of the basic instructions for Modernism, which included clear and precise language and suggestive and visual imagery. Modernists would experiment with ways in which to relate poetry to the other arts.

Modernism implied that the population was tired of the past and wanted to see things as they really were in the present or to think about how they might be in the future. The past was old, and the ancient casts should be broken and discarded. Modernists wanted to create something new. Experimentation and exploration were the new focus. There was a breaking away from patterned responses and predictable forms. Modernist themes often included the feeling of alienation: the individual having difficulty placing him- or herself in time because the traditional has been discarded and the present is in a state of redefinition. Other themes of the modernists were the beginnings of an exploration of the inner self, life as experienced in large urban centers, and the effects of rampant materialism and industrialization.

World War I

World War I was a traumatic event for Europe and the United States. Previous wars had involved the upper social classes more so than the general population. World War I was also the first war to involve gas warfare and heavy artillery. The physically and emotionally wounded soldiers were brought home, most of them in shellshock, most of them filled with bitterness. They found themselves alienated from their own optimistic views of the promises of the machine age that they had held prior to the war. European and American authors writing during and after the war spoke about the horror of war and its attendant disillusions more than any generation had before them. Their styles became more introspective, less idealistic, and more cynical. In an attempt to heal their inner wounds, they tried to explain the effects that the war had upon them and to analyze and criticize the society that had sent them there.

Women's Rights

In 1903, the women's suffrage movement in Britain took a turn toward the militant under the leadership of Emmeline Pankhurst and her daughters. They had grown tired of being silenced and were determined to grab headlines with their acts of arson, destruction, and general mayhem in the streets. Many of the leaders of this group were often imprisoned, at which time they would then go on hunger strikes. After World War I, limited suffrage was granted to them. In 1928, eight years after their American sisters, British women were granted the right to vote.

With political awareness of their rights, women also gained the courage to speak out not only for public freedoms but also for independence in their personal lives. Everything from clothing to sexual relations was undergoing close examination as women began defining their lives in terms of what they needed and wanted rather than what the male-dominated society dictated for them. This can be seen in terms of Lowell's mannerisms, in particular. She liked to wear men's clothes and often smoked cigars. She, like Doolittle, was involved in a lesbian relationship. Doolittle was also very free in determining her relationships with men. While married to Aldington, she had affairs with other men, one of them resulting in her getting pregnant. Although both these women were courageous enough to demand their rights, Doolittle often suffered mentally from the emotional impact of her actions. She was well ahead of her time in terms of women's liberation and often sought the care of

Compare & Contrast

- **Early Twentieth Century:** Women win the right to vote after a long period of political activism in both Britain and in the United States.

  Middle Twentieth Century: Gloria Steinman, Bella Abzug, Shirley Chisholm, and Betty Friedan join forces to establish the National Women's Political Caucus, encouraging women to use their political power to gain equal rights.

  Today: Although proposed at the beginning of the twentieth century, the Equal Rights Amendment has failed to be ratified in a majority of state legislatures in the United States.

- **Early Twentieth Century:** China and Japan open their cultural doors to the West, influencing Western literature with various forms of classical Asian poetry.

  Middle Twentieth Century: After the musical group the Beatles are influenced by the Eastern practice of meditation, Asian spiritual practices such as Buddhism spread across the United States.

  Today: The Japanese economy reaches its highest point as Japanese cars and electronic devices flood the U.S. markets.

- **Early Twentieth Century:** Over 57,000 American troops are killed in World War I.

  Middle Twentieth Century: Over 55,000 American troops are killed in World War II; over 33,000 troops are killed in Korea; over 58,000 are killed in Vietnam.

  Today: Over 300 troops are killed in the Gulf War. America's "War on Terrorism" follows the September 11, 2001, attack on the World Trade Center in New York, where more than 3,000 were killed or remain missing.

psychiatrists, including Sigmund Freud, to help her come to terms with her emotional needs and the social confines of the early era of women's rights.

Critical Overview

In the chapter "Critical Reaction," Hughes makes the statement that "few comments on the [imagist] movement have appeared in English periodicals. The effect is that of a conspiracy of silent scorn." Hughes wrote this in 1931, but his book remains today, one of the standard studies of the imagist movement, so his seventy-year-old opinion seems to be still standing. Hughes claims that the critics who did write about Imagism were usually either the imagist poets themselves or else their friends.

The only comments that were made were either brief sarcastic remarks or "mutual back-scratching," Hughes concludes. Of the sarcastic remarks, he mentions Harold Monro, who wrote an article in the *Egoist*, a largely imagist publication. Monro writes, "the imagists seem to have been struck partially blind at the first sight of their new world; and they are still blinking."

Ford Maddox Ford (using his German last name, Hueffer, for this article) is quoted by Hughes as commending Doolittle and Flint for their writing, praising them as the only two poets in the movement who wrote well enough to be called imagists. Ford then continues: "Mr. John Gould Fletcher, Mr. Aldington, and Miss Lowell are all too preoccupied with themselves and their emotions to be really called Imagists." Ford concludes by stating that the imagist movement is the only thing that was happening in literature during that time.

Hughes then goes on to discuss the critical response that the imagists received in America. He begins with a statement from a reviewer writing for the *Chicago Tribune*. The writer concluded the review by stating that Imagism should be established as a constitutional amendment and that anyone who writes anything other than in the imagist mode should be imprisoned. Later, after the publication of *Some Imagist Poets* (1915), Conrad Aiken, an American poet himself and friend of Pound, wrote a poem for the imagists and had it published in the *Boston Transcript*. The poem was not at all flattering, and as presented in Hughes's book, Aiken ended each stanza with the question: "Where in a score years will you be," making an allusion to the fact that he thought Imagism was but a mere fad.

Aiken later wrote an article for the *New Republic*, in which he praised Fletcher at the other imagist poets' expense, stating that only Fletcher was able to express enough emotion to move the reader. W. S. Braithwaite, in response to Aiken's attacks, also published an article in the *New Republic*. His opinion of the imagists was more generous, praising the poets for their courage to break out of the old poetry molds. As quoted in Hughes's book, Braithwaite writes, "The final test of poetry is not that it stirs one . . . but that it haunts one."

In 1915, William Ellery Leonard, a professor at the University of Wisconsin, took upon himself the task of critiquing the imagists. His analysis was not very favorable. Hughes describes Leonard's remarks as "the most scholarly, sarcastic, and seriously-considered attempt at the annihilation of imagism yet recorded." Leonard disliked the imagists' allusions to Japanese poetry, although Hughes points out that at the time of the criticism none of the imagists had yet written any poetry that was influenced by haiku. Leonard also criticized their use of classical Greek and Latin poets, assuming (wrongly) that none of the poets had a real understanding of the classics. Hughes sums up his views about the Leonard attacks on the imagists by stating that Leonard was correct in pointing out some of the weak points of some of the poets but that to condemn the whole movement without mentioning any of their strengths was a "cheap trick."

Other critics did not like the egoism that the imagist poets appeared to flaunt. Some felt that the imagist poet made him- or herself more important than the poem. Hughes then writes that Lewis Worthington Smith, writing for the *Atlantic Monthly*, believed that the imagists were only pretending to revolt from all literary forms but were, actually, "doing nothing of the kind: they are minor poets who cannot stand the strain of the sophisticated and complex world in which they find themselves." Smith concludes that Imagism is merely a "freakish and barren cult" and a sign that Romanticism will bounce back with a much "fuller and more vital poetry."

John Gould Fletcher

These were the early reviews. Later, Hughes writes, the critics were "more favorable, owing to the continuous propaganda of the imagists themselves and to the natural decline of prejudice toward something new."

Criticism

Joyce Hart

Hart has degrees in English literature with a minor in Asian studies and focuses her writing on literary topics. In this essay, Hart considers the influence of the Japanese poetic form of haiku on imagist poetry.

The Imagism movement, although short-lived and complicated by some basic contradictions and controversies, definitely left its mark on the literature of its time as well as on many works that would follow. Included in the contradictions was the dictate from the movement's founders to break the chains of tradition, while two of its most loyal poets wrote their imagist poems with allusions to classical Latin and Greek poetry. Another contradiction was the call for freedom in writing, and yet the leaders of the movement sat down and wrote an imagist manifesto, delineating rules for anyone

What Do I Study Next?

- *Imagist Poem*, edited by William Pratt and revised in 2001, is an expanded anthology of imagist poetry first published in the 1960s. This collection is a good place to start for getting to know and understand imagist poetry.
- A comprehensive collection of Japanese haiku from the seventeenth to the nineteenth century can be found in *The Essential Haiku: Versions of Basho, Buson, and Issa* (1995), edited by Robert Hass. Basho, Buson, and Issa are the most proficient poets of haiku. This anthology contains three hundred of their poems.
- *The Women's Movements in the United States and Britain from the 1790s to the 1920s* (1993), by Christine Bolt, offers an extensive historical perspective of the women's rights movement seen through the more modern vision of feminism. This book offers a good understanding of the environment in which the men and women of Imagism were writing.
- Marjorie Perloff, a professor of comparative literature, has spent her professional career fighting for inclusion of a broader range of literary works in the list of books that are usually taught on college campuses. In her *Poetic License: Essays on Modernist and Postmodernist Lyric*, she discusses poems by authors who have often been ignored. In this book, she includes Doolittle and Fletcher, as well as the more well-known poets associated with Imagism, such as Ezra Pound and D. H. Lawrence.
- *The Lost Voices of World War I: An International Anthology of Writers, Poets, and Playwrights* (1989), edited by Tim Cross, includes the poems of T. E. Hulme, the man most responsible for creating the philosophical foundation of Imagism. Hulme, who wrote very few poems in his lifetime, died in World War I, as did most of the authors included in this collection.
- *British Poets of the Great War* (1988), by Fred D. Crawford, contains a chapter on the imagists. Crawford offers a literary background for the movement and discusses the imagist poets and their poems.

who would write imagist poems. Added to the contradictions was the confusion that many readers (and critics) experienced as they tried to understand free verse, which to them read more like prose than poetry. And, finally, even though the basic tenet of this group of poets was that the *image* was the poem, no one was able to offer a definitive explanation of what the word *image* meant to them, despite the fact that, quite obviously, the most influential element of this movement was just that—the concept of the focused image. However, despite this latter problem, the imagists did discover a model upon which they could build their images, and that was the Japanese poetic form referred to as haiku.

It was in the form of the haiku, or, if not the exact form, at least in the general concept of it, that many of the tenets of the imagist manifesto were best expressed. The manifesto, in short, expected imagist writers to use common speech, words from daily dialogue. The language should be precise and concrete. Rhythm should be free, and rhyming was not only unnecessary, it was practically discouraged. The poem should be concentrated and definite; and, most important, the poem should present an image. Matching this explanation of Imagism are the descriptions of the Japanese poem, which state that haiku should be true to reality and written as if it represented a first impression of subjects taken from daily life or as seen with fresh eyes. The language should be simple, and the focus should be on one image. In both the haiku and the imagist poem, two images are often juxtaposed and the meaning of the poem is understated.

Despite the fact that critics argue that the imagists never truly mastered the haiku form, the influence of the Japanese haiku is very evident in many of their poems. Pound, being the initial leader of the movement, tried his hand at the haiku with his often quoted poem "In a Station of the Metro," taken here from Harmer's book:

The apparition of these faces in the crowd;
Petals, on a wet black bough.

Compare Pound's poem to one from Japan's more famous haiku masters, Yosa Buson (1715–1783), and the similarities are easy to see. Buson's poem is also taken from Harmer.

Alone in a room
Deserted—
A peony.

In both poems, the wording is sparse. The language is simple. There are two very clear images woven together by a subtle reading, that is left to the reader to decipher. In Pound's poem, the image of the petals of a flower that have been momentarily pasted to the limb of a tree after a rainfall is something that almost all readers could relate to no matter where they lived, what culture they were brought up in, or what language they spoke. By using this image, Pound gives the reader a hint of his feelings, as the speaker stands, possibly leaning against some far wall, watching the crowd of temporary faces pass by him. Just as the petals of the flower are temporarily pasted against the wet limb, the people who are passing are only momentarily fixed in the speaker's mind. He juxtaposes the crowded station with a beautiful, understated scene from nature—a few wet petals.

Japanese art, whether a painting or a flower arrangement, is an expression as much of what is not there as of what is presented. A single flower placed with an interestingly formed stick allows space around its images, thus encouraging the imagination to fill in the emptiness. The beauty is in the simplicity. Pound senses this and even plays with it as he first takes his readers to a crowded and busy center of transportation in some unnamed city, then suddenly plants them in a quiet place where they can meditate on a single bough. Buson makes a similar surprising movement. He first implants the feelings of loneliness. The reader is made to believe that a person is sitting in a room by him- or herself, although the reader does not know for sure why. The next line adds the emotion. The loneliness gives way to the more incredible feeling of abandonment and neglect. Then Buson adds nature, and the image softens; it becomes pristine and beautiful in its aloneness. It is in the starkness of the single peony that an image of art is created. The lone flower in a vase is turned into a pure, focused image, because there is nothing else in the room to distract the eye.

One more example from the Japanese is the following, also taken from Harmer, and credited to Moritake:

A fallen petal
Flies back to its branch:
Ah! A butterfly!

In comparison to this haiku is one written by Amy Lowell. Although Lowell's is not as humorous, she wrote a poem that contains a very similar rhythm. This poem is taken from Hughes's book:

My thoughts
Chink against my ribs
And roll about like silver hailstones

In Moritake's poem, there is surprise in the last line, as there is in Lowell's. The surprise in Moritake's is more evident. The reader feels the jolt, just as the poet must have experienced it, watching one image turn into quite another, from a dead, falling petal to a live and beautiful butterfly. Lowell's surprise is more subtle. The image of thoughts hitting, albeit lightly, against the speakers ribs is somewhat uncomfortable. The concept makes the speaker appear agitated and possibly hungry, if not for food, then for a solution of some kind. Then she adds the final line, having the thoughts roll now, a much more comforting feeling, and they are also turned into silver—smooth and shiny. Iinstead of being bothersome, they now appear somewhat precious.

There are many examples of the influence of haiku upon the imagists, as all of them tried their hand at the Japanese form, some of them more successfully than others. Even T. E. Hulme, who wrote very few poems and was not directly considered an imagist poet, even though it was his philosophy of poetry that began the movement, was able to create a type of haiku. In his poem "Autumn," taken from Hughes's book, Hulme writes a somewhat longer version, but the rhythm and the form are still there:

A touch of cold in the Autumn night—
I walked abroad,
And saw the ruddy moon lean over a hedge
Like a red-faced farmer.

In this stanza of his poem, Hulme juxtaposes images of nature with the figure of a person. There is a similar surprise in Hulme's poem, as there is in Moritake's, in which the petal suddenly turns into a butterfly. With Hulme, the moon suddenly turns into the face of a farmer. The picture in the poem jumps from one image to the other, as Hulme superimposes the moon and the farmer in such a quick motion that the reader witnesses the blending of the two images into one.

One of the best examples of haiku poetry from Richard Aldington comes from his collection *Images of Desire*. It is quoted here from Hughes's book:

> Like a dark princess whose beauty
> Many have sung, you wear me,
> The one jewel that is warmed by your breast.

Here Aldington focuses on one image, that of a beautiful princess, bejeweled. What is interesting in this poem is that Aldington embeds the speaker in that "one jewel," creating a double image in one object. The attention remains on the princess and her beauty, while the speaker sneaks in and prevails over the throngs of men who clamor for her attention. This is a clever poem, whose image changes the more it is thought about. The picture first appears as a solitary figure, then slowly grows more complex as more people crowd into the image, first the other admirers, then the jewel that takes on the personification of the speaker.

John Gould Fletcher wholly engaged Japanese art in many of its forms, and in the following two lines, taken again from Hughes, he captures a beautiful Japanese image in very few words:

> Uneven tinkling, the lazy rain
> Dripping from the eaves.

This short poem not only provides an image, it adds music. Raindrops splashing down on the roof, "tinkling" like the sounds of tiny bells or like a wind chime. Then he slows down the rhythm, as he describes the rain as lazy, and the reader can again see the sluggish drops leisurely slithering down from the eaves. This is imagist poetry imitating haiku at its best, with several of the senses drawn in, with such spare and simple words, to create one exquisite image.

Fletcher is successful again in one of his poems taken from his collection *Ghosts and Pagodas*. This one comes from the first section, "The Ghosts of an Old House," and as quoted from Hughes, it reads in part:

> The windows rattle as if someone were in
> them wishing to get out
> and ride upon the wind.

Knowing the context of this poem gives it more meaning. Fletcher has gone back to his family home, after having been away for a long time. His family is gone. All that remains for him are the memories of having once lived there. When the wind rattles the windows, he imagines the ghosts of his memories, trying to release themselves from his mind. Fletcher builds the image by bringing in various senses. Not only can the reader envision what this might look like, or feel like, but the sound of the wind and the rattling of the window are also very easy to imagine. The surprise element is also present. The normal impression might be that if there were ghosts inside the window, and they were trying to get out, that the ghosts would then come after the speaker of the poem. Instead, Fletcher has them wanting to ride the wind, to fly away from him, to return to nature. He has captured the essence of the haiku in his own way, imbuing the image with past emotions conjured in the present moment, all illustrated realistically and concretely.

Closing this essay is a poem from William Carlos Williams (1883–1963), who was not considered one of the major imagist poets, but he is often referred to as one of the major poets of that time who was affected by the Imagism movement. His poem "Red Wheelbarrow" is often used as a classic representation of both the perfect imagist poem as well as one that demonstrates the influence of the haiku. The image of the red wheelbarrow, on which, as the poem reads, "so much depends" visually, is so vivid that it could almost be framed and hung on the wall as a painting. The rhythm is slightly less Japanese, but the picture that is created is very much in line with haiku.

This poem is so visual that the reader feels as if standing in a museum, staring at an oil painting. The first line focuses on the brightest color, the red of the wheelbarrow. Added to this image is the simply stated observation that the wheelbarrow is "glazed with rain," a concise detail that further elaborates the scene with so few words that it seems understated. (Note the painting terminology in the word *glazed*, thus reinforcing the impression of this poem as a painted image.) Finally, the lustrous, red wheelbarrow is situated near white chickens, which were at first unseen but now stand out, their whiteness exaggerated in contrast to the color red. What, if any, meaning Williams intended in this poem is practically unimportant. However, as a poem of meditation, which is one of the reasons that the Japanese haiku is written, this poem has excelled. When read for purely imagist terms, this poem is still a prizewinner. Who could read this poem and not take with them an extremely vivid, focused image impressed upon their minds?

The imagist manifesto wanted the poets to create images rather than to moralize or preach as many of their poetic Victorian predecessors had done. It also wanted poets to minimize their language. It is no wonder that they were attracted to and influenced by the Japanese haiku, which had been perfected many hundreds of years before them. The Imagism movement was short, and most of the poets who were involved in the movement quickly passed either into obscurity or moved on to create different forms of poetry. However, despite the brevity of their involvement, they left an indelible mark on poetry of the English language by introducing the form and facility of haiku to American and British audiences.

Source: Joyce Hart, Critical Essay on Imagism, in *Literary Movements for Students*, The Gale Group, 2003.

"The imagist manifesto wanted the poets to create images rather than to moralize or preach as many of their poetic Victorian predecessors had done."

Patricia Clements

In the following essay excerpt, Clements explores the influence of Baudelaire on the work of the Imagists.

> Lexicon of beautiful is elastic, but
> walla-walla not yet poetically possible.
> —T. E. Hulme, "Notes onLanguage and Style"

For a long time, supported both by Eliot's remark that the Imagists were the *point de repère* of modern poetry and by anthologists of Imagist verse, literary historians took the "modernism" of that English school as given. William Pratt, anthologizing Imagist poems in 1963, adopted Eliot's line: they wrote, he said, "the first 'modern' poems in English." Peter Jones, presenting them anew for Penguin ten years later, said that their ideas "still lie at the centre of our poetic practice." The Imagists themselves, of course, made "modernism" a key element in their platform, and they defined it largely as reaction. T. E. Hulme dismissed virtually the whole of the last century when he named Henley as the single English poet who was "perhaps" a worthwhile model for what he wanted to do, and Richard Aldington voiced a common view with uncommon frankness when he said that "the majority of the poetry of the last century had nothing to do with life and very little to do with poetry . . . except for Browning and a little of Swinburne there was no energy which was not bombast, no rendering of life without an Anglican moral, no aesthetic without aesthetic cant" and when he acknowledged that he was "out to destroy . . . to a certain extent" the reputations of Shelley and Tennyson.

The outpost the Imagists established, however, was nothing like so securely held as historians were for so long willing to believe. Like Murry and Mansfield in *Rhythm*, or the Sitwells and Huxley in *Wheels*, the Imagists named their "modernism" before they knew what it was. Their poetics gather borrowed materials into uneasy equilibrium, and if, as Peter Jones says, we are sometimes struck by the differences between their theories and their practice, that is partly because the materials they borrowed were not always compatible with one another. They did not, however, merely "rummage among a variety of sources," and they were not merely "muddled." They articulated precisely, in both their theories and their poetry, the central conflicts of modern verse. In their theories, they attempted to recover the nineteenth-century synthesis, the accommodating double emphasis of "The School of Giorgione"; in their poetry, they struggled for sincerity, as Hulme defined it: "Each age must have its own special form of expression," he wrote, "and any period that deliberately goes out of it is an age of insincerity." On most important matters, however, the Imagists looked resolutely in two clearly defined and opposed directions: they began by imitating the very models they thought they should reject; they constructed a theory that is based on mutually hostile positions; they cultivated influences that pushed their poetry toward antithetical ideals. These conflicts do not make Imagism any less significant a workshop for modernism—on the contrary, they demonstrate the difficulty of the enterprise and underline the significance of what was achieved—but they do account for the Imagists' failure to accomplish at a stroke what they took

Images such as these from World War I influenced Richard Aldington

to be their chief task, "the reform of poetic style and, above all . . . the assimilation by poetry of modern thought and the complex modern mind." When the Imagists confronted what they came to see as their most important subject matter, the life of great cities, they were paralyzed by their self-contradictions. Aldington's "Xenophilometropolitania," which appeared in the *Egoist* in January, 1914, cover the conflicts with parody, but the "Strange Love," the "foreign" objects of this oddly amorous poetry, emerged as a central problem for the Imagist poets. Aldington's assertion that his "Metropolitania" were "penultimate poetry" was not entirely whimsical.

In all of this, Baudelaire is deeply implicated. He is an aspect of each of the Imagist antitheses—a part of their parentage, an affiliate of their theoretical dilemmas, a model for their precisely defined "modernism." In their work it is possible to observe both the process of his modernizing in England and some of its causes. Moreover, in an account of Baudelaire's shifting English identity, the Imagists are crucial: they redid some of the critical work of Swinburne and Pater, importing massively from modern French writers and so reversing once again the notion that the French could be ignored; they devised a literary classicism which turned the attention of English writers back beyond

Mallarmé and Verlaine to the originating double visage of Baudelaire, who carried, as Valéry was to write some time later, his own critic within him; and they articulated a problem for "modernism" that made him seem, inevitably, "the greatest exemplar in *modern* poetry in any language," as Eliot would put it years later, when all of this Imagist activity had subsided into history.

The Imagists' transactions with French poetry in general and with Baudelaire in particular reflect their characteristic self-contradiction. On the one hand, they placed the French at the heart of their reforming modernism, and for them poets from Villon to Remy de Gourmont represented escape from what they saw as all of that English staleness. But, on the other hand, in rejecting the English mainstream, the Imagists drew heavily on the counter-tradition: their approach to the French was shaped precisely by their English predecessors, and what they sought from their French models was often what had already been domesticated. Although in their later work the Baudelaire who is recognizable as a contributing voice is also recognizably the figure who speaks in *The Waste Land*, in their earlier work he echoes from the 'nineties.

"The Imagists' transactions with French poetry in general and with Baudelaire in particular reflect their characteristic self-contradiction."

There were powerful reasons for the Imagists' imitations of their predecessors, of course. The poets of the later nineteenth century had neatly prefigured the Imagists' major concerns, proffering the lyric as a corrective to the long Victorian narrative, seeking to purge the language, focussing on "intense" moments, and emphasizing sensation and individuality. Symons's concern for a "revolt from ready-made impressions and conclusions, a revolt from the ready-made of language, from the bondage of traditional form, of a form become rigid," for instance, could settle with smooth consistency into Hulme's "Notes on Language and Style." After the noise of Imagism's opening battles had stilled, its blood relation to the later nineteenth century became clear to some of its members. Pound wrote in 1928 of the "Rapports fr. > eng. via Arthur Symons etc. 1890 Baudelaire, Verlaine, etc." and John Gould Fletcher confessed in 1937 that he and Amy Lowell had agreed from the beginning that there

> was nothing . . . particularly new about imagism. It was but a more lyrical, a saner and more intelligible, development of the aesthetic theories of the English Pre-Raphaelite poets, the Parnassians and the symbolists in France.

There *was* something new in Imagism, however, and Harold Monro more accurately described its relationship to the nineteenth century: "We in the twentieth century," he wrote, "are on the treetops of the poetic growths represented by the Pre-Raphaelites and the 'Nineties."

T. E. Hulme, who so immoderately dismissed almost all of his English predecessors, was by no means oblivious to complexity and contradiction in the process of literary reform. He said that he had "no reverence for tradition" and that he "started from a standpoint of extreme modernism," but, like Pater, he was fascinated by this fact of transition itself. "Wonder," he said in the conclusion of his essay on "Romanticism and Classicism," "can only be the attitude of a man passing from one stage to another." Like a belated Gautier, delivering a luxurious account of the decomposed language of *Les Fleurs du Mal*, Hulme adopts a violent figure of decay (adding to it the brass knuckles of his misogyny) to represent the present stage in the history of poetic form: "The carcass is dead," he writes, "and all the flies are upon it. Imitative poetry springs up like weeds, and women whimper and whine of you and I alas, and roses, roses all the way. It becomes the expression of sentimentality rather than of virile thought." But Hulme insisted at the same time on the limitations imposed by inheritance: "Just as physically you are not born that abstract entity, man," he wrote, "but the child of particular parents, so you are in matters of literary judgment." He observed a similar lag in the development of poetic expression: it was one thing to be in revolt, he suggested, and quite another to produce a new order:

> What happens, I take it, is something of this kind: a certain change of direction takes place which begins negatively with a feeling of dissatisfaction with and reaction against existing art. But the new tendency, admitting that it exists, cannot at once find its own appropriate expression. But although the artist feels

> that he must have done with contemporary means of expression, yet a new and more fitting method is not easily created. Expression is by no means a natural thing. It is an unnatural, artificial and, as it were, external thing which a man has to install himself in before he can manipulate it... A man has first to obtain a foothold in this, so to speak, alien and external world of material expression, at a point near to the one he is making for. He has to utilise some already existing method of expression, and work from that to the one that expresses his own personal conception more accurately and naturally.

For most of the Imagists, the point closest to the one they were making for was the poetry of the 'nineties. Most of them had, after all, grown up on the products of the Aesthetic Movement. Aldington began his career by reading Wilde, whose voice echoes frequently in his poetry, and he conceived for him in youth an admiration he never lost, even though he laced it later with resentment. He edited selections from Wilde and from Pater, and as late as 1950 he produced an anthology of writings of the Aesthetes. Pound's modernism was similarly based, and Aldington complained about that when he reviewed his contributions to *Blast*: "It is not that one wants Mr. Pound to repeat his Provençal feats," he wrote, "to echo the 'nineties—he has done that too much already." Although he always knew what was the last word in Paris, F. S. Flint shaped his own verse to the pattern of the recent English past; and the early work of John Gould Fletcher is devoted exclusively to what Eliot later scorned as the last fashion but one.

Fletcher was not one of the earliest Imagists, but by the time of the *Egoist*'s special number on Imagism, on 1 May 1915, he had established his credentials. In the special number, he reviewed the poems of Amy Lowell, praisingly of course, and his own poems in turn were reviewed by Ferris Greenslet, Amy Lowell's publisher, who found them "in the highest degree vivid, original, and provocative." Pound, too, reviewed Fletcher's early poems, in *The New Freewoman*: he found in them promise of great talent and an admirable French influence, and he urged Harriet Monroe to publish him in *Poetry*. Fletcher continued for some time to enjoy the reputation of an *avant-gardist*: his poems appeared in *The Chapbook* and *Coterie*; Eliot printed his work in *The Criterion*; and the whole of *The Chapbook* for May 1920 was given over to his article on "Some Contemporary American Poets." "In England," says a summary of his life, "he was a leader of the Imagists."

Yet, at this stage in his career, Fletcher's "modernism" was a wholly reflected light. His early poems exemplify the inheritance that was the Imagists' first expression and they identify some of the ways in which Baudelaire was an element in that. Glenn Hughes writes that Fletcher's interest in "the new French poetry, particularly in its wilder manifestations," developed after his arrival in England, but, in fact, Fletcher, like Eliot, encountered modern French poetry while he was at Harvard, as a consequence of reading the later nineteenth-century English poets. A year after experiencing what he calls in his memoirs "the heady and passing intoxication of Swinburne, Rossetti, and the poets of the nineties," he came upon Symons and so learned of Baudelaire and the French Symbolists, who "held me for unforgettable hours." Baudelaire, Gautier, and Flaubert, translations of whose work he found not in the Harvard Union but in the Boston Public Library, became his models: these could be "read and reread for the sake of their perfect craftsmanship alone, their supreme aesthetic delight, rather than for their social value or for any message of importance they may speak to mankind." In Flaubert's *Trois Contes*, Gautier's *Emaux et Camées*, and "in Baudelaire's incomparable *Fleurs du Mal*," Fletcher found "a world of intense aesthetic sensation." When he came to England in 1913, three years after discovering these poets, he found himself in what now appeared to be the mainstream. "I had rushed headlong via English romanticism and French symbolism into modernity," he remembered.

Shortly after he arrived in London, Fletcher published his first five volumes of verse. These identify his own point of departure. They are virtually handbooks of "baudelairism." Fletcher and Squire, who were to take up opposite sides in the poetic wars of the early twentieth century, set out, though in different countries, from the same texts. Fletcher's books—*Fire and Wine Fool's Gold*, *The Book of Nature*, *The Dominant City* (1911–1912) and *Visions of the Evening*—are enthusiastically and openly derivative. They make *his* tradition their most prominent feature. *Fool's Gold* is dedicated to "Mes 'Poetes [sic] Maudits'" and *The Dominant City* to "The French Poets of To-Day." *Visions of the Evening*, which announces that its author is "a symbol of perverse art," opens with a poem dedicated "To The Immortal Memory of Charles Baudelaire." It takes its imagery and themes from Swinburne:

> Baudelaire, green flower that sways
> Over the morass of misery
> Painfully, for days on days,
> Till it falls, without a sigh.

Les Fleurs du Mal are a "clarion call, / To the Judgment held on high." The emotional temperature in these poems is elevated, and several of them—"Blasphemy," "Sin," "Revolt," "Midnight Prayer," "The Descent into Hell"—manifest their ancestry in their very titles: it was of course not Fletcher, but Baudelaire, who had become "a symbol of perverse art." And for Fletcher, just after he arrived in London, as for Symons, until the end of his life, Baudelaire, the perverse, *was* the modern poet. When, in *The Dominant City*, Fletcher writes, "Last night I lay disgusted, sick at heart, / Beside a sodden woman of the street: / Who drowsed, oblivious of the dreadful mart, / Her outraged body and her blistered feet," he is reviving the vocabulary and the iconography of "Une nuit que j'étais près d'une affreuse juive," the thirty-second poem of *Les Fleurs du Mal*, to which the young Squire had been intensely attracted, which he had translated, and which he had subsequently rejected, in middle-aged embarrassment.

Fletcher, like Squire, withdrew his earliest volumes from circulation shortly after they had been published, and so he extended the list of English "Baudelairean" books that had retreated from the public gaze. The books, however, index a well-established convention of Baudelaire borrowings, and what is most important about them in the present context is that their precisely derivative character passed unnoticed by some of Fletcher's most innovating contemporaries. Pound took pains to point out that Fletcher was above all not an imitator: he had faults, Pound said, but these at least were "mostly his own" and they gained him "such distinction as belongs to a man who dares to have his own faults, who prefers his own to those of anyone else." He was, Pound insisted, a man of his time: "I do not think Mr. Fletcher is an imitator, he is influenced, if you like, as all the younger Frenchmen are influenced. If you ask south of the channel *à quoi rêvent les jeunes gens?* you might find that their reveries are not unlike those of Mr. Fletcher."

A similar retrospective rebellion appears in the poems of F. S. Flint, and it is, like Fletcher's, precisely rooted. More than any other Imagist, Flint held the French to be the touchstone of modernity; more than any other Englishman, he was in touch with the French modernists. His works commanded the highest respect of his contemporaries. The Poetry Bookshop published his *Cadences* and advertised his work alongside that of Aldington and Harold Monro; Amy Lowell's Imagist anthologies gave him more space than any other poet save Aldington; *The Egoist*, *The Anglo-French Review*, *The English Review*, *The New Age*, and *Poetry and Drama* published his poems. May Sinclair thought that *Otherworld Cadences* was a landmark in the development of modern poetry; Ford Madox Hueffer found Flint's poems more compelling than those of any other Imagist; and Harold Monro wrote that his sincerity "of thought, originality of mind, and fertility of imagination make his work important to the student of modern poetry."

But Flint's poems, too, like Fletcher's, are striving to be born. "Yet still we are troubled and torn," he might have said with Dowson, "By ennui, spleen and regret." The world of his poems is often a "mephitic hell of dullness and stagnation," and he frequently seeks to convey a familiar, tormenting *ennui* in figures of enclosure, paralysis, rain, decay, débris, and death. The stock of images comes to him from Baudelaire's *spleen* poems, which document the settling in of solipsism, the imprisonment of the mind. "Silence sings all around me;" Flint writes. "My head is bound with a band; / Outside in the street, a few footsteps; / A clock strikes the hour." The central formal feature of Flint's poetic thought, a characteristic contrast between the deathly solitude of the isolated poet and a dreamed, paradisal escape, comes from the same source, and Flint, like Baudelaire, makes the contrast underline the bitterness of the poet's real circumstances. But while Baudelaire uses it to expose the double nature of the imagination, which turns the poet into a "matelot ivrogne, inventeur d'Amériques / Dont le mirage rend le gouffre plus amer," Flint makes it serve the purposes of his social protest, his anguished attack on what Robert Graves, discussing Aldington, called "the dreariness, obscenity and standardisation . . . [of] the present structure of society." Flint's ironically titled "Unreality," for instance, pits his "dream" ("bloom on the bramble and the wild rose") against the "reality" (a "dull, drab room, in a drab, noisy street") of a degraded world; and his "Once in Autumn," which echoes in its opening line the first stanza of "Une Charogne," establishes a similar contrast for a similar, bitterly critical, effect.

What Richard Aldington took from his predecessors—an idea of the beautiful and an attitude toward the relationship of the poet to society—confirmed him in an idea of aesthetic isolation. He identified himself explicitly with the "aesthetes," as he called them, and throughout his career he defended their causes. He saw Dowson as a heroic example of the "sensitive, almost over-sensitive type of artist" that society cannot tolerate; he attacked "commercial democracy" for its imperviousness to beauty; and he frequently defended poetry against the moralists. "When you find a man whole-heartedly condemning generally every one from Verlaine to Guy-Charles Cros," he wrote, "you can bet your life that that man is an ignoramus who is concealing his ignorance under that easiest of all poses—moral indignation." Often Aldington's early poems show their ancestry proudly. His "Happiness," which is dedicated to "F.S.F.," invokes Dowson in its enumeration of the benefits especially reserved for poets, and his famous "Evening," which is frequently cited as an example of the small perfection sought by the Imagists, borrows its central image—of the moon "With a rag of gauze about her loins"—from Wilde's "Fuite de la Lune." His overriding early theme is that of lost beauty, his dominant tone is lament. Both come to him, filtered through the 'nineties, from Baudelaire and Gautier. In "Beauty Thou Hast Hurt Me Overmuch," for instance, Aldington takes up the question of "Hymne à la Beauté," and he replies with the answer of "La Beauté" (both of which are quoted above. Aldington's borrowings are pointed:

Where wert thou born
O thou woe
That consumest my life?
Whither comest thou?

Toothed wind of the seas,
No man knows thy beginning.
As a bird with strong claws
Thou woundest me
O beautiful sorrow.

That borrowed, cruel, Baudelairean beauty was part of Aldington's *English* inheritance.

Although the Imagists may have written the first "modern" poems in English, then, the "already existing method of expression" that they "utilized," as Hulme put it, their own *point de repère*, was the poetry of the 'nineties. Their beginnings constituted for them a limitation they could not ignore: what they derived from the 'nineties bound them to a paralyzing ideal of artistic isolation and an outworn convention of the beautiful.

The Imagists' earliest sympathies comprise one element in what came to be their modernist dilemma. Their theories added another. In their attempts to gain a foothold in the "alien and external world of material expression," they became uncommonly theoretical: they are remembered more for their "Rules" than for their verse. Their theories, however, failed in coherence. The Imagists worked earnestly in two directions: Flint was proposing an orthodox, intensely romantic symbolism, a mystical view of poetry which was compatible with the oriental and Greek influences at work in the Imagist group; at the same time, Hulme was arguing for a "classicism," which, while it leaned heavily on French symbolism for some of its terms, was in effect a new realism, a poetic positivism fundamentally at odds with the views Flint had derived from Mallarmé. Imagist theory was the marriage of those two views: "Image from T.E.H.; ism from August, 1912, number of The Poetry Review," Flint wrote in the margin of Eliot's copy of René Taupin's study of the movement. But the theory was a miracle of contradiction, and the strain of its internal conflicts shows in the poetry. Of the first Imagists, only Pound, who came down solidly on the side of "the prose tradition," and H.D., who opted wholeheartedly for the pure poetry, were able to resolve them. In Imagist theory, the double focus of Pater dissolves into mutually excluding viewpoints: the nineteenth-century synthesis fails. But in articulating those conflicts or problems in poetry, the Imagists created a context in which Baudelaire seemed more modern, more usefully a model for modernists, than his great symbolist successors.

Source: Patricia Clements, "The Imagists," in *Baudelaire and the English Tradition*, Princeton University Press, 1985, pp. 260–99.

David Perkins

In the following essay excerpt, Perkins examines Pound's and Addington's definitions of Imagism, and looks at representative Imagist poetry.

The Imagist Doctrine

The first public statement of Imagist principles was that printed by *Poetry* in March 1913. Written by Pound, the statement was signed by Flint, who said he had obtained the three-fold program by interviewing an Imagiste:

1. Direct treatment of the "thing," whether subjective or objective.

2. To use absolutely no word that did not contribute to the presentation.

3. As regarding rhythm: to compose in sequence of the musical phrase, not in sequence of a metronome.

The list illustrates that so far as doctrine was concerned, Imagisme, as Pound conceived it, was not so much a special type of poetry as a name for whatever he had learned (from Hulme, Hueffer, Yeats, and others; see Chapter 20) about "HOW TO WRITE" since coming to London in 1908. He was in the habit of scribbling such recipes. In 1916, for example, "the whole art" of poetry was divided (with no reference to Imagisme) into:

a. concision, or style, or saying what you mean in the fewest and clearest words.

b. the actual necessity for creating or constructing something; of presenting an image, or enough images of concrete things arranged to stir the reader.

The historical importance of Imagism, in other words, does not lie in the formulation of a poetic doctrine, for Pound had developed his ideas with no reference to Imagism and continued to hold them after he disowned the movement. The importance was, rather, the extent to which the name, movement, and attendant controversies caused these values to be effectively disseminated.

So far as Pound endowed Imagism with a program distinct from his principles of effective writing in general, it must be sought in the special role assigned to the "image." Pound defined his key term only vaguely. An image is, he said in the same issue of *Poetry*, "that which presents an intellectual and emotional complex in an instant of time. . . It is better to present one Image in a lifetime than to produce voluminous works." Whatever else the "doctrine of the image" might include was not to be published, readers were told, for "it does not concern the public and would provoke useless discussion."

The March 1913 issue contained further admonishments from Pound, "A Few Don'ts by an Imagiste," which helped interpret the program: for example, "Use no superfluous word, no adjective, which does not reveal something"; "Go in fear of abstractions"; "Let the candidate fill his mind with the finest cadences he can discover, preferably in a foreign language so that the meaning of the words may be less likely to divert his attention from the movement"; "Don't be 'viewy'—leave that to the writers of pretty little philosophic essays"; "Don't chop your stuff into separate *iambs*." Such tips were admirably practical, and the offhand phrasing enhanced their authority.

In June 1914 in *The Egoist* Aldington again explained what Imagism was, but the most influential single statement produced in the whole course of the movement was his Preface to the Imagist anthology for 1915. It listed six points, "the essentials of all great poetry, indeed of all great literature":

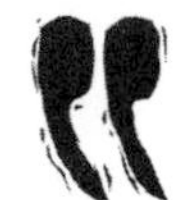

The historical importance of Imagism, in other words, does not lie in the formulation of a poetic doctrine, for Pound had developed his ideas with no reference to Imagism and continued to hold them after he disowned the movement."

1. To use the language of common speech, but to employ always the *exact* word, not the nearly exact, nor the merely decorative word.

2. To create new rhythms—as the expression of new moods—and not to copy old rhythms, which merely echo old moods. We do not insist upon "free-verse" as the only method of writing poetry. We fight for it as a principle of liberty. We believe that the individuality of a poet may often be better expressed in free-verse than in conventional forms. In poetry, a new cadence means a new idea.

3. To allow absolute freedom in the choice of subject. It is not good art to write badly about aeroplanes and automobiles; nor is it necessarily bad art to write about the past. We believe passionately in the artistic value of modern life, but we wish to point out that there is nothing so uninspiring nor so old-fashioned as an aeroplane of the year 1911.

4. To present an image (hence the name: "Imagist"). We are not a school of painters, but we believe that poetry should render particulars exactly and not deal in vague generalities, however magnificent and sonorous. It is for this reason that we oppose the cosmic poet, who seems to us to shirk the real difficulties of his art.

5. To produce poetry that is hard and clear, never blurred nor indefinite.

6. Finally, most of us believe that concentration is of the very essence of poetry.

The statement was directed against undemanding techniques and against conventional, though not necessarily conservative attitudes. Instead of many adjectives and statements, there would be an image rendered in concentrated, exact, idiomatic speech. Instead, for example, of the looseness of Masefield's "The West Wind"—

It's a warm wind, the west wind, full of bird's
cries;
I never hear the west wind but tears are in my eyes.
For it comes from the west lands, the old brown
hills,
And April's in the west wind, and daffodils—

there would be Aldington's "New Love":

She has new leaves
After her dead flowers,
Like the little almond-tree
Which the frost hurt.

As opposed to frequent demands at this time for a specifically contemporary subject matter, Aldington implicitly defended the "Hellenism" of himself and H.D. by invoking the poet's right to "absolute freedom in the choice of subject," a principle to which all would-be Modernists subscribed. Against the expectation that poetry would be metrical, he adopted a point of view that legitimized free verse without decrying meters. Whether verse was traditional or free, there should be "new rhythms" as the expression of "new" and individual moods.

Against the poets and poetic habits Aldington implicitly criticized, his points were effectively made. On the other hand, though this Preface was so strongly influenced by Pound that it seemed mainly a restatement of his views, one finds, if one compares it with Pound's earlier statement, that a vulgarization has set in. "Concentration," the "*exact* word," and "hard and clear" style do not impose quite so severe a standard as Pound's second article, "To use absolutely no word that did not contribute to the presentation" (and this was the essential article in Pound's opinion). Moreover, although Pound was probably not quite sure what he meant by an "Image," he thought of it as a "complex" concretely presented. In Aldington's Preface the concept of the Image is wavering toward a much simpler notion, that of a clear, quick rendering of particulars without commentary. Imagist poems of this kind would of course be much easier to write.

The attacks on Imagism that followed in 1915 raised only two important issues. The controversy over free verse—is it poetry?—was discussed in Chapter 14. Secondly, it was immediately pointed out that Imagist successes could only be small-scale. As Conrad Aiken put it, the Imagists

> give us frail pictures—whiffs of windy beaches, marshes, meadows, city streets, disheveled leaves; pictures pleasant and suggestive enough. But seldom is any of them more than a nice description, coolly sensuous, a rustle to the ear, a ripple to the eye. Of organic movement there is practically none.

One could not write a long Imagist poem. Quite apart from particular issues, however, controversy gradually caused the doctrine of Imagism to become less definite. For the battle on behalf of Imagism was fought by Amy Lowell. Since her temperament was not ideological but political, she compromised doctrine, like many another politician, in order to prevail in the field. In *Tendencies in Modern American Poetry* she characterized the Imagist principles as "Simplicity and directness of speech; subtlety and beauty of rhythms; individualistic freedom of idea; clearness and vividness of presentation; and concentration." With such generalities no one could quarrel, but neither could anyone be arrested by them, as poets had been by Pound's statement in *Poetry* four years before.

The Imagist Poem

Once the Imagist poem was established as a type, it was written occasionally by many poets who were not members of the original Imagist group. Familiar instances are Sandburg's "Fog" and Williams' "El Hombre." Many other poets, such as Marianne Moore, e.e. cummings, and Archibald MacLeish, were strongly influenced by Imagist principles and style, even though they did not write specifically Imagist poems. Because the poems of T. E. Hulme were the first examples of Imagism offered to the world (by Pound in October 1912), his "Autumn" may be used to exemplify the mode:

A touch of cold in the Autumn night—
I walked abroad,
And saw the ruddy moon lean over a hedge
Like a red-faced farmer.
I did not stop to speak, but nodded,
And round about were the wistful stars
With white faces like town children.

The poem was probably written in conscious contrast with Shelley's famous "To the Moon," for Shelley's poem also contrasts the moon to the stars and thinks about companionability or the lack of it:

Art thou pale for weariness
Of climbing heaven, and gazing on the earth,
Wandering companionless
Among the stars that have a different birth,—
And ever-changing, like a joyless eye
That finds no object worth its constancy?

Whether or not Hulme recalled Shelley, his verses are anti-Romantic. Within the Romantic tradition to view the cold and starry heavens in autumn would predictably evoke feelings of melancholy, loneliness, and death. If such feelings are present here, it is only in a complex, indirect, and controlled way. Hulme's "red-faced farmer," unlike Shelley's pale moon, seems well fed, healthy, comfortable, and neighborly, and is humorously regarded. What is conveyed by the poem is not, as with Shelley, a comparison that projects the poet's "moan" (as Hulme would have put it) into the moon but a comparison in altogether unexpected terms. If we ask what is communicated in Shelley's poem, "the poet's feeling of loneliness" would be an inadequate, though not incorrect generalization. In the case of Hulme's poem, the "meaning" cannot be conveyed by a generalization.

Another modal poem, often cited, was H.D.'s "Oread":

Whirl up, sea—
Whirl your pointed pines,
Splash your great pines
On our rocks,
Hurl your green over us,
Cover us with your pools of fir.

The perception of the sea as a pine and fir forest is fresh and apt; the cadenced lines enact an emotional transition; the effect is complex, immediate, and made wholly by concrete means; the poet avoids discursive or generalizing comment. As a final example we may turn to MacLeish's "Ars Poetica," which illustrates much that the Imagist movement taught other poets. A poem, MacLeish writes, should be "palpable and mute"; it should not tell a "history of grief" at length but should evoke it through concrete particulars:

For all the history of grief
An empty doorway and a maple leaf

For love
The leaning grasses and two lights above the sea—

A poem should not mean
But be.

Source: David Perkins, "Imagism," in *A History of Modern Poetry: From the 1890s to the High Modernist Mode*, Belknap Press, 1976, pp. 329–47.

Sources

Crawford, Fred D., *British Poets of the Great War*, Susquehanna University Press, 1988.

DuPlessis, Rachel Blau, *H. D.: The Career of That Struggle*, Indiana University Press, 1986, pp. 12–13.

Friedman, Susan Stanford, "Hilda Doolittle (H. D.)," in the *Dictionary of Literary Biography*, Vol. 45: *American Poets, 1880–1945*, Gale Research, 1986, pp. 115–49.

Harmer, J. B., *Victory in Limbo, Imagism 1908–1917*, St. Martin's Press, 1975.

Hughes, Glenn, *Imagism and the Imagists*, Humanities Press, 1960.

Perkins, David, *A History of Modern Poetry: From the 1890s to the High Modernist Mode*, Harvard University Press, Belknap Press, 1976.

Smith, Richard Eugene, *Richard Aldington*, Twayne Publishers, 1977.

Further Reading

Bergson, Henri, *An Introduction to Metaphysics*, translated by T. E. Hulme, Liberal Arts Press, 1949.

Hulme is credited with creating the initial philosophy behind the Imagism movement. His inspiration came from two sources, the symbolist poets in France and Bergson's metaphysics philosophy. This could be considered the book that started it all.

Carpenter, Humphrey, *A Serious Character: The Life of Ezra Pound*, Houghton Mifflin, 1988.

After meeting with T. E. Hulme, Pound formulated Hulme's ideas and organized the Imagism movement around them. Although Pound's poetry is not totally representative of the imagist tenets, his writing was influenced by the movement that he started. As one of the most noted American poets, the reading of his life story offers an interesting background for the study of American poetry.

De Chasca, Edmund S., *John Gould Fletcher and Imagism*, University of Missouri Press, 1978.

De Chasca studies Fletcher's poetry and offers his interpretations and criticisms of this American imagist poet.

Doolittle, Hilda, *HERmione*, W. W. Norton and Company, 1981.

This is a semi-autobiographical novel about Doolittle's life during her twenties. At this time she was torn between old definitions of herself and her newfound world that included living in a foreign land, working with very powerful poets, and experimenting with sexuality. In this work, she discusses her relationship with Ezra Pound and her bisexuality and offers a vivid portrayal of her inner psychology.

Eliot, T. S., Aldous Huxley, and F. S. Flint, *Three Critical Essays on Modern English Poetry*, 1920, reprint, Folcroft Library Editions, 1974.

The word *modern* in the title of this book can not be taken at face value as it was originally written in 1920. When these three exceptional and well-respected writers refer to modern poetry, they mean the beginning of the modernist period, which means that imagist poetry is discussed. Eliot offers a brief criticism of poetry in general; Huxley discusses the subject matter of poetry; and Flint writes about the art of writing, especially as affected by the tenets of imagism.

Healey, E. Claire, and Keith Cushman, eds., *Letters of D. H. Lawrence and Amy Lowell, 1914–1925*, Black Sparrow Press, 1985.

Lowell was the major spokesperson for the Imagism movement, and Lawrence, although not one of the major imagists, was affected by the imagist poets. Their correspondence offers the reader an inside look into their private discussions about American and British poetry at the turn of the century as well as their reflections on the movement.

Kirby-Smith, H. T., *Origins of Free Verse*, University of Michigan Press, 1996.

One of the major controversies both in Britain and in the United States concerning the Imagism movement was the discussion of the use of free verse. This book offers an overview of the use of this form and tries to answer some of the questions that free verse has aroused: can free verse be categorized? or what is a prose poem?

Quennell, Peter, *Baudelaire and the Symbolists*, Weidenfeld and Nicolson, 1954.

To better understand what Imagism was all about, it is best to comprehend the forces and influences that preceded this movement. Most of the imagist poets were heavily influenced by the French poets, and this book offers a historic perspective of some of the best of the nineteenth-century French poets and their Symbolism movement.

Magic Realism

Movement Origin

c. 1940

Magic Realism is a literary movement associated with a style of writing or technique that incorporates magical or supernatural events into realistic narrative without questioning the improbability of these events. This fusion of fact and fantasy is meant to question the nature of reality as well as call attention to the act of creation. By making lived experience appear extraordinary, magical realist writers contribute to a re-envisioning of Latin-American culture as vibrant and complex. The movement originated in the fictional writing of Spanish American writers in the mid-twentieth century and is generally claimed to have begun in the 1940s with the publication of two important novels: *Men of Maize* by Guatemalan writer Miguel Angel Asturias and *The Kingdom of This World* by Cuban writer Alejo Carpentier. What is most striking about both of these novels is their ability to infuse their narratives with an atmosphere steeped in the indigenous folklore, cultural beliefs, geography, and history of a particular geographic and political landscape. However, at the same time that their settings are historically correct, the events that occur may appear improbable, even unimaginable. Characters change into animals, slaves are aided by the dead, time reverses and moves backward, while other events occur simultaneously. Thus, magic realist works present the reader with a perception of the world where nothing is taken for granted and where anything can happen.

The fantastical qualities of this style of writing were heavily influenced by the surrealist movement in Europe of the 1920s and literary avant-gardism

as well as by the exotic natural surroundings, native and exiled cultures, and tumultuous political histories of Latin America. Although other Latin America writers such as Jorge Luis Borges, Carlos Fuentes, and Julio Cortazar used elements of magic and fantasy in their work, it was not until the publication of Gabriel García Márquez's *One Hundred Years of Solitude* in English in 1970 that the movement became an international phenomenon. Subsequently, women writers like Isabel Allende from Chile and Laura Esquivel from Mexico have become part of this movement's more recent developments, contributing a focus on women's issues and perceptions of reality. Since its inception, Magic Realism has become a technique used widely in all parts of the world. Thus, writers such as Salman Rushdie, Toni Morrison, and Sherman Alexie have recently been added to the magic realist canon of writers because of their use of magical elements in real-life historical settings.

Representative Authors

Isabel Allende (1942–)

Isabel Angelica Allende was born on August 2, 1942, in Lima, Peru, the daughter of a Chilean diplomat, Tomas, and his wife, Francisca. They later moved to Chile, where Isabel attended a private school. Afterwards, she worked for a United Nations development organization before becoming a journalist in Santiago. Allende's most notable family member was her uncle, the Chilean president Salvador Allende, who was assassinated in 1973 as part of a military coup. This event heavily influenced Allende, who commented in an interview later that she divided her life before and after the day of her uncle's assassination. Her first novel, *La casa de los espíritus* (*The House of the Spirits*), published in 1982, won a number of international awards in Mexico, Germany, France, and Belgium. In the mid-1980s, Allende moved to the United States where she has taught creative writing at various universities. In 1985, an English translation of her first novel, *The House of the Spirits*, was published by Knopf. Since then, she has written a number of other well-known novels, including *De amor y de sombra* (*Of Love and Shadows*), translated in 1987, *Eva Luna*, translated in 1988, which won a number of national book awards including the Before Columbus Foundation award, the Freedom to Write Pen Club Award in 1991, and the Brandeis University Major Book Collection Award in 1993. Allende's most recent novels include *Daughter of Fortune: A Novel* (1999) and *Portrait in Sepia* (2001).

Miguel Ángel Asturias (1899–1974)

Born in Guatemala City, Guatemala, on October 19, 1899, Asturias was the son of a supreme court magistrate, Ernesto, who later became an importer, and his wife, Maria Asturias. He became a lawyer in 1923 and left Guatemala for political reasons, residing in Paris and studying the history of ancient Mesoamerican cultures at the Sorbonne in Paris from 1923 to 1928. In Paris, he associated with members of the surrealist movement, such as Andre Breton and Paul Valery. His exposure to Surrealism as well as his intellectual and political interests in Central American indigenous cultures would later influence his own writing. Returning to Guatemala in 1933, Asturias worked as a journalist, publishing books of poetry in small presses. In 1942, he was elected deputy to the Guatemalan congress and later became a diplomat under Jose Arevalo's presidency. In 1946, he published his first novel, *El señor presidente*, translated in English as *Mr. President*, which garnered praise from both South and North American critics. His next novel, *Los hombres de maize* (*Men of Maize*), published in Spanish in 1949, was not as highly praised but has come to be viewed as his masterpiece. In 1954, Asturias was exiled again due to the establishment of another repressive Guatemalan regime. He worked as a journalist in South America and later returned in 1966, becoming the French ambassador under Carlos Montenegro's moderate government. He was awarded the 1967 Nobel Prize for literature for his commitment to writing about the injustice and oppression of Guatemalan people, particularly working class and peasants. He died on June 9, 1974, in Madrid, Spain.

Jorge Luis Borges (1899–1986)

Born on August 24, 1899, in Buenos Aires, Argentina, Jorge Luis Borges was the son of a lawyer and a translator. He was born of mixed European and Spanish-American heritage and was educated in Switzerland, England, and Argentina. In 1919, the Borges family moved to Spain. However, young Borges moved back in 1921 and began to write poetry and essays for literary journals. He also cofounded a number of magazines before publishing his first book of poetry in 1923. His current reputation is based more on his short stories than his poetry, and it was the publication of *Historia universal de la infamia* (*A Universal History of In-*

famy) in 1935 that heralded his career as a well-known writer of a hybrid genre that was part fiction, part essay. In 1941, his magic realist tales *El jardín de senderos que se bifurcan* (*The Garden of Forking Paths*) were published, and a few years later, it was followed by *Ficciones*, 1935–1944 (*Fictions*, 1935–1944) and *El Aleph* (*The Aleph*). For many years, he worked as a municipal librarian in Buenos Aires, as well as a teacher. In 1955, he was appointed director of the Biblioteca Nacional (National Library) where he served until 1970. By the late 1950s, he was completely blind but continued to publish in a variety of genres: poetry, essays, and stories. Borges died of liver cancer on June 14, 1986, in Geneva, Switzerland.

Alejo Carpentier (1904–1980)

Cuban writer Alejo Carpentier y Valmont was born on December 26, 1904, in Havana, Cuba, to a Russian mother and a French father. He attended the Universidad de Havana until dropping out due to economic circumstances. For many years afterward, he worked as a journalist, editor, educator, musicologist, and author. Involved in revolutionary activities against the dictator Gerardo Machado y Morales, Carpentier was forced to leave Cuba after he had been imprisoned and subsequently blacklisted. He lived in France for many years, publishing his first novel in 1933, *Ecue-yamba-o!*, which faded quickly into obscurity. In 1939, Carpentier returned to Cuba, where he began to write fiction again. This time, with the publication of novels such as *El reino de este mundo* (*The Kingdom of This World*) in 1949, *Los pasos perdido* (*The Lost Steps*), and *El Acoso* (*Manhunt in Noonday*), Carpentier became an established and world-renowned writer. He continued to write short stories, novels, essays, and criticism until his death, from cancer, in Paris, France, on April 24, 1980, where he served as Cuba's cultural attache.

Laura Esquivel (1951–)

Born in Mexico in 1951, Laura Esquivel began her writing career as a screenwriter. Married to the Mexican director Alfonso Arau, Esquivel wrote a screenplay for a 1985 film, *Chido One*, that he directed. They continued to collaborate on projects, culminating in Arau's directing of Esquivel's first novel, *Like Water for Chocolate*. Published in Mexico in 1989 as *Como agua para chocolate*, the book became a best-seller and was soon translated into numerous languages, including an English translation in 1993. The film's release in the United States brought record-breaking attendance to a foreign film. Subsequently, Esquivel has published *The Law of Love* and *Swift as Desire*, in 2001, and a book of autobiographical writings, *Between Two Fires: Intimate Writings on Life, Love, Food & Flavor*. She currently lives in Mexico City.

Isabel Allende

Carlos Fuentes (1928–)

Mexican writer Carlos Fuentes was born in Panama City, Panama, on November 11, 1928. The son of a Mexican diplomat, from an early age, Fuentes was exposed to a number of South-American literary giants, such as the Brazilian poet Alfonso Reyes and the Chilean novelist Jose Donoso. He attended Henry D. Cooke, a public school in Washington, D.C., where he learned to speak English. He later went on to study in Geneva, Switzerland, and followed up by receiving a law degree from the National University of Mexico. Fuentes has written a number of influential and deeply provocative novels that interrogate the notion of Mexican identity. In 1958, he published his first novel, *La región más transparente (Where the Air Is Clear)*, translated in 1964 to international acclaim. With the publication of *La muerte de Artemio Cruz* (*The Death of Artemio Cruz*), translated in 1964; *Aura*, translated in 1968; *Terra Nostra*, translated in 1976; and *Gringo Viejo* (*The Old Gringo*), translated in 1985, Fuentes is currently seen as Mexico's premier author, winning a host of literary prizes in Spanish-speaking countries such as Venezuela, Mexico, Nicaragua, and Chile, as well as making the *New York Times* best-seller list for *The Old Gringo*. He currently lives in London, England.

Gabriel García Márquez (1928–)

Born in Aracataca, Colombia, on March 6, 1928, Gabriel García Márquez is South America's most renowned author. Many of García Márquez's novels are set in a mythical town based on the town of Aracataca where he was raised by his maternal grandparents. For many years, García Márquez worked as a journalist, first in Colombia, then later in Paris, London, and Caracas, Venezuela until pursuing his writing career full-time in the 1960s. In 1967, García Márquez published his most famous novel *Cien años de soledad* (*One Hundred Years of Solitude*), translated in 1970. The publication put Latin-American fiction on the world's literary map, particularly those works related to the movement known as Magic Realism. Although primarily known as a fiction writer of novels such as *El otoño del patriarca* (*The Autumn of the Patriarch*) and *El Amor en el tiempo de colera* (*Love in the Time of Cholera*) and short story collections *El coronel no tiene quien le escriba* (*No One Writes to the Colonel*), García Márquez continues to produce reportage for both Spanish- and English-speaking periodicals. In 1982, he won the Nobel Prize for literature. He has also won the Los Angeles Times Book Prize for fiction in 1988 for *Love in the Time of Cholera*. He currently lives in Mexico City.

Representative Works

Aura

Aura, a novella by Fuentes, was published in its original Spanish in 1962 and later translated into English in 1968. Narrated by a young scholar who has been hired by an elderly woman to write the memoirs of her husband, a deceased general, the novella reveals how the past and present are often interlocked and how time is fluid, rather than progressive, through the figure of Aura, who is a projected ghostlike image of the general's widow at her most beautiful. In this novella, Fuentes's use of the second person "you" is meant to pull the reader into the web-like reality that the scholar is caught up in. He cannot escape the past nor extricate himself from others as his identity slowly transforms into that of the dead general. Because of its accessibility and brevity, *Aura* has been anthologized widely as a classic example of Magic Realism's ability to transform what people think of as reality into something mysterious and grounded in the supernatural.

Fictions

Originally published in Spanish in 1944 as *Ficciones*, Borges's collection of short stories could more aptly be described as essays and parables rather than fiction. Embroidered with images of mirrors, circular towers, mazes, gardens, swords, and ruins, these concise, broadly imaginative sketches are meant to be viewed as allegories of different states of consciousness. Rather than creating fully developed characters and traditional narratives, Borges creates characters who appear to have no relation to contemporary reality but who are, for different reasons, on a quest for some kind of knowledge. Unlike García Márquez, who views the specific historical and political reality of South America as having certain magical or "unreal" aspects to it, Borges uses different settings, historical characters, and fantastical plots as a way of exploring ideas about politics, philosophy, world events, art, and above all the limitless power of magic to envision a better world. *Fictions* offers readers a series of inventive worlds that are intellectually challenging but are not situated in current Latin-American politics and history. Both in its maze-like narratives that often pose questions that are never answered and in its excessive use of details, *Fictions* presents reality as a linguistic puzzle that needs to be obsessively figured out.

The House of the Spirits

Allende's 1982 novel, *La casa de los espíritus*, published in English in 1985, immediately became an international best seller among the literary crowd who had followed the older "Boom" writers like Marquez, Fuentes, and Borges. The narrative follows four generations of an upper-class family in Chile, revealing the political and social upheaval of that country as witnessed by various members of the family. The novel is a reconstruction of history that has been undertaken by Alba, who is a recent descendent of the family and its current social commentator. Its fierce political critique of the Pinochet dictatorship as well as its use of fantastical description and supernatural acts places it well within the parameters of magic realist fiction. As many critics have noted, in tone and content this novel is similar to García Márquez's *One Hundred Years of Solitude*, yet its focus on women as agitators and writers of history demands that it be viewed as a work that is not completely derivative of García Márquez's. Feminist critics have applauded the novel's ability to portray women not as passive victims of political and social injustice but as active resisters to political and sexual oppression through their desire to write about these experiences.

The Kingdom of this World

The Cuban writer Carpentier, one of the earliest writers of Magic Realism, is best known for his novel, *El reino de este mundo*, published in 1949, and later translated into English in 1957. This seminal work, set in both Cuba and Haiti, follows the story of Ti Noël, a slave who recounts the numerous insurrections by slaves who were aided by magic and the natural world against their oppressors from the mid-eighteenth to the early nineteenth century. Its emphasis on Afro-Caribbean life, with its roots in African spiritualism, music, magical and healing practices, reveals the vitality of a culture that refused to be completely assimilated into Western cultural practices. Critics claim that this novel paved the way for a new generation of Spanish American writers who used the novel as a form of social protest that related particularly to the political, social, and physical conditions found in Latin America. The novel can be seen as a fictive extension of Carpentier's essay on "the marvelous real," an essay that argues that the rich cross-fertilizing of different cultures in South America engendered the literature that has come to be called Magic Realism.

Love in the Time of Cholera

Originally published in 1985 as *El amor en los tiempos del cólera*, this novel is another lavishly drawn epic written by García Márquez. However, unlike many of his previous novels and short stories that focus on the political and social upheavals in Latin America, *Love in the Time of Cholera* relates the intricacies of Florentino Ariza's love for Fermina Daza, a love that is requited after nearly sixty years. The novel is a tribute to the long-lasting abilities of love to succeed in a corrupt and unpredictably violent world. The bizarre and unlikely political and social events that become commonplace in *One Hundred Years of Solitude* take a backseat in this novel to a lyrical and deeply affecting portrait of the everyday lives of a group of people who are intimately connected to each other.

Alejo Carpentier

Because this novel lacks some of the political punch and narrative improbability that much of his previous work had, it has not received as much critical attention, yet for many *Love in the Time of Cholera* reveals the same intelligent and forceful wit at work that emphasizes the magic inherent in the everyday.

Men of Maize

In 1949, Asturias published his novel *Hombres de Maize*, which was later translated into English as *Men of Maize*. Although the book may be viewed as too early to be part of the Magic Realism movement, the novel's focus on politics, the effects of colonialism, and the fantastical qualities of reality certainly shares characteristics with many later novels. Influenced by both European Surrealism and the indigenous myths of pre-Columbian Latin America, Asturias's novel reveals the plight of indigenous Guatemalans as their world becomes increasingly subjected to exploitation by the encroachment of whites. The novel's magical qualities invoke indigenous myths of the power of transformation through humans' ability to assume animal shapes. Critics have pointed out that its narrative nonlinearity, shifting points of view, and magical aspects were informed by the sacred Mayan book *The Popol-Vuh*.

Media Adaptations

- On its release by Miramax in 1993, the Spanish-language film *Like Water for Chocolate*, based on the novel by Laura Esquivel, was an instant international success. Revised as a screenplay for film by Esquivel and directed by her husband, Mexican director Alfonso Arau, the film effectively translates the fantastical qualities of Magic Realism to cinema.
- As a series of cassettes produced by National Public Radio in 1984, *Faces, Mirrors, Masks* provides a good introduction to twentieth-century Latin-American fiction writers. Authors represented include Gabriel García Márquez, Jorge Luis Borges, Miguel Ángel Asturias, and Alejo Carpentier. Each tape provides an in-depth discussion of an individual author that includes interviews, music, and excerpts from stories and novels.
- *Gabriel García Márquez: Magic and Reality* is a an hour-long biopic on the life and times of the Colombian author and Nobel Prize winner. The film (written, produced, and directed by Ana Christina Navarro) is distributed by Films for the Humanities and Sciences and was released in 1995. It covers Márquez's life, the sources of his books, his development of Magical Realism, and a history of Colombia. Interviews with him, his friends, and critics are an integral part of the presentation.
- The Modern Word, an Internet resource for contemporary authors, has an informative web site on Gabriel García Márquez at http://www.themodernword.com/gabo/index.html with many links to other related sites and sources.

One Hundred Years of Solitude

A book that put the term Magic Realism into circulation, García Márquez's *Cien años de soledad* was first published in 1967 and later translated into English as *One Hundred Years of Solitude* in 1970. The book, amazing in its ability to cover the intricate lives of several generations of the Buendia family, has sold more than thirty million copies worldwide and has been translated into over thirty languages. Through his penetrating analysis of Colonel Aureliano Buendia and his subsequent descendents, García Márquez provides the reader with a micro-history of Latin America that pushes the limits of what readers think of as reality. His ability to mix historical and political events with fantastical and often outlandish events in the village of Macondo on the Colombian coast has given this book the title of a masterpiece. Although the novel ponders serious questions about the nature of reality and the effects of colonialism, progress, and imperialism on so-called Third World countries, it is also comical and ironic in tone.

Themes

Exploration of Latin-American Identity

A theme that runs through nearly every magic realist text is the urge to redefine Latin-American identity by forging a point of view specific to the events, history, and culture of that region. Therefore, its history of colonization, the importation of slaves and influx of immigrants, the political tumult after independence, and economic dependency on imperial powers like the United States and England that positioned Latin America as inferior and backwards become subjects of investigation that are rewritten and retold from an alternative point of view. For example, Carpentier's *The Kingdom of this World* is told by a slave who is witness to numerous catastrophic and traumatic events occurring in Haiti during the eighteenth and nineteenth centuries. Likewise, in *The House of the Spirits*, Allende attempts to forge a feminine identity within a social and historical framework that covers nearly a century of political conflict. For many writers, magic realist techniques were used as an attempt to break with many of their inherited representations by engaging with oral histories of indigenous people, as found in Asturias's *Men of Maize*.

Importance of Magic and Myth

A defining aspect of magic realist texts is the powerful capabilities of myth and magic to create a version of reality that differentiates itself from what is normally perceived as "real life." This approach to narrative relies on legends and myths from oral pre-Columbian cultures, family histories (both García Márquez and Allende note the influence of their respective grandmother's yarn-spinning on their writing), the narratives of early explorers and clergy to Latin America, and the spiritual magic of African slaves to the Caribbean region. Drawing from these various influences, magic realist writers redraw the parameters of what is possible by invoking legends and myths that have been passed from one generation to the next and that invoke a loss of some kind with the onset of the modern age. Sometimes it is the loss of traditional values, as in *One Hundred Years of Solitude*; other times it is the loss of the intimate relationship between humans and animals. These mythical influences form a collective voice that often acts as it does in *Men of Maize* and *The Kingdom of this World*, as a resistant force against oppression and exploitation.

A Critique of Rationality and Progress

The use of magic and myth in magic realist fiction can be viewed as a critique of rationality and progress. Because many South American countries were economically exploited by countries in the industrialized West, first through slavery and exploration and then through economic imperialism, magic realist writers attempt to subvert the values that dominating cultures privilege in order to justify their exploitation of other cultures. Thus, logic, progression, and linearity are cast aside for a reliance on emotions, the senses, circularity, and ritual. For example, Asturias's *Men of Maize* consistently thwarts the notions of progress and rationality by presenting the perspectives of indigenous peoples as being outside of what most consider traditional concepts of time. Rather than present the reader with a linear narrative, Asturias divides his book into six chapters, each exploring an aspect of indigenous beliefs that counter Western conceptions of time, rationality, and progress. Similarly, *One Hundred Years of Solitude* begins with a sentence that disrupts the sense of time being a logical progression with a distinct past, present, and future: "Many years later, as he faced the firing squad, Colonel Aureliano Buendía was to remember that distant afternoon when his father took him to discover ice." The fast-forwarding of time as well as the memory embedded in this future scene reveals time as occurring simultaneously. The notion of progress and its relation to technology is also critiqued in *One Hundred Years of Solitude*, particularly in its relationship to economic imperialism. For example, the railroad that is finally established in Macondo is viewed as both a sign of Macondo's assimilation into the modern world as well as a metaphor for its eventual exploitation by the North American Banana Company.

Questioning of Reality

Many magic realist writers use language in innovative ways that raise doubts about the concept of reality as well as art's ability to imitate it. For many writers who work within the magic realist paradigm, reality is much more ambiguous and complicated than meets the eye. Rather than create a realistic fiction that attempts to mimic the events and outward appearance of the external world, magic realists use a variety of techniques that force the reader to question the nature of reality. For writers like García Márquez and Allende, reality constitutes both real and imagined acts. Thus, a levitating priest, appearances of the dead, and animals that have transcendent powers all take on a matter-of-factness by those who observe these phenomena. For Borges, reality becomes an exploration of multiple universes and existences that tear away assumptions most people share about observed reality. Reality in *Fictions* is never taken for granted but in fact is often distorted so that what the reader thinks he or she knows is cast into doubt. This approach to understanding the nature of reality assumes that reality is not external from human thought but is created by humans. In this respect, reality and selfhood itself become fragile concepts. For many magic realist writers, existence is a concept that does not have a one-to-one correspondence with observed reality. By subverting the assumption of an observed reality through innovative forms and devices that address the fantastical, magic realist writers relay the message that language itself is unable to provide an accurate depiction of reality.

Topics for Further Study

- Compare Allende's *The House of the Spirits* to Garcia Marquez's *One Hundred Years of Solitude* by researching the histories of Chile and Colombia respectively. How does the use of Magic Realism evoke the specific political and social realities of these countries? What do the histories of these countries tell us about the formation of Magic Realism as a literature of protest?
- Read Toni Morrison's *Beloved* in light of Carpentier's notion that magic realist texts are specifically related to Latin-American history and culture and that the term cannot address imaginative works outside of this context. State whether you agree with his argument by making a case for or against *Beloved* as a magic realist text.
- Many magic realist writers incorporate indigenous people's legends, myths, and rituals into their fiction as a way to disrupt traditional notions of time and space. Read Asturias's *Men of Maize* in light of the Guatemalan oral text *The Popol-Vuh*. What structural and conceptual elements does he borrow from this traditional text to enhance the "ethnographic" elements of his novel?
- The natural world plays a large part in magic realist texts, often providing a richly textured backdrop to the social and political aspects of these works. Research the natural resources of one or two Latin-American countries. What minerals, plants, cash crops, natural formations, and ecosystems are most common in these countries? How have these natural resources become a source of conflict as well as of value to the various inhabitants and outsiders of these countries? Use examples from magic realist texts to help formulate your argument.

Style

Genre

An innovative technique of magic realist writers is to experiment with incorporating different kind of genres into the novel and short story form. Genres are different kinds of literary forms that share certain characteristics. Thus, plays, short stories, novels, biographies, and poems can all be seen as having specific characteristics that set them apart from each other. In magic realist fiction, genres such as the epic, autobiography, historical documents, essay, and oral storytelling are used as a way of blurring the lines between fact and fiction. One of the earliest magic realist writers, Borges, is known for his use of the short story form that uses elements of the essay and autobiography to question the ability of language to represent observed reality. His stories also make use of the parable, a genre found most frequently in the Bible, in which brief narratives stress a philosophic statement about existence through the telling of a story. Other magic realists, such as Asturias, rely on older storytelling traditions from pre-Columbian times and thus incorporate tall tales, nonlinear narrative sequences, and repetitive phrases that are also onomatopoeic: they attempt to imitate sounds they denote. A genre used by Carpentier in *The Kingdom of this World* is the travel narrative, specifically those written during the centuries of exploration in the New World that described in detail the flora and fauna found in Latin America.

Hyperbole

Hyperbole, or overstatement, is a figure of speech, or trope, that makes events or situations highly unlikely or improbable due to its gross exaggeration. Hyperbole is often associated with the folk tale to make an event that may be commonplace appear larger than life. It is often used for dramatic affect, such as to invoke comedy or irony, yet it may also have serious underpinnings. Magic realist texts tend to use hyperbole for both comic and serious effect. In engaging the reader with bizarre and catastrophic historical events that have occurred in Latin America, magic realist authors use hyperbole to dramatize the emotional and traumatic effects these events had on the people affected. At other times, hyperbole may be used to make what is commonplace seem extraordinary and magical. This is a technique that García Márquez uses quite effectively to convey the mystery that ordinary objects, such as ice, for example, can have for those who have never been exposed to them: "When it was opened by the giant, the chest gave off a glacial exhalation. Inside there was only an enormous, transparent block with infinite internal needles in which the light of the sunset was broken up into colored stars." Thus, hyperbole has the effect of making the ordinary appear extraordinary through excessive and outlandish description.

Imagery

Imagery is an essential stylistic device used in magic realist works since the attempt to create aspects of reality that are unfathomable must appear likely through the development of convincing images. Thus, the use of concrete language in detailing supernatural events and conjuring a sensual world that is both mysterious and based in material reality is key. Allende, García Márquez, and Carpentier use extensive description in their works, detailing the worlds they create with sensory images that communicate the mysteries of the natural world. In *The Kingdom of this World*, a description of the sea is like peering into a kaleidoscope: "It was garlanded with what seemed to be clusters of yellow grapes drifting eastward, needlefish like green glass, jellyfish that looked like blue bladders." The wonder and amazement at the varied diversity of life forms found in the New World is part of Carpentier's construction of "the marvelous real." Images of the natural world also pervade *Men of Maize*, in which, as the title indicates, maize is an essential life-force for the people who grow it. Thus, as the maize's sacred powers are destroyed by outsiders, the traditional ways of the Indians are eroded.

Point of View

A main feature of magic realist writing is its attempt to incorporate numerous points of view into their narrative, many of which are drawn from popular or folk tales and are thus based more on popular understanding of events rather than originating from a specific character. Point of view traditionally investigates the formal dimensions of how a story is told and who is telling it. Magic realist texts often subvert these traditional notions of who is telling a story by presenting different versions of a particular event through a collective perspective, thus raising the question of which version is true. For example, in *One Hundred Years of Solitude*, the disappearance of Remedios the Beauty is described as having two versions. The more descriptive one that is promoted by Remedios's family is that she ascended into heaven, holding her bed sheets tightly in her hand, whereas the more mundane story has Remedios running off with a suitor. However, because the village people of Macondo believe the family's story, it is that version that becomes privileged despite its outlandish cast. Thus, point of view in this context suggests that reality is ascribed not by any sense of rationality but by what people tend to believe.

Movement Variations

Once writers like Asturias and García Márquez began using magic realist narratives to critique the role of imperialism (especially U.S. imperialism), it should not be surprising that the style became well known and popular in other regions of the world where writers, readers, and thinkers found themselves in similar political and social predicaments. Thus, Magic Realism has emerged in fictions in various parts of the postcolonial world such as South Asia, Africa, and the Middle East while also influencing many writers in the United States and England. In turn, it has reemerged in Latin America with a particular focus on women's writing.

In the years between the end of World War II and the fall of the Berlin Wall, the political predicament of imperialism and the social catastrophes of dictatorship and underdevelopment were very common throughout developing regions such as South Asia, the Middle East, and Africa. For example, in Salman Rushdie's second and most celebrated novel, *Midnight's Children*, the Indian-born author creates a narrator who is born at the very moment that the British leave the subcontinent and when India and Pakistan are partitioned on midnight, August 14, 1947. This point of departure allows the narrative to relate a series of accounts of the climactic events in India's colonial and postcolonial history from the perspective of a very ordinary Indian family. The resulting effect suggests that free movement of South Asian history does not obey the narrow empirical rules of European historiography and that history is rewritten from the perspective of one born into the legacy left by the

British colonial enterprise. In other well-known works such as V. S. Naipaul's *The Bend in the River* and Ben Okri's *The Famished Road*, narratives are infused with narrative surprises and events that jar the reader's sense of reality.

Meanwhile, in Latin America female novelists revised the traditional genre with a feminist slant in Allende's *The House of the Spirits* and Esquivel's *Like Water for Chocolate*, two novels that focus on the experiences of women and their roles within the family and state. Feminist Magic Realism was combined with a connection between Third World oppression and oppression of African Americans in the works of Toni Morrison and Ntozake Shange and also among Native-American and Latino writers such as Sherman Alexie, Leslie Marmon Silko, and Rudolfo Anaya. In her book *Show and Tell: Identity as Performance in U.S. Latina/o Fiction*, literary critic Karen Christian notes that magic realist approaches to Latino fiction are found in the 1971 novel *Bless Me, Ultima* by Anaya: "Anaya's novelistic portrayal of rural Chicana/o life and folkore, set in northern New Mexico, offered readers access to mythical, magical, and spiritual aspects of Chicana/o culture." However, Christian is quick to note that although influences of Magic Realism are found in contemporary U.S. Latino fiction, it does not necessarily mean that there is a Latino "mystical essence" that derives from Latinos connection to their ethnic roots. Instead, she claims that these magic realist tendencies are used to perform a certain kind of Latino identity that in fact may parody magic realist techniques rather than imitate them.

In another recent incarnation, the magic realist movement has begun to influence Western writers in what is seen as an ironic circling back to Surrealism in the work of Czech writer Milan Kundera in such works as *The Joke* and the Italian writer Italo Calvino in a Borges-like blurring of genres book called *Cosmicomics*.

Historical Context

As a literary movement, Magic Realism was part of a larger cultural development in the mid-twentieth century among a group of Latin-American writers in the Caribbean, South America, and Mexico who contributed to the creation of an innovative approach to writing called "the new novel." Some generic aspects of the "new novel," as defined by Philip Swanson in his introduction to the anthology *Landmarks in Modern Latin American Fiction*, are interior monologues, multiple viewpoints, fragmented or circular narrative structures, and an overall distorted sense of reality. Thus, to understand the social, political, and cultural climate that engendered magical realist fiction, one must first view it as being a reaction to the narrative Realism that attempted to mimic reality. At the same time, "the new novel" arose as a response to the increasing understanding that Latin-American society was changing, particularly as it became increasingly urban and modernized by new technological innovations. Thus, many writers responded to these changing conditions by experimenting with new forms and genres that presented reality as ambiguous, complex, and disorganized rather than orderly and meaningful. This style of writing reached its height in the Boom period of Latin-American literature, a period from the early 1960s to the mid-1970s, in which a number of extremely important works, most notably Marquez's *One Hundred Years of Solitude* and Cortazar's *Hopscotch*, became internationally recognized.

As one literary development among many occurring at the time, Magic Realism focused on the fantastical elements of everyday life as found in imagined communities situated primarily in Latin America. Its specific influences are found in the surrealist movement in Europe during the 1920s and 1930s of which Asturias, Borges, and Carpentier, three early magic realist writers, were exposed to while studying in Europe. In fact, the first magic realist movement was centered in Europe, especially Germany and France where the major exponents of Surrealism were Franz Roh and Andre Breton, respectively. During the 1920s, these critics and their cohorts declared the "marvelous" not only an aesthetic category but a whole way of life. These critics influenced and learned from artists like Max Ernst, whose painting *Two Children are Threatened by a Nightingale* brings together a random association of images to jar the viewer's conventional sense of what the contexts for the images should be. Ultimately, the work of Ernst, Joan Miro, Salvador Dali, and others, as well as the writings of Breton and other surrealist thinkers, sought to utterly confuse the distinctions between art, thought, ideas, and matter.

This interest in an ultimate union of all things was not shared by the first major proponents of Magic Realism in Latin America. This second movement, whose best known figures were Borges

Compare & Contrast

- **1950s–1960s:** Many Latin-American writers rely on aspects of indigenous cultures, especially their customs and beliefs that flourished before the Conquistadors arrived in America, as material for their writing.

  Today: Many indigenous cultures of Latin America are celebrated all over the southern hemisphere through the reenactment of traditional songs, dancing, and music by national and international groups and organizations.

- **1950s–1960s:** The Magic Realism writers mix elements of fantasy and fact, history and mythology as a way of capturing the social and cultural complexity of Latin America and exposing social injustices and political instability.

  Today: A new generation of Latin-American writers such as Elena Poniatowska and Carlos Montemayor rely on documentary realism to expose the contradictions and corruption that make up the contemporary urban realities found in Latin-American countries.

- **1950s–1960s:** Very few Spanish-American writers are translated or taught in English classes in high schools and college classrooms in English-speaking countries such as the United States and England.

  Today: Teaching literatures from India, Nigeria, Latin America, Egypt, and East Asia has become a staple of the English classroom as more and more novels by non-Western or non-English speaking writers are translated and become part of the literary canon.

- **1950s–1960s:** Many Latin-American countries are controlled by military dictatorships that often resort to violence, suppression of rights, and censorship to maintain their power.

  Today: Most Latin-American countries have moved toward democratic forms of government, although corruption and human rights violations continue to exist, especially in countries such as Mexico, Colombia, and Ecuador where drug trafficking creates regional and national conflicts.

---

and Carpentier, both of whom lived as young men in Europe, borrowed from the surrealists' style and shared in their fascination with the fact that a banal everyday object could become magical simply by having extra attention called to it. But these writers practiced their versions of Magic Realism almost exclusively in narrative fiction rather than visual arts, and each had his philosophical difference with the European movement. Borges, a staunch philosophical idealist, rejected the attempt to unify all categories. Instead, he wrote stories and essays that consistently embraced the notion of an orderly universal realm of thought that was confused by a flawed (and utterly separate) world of matter. Carpentier also rejected the surrealists' attempt to impose the magical on everything. But in his rejection of surrealist unity, he went in the opposite direction from Borges. In his 1949 essay, *On the Marvelous Real in America*, which was a prologue to his novel *The Kingdom of this World*, Carpentier argues that the very material history of the Americas is essentially magical (or "marvelous," in his own terminology). Specifically for Carpentier, this magical element comes from the rich religious mixture, heavily invested in magic, which manifests in Afro-Carribean culture. This essay by Carpentier is considered a landmark because it is the first attempt to describe Magical Realism as uniquely Latin American. Thus, whereas Surrealism focused on dreams and the unconscious in creating new kinds of images and experimental writing styles through the juxtaposition of unrelated objects, both Asturias and Carpentier returned to their homelands in Latin America and infused their writing with mythic, historical, and geographical elements found in their local environments.

The historical and political currents that are often an indelible aspect of magic realist writing reflected a variety of social and political ills that individual countries were undergoing or had undergone at some prior time. More specifically, Latin America's history of conquest, slavery, imperial domination, and subsequent attempts to self-govern become the backdrop as well as the primary "raw" materials for many magic realist writers. For example, Carpentier in *The Kingdom of This World* focuses on the slave uprisings in Haiti, which occurred in the seventeenth and eighteenth centuries. Other writers, like Fuentes in *Where the Air is Clear*, probe the issue of national identity in contemporary urban societies like Mexico City or Havana. In Allende's and García Márquez's work, historical events of the recent past tend to appear as pivotal scenes. For example, American multinational companies' entrance into Latin America economies in the late nineteenth century resulted in exploitation, alienation, and sometimes death of workers. The consequences of American economic imperialism is referred to in the massacre scene at the banana plantation in *One Hundred Years of Solitude* in which hundreds of demonstrating workers are killed and thrown into the sea. This scene is based on the 1928 banana strike by United Fruit Company workers in Colombia, many of whom were gunned down by the army. Similarly, both *The House of the Spirits* and *One Hundred Years of Solitude* reveal the rise of military dictatorships that created an endless succession of civil wars and political coups in countries like Colombia and Chile.

On the other hand, a much-lauded event in Latin-American countries, where divisions between the rich and the poor were and still are extreme, was the socialist revolution in Cuba in 1960. The overthrow of a long-standing despot ushered in an optimistic era among socially minded Latin-American artists and intellectuals who were fueled by the socialists' hopes for an egalitarian, classless, and safe society. Thus, despite the many horrific atrocities that many magic realist works depict, the movement's adherents have often been seen as delivering a hopeful message in their work, revealing at its roots a joyful engagement with life that is bound together with the utopian vision that destruction and violence will be overcome.

Critical Overview

As a literary movement whose most well-known writers are from Latin America, Magic Realism played an important role in placing Latin-American fiction on the international literary map in the 1960s, particularly in the United States. As Jean-Pierre Durix points out in his book *Mimesis, Genres, and Post-Colonial Discourse*, the term Magic Realism "came into common usage in the late 1960s, a time when intellectuals and literary critics were often involved in Third-Worldism, civil rights, and anti-imperialism." Propitiously, these same issues are often the underlying themes of many magical realist novels, and thus they were widely read and discussed as significant testimonies that "evoke the process of liberation of oppressed communities." However, it was not just these novelists' politics and commitment to social justice that made their works so well received. In their article, Doris Sommer and George Yúdice claim that Magic Realism's popularity could not be summed up as response to one particular aspect of the works but instead to an array of characteristics:

> Latin Americans dazzled the reader with crystalline lucidities (Borges), moving renderings of madness (Sábato, Cortázar), and violence (Vargas Llosa), larger than life portrayals of power and corruption (Fuentes, García Márquez), ebullient baroque recreations of tropical culture (Carpentier, Souza, Amado, Cabrera Infante, Sarduy).

However, for Latin-American critics, the concept of Magic Realism had been debated for quite some time. In his famous 1949 essay, "On the Marvelous Real in America," Carpentier discusses the importance of "lo real marvilloso" (the marvelous real) as an artistic movement that had sprung from the soil of Latin-American history, myth, and geography. The richness one finds in Latin America due to its unique history and fecund landscape acts as a catalyst for the imagination in Latin-American writers. However, other critics such as Angel Flores disagree. In his 1955 essay, *Magical Realism in Spanish American Fiction*, Flores argues that (Latin) American Magical Realism is distinguished by a transformation of "the common and everyday into the awesome and the unreal." Flores locates magic realist's roots in the aesthetics of European art, particularly Surrealism. Interestingly enough, Flores does not even mention Carpentier's earlier essay on marvelous Realism, which later became influential. However, much later in 1967, Luis Leal put forward a thesis in his essay "Magical Realism in Spanish American Fiction" that resonated with Carpentier's. His claim that Magic Realism is not "the creation of imaginary beings or worlds but the discovery of the mysterious relationship between man and his circumstances" coincides with Carpentier's material definition of Magic Realism as being a confrontation with a specific sociohistorical reality rather than an escape. Thus, a large part of the critical reception of magic realist fiction has been defining what exactly it is in terms of origins and philosophy.

For the most part, critics tend to fall into two camps: those that view Magic Realism as being specifically tied to the formation of a Latin-American literature and others who view Magic Realism as being less about geography, history, and culture and more about rendering a specific version of reality that can be adapted across cultures. For example, whereas Chilean literary critic Fernando Alegría, in "Latin America: Fantasy and Reality," reads magic realist works as a political critique in which "we come to realize [that their realism] is a truthful image of economic injustice and social mockery which passes off as authoritarian democracy in Latin America," for other critics, such as Zamora and Faris, authors of *Magical Realism: Theory, History, Community*, Magic Realism "is a mode suited to exploring—and transgressing—boundaries, whether the boundaries are ontological, political, geographical, or generic." What is most impressive about Zamora and Faris's book is the liberty it takes in presenting Magic Realism as a device utilized by writers worldwide yet at the same time publishing key articles such as Carpentier's and Leal's that argue against this global approach.

Other recent critical approaches to Magic Realism that fall within the two poles mentioned are also worth mentioning for what can be seen as unorthodox approaches. For example, the most radical view is taken by González Echevarría, who represents the skepticism that is part of post-structuralism. He states, "The relationship between the three moments when magical realism appears is not continuous enough for it to be considered a literary or even a critical concept with historical validity." Others such as José David Saldívar in *The Dialectics of Our America: Genealogy, Cultural Critique, and Literary History* attempts to forge a pan-American approach to Magic Realism that includes the diaspora of slaves and Mexican immigrants in North America as being part of the collective voice that situates specific histories in a magic realist moment. Lastly, Durix's book *Mimesis, Genres and Post-Colonial Discourse* probes Magic Realism as a specific genre that developed within a sociohistorical postcolonial moment in which writers and intellectuals in former colonized countries began to question the representations and realities handed to them by the colonizers. Thus, Durix is attempting to broaden the concept of Magic Realism by viewing it as an artistic manifestation of the psychological and ontological conditions posed by the European colonial era.

Miguel Ángel Asturias

Criticism

Doreen Piano

Piano is a Ph.D. candidate in English at Bowling Green University in Ohio. In this essay, Piano analyzes the literature of the Magic Realism movement as a new form of social protest to oppressive governments and imperial powers through the use of history and myth, supernatural events, and folkloric tropes as an antidote to narratives of progress and rationality.

In the mid-twentieth century, a literary movement developed in Latin America that expressed a new form of writing that was deeply embedded in the cultural, physical, and political landscape of Latin America. This movement known as Magic Realism has been interpreted as both a literary device in terms of infusing realistic narrative with fantastical qualities and hyperbolic descriptions such as those found in the works of García

What Do I Study Next?

- *The History of Surrealism*, written by Maurice Nadeau and published in 1944 in French, is a classic text on this avant-garde movement. It provides an overall account of the movement and its evolution as well as internal debates about the meaning of artistic production. Leading surrealist proponents like Breton, Tzara, and Aragon are quoted extensively.
- Published in 1967, Luis Harss and Barbara Dohmann's book *Into the Mainstream: Conversations with Latin American Writers* is one of the first books to present interviews with the leading writers of the Spanish-American Boom period. Interviews with Asturias, Borges, Cortazar, Fuentes, García Márquez and Vargas Llosa are included.
- *Landmarks in Modern Latin American Fiction*, edited by Philip Swanson, provides a variety of essays on notable twentieth-century Latin American authors. Included are essays on magical realist authors like García Márquez and Borges as well as on avant-garde writers like Cortazar and Rulfo. This collection reveals a range of Latin-American literary styles and traditions that Latin American writers were working in during the Boom period.
- Based on an exhibition of Latin-American art at the Museum of Modern Art in 1993, the book *Latin American Artists of the Twentieth Century*, edited by Waldo Rasmussen, reveals a range of essays that focus on the previous century's visual trends found in different parts of Latin America. Particularly relevant may be the essays that focus on Surrealism and its connection to artistic movements in Latin America.
- Twenty five years ago, Paraguayan writer Eduardo Galeano wrote a highly engaging social and political analysis of Latin-American history entitled *Open Veins of Latin America* that is still a definitive poetic and historical work on the area's colonial and postcolonial past, particularly as it relates to United States foreign policy.
- A 1999 article by Jon Anderson in the *New Yorker Magazine* titled "The Power of Gabriel García Márquez" provides a current profile of this prolific author within the current political and social context of his homeland, Colombia.
- Naomi Lindstrom's book of literary criticism, *Twentieth-Century Spanish American Fiction* (1994), covers each period of Latin-American literature extensively from the beginning to the end of the century. She reveals important works in their historical context while providing in-depth discussions of adherents to specific movements such as Realism, Modernism, Magical Realism, Avant-Gardism, Boom and Post-Boom literature.

Márquez, Allende, and Carpentier as well as an attitude that, as critic John Brushwood notes, is the reaffirmation of the novelist's right to invent reality, to make up his story rather than copy what he has observed. Thus, Magic Realism can be viewed as both a political and aesthetic movement in its attempt to forge new formalistic developments in literature at the same time that it addresses social and political issues.

One of the most daring innovators of magic realist fiction is Borges, author of *The Garden of Forking Paths* and *Fictions*, who not only questions the limits of what is known as reality but who questions the possibility of language to depict it accurately. His wide-ranging experimental forms of writing explore chance, coincidence, and fate as essential elements of a reality that needs to be figured out. Thus, his preoccupation with images such as labyrinths and mazes attest to his construction of a puzzling universe that has an order to it, but one that must be figured out. His numerous short fictions, however, are less concerned with the physical geographies and political landscape of Latin America than other magic realists' works are. In fact, although he is viewed as part of the magic realist movement, he is more concerned with different kinds of settings as a way to probe metaphysical questions about the nature of reality. Thus, although he shared many of the aesthetic aspects of Magic Realism such as innovative structure and uses of time, fragmented narratives, and shifting points of view, it is the later writers such as Asturias, Carpentier, Fuentes, and García Márquez who were more involved in invoking fantastical elements within a realist depiction of Latin America.

Therefore, although the fantastical elements of Magic Realism are its most notable feature, the importance of setting, particularly the social and political climate of Latin America, is not to be dismissed. In his introduction to *Landmarks in Modern Latin American Fiction*, editor Philip Swanson argues that "Magical realism is based around the idea that Latin American reality is somehow unusual, fantastic, or marvelous because of its bizarre history and because of its varied ethnological make-up." The observation that Magic Realism was a literature that stemmed specifically from Latin America was first delineated in Carpentier's ground-breaking essay "The Marvelous Real in America," which ends on this note: "After all, what is the entire history of America if not a chronicle of the marvelous real?" Thus, the fantastical elements these writers use are intimately situated in the physical and historical realities in which their works take place. García Márquez makes this clear in *The Fragrance of Guava* when he states:

> The history of the Caribbean is full of magic—a magic brought by black slaves from Africa but also by Swedish, Dutch and English pirates who thought nothing of setting up an Opera House in New Orleans or filling women's teeth with diamonds.

His comment intimates how the particular ambience of Latin America engendered acts of radical imagination that were not confined to the literary.

That Latin-American culture is a product of numerous cultural influences and powerful forces is revealed most powerfully in García Márquez's *One Hundred Years of Solitude*, a work that probes the very question of what is real and what is not. His use of traditional storytelling techniques and reliance on historical events points to an implicit conclusion that it is more a matter of point of view than the existence of facts that constitutes reality. For example, although the massacre of thousands of banana strikers in Macondo that takes place in the novel, based on a historic confrontation between the American multinational company United Fruit Company and the local workers, is witnessed by the sole survivor Jose Arcadio Segundo, his story is discredited, the event erased from history because of the power of the military to determine which version of history should be written.

That power has been dictated from the top down in Latin-American history, first through the conquistadors, then the colonizers, and more recently through the rise of military dictatorships, has inspired writers such as Carpentier, Asturias, Allende, and García Márquez to use literature as a method of telling a different version of history, one that critiques progress and rationality and that protests social injustices, especially as it is directed toward those most vulnerable—the working poor, peasants, indigenous peoples, and slaves. David Danow's observation that Magical Realism manages to present a view of life that exudes a sense of energy and vitality in a world that promises not only joy but a fair share of misery as well reveals the importance of understanding Magic Realism not as simply a way to make stories appear fantastical like traditional ghost stories emerged as a radical artistic response to the complex history that envelopes Latin America. In fact, another form of novelistic genre that magic realist writers engage in is called "the dictator novel," which may or may not invoke magical elements. García Márquez's *The Autumn of the Dictator*, Asturias's *Mr. President*, and Carpentier's *Reasons of State* are all examples of another form of "protest" novel that has emerged in Latin-American literature.

Magic realist writers incorporate innovative narrative techniques to convey an alternative view of history by borrowing aspects of traditional storytelling devices as well as avant-garde experimental writing. James Higgins, in his essay "Gabriel Garcia Marquez," poses the theory that magic realists' use of hyperbole and/or linguistic exaggeration is linked to traditional forms of storytelling such as the "folk tale" and preliterate forms like the epic. Using the "tall tale" provides an alternative perspective of historical events from the point of view of "the people." In other words, "it permits a rural society to give expression to itself in terms of its own cultural experience." Creating a "people's history" has the effect of raising doubts about historical accounts that appear rational and sequentially ordered by providing a point

"Emphasizing the fantastical qualities of reality allows for a blurring of fact and fiction where the quest for truth is discerned as being beyond the mere surface of things."

of view that may disrupt the appearance of an orderly universe.

Although the narrative's point of view may shift from one character to another through omniscience, by focusing on local settings or specific histories, these writers project a version of history that is polyphonic, using a number of points of view to create multiple and sometimes conflicting histories. In Asturias's *Men of Maize*, the narrative structure of the novel is divided into six parts and an epilogue that creates a shifting point of view. The disruptive breaks in point of view prohibit traditional notions of cause and effect and reveal a concept of time that is recursive, revealing that the injustices occurring to indigenous peoples continue despite occasional moments of resistance. Thus, the history of conquest and colonization is one that continues to be present in the lives of indigenous people who are supposedly "free" of this history.

This presentation of time as nonlinear raises questions about the art of storytelling, particularly as it relates to the construction of a collective, and not individual, voice. García Márquez, Allende, and Asturias tend to view the stories told by families and communities as true rather than to weigh their truth-value against objective notions of reality. In many magic realist works, truth lies in a community's agreement of what constitutes reality rather than its ability to convey logical reasoning about certain events. Thus, extraordinary events in *One Hundred Years of Solitude* such as the levitation of Father Nicanor Reyna, the ascension of Remedios the Beauty into heaven, and the birth of a child with a pig's tail are as common as ice that is discovered and delighted over in Macondo. As Zamora and Faris note:

> Texts labeled magical realist draw upon cultural systems that are no less than those upon which traditional literary realism draws—often non-Western cultural systems that privilege mystery over empiricism, empathy over technology, tradition over innovation.

Emphasizing the fantastical qualities of reality allows for a blurring of fact and fiction where the quest for truth is discerned as being beyond the mere surface of things.

What becomes most clear in reading the works of magic realists is that a reconfiguration of the relationship between artists and society has occurred. A more recent fictional work by Allende, *The House of the Spirits*, illustrates this point succinctly by having one of the narrators of the novel, Alba, chronicle not just her family's history over four centuries, but the history of a nation that has not yet been told. In her book *Twentieth-Century Spanish American Fiction*, Naomi Lindstrom claims that "[t]he long-standing association between social criticism in literature and realistic representation began to be questioned by writers who found stylized, mythical, and magical modes the best vehicle for their artistic statements about society." Thus, although magic realist writers were, like their narrative realism predecessors, social critics particularly concerning freedom from oppression, their approach incorporated elements of traditional forms of storytelling as well as new technical innovations that engaged in questioning the assumptions of an observed reality and that embarked on a new form of social criticism.

Source: Doreen Piano, Critical Essay on Magic Realism, in *Literary Movements for Students*, The Gale Group, 2003.

William Spindler

In the following essay, Spindler explores the origination of the term "Magic Realism," and attempts "to put forward a framework that will incorporate the different manifestations of Magic Realism into one single model."

Magic realism is commonly associated with Latin American novelists such as Gabriel García Márquez, Alejo Carpentier, Isabel Allende and Miguel Angel Asturias. The term, however, originated in Europe in the 1920s when it was applied not to literature, but to painting. Since then, critics have made use of the term when dealing with various art forms including, more recently, cinema. The lack of an agreed definition and the proliferation of its use in various contexts have resulted in confusion. This, in turn, has led to the indiscriminate use of the term to describe almost any work of literature or art that somehow departs from the established canons of realism.

Despite terminological and conceptual problems, which have persuaded a number of critics to abandon it, the term continues to have, in Fredric Jameson's words, "a strange seductiveness." Furthermore, it can be argued, as I do, that Magic Realism, properly defined, is a term that describes works of art and fiction sharing certain identifiable thematic, formal and structural characteristics, and that these characteristics justify it being considered an aesthetic and literary category in its own right, independent of others such as the Fantastic and Surrealism, with which it is often confused. This article attempts to put forward a framework that will incorporate the different manifestations of Magic Realism into one single model, and in this way, help to clarify the present confusion by distinguishing between different types of Magic Realism, while maintaining the links and points of contact between them.

The first to use the term was the German art critic, Franz Roh. He applied it to a group of painters living and working in Germany in the 1920s who, after the First World War, rejected what they saw as the intensity and emotionalism of Expressionism, the tendency that had dominated German art before the War. These artists, who included painters such as Carl Grossberg, Christian Schad, Alexander Kanoldt, Georg Schrimpf, Carlo Mense and Franz Radziwill, prescribed a return to the representation of reality, but under a new light. The world of objects was to be approached in a new way, as if the artist was discovering it for the first time. Magic Realism, as it was then understood, was not a mixture of reality and fantasy but a way to uncover the mystery hidden in ordinary objects and everyday reality.

In 1927 the Spanish writer and philosopher José Ortega y Gasset had Roh's book translated and published in his influential journal *Revista de Occidente*. The term Magic Realism soon became widely used by Latin American critics in the context of literature. The Argentinian writer and critic Enrique Anderson Imbert, for example, writes that the term was used in the cultural circles of Buenos Aires in the 1930s to refer to European writers such as Kafka, Bontempelli, Cocteau and Chesterton. The first to apply the term to Latin American literature was the Venezuelan writer Arturo Uslar Pietri. At that time, the generally accepted meaning of Magic Realism was still based on Roh's definition.

This painting by Roberto Montenegro is representative of Mayan art

In 1949 Alejo Carpentier published his novel *El reino de este mundo*. In its prologue the Cuban novelist introduced his concept of "lo real maravilloso americano", by which he referred not to the fantasies or inventions of a particular author, but to the number of real objects and events which make the American continent so different from Europe. In Carpentier's view, America's natural, cultural and historical prodigies are an inexhaustible source of real marvels: "¿qué es la historia de América toda sino una crónica de lo real maravilloso?" Furthermore, this marvellous reality was supposed to be qualitatively superior to "la agotante pretensión de suscitar lo maravilloso que caracterizó ciertas literaturas europeas de estos últimos treinta años." In this way Carpentier manifested his disillusion with Surrealism, a movement he had joined while living in Paris.

Surrealism was, to a large extent, a reaction against the excessive emphasis on a rational outlook demanded by the Western traditions of empiricism and scientific positivism. It aimed at liberating the creative forces of the unconscious and the imagination, and was profoundly influenced by the work of Freud. It was the product of a highly developed industrial society where the

> "Carpentier's sense of amazement at the 'marvellous' reality of America, however, can be seen as a reflexion of the European myth of the 'New World' as a place of wonders."

ability to be amazed and enchanted by mystery had been lost. Carpentier's "lo real maravilloso", on the other hand, while taking the Surrealists' fascination with "le merveilleux" as a departure point, presents two contrasting views of the world (one rational, modern and discursive; the other magical, traditional and intuitive) as if they were not contradictory. In Latin America, for example, the rational mentality that accompanies modernity often coexists with popular forms of religion largely based on the beliefs of ethno-cultural groups of non-Western origin such as the Native and Afro-Americans. Instead of searching for a "separate reality", hidden just beneath the existing reality of everyday life, as the Surrealists intended, "lo real maravilloso" signals the representation of a reality modified and transformed by myth and legend. In this, it comes closer to the ideas of Jung, especially his concept of the "collective unconscious", which relates to the fabrication of myth, than to Freudian psychoanalysis with its emphasis on the individual unconscious, neurosis and the erotic, which attracted the Surrealists.

Carpentier's sense of amazement at the "marvellous" reality of America, however, can be seen as a reflexion of the European myth of the "New World" as a place of wonders, based on a constant reference to European experience as a measure for comparison. This is clearly seen in the chronicles of discovery and conquest, from Columbus' diary to Bernal Diaz del Castillo's history of the conquest of Mexico, which according to Carpentier is "el único libro de caballería real y fidedigno que se haya escrito."

Also in the 1940s, the Guatemalan writer Miguel Angel Asturias was moving away from Surrealism towards ideas and concerns similar to Carpentier's. Asturias was interested in how the Maya of Guatemala conceive of a reality coloured by magical beliefs:

> Las alucinaciones, las impresiones que el hombre obtiene de su medio tienden a transformarse en realidades, sobre todo allí donde existe una determinada base religiosa y de culto, como en el caso de los indios. No se trata de una realidad palpable, pero sí de una realidad que surge de una determinada imaginación mágica. Por ello, al expresarlo, lo llamo "realismo mágico".

A few years after Carpentier's formulation of "lo real maravilloso", Angel Flores delivered a lecture on "Magical Realism in Spanish American Fiction" to the 1954 Congress of the Modern Languages Association in New York. Published in a subsequent article, it contributed to popularise the term Magic Realism among critics to the extent that it came to overshadow "lo real maravilloso". Flores departed from Roh's original formulation as he considered Magic Realism an "amalgamation of realism and fantasy." He included in this category all those narratives which achieved a "transformation of the common and everyday into the awesome and the unreal" and where "time exists in a kind of timeless fluidity and the unreal happens as part of reality." These included, according to him, the works of Jorge Luis Borges, Adolfo Bioy Casares, María Luisa Bombal, Juan José Arreola, and others. Based on Flores' definition, Magic Realism began to be associated with a certain type of narrative which employs apparently reliable, realistic descriptions of impossible or fantastic events (the exact opposite, in fact, of what the original term signified). The terms Magic Realism and "realismo maravilloso" became more or less interchangeable and were applied to an increasing number of Latin American writers associated with the post-Second World War "New Novel".

In 1967 the Mexican critic Luis Leal attempted to return to Roh's original formula of making the ordinary seem supernatural. According to Leal, the writer of magic realist texts deals with objective reality and attempts to discover the mystery that exists in objects, in life and in human actions, without resorting to fantastic elements: "lo principal (en el realismo mágico) no es la creación de seres o mundos imaginados, sino el descubrimiento de la misteriosa relación que existe entre el hombre y su circunstancia." Similarly, the Argentinian Enrique Anderson Imbert rejected the presence of the supernatural in Magic Realism. The latter, for Anderson Imbert, is preternatural rather than supernatural, in other words, it exceeds in some way what is normal, ordinary or explicable, without transcending the limits of the natural. Instead of creating a text where the principles of logic are rejected and the laws of nature reversed, magic realist narratives, in his view, give real events an illusion of unreality.

At this point it will have become apparent that the debate between critics has been provoked, to a large extent, by the existence of two different, and even apparently contradictory, understandings of the term: (i) the original one, which refers to a type of literary or artistic work which presents reality from an unusual perspective without transcending the limits of the natural, but which induces in the reader or viewer a sense of unreality; and (ii) the current usage, which describes texts where two contrasting views of the world (one "rational" and one "magical") are presented as if they were not contradictory, by resorting to the myths and beliefs of ethno-cultural groups for whom this contradiction does not arise.

Usage (i) comprises the definitions proposed by Roh, Leal, Anderson Imbert, and the United States critic Seymour Menton. As a style, it presents the natural and the ordinary as supernatural, while structurally excluding the supernatural as a valid interpretation. Usage (ii), which is the one most commonly employed by critics of Latin American fiction and has now largely replaced the previous one, is based, to a considerable extent, on "lo real maravilloso". In fact, in the Latin American context, Magic Realism and "lo real maravilloso" have now become synonymous and have been mentioned not only in connection with Carpentier's and Asturias' novels but also with the work of writers such as Gabriel García Márquez, Juan Rulfo, Carlos Fuentes, Rosario Castellanos, Juan José Arreola, Manuel Scorza, Isabel Allende and José Maria Arguedas. Usage (ii) refers, stylistically, to texts where the supernatural is presented as normal and ordinary, in a matter-of-fact way. Structurally, it considers the presence of the supernatural in the text as essential for the existence of Magic Realism. A. B. Chanady, for example, proposes three criteria to determine whether a text belongs to Magic Realism or not: firstly, the presence in the text of two conflicting views of reality, representing the natural and the supernatural, the rational and the irrational, or the "enlightened" and the "primitive". Secondly, the resolution of this antinomy through the narrator accepting both views as equally valid. Thirdly, authorial reticence in the absence of obvious judgements on the veracity or authenticity of supernatural events.

Neither usage (i) nor usage (ii) on its own is sufficient to account for all the different examples of magic realist works. Usage (i), for example, leaves out key novels such as *Cien años de soledad* (1967) by Gabriel García Márquez and *Hombres de maiz* (1949) by Miguel Angel Asturias, because of their descriptions of impossible or fantastic events; while usage (ii) excludes equally important novels such as *Crónica de una muerte anunciada* (1981), also by García Márquez, and *Los pasos perdidos* (1953) by Alejo Carpentier, for they do not include supernatural or fantastic occurrences. Given the existence of these two different interpretations of Magic Realism corresponding to two different traditions, one pictorial and mainly European, the other literary and mainly Latin American, I propose the following typology which will unify the definitions put forward by critics in both continents. Instead of two completely different conceptions of Magic Realism, the two understandings should be seen as two sides of the same coin. There is, indeed, the possibility of a third type of Magic Realism, which I will discuss below. It has to be stressed that there are many points of overlap between the three types proposed, and that they are by no means mutually exclusive. Works by the same author, furthermore, might well fall into different categories. These categories correspond, moreover, to three different meanings of the word "magic".

Metaphysical Magic Realism

This form of Magic Realism corresponds to Roh's ideas and the original definition of the term. Examples of this type of Magic Realism, consequently, are common in painting, where unsettling perspectives, unusual angles, or naive "toy-like" depictions of real objects produce a "magical" effect. "Magic" here is taken in the sense of conjuring, producing surprising effects by the arrangement of natural objects by means of tricks, devices or optical illusion. This approach can be observed in some of the works of Giorgio de Chirico, a painter who had the most important, direct and acknowledged influence on the German painters studied by Roh.

Together with Carlo Carrà, who would later found in Italy a movement called *Realismo Magico*, De Chirico established a style known as *Pittura Metafisica*, which was characterised by its sharp lines and contours, and by the airless and static quality and eerie atmosphere of the scenes portrayed. De Chirico explained the use of the term "metaphysical" for his work:

> it is the tranquil, flawless beauty of matter that seems metaphysical to me, and things appear metaphysical to me when through their clarity of color, the precision of their dimensions, they form contrasts with each "shadow".

In literature, Metaphysical Magic Realism is found in texts that induce a sense of unreality in the reader by the technique of *Verfremdung*, by which a familiar scene is described as if it were something new and unknown, but without dealing explicitly with the supernatural, as for example, in Franz Kafka's *Der Prozeß* (1925) and *Das Schloß* (1926); Dino Buzzati's *Il deserto dei Tartari* (1940) and Jorge Luis Borges' stories "Tema del traidor y del héroe", "La secta del Fénix" and "El Sur". The result is often an uncanny atmosphere and the creation within the text of a disturbing impersonal presence, which remains implicit, very much as in Albert Camus' *La Peste* (1947), Joseph Conrad's *Heart of Darkness* (1902) or Henry James's *The Turn of the Screw* (1898). Also belonging to this type of Magic Realism are those works that present phenomena of the preternatural kind, in Anderson Imbert's characterisation. Examples of this are Borges' "Funes el memorioso", about a man who could remember literally everything; and Patrick Süskind's *Das Parfum* (1985), where the protagonist is endowed with a monstrously developed sense of smell.

Dino Buzzati's novel *Il deserto dei Tartari* has often been compared to Kafka's *Das Schloß*. It is the story of Giovanni Drogo, a young lieutenant who is commissioned to Fort Bastiani, a fortress that guards the Northern Frontier against a mythical enemy which has not been heard of for centuries. Buzzati describes the monastic regime of the fort where soldiers and officers remain in strict readiness for battle, constantly waiting for the invisible enemy that would justify their and the Fort's existence. Like Kafka, Buzzati presents a world recognisable as within the boundaries of the real. Despite its superficial similarities with the world of the reader, however, the latter cannot help finding it alien and disconcerting. The time and the geography of the events are uncertain. A serene and melancholy atmosphere similar to that of De Chirico's paintings contributes to produce an effect of mystery which is achieved without resorting to the irruption of the supernatural in the narrative. Buzzati's novel, like Kafka's, opens in the reader's mind the suspicion of being confronted with an allegory or a metaphor of something which remains almost within grasp and yet, unknown.

Anthropological Magical Realism

In this type of Magic Realism the narrator usually has "two voices". Sometimes he/she depicts events from a rational point of view (the "realist" component) and sometimes from that of a believer in magic (the "magical" element). This antinomy is resolved by the author adopting or referring to the myths and cultural background (the "collective unconscious") of a social or ethnic group: the Maya of Guatemala, in the case of Asturias; the Black Haitian population, in Carpentier; and small rural communities in Mexico and Colombia, in Rulfo and García Márquez. The word "magic" in this case is taken in the anthropological sense of a process used to influence the course of events by bringing into operation secret or occult controlling principles of Nature. This is the most current and specific definition of Magic Realism and it is strongly associated with Latin American fiction. European critics such as Jean Weisgerber reserve the term "realismo maravilloso" exclusively for the Latin American variety, in order to distinguish it from European Magic Realism, which generally approximates to the metaphysical type. Although this type of Magic Realism is, in my view, synonymous with "lo real maravilloso", Anthropological Magic Realism is a more exact and useful term, as it places it within a larger category (Magic Realism) of which it is a part, as well as not confining it to Latin America, as "lo real maravilloso (americano)" does.

In Latin American literature, Anthropological Magic Realism forms part of a more general trend reflecting a thematic and formal preoccupation with the strange, the uncanny and the grotesque, and with violence, deformity and exaggeration. This tendency, apparent in writers as diverse as Andrade, Arreola, Asturias, Borges, Cabrera Infante, Carpentier, Cortázar, Fuentes, García Márquez, Lezama Lima, Marechal, Onetti, Puig, Roa Bastos, Rulfo, Sábato and Vargas Llosa, has been named *neobarroquismo* by some critics to emphasise its roots in the Latin American tradition of Baroque art and literature. Similar concerns, however, were to be found in the "modernista" movement and especially in the short stories of the Uruguayan Horacio Quiroga (1878–1937). "Modernismo" has had a profound impact on writers such as Borges, Paz, Cortázar and Lezama Lima. Latin American Magic Realism draws on these two literary traditions, but also on that represented by other writers such as William Faulkner and Jorge Amado who, in their writings, show the contrast between the claustrophobic and stagnant atmosphere of provincial or rural communities and the vivid imagination of those who live in them. In both Faulkner and Amado, the lives of the characters are subtly but constantly overshadowed by the slave-holding past of their societies (the Southern United States and North-Eastern Brazil, respectively). In the culture of the descendants of the slaves and other groups that live in contact with them, there are echoes of magical beliefs, half-forgotten but still powerful enough to influence attitudes and behaviour.

Juan Rulfo's *Pedro Páramo* (1955) and Gabriel García Márquez's *La mala hora* (1962) also depict the asphyxiating atmosphere of provincial life. In this, however, they depart from previous Latin American realist novels such as Rómulo Gallegos' *Doña Bárbara* (1929), Jorge Icaza's *Huasipungo* (1934) and Graciliano Ramos' *Vidas sēcas* (1938). An important difference is the existence of a "magical consciousness" in the characters, which is regarded by the author as equal or superior to Western rationalism. This feature links Anthropological Magic Realism to popular culture.

The survival in popular culture of a magical and mythical *Weltanschauung*, which coexists with the rational mentality generated by modernity, is not an exclusively Spanish-American phenomenon. It can be found also in areas of the Caribbean, Asia and Africa where writers such as Wilson Harris (Guyana), Simone Schwarz-Bart (Guadeloupe) and Jacques Stephen Alexis (Haiti) in the Caribbean, the Indian-born Salman Rushdie, and Amos Tutuola and Olympe Bhêly-Quénum in Africa, have resorted to Magic Realism when dealing, in English or French, with similar concerns to those of Spanish American writers.

> La littérature la plus contemporaine des Antilles et de l'Amérique Latine parvient, semble-t-il, à se fixer à la fois dans un contexte national et dans un contexte universel, en faisant appel à des archétypes hérités de la culture traditionnelle, mais aussi en découvrant d'autres au cœur de la réalité moderne.

In fact, the strength of Magic Realism in the "periphery" (Latin America, Africa, the Caribbean) and its comparative weakness in the "core" (Western Europe, the USA), could be explained by the fact that collective myths acquire greater importance in the creation of new national identities, as well as by the more obvious fact that pre-industrial beliefs still play an important part in the socio-political and cultural lives of developing countries. Magic Realism gives popular culture and magical beliefs the same degree of importance as Western science and rationality. In doing this, it furthers the claims of those groups which hold these beliefs to equality with the modernising elites which govern them.

Ontological Magic Realism

Unlike anthropological Magic Realism, ontological Magic Realism resolves antinomy without recourse to any particular cultural perspective. In this "individual" form of Magic Realism the supernatural is presented in a matter-of-fact way as if it did not contradict reason, and no explanations are offered for the unreal events in the text. There is no reference to the mythical imagination of pre-industrial communities. Instead, the total freedom and creative possibilities of writing are exercised by the author, who is not worried about convincing the reader. The word "magic" here refers to inexplicable, prodigious or fantastic occurrences which contradict the laws of the natural world, and have no convincing explanation.

The narrator in Ontological Magic Realism is not puzzled, disturbed or sceptical of the supernatural, as in Fantastic Literature; he or she describes it as if it was a normal part of ordinary everyday life. Formally, the factual style employed in Ontological Magic Realism, where impossible situations are described in a very realistic way, represents the exact opposite of the technique of *Verfremdung* used in Metaphysical Magic Realism.

Examples of the ontological type are Kafka's *Die Verwandlung* (1916), Carpentier's "Viaje a la semilla", and some of Julio Cortázar's stories such as "Axolotl" and "Carta a una señorita en París". This type of text can be interpreted sometimes at the psychological level, and the events described seen as the product of the mind of a "disturbed" individual, as in Gogol's "Diary of a Madman". They should be regarded as magic realist, however, for these "subjective" views are endorsed by the "objective" impersonal narrator, by other characters or by the realistic description of events that take place in a normal and plausible framework. Instead of having only a subjective reality, therefore, the unreal has an objective, ontological presence in the text.

Julio Cortázar's short stories often deal with strange, unexpected or unexplained occurrences. Antinomy, in most of them, is left unresolved in order to produce a disturbing effect on the reader, as in "La noche boca arriba", "El ídolo de las Cícladas", "Continuidad de los parques" and "La isla a mediodía". These stories belong not to Magic Realism but to the related mode of Fantastic Literature. In some of Cortázar's stories, however, antinomy is underplayed by presenting a supernatural event as if it did not contradict reason. In "Axolotl", for example, the narrator explains at the beginning of the story that he is an axolotl, an amphibious creature from Mexico, and then proceeds to recount how he became one. He used to be a man who became obsessed with the axolotls when he visited the aquarium. After studying them intensely for many days, he actually became transformed into an axolotl. No surprise is expressed by the narrator in the face of such an unusual occurrence:

> [. . .]no hubo nada de extraño en lo que ocurrió. Mi cara estaba pegada al vidri del acuario, mis ojos trataban una vez más de penetrar el misterio de esos ojos de oro sin iris y sin pupila. Veía de muy cerca la cara de un axolotl inmóvil junto al vidrio. Sin transición, sin sorpresa, vi mi cara contra el vidrio, en vez del axolotl vi mi cara contra el vidrio, la vi fuera del acuario, la vi del otro lado del vidrio. Entonces mi cara se apartó y yo comprendí.

As in Kafka's *Die Verwandlung*, where in the first paragraph the protagonist, Gregor Samsa, wakes up to find himself transformed into a giant insect, the horrific transformation is described almost incidentally. There is no apparent antinomy between the natural and the supernatural. The statement that the narrator is an axolotl ("Ahora soy un axolotl") is made in the same tone used to describe an ordinary action ("Dejé mi bicicleta contra las rejas y fui a ver los tulipanes"). The ordinary and the extraordinary are portrayed on exactly the same level of reality. Cortázar does not want to titillate his reader with mystery or suspense. No explanation is called for, or put forward, for the incredible occurrence. The reader is simply invited to accept the ontological reality of the event.

Conclusions

Magic Realism is a label that has been applied to a number of works of art and literature at different points in time. At first, it appears that those who have used the term, or continue to use it, have in mind widely different concepts. On closer inspection, however, it is possible to detect similarities and links between the different usages. This makes it necessary, for the sake of clarity, to differentiate between the various types of work being categorised as magic realist. The fact that there is a degree of overlap between the three types of Magic Realism suggested here, and the fact that works by the same author can belong to different types, demonstrate that they are all related in different ways.

The magic realist novels belonging to Italo Calvino's trilogy *I nostri antenati*, for example, are difficult to categorise. Two of them, *Il visconte dimezzato* (1951), where a man is bisected by a cannonball and continues to live in two separate halves, and *Il cavaliere inesistente* (1959), about an empty suit of armour which moves as a result of its own will power, are close to the ontological variety because they depart from an initial absurd situation and then proceed methodically to explore the practical problems caused by it, moving towards a logical outcome (as in Kafka's *Die Verwandlung*). They, however, borrow elements from popular sources such as fairy tales, the Sicilian puppet theatre and the medieval romances of chivalry and, in that way, approximate also to the anthropological type. The other novel, *Il barone rampante* (1957), tells a strange but not utterly impossible story, that of a boy who climbs up the trees and refuses to come down for the rest of his life. Despite its unusual departing point, the novel does not narrate any supernatural events. For this reason alone, it should be included in the metaphysical type, in spite of the fact that its tone evokes the playful and cheerful mood of adventure stories (Stevenson is frequently alluded to), instead of the eerie and melancholy atmosphere of most metaphysical magic realist novels and paintings.

García Márquez's *Crónica de una muerte anunciada*, again, is characterised by the absence of the supernatural. The inevitability of its plot has some of the qualities of classical Greek tragedy. Although this points to the metaphysical, it also fits well with the anthropological, for it takes the view that reality is a collective construction. Some critics have drawn attention to the structural similarity between Magic Realism and the detective story, and although they typically have in mind Argentinian writers like Borges, Bioy Casares and Anderson Imbert, *Crónica*'s concise, perfect, well-knit plot provides a good example of this relationship, being in fact a detective story, albeit in reverse. Finally, the fact that anthropological magic realist novels such as *Cien años de soledad* and Salman Rushdie's *Midnight's Children* (1981) also make use of the stylistic device of *Verfremdung*, characteristic of Metaphysical Magic Realism, points to a formal relationship between the two types. The most memorable example is the scene in *Cien años de soledad*, where Aureliano is taken by his father to see the ice for the first time. Something very ordinary is presented as if it were a real prodigy by describing it through the eyes of a character for whom this is the case.

Source: William Spindler, "Magic Realism: A Typology," in *Forum for Modern Language Studies*, Vol. XXIX, No. 1, January 1993, pp. 75–85.

Sources

Alegría, Fernando, "Latin America: Fantasy and Reality," in *Americas Review*, Vol. 14, No. 3, 1986, pp. 115–18.

Allende, Isabel, *The House of the Spirits*, translated by Magda Bogin, Bantam, 1985.

Anderson, Jon, "The Power of Gabriel García Márquez," in *New Yorker Magazine*, September 27, 1999.

Asturias, Miguel Ángel, *Men of Maize: The Modernist Epic of the Guatemalan Indians*, translated by Gerald Martin, University of Pittsburgh Press, 1993.

Brushwood, John, *The Spanish American Novel: A Twentieth Century Survey*, University of Texas Press, 1975, pp. 157–304.

Carpentier, Alejo, *The Kingdom of This World*, translated by Harriet de Onis, Noonday Press, 1989.

———, "On the Marvelous Real in America," in *Magical Realism: Theory, History, Community*, edited by Lois Parkinson Zamora and Wendy B. Faris, Duke University Press, 1995, pp. 75–88.

Christian, Karen, *Show and Tell: Identity as Performance in U.S. Latina/o Fiction*, University of New Mexico Press, 1997, pp. 121–28.

Danow, David K., *The Spirit of Carnival: Magical Realism and the Grotesque*, University Press of Kentucky, 1995, pp. 65–101.

Durix, Jean-Pierre, *Mimesis, Genres, and Post-Colonial Discourse: Deconstructing Magic Realism*, Macmillan Press, 1998, pp. 102–48.

Esquivel, Laura, *Like Water for Chocolate*, Doubleday, 1991.

Flores, Angel, "Magical Realism in Spanish American Fiction," in *Magical Realism: Theory, History, Community*, edited by Lois Parkinson Zamora and Wendy B. Faris, Duke University Press, 1995, pp. 109–17.

Galeano, Eduardo, *Open Veins of Latin America: Five Centuries of the Pillage of a Continent*, translated by Cedric Belfage, Monthly Review Press, 1998.

García Márquez, Gabriel, *One Hundred Years of Solitude*, translated by Gregory Rabassa, HarperCollins Publishers, 1998.

González Echevarría, Roberto, *Alejo Carpentier: The Pilgrim at Home*, Cornell University Press, 1977, pp. 107–29.

Graham-Yooll, Andrew, *After the Despots: Latin American Views and Interviews*, Bloomsbury Publishing, 1991.

Harss, Luis, and Barbara Dohmann, *Into the Mainstream: Conversations with Latin-American Writers*, Harper & Row, 1967.

Higgins, James, "Gabriel García Márquez," in *Landmarks in Modern Latin American Fiction*, edited by Philip Swanson, Routledge, 1990.

James, Regina, *"One Hundred Years of Solitude": Modes of Reading*, Twayne Publishers, 1991.

Leal, Luis, "Magical Realism in Spanish American Literature," in *Magical Realism: Theory, History, Community*, edited by Lois Parkinson Zamora and Wendy B. Faris, Duke University Press, 1995, pp. 119–24.

Lindstrom, Naomi, *Twentieth-Century Spanish American Fiction*, University of Texas Press, 1994.

Mendoza, Plinio Apuleyo, and Gabriel García Márquez, *The Fragrance of Guava*, Verso, 1983.

Nadeau, Maurice, *The History of Surrealism*, translated by Richard Howard, Belknap Press, 1989.

Saldívar, José David, *The Dialectics of Our Americas: Genealogy, Cultural Critique, and Literary History*, Duke University Press, 1991, pp. 90–96.

Sommer, Doris, and George Yudice, "Latin American Literature from the 'Boom' On," in *Theory of the Novel: A Historical Approach*, edited by Michael McKeon, Johns Hopkins University Press, 2000, pp. 859–81.

Williams, Raymond L., *Gabriel García Márquez*, Twayne Publishers, 1984.

Zamora, Lois, and Wendy Faris, Introduction, in *Magical Realism: Theory, History, Community*, edited by Lois Parkinson Zamora and Wendy B. Faris, Duke University Press, 1995, pp. 1–11.

Further Reading

Asturias, Miguel Angel, *Men of Maize: The Modernist Epic of the Guatemalan Indians*, translated by Gerald Martin, University of Pittsburgh Press, 1993.

This critical edition of an early magic realist masterpiece includes a series of critical essays by well-known critics and writers of Latin-American literature that cover a variety of topics related to Asturias's work.

Bruner, Charlotte H., *Unwinding Threads: Writing by Women in Africa*, Heinemann, 1994.

This is a collection of short stories by African women from all parts of the continent. Divided by region, the book provides a comprehensive view of the variety and diversity of African women's approaches to imaginative writing. Many well-known and new writers are represented.

Graham-Yooll, Andrew, *After the Despots: Latin American Views and Interviews*, Bloomsbury Publishing, 1991.

Collected in this book are interviews, observations, and political analyses about Latin America by an Argentine journalist. Written in a style á la the *New Yorker*, Graham-Yooll has his finger on the pulse of the current literary and political currents of his time. A number of pieces focus on Latin America's leading writers: Allende, García Márquez, Borges, and Fuentes.

James, Regina, *"One Hundred Years of Solitude": Modes of Reading*, Twayne Publishers, 1991.

This informative book engages in a number of readings of García Márquez's masterpiece. It provides biographical and historical context as well as a good discussion of the novel's form and content.

Owomoyela, Oyekan, ed., *A History of Twentieth-Century African Literatures*, University of Nebraska Press, 1993.

A range of bibliographic articles covering African literary production in all European languages represented on the continent. In particular, chapters on women's literary production and on East African English-Language fiction are particularly relevant to Ogot's work.

Parekh, Pushpa, ed., *Postcolonial African Writers*, Greenwood Publishing, 1998.

This is a reference book that covers individual authors of postcolonial Africa, including biographical information, a discussion of themes and major works, critical responses to the works, and bibliographies.

Williams, Raymond L., *Gabriel García Márquez*, Twayne Publishers, 1984.

Williams's book is a literary and biographical account of García Márquez, discussing not only his career as a journalist and writer but providing an in-depth account of his literary output over a period of thirty years.

Zamora, Lois, and Wendy Faris, eds., *Magical Realism: Theory, History, Community*, Duke University Press, 1995.

This recent collection of essays provides an historical overview of the various scholarly approaches to interpreting Magic Realism. Of particular importance are the essays by Carpentier that describe the importance of Magic Realism to the geographic and political climate of Latin America.

Modernism

Movement Origin

c. 1900

"On or about December 1910 human nature changed." The great modernist writer Virginia Woolf wrote this in her essay "Mr. Bennett and Mrs. Brown" in 1924. "All human relations shifted," Woolf continued, "and when human relations change there is at the same time a change in religion, conduct, politics, and literature." This intentionally provocative statement was hyperbolic in its pinpointing of a date, but almost anyone who looks at the evolution of Western culture must note a distinct change in thought, behavior, and cultural production beginning sometime in the late nineteenth century and coming to full fruition sometime around the Second World War. This change, whether art, technology, philosophy or human behavior, is generally called Modernism.

Modernism designates the broad literary and cultural movement that spanned all of the arts and even spilled into politics and philosophy. Like Romanticism, Modernism was highly varied in its manifestations between the arts and even within each art. The dates when Modernism flourished are in dispute, but few scholars identify its genesis as being before 1860 and World War II is generally considered to mark an end of the movement's height. Modernist art initially began in Europe's capitals, primarily London, Milan, Berlin, St. Petersburg, and especially Paris; it spread to the cities of the United States and South America after World War I; by the 1940s, Modernism had thoroughly taken over the American and European academy, where it was challenged by nascent Postmodernism in the 1960s.

Modernism's roots are in the rapidly changing technology of the late nineteenth century and in the theories of such late nineteenth-century thinkers as Freud, Marx, Darwin, and Nietzsche. Modernism influenced painting first (Impressionism and Cubism are forms of Modernism), but in the decade before World War I such writers as Ezra Pound, Filippo Marinetti, James Joyce, and Guillaume Apollinaire translated the advances of the visual arts into literature. Such characteristically modernist techniques as stream-of-consciousness narration and allusiveness, by the late 1930s, spilled into popular writing and became standard.

The movement's concerns were with the accelerating pace of society toward destruction and meaninglessness. In the late 1800s many of society's certainties were undermined. Marx demonstrated that social class was created, not inherent; Freud boiled down human individuality to an animalistic sex drive; Darwin provided evidence that the Bible might not be literally true; and Nietzsche argued that even the most deeply-held ethical principles were simply constructions. Modernist writers attempted to come to terms with where humanity stood after its cornerstones had been pulverized. The movement sifted through the shards of the past looking for what was valuable and what could inspire construction of a new society.

Representative Authors

T. S. Eliot (1888–1965)

Thomas Stearns Eliot was born in St. Louis, Missouri, on September 26, 1888. He attended Harvard, the Sorbonne and Oxford, studying philosophy and writing a dissertation on the logician F. H. Bradley. While in college, Eliot began writing poetry, but in 1908 he discovered French Symbolist poetry and his whole attitude toward literature changed. Ezra Pound read some of Eliot's poetry in the 1910s and immediately decided that Eliot would be a member of his own literary circle. Pound advocated for Eliot with Harriet Monroe of *Poetry* magazine and got Eliot's poem "The Love Song of J. Alfred Prufrock" published in that journal in 1915. Eliot had settled in London at the same time, and married the emotionally unstable Vivian Haigh-Wood. Eliot struggled to make a living, working as a teacher and later at Lloyd's Bank until 1925.

In 1922 Eliot broke through with his brilliant and successful poem "The Waste Land, " although the manuscript of the poem demonstrates that Ezra Pound played a large role in the editing of the poem. "The Waste Land" brought Eliot fame and a place at the center of the burgeoning modernist movement. For the rest of the 1920s and 1930s, Eliot used his fame and his position as editor of a prominent literary journal (*The Criterion*) and as managing editor of the publishing house Faber & Faber to argue for a new standard of evaluating literature. In critical essays and his own poetry, he denigrated the romantics and neoclassicists and celebrated Dante and the Elizabethan "metaphysical" poets. He argued for the central role of "Tradition" in literature and downplayed the cult of individual genius created by the romantics.

For the remainder of his life, Eliot occupied the role of literary elder statesman. He continued to produce poems such as the *Four Quartets* but was never prolific. He became the very model of the conservative, royalist, High Church English gentleman. He died January 4, 1965, the very embodiment of the literary establishment.

William Faulkner (1897–1962)

William Faulkner was born in New Albany, Mississippi, on September 25, 1897, to a family with deep Mississippi and Confederate roots. He grew up in Oxford, Mississippi, and briefly attended the University of Mississippi before leaving the state to seek his fortune as a writer. Settling briefly in New Orleans, Faulkner came under the tutelage of Sherwood Anderson and published his first book, *The Marble Faun*, a collection of short stories, in 1924. In 1929 he published the novel *Sartoris*, his first work set in the fictional Mississippi county of Yoknapatawpha. Others followed, including his masterpieces *The Sound and the Fury* and *As I Lay Dying*.

In the 1930s and 1940s, Faulkner received a great deal of critical attention for his works, but he never obtained the kind of financial success that he sought. Attempting to remedy this, he wrote two sensationalistic books (*Sanctuary* and *Requiem for a Nun*) and briefly moved to Los Angeles to work as a screenwriter in Hollywood. Faulkner died on July 6, 1962, in Byhalia, Mississippi.

James Joyce (1882–1941)

James Joyce is the most important writer of the modernist movement. He produced relatively few works, but these books ranged from poetry to drama, to short stories to the novel that the Modern Library publishing imprint named the most important novel of the twentieth century. His life, too, became the embodiment of many of Modernism's most central themes: exile, the presence of the past in one's life, familiarity with a broad range of cultures and historical periods, and self-destruction.

Joyce was born in Dublin, Ireland, on February 2, 1882, to a lower middle-class Catholic family. His father died when Joyce was young. Joyce attended Catholic schools in Ireland and matriculated at University College, Dublin. During his youth and college years, he struggled with the rigid structures of Catholic school and Irish nationalism. In 1902 Joyce left Dublin for Paris, but was called back to Ireland when his mother fell ill. He left Dublin again in 1904, bringing with him his companion Nora Barnacle, an uneducated but vivacious young woman (whom he did not marry until 1931). For many years Joyce struggled to make a living and to provide for his growing family. Settling first in Trieste and then in Zurich, he taught literature and enjoyed an occasional monetary grant.

During this time Joyce wrote and published stories, poems, and a novel, *A Portrait of the Artist as a Young Man. Dubliners*, his collection of stories, was published in 1914 and immediately obtained the notice of the Anglo-American avant-garde and the disapproval of the Irish literary establishment. *A Portrait of the Artist as a Young Man* (1916) was just that, a stream-of-consciousness narrative of Joyce's own life (barely fictionalized as "Stephen Dedalus") up to the point that he left Ireland. In 1922 Joyce published his masterpiece and the single greatest work of Modernism, *Ulysses*. This retelling of the Odysseus myth through the persona of a Jewish advertising salesman in Dublin is a triumph on every level. The book was immediately banned in England and America for blasphemy and obscenity; it was not until 1934 that it became legal in the United States.

After *Ulysses*, Joyce began work on another long novel, which was simply called *Work in Progress* during its composition. Joyce, by now the leading modernist writer, was living in Paris and had the worshipful admiration of the Lost Generation Americans as well as the more established writers of the city. Celebrations of *Work in Progress* appeared even before any of the work appeared in print. When it finally was published as *Finnegans Wake* in 1939, it shocked readers with its incessant wordplay. It is a very difficult novel, barely recognizable as English in many places, but its intricate structure and brilliant use of all of the English language's possibilities ensure that readers will attempt to decipher it for decades to come. After finishing *Finnegans Wake*, Joyce and Nora moved back to Zurich to avoid being caught in the Nazi occupation of Paris. Joyce died in Zurich on January 13, 1941, following surgery for a perforated ulcer.

Ezra Pound (1885–1972)

In many ways, Ezra Pound was the father of literary Modernism. If nothing else, he almost single-handedly brought the techniques of Modernism to American poets, while at the same time bringing the talents of American modernist poets to the notice of the avant-garde establishment. Pound was born in Hailey, Idaho, on October 30, 1885, but soon after his birth his family moved to the suburbs of Philadelphia. He grew up in that area and attended the University of Pennsylvania (where he met William Carlos Williams and another important American modernist poet, Hilda Doolittle) and Hamilton College. After a short stint teaching at a small college in Indiana, Pound grew tired of what he saw to be American small-mindedness and moved to Venice, Italy.

In Venice, Pound resolved to become a poet. He published a book there, but soon relocated to London. In the decade he spent in London, Pound, through the strength of his own will, created movements and forced himself into the center of those movements. Probably the most important of those movements was Imagism, a school of poetry that explicitly rejected Victorian models of verse by simply presenting images without authorial commentary. In 1920 Pound left London for Paris, where he spent a few years before becoming frustrated by the dominance of Gertrude Stein in the avant-garde scene there. In 1925 he moved to Rapallo, Italy, where he developed a strong affinity for Mussolini and Italian fascism. At this time he also began working in earnest on *The Cantos*, the epic poem that would become his life's work.

Pound stayed in Italy for more than twenty years. During World War II he spoke on Italian state radio broadcasts aimed at American soldiers; in 1943 he was indicted for treason as a result of these activities and in 1945, returned to the United States to face trial. Found mentally unfit to defend himself, Pound was incarcerated in St. Elizabeth's Hospital for the Criminally Insane in Washington, D.C. for thirteen years. Because of the intercession of such luminaries as T. S. Eliot, Robert Frost, and Ernest Hemingway, in 1958 Pound was released

Virginia Woolf

from his incarceration and allowed to return to Italy. Settling in Venice, he published a few more books but by the mid-1960s he fell into a silence. He died in Venice, Italy, on November 1, 1972.

Virginia Woolf (1882–1941)

Born January 25, 1882, Woolf met many eminent Victorians during her childhood. In 1904 she moved to the Bloomsbury district of London, a neighborhood that gave its name to Woolf's literary and intellectual circle. She married the journalist Leonard Woolf and in 1917 she and her husband founded the Hogarth Press, an important literary and cultural publishing firm that published the first English-language editions of Freud's work and T. S. Eliot's early collection *Poems* (1919).

Beginning in the late 1910s, Woolf began to write. She quickly internalized the discoveries of Freud and the literary advances of the modernists and produced a number of novels striking in their sophistication: *Jacob's Room* (1922), *Mrs. Dalloway* (1925), and *To the Lighthouse* (1927). Her novels brought the "stream-of-consciousness" style a new depth and possibility. In addition to her activity in the literary world, she brought her feminist orientation and bisexual lifestyle to the forefront of her writing. In such works as *Three Guineas* (1938), *A Room of One's Own* (1929), and *Orlando* (1928) she expressed opinions revolutionary for her time. However, her own life was not entirely happy. During the 1930s she grew increasingly fearful that she was suffering from a mental illness and would become a burden on her husband and friends. Spurred on by this fear and by her dread of World War II, she committed suicide by drowning on March 28, 1941.

Representative Works

Call It Sleep

Perhaps the most notable example of Joycean prose in American literature is this novel, written in 1934 by Henry Roth, the son of Jewish immigrants to New York. The novel tells the story of David Schearl, an immigrant boy in New York. Using the stream-of-consciousness technique perfected by Joyce in his *A Portrait of the Artist as a Young Man*, readers hear the interior voice of this boy as he grows up poor, watches his parents fight, and struggles with persecution from neighborhood bullies. The novel gained critical acclaim upon publication but was quickly forgotten until its paperback republication in 1964. By this time Roth had given up writing and moved to New Mexico. In the early 1990s, near the end of his long life, Roth returned to writing, producing four sequels to his masterwork.

The Cantos

If *Ulysses* is the most successful and greatest work of the modernist movement, Ezra Pound's long poem *The Cantos* is perhaps its most characteristic. Its composition and contents mirror the ideas of the modernists. It is composed of fragments, of different voices from different times and places. It attempts to diagnose the ills of the modern world, comes up with an ultimately failed solution, and imagines a better world that existed once and could exist in fragmentary form again.

Pound began writing his "poem including history," as he called it, in 1917, when he published early versions of three of the cantos in a litterary magazine. He began working in earnest on the poem in the 1920s after he moved to Italy, and continued working on it, eventually publishing eight installments, until the late 1960s. The poem is an epic, attempting to tell "the tale of the tribe" (civilized humanity) from ancient times to today.

Structured to mirror and include characters from two of history's great epics (Homer's *Odyssey* and Dante's *Divine Comedy*), the poem was originally planned to include 120 "cantos," or shorter chapters. There is no plot to speak of, but the poem broadly moves from hell (literally but also in the sense of an utterly fallen civilization) to purgatory, where historical figures such as Confucius, Sigismondo Malatesta, Thomas Jefferson, John Adams, and Mussolini are introduced. Pound wanted to highlight moments in history where a just and aesthetically appreciative society existed or could have existed. The poem veered sharply back to Pound's own life during the 1940s, when Pound found himself working for the Fascists and ultimately was incarcerated in a mental hospital in the United States. As Pound neared the end of his life and of the poem, he discovered and recorded glimpses of paradise on earth.

Public opinion of the work varies dramatically. Many readers can make no sense of the poem; others find that it contains some of the most remarkable passages in English-language poetry. Critics have been similarly divided. Although the poem is solidly in the canon of American literature and is considered one of the central works of modernist literature, many scholars and academics dismiss it as a failed, obscure, and ultimately fascist poem.

William Carlos Williams

A Farewell to Arms

Ernest Hemingway published *A Farewell to Arms* in 1929. He was already famous for his portrait of dissolute youth in Paris, *The Sun Also Rises*, but this novel was a great step forward in terms of sophistication and importance. It tells of Hemingway's own experiences as an ambulance driver during the last days of World War I; his wounding and convalescence and affair with a nurse. More important, though, was Hemingway's revolutionary technique. His prose was journalistic, stripped of adjectives and any construction that might call attention to itself. Such narration achieved a numbness that reflected the mental brutalization the war visited upon the hero—and the author. Hemingway eschews abstract concepts such as glory, duty, and honor because, like his hero's, his own experience during the war showed him that these were weapons used by people in power to manipulate ordinary people.

After the popular and critical success of this novel, Hemingway became an international celebrity with literary credibility. He continued to write for much of the rest of his life and produced at least two great novels (*For Whom the Bell Tolls* and *The Old Man and the Sea*) before committing suicide in 1961.

Harmonium

The popularity of the work of poet and insurance lawyer Wallace Stevens has continued to grow even as the work of other modernists has fallen in favor. Stevens's first book of poetry was *Harmonium*, published by Alfred A. Knopf in 1923. While modernist poetry written by Pound and Eliot was allusive, drenched in the fragments of previous cultures and other languages, and overwhelmed by an almost angry melancholy, Stevens's work was light and lyrical. In *Harmonium*, Stevens exhibited a verbal dandyism, delighting in the sounds of words and in Elizabethan definitions. He was a direct descendant of Keats and Marvell, whereas other modernists saw Browning, Shakespeare, and Dante as their ancestors.

But Stevens cannot be dismissed as a writer of light verse. His poems exhibit the characteristic modernist fear of nihilism while entertaining the fear that the entire world is simply a projection of his mind. In "The Snow Man," for instance, Stevens listens to "nothing that is not there and the nothing that is," and in "Tea at the Palaz of Hoon" the narrator questions whether "I was the world in which I walked." In his later books, Stevens produced longer, philosophical poems that questioned art's place in human cognition, and by the 1970s and 1980s, Stevens, not Eliot or Pound, was cited as an influence by hundreds of practicing American poets.

The Sound and the Fury

William Faulkner, a Mississippian, began his career as a writer heavily influenced by the regionalist Sherwood Anderson, with whom he worked in New Orleans (in the 1920s, the home of American Bohemianism). But Faulkner quickly outdid his teacher. He created an entire fictional world in which almost all of his fiction was set: Yoknapatawpha County, Mississippi. In this world the past always impinges upon the present, and Faulkner's fiction is full of narrative devices intended to outflank language's need to be based in time. His 1929 *The Sound and the Fury* contains Faulkner's most successful experiments with time.

The novel is the story of the fall of the Compson family that culminates in the suicide of son Quentin. Told by a series of narrators, the stories in the book provide different perspectives on the same events and the reader must compare all of the different versions in order to understand what "really" happened. Most difficult is the narration of Benjy, a retarded boy who has no conception of time. In his narration there is no differentiation between what happened years ago, what happened yesterday, and what is happening now. Faulkner's experiments did not gain him a large audience in the United States (in search of income, he moved to Hollywood in a failed attempt to be a screenwriter) but his influence was vast among Latin American writers, especially such "magical realists" as Gabriel García Márquez.

To the Lighthouse

Virginia Woolf perfected the stream-of-consciousness or interior monologue style in her novels of the 1920s. Her 1927 novel *To the Lighthouse* depicts the Ramsay family, who is spending the summer in a vacation house on the Isle of Skye. Assorted guests, including the painter Lily Briscoe (a character many readers feel is a stand-in for Woolf herself), also come and go. The novel moves from a focus solely on the personal level of the family to a wider focus; the impending world war appears as a dark cloud on the horizon. The novel then shifts time to ten years later as the family deals with the death of one of its members.

Woolf's novel delicately and insightfully pulls apart memory, family relationships, and the effects of death. In a movement such as Modernism, generally so focused on the big picture often to the exclusion of the personal, *To the Lighthouse* stands out as an example of how modernist technique can be applied to the examination of emotion.

Ulysses

James Joyce's novel *Ulysses*, first published in 1922, is the single greatest work of modernist literature and is considered by many to be the finest novel ever written. Joyce spent ten years writing this book, a meticulously detailed day in the life of three Dubliners. The main characters are Leopold Bloom, a Jewish advertising salesman; Molly Bloom, Leopold's wife, a singer who is planning to cheat on her husband; and Stephen Dedalus, a dissipated young intellectual. The story parallels Homer's *Odyssey* but translates that epic journey of ten years to eighteen hours and one city.

Upon its publication—and even before, when fragments were published in magazines—the book was immediately hailed as a work of genius. Joyce's endless erudition, his command of languages and literature and history, his love and intimate knowledge of one small place at one specific time, are all on display in this book. More than just an intellectual enterprise and a small gem of engineering, though, *Ulysses* is a genuinely moving story of conjugal and parental love. Because of its frank treatment of sex and its, at times, insulting portraits of religion and Irish nationalism, the book was banned in Ireland and America. In the United States, it took twelve years for the book to be allowed in the country; until then, travelers to Paris would have to hide the book in their luggage from customs inspectors (who were warned to look for its characteristic blue-green binding).

"The Waste Land"

T. S. Eliot's "The Waste Land," published in 1922, is the single most important modernist poem. Essentially plotless, the poem instead attempts to capture historical development to the present day by use of allusion. Characters such as Tiresias, the Smyrna merchant, and an East London housewife, wander through the poem. London, the "Unreal City" in the fog, becomes the synecdoche for the fallen world as a whole. The poem moves from Elizabethan times to the ancient world to the present and ends, finally, with a small failing voice speaking Sanskrit.

Interestingly, in its original version the poem was six times as long and titled "He Do The Police in Different Voices." When he was still a struggling poet, T. S. Eliot showed the poem to Ezra Pound, asking for his advice. Pound performed what he called a "Caesarean operation" on Eliot's manuscript, telling him to cut the links between the vignettes so that the poem appeared as a series of fragments. Eliot never called attention to Pound's central role in creating "The Waste Land" and it was not until the 1960s, when the original manuscript was found, that Pound's true role became publicly known.

Most critics have seen the poem as expressing a fundamental despair at the sense that, with the loss of all certainties, the world was nothing but "fragments" that are "shored against [our] ruin." It continues to vex students with its difficulty, but even the most basic reading evokes a sense of desperation and loss.

Themes

Technology

In very real terms, the entire world and the way that humans understood that world changed between 1860 (when the modernist period is generally understood to have begun) and 1940. In 1860 the idea of travelling at a mile a minute was but a dream, as was the notion of human beings flying. The photograph was new; moving pictures, much less moving pictures that talked, were only fantasies. Electrical signals being sent through wires was a possible dream, but the idea that voices could be transmitted was fantastic. The idea that voices could be transmitted without wires, through the air, was utterly preposterous.

In 1940 the world was a different place. Machines allowed people to see moving, talking pictures; to travel at more than one hundred miles an hour; to fly through the air; to transmit both voices and images without wires; to talk, in real time, with someone at the other side of the Atlantic Ocean. Humans relied on machines to a much greater extent than they ever had. It is hard today to conceive of a world without powered machines, but in 1860 many people in the United States lived their entire lives without ever encountering a powered machine. By the 1940s machines had made it possible to communicate or travel—or destroy—with much greater speed and efficiency than anyone had ever dreamed in 1860.

The modernist writers, almost as a rule, feared the new technology and left it out of their writing. Joyce set his masterpiece *Ulysses* in 1904, before motorcars had become widespread. Eliot and Pound move easily between historical periods but rarely mention the technological advances that had permeated all aspects of urban life by 1920. Rather, they look back to the classical or medieval or Renaissance periods, fearing that dependence upon machines will cloud their minds, make them less able to understand what is truly important about being human. The only modernist writer who really engaged with technology, in fact, is the Italian futurist writer Filippo Marinetti. Marinetti was a Milanese who came to London to perform spoken-word pieces that celebrated machines. The glory of airplanes, cars, factories, and machine guns was always the subject of Marinetti's verse. Blinded by his fascination with the clean efficiency of machines, Marinetti ended up advocating the horrific violence of World War I and, in the mid-1920s, became an apologist for Mussolini.

Freud

Modernist novelists had no more important influence than the Viennese psychiatrist Sigmund Freud. Although he did not actually invent the discipline, Freud is considered the father of psychoanalysis. His writings propose a three-part model of the psyche consisting of the id (or the primitive drives), the ego (the sense of the self), and the superego (or the moral lessons and codes of behavior we are taught). Freud believed that human behavior and "neuroses" have causes of which people are unaware, causes that stem from childhood experiences or from the thwarting of certain basic urges. Psychoanalysis was predicated on the idea that an analyst could pick out certain ideas and reactions in a patient that would indicate the real problem.

Such writers as Woolf and Joyce took this idea and turned it into the basis for fiction. They were reacting against "realist" writers, who sought to simply record the unadorned facts of the world around. This is impossible, the modernists said; the psyche of the narrator will always be affected by unknown forces and thus is never able to capture reality without any kind of bias or alteration. Rather, people should attempt simply to record thoughts, for by this the reader can understand things about the narrator that the narrator him- or herself does not. Joyce's first novel, *A Portrait of the Artist as a Young Man*, records the thoughts of Stephen Dedalus from the time he is a "nicens

Media Adaptations

- Historically, most modernist works have not translated well into film or television adaptations. Of the modernist writers, it is Hemingway whose work has been most often filmed. Hollywood produced two versions of *A Farewell to Arms*, one in 1932 (starring Gary Cooper and Helen Hayes, directed by Frank Borzage) and the other in 1957.
- Other modernist writers have seen their novels turned into films. A few attempts have been made to produce Joyce's work, for instance. In 1967 the director Joseph Strick filmed a version of *Ulysses* that depicted a bare-bones version of the story. However, since most of the book takes place on a linguistic and allegorical level, most viewers have found the film unsatisfying.

little boy" to the time he is a college student. In her short story "The Mark on the Wall," Virginia Woolf captures a moment in time as a woman looks at a mark on the wall. The narration follows her mind as she extrapolates all of the possibilities of what the mark could be and follows all of the subconscious connections her mind makes with seemingly unrelated topics. Modernist writers felt that the "interior monologue" or the stream-of-consciousness technique gave readers access to the character's subconscious.

The "Unreal City"

In "The Waste Land" Eliot describes London as an "Unreal City," a city through which shades of the dead troop over the bridges. Modernism was the first literary movement to take urban life as a given, as a form of experience that was categorically different from any other kind of life. The French symbolist poet Charles Baudelaire was fascinated by the "flaneur," the man who strolls the city aimlessly as a way of life. The anonymity of the city, its darkness, its mechanization, its vast power, all inspired the modernists; it attracted and repelled them in equal measure. Modernist writers (most of them, interestingly enough, from suburbs or small cities) gravitated to London and Paris, St. Petersburg and New York, where they found each other, formed movements, drank and fought together, and broke apart.

London was the first home of Anglo-American Modernism, but the city's essentially commercial character eventually sent most of the writers elsewhere. By the 1920s, Paris was the home of one of the greatest concentration of artists in history. In the 1930s, with war looming in Europe, the artistic energy moved west to New York. But no matter what city, the city was almost always the subject of modernist literature. Although he could not stay there and moved between Paris, Trieste, and Zurich during his "exile," everything James Joyce ever wrote was about the vibrant urban life of Dublin. The poet Hart Crane composed his epic poem "The Bridge" about the Brooklyn Bridge, the monument of engineering and architectural beauty that made New York City the center of American urban life. Eliot's melancholy poems point out the loneliness and lack of meaning city-dwellers often feel. The city, where technology and masses of people and anonymity come together, became the master trope of Modernism itself.

Alienation

Alienation is defined as the sensation of being alien, or of not belonging, to one's own milieu. It can also mean separation from something. If the city is the master trope (or image) of Modernism, alienation is its master theme. Almost all modernist writing deals with alienation in some form.

The primary kind of alienation that Modernism depicts is the alienation of one sensitive person from the world. The stream-of-consciousness technique of narration is particularly well suited for this, because readers can see the inner feelings of a person and witness his or her essential self along with the actions of the world outside. Stephen Dedalus, Joyce's protagonist and stand-in, is alienated from his family, his friends, his religion, and his country because of devotion to art and his certainty that nobody can understand and accept him. Woolf's heroines are doubly alienated from the world because of their status as women; because of their sex, they are not allowed to participate in the world of politics, education, or economics. Eliot's narrators (most notably Prufrock in "The Love Song of J. Alfred Prufrock") are confronted by a world that is just broken shards of a discarded whole; everyone else seems to walk through the world calmly but they cannot. And for Ezra Pound, it is the world itself that has been alienated, by the forces of greed, from what should truly be historical heritage.

The Presence of the Past

Surrounded by the debris of all of the smashed certainties of the past, modernist writers looked at the contemporary world as a directionless place, without center or certainty. These past certainties, although oppressive and constructed on specious values, were at least some kind of foundation for the world. The modernist age set out to break apart these certainties; World War I then finished the job and horrified the world by demonstrating what humanity was capable of. Writers in the modernist age often felt that they were at the end of history. Because of this, modernist poems and novels often incorporate and mix together huge swaths of history. Allusion—brief references to people, places, things, or even languages and literatures—was the characteristic modernist technique for including history. Partly because of their profound uneasiness in the modern world, modernist writers alluded constantly to the past.

This is not to say that the modernists were uncritical admirers of the past. In his poem "Hugh Selwyn Mauberley," Ezra Pound wrote that World War I's vast slaughter was ultimately for the purpose of defending "an old [b——] gone in the teeth . . . a botched civilization . . . two gross of broken statues . . . [and] a few thousand battered books." Joyce's Stephen Dedalus says that "history is a nightmare from which I am trying to awake" and the Irishmen who live in past glories are portrayed as buffoons and fools. But both of these writers' works are filled with allusions to the past. And almost all of the important modernist writers, as well, structure their work around the presence of the past.

Pound, for instance, called his *The Cantos* "a poem including history" and the list of allusions in that poem has over ten thousand entries.

Style

Narration

Modernism sought to accurately portray the world not as it is but as humans actually experience it. Modernist literature, then, relied especially heavily on advances in narrative technique, for narration (a voice speaking) is the essential building block of all literature. Interestingly, the narrative techniques in modernist poetry and modernist fiction illustrate the same ideas about experience, but they do so in very different ways.

Modernist fiction tends to rely on the stream-of-consciousness or "interior monologue" techniques. This kind of narration purports to record the thoughts as they pass through a narrator's head. The unpredictable connections that people make between ideas demonstrates something about them, as do the things they try to avoid thinking about. In *Ulysses*, Leopold Bloom attempts not to dwell on his knowledge that his wife will cheat on him as he wanders the city, so thoughts of his wife, of Blazes Boylan (her lover), or of sex make him veer quickly in another mental direction. Also, a number of small ideas and images recur throughout the book: an advertisement for Plumtree's Potted Meat, for instance, and the Greek word *metempsychosis*. These ideas crop up without any apparent pattern and get stuck in Bloom's head, just as a song or a phrase might resonate through people's minds for hours and then just disappear. This narrative technique attempts to record how scattered and jumbled the experience of the world really is, and at the same time how deeper patterns in thoughts can be discerned by those (such as readers) with some distance from them. That humans are alienated from true knowledge of themselves is the implicit contention of the stream-of-consciousness form of narration.

Modernist poets such as Ezra Pound or T. S. Eliot, on the other hand, did not delve deeply into the individual consciousness. Rather, they attempted to model the fragmented nature of minds and civilization in their narratives. Eliot's "The Waste Land" has dozens of speakers that succeed each other without warning: the poem opens with the voice of the dead speaking from underground, then shifts quickly to the unattributed voice of Countess Marie Larisch of Bavaria, then shifts just as quickly to a stentorian, priestly voice. The effect is a cacophony of voices, a mass of talking devoid of connection.

In Ezra Pound's *The Cantos* or William Carlos Williams's *Paterson*, this array of voices is taken to its logical conclusion. The poet speaks in many different voices, but historical figures speak, artworks speak, ordinary people speak. In both of these long poems, the poets transcribed letters (Pound used letters of Thomas Jefferson and John Adams, while Williams used the letters of his friends and admirers) and included them in the

Topics for Further Study

- Modernism evolved as an artistic reaction to dramatic changes in politics, culture, society, and technology. Research some of the technologies that were developed in the late 1800s and early 1900s that might have literally changed the world. Some of the inventions you might want to investigate might be the technologies that captured and recorded reality (photography, sound recording, film), the technologies of communication, the technologies of transportation, and the technologies of weaponry.
- The two world wars of the twentieth century had an enormous effect on the modernist movement. Many critics feel that the movement hit its height just after World War I and was effectively killed by World War II. Research the wars' effects on writers of the modernist movement. What did they do during the war years? How did the war change their lives? You might want to look at lesser-known writers such as Rupert Brooke or Wilfred Owen who actually served in the conflict.
- Most of the important modernist writers were born between 1880 and 1900, and most of them died in the 1960s. The world changed dramatically in the intervening period. In 1890 what were the world's great powers? Who were its important leaders? What were the important issues in international relations? What products did people use? How did people travel from place to place? Compare the answers to these questions to what the world looked like in 1965.
- In addition to being a reaction to changes in technology and politics, Modernism was a reaction to important developments in Western thought. Dozens of philosophers and scholars of the late nineteenth century rejected the accepted explanations about the world and proposed their own. Of these, the thinkers who had the greatest effect on Modernism were the economist Karl Marx, the naturalist Charles Darwin, the philosopher Friedrich Nietzsche, and the psychiatrist Sigmund Freud. Research any one of these thinkers. What were their most important insights? What previous explanations did their writings reject? How do their ideas affect the world today?

poem. The poet, in this case, is less a writer than a compiler of voices; it is the arrangement of pieces, not the content of each individual piece that is important. The effect is to "decenter" the reader. Readers are no longer sure where the poet (with his or her implicit authority over the text) exists in the poem.

Allusion

An allusion is a brief reference to a person, place, thing, idea, or language that is not actually present. Because of modernist theories about the omnipresence of the past, allusions are difficult to avoid in modernist literature. Joyce, Eliot, and Pound—the three authors generally acknowledged as the leaders of the modernist movement in English—included allusion as perhaps the central formal device in their writing. The past is everywhere in the writing of these three, and indeed this is the case with most of the other modernist writers.

But it is in Joyce, Eliot, and Pound that the allusion is particularly important. Indeed, it is essentially impossible to understand their work without tracking down their more important allusions, and scholars have compiled long volumes explaining each reference in *Ulysses* and *The Cantos*. Some of their allusions are quite clear: for instance, in "Canto IV," Pound includes the lines "Palace in smoky light, / Troy but a heap of smouldering boundary stones." Most readers would be able to identify those lines as a reference to Homer's *Iliad*, which tells the story of the end of the Trojan War. But not all of Pound's allusions are so clear: "Canto VIII" begins "These fragments you have shelved (shored)"; the allusion is to Eliot's famous line "These fragments I have shored against my ruins" at the end of "The Waste Land." Eliot's line is well-known, but only those who have studied poetry would know it. And many of Pound's allusions, indeed most of them, are frankly inaccessible. Pound spends a number of cantos alluding to Sigismondo Malatesta, an obscure Italian warrior-prince from the Renaissance. Only because Pound made him famous does anyone recognize his name.

Joyce structured *Ulysses* to work on numerous levels. All of the mundane events in Bloom's day correspond to episodes in Homer's epic *Odyssey*, for instance, but the book also works as a retelling of Irish history, of the growth and development of the human fetus, and of the history of the Catholic Church. Eliot's "The Waste Land" can be read simply as a collection of allusions or "fragments" as he calls them in the last section: appearing in the poem are the Greek seer Tiresias, a pair of working-class women in East London, a number of Hindu deities, Dante, and an American ragtime singer. None of these references are explained; they just appear and the reader must make what sense of it he or she can. In the critical reevaluation of Modernism that has been taking place over the last decade, one of the central questions has been whether one must understand all of the allusions in order genuinely to appreciate the work.

Movement Variations

Imagism

Imagism is the best-known of the dozens of small movements in modernist poetry in the years leading up to World War I. Ezra Pound formulated the "rules" of Imagism, which were essentially a rejection of Victorian poetry. Imagist poets were encouraged to "simply present" an image; the poet "does not comment." Excessive adjectives and the voice of the poet were anathema. Finally, Pound urged imagists to use the rhythm of the metronome.

From his base in London, Pound published the anthology *Des Imagistes* in 1914. Other poets in the movement included H. D., William Carlos Williams, Richard Aldington, and Amy Lowell; H. D.'s poem "Oread" embodies the imagist project. Pound soon moved on from Imagism but Lowell, from Boston, continued to publish imagist anthologies for years after the movement had become irrelevant.

Vorticism

After Imagism, Pound moved on to Vorticism. This movement (which consisted primarily of Pound, the writer T. E. Hulme, and the painter/novelist Wyndham Lewis) was published in their magazine *Blast: A Review of the Great English Vortex.* It took the basic tenets of imagism, combined them with the painting style of Cubism, and injected an aggressive anger. At this time Pound had discovered the Chinese written character and had decided that its unique combination of sound, text, and image created a luminous "vortex" of energy. The movement fell apart as World War I began, for its anger and violence seemed very small and ineffective when compared to the real destruction of the war.

The Objectivists

The objectivists were a group of modernist poets who formed relatively late during the modernist period. In a way, they can be considered the descendants of the imagists, but their poems tend to be even starker and flatter. The objectivists drew their inspiration from William Carlos Williams but most of the members of the movement were of the younger (born after 1900) generation. George Oppen, Louis Zukofsky, Charles Reznikoff, and a few others are the best-known poets of the objectivist movement.

The Lost Generation

The Lost Generation was a name given by Gertrude Stein to the group of young Americans who migrated to Paris in the 1920s. Ernest Hemingway is the most famous of these Americans (in fact, it was to him that Stein said, "you are all a lost generation"), but there were dozens. Many of these Americans were artists and writers, but just as many were not and were attracted to Paris because of the strong dollar and the bohemian lifestyle. Hemingway's first novel, *The Sun Also Rises*, is the enduring portrait of this group as they wander from Paris to Spain and back, looking for thrills and occasionally working.

The Lost Generation's members constantly crossed paths with the European artists who were already living there. Pablo Picasso, Ezra Pound, James Joyce, Stein, Constantin Brancusi, and many others had made Paris their home and had made it into one of the great centers of artistic activity. When the "Lost Generation" arrived, many of the established artists befriended these Americans, took advantage of them, or even worked with them. By the end of the 1920s, though, most of these Americans returned home.

Historical Context

World War I

Modernism took place over many decades, and almost no facet of life in the West was not profoundly transformed by the changes that took place between 1860 and 1939. But if Modernism centered around one historical event, it was the unthinkable catastrophe that became known later as World War I. In the years leading up to World War I, the modernist writers thought of themselves as rebels, ruthlessly breaking apart all of the societal certainties of the Victorian age. The American modernists sneered at American middle-class acquisitiveness, while the British modernists chafed at the smug, self-assured conservatism of the Victorian and Edwardian age. Modernist writers broke convention by writing frankly about sex, by insulting religion, and by arguing passionately that the poor were not poor simply because of a moral failing. By breaking these societal taboos, modernist writers found themselves cast in the role of rebels, pariahs, even dangerous men and women. And such writers as Ezra Pound and Wyndham Lewis began to believe their own hype about being dangerous to society.

The coming of World War I fulfilled the modernist predictions of a coming fragmentation and destruction beyond anything they could have imagined. The war itself came upon an unsuspecting Europe almost in a way that the modernists might have envisioned, for it was society's faith in its own structures that ended up destroying it. Specifically, the complicated network of alliances dividing Europe into two moderately hostile camps (one consisting largely of democracies such as Great Britain and France, the other consisting of monarchies or dictatorships such as Germany and the Austro-Hungarian Empire, but even these categories had exceptions—Czarist Russia fought on the democracies' side) became not a means of stability but the mechanism of Europe's destruction.

The war began when the Serbian rebel Gavrilo Princip assassinated the Austro-Hungarian Archduke Franz Ferdinand in Sarajevo in 1914. Austro-Hungary sought reprisals against Serbia, the Russians came to the Serbian defense, the Germans came to the assistance of the Austro-Hungarians, and Eastern Europe was at war. At the same time, the Germans took this opportunity to try out a plan they had been developing for years. The German strategic command had worked out a way to march across Belgium and northeastern France and take Paris in six weeks, and in 1914 they attempted to do just this. The plan bogged down and soon the English came to the assistance of the French and Belgians. Pushing the Germans back from the very suburbs of Paris, the Allied forces managed to save the French nation but the armies soon found themselves waging trench warfare in the forests and fens of northern France, Alsace, and Belgium. Millions died in futile attempts to move the line forward a few yards. Among these were a number of modernist artists and writers, including the French sculptor Henri Gaudier-Brzeska, Ezra Pound's friend.

The tone of excitement about violence that characterized earlier modernist writing disappeared after the war, for the writers who exalted in the promise of destruction were utterly numbed by the effects of real destruction. Although the soldier-writers like Rupert Brooke and Siegfried Sassoon have left readers with vivid, horrifying pictures of combat, perhaps the enduring modernist imagery of the war is contained in two poems: Eliot's "The Waste Land" and Pound's "Hugh Selwyn Mauberley." Pound's poem addresses the war directly, saying that "There died a myriad, / And of the best, among them, / For an old [b——] gone in the teeth, / For a botched civilization." Eliot's poem is more evocative of the psychological effects of the war, for it is a collection of fragments, of pieces of culture and society broken apart and without meaning. The poem is perhaps the best verbal portrait ever created of civilized man confronting the possibility that everything has been destroyed.

Critical Overview

Modernism did not exist until it was almost dead. That is, until the 1930s or later the term "Modernism" simply did not mean what it means today: a group of writers, an arsenal of literary devices, a number of characteristic themes. Interestingly, in the 1910s and 1920s—the height of Modernism as it is understood today—the word "Modernism" referred to a particular strain of thought in the Catholic Church. At that time, the modernist writers did not see themselves as a unified movement. Instead, the writers now called modernists were members of dozens of different smaller movements: the Lost Generation, the dadaists, the imagists, the vorticists, the objectivists, the surrealists, and many others. What is identified as the characteristic themes or concerns of the modernist period (a general pessimism about the state of the world, a rejection of society's certainties, a sense that only the rebel

Compare & Contrast

- **1890s:** The United States' economy expands rapidly as the nation exploits its natural resources. Large corporations in the transportation, steel, oil, meat-packing, and financial industries establish monopolies; as a result, Congress passes the Sherman Anti-Trust Act intended to break up such monopolies.

  Today: Dozens of states and the federal government go to trial with the Microsoft corporation. Charged with being a monopoly, the company defends itself on the grounds that standardization is better for consumers than variety.

- **1914:** World War I breaks out when Archduke Franz Ferdinand of the Austro-Hungarian Empire is assassinated in Sarajevo. The system of interlocking alliances among Europe's great powers compels these nations to go to war on each other's behalf. The war drags on until 1918; millions are killed.

  Today: After a terrorist attack destroys the World Trade Center in New York, President George W. Bush calls for a war against terrorism and especially against Osama bin Laden. In the first stage of the war, American and British submarines and airplanes bombard Afghanistan, where bin Laden is said to reside.

- **1915:** During the first years of World War I, the United States refuses to join the fighting. In 1915, though, the passenger ship *Lusitania* is sunk by the German navy, killing thousands of Americans. This incident plays an important part in swaying American public opinion toward joining the war.

  Today: After terrorists pilot jetliners into American targets, killing thousands of people, President George W. Bush calls for a "war on terrorism" and begins bombing targets in Afghanistan. As the campaign to find and punish the terrorists responsible continues, American troops fight alongside the local militias to defeat Afghanistan's Taliban government.

- **1927:** Al Jolson stars in *The Jazz Singer*, the first "talkie" motion picture. The conjunction of recorded sound and recorded image, revolutionary in its time, follows the instantaneous broadcast of sound by radio, which achieved its first transatlantic broadcast in 1901. It is followed by the instantaneous broadcast of sound and images by television in 1939.

  Today: The advent of computers in the 1960s has by now changed the nature of recorded sound and images. All of the pre–Worlds War II technologies such as film, magnetic tape, vinyl records, and radio broadcasts are what is known as "analog" information. Modern technologies like compact disks, digital cameras, computer hard drives, and even cable television feeds are based on digital information—a series of instructions to a computer. Many people suspect that this change from analog to digital will change our relationship to reality just as profoundly as did the development of recorded sound and images.

- **1929:** After many years of what is now known as the Roaring Twenties, a period in which the American economy expands rapidly and the United States begins to develop the consumer culture popular today, the stock market crashes on October 29, 1929. The crash is caused by many factors including dramatic economic troubles in Europe and Asia and the tendency, among American consumers, to buy items on credit and then default on payment. The crash leads to the terrible Great Depression of the 1930s.

  Today: After many years of unprecedented economic expansion (largely driven by the high-technology sector of the economy), these seemingly endless good times begin to dramatically slow. Paper fortunes are wiped out overnight as stock options become worthless. Hundreds of Internet companies go out of business, but the slowdown also affects "brick and mortar" industries like automobiles, construction, and travel.

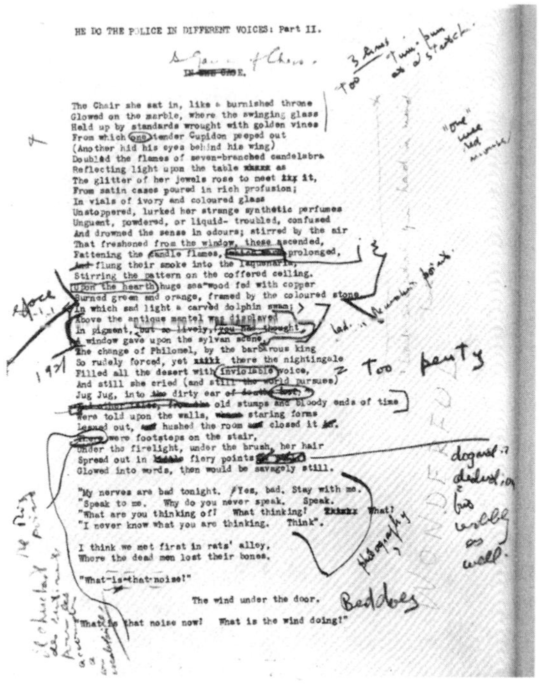

HE DO THE POLICE IN DIFFERENT VOICES: Part II.

IN THE CAGE.

The Chair she sat in, like a burnished throne
Glowed on the marble, where the swinging glass
Held up by standards wrought with golden vines
From which one tender Cupidon peeped out
(Another hid his eyes behind his wing)
Doubled the flames of seven-branched candelabra
Reflecting light upon the table as
The glitter of her jewels rose to meet it,
From satin cases poured in rich profusion;
In vials of ivory and coloured glass
Unstoppered, lurked her strange synthetic perfumes
Unguent, powdered, or liquid- troubled, confused
And drowned the sense in odours; stirred by the air
That freshened from the window, these ascended,
Fattening the candle flames, prolonged,
flung their smoke into the laquenaria,
Stirring the pattern on the coffered ceiling.
Upon the hearth huge sea-wood fed with copper
Burned green and orange, framed by the coloured stone,
In which sad light a carved dolphin swam;
Above the antique mantel was displayed
In pigment, but so lively, you had thought
A window gave upon the sylvan scene,
The change of Philomel, by the barbarous king
So rudely forced, yet there the nightingale
Filled all the desert with inviolable voice,
And still she cried (and still the world pursues)
Jug Jug, into the dirty ear of
old stumps and bloody ends of time
Were told upon the walls, staring forms
Leaned out, hushed the room closed it.
There were footsteps on the stair,
Under the firelight, under the brush, her hair
Spread out in fiery points
Glowed into words, then would be savagely still.

"My nerves are bad tonight. Yes, bad. Stay with me.
"Speak to me. Why do you never speak. Speak.
"What are you thinking of? What thinking? What?
"I never know what you are thinking. Think".

I think we met first in rats' alley,
Where the dead men lost their bones.

"What is that noise?"

The wind under the door.

"What is that noise now? What is the wind doing?"

T. S. Eliot's corrected proof for his poem "The Waste Land"

artist is telling the truth about the world) were simply "in the air" of the times; everyone was thinking and writing about the same ideas, so it did not seem necessary to name their commonalities.

Literary critics of the early twentieth century were generally hostile to the writers now called modernists. The Victorian ethos held that literature's purpose was to identify "sweetness and light" and "the best that has been thought and said" (in the words of Matthew Arnold, one of Victorian England's most important critics) in order to make better citizens. Literature and art, for the Victorians, were meant to be "edifying"—educational. Literature was read to learn how one should behave. By that same token, literature that did not put forth edifying models was simply bad literature. This attitude is shown especially well in the hostile response to Gustave Flaubert's 1857 *Madame Bovary*, a novel that depicted, without comment or condemnation, the adulterous behavior of a middle-class woman. The Arnoldian attitude toward literature persisted well into the twentieth century, and in the United States was personified by the writers and editors of the *Saturday Review of Literature*, especially Henry Seidel Canby.

For these critics, modernist literature was both incomprehensible and dangerous. Its stylistic experiments made it difficult to digest easily—readers had to work to make it through *Ulysses* or *The Sound and the Fury*, not to mention *The Cantos* or "The Waste Land"—and its pessimistic, negative attitude toward society could hardly be expected to make better citizens. In fact, modernist literature celebrated those people, artists especially, who rebelled against society. Where the late Victorian critics and their intellectual descendants wanted edifying, socially-uplifting literature, modernist literature sought to create independent, critical, alienated subjects.

As a result, Modernism had to create its own critics and to a remarkable extent it succeeded. At first, modernist writers simply started their own magazines and reviewed each other's work. Ezra Pound, through the journals *Poetry* and *The Egoist*, was especially productive in this. Later, T. S. Eliot became Modernism's leading critic. In his journal *The Criterion* and, later, from his post as managing editor of the publishing house Faber & Faber, Eliot advanced his own vision of good literature. He denigrated the neoclassicists and the romantics and praised the Elizabethans; he argued for a literature steeped in the "Tradition"; he valued tension, ambiguity, and allusion. Not coincidentally, his own poetry seemed to be the height of "Good Literature" as he defined it.

After Eliot defined a modernist aesthetic, other critics began to agree with him. Difficulty, resistance, ambiguity, irony, and the sense of an ending to something were all qualities praised by critics ranging from the political right wing (the New Critics) to the far left (the New York Intellectuals). By the 1930s and 1940s the modernist aesthetic was taking over Anglo-American literary criticism. The old guard of critics defending the edifices of Western civilization seemed less and less relevant after a war, a depression, and another war. The pessimistic modernist view of the world began to seem correct. By the 1950s, Modernism and its aesthetic standards were almost unquestioned in American criticism and education.

During the 1950s and 1960s, Modernism remained dominant in American literature. Literary histories were rewritten to reflect Modernism's new importance; earlier, forgotten writers such as Herman Melville were rediscovered as important ancestors. And the modernist aesthetic of alienation, separation from the world, and profound pessimism became almost synonymous with literature.

This all changed in the 1970s and 1980s. Because of the political upheavals of the 1960s, relevance again became an important virtue of literature. Readers wanted literature to be politically engaged, to tell the stories of the struggles of oppressed groups (women, African Americans, Chicanos, gays and lesbians), and most importantly to take a political stand on issues. The modernist aesthetic denigrated works that sought to be politically relevant; this dated the works and made them less timeless and universal. But again, as in the 1940s and 1950s, a new generation of critics and teachers reevaluated Modernism and found it to be lacking in many virtues. It did not help that many modernist writers held political and social beliefs that ranged from extremely conservative to outright Fascist.

Over the last decade or so, a new generation of scholars has sought to again reevaluate Modernism. These scholars no longer look at Modernism according to Eliot's own opinions of what is important in literature. In a sense, these new scholars read Modernism against its own grain, trying to find buried content in the literature. And while Eliot's reactionary beliefs and Pound's anti-Semitism still exist, even the most left-wing critics often find something to admire in their works, something that often Pound or Eliot explicitly urged readers to ignore. Perhaps the most notable example of this "against-the-grain" reading of Modernism is the reconsideration of "The Waste Land" after Pound's central role in the poem's composition was discovered. Eliot's cult of the solitary, alienated artist standing apart from all of his peers and creating suddenly seemed questionable after readers discovered that Eliot's greatest poem was, in fact, the product of a collaboration that he tried to hide for decades.

Criticism

Greg Barnhisel

Barnhisel directs the Writing Center at the University of Southern California in Los Angeles. In this essay, Barnhisel describes the process by which Modernism became the dominant literary movement of the twentieth century.

In its heyday (the 1910s and 1920s), Modernism did not exist. That is to say, the word Modernism did not have the meaning that it has today. Modernism referred to technology, to an openness to the new commercially-driven society that was coming about, and to changes in Catholic theology. The literary themes and concerns and stylistic innovations that today are called modernist belonged, in their time, to dozens of different writers who lived in different places, spoke different languages, were members of different groups, and very often were hostile toward each other and their work. It was only in the 1950s and 1960s, years after the movement ended, that the term Modernism came to designate a group of writers preoccupied with alienation and the destruction of old certainties. It can be instructive to look at the ways that large trends in literature and culture are examined, classified, and codified into a movement by readers and critics. Modernism was produced long after the movement's height by critics; Modernism was not produced by the modernist artists themselves.

In a very real sense there is no one Modernism; there are many modernisms. Some critics have identified Modernism as far back as the French writer Gustave Flaubert, who wrote in the 1850s, and many critics see a number of works of the 1970s (Thomas Pynchon's novel *Gravity's Rainbow*, for instance) as late examples of Modernism. The themes now understood as characteristically modernist existed in many works of the nineteenth century. By the early 1900s, an explosion of artistic subgroups whose members crossed between music, painting, sculpture, dance, photography, and literature rapidly coalesced and just as quickly disappeared. Almost all of these groups—the surrealists, the imagists, the cubists, the vorticists, the dadaists, the futurists, and many others—are considered components of Modernism.

It was only near the end of the movement that critics came to a consensus about what constituted Modernism in literature, and these critics set the rules for who should be considered a central member of the movement and who would remain only a minor figure. Perhaps more important in the long run, these critics codified a way of reading and criteria for evaluation of literature, both of which, not coincidentally, were particularly friendly to Modernism.

These critical developments of the 1950s were a direct reaction against the climate of earlier decades. In the 1930s and 1940s, art and politics were linked together very closely. Artists were expected to weigh in on the political issues of the day, and especially in the 1930s they allied themselves with left-wing causes. Dozens of artists and writers joined the Communist Party, feeling that only

What Do I Study Next?

- There was almost no facet of life that was not fundamentally transformed by the technological advances of the modernist period. Stephen Kern's 1983 book *The Culture of Time and Space 1880–1918* (1983) is an excellent meditation on how technology changed human life and perception.
- A movement that was not similar to Modernism in its formal features but provided many modernist writers with a model of artistic rebellion was the so-called Decadent movement of the 1890s. The best-known Decadent writers were the Anglo-Irish poet and playwright Oscar Wilde and the French novelist J. K. Huysmans, but dozens of other writers were loosely affiliated with this group. Reading Wilde's *Importance of Being Earnest* (1895) gives a good idea of the nature of Decadent literature.
- World War I was the central historical event affecting Modernism. Paul Fussell's study *The Great War and Modern Memory* (1975) provides a detailed and often moving discussion of this war and its effects on contemporaries.
- Out of the armistice that settled World War I grew the seeds that would eventually mature into World War II. The "belligerents," or the losing powers, were forced to pay vast sums to the victors and give up large amounts of territory. Even in Italy, a poor country that was dragged into World War I, the effects of the war led directly to the ascension of Benito Mussolini to power. Dennis Mack-Smith's 1983 biography *Mussolini* gives a detailed portrait of post–World War I Italy.

a worker-centered movement could save America from the depression and from vast concentrations of wealth. Other, albeit fewer, writers and artists allied themselves with the other side: of these, the most notorious were the English painter and novelist Wyndham Lewis, the Norwegian novelist Knut Hamsun (who praised Hitler), and the American poet Ezra Pound, who admired Mussolini and held anti-Semitic beliefs. T. S. Eliot, although he never supported fascism, had extremely conservative political views as well.

Writers have never become famous only by their own efforts. It takes dozens of people to bring a work from the mind of the writer to the hands of the reader. And in an age such as the mid-twentieth century, when thousands of works of literature were published every year, the role of the critic became especially important in establishing whether a writer was important and why. In the 1930s, when the modernist writers had already produced a solid body of work to be explained and evaluated, two groups of critics with drastically different backgrounds and political inclinations set their sights upon Modernism. Together, these groups defined the sprawling movement, telling readers what it meant and, most importantly, arguing that Modernism should be read without concern to any political beliefs expressed in the works or held by the writers. Their consensus about Modernism eventually made the movement the great movement of twentieth-century literature.

The first of these two groups came together in the American South in the 1920s. This "Fugitive" or "Agrarian" group included writers Cleanth Brooks, Robert Penn Warren, John Crowe Ransom, and Allen Tate (most of whom were poets or novelists as well as critics) who were inspired by the antebellum South and its Elizabethan English heritage. They yearned for a preindustrial world where cultured aristocrats cultivated the land and wrote subtle, accomplished verse. In the 1920s they read the influential critical writings of T. S. Eliot, which meshed well with their own ideas about literature and led them to appreciate Eliot's (and by extension other modernists') works.

Eventually, these writers obtained academic posts and developed a method of literary analysis called "New Criticism." The New Criticism valued such formal devices as tension, ambiguity, wordplay, and irony. It had absolutely no interest in questions of what a work can tell about history or about an author's life or what political meaning a work holds. People who read works for what they had to say about society were Philistines to the New Critics; the goal of reading literature was to refine one's sensations and to make ever-finer distinctions about the excellence of language. In such works as Brooks's *The Well-Wrought Urn* and Ransom's *The New Criticism*, these critics provided a model for reading literature apolitically.

This apolitical attitude was anathema to the New Critics' counterparts, the New York Intellectuals. The New York Intellectuals were urban, immigrants or the children of immigrants, largely Jewish, and adamantly left-wing (many of them were briefly Communist Party members). They came together writing for *Partisan Review*, the leading intellectual journal of postwar America. And for these critics—Philip Rahv, Delmore Schwartz, Diana Trilling, Irving Howe, and many others—Modernism's value was that it undermined the simplistic happy-ending narratives produced by capitalism and "mass culture." Modernism, with its fragmented visions of the world and its insistence that there is no such thing as an objective perspective, was a blow against the smug capitalist structure of advertising and consumption. Modernism accomplished this not by means of the content of the writing, but by means of the form. The complicated combination of allusions, the decentralizing interior monologue, and the often jarring sense of time take away all certainties and call attention to the ways that minds create the world.

During most of the 1930s, these two groups had little to do with each other. The New Critics, from their posts at universities and colleges, taught students how to read and appreciate literature. The New York Intellectuals wrote for journals and lived as public intellectuals; few of them had any affiliation with schools and most of them mistrusted universities. But both argued to different audiences that the type of writing now called modernist was the highest form of literature in the contemporary world.

In 1949, though, these two groups were forced to directly confront Americans' refusal to ignore literature's political meanings. The great American Modernist poet Ezra Pound had lived in Italy for

"Modernism, with its fragmented visions of the world and its insistence that there is no such thing as an objective perspective, was a blow against the smug capitalist structure of advertising and consumption."

over two decades, during which time he had expressed his admiration for Mussolini as well as for a growing anti-Semitism. During World War II, Pound broadcast radio programs on Fascist state radio and, as a result, was indicted for treason in 1943. In 1945 Pound was arrested and brought back to Washington to face trial. Broken and unstable, he was found mentally unfit to stand trial. He was sentenced to an indefinite period in St. Elizabeth's Hospital for the criminally insane.

But Pound was not finished. During his term in the army's detention center in Pisa, Italy, Pound composed a series of cantos (individual installments of his epic poem *The Cantos*). Published in 1948 as *The Pisan Cantos*, the book was Pound's most personal work in decades and perhaps his greatest single book of poems. It won the first Bollingen Prize, an award given by the Library of Congress, in 1949. Immediately, a storm of controversy arose. The American press and large numbers of American citizens were angered and insulted that a man who had supported an enemy power only a few years before, and who could have been executed for treason, was now being honored by the United States government.

The Bollingen Prize committee included members associated with the New Critics and the New York Intellectuals as well as the poets W. H. Auden, Conrad Aiken, and T. S. Eliot. Called upon to defend their decision, the committee members did so in very different ways. The Jewish poet Karl Shapiro frankly stated that he voted against Pound because he could not abide anti-Semites. Allen Tate argued that poetry must be judged without reference to the personal life of the poet. The committee as a whole released a statement to the press arguing that their decision was grounded on "that objective perception of value on which civilized society must rest."

Where the New Critics would have been expected to defend the prize, many assumed that the left-wing, anti-Fascist, Jewish New York Intellectuals would oppose any award being granted to Pound. *Partisan Review* convened a symposium in its pages to discuss the award, and although a range of points of view were expressed, the editors of the notably leftist journal (Philip Rahv and William Barrett) came out in support of the award. They feared what they termed the "Stalinoid" tendency of governments and societies to judge art only by the criteria of whether it advances that society's interests. To the New York Intellectuals, art must spur challenge of society's assumptions, not uphold them; art must demand thinking and questioning. By no means did the New York Intellectuals endorse Pound's ideas; on the contrary, many of them made a point to condemn him even when defending his award.

If World War I was the vortex out of which Modernism was truly born, the Bollingen Prize controversy became the event that transformed Modernism from an avant-garde movement into the literary establishment. During the 1950s, literary critics of the left and the right agreed about literature, at least in broad strokes. And while they each admired different things about Modernism (the New Critics liked its formal intricacy, while the New York Intellectuals endorsed its demands on the reader), their consensus about the movement defined it and ushered it into the center of the American literary canon, where it has remained ever since.

Source: Greg Barnhisel, Critical Essay on Modernism, in *Literary Movements for Students*, The Gale Group, 2003.

Richard Sheppard

In the following essay excerpt, Sheppard explores the problems inherent in fully defining of European Modernism and its impetus.

Methodological Introduction

In one of the earliest attempts to come to terms with modernism as a total phenomenon, the Czech Formalist, Jan Mukarovsk˝, began by stating that 'the notion of "modernism" is very indefinite'. Thirty-five years later, Monroe K. Spears echoed that sentiment when he prefaced an important book on the same subject by observing that 'Modernism is, of course, an impossible subject'. Shortly after that, the editors of one of the most widely disseminated anthologies of essays on the topic wrote in their introduction:

> The name [i.e. modernism] is clear; the nature of the movement or movements . . . is much less so. And equally unclear is the status of the stylistic claim we are making. We have noted that few ages have been more multiple, more promiscuous in artistic style; to distil from the multiplicity an overall style or mannerism is a difficult, perhaps even an impossible task.

And a decade later, two other influential commentators tacitly admitted that they were still encountering the same difficulties in finding 'the core of Modernism' by opting, as they were finally forced to concede, for an unsatisfactorily reductionist definition of the concept. Indeed, the most obvious index of the difficulties involved in discussing the subject is its lack of clear chronological boundaries. Although the broad consensus agrees on 1885–1935, some critics set its starting-date as early as 1870 (so as to include Nietzsche and Rimbaud), while others, notably North American critics, set its ending in the 1950s (so as to include the early novels of Vladimir Nabokov, the late poetry of William Carlos Williams, the abstract Expressionists, and work produced under the impact of *émigré* European modernists).

As three basic bibliographies clearly indicate, a huge amount of secondary literature on modernism exists, and in adding to it, I am aware that I may have neglected a key work which either anticipates or counters my argument. However, because critical understanding of modernism has developed so much ever since academic literature on the subject began to snowball in the early 1960s, it is not totally foolhardy to attempt, on the basis of that development, to try and elaborate a more differentiated understanding of the phenomenon.

On the whole, critics have tried to comes to terms with modernism via one of three strategies. First, a large number have tried to define it by pinpointing one or more key features, concerns or 'common traits'. These have included an 'uncompromising intellectuality', a preoccupation with 'Nihilism', a 'discontinuity', an attraction to the Dionysiac, a 'formalism', an 'attitude of detachment', the use of myth 'as an arbitrary means of ordering art' and a 'reflexivism', an 'anti-democratic' cast of mind, an 'emphasis on subjectivity', a 'feeling of alienation and loneliness', the sense

A scene from the film The Dead, *based on the story by James Joyce*

of 'the ever-present threat of chaos ... in conjunction with the sense of search' and 'the experience of panic terror', a particular form of irony which derives from 'the rift between self and world', 'consciousness, observation and detachment', and a commitment to metaphor as 'the very essence of poetry itself'. In the early 1970s, when this strategy was most prevalent in critical literature, two Marxist critics aptly remarked: 'On the question of what Modernism is, no two critics agree...' Three years after that, Bradbury and McFarlane outlined the limitations of this approach, and as late as 1984, the reductionism of Fokkema and Ibsch (who excluded a range of classically modernist texts from the category on the basis of an excessively narrow definition) highlighted these limitations even more starkly. But it is, perhaps, Chapters 4 and 5 of *Les Avant-gardes littéraires au XXe siècle* (in which a large number of allegedly defining characteristics of modernist art are isolated and discussed at great length) that bring several basic weaknesses of this strategy into the clearest relief. Once torn out of the context which generated them, it becomes evident that almost none of these characteristics, whether formal or experiental, is specific to the modernist period. It also becomes clear that more than one of them, depending on which author, works or culture one selects, could arguably be privileged in any reductionist account of modernism. And from this it follows that to breathe life back into this collection of dead concepts, it is necessary to reconstruct the dynamic, not to say cataclysmic context which generated them in their specifically modernist *combinatoire*. As one of the editors of a recent collection of essays on German modernism clearly saw, it is time both to stop 'reducing modernism to this or that set of criteria' and to pose 'the question of history and politics in the [modernist] text ... with renewed vigor'.

Given the limitations of this first approach, more than a few critics have felt the need to develop a second, more broadly-based strategy—quite often as a spin-off from the first. Having identified one or more allegedly key features of modernism or the modernist avant-garde, critics then attempt to bring these into sharper focus by setting them in a one-dimensional historical, literary-historical or sociological context. Thus, modernism has been viewed as a continuation of or a contrast with Romanticism; as a reaction, in its extreme avant-garde forms, against Aestheticism; as an inversion of the conventions of Realism; as a contrast with Expressionism, Futurism and Surrealism; as a precursor of postmodernism; as a product of the megalopolitan experience and/or the Great War; and as a result of the 'serious arts' being forced to cede their 'utilitarian function' to the 'mass media of communication and entertainment'. All of these positions are more or less tenable, but none is exclusively so. Precisely because, as Alan Wilde observed, the modernists were 'heirs to a tradition they revolted against', they simultaneously used *and* reacted against aesthetic conventions which marked several earlier and contemporary artistic movements. Moreover, fused with such purely aesthetic considerations, the experience of modernity (of which the mass city is but one, major aspect) is equally important to most, if not all, important modernist texts: either visibly or as the equally significant 'repressed Other' in such works as Rilke's *Neue Gedichte* (*c.* 1903–8) (translated as *New Poems* (1964)), most of Kandinsky's pre-1914 visual work, or E. M. Forster's *A Passage to India* (1922–4). Furthermore, as Spears so clearly saw, the Great War did not of itself generate modernism, but rather foregrounded that awareness of the darker side of reality and human nature which had already been present in the work of several major non-modernist writers of the nineteenth century. And while modernism and postmodernism overlap to such an extent that a large number of *surface* features are common to both phenomena, there are, as Wilde's and Hassan's books show, basic ontological differences between the two modes. Bathrick and Huyssen are right to reject simple categorical contrasts, but their own work, speaking as it does of 'the modernist aesthetic of transcendence and epiphany', points to a nostalgia or desire for epiphany, transcendence and closure which has no place within the flat surfaces and eternal present of postmodernism. As with the movements which preceded modernism, its relationship with its successor is far from simple. What Fredric Jameson said of any cultural or historical period is especially true of modernism, given that modernism is more a transitional phenomenon than a period or a movement. What is designated by the label does not '"express" some unified inner truth—a worldview or a period style or a set of structural categories which marks the whole length and breadth of the "period" in question'. Modernism not only evolved from, reacted against and anticipated a multiplicity of other artistic phenomena, it also developed out of a complex of socio-historical experiences, of which the shocks caused by the modern megalopolis and the Great War were simply the most violent.

We shall, I suggest, get further with the problem by developing a third strategy which is more or less manifest in works on modernism or the modernist avant-gardes by Schwartz, LeRoy and Beitz, Bürger, Jameson, Renate Werner, Jeffrey Herf, and Huyssen and Bathrick, and if we then combine their insights with the central thesis of Horkheimer's and Adorno's *Dialektik der Aufklärung* (1947) (translated as *Dialectic of Enlightenment* (1972)). Basing his argument on a concept borrowed from the American scientist Thomas S. Kuhn, Schwartz argues that the modernist epoch involved a 'global shift' across a range of disciplines, and that to understand this shift, we need to develop a 'matrix approach' which 'makes it possible ... to compare individuals who have no direct ties to one another but exhibit similar patterns of thought.' Like the much looser matrix which is used in *Les Avant-gardes littéraires au XXe siècle*, the matrix established by Schwartz to investigate the poetry of Pound and Eliot derives primarily from the natural sciences, mathematics and philosophy. But the work of the other writers named above implies that the paradigm shift which those disciplines, like the arts, underwent during the modernist period derived from a much more fundamental seismic upheaval. In 1974, Bürger, following Adorno, connected that upheaval (which generated both Aestheticism and the avant-garde reaction against it) with imperialism. And in 1973, LeRoy and Beitz were even more precise about that generative source when they described it as 'the transition to the epoch of imperialism', which they then analysed as follows:

> Turning then to some changes brought about by the transition to imperialism, we can say first that the ideals of the French Revolution, which had held up reasonably well during two thirds of the nineteenth century (in England and the United States, at any rate), become markedly less tenable. The same thing happens to the notion associated with Adam Smith that the existing economic system has the capacity to correct its own ills and bring about an equitable distribution of the wealth. Profound doubts now arise as to whether man has the capacity to dominate the historical process. With a suddenness that would be surprising if one knew nothing about the causes, the idea of progress collapses. When we seek an explanation for these changes, it is relevant to note how in the epoch of monopoly the decision-making process becomes invisible, the real decisions coming to be made more and more by those in command of the monopolies; ordinary people, even those in somewhat privileged positions, come to feel—and justifiably—that they lack the kind of leverage that the humanist tradition had always made one feel entitled to command. A further cause lies in the intensifying irrationalities in the existing order, the vast increase in productive capacity along with economic stagnation, technological progress, and the neglect of human needs, breathtaking scientific advances that seemed to promise a solution to the age-old problem of human want, but

> with no mechanism for connecting these advances with the demand which in theory they ought to be able to meet . . . Still another cause of the new doubts about the existing order is a new kind of alienation from work. This results in part from gigantism in industrial development and corresponding efficiency in techniques for managing the work force.

For all its perceptiveness, monocausalism never lurks far behind the surface of this avowedly Marxist account of the origins of modernism, and in 1981, Jameson offered a corrective to that tendency when he warned against viewing modernism as 'a mere reflection of the reification of late nineteenth-century social life.' More importantly still, Jameson, like Bürger seven years before, saw modernism in dialectical terms: its works are not just reflexes, transcriptions or symptoms of a profound cultural upheaval, but, *simultaneously*, responses through which the authors of those works try to pictorialize their understanding and so make sense of that upheaval. Bürger had asserted that the literary work was not just an 'Abbild, d.h.. . . Verdoppelung der gesellschaftlichen Realität' ('image, that is to say . . . replication of social reality'), but the 'Resultat einer Tätigkeit, die auf eine als unzulänglich erfahrene Wirklichkeit *antwortet*' ('product of an activity which *responds* to a reality that is experienced as inadequate'). And Jameson implied a similarly dialectical conception of modernism when he wrote:

> we are first obliged to establish a continuity between these two regional zones or sections—the practice of language in the literary work, and the experience of *anomie*, standardization, rationalizing desacralization in the *Umwelt* or world of daily life—such that the latter can be grasped as that determinate situation, dilemma, contradiction, or subtext, to which the former comes as a symbolic resolution or solution.

Indeed, towards the end of the same work, Jameson broadened out that dialectical conception by indicating that it was necessary to understand modernism not as a single, unified response, but as a range of responses to a perceived crisis. In doing this, he implied that it was possible to account coherently for the diverse phenomena which the concept involves, but without falling prey to the reductionism and over-simplification which the first two strategies described above involve. Because, Jameson suggested, modernism was the product of an age in a process of radical change, it was not simply, but multiply Janus-faced (and in the case of Dada, anus-faced into the bargain), with the result that any account of it has to look not just in two, but in several directions at once. And it is this dual awareness that modernism is both an active response to a seismic upheaval and a heterogeneous phenomenon which constitutes one of the greatest strengths of the major essays in Huyssen's and Bathrick's recent book.

Werner and Herf enable us to go further still. Herf noted that many (conservative) German modernists were born between 1885 and 1895 into a country which was modernizing rapidly (i.e. rationalizing its institutions and industrializing), and in which the humanist, liberal democratic tradition was relatively weak. And Werner pointed out that in common with most other major artists and intellectuals in nineteenth-century Germany, most German modernists had come from one class (the 'Bildungsbürgertum'—'educated middle class') and attended one educational institution (the 'Gymnasium'—'classical grammar school'). This latter was dominated by 'ein klassizistischer Normenkanon, die doktrinäre Verfestigung der klassisch-idealistischen Ästhetik, die Vorstellung, dem Kunstwerk als einem in sich harmonisch gegliederten Organismus komme die symbolische Repräsentanz einer göttlich geordneten Welt zu' ('a quasi-classical set of norms, the canonical institutionalization of a classical-idealist aesthetic, the notion that a work of art could stand symbolically for a divinely ordered world to the extent that it itself was a harmoniously structured organism').

Similar things could be said, *mutatis mutandis*, of modernists from other European cultures. Consequently, it can be argued that at one level, the concept of modernism designates a heterogeneous range of responses to a global process of modernization by a generation which had internalized a set of assumptions in conflict with the values inherent in that process, and which, as a result, experienced modernization as a cultural cataclysm. It should, however, be stressed that the nature and intensity of the conflict varies from culture to culture, in Germany, for example, the classical ideal described by Werner was particularly remote from reality; the process of modernization was exceptionally rapid; and the liberal democratic, humanist ideal had a comparatively weak hold in the public domain. Consequently, many German modernists experienced the conflict particularly intensely. In England, however, the Arnoldian ideal was more robustly ethical than its German counterpart; the process of modernization, having begun much earlier, had been less rapid than in Germany; as Dagmar Barnouw has argued, the liberal democratic, humanist ideal continued to play a comparatively important role in the public domain throughout the modernist period; and the Great War did not produce the same social upheaval as it did on the Continent. Consequently, it was easier for intellectuals in Britain to find more common ground with their societies so that what was in essence the same conflict was, on the whole, experienced less apocalyptically. As a result, it generated much smaller, less radical and less threatening avant-gardes (i.e., the Georgians, Imagists and Vorticists) than was the case on the Continent. So, for all the criticisms which can be levelled at Bürger's theory of the avantgarde, he was fundamentally correct in describing its work as the 'Ausdruck der Angst vor einer übermächtig gewordenen Technik und einer gesellschaftlichen Organisation, die die Handlungsmöglichkeiten des Einzelnen extrem einschränkt' ('expression of a profound anxiety in the face of a technological system which had become excessively powerful and a social system which imposes extreme limitations on the individual's freedom of action').

It is no accident that Georg Heym's first use of the neologism 'Weltstadt' ('world city'—i.e. 'city which has become the whole world') should have occurred in a poem, 'Berlin VIII', which was written in December 1910—that precise juncture when, according to Virginia Woolf, 'human nature' and 'all human relations' changed. By late 1910, a significant number of major modernist artists and intellectuals were foregrounding a powerful sense that a global process was affecting *all* areas of human life. But modernism was more than just a reflex, it also involved an active attempt to understand and pictorialize the complexities of that process. More importantly still, modernism, in its extreme forms, involved the prophetic urge to investigate the long-term implications of those complexities—both for the individual and society in general. Consequently, Horkheimer and Adorno, writing from America in the 1940s, enable us to add a final dimension to our understanding of the context which generated modernism via their analysis of the dialectical turn which, they contend, the central project of the Enlightenment had taken by the mid-twentieth century. In their view, those very constructs of human reason whose original purpose was to free mankind from its thralldom to Nature and feudalism, had turned into an autonomous system which was running madly out of control, depriving its creators of any real autonomy, and enslaving them more effectively than ever Nature or feudalism had done:

> Die Herrschaft des Menschen über sich selbst, die sein Selbst begründet, ist virtuell allemal die Vernichtung des Subjekts, in dessen Dienst sie geschieht, denn die beherrschte, unterdrückte und durch Selbsterhaltung aufgelöste Substanz ist gar nichts anderes als das Lebendige, als dessen Funktion die Leistungen der Selbsterhaltung einzig sich bestimmen, eigentlich gerade das, was erhalten werden soll.
>
> Man's self-mastery, in which his sense of selfhood is grounded, almost always involves the destruction of that very subject in whose name the process of self-mastery is undertaken. For the substance which is thereby mastered, suppressed and dissolved is that selfsame vital force from which all that is achieved in the name of self-preservation uniquely derives—i.e. precisely that element which is supposed to be preserved.

Viewed in this context, modernism ceases to be merely the artistic manifestation of a conflict between conservative, humanist sensibilities and a modernizing, non-humanist world, and becomes the manifestation of a more or less shocked realization that modernization required more than the development of a new, appropriate sensibility. Rather, a significant number of modernists saw that for all its ideology of scientific rationality, the process of modernization was, like the Golem of Paul Wegener's expressionist film *Der Golem* (1920), the monstrous product of an originally emancipatory impulse which was now running amok. Many of the modernists had, during their youth, been imbued by their liberal humanist background with the Enlightenment belief that it was possible for Man increasingly to understand, rise above, dominate and utilize the external world by means of his *logos*—understood either as a purely secular faculty or as one which was grounded in the divine *logos*. But, paradoxically, that very generation which had grown up amid the triumphant achievements of increasingly confident nineteenth-century science, technology and economics, now felt that these systems were becoming dysfunctional and potentially totalitarian. Moreover, by virtue of the law by which the repressed always returns in a destructive form, they also felt they were in danger of turning into their opposite: the entropic chaos which the sociologist Emile Durkheim had, in *Le Suicide* (1897) (translated as *Suicide* (1952)) and *De la Division du travail social* (1902) (translated as *Division of Labour in Society* (1933)), called *anomie*. And it was this feeling of normlessness (which, according to Durkheim, was induced by modernity's destruction of traditional communities) that generated the 'panic terror' which informs so many modernist works.

Marcel Duchamp's *La Mariée mise à nu par ses célibataires, même* (*The Bride Stripped Bare by her Bachelors, Even*; also known as the *Large Glass* (1915–23)); the dystopic vision of Yevgeny Zamyatin's My (1920) (translated as We (1924)); Breton's claim in the first Surrealist Manifesto (1924) that we are increasingly being forced to live in a rationally constructed cage from which, 'sous couleur de civilisation, sous prétexte de progrès' ('using civilization and progress as pretexts'), everything is banished which does not conform to convention; and such paintings from the 1930s by Max Ernst as *La Ville entière* (*The City as a Whole*) (1935–6 and 1936) and *La Ville petrifiée* (*The Petrified City*) (1935) catch the first movement of the dialectic described by Horkheimer and Adorno, as does Balázs's and Bartók's image of Duke Bluebeard's Castle. In their opera the triumph of (male) rationality is shown to bring immense wealth and power, but at a terrible cost. Against Duke Bluebeard's intention and despite his desire to be redeemed from his own creation by Judith, his castle holds him more securely captive than ever Nature could do. It induces in him a sense of powerlessness; turns the female and the elemental into dead things locked behind the seventh door of his castle and so divorces him from those powers which might save him from himself.

But Franz Kafka's 'In der Strafkolonie' (1914) (translated as 'In the Penal Colony' (1914)); Henri Barbusse's *Le Feu* (1915–16) (translated as *Under Fire* (1917)); Georg Kaiser's *Gas* trilogy (1916–19) (translated by various hands 1924 and 1971); the concluding pages of Italo Svevo's *La Coscienza di Zeno* (1919–22) (translated as *Confessions of Zeno* (1930)); the war paintings of Otto Dix from the 1920s and 1930s (one of which, *Flandern* (*Flanders*) (1936), was inspired by the concluding pages of *Le Feu*); Alfred Döblin's *Berge Meere und Giganten* (*Mountains Seas and Giants* (1921–3)), especially Books One and Two; and the slaughterhouse chapters from Book Four of Döblin's *Berlin Alexanderplatz* (1927–9) (translated 1931) transcribe both movements of Horkheimer's and Adorno's dialectic. In all six cases, a rationally constructed system—a machine for executing convicts; the military-industrial complex; mechanized warfare; the technological megalopolis; and a food production process—has turned or is in danger of turning into its opposite. In all six cases, an elemental, irrational system is running out of control, treating people as though they were animals or reducing them to dead primal matter, and threatening to destroy both its creators and itself as it does so.

"... [I]t was this feeling of normlessness (which, according to Durkheim, was induced by modernity's destruction of traditional communities) that generated the 'panic terror' which informs so many modernist works."

Indeed, because of the very tenacity with which Western Man clung to the fiction of the rationality of the process which was enslaving him, many modernists felt that he was all the more perilously exposed to those anti-rational powers which the Enlightenment had thought it possible, in some final sense, to subdue, harness and control: psychopathological urges and demonic Nature. Kandinsky, whose seven *Compositionen* (*Compositions*) (1909–13) are marked by a violent sense of impending Apocalypse, put that sense into words when, in *Über das Geistige in der Kunst* (1900–10) (translated as *The Art of Spiritual Harmony* (1914)), he wrote as follows on the state of contemporary civilization: 'Der alte vergessene Friedhof bebt. Alte vergessene Gräber öffnen sich, und vergessene Geister heben sich aus ihnen' ('The old forgotten graveyard is quaking. Old forgotten graves are opening and forgotten spirits/ghosts are rising up from them'). And Hugo Ball, one of the founders of Dada in Zurich in February 1916, echoed the diagnosis when lecturing on Kandisky in Zurich on 7 April 1917: 'Die Titanen standen auf und zerbrachen die Himmelsburgen' ('the Titans rose up and smashed the celestial castles into pieces'). Thus, it is precisely because Mann's Gustav von Aschenbach clings so stubbornly to the illusion that his attraction for Tadzio derives from high, Apollonian motives that he falls prey so destructively to Dionysiac obsession. And it is precisely because the utopian Dream Kingdom of Perle in Alfred Kubin's *Die andere Seite* (1908) (translated as *The Other Side* (1967)) has been created so artificially that its final collapse into anarchy is so violent and so total. The same sense also explains why madness and the city are so closely connected in so many modernist texts. As Spears put it, that institution which had originally been constructed as 'a society of individuals who subscribe to an ideal of rational order' was felt to be turning dialectically into the 'Weltstadt', the insane megalopolis which, in all major pre-war Expressionist poetry and painting, is associated with darkness, demonic ingression, elemental inundation and the dystopic machine. It is not simply, as Bathrick suggests, that 'quotidian modernity' is felt to *cause* madness. Rather, for all its claims to rationality, the modern city itself is perceived to have 'den charakter des offenen Wahnsinns' ('to be characterized by public insanity'). One work which graphically demonstrates this connection *in extenso* is Rilke's novel *Die Aufzeichnungen des Malte Laurids Brigge* (1910) (translated as *The Notebook of Malte Laurids Brigge* (1930)). In this text, the central character is so profoundly affected by the dislocated insanity of modern Paris that, as Huyssen has shown (see note 33), the shock uncovers the fragmentary nature and latent paranoia of his own personality: insane city and unhinged self are mirror images of one another. By the same token, Michael Fischer in Döblin's *Die Ermordung einer Butterblume* (*The Murder of a Buttercup*) (*c.* 1905), a small-scale entrepreneur; the madman in Heym's story. *Der Irre* (*The Head-case*) (1911), a psychopath who is associated with an industrial landscape; and Anton Gross in Franz Jung's *Der Fall Gross* (*The Case of Anton Gross*) (*c.* 1920), a draftsman, are metonymic. While convinced of their sanity, all are motivated by pathological drives which they cannot control, and these lead them to do violence to the natural, the innocent and the female, and, ultimately, to destroy themselves.

Because we can, with hindsight, understand modernist texts in a total context in a way which many of their creators could not, Althusser's concept of a 'problématique' is of relevance. In *Pour Marx* (1965) (translated as *For Marx* (1977)), Althusser argues that any 'problématique' as that is perceived subjectively will be more or less mismatched with the objective state of things, and so will tend to de-form, obscure or repress factors which are not compatible with the epistemological position of the perceiver. If we apply this idea to modernism, it becomes easy to see why the phenomenon is so diverse. First, because of the subjective elements involved in the dialectic encounter from which any given text is generated, two texts which derive from the same objective 'problématique' may appear to be unconnected at the surface level. Second, texts will vary greatly in the manner in which they transcribe and foreground the objective 'problématique' from which they have been generated. Where some will display an 'explicit consciousness of their own ideologies', others will distort, simplify or repress those ideologies and the objective 'problématique' which underpins them—'manage' them, 'forget' them, drive them underground. Thus, some modernist texts, like Hugo von Hofmannsthal's 'Vorfruhling' ('Early Spring') (1892), the early work of Gustav Klimt, or the poems of Georg Trakl (1910–14) allow the objective 'problématique' of modernism to manifest itself only as more or less dark intimations of an impending threat. Others, like Musil's *Die Verwirrungen des Zöglings Törless* (1902–3) (translated as *Young Törless* (1955)) naturalize that 'problématique' into something more manageable (an adolescent crisis in this particular case). Others, like Egon Schiele's paintings *Selbstbildnis mit Lampionfrüchten* (*Self-portrait with Chinese Lanterns*) (1912), *Mutter und Tochter* (*Mother and Daughter*) (1913) and *Liesbesakt* (*Act of Love*) (1915), show terrified human figures in contorted and defensive postures but provide no background which indicates what is causing their terror. Others, like Andrey Bely's *Petrburg* (1911–13) (translated as *Petersburg* (1959; revised and improved in 1978)), Balász's and Bartók's *A Kékszakállá herceg vára* (*Duke Bluebeard's Castle*) (1911), Thomas Mann's *Der Tod in Venedig* (1911) (translated as *Death in Venice* (1928)), or Franz Kafka's *Der Proceß;* (1914) (translated as *The Trial* (1929)), foreground a very powerful sense of the objective 'problématique', but do so in terms which are mythological, quasi-mythological or surreal rather than overtly modern. And others, like Ludwig Meidner's *Apokalyptische Landschaften* (*Apocalyptic Landscapes*) (1913–14), or the major poetry of the German Expressionists, foreground the objective 'problématique' using images which are derived from the modern, i.e. urban/technological world.

Furthermore, modernist texts vary greatly in the degree of complexity with which they present the 'problématique' which they are confronting and trying to resolve. Some, like the poetry of the German Expressionist August Stramm, evince a sense that the 'problématique' is so tangled, so multidimensional, that it vitiates the very medium—in Stramm's case language—which is being employed. While others, like the poetry of the German Activists (1914–20), such late novels by Lawrence as *The Plumed Serpent* (1923–5), or Heidegger's *Einführung in die Metaphysik* (1935; second (revised) edition 1953) (translated as *An Introduction to Metaphysics* (1959)), involve a subjective 'problématique' which is relatively simple, notwithstanding the portentous weight of their rhetoric. Finally, modernist works vary extensively in the nature and complexity of their response to the perceived 'problématique'. On the one hand, it is perfectly possible for important modernist works—like many of Rilke's *Neue Gedichte* or Kandinsky's post-1910 visual work—to involve a highly complex response to a perceived 'problématique' which is so repressed, concealed or 'veiled' that we seem to be dealing with Art for Art's sake in its purest form. While on the other hand, an excessively simple perception of the 'problématique' can, and indeed tends to provoke a correspondingly simplistic response and so generate works which, although modernist, are utopian, and even totalitarian in one form or another.

These variables have been the (often unrecognized) source of critical debate along at least two axes: which works belong in the modernist canon and how important is any given modernist work or author? Although such debates are important, I wish, in this essay, to sidestep them for the sake of two more descriptive aims. First, I wish to chart the major aspects of the modernist 'problématique' within the context established above. And second, I want to chart some of the major ways in which a range of modernists responded to and attempted to resolve that 'problématique' as they perceived it. The point of drawing such a map is not to make it unnecessary to explore individual texts. Rather, the point is to bring those texts into some kind of relationship with one another and so give readers some kind of idea of the issues they may expect to find there when they throw away the map and engage with the texts themselves...

Modernism as Response

By the early 1930s, it was a commonplace among artists and intellectuals, especially on the Continent, that European civilization was at a crossroads. C.G. Jung's *Seelenprobleme der Gegenwart* (*Spiritual Problems of the Present Day*) (1931), especially the chapter entitled 'Das Seelenproblem des modernen Menschen'; Karl Jaspers's *Die geistige Situation der Zeit;* Edmund Husserl's lecture of 7 and 10 May 1935 'Die Krisis des europäischen Menschtums und die Philosophie' (translated as 'Philosophy and the Crisis of Modern Man' (1965)); and, of course, Heidegger's *Einführung in die Metaphysik* all evince a more or less pronounced awareness that Western humanist and/or idealist culture was in a state of crisis. The scientist Max Planck put it thus:

> We are living in a very singular moment of history. It is a moment of crisis, in the literal sense of that word... Many people say that these symptoms mark the beginnings of a great renaissance, but there are others who see in them the tidings of a downfall to which our civilization is fatally destined.

But the art of modernism had anticipated and gone beyond such a straightforwardly optimistic/pessimistic reaction to the perceived crisis, and at the risk of excessive categorization, it is possible to identify at least nine fairly well distinguished types of response to that crisis which recur throughout modernist art.

First, and most negatively, there is the nihilist response. Faced with a situation which Durkheim had, in *Le Suicide* and *De la Division du travail social*, described as one *of anomie*, more than a few modernist artists and intellectuals succumbed to the feeling that an apocalyptic end was approaching beyond which there was only the 'endless darkness . . .' with which *A Kékszakállá herceg vára* concludes, or that human relationships were irredeemably locked into that sado-masochistic double bind which marks Kafka's early writings and Georg Kaiser's *Von morgens bis mitternachts* (1912) (translated as *From Morn to Midnight* (1920)). Consequently, a significant number either went insane (Nietzsche, van Gogh, Jakob van Hoddis, Antonin Artaud); or took their own lives (Virginia Woolf, Jacques Vaché, Jacques Rigaut, René Crevel, Georg Trakl, Ernst Toller, Kurt Tucholsky, Vladimir Mayakovsky, Sergey Yesenin); or died prematurely in a state of near total despair (Rimbaud, Alfred Lichtenstein, August Stramm).

Second, several modernists—and this response is particularly typical of the early Expressionists—sought to relieve their sense of crisis by means of the experience of ecstatic release, sometimes aided by drugs, alcohol or violent experience. Following Rimbaud's stated aim in his letters of 13 and 15 May 1871 of arriving at the Unknown by deranging all his senses, several early Expressionists, not to mention the *alter egos* who form the mid-point of their so-called *Ich-Dramen*, would have assented to the view which Georg Heym recorded in his diary on 6 July 1910 and 15 December 1911: that one instant of intoxicated enthusiasm, even though it may lead to death, is preferable to the suffocating banality and oppression of everyday modern life. And Ludwig Rubiner's highly influential essay of mid-1912, 'Der Dichter greift in die Politik' ('The Poet intervenes in Politics'), with its call for dynamism, intensity, ecstasy and the will to catastrophe, was almost certainly one of the immediate stimuli for such hymns to ecstasy as Bean's 'Untergrundbahn' ('Underground Train/Railway') (1913), Stadler's 'Der Aufbruch' ('The Beginning'/'The Break-Out') (*c.* 1912) and 'Fahrt über die Kölner Rheinbrücke bei Nacht' and Ernst Wilhelm Lotz's 'Aufbruch der Jugend' ('Youth Bursts Out') (*c.* 1913–14). In these and similar works, no attempt is made to analyse or understand. The threatened ego seeks to overcome its sense of isolation and constriction by tapping the irrational powers of the psyche and inducing what Freud called the 'oceanic feeling', regardless of where that might lead. And in several cases, it led, via the war hysteria of 1914, to the trenches and an early death (Lotz, Stadler, Hans Leybold, Franz Marc and August Macke) or to rapid disillusion with ecstatic irrationalism (Ludwig Rubiner, Oskar Kokoschka, Wilhelm Klemm, Hugo Ball and Rudolf Leonhard). As Freud was to argue in *Jenseits des Lustprinzips* (XIII) (translated as *Beyond the Pleasure Principle* (XVIII)) which he published in 1920 in the wake of the Great War: if you open up the Unconscious, you are as likely to release the destructive power of the Death Instinct (*Thanatos*) as the creative power of the Life Instinct (*Eros*).

Third, a significant number of Modernists turned to mysticism as a way of resolving their sense of crisis. This might take the form of a latter-day Platonism (like that of Kandinsky's *Über das Geistige in der Kunst*); a panentheism (like that informing the theory and practice of Hans Arp and Paul Klee); an esoteric hermeticism (like that of Yeats); or a more or less westernized Eastern mysticism (like that embodied in the blue-eyed people who preside over and survive the concluding apocalypse of *Die andere Seite;* or that implied by the concluding (Sanskrit) words of Eliot's *The Waste Land;* or that involved in Hesse's *Siddhartha* (1919–22) (translated 1954) and *Narzibeta; und Goldmund* (1927–9) (translated as *Death and the Lover* (1932)). But the mysticism might also take more secular forms like Chandos's final openness to inexplicable epiphanic moments; Breton's alchemically inspired quest for 'le merveilleux' ('the marvellous') in *Nadja* (1927–8) (translated 1960); the importance of music in Symbolist and Symbolist-derived aesthetic theory; the use of music imagery throughout *A Passage to India* and in the concluding pages of *La Nausée, Dr Faustus* and Kafka's 'Die Verwandlung' (1912) (translated as 'The Metamorphosis' (1937)); or what has been variously termed the 'individualist mysticism' and 'the aesthetic of transcendence and epiphany' of such works as *Die Aufzeichnungen des Malte Laurids Brigge, My, Das Schloß, Der Steppenwolf and Berlin Alexanderplatz.* In all cases, we are dealing with an attempt, albeit one which expresses itself in very different ways and with varying degrees of confidence, to arrive at a sense which is deeply repugnant to those critics who have accepted the (anti-)ontology of postmodernism. Beyond or within what looks like entropic chaos or unresolvable conflict, there exists a firm spiritual substratum. This substratum may be either psychological or metaphysical, but it permits what Jung termed 'integration' and the emergence of what the Existentialists were to call a sense of Being out of Nothingness: it is a melody, as Roquentin puts it in the final pages of *La Nausée*, which persists even after the record has been broken.

Fourth, and closely related to the mystical response, is the aestheticist one. As Bürger has shown, the attempt to establish art as something autonomous, a-historical and removed from the realm of rationalization and commercialization goes back to the end of the eighteenth century. But towards the end of the nineteenth century the sense intensified that the world had not only been desacralized, but was also being increasingly afflicted by the radical sense of uncertainty generated by the dialectical turn taken by the central project of the Enlightenment. Consequently, such practitioners of Art for Art's sake and aestheticism as the Symbolists, the Decadents, the George Circle and the Imagists felt the ever more urgent need to proclaim the sacral nature of art and thereby hold on to an allegedly a-temporal enclave of meaning, stability and transcendence. It is this desire which informs Mallarmé's essay 'Averses ou Critique' ('Rainshowers or Criticism') (1886–95); better known as 'Crise de vers' 'Crisis in Poetry' (1897)); Rilke's book on Rodin (1903–7) (translated 1946) and Hofmannsthal's essay 'Der Dichter und diese Zeit' ('The Poet and this Age' (1906)). In an age when, as Hofmannsthal puts it, the representative things lack spirit and the spiritual things do not stand out in relief; which has no Eleusinian Mysteries or Seven Sacraments with which people can lift themselves above everyday life, it is the artist's task to redeem the world by recapturing that lost sense of mystery.

From here, it is only a short step to the fifth response, the decision to turn one's back on the modern age. After the Great War, for instance, Rilke, Yeats and Ball expressed that decision in a 'flight out of time'—the emigration to a 'still point' or the fixed centre of a 'gyre' which was geographically as far removed as possible from the confusions of the modern age. In Rilke's case, this meant the little château at Muzot; in Yeats's case, the tower in Galway; and in Ball's case, Montagnola in the Tessin (where he became Hesse's secretary and biographer) and the certainties of ultra-orthodox Catholicism. Eliot and Pound (whose early thinking about art and poetry, especially in respect of the need for impersonality, owed much to Symbolism) expressed a very similar decision in a somewhat different way. After the Great War, both moved backwards in time to associate themselves with a pre-modern consciousness and system of beliefs which, they felt, were free from the uncertainties, instability and sense of meaninglessness which marked the modern age. In *The Waste Land*, Eliot came to the conclusion that the modern world was an arid desert full of broken images and that all he could do about it was to put his own lands in order. And he rationalized that conclusion in his essay 'The Metaphysical Poets' (1921) by means of the extremely influential notion of the 'dissociation of sensibility' according to which English culture had undergone a historical fall from grace during the seventeenth century from which it had never recovered. On the basis of that conclusion, Eliot committed himself publicly, in his preface to *For Lancelot Andrewes* (1928), a book dedicated to an English divine who had died in the pre-lapsarian year of 1626, to classicism in literature, royalism in politics and Anglo-Catholicism in religion—i.e. to those attitudes which Eliot believed to have been most finely developed in the last part of the sixteenth century, before the historical fall. And it was the quintessential spirit informing those attitudes which Eliot sought to celebrate in *Little Gidding* (1941–2), the last of the *Four Quartets*, which takes as its starting point a religious community near Huntingdon founded one year before Andrewes's death by Nicholas Ferrar, but looted and dissolved by the Roundheads in 1646. Pound voiced a similar disgust with contemporary European civilization in *Hugh Selwym Mauberly* (1919–20), describing it as 'an old b____ gone in the teeth,/ . . . a botched civilization'. He then left England, and after a stay in Paris, finally settled in 1924 in Mussolini's Italy (which he saw as a modern version of the corporate medieval state and hence free from the mechanization, systematization and 'the black death of the capitalist system') in order to write his own, latter-day version of the *Divine Comedy*: the *Cantos*. These were, as Schwartz put it, 'designed to challenge the corrupted values of Western civilization and to inspire reverence for the highest values—the "eternal state of mind"—which will lay the groundwork for a new and more humane society.' Likewise, Hofmannsthal and George went down their own, not dissimilar paths leading from Aestheticism to various forms of high conservatism.

Where Pound and Eliot turned their backs on the complexities and confusions of the present in the name of an ideal, hieratic past, other modernists, especially during the immediate post-war years, turned their back on the same complexities and confusions in the name of an ideal, socialist future. Thus, the more or less short-lived left-wing utopianism of, for instance, Ernst Toller, Johannes R. Becher, RudolfLeonhard, Kurt Hiller, Ludwig Rubiner, Lyonel Feininger, Bruno Taut and the members of the *Arbeitsrat für Kunst* in Germany, or of Kandinsky, Mayakovsky, Alexander Blok, El Lissitzky, Vladimir Tatlin and Alexander Rodschenko in Russia, was the obverse of the right-wing nostalgia of Eliot, Pound, Hofmannsthal and George. Both groups of modernists were marked by a deep yearning for a total, centred world in which the New Man under socialism or redeemed humanity under God could rediscover a secure identity and transcendent sense of purpose. It is wrong to say, as some critics have, that all modernist utopianism issued in a totalitarian commitment. However, Pound's extreme right-wing illusions did lead him to become the propagandist for a fascist state; and Becher's extreme leftwing illusions did lead him to become the first Minister of Culture of a Stalinist state, the GDR, and the composer of its national anthem. In both cases, a flawed sense of 'problématique' ultimately generated a frighteningly simple, totalitarian response.

The sixth response can be broadly described as a 'primitivism'. Non-European or pre-modern cultures are used not just as sources of aesthetic inspiration, but as a cultural model for emulation. Hence the importance of the Hindu philosopher Professor Godbole in *A Passage to India* and the black community of Harlem in Section II of Lorca's *Poeta in Nueva York* (1929–30) (translated as *Poet in New York* (1940)). Godbole's intuitive, non-rational cast of mind makes him the character who is best adapted to the mysteries, ambiguities and open-ended fluidity which Forster designated with the non-topographical shifter 'India'. And in Lorca's poem, it is the elemental, mythological, 'great and desperate' King of Harlem (whose beard is said to stretch down to the sea) who offers the inhabitants of New York, especially its black community, their only hope of redemption from the anguished frustration and cancered blood which derive from their enslavement by the banality and materialism of industrial civilization.

The seventh response, aptly characterized by Pär Bergman as 'modernolatry', is characteristic of Italian Futurism, early Vorticism and that group of writers, of whom Ernst Jünger is the best known, described by Herf as 'reactionary modernists'. Where the first six responses described above all, in various ways, involve a withdrawal from or transcendence of the contemporary world, the three latter groups celebrated their unreserved commitment to it. The Futurists and the reactionary modernists did so because of the speed, energy, size and sheer modernity of industrial society, and, conversely, its ability to destroy what had been inherited from the past. The Vorticists did so because of the tension they perceived between the massively static, abstract machine forms of modernity and the violence which was stored up within them. But where the Futurists' hymn to the machine, the city and material energy led several of the major members of the movement towards 'embarrassingly reactionary' attitudes—the inhuman celebration of mechanized warfare, Man's ability to master his environment by machine brutality and, ultimately, Mussolini's fascism—most of the Vorticists moved away from their early attitudes and towards less abstract and more humane modes of art. Indeed, Jacob Epstein (who belongs stylistically to the Vorticist group even though he refused to exhibit with them in June 1915) went so far as to destroy what is arguably the major example of Vorticist sculpture, his massive *Rock Drill* (1913–15), probably because he felt that it celebrated the machine violence which had issued in the Great War. Unlike Epstein, but like several major Futurists, Jünger failed to learn more humane attitudes from his war experience. And in books like *In Stahlgewittern* (1920; second (revised) edition 1924) (translated as *The Storm of Steel* (1929)) and *Der Arbeiter* (*The Worker*) (1932), he actually seems to approve of the process by which human beings lose their autonomy and become aspects of a supra-human military or industrial machine. But like the early Vorticists, it was the staticness and stability of huge machines which attracted him; and this, together with his ingrained aristocratism, generated in the late 1930s the totalitarian (albeit anti-Nazi) 'static hierarchy of value' and 'haven of paradisaical permanence' which forms the resolution of his novel *Auf den Marmorklippen* (1939) (translated as *On the Marble Cliffs* (1947)).

The change of heart on the part of most of the Vorticists forms an obvious bridge to the eighth response. Utopian and messianic socialism was doomed to disillusion as the real nature of the German and Russian revolutions became apparent; and Futurist affirmation of the modern was unacceptable to many modernists because of its blindness to or indifference towards the reality and implications of machine violence. So, in order to avoid these pitfalls, those modernists who suffered from a sense of cultural crisis but who wished to stay with the contemporary world had to develop more modest, more ambiguous and more ironic attitudes to the complexities of modernity. It was this desire to negotiate a middle way which generated Constructivism and *Neue Sachlichkeit* (New Objectivity), with their assertion of the need for a modern classicism, their commitment to modern materials and their desire to rescue Western civilization from the barbarism to which it had succumbed over the previous decade. But above all, whether they understood it in these terms or not, the proponents of both movements were trying to reverse the dialectical turn which the central project of the Enlightenment had taken and bring it back onto its central and proper course. Hence their attempts to bring technology back to manageable human dimensions through the design and construction of aesthetically pleasing cities where imperialist capitalism was not permitted to turn into a chaotic, autonomous system, but was, instead, subject to reasonable and humane control. One might describe this general attitude as a pared-down humanism: Man was reinstated at the centre of things but not necessarily regarded as the measure of all things. And human reason, while retaining its centrality, was not overestimated vis-à-vis the powers of unreason inside and outside human nature. Such was the spirit informing Bruno Taut's move away from utopianism and acceptance of the post of City Architect in Magdeburg; Sartre's Existentialism; Jung's central doctrine of 'integration'; Ernst Bloch's *Spuren* (Traces) (1930); Döblin's revision of his apocalyptic *Berge Meere und Giganten into Giganten* (*Giants*) (1932) (in which human autonomy and technological ability were celebrated); and, perhaps of all literary works, Thomas Mann's *Joseph* tetralogy (1926–42) (translated as *Joseph and his Brothers* (1934–45)). Here, as Ritchie Robertson has perceptively observed, Mann, instead of 'surrendering blindly to the primitive or trying to deny its power', sought to 'explore and understand it with the aid of his modern consciousness' and so developed an ironic stance as 'a means of keeping the primitive at bay while acknowledging its authority and appeal'.

And finally, one can identify a strand in modernism which points forward very clearly to McHale's definition of the postmodernist condition as an acceptance of 'an anarchic landscape of worlds in the plural' in which artists renounce the nostalgia or desire for epiphany, transcendence and closure. From the modernist point of view, this double attitude of acceptance and renunciation can be experienced either as a loss (as in Virginia Woolf's last, posthumously published *Between the Acts* (1938–41), and, less tragically, in *Ulysses* and *Watt*). Or it can be experienced as a liberation (as in *Finnegan's Wake* and *Der Mann ohne Eigenschaften*). Or it can be experienced as both at the same time. The best example of this latter, ambiguous response is undoubtedly provided by Dada with its anarchist roots, plurality of poetic registers (including deliberate banality), wide-ranging use of various kinds of collage components, recognition that the cinema rather than the printed word is the art form of modernity, aggressive challenging of classical humanist assumptions, metaleptic mistrust of hierarchies, disrespect for allegedly impermeable boundaries (like that between 'Art' and 'life'), hostility to final solutions and closures, parodic use of machinery, experimentation with heteroglossia via the simultaneous poem, carnival imagery, willingness to accept its own disposability/death, anti-illustrations and repeated insistence that Dada involves the ability to say 'yes' and 'no' at the same time. It can be argued that Dada left too many of the tragic aspects of life out of account, and in his later years, Arp came to see this. Nevertheless, Dada involves the 'suspensive irony', the 'more comprehensive "both-and"', the 'willingness to live with uncertainty, to tolerate and, in some cases, to welcome a world seen as random and multiple, even, at times absurd' and the ability to accept 'the gaps and discontinuities' which Wilde identified as central features of postmodernism. Dada also evinces virtually all the characteristics which, in McHale's view, typify postmodernism—so that it comes as something of a surprise to discover that neither of these critics accords Dada so much as a mention!

It is an artistic landscape like that constructed by Dada in which Ulrich, Musil's 'Möglichkeitsmensch' (literally 'possibilitarian') lives and moves: 'without the fiction of the self as entelechy unfolding and growing according to some inner law'; untroubled by 'the futile and frequently self-destructive searches for selfhood as wholeness, which neglect the potential rewards of openness toward the other'; and without the need for certainty. Indeed, Ulrich's refusal to look for any final solution outside his situation, his ability to hold an ironic balance between the conflicting, overlapping and fluctuating possibilities which inform his situation, and his preparedness to live without any final certainty in an elastic situation where reason is of limited help all make him an example of that 'non-Euclidian humanity' which can live in a 'Lobatchevskyan' universe. Eliot glimpsed precisely this possibility when he published his essay on Ben Jonson in the *TLS* on 13 November 1919, but having achieved his own sense of centred, 'Euclidean' certainty, he repressed that awareness when he published his *Selected Essays* in 1932. Ulrich's attitudes also put him in the same category as those quintessentially modernist heroes Chaplin and Keaton—little men who, when everything is ranged against them, manage to keep their balance in an insane modern universe.

Because the modernists could see, with varying degrees of clarity, complexity and acceptance, the implications of an accelerating process which, in our own era, has turned the world into an electronic stage, or, as Wilde put it, a global shopping mall, they constituted in the literal sense an avant-garde scouting out an unknown territory. But because that process had not yet turned into a total and accepted way of life legitimized by what Horkheimer and Adorno were to call the 'culture industry', it was still possible for the modernists to respond to it in ways which are closed to the postmodernists. Hence the frequent and hotly debated charge that postmodernism is not an oppositional phenomenon. The modernists were still able, either literally or imaginatively, to seek out alternative or geographical enclaves which had not yet been colonized by the media or the leisure industry. They could call to mind a past which was in danger, but not irrevocably so, of being lost and had not been reified by the nostalgia or heritage industries. They could hope in a hieratical or socialist utopia which had not been discredited by Nazi or Stalinist atrocities. They could withdraw into arcane areas of the mind which had not been invaded by the religious or the fantasy industries. And they could use a variety of innovative artistic techniques and psychological ploys which enabled them to retain a greater or lesser sense of selfhood and autonomy, but which had not yet been assimilated by the advertising, fashion and lifestyle industries. Although modernism anticipated what McHale has called 'the pluralistic and anarchistic ontological landscape of advanced industrial cultures', most modernists disliked what they espied from their advanced position. As Barnouw and Wilde suggest, this was partly because of a nostalgia for a (probably imaginary) ideal stability, but partly, too, because of three more serious reasons. First, many modernists suspected that what McHale describes as 'pluralism' might actually be nothing more than a multicoloured surface concealing a commodified uniformity. Second, the more socially aware realized that that 'anarchistic' landscape was not a flat one, but involved large, possibly growing areas of systematically created physical and psychological misery. And third, the more psychoanalytically aware feared that the abolition of metaphors of depth—one of the central features of the postmodernist imagination—inevitably involved a blindness to or the repression of those dark, Dionysiac powers which return from the forgotten depths all the more potently and destructively for being ignored.

Given the unmistakeable consequences which are now issuing from the dialectical turn taken by the central project of the Enlightenment— escalating environmental problems, the growing gap between the haves and the have-nots, the boredom, violence and alienation which haunt our advanced societies, the difficulties involved in making relationships within a system which is inherently hostile to *Gemeinschaften*—the anxiety of modernism may well be a more appropriate response to that turn than postmodernism's ludic acceptance. Ever since Kierkegaard, the Existentialists, with the exception of the later Sartre, have been telling us that our capacity to experience *Angst* betokens a very deep realization that the prevailing system which constructs what Lawrence called the 'old stable *ego*' is at odds with the profoundest stratum of the personality. And the central project of German aesthetics since Kant, admirably analysed by Andrew Bowie in terms of the 'concern with those aspects of subjectivity which are incompatible with wholesale rationalisation', points to the same awareness. We may not be able to return in good faith to the security of religious orthodoxy, cling on to the centred categories and confident correspondences of classical humanism, or find refuge in any of the enclaves still available to many of the modernists. But in the face of the massive problems faced by Western or westernizing humanity, all of which can, ultimately, be understood in terms of Horkheimer's and Adorno's analysis, it has become a matter of urgency to undertake a transvaluation of values. And that means defying the massively oracular authority of the patriarchs of the 1980s like Lacan and Derrida; finding a power with which to fill the gap at the heart of postmodernist aesthetics and psychology; undoing the post-Enlightenment equations of Geist-as-spirit with Geist-as-ego and self with ego; relegitimizing metaphors of depth; and rediscovering that decentred fluidum at the heart of the human personality which many ancient cultures referred to by means of metaphors of breath. The problematics of modernism are still with us, albeit in a more drastic form. Thus, by studying the variety of ways in which modernist writers, thinkers and artists responded to them and understanding the implications and end results of those responses, we are given the means of avoiding the modernists' mistakes and making decisions about the nature of reality, our relationship with reality and our relationship with ourselves which can, in some measure at least, help us to look for a way out of the *impasse* into which our civilization seems currently to be heading.

Source: Richard Sheppard, "The Problematics of European Modernism," in *Theorizing Modernism: Essays in Critical Theory*, edited by Steve Giles, Routledge, 1993, pp. 1–51.

Sources

Arnold, Matthew, *Culture and Anarchy*, Yale University Press, 1994.

Brooks, Cleanth, *Modern Poetry and the Tradition*, University of North Carolina Press, 1939.

———, *The Well-Wrought Urn*, Harvest Books, 1956.

Eliot, T. S., *Selected Prose of T. S. Eliot*, edited by Frank Kermode, Harvest Books, 1975.

Ransom, John Crowe, *The New Criticism*, New Directions Press, 1939.

Further Reading

Bradbury, Malcolm, and James McFarlane, *Modernism: A Guide to European Literature 1890–1930*, Penguin, 1991.

This anthology provides more than two dozen essays by the most eminent critics of Modernism. Topics range from the artistic scenes in various cities to the formal characteristics of modernist poetry to discussions of some of the smaller movements within Modernism.

Charters, Jimmie, *This Must Be the Place*, Herbert Joseph, 1932.

Jimmie Charters—"Jimmie the Barman"—tended bar at the Dingo in the Paris neighborhood of Montparnasse, a notorious haunt for such modernist writers as Ernest Hemingway and James Joyce. The book provides a portrait of these writers in their leisure hours, written by a man with very little interest in their art but a great appreciation for their personalities.

Douglas, Ann, *Terrible Honesty: Mongrel Manhattan in the 1920s*, Farrar, Straus, and Giroux, 1995.

The artistic scene in New York in the 1920s was a "mongrelized" blend of black and white, urban and rural, male and female, according to Ann Douglas, who suggests that there is a need to understand the important contribution that marginalized groups made to American Modernism. In her book, she portrays the rise of New York City to cultural preeminence and balances the stories of traditional modernist heroes such as Ernest Hemingway with discussions of Harlem Renaissance figures such as Langston Hughes.

Hemingway, Ernest, *A Moveable Feast*, Touchstone, 1996.

Hemingway's casual memoir of the Lost Generation is the most famous description of Paris in the 1920s. Artists and writers from Picasso to Gertrude Stein to Man Ray appear in this amiable and fascinating book.

Kenner, Hugh, *The Pound Era*, University of California Press, 1973.

Controversial and idiosyncratic, Hugh Kenner is the most famous critic who deals with Modernism. In this book, he argues that Ezra Pound, not T. S. Eliot or James Joyce, is the central figure of Modernism and that all of Modernism's themes and formal devices can be found in Pound's writings.

Naturalism

Movement Origin

c. 1860

Naturalism applies both to scientific ideas and principles, such as instinct and Darwin's theory of evolution, and to fiction. Authors in this movement wrote stories in which the characters behave in accordance with the impulses and drives of animals in nature. The tone is generally objective and distant, like that of a botanist or biologist taking notes or preparing a treatise. Naturalist writers believe that truth is found in nature, and because nature operates within consistent principles, patterns, and rules, truth is consistent.

Because the focus of Naturalism is human nature, stories in this movement are character-driven rather than plot-driven. Although Naturalism was inspired by the work of the French writer Émile Zola, it reached the peak of its accomplishment in the United States. In France, Naturalism was strongest in the late 1870s and early 1880s, but it emerged in the United States at the end of the nineteenth century and extended up to the first world war.

The fundamental naturalist doctrine is presented in Zola's 1880 essay "Le roman experimental" (meaning the experimental—or experiential—novel). In it, Zola claims that the naturalist writer should subject believable characters and events to experimental conditions. In other words, take the known (such as a character) and introduce it into the unknown (such as an unfamiliar place). Another major principle of Naturalism that Zola explains in this essay is the idea of determinism, which is the theory that a person's fate is determined solely by heredity and environment.

While the French initiated and began to develop Naturalism, Americans are credited with bringing it to fruition. American Naturalist writers include the novelists Theodore Dreiser, Stephen Crane, Frank Norris, Hamlin Garland, and Jack London; the short story writer O. Henry (William Sydney Porter); and the poets Edwin Arlington Robinson and Edgar Lee Masters. Dreiser's *An American Tragedy* is considered the pinnacle of naturalist achievement. Other representative works are Dreiser's *Sister Carrie*, London's *The Call of the Wild*, Norris's *McTeague*, and Crane's *The Red Badge of Courage*.

Jack London

Representative Authors

Stephen Crane (1871–1900)

Best remembered for his Civil War narrative, *The Red Badge of Courage*, Stephen Crane was born on November 1, 1871, six years after the war ended. He was born in Newark, New Jersey, and later launched his career in New York as a journalist for the *New York Herald, New York Tribune*, and *New York Journal*. His first story, the novella, *Maggie: A Girl of the Streets*, was self-published when he was twenty-two years old. In 1895 *The Red Badge of Courage* was published, making Crane internationally famous and enabling him to focus on writing fiction for the rest of his short life. Crane died of tuberculosis on June 5, 1900, in Badenweiler, Germany. He is buried in Hillside, New Jersey.

Crane's major contribution to American literature is *The Red Badge of Courage*. It is the story of Henry Fleming, a young man who enlists to fight in the Civil War. Through his experiences, he discovers that he possesses courage and that war is less glamorous than he imagined it would be. With this narrative, Crane takes the characteristics of Naturalism and applies them to a critical period in American history. The result is a work that was immediately embraced by Americans at the time of publication and continues to be admired and taught today.

Theodore Dreiser (1871–1945)

Born in Terre Haute, Indiana, on August 27, 1871, Theodore Dreiser enjoyed a career as a respected journalist and novelist. Dreiser left Indiana as a young man and found work in Chicago as a journalist. When his first novel, *Sister Carrie*, was a failure, he was plagued by self-doubt. His doubt proved to be unfounded, however, as he rose to prominence in literary circles, was a finalist for the Nobel Prize for literature in 1930, and received an Award of Merit from the Academy of Arts and Letters in 1945. Dreiser died of a heart attack in Los Angeles, California, on December 28, 1945.

In *An American Tragedy* and *Sister Carrie*, Dreiser depicts the dark side of the myth of the American dream. This is a recurring theme in his work. Both novels feature tragic characters who are the victims of their own desires. In any discussion of Naturalism, *An American Tragedy* is generally held up as the best example. But *Sister Carrie* is also a strong representative of the movement and, as Dreiser's first novel, demonstrates how naturally the style came to him.

Frank Norris (1870–1902)

Benjamin Franklin Norris, Jr. was born in Chicago, Illinois, on March 5, 1870. He was an artistic and well-educated man, having studied painting in 1887 at the Atelier Julien in Paris and attended the University of California at Berkeley (1890–94) and Harvard University (1894–95). Like many of the naturalist writers, he worked in journalism as a foreign correspondent. Norris wrote from South Africa for *San Francisco Chronicle* from 1895 to 1896, and from Cuba for S. S. McClure Syndicate of New York City as a war correspondent in 1898. He died of appendicitis in San Francisco, California, on October 25, 1902.

Norris is respected as one of the major writers who developed American Naturalism. Critics regard his work as being the closest to the pure Naturalism described by Zola. His most notable works are *McTeague: A Story of San Francisco*, *The Octopus: A Story of California*, and *The Pit: A Story of Chicago*. Although *McTeague: A Story of San Francisco* was written early in Norris's career, many scholars consider it his masterpiece despite its violent content. *The Octopus: A Story of California* and *The Pit: A Story of Chicago* are two volumes of an unfinished trilogy. In addition to novels, Norris wrote numerous short stories that appeared in publications for a wide range of audiences.

Émile Zola (1840–1902)

Émile Zola was born in Paris, France, on April 2, 1840. During his career Zola wrote novels, short stories, plays, translations, and criticism. He was awarded the position of Officer of Legion d'Honneur in 1888–89. This position was revoked, however, because of Zola's disputes with the French government. Always a controversial figure, Zola had a wide audience among his contemporaries and remains a major figure in French literature today. He died of accidental asphyxiation on September 29, 1902, in Paris. Although he was buried in Paris, his ashes were later moved to the Pantheon in Rome, Italy, home to the tombs of many of the greatest thinkers in the world.

Considered the most prominent theorist of Naturalism, Zola wrote the essay "Le roman experimental" (meaning "the experimental—or experiential—novel") in 1880. In it, Zola explains that the role of the naturalist is to subject believable incidents to experimental conditions in the novel in order to find truth. The author, in a sense, becomes a scientist. Zola also claims that character is conditioned and determined by heredity and environment. Although Zola is credited as the father of Naturalism, his views are often considered to represent the extremes of the style.

Representative Works

An American Tragedy

Published in 1925, *An American Tragedy* is loosely based on a true story and is considered the best example of American Naturalism. It is the story of Clyde Griffiths, whose desire to see the American dream made manifest in his life almost leads him to commit murder. In just one of the novel's examples of irony, Clyde is found guilty of committing murder, even though his intended victim died accidentally.

An American Tragedy is typical of Dreiser's work in demythologizing the American dream. Dreiser felt that believing in the American dream led to heartbreak, disappointment, and cynicism. *An American Tragedy* typifies Naturalism because it concerns an ordinary middle-class man whose circumstances push him to make extreme choices. Having always dreamed of a better life and having always been told he could create that life, he is finally on the brink of entering the upper echelons of society when a wealthy woman becomes romantically interested in him. The problem is that he already has planned to marry a poor woman who has had his child. This situation is devastating for Clyde because he sees his long-awaited opportunity to fulfill his dreams slipping away. The lure of the American dream proves too strong, and he plans to kill his betrothed.

Upon publication, *An American Tragedy* received popular and critical acclaim. Some critics suggest that the novel's popular success was due to the post-World War I public's desire to read about individual accountability in society. After all, Clyde is found guilty of a crime he intended to commit. Critically, the novel is declared a masterpiece and is deemed Dreiser's best work. Although some reviewers claim that the book is inelegantly written, contains bad grammar, and is overly melodramatic, most enthusiastically recommend it.

The Call of the Wild

Although it started as a short story, London's *The Call of the Wild* (1903) soon became a wildly popular novel. The money London made by selling the rights to the novel enabled him to purchase a boat on which he could disappear and write without distraction. Read all over the world and taught in schools, *The Call of the Wild* is now considered a classic of American fiction.

The Call of the Wild is about a dog named Buck who is taken from his home in California and put on a dog team in the Yukon. In his new environment, he must assert himself among the other dogs to survive. He is eventually adopted by a loving man named John Thornton, whose patience and kindness teach Buck to trust and love. This novel is unique among naturalist novels because its main character is not a person, but this is also why it is a good example of Naturalism. The laws and forces of nature are laid bare in the story of Buck. His interaction with the pack, nature, and people reveals the laws of nature.

McTeague: A Story of San Francisco

In *McTeague: A Story of San Francisco* (1899), Norris disputes the image of the self-reliant American in charge of his or her own fate. Instead, Norris takes a typically naturalist approach and portrays people as the products of their environments, genetic traits, and chance occurrences. Norris took almost a decade to complete this novel, and it stands as his most prominent work. In *McTeague: A Story of San Francisco*, the title character is an unlicensed dentist of below average morality and intelligence. He is an ideal naturalistic character because he is guided by his impulses rather than by careful deliberation or acts of will. In the end, he loses his practice and beats his wife to death when she refuses to tell him where she has hidden money she inherited. Both characters are portrayed as victims. While she is the victim of violence, he is the victim of his own bestial nature.

Readers and critics found the book to be unnecessarily violent in its pessimistic portrayal of what human beings are capable of doing. While other naturalist books included violence (most notably *The Red Badge of Courage*), none were as descriptive or explicit. The novel is important, however, as a key work of the naturalist movement and as the masterpiece of one of its dominant figures.

The Red Badge of Courage

The Civil War narrative, *The Red Badge of Courage* (1895) made Crane internationally famous. The style and the stirring, emotional voice of a young soldier captivated critics and readers alike. Veterans of the Civil War praised the book's realistic account of the experience. Although numerous books containing Civil War narratives had been published since the 1860s, *The Red Badge of Courage* stood out for Crane's contemporaries. The book's ability to capture such a vivid time in American history is evident in the fact that it is still read today in classrooms all over the country. The book is not only a classic of Naturalism, but it is also a testament to Crane's imagination; born in 1871 (six years after the war's end), he never served in the war, and everything he knew of it was from secondary sources.

Émile Zola

The story is about a young man named Henry Fleming who is full of youthful adventure and longing to be part of the war. He enlists, only to face doubts about his own courage and romantic attitudes. Crane uses the war as the fictional "laboratory" into which he places his young protagonist. The war is an extreme set of environmental variables, and Henry's experiences lead him from uncertainty to confidence in his own character. In the true spirit of Naturalism, Crane portrays Henry's fate as a set of outcomes based on his inborn traits (his drive to be a part of the adventure) and his new environment (the pressures of the war). Crane utilizes many typical naturalist techniques such as symbolism, third-person point-of-view, and use of detail.

Sister Carrie

Dreiser's first novel, *Sister Carrie*, was published in 1900. After publication, there was controversy surrounding the novel because of the lack of morality of the main character and the fact that the outcome suggests that she is rewarded for her sinful ways. Still, many readers and critics find it to be a moving and honest portrayal of a young woman who leaves her rural home to make a life for herself in Chicago. After briefly working in a factory, she moves in with a well-to-do salesman and becomes his mistress. Soon, however, she catches the eye of a wealthier older man who leaves his wife and career in order to run away with Carrie. They end up in New York, where they part ways and Carrie successfully pursues a stage career.

As a naturalist writer, Dreiser sought to reveal the harshness of life and the ways in which individuals can seize opportunities to alleviate much of that harshness. While some of Dreiser's contemporaries found the depiction of Carrie's amoral life inappropriate, others found it refreshingly realistic. This novel is also important because it shows Dreiser's early tendencies toward the naturalist style. For example, he takes Carrie out of her comfortable environment (the Midwest) and places her in the unfamiliar big city of Chicago to see how her wants and needs will affect her decision-making. The setting, in essence, becomes a set of conditions in which the reader can observe the changes taking place in the character. Other aspects of the novel, such as Dreiser's attention to detail and his portrayal of the struggling lower class, are consistent with the naturalist style.

Themes

Scientific Principles

Naturalist writers apply scientific principles and methods to the writing of fiction. Like scientists conducting experiments, they introduce readers to a character or characters and then set the events of the novel in motion to see how the characters' inherited traits and environmental influences will determine their outcomes. In some cases, an unexpected opportunity is also introduced to give the character a chance to take it or to ignore it. Given extreme circumstances or desires or needs, characters make decisions they would not otherwise make. The naturalist writer believes that the characters' true natures emerge in these situations.

Another scientific idea used in naturalist writing is conditioned behavior. Characters learn how to behave when they are exposed repeatedly to the same environmental influences. A character such as Henry in *The Red Badge of Courage* quickly learns how to behave in order to survive in the extreme circumstances of war. Buck in *The Call of the Wild* is first conditioned to hate people but later learns to trust the right man.

Darwinian processes are sometimes evident in naturalist writing. In *Sister Carrie*, for example, Carrie is inherently stronger than Hurstwood; as a result of his weakness, he abandons all of his comforts and ultimately commits suicide, while Carrie enjoys a successful stage career and self-reliance. Society is unforgiving and harsh toward the weak but offers rewards to the strongest members of society. This suggests that civilized society is as much a forum for competition among its members as nature is for animals.

Ordinary People in Extraordinary Circumstances

Novels of the naturalist movement feature common, everyday people. There are no members of royalty, titans of the business world, or great minds. Instead, naturalist authors choose protagonists like McTeague, a would-be dentist; Carrie, a rural Midwestern girl; and Buck, a mixed-breed dog. These characters lead simple lives, uncluttered by the good fortune and distractions of glamour, wealth, or adventure. They are left only with their limited resources and their innate natures. In rare cases such as Carrie's, a character attains an extraordinary life but finds it ultimately unsatisfying. These characters learn that there are more similarities than differences between the common and the uncommon.

Naturalist authors place these ordinary characters in extraordinary situations. Carrie finds herself first in the big city of Chicago and eventually in New York City, enjoying a glamorous career as an actress. In contrast, her lover, Hurstwood, descends from a lavish lifestyle to living on the street. In the end, his dramatic decision to take his own life is in sharp contrast to the cheap motel where he does it.

Henry in *The Red Badge of Courage* is an ordinary young man who makes a decision to seek out the extraordinary by enlisting to fight in the Civil War. He discovers that it is he who is extraordinary in his courage and that war consists of common ugliness.

By placing ordinary people in extreme situations, naturalist writers show their readers that they, too, could find themselves in extraordinary situations. They also show that while some people become extraordinary due to their circumstances, others are destined to remain common.

Media Adaptations

- *The Call of the Wild* was adapted to audio by Naxos Audio Books (abridged) in 1995, read by Garrick Hagon; and by Dercum (unabridged) in 1997, read by Samuel Griffin.
- *The Call of the Wild* was adapted to film in 1908 by Biograph Company; in 1923 by Hal Roach Studios; in 1935 by 20th Century Pictures, starring Clark Gable; and in 1972 by Metro-Goldwyn-Mayer, starring Charlton Heston.
- *The Call of the Wild* was also adapted for television movies in 1976 by Charles Fries Productions; in 1993 by RHI Entertainment, starring Rick Schroder; and in 1997 by Kingsborough Greenlight Pictures. It was adapted as a television series in 2000 by Cinevu Films and Call of the Wild Productions.
- *Sister Carrie* was adapted to audio by Books on Tape in 1997, read by Rebecca Burns; and in 2000 by Blackstone Audio Books, read by C. M. Herbert.
- *McTeague: A Story of San Francisco* was adapted to audio by Audio Book Contractors in 1994.
- *McTeague: A Story of San Francisco* was adapted to film in 1915 by William A. Brady Picture Plays, Inc., and was adapted as a television opera by Robert Altman in 1992 in a production by The Lyric Opera of Chicago aired on Public Broadcasting Station.
- *The Red Badge of Courage* was adapted to audio in 1993 by Bookcassette Sales, read by Roger Dressler.
- *The Red Badge of Courage* was adapted to film in 1951 by Metro-Goldwyn-Mayer, directed by John Huston and starring Audie Murphy.
- *The Red Badge of Courage* was also adapted as a television movie in 1974 by 20th Century Fox Television.
- *An American Tragedy* was adapted to film in 1931 in a production by Paramount. It was again adapted in 1951 as *A Place in the Sun.*

Style

Symbolism

Naturalist authors use symbolism to subtly convey a wealth of meaning in a few words or images. In *McTeague: A Story of San Francisco*, Norris uses McTeague's tooth-shaped sign as a symbol of how the character would like to perceive himself and be perceived by others. Although he has no license to practice dentistry, he wants the respectability such a profession would bring him. The tooth is gold, which symbolizes McTeague's drive to acquire wealth. In *Sister Carrie*, Dreiser introduces the rocking chair as a symbol during key moments in Carrie's life. Her rocking in it symbolizes her solitude in the world. As she rocks, she thinks about the state of her life, and the chair moves but never goes anywhere. Still another example of naturalist symbolism is the mountain in *The Red Badge of Courage*. It is ominous and immovable, and represents the power and permanence of nature.

Details

Naturalists are similar to realists in their attention to detail. Naturalist works contain detailed passages describing settings, backgrounds, appearances, and emotions. This helps the reader get a specific and fully formed perception of the characters' lives. Details also give the work a realistic feeling. Naturalists include details of every kind, not just those that are considered artistic or beautiful. If a character's attire is shabby, the naturalist author will describe it as shabby, not cast in a romantic or sentimental light. The objective is to depict a subject wholly and factually. Dreiser uses details to give the reader insight into his characters in *Sister Carrie.* By describing Carrie's clothing and furnishings in detail, he suggests to the reader how important appearance is to Carrie and to her first lover, Drouet.

A common naturalist pattern is to present a great deal of information at the beginning of the novel and then let the events unfold. *McTeague:*

Topics for Further Study

- Consider the main identifying characteristics of Naturalism, and choose three films that you believe reflect naturalistic ideas. Write a review of each film, explaining the characteristics of Naturalism that you see in it.
- After Naturalism came Modernism, a period that produced fiction, drama, and poetry expressing the experiences and attitudes of wartime and postwar writers. Research this period and its major contributors and create a presentation in which you demonstrate how Modernism grew out of, or in reaction to, Naturalism. Be sure to consider historical influences.
- The photography of Edward Curtis is often associated with the naturalist movement. His subject matter was primarily the dwindling Native-American population and culture. Examine some of his photographs and decide if you would classify him with the naturalists or with the romantic Western writers. (You will need to learn a little about the characteristics of romantic Western writing.) Explain your position in a well-organized essay that makes references to specific photographs.
- Read a naturalist work of your choice, paying particular attention to the author's use of symbolism. Write an essay discussing examples of symbolism in the work and how the symbols used relate to Naturalism.

A Story of San Francisco adheres to this pattern. Norris provides a great deal of information at the beginning, and the events of the story flow from this information. There are no plot twists, shocking turns of events, or unexpected characters. Further, the information given at the beginning is reliable, so the reader is a fully informed observer from the start.

Movement Variations

France

Naturalism began in France in the mid-nineteenth century and lasted until the early 1880s. The principal figure of French Naturalism is Zola, whose 1880 essay "Le roman experimental" was instrumental in the spread of Naturalism to the United States. Zola describes human existence as being determined by environment and genetics, and he adheres to the belief that people behave basically as animals in nature do.

Edmond and Jules de Goncourt were brothers who also wrote in the naturalist style in France during Zola's time. The Goncourt brothers adhered to certain tenets of Romanticism, such as the elite status of the artist, as they explored the realistic tone of Naturalism. Their application of scientific ideas in fiction was a major contribution to the naturalist movement.

England

The term naturalist is not generally used to describe English literature during the American naturalist period. The Edwardian period (1901–14), however, shares certain characteristics of Naturalism, indicating that attitudes and reading habits were similar among Americans and the British in the years leading up to World War I. Edwardian writers were cynical and questioned authority, religion, art, and social institutions. This is akin to the naturalist method of observing and testing human behavior in an inquisitive manner rather than accepting traditional beliefs uncritically. Both Naturalism and the Edwardian period were dominated by fiction writers rather than by dramatists or poets.

Drama

Naturalism in drama was a minor movement that emerged in the late nineteenth century. Playwrights of this style paid special attention to detail in costume, set design, and acting in order to re-

Compare & Contrast

- **Early 1900s:** In 1907, Paris is the site of the first cubist painting exhibition in the world. Pablo Picasso and Georges Braque spearhead the movement. An artistic manifestation of the age's rationalism, Cubism is embraced by some and staunchly rejected by others. It will be years before it is recognized as a legitimate artistic movement and its influence fully appreciated.

  Today: Modern art includes a wide variety of media and styles. Although art lovers are more accepting of innovations and radical new approaches, many artists continue to struggle with society's preconceived notions of what constitutes art. This tension between the artist and society keeps alive the fundamental question: "What is art?"

- **Early 1900s:** In 1903 Henry Ford founds the Ford Motor Company and creates an efficient assembly line ten years later. This revolutionizes both transportation and manufacturing, making it possible for many more people to own cars.

  Today: Owning a car is quite common, and prices range from the affordable to the lavish. Car buyers are no longer limited to the "basic black" first offered by Ford or even to American-made vehicles; automobiles are imported from all over the world. Innovations in design often dictate innovations on the factory floor.

- **Early 1900s:** Max Planck and Albert Einstein make major contributions to physics, publishing theories that radically change the way scientists look at the universe.

  Today: In 2000 three scientists share the Nobel Prize for physics. For their contributions to the field of modern information technology, Zhores I. Alferov, Herbert Kroemer, and Jack S. Kilby are honored.

move as much artificiality as possible. They sought to break down barriers between the audience and the stage, and they were especially opposed to the melodrama that was so popular with audiences at the time. Some naturalist playwrights embraced social causes of the day, preferring to inform and alarm audiences rather than to provide them with mindless entertainment. As a result of removing artifice from the theater, they hoped that the audience would have a sense that they were watching and learning from real people. Playwrights associated with this style include Henri Becque (French), Eugene Brieux (French), Gerhart Hauptmann (German-Polish), and Maxim Gorky (Russian).

Historical Context

Realistic Period in American Literature

Realism preceded Naturalism in American literature, and the two are closely related. Both aim for realistic portrayals of everyday life, and both incorporate a great deal of detail. Realism arose after the Civil War, a traumatic period in history in which Americans fought one another over basic issues such as unity and freedom. After the Civil war, Americans were less idealistic and more interested in politics, science, and economics. A new kind of American fiction had to emerge in the wake of widespread disillusionment.

The expansion of education created a broader readership, and new laws helped protect copyrights. These developments meant that more writers could enjoy viable careers. Authors of fiction found ready audiences for their unsentimental works. Within Realism, minor movements such as pragmatism and historical novels emerged. The prominent authors during the realistic movement included Mark Twain, William Dean Howells, and Henry James. In poetry, Walt Whitman, Emily Dickinson, and Sidney Lanier are considered the prominent writers of the time. In drama, little change was evident. The melodrama and fanfare that typified drama prior to Realism continued to find audiences.

Technology and Science

The early 1900s was a period marked by advances in technology and science, creating a social environment in which the intellect was considered superior to emotions and to traditional, blindly accepted beliefs. In 1900 Max Planck opened up a new world of physics when he discovered the quantum nature of energy. Five years later, Albert Einstein developed the Special Theory of Relativity, and in 1915 he developed the general theory. Together, these advances in physics revolutionized scientific thought. This new way of thinking shaped not only the sciences but also the arts, economics, and politics. By the turn of the century, America was well on its way to being an industrialized nation. After the Civil War, the spirit of industrialism that had been born in the North took on new fervor. It was time to repair the nation and its economy. Progress was made in the fields of communication, transportation, and manufacturing. In transportation, Henry Ford founded Ford Motor Company in 1903 (the same year that Orville and Wilbur Wright successfully flew the first motorized plane) and opened the first automotive assembly line in 1913. As a result of the competition encouraged by free market economics, General Motors Corporation was founded in 1908.

In the intellectual world, new thinkers revolutionized the ways in which people understood their world. Charles Darwin challenged the traditional religious concept of the origin of human beings; Karl Marx challenged traditional views on economics and social class; and Auguste Comte initiated the philosophy of positivism (which claims that the purpose of knowledge is merely to describe, not to explain, the world) and the field of sociology (which focuses on observing, quantifying, and predicting social phenomena).

Advances in science and technology led to widespread acceptance of rationalism and scientific inquiry. Among the arts, this attitude was especially noticeable in literature. Moving away from the realms of feelings and relationships, writers approached their craft as a medium for understanding the human psyche. Writers were inspired less by the desire to provide readers with escape and and more by a desire to find truth.

Critical Overview

Although naturalist novels such as *The Red Badge of Courage* and *The Call of the Wild* are now considered classics, critics are often torn on the merits of the movement as a whole. The movement was initially met with suspicion because it was regarded as irrelevant to the American culture and its values. Perhaps because of its French roots, Naturalism was perceived as having little to offer an American readership. The lack of a strong morality presented in many naturalist novels further alienated critics and readers who looked to literature to enlighten and inspire. In his book *Realism and Naturalism in Nineteenth-Century American Literature*, Donald Pizer provides a retrospective comment: "We are coming to realize that a generation of American critics has approached American literary Naturalism with beliefs about man and art which have frequently distorted rather than cast light upon the object before them." Conservative reviewers denounced the works of Dreiser, for example, for his unfavorable depiction of the modern American man and woman. Still others, like Joseph Warren Beach in his book *The Twentieth Century Novel: Studies in Technique*, praise Dreiser for his negative depictions. Beach commends Dreiser's "fearlessness, his honesty, his determination to have done with conventional posturings and evasions."

In the 1940s and 1950s, critics were quick to distance themselves from naturalist writers because some of them (such as Dreiser) were associated with the Communist Party. During that time, there was intense distrust of anyone with communist leanings. Today, critics legitimize the movement on its own terms, crediting it as a significant and coherent movement that resulted in great literary works.

Many critics have difficulty discussing Naturalism without reference to its predecessor, Realism. The two movements share many characteristics (such as attention to detail, common people as subjects, and portrayals of harsh circumstances), but most scholars see Naturalism's reliance on the principle of determinism as its main distinguishing feature. This refers to the belief among naturalist writers that people's fates are determined by their environments and/or their genetics. Pizer declares:

> The common belief is that the naturalists were like the realists in their fidelity to the details of contemporary life but that they depicted everyday life with a greater sense of the role of such causal forces as heredity and environment in determining behavior and belief.

Critics find Naturalism to be the more pessimistic of the two movements. Pizer comments that another important difference is the way human nature is perceived. He explains:

> A naturalistic novel is thus an extension of Realism only in the sense that both modes often deal with the local and contemporary. The naturalist, however, discovers in this material the extraordinary and excessive in human nature.

Critics like Pizer find Naturalism to be empowering because it reveals the humanity, experiences, and emotional states of common and lowly characters.

Criticism

Jennifer Bussey

Bussey holds a master's degree in interdisciplinary studies and a bachelor's degree in English literature. She is an independent writer specializing in literature. In the following essay, Bussey asserts that Theodore Dreiser's Sister Carrie *is important because it makes Naturalism accessible and relevant to American women.*

A survey of Naturalism reveals that women are underrepresented in this movement, both as authors and as protagonists. Of the major authors—Theodore Dreiser, Stephen Crane, Jack London, Frank Norris—none are women. Previous movements, most notably Romanticism, included women as contributors and as heroines, yet Naturalism is almost exclusively masculine. This is not to imply that the omission of women was intentional but rather that something about the movement itself spoke to men more meaningfully than to women. Some of the best-known naturalist works represent experiences that, at the time, were exclusive to men. Crane's moving Civil War story, *The Red Badge of Courage*, is set during the war and relates a soldier's experiences. London's *The Call of the Wild* is about a dog in the Yukon, where living conditions are harsh and the culture revolves around heavy drinking, gambling, and dog fights. Where in all of this is there a place for women? The answer, ironically, comes from one of the male authors, Theodore Dreiser, in his novel *Sister Carrie*.

Sister Carrie is unique among the prominent naturalist works because it is about a woman and it speaks to the difficult decisions many women were forced to make in turn-of-the century urban America. The story concerns Caroline Meeber, known as Carrie or Sister Carrie by her friends and family. She leaves her rural home to live with her sister in Chicago, where she hopes to find work and establish her independence. This change of scenery embodies the Naturalist technique of transplanting a character to create a fictional laboratory in which the reader can observe the character's behaviors and reactions.

Cover of The Red Badge of Courage *by Stephen Crane*

After working briefly in a factory she becomes a salesman's mistress, sharing an apartment with him and enjoying a nicer lifestyle than she had with her sister. While this choice is not the most moral one, it enables her to get what she wants (a better way of life) by providing what someone else wants (the company of a pretty girl). Given Carrie's standing as a woman in turn-of-the-century Chicago, she reacts to her new environment within her limited choices. When a wealthier man shows interest in her, she readily transfers her loyalties to him. He eventually disappoints her, however, and having moved to New York with him, she finds that she has more options. She makes a career for herself in the theater, and no longer needing the security of a

What Do I Study Next?

- Crane's *Maggie: A Girl of the Streets* (1893) is the startling story of a pretty girl whose life of violence and poverty leads her to prostitution and suicide. Although less well-known than *The Red Badge of Courage*, *Maggie* is considered an excellent example of the naturalist novel.
- *A Sourcebook on Naturalist Theater* (2000), by Christopher Innes, introduces students to the influences of Naturalism on modern theater. He visits Naturalism's roots and analyzes six plays by three playwrights, including full chapters on each play's historical and theatrical context.
- Mary Lawlor's *Recalling the Wild: Naturalism and the Closing of the American West* (2000) summarizes early American attitudes about the West and the literature that came out of those perceptions. Lawlor then shows how Naturalism stripped the West of its romantic overtones and forever changed the way it was understood.
- Edited by Donald Pizer, *The Cambridge Companion to American Realism and Naturalism* (1995) explores Realism and Naturalism in American literature. Pizer addresses the conflict over terminology before providing an overview of critical approaches to these two movements. He also offers in-depth analysis of various texts with reference to their importance to the movements and their historical influences.

---

man, she leaves him. In the end, Carrie has all the things she thought she wanted, but she remains vaguely unsatisfied with the trappings of her new, independent life.

Carrie is an important character in American literature because she begins as typical of many women of her time: average and faced with few opportunities. Because she is ordinary, she was accessible to women readers at the time and is accessible to women today. She is also a believable character. Dreiser gives her a share of virtue and principle but does not hide her weaknesses and flaws. She is ambitious, unwilling to be involved with a married man, and ultimately self-sufficient, but she is also materialistic, selfish, and jaded. She is, in many ways, a typical naturalistic character, and in this way she has much in common with her male counterparts in other prominent naturalist novels.

In *An American Tragedy*, Dreiser introduces Clyde Griffiths, whose lack of emotional attachments (even in his romantic life), desire to be a social climber, and opportunism are also manifest in the character of Carrie. Both characters make morally questionable decisions, and while Carrie's decision-making does not have criminal intent as Griffiths's does, she is ultimately rewarded for it rather than punished.

In Frank Norris's *McTeague: A Story of San Francisco*, the title character loves money, acts impulsively and selfishly, and sustains false appearances to try to recreate himself. He is also quick to sacrifice actual respectability for the appearance of respectability. All of these characteristics are seen in Carrie as well. She longs for a better life, which she defines as a life of material wealth and societal approval. She, however, realizes what McTeague does not: that a better life is only attained when a person's inner world is content and fulfilled. Carrie and Henry Fleming from Stephen Crane's *The Red Badge of Courage* share qualities, too. Both are innocents introduced into environments that are totally foreign to them, and they both have romantic ideals at the onset. The harshness of their new environments soon becomes evident, however, and these characters surprise themselves by how they react to, and function in, their new realities. Both are, in their own ways, heroic in the end.

Carrie even has something in common with the canine protagonist, Buck, in Jack London's *The Call of the Wild*. Both experience a dramatic change of environment and are highly distrustful as a result. Unfortunately for Carrie, she does not encounter someone whom she can learn to trust, as Buck does when he is adopted by John Thornton.

Despite the common threads that unite Carrie with the male protagonists of Naturalism, she is unique because of the realities of being a woman. She faces a different array of choices than the male characters face. She cannot learn basic dentistry and practice as an unlicensed dentist like Norris's title character in *McTeague: A Story of San Francisco*, and she cannot decide between staying home to seek work or becoming a soldier like Henry Fleming in Crane's *The Red Badge of Courage*. Her choices are to become a rural housewife or to move to the city and work in a factory or find a wealthy man.

"Despite the common threads that unite Carrie with the male protagonists of Naturalism, she is unique because of the realities of being a woman. She faces a different array of choices than the male characters face."

What is heroic about Carrie is that she accepts her limited choices and through them creates a new set of choices for herself. Her relationships with Drouet and Hurstwood ultimately lead her to becoming a successful stage actress in New York, which enables her to provide for herself in a career she genuinely enjoys. She is inspiring as a woman because of whom she becomes and the circumstances she seeks out, not because she displays nobility in the narrow confines of her given circumstances.

In contrast to Carrie is Crane's title character in *Maggie: A Girl of the Streets*. Maggie comes from a poor and violent background, but rather than find her way out of it, she becomes a victim of it. Maggie becomes a prostitute and commits suicide in the end. She does not seek self-sufficiency but rather survival. Granted, Maggie's situation is more dire than Carrie's is, but Maggie's character is one who would not seek out or, possibly, even recognize an opportunity for something better. In the eyes of readers at the turn of the century, both characters trade on their feminine wiles to get what they need from men, and although Carrie remains more socially respectable than Maggie does, the premise is the same. Both characters were seen as leading immoral lives for material gain. This may be true, but judgments aside, Carrie finds a way to provide for herself so she no longer has to trade on her virtue to have what she needs. Maggie, on the other hand, loses her battle with hopelessness and ends her life.

Without Carrie, the only major female protagonist in Naturalism might have been Maggie. How unfortunate if the portrayal of women and their experiences in turn-of-the-century America had been limited to Maggie. Although Carrie's story has its share of sorrow, it is hopeful and as optimistic as such a story can realistically be. In the end, she still feels empty; the objects and luxuries she longed to have do not fill her heart or nurture her spirit. She has come to understand this, however, which means there is the possibility that she will seek out what she truly needs as fervently as she sought out what she thought she needed. These feelings of loneliness and confusion are common, and women can certainly relate to them now just as they could then. Carrie is a new kind of heroine in American literature. She is flawed, fallen, and lost, but knows herself better at the end of the story. In this light, she is as important a character to the naturalist movement as the men who dominate it.

Source: Jennifer Bussey, Critical Essay on Naturalism, in *Literary Movements for Students*, The Gale Group, 2003.

Roger Sherman Loomis

In the following essay, Loomis defends the major points of Naturalism and argues that its impact on morality and human feeling can be seen more than ever today.

Naturalism is a word with as many phases of meaning as pacifism or patriotism, and about it rages nearly as fierce a conflict. When Zola issued his well-known pronunciamento that Naturalistic art was Nature seen through a temperament, he stressed the word "Nature." Nature and Nature only must be the subject of art: to face Nature frankly and openly, to present her dulnesses and stupidities and shames with scrupulous impartiality must be the aim of the artist. Now modern English criticism has preferred to call such full-length and unflattering portraiture of Dame Nature, even the emphasis upon her wry neck, bow legs, and squint eyes, by the name of Realism. Accordingly, when the critic nowadays quotes Zola's definition of Naturalism, he stresses the word "temperament." Naturalistic art

A scene from A Place in the Sun *based on* An American Tragedy *written by Theodore Dreiser*

is Nature seen through a certain temperament, or through a certain formula created by that temperament. Naturalism, we are told, is not simply a reproduction of the homely and repulsive side of Nature's physiognomy, but an attempt to read in it a certain character.

With Zola's profession faithfully to portray Nature the critics have now no quarrel, but with his practice of giving a certain interpretation of her character they and a great body of readers beg leave, more or less politely, to differ. Realism, though not admitted to so high a seat as idealizing poetry and romance, has been received into the company of the immortals, and Howells and Bennett are permitted to sit down to dinner with self-respecting critics. But Naturalism, Zola's interpretation of Nature, the high priests of criticism hold up to mocking and execration. Flaubert, Ibsen, Hardy, Moore, Brieux, and Masters were all at first denounced in the reputable journals as devils from the pit: and they are still ostracized by good society as if a sulphurous vapor hung around them.

To the question, "What is this interpretation, this formula which brings down upon its enunciators the formidable wrath of the critics?" we are likely to receive several answers. The first genial and rubicund gentleman of letters whom we interrogate over a bottle of Burgundy is apt to reply simply: "These fellows are arrant pessimists. They do not assure us that 'God's in his heaven all's right with the world.' They are notoriously addicted to depressing surroundings and unhappy endings. Literature should not upset one's ideas about anything, and should be either soothing, inspiring, or funny." Apparently, for all his assumed superiority the genial critic demands just about the same remoteness from the workaday world and the same comfortable ending as the tired business man, whom he professes to despise.

If we approach some gentleman who has perhaps felt a little more than our genial friend the brunt of pain and perplexity, we are likely to get a somewhat more illuminating answer. "Naturalism is Bestialism. Man is not a beast." To be sure, Zola has much to say of the Bête Humaine, and undoubtedly does stress in us the ape and tiger strains. But will anyone deny that the strains are there? Now and then a human being sprouts an atavistic tail or fell of hair. So, too, now and then, human beings commit atrocities at Louvain or East St. Louis. Let him that is without a streak of the beast in him cast the first stone at the Bête Humaine. After all, what most critics of this class object to is not the recognition of the animal, but the recognition of the animal as a serious problem. The emphasis on the beast in *L'Assommoir*, *Jude the Obscure*, and *Spoon River* shocks the conventional critic, who is accustomed to hear such things mentioned only over his after-dinner cigar: he feels it very deeply when he sees them in print where they can be read by ladies, and where apparently they are treated not as jests to roll under his tongue but as grit to break his teeth on. He is ready enough to recognize the beast, but only as a joke or a German. So long as it can be laughed away or blown to bits with high explosive, he is quite ready to appreciate it in his Boccaccio or his Bryce reports. But when the naturalistic author shows him the beast everywhere about him, in the office, the church, and the home, and by no means to be got rid of by such simple methods as laughter or trinitrotoluol, and he realizes that only a reorganization of all his ideas in the light of what sociological, economic, and psychological experts tell him can make this abundant *èlan vital* galvanize rather than blast our society, he kicks like a Missouri mule and refuses to recognize the Bête Humaine.

Perhaps, however, we have put our question to some more rational critic and he replies that he confesses the beast in man, but that he also finds a demigod: Naturalism denies the demigod. True enough, if by the demigod is meant some infusion of a supernatural or mystical element into the beast. But if by the demigod be meant simply those qualities which men have ascribed to gods as their chief and worthiest title to worship—justice and love, beauty and reason—then, of course, the Naturalist does not deny the demigod, though like the Nazarene he often discovers him in the less reputable circles of society. Furthermore, he finds embryonic even in the beast all that is popularly considered peculiar to man—art, altruism, remorse, some of the simpler forms of reasoning and foresight. In the most primitive types of humanity he finds a religion claiming as much supernatural sanction as the Roman Church or Bahaism. When confronted, then, with the fact that even animals possess the supposedly divine traits, and that as divine revelation the totem pole and the Cross claim equal authority, the Naturalist comes to the conclusion that the supernatural is only a development of the natural, and that mystical experience, however valuable as a dynamic, is worthless as a directive. Only reason acting upon the facts supplied by experience can guide us to the truth.

Accordingly the Naturalist discards as obsolete three supernaturalistic concepts—Providence, absolute morality, and freedom of the will. In his novels and plays Providence is represented as a blind bungler, conventional morality is scouted and even flouted and man is displayed as a puppet worked by the forces of Heredity and Environment. It is about these three phases of the Naturalistic interpretation of Nature that the battle of the critics still rages. What may be said in defense of these tenets of Naturalistic doctrine trine—a cosmic order without justice, a morality without sanction or stability, and a will, free within limits to choose what it likes best, but determined as to what it likes best?

"The Naturalist discards as obsolete three supernaturalistic concepts–Providence, absolute morality, and freedom of the will. In his novels and plays Providence is represented as a blind bungler, conventional morality is scouted and even flouted and man is displayed as a puppet worked by the forces of Heredity and Environment."

The idea of a Providence in the affairs of men, working out a sort of poetical justice, has, to be sure, a certain basis in fact. No one can help observing that certain acts cause pain, directly to himself or indirectly through others. The relation is far from being uniform and inevitable, but despite the exceptions certain general causal relations are recognized. It is obvious that to overindulge in Welsh rarebit to spoil a child with petting brings its own retribution with it. But Nemesis as an instrument of God's jealous vengeance upon the mortal who dares disobey his fiat seems a superfluous explanation of these facts. For it occurs to the Naturalist that a sane ethics calls only those deeds evil which generally bring suffering in their train: and if occasionally that suffering falls upon the evildoer there is no occasion for seeking an explanation in some mysterious Nemesis. Surely never was an absurder piece of writing than Emerson's dithyramb on *Compensation*. To him it would be a cause for wonder and awful speculation that Providence had provided a dark brown taste in the mouth to balance the exhilaration of drunkenness, and had made fire burn to punish the child for putting its finger in the flame. The fundamental idea is worthy of the good old lady who thanked the dear Lord for providing such excellent harbors where the cities of New York and San Francisco were to spring up. Nemesis is a law, just as gravitation is a law; but like gravitation it is offset a billion times a minute by other laws: and inasmuch as it is therefore less successful than any human penal system in saddling the heaviest penalty on the worst offender, it scarcely deserves all the mystified veneration that has been lavished upon it.

Let us turn next to the Naturalist's morality. We have noted that whether an act is right or wrong depends upon whether joy or pain the long run follows. This, in turn, depends upon the human and other sentient beings involved. These, in turn, will be affected by climate, heredity, education, and a thousand other things. Naturalistic morality differs, then, from orthodox morality in its relativity. The notion of an eternal code, confided by Infallible Wisdom to the visions of seers and the conscience of every individual, does not appeal to the Naturalistic thinker. If conscience be an infallible guide to right conduct, why did the conscience 1700 encourage duelling, the conscience of ancient Sparta stealing, the conscience of the devout Mohammedan polygamy, and why was what we now regard as a loathsome sexual perversion practised unblushingly in Periclean Athens? The Naturalist has come to believe that conscience, an emotional assurance of the rightness of one's action, varies so uniformly with the social conventions about it that it can no more be relied on than a compass in the neighborhood of masses of iron. If the moral law is carved on tables of adamant for all times and all places, why is it that when the moral law interferes too severely with the right to life or happiness, we all by common consent make and approve exceptions thereto? We agree that the starving child cannot be blamed for stealing, the invalid must be kept alive by falsehoods, self-defense justifies killing, a noble purpose takes the taint from suicide. I know a clergyman, who had one of the greatest shocks of his life when I wrote him that I believed in comparative freedom of divorce, who yet not long after met with a case of domestic unhappiness, which not only led him to approve a divorce but actually to officiate at the remarriage of the divorced wife. The unpardonable sin, to use a manner of speaking, for the Naturalist is to let a taboo stand in the way of human happiness.

Naturalistic ethics, then, are hedonistic. The greatest happiness of the greatest number is the end and criterion of action. But the Naturalistic thinker does not believe that to obey each moment's passing whim brings the maximum of happiness either for the individual or for the group. He perceives that man is a highly complex organism, whose nature includes, besides the passions, a social instinct, an artistic instinct, and a reason. In the harmonizing of all these factors lies happiness. To give controlled expression to the passions and to sublimate them, to enjoy the pleasures of social intercourse and social approval, to do all things beautifully, and viewing all these things in their relation, to harmonize them by reason,—this is the art of living. Individuals here and there may attain degrees of happiness in spite of, even by the partial denial of one or another of these four elements. One may even kill the artistic impulse and yet live in moderate pleasure. But to deny the fundamental passions or the claims of society or of reason is to court destruction. On the other hand, to follow too eagerly the seductions of any one is to distort the growth of the organism, and evil results appear either in the later development of the individual or in the society which imitates him.

What does duty mean to the Naturalistic thinker? The root of the word supplies the key. Duty is simply the debt which the individual owes to society. If society gives him much,—wealth, power, education,—society has a right to demand much. If it gives him little, it should demand little. The product of the slum, the ten hour day, and the gin palace, owes nothing to society. Society's demand that he make himself an intelligent human being and refrain from burglary, rape, and murder is an impossible impertinence on the part of society; though society will doubtless continue to enforce the payment of loans which it never made. Duty, then, is simply a claim by society upon the individual.

Since, however, the individual craves happiness and the way to complete happiness does not lie in antagonism to society and wholesale infringement of social interests, it will always be expedient for him, no matter how little society has done for him, to work for social ends. On the whole, it pays to cash up when society sends in a bill.

What have the Naturalistic writers done for morality? We may admit at once that they have done more to throw down rotting conventions than to build up new moral and social laws. But the former service is not to be minimized. Zola built his ponderous engines of destruction up against the walls of clerical imposture and vice in many forms; Hardy battered at the undemocratic walls of Oxford colleges and laid bare the shallowness of revivalism; Wells in his Naturalistic period exploded the bladder of the patent medicine and the whole vast imposture of advertising; Galsworthy attacked a jingoistic patriotism, and enacted for us the farce-tragedy that is sometimes played under the title of "Justice"; and Masters in his *Spoon River Anthology* has pierced to the root of nearly every wrong and folly and sham that festers in the modern social body.

Greatest has been the service of the Naturalistic school to the cause of labor and the cause of women. There are Naturalists who have been indifferent or hostile to both, but they form a small minority. From Zola to Verhæren, from Arthur Morrison to Ernest Poole, the majority of Naturalists have insistently claimed or labor that right to the pursuit of happiness which is so tantalizingly offered in our revolutionary Declaration of Independence.

For women Naturalistic literature has done the enormous service of telling the truth and the whole truth about sex. Conventional literature gave glimpses of purple mountain peaks, encircled with clouds of gold; it told besides of a vast tract hidden by sulphurous vapors, where the unwary wanderer felt the earth's crust crumble beneath him, and sank into a seething cauldron. Conventional literature charted only the most obvious parts of this region: where the concealed dangers were perhaps greatest it gave no direction. It prescribed for women one entrance only, a gate called marriage, and gave many details of the route thither. But for all the tract that lay beyond or outside of it the details were meagre and sometimes false. Now all this region has been faithfully charted and published abroad. I venture to say the reading of half a dozen novels of the Naturalist school will exhibit more of the rationale of sex than any other body of literature ever written. Wifely subjection, the double standard of morals, prostitution, the seduction of working-girls, long sanctioned or condoned in much conventional literature, have received no quarter here. Among what school of writers are we to find one particular form of criminal folly so scarified as in *Ghosts, Damaged Goods*, and "Willard Fluke" of the *Spoon River Anthology*? Burke's famous generalization that no discoveries are to be made in morality breaks down before such a case. For while, doubtless, the ethical principle of which this is an application is as old as society, yet the perception of its application and the forcible presentation of the evil and its consequences, leading at last to recognition in our legislatures, is new and may be placed in large measure to the credit of the Naturalists.

Look at Tom Jones, the hero of what has been called by the conventionalists the greatest English novel. Tom is scarcely more than a slave of the moment's appetite. To be sure, he has too much sense of fair play ever to seduce women, but women have not the slightest difficulty in seducing him. The possibility that any of his adventures may have dire consequences is never faced, except when the sensational possibility of committing incest for a time horrifies him. This amiable gentleman, rather than soil his hands, resolves to sell himself to a lady in return for his keep. At last, he marries the chaste Sophia and rears a lusty brood. I should like to know what those who charge the Naturalistic novel with a predilection for feeble heroes and heroines have to say for this flabby protagonist of their greatest English novel. As a picture of random sex relations it betrays a facile optimism that no realist would be capable of.

Now by way of contrast let us look at a novel of the Naturalistic extreme,—*Sanine*, by Artzybasheff. The book is not a typical example of Naturalism, for the author derides the exercise of reason and humanitarian effort. But even though in these respects it falls short of the saner Naturalism characteristic of Zola, Ibsen, Hardy, and Masters, even though it glorifies sexual experiences as the greatest thing in the world, yet it is so far superior to *Tom Jones* as a criticism of life that it does not flinch from the tragic possibilities in such experience, and it makes a sharp differentiation between the putrescent koprophagy of the garrison town and the artistic expression of a healthy desire. While in my opinion the author does not sufficiently recognize that human nature has other summits than those reached in the culmination of the mightiest elemental passion, and does not realize the limitations which society has a right to place upon mating, yet in his demand that passion be beautiful as a Greek statue is beautiful, and in his recognition of the woman, not as a plaything but as a personality, he admits the place of the artistic and social impulses and justifies his classification as a Naturalist. Neither *Sanine* nor *Tom Jones* gives us anything like an exhaustive study of sex, but *Sanine* penetrates beneath the crust of convention; *Tom Jones* does not: *Sanine* has an idealism of sex; *Tom Jones* has none.

The larger Naturalism, then, founded upon the view of happiness as the goal of life, of the all round development of the individual as the way, and of the golden mean as the guiding principle, has been gradually making over our morality, ridding it of the relics of primitive taboos, and establishing it upon the demands of human nature.

But the third fundamental principle of Naturalism, determinism, is a stumbling block to many. The conventionalist is sure to object. "Granted that Naturalism has laid bare the ulcers and cancerous growths in the body of society, and has been as plain-spoken as the Old Testament or Shakespeare about things that are never mentioned in polite society, it destroys all incentive to salve those sores because it denies the freedom of the human will. It so impresses on us the thorough corruption of society that we feel that it is condemned to an eternity of disease. We see these men, as one reverend critic phrases it, 'concentrating attention on the shadiness and seaminess of life, exploiting sewers and cesspools, dabbling in beastliness and putrefaction, dragging to light the ghastly and gruesome, poring over the scurvy and unreportable side of things, bending in lingering analysis over every phase of mania and morbidity, going down into the swamps and marshes to watch the phosphorescence of decay and the jack-o'-lanterns that dance on rottenness'; and we conclude forsooth that if this is life, there is no hope for the world."

Naturalism may at once plead guilty to the doctrine of determinism: but it does not admit that the doctrine is inconsistent with optimism of the future or that it robs man of incentive to moral action. The argument that optimism can be justified only by belief in an outside power pumping virtue into humanity by slow degrees is not convincing to anyone who realizes what is meant by potential energy. It is not necessary to believe that if a pound of radium could emit electrical energy for thousands of years it must be connected with a celestial dynamo. Neither is it necessary to believe that the human race is incapable of improving itself, however unhappy its present condition. No man can tell the potential energies latent in the human race, energies that may express themselves through reason, social feeling, and the love of beauty to make the superman. Determinism is no foe to an optimism of the future. Professor Santayana puts the theory admirably: "We are a part of the blind energy behind Nature, but by virtue of that energy we impose our purposes on that part of Nature which we constitute or control. We can turn from the stupefying contemplation of an alien universe to the building of our own house, knowing that, alien as it is, that universe has chanced to blow its energy also into our will and to allow itself to be partially dominated by our intelligence. Our mere existence and the modicum of success we have attained in society, science and art, are the living proofs of this human power. The exercise of this power is the task appointed for us by the indomitable promptings of our own spirit, a task in which we need not labor without hope."

The conventionalist pursues his point. "This all sounds mighty fine. But experience shows that a belief in the freedom of the will and moral responsibility is all that keeps us from wallowing in a sensual sty." As the Rev. Dr. S. Law Wilson puts it, "What, we ask, would be the effect of persuading the masses of mankind to believe that all the evil of which they are guilty is necessitated, and all the blame must be laid to the door of blood, or birth, or environment, or the tyranny of impulse? Indoctrinate the masses of our population with this pestiferous teaching, and there be some of us who shall not taste of death till we see the reign of moral anarchy and disintegration set in."

Now let us see what the real effect of acting upon the doctrine of free will is as contrasted with the effect of acting upon its denial. The theory of the freedom of the will, apart from its incompatibility with the generally accepted law of causation as implying an agent that, without being itself caused, initiates or causes action, involves the doctrine of complete responsibility. For if the will could have refrained just as well as not from the immoral act, no matter how powerful the pressure of heredity and environment, the man is absolutely responsible. His guilt has no extenuation. Punishment heavy and merciless is but his due. The only thing for society to do is impress upon him the enormity of his crime and urge him to repentance.

Now the old penal methods were in entire accord with this theory. Criminals were in prison to be punished. No treatment was too bad for them. The prison chaplain dilated on their essential wickedness, and told them that they had only themselves to thank for the plight in which they found themselves. If they would freely confess their guilt and accept the inspiration of religion, though society would not forgive them, God would. Now the results of such a logical application of the doctrine of moral responsibility to the criminal class are notorious. Everyone knows that the men who went to the penitentiary did not come out penitent, far less did they come out with any propensity to good. These men had learned what the doctrine of free will was in its application to them. Somehow there seems to have been a perverse conspiracy among criminals throughout the world to discredit the doctrine of free will and its corollary, moral responsibility.

What, however, are the results of determinism as applied to these same men? Mr. Osborne, whose work at Sing Sing we all know, has without knowing it acted upon this principle. He has brought into the prison pleasure and social life and a system of stimuli in the form of rewards. He has created a society where the criminal naturally did his duty to society because society had done something for him. He has taught the men trades and made openings for them in the world, and as a result he has made citizens out of outlaws. Of his success there can be no question. What here the individual could not do for himself, enviromnent did for him. It mattered little whether he thought his will free or not: it responded inevitably to the right stimuli. Little need have we to fear the spread of the determinist theory among the masses, if only we have intelligence enough to practice as well as to preach it.

The conventionalist once more objects. "But turn away from life to your own Naturalistic novels. Are they not shrieking in our ears that man is feeble and doomed to failure? Are not their heroes and heroines weaklings who fall unresisting under the bludgeonings of Fate?"

Now it may well be admitted that the Naturalists, in order to show where the rocks lie, have usually represented their human barks as breaking upon the reefs rather than gliding smoothly into harbor. But in doing so the Naturalists have done only what every tragic writer has done. If the Mayor of Casterbridge or Madame Bovary fell through a combination of defects of character with adverse circumstances, what else may we say of Hamlet and Lear? Are we to despise Tess of the D'Urbervilles because though she often showed great strength of character, at certain crises of her fate timidity prevailed over purpose? When the conventionalists begin to call the great tragedies decadent on the same grounds that they condemn the Naturalistic novels; when they scorn Desdemona because when her husband suspected her she did not call up the Pinkerton's detective agency of Cyprus and probe the matter to the bottom, and because on her deathbed she did not wrestle courageously, but murmured merely, "A guiltless death I die," then we may listen patiently when they apply these standards to works not in the classic tradition. Until then some of us are inclined to believe that these critics unconsciously act upon the principle that any stick is good enough to beat a dog with.

Dr. Johnson once said that if he had no duties and no reference to futurity he would spend his life in driving briskly in a post-chaise with a pretty woman. To such a declaration the appropriate Johnsonian reply is, "You lie, sir." If the Doctor would permit of any further explanation, we might go on to say: "In the first place Fate might refuse. Fate, in the form of the pretty woman, might politely decline the invitation. She might prefer other company to that of the hectoring oracle of the Mitre, the polysyllabic proser of the *Rambler* papers: she might object to being referred to as an unidea-ed girl. In the second place, if the woman found it agreeable, the Doctor himself would soon have found it disagreeable. It may be an impertinence to presume that we know the Doctor better than he knew himself, but Boswell has made the claim possible. Now the Doctor had certain hereditary traits that would never have been satisfied for long with sitting in a post-chaise beside a pretty woman. He had too active a brain, he was too much of a clubman and, as a matter of fact, despite all his complaints of indolence, he had an instinct for work. Moreover, it is difficult to imagine that Samuel Johnson would have let the American Revolution go by without leaping from the post-chaise and scratching off *Taxation No Tyranny*. At the very least, he would have had to stop for a moment, stretch his limbs, and perhaps roll down a hill for the fun of it. Without disparaging the worthy Doctor's sincerity, one may say that, granted his pecuniary and other restrictions, he would have lived much the same life if he had had no theories duty beyond what every social being holds, and no more reference to futurity than the desire that the rest of life contain as much happiness as he could put into it.

Moreover, one cannot help thinking that if Doctor Johnson had exerted his great influence, not as a conventionalist and Tory, but as a Naturalist and democrat, the whole course of events in Europe might have been changed. His posthumous power might have offset the Bourbonism of Burke; England might not have thrown her strength on the side of that Holy Alliance of Prussian, Austrian and Russian despotisms; the contagion of a liberal England and France might have liberalized Europe; and the world might have been made safe for democracy a hundred years ago. But it was not to be.

There are people who see in Naturalism the origin of this war and in the triumph of the Allies the vindication of Providence. Such a view is only possible through a misconception of the facts. The insane policies of German imperialism found ready support throughout the ranks of the German supernaturalists, and palliation in that inviolate citadel of supernaturalism, the Vatican. On the other hand, the bitterest and most courageous of the foes of German imperialism were a small group of atheistic socialists in Germany, whose creed was the creed of Naturalism. As for the victory of the Allies I can see nothing but a confirmation of the blunt statement erroneously attributed to Napoleon that God is always on the side of the heaviest battalions. The feeble succor afforded by St. Michael at Mons hardly leads one to rely much upon the heavenly powers for aid. The despairing prayers of millions went unheeded until material force came to the aid of spiritual yearnings. One who can believe in supernaturalism after this war possesses, indeed, a faith which serves as an evidence of things not seen. Let him have his angels of Mons and be happy. But the rest of us, in this time momentous and critical as scarcely any other time in the world's history, can hardly afford to base our hopes for the future on any efforts but our own, or afford to direct those efforts by any but Naturalistic principles: for these must bring happiness in their wake, or *ipso facto* cease to be the principles of Naturalism.

Source: Roger Sherman Loomis, "A Defense of Naturalism," in *Documents of Modern Literary Realism*, edited by George J. Becker, Princeton University Press, 1963, pp. 535–48.

Sources

Beach, Joseph Warren, *The Twentieth Century Novel: Studies in Technique*, Appleton-Century-Crofts, 1932.

Pizer, Donald, *Realism and Naturalism in Nineteenth-Century American Literature*, Southern Illinois University Press, 1984.

Further Reading

Brown, Frederick, *Zola: A Life*, Johns Hopkins University Press, 1995.

This detailed account of Émile Zola's life demonstrates his importance as a writer, thinker, and political figure. This biography took fifteen years to compile and includes information from Zola's personal correspondence.

Fast, Howard, ed., *The Best Short Stories of Theodore Dreiser*, Elephant Publishers, 1989.

Although he is known mainly for his novels, Dreiser was also a short-story writer. Here, Fast collects the best examples of Dreiser's short fiction.

Kershaw, Alex, *Jack London: A Life*, Griffin, 1999.

Kershaw examines London's exciting, short life in this fast-paced biography. He includes London's literary efforts, his adventurous spirit, his social and environmental concerns, and his unpopular views.

Norris, Frank, *The Best Short Stories of Frank Norris*, Ironweed Press, 1998.

This is the first collection of Norris's short fiction, and critics praise the publisher's selection of these fourteen stories from the more than sixty available. Norris's naturalistic tendencies are evident, even though these stories are a departure from the novels for which he is better known.

Wertheim, Stanley, *A Stephen Crane Encyclopedia*, Greenwood Publishing, 1997.

In this single volume, students will find information about Crane's short life along with analysis of his works, characters, settings, and prominent issues of his work and times.

Postcolonialism

Movement Origin

c. 1960

The term "Postcolonialism" refers broadly to the ways in which race, ethnicity, culture, and human identity itself are represented in the modern era, after many colonized countries gained their independence. However, some critics use the term to refer to *all* culture and cultural products influenced by imperialism from the moment of colonization until today. Postcolonial literature seeks to describe the interactions between European nations and the peoples they colonized. By the middle of the twentieth century, the vast majority of the world was under the control of European countries. At one time, Great Britain, for example, ruled almost 50 percent of the world. During the twentieth century, countries such as India, Jamaica, Nigeria, Senegal, Sri Lanka, Canada, and Australia won independence from their European colonizers. The literature and art produced in these countries after independence has become the object of "Postcolonial Studies," a term coined in and for academia, initially in British universities. This field gained prominence in the 1970s and has been developing ever since. Palestinian-American scholar Edward Said's critique of Western representations of the Eastern culture in his 1978 book, *Orientalism*, is a seminal text for postcolonial studies and has spawned a host of theories on the subject. However, as the currency of the term "postcolonial" has gained wider use, its meaning has also expanded. Some consider the United States itself a postcolonial country because of its former status as a territory of Great Britain, but it is generally studied for

its colonizing rather than its colonized attributes. In another vein, Canada and Australia, though former colonies of Britain, are often placed in a separate category because of their status as "settler" countries and because of their continuing loyalty to their colonizer. Some of the major voices and works of postcolonial literature include Salman Rushdie's novel *Midnight's Children* (1981), Chinua Achebe's novel *Things Fall Apart* (1958), Michael Ondaatje's novel *The English Patient* (1992), Frantz Fanon's *The Wretched of the Earth* (1961), Jamaica Kincaid's *A Small Place* (1988), Isabelle Allende's *The House of the Spirits* (1982), J. M. Coetzee's *Waiting for the Barbarians* and *Disgrace* (1990), Derek Walcott's *Omeros* (1990), and Eavan Boland's *Outside History: Selected Poems, 1980–1990.*

Representative Authors

J. M. Coetzee (1940–)

John Michael Coetzee was born on February 9, 1940, in South Africa. His father, a government worker who lost his job because he disagreed with South Africa's apartheid policies, was an early influence in the writer's life. Coetzee took a bachelor of arts degree in 1960 from the University of Cape Town and a master of fine arts degree in 1963. In 1969, he received his Ph.D. in English from the University of Texas at Austin. He has worked in academia for most of his adult life, holding teaching positions at the University of Cape Town, the State University of New York in Buffalo, Johns Hopkins University, and Harvard University. Coetzee is currently professor of general literature at the University of Cape Town.

As a white writer living in South Africa during apartheid, Coetzee developed powerful anti-imperialist feelings. His novels, deeply influenced by postmodern ideas of representation and language, illustrate the insidious ways in which dominant groups seek to impose their culture and thinking on conquered peoples. For example, his first novel, *Dusklands* (1974), tells two distinct but parallel stories: one of the workings of the United States State Department during the Vietnam war and the other Jacobus Coetzee's conquest of South Africa in the 1760s. Coetzee's own alienation from his fellow Afrikaners is evident in his novels, most of which focus on the thoughts and actions of a single character put in an untenable situation. Coetzee's Booker Prize-winning novel, *The Life and Times of Michael K* (1984), set in racially divided Cape Town, tells the story of gardener Michael K who, after taking his dying mother to the farm on which she was raised, lives happily until he is accused by the government of aiding guerillas. Coetzee's early novels, however, are not polemical. Rather, they are allegorical, underscoring the timeless nature of human cruelty.

Coetzee's other novels include *From the Heart of the Country* (1977), *Waiting for the Barbarians* (1982), *Foe* (1987), *Age of Iron* (1990), *The Master of Petersburg* (1994), and *Disgrace* (1999), for which he received his second Booker Prize. In addition to the Booker Prizes, Coetzee has been awarded the James Tait Black Memorial Prize and the Faber Memorial Award in 1980, the Jerusalem Prize in 1987, and the Mondello Prize in 1994. Coetzee is also a fellow of the Royal Society of Literature. In addition to his novels, Coetzee has written collections of essays and edited and translated a number of other books. His memoir, *Boyhood: Scenes from Provincial Life* was published in 1997.

Frantz Fanon (1925–1961)

Frantz Fanon was born July 20, 1925, in the French colony of Martinique and left in 1943 to fight with the Free French in World War II. A psychiatrist, Fanon was interested in the emotional effects of racism and colonization on blacks. Fanon considered himself French, but his experience as a black man in France caused him to rethink his ideas about culture and identity. In 1952, he published *Black Skin, White Masks*, originally titled "An Essay for the Disalienation of Blacks." With the publication of *The Wretched of the Earth* in 1961, Fanon established himself as a leading critic of colonial power and a voice for violent revolution. As head of the psychiatry department at Blida-Joinville Hospital in Algeria in 1953, Fanon saw firsthand the kind of psychological damage done to the tortured and the torturers during the Algerian war for independence. Fanon resigned his post and worked openly with the Algerian independence movement in Tunisia. He was an important influence on thinkers such as Jean-Paul Sartre, Homi Bhabha, and Edward Said. Fanon died December 6, 1961, of leukemia at the National Institute of Health in Bethesda, Maryland, where he had sought treatment.

Jamaica Kincaid (1949–)

Born Elaine Potter Richardson on the island of Antigua, May 25, 1949, Jamaica Kincaid was educated in the British school system of the colony.

In 1967, Antigua achieved self-governance, and in 1981 it became an independent country of the Commonwealth. Kincaid moved to New York City, where she studied photography at the New York School for Social Research and began writing for magazines including *Ingenue* and *The New Yorker*. Much of her writing displays her disdain for all things English and the inability of native Antiguans to resist British cultural imperialism. In her book about Antigua, *A Small Place* (1988), Kincaid describes the island as follows:

> Antigua is a small place, a small island . . . . It was settled by Christopher Columbus in 1493. Not too long after, it was settled by human rubbish from Europe, who used enslaved but noble and exalted human beings from Africa . . . . to satisfy their desire for wealth and power, to feel better about their own miserable existence, so that they could be less lonely and empty—a European disease.

In addition to *A Small Place*, Kincaid has published a number of novels including *Annie John* (1986); *At the Bottom of the River* (1992); *The Autobiography of My Mother* (1996); *Lucy*; (1990); *My Brother* (1997); and, with Eric Fischl, *Annie, Gwen, Lilly, Pam and Tulip* (1986). Invariably, Kincaid writes about women's experiences with other women and the effects of colonialism and patriarchy on women's self-image.

Li-Young Lee (1957–)

Li-Young Lee is one of the leading poetic voices of the Chinese diaspora writing in America. A profound sense of loss and nostalgia and a questing for and questioning of one's national or ethnic identity often characterize diasporic writing. Lee was born August 19, 1957, in Jakarta, Indonesia, to Richard K. Y. Lee and Joice Yuan Jiaying, the granddaughter of China's provisional president, Yuan Shikai, elected in 1912 during the country's transition from monarchy to republic. Before moving to Indonesia, Lee's father was China communist leader Mao Zedong's personal physician. In 1959, the Lees left Indonesia after President Sukarno, for whom Lee's father had been a medical advisor, began openly persecuting the country's Chinese population. After wandering through the Far East for five years, the family immigrated to the United States, settling in Pennsylvania. With publication of his first collection of poems, *Rose*, in 1986, Lee garnered widespread attention from critics, who were moved by the mix of tenderness, fear, and longing in his portraits of his family, especially his father. *Rose*, for which Lee received New York University's Delmore Schwartz Memorial Poetry Award, was followed in 1990 by *The City in Which I Love You*, which was the 1990 Lamont poetry selection of the Academy of American Poets. In addition to the two titles mentioned above, Lee has written a critically acclaimed memoir, *The Winged Seed* (1995), which reads like an extended prose poem. His most recent collection of poems is *The Book of My Nights* (2001).

Michael Ondaatje (1943–)

Born on September 12, 1943, in Colombo, Ceylon (now Sri Lanka), to Mervyn Ondaatje and Doris Gratiaen, Michael Ondaatje was educated at St. Thomas College in Colombo and Dulwich College in London, where he moved with his mother. Between 1962 and 1964, Ondaatje attended Bishop's University in Lennoxville, Quebec, and eventually took his bachelor of arts degree at the University of Toronto in 1965. In 1967, he received an master of fine arts degree from Queen's University in Kingston, Ontario, Canada. Ondaatje taught at the University of Western Ontario, London, between 1967 and 1971, and has been on the English faculty at Glendon College, York University in Toronto, Ontario, since 1971.

A novelist, critic, and poet, Ondaatje is best known for his 1992 novel, *The English Patient*, which details the interactions of characters of various nationalities during the last days of World War II. The novel explores the relationships between past and present, individual and national identity, and how those relationships shape a person's idea of "home." The novel was adapted into an internationally acclaimed film in 1996. Ondaatje has received a number of awards for his writing, including the Ralph Gustafson Award, 1965; the Epstein Award, 1966; and the President's Medal from the University of Ontario in 1967; and the Canadian Governor-General's Award for Literature in 1971 and again in 1980. In 1980, he was awarded the Canada-Australia Prize, and in 1992 he was presented with the Booker Prize for *The English Patient*. Ondaatje's most recent work is the novel *Anil's Ghost*, which is set in Sri Lanka, in the middle of the island country's violent civil war.

Salman Rushdie (1947–)

Born into a prosperous Muslim family in Bombay, India, on June 19, 1947, Ahmed Salman Rushdie was raised in a liberal atmosphere in which education was valued. His parents, Anis Ahmed Rushdie, a Cambridge-educated businessman, and his mother, Negin, a teacher from Aligarh, India,

Salman Rushdie

migrated from Kashmir before Rushdie was born. Rushdie grew up reading Western comic books and watching Disney movies as well as films made in Bombay. By his tenth birthday, he knew he wanted to be a writer. Rushdie attended Rugby in England at age thirteen and in 1965 enrolled in King's College, Cambridge. In 1968, he graduated with a master of fine arts degree in history. After graduation, Rushdie moved to Karachi, Pakistan, to join his family, who had moved there in 1964.

In Karachi, Rushdie wrote advertising copy by day and worked on his fiction at night. His first major success as a writer was his novel, *Midnight's Children*, which won the prestigious Booker Prize in 1981 and brought Rushdie international fame. Weaving personal experience with history, Rushdie traces Indian history from 1910 until 1976. His 1983 novel, *Shame*, a satire of the Pakistani elite, was short-listed for the Booker Prize in 1984. In 1988, Rushdie published his most well-known work, *The Satanic Verses*. Calling the book "blasphemous," many governments banned the novel, and Muslims throughout the world protested. Ayatollah Khomeini, Iran's spiritual leader, declared a judicial decree, known as a fatwa, sentencing Rushdie to death. Rushdie immediately went into hiding. In 1998, the Iranian government withdrew the fatwa against Rushdie.

Rushdie has continued to write, exploring the intersections of history, culture, religion, and identity. In 1990, he published *Haroun and the Sea of Stories* and, in 1994, *East, West*, a collection of his short stories. His most recent fiction includes *The Ground Beneath Her Feet* (1991) and the novel *Fury* (2000).

Gayatri Chakravorty Spivak (1942–)

Gayatri Chakravorty Spivak is one of the leading theorists of postcolonial literary theory. Born February 24, 1942, in Calcutta, West Bengal, Spivak took a bachelor of arts degree in English from the University of Calcutta and then left India for graduate work at Cornell University, from which she received both her master's degree and Ph.D. in comparative literature. Spivak's dissertation director was Paul de Man, one of the leading scholars of deconstructionist theory. Spivak's academic career was launched after she translated Jacques Derrida's *Of Grammatology* (1976) into English and wrote its preface. In addition to her work on Derrida, Spivak has authored a number of critical texts and edited numerous collections of essays including *In Other Worlds: Essays in Cultural Politics* (1987); *Outside in the Teaching Machine* (1993); and, most recently, *A Critique of Post-Colonial Reason: Toward a History of the Vanishing Present* (1999). Spivak has given numerous interviews on her thinking about Postcolonialism and teaching. These interviews are more accessible than her own writing, which her critics often call "unreadable."

Derek Walcott (1930–)

Born January 23, 1930, on St. Lucia, a former British colony of the Windward Islands in the Lesser Antilles, Derek Walcott was educated in the British school system but lived the life of an impoverished colonial. The son of an English father and an African mother, Walcott's mixed racial heritage provides him with a unique understanding of postcolonial culture. Already a practicing poet, Walcott began writing drama after graduating from the University College of the West Indies. Walcott's writing grafts Caribbean, African, and Latino sources onto European traditions of poetry and drama to elegantly express the complexities of the postcolonial condition. Indeed, critics have sometimes faulted him for relying *too* much on Western literary traditions. Walcott's themes include the injustices of racism, colonial oppression, and the search for a coherent and stable identity and past. More recently, Walcott, who has held a teaching appointment at Boston University since 1981, has begun to explore the theme of exile in his writing. When the Swedish Academy awarded him the Nobel Prize in 1992, it noted Walcott's contributions to Caribbean theater and praised his book-length poem, *Omeros* (1990), which retells Homer's *Odyssey* from a Caribbean perspective, using native characters to explore events in colonial history. Walcott's numerous collections of poetry include *The Castaway, and Other Poems* (1965), *The Bounty* (1997), and *Tiepolo's Hound* (2000). A few of his best-known plays include *Henri Christophe: A Chronicle in Seven Scenes* (1950), *Dream on Monkey Mountain* (1967), and *Viva Detroit* (1990).

Representative Works

Breath, Eyes, Memory

In her 1994 novel, *Breath, Eyes, Memory*, Haitian-born Edwidge Danticat examines themes of migration, gender, sexuality, and history, common themes of postcolonial literature. The novel follows the exploits of Sophie in her battles to carve an identity out of disparate languages and cultures, such as Creole, French, and English and to adapt to American ways in the Haitian diaspora after she arrives in Brooklyn, New York. Danticat's emphasis on women's experience makes her a leading younger voice of postcolonial feminism. *Breath, Eyes, Memory* was an Oprah Book Club selection and helped Danticat to be named one of the Best Young American Novelists by *Granta* magazine in 1996.

Ceremony

Leslie Marmon Silko's 1977 novel, *Ceremony*, is widely considered to be one of the most important works of Native-American literature written. Silko's novel celebrates the traditions and myths of the Laguna Pueblo people while examining the influence of white contact on Pueblo storytelling. As a people who continue to live under a form of colonial rule (i.e., the United States) yet who have achieved a degree of autonomy, Native Americans occupy a special place in postcolonial discourse.

Decolonizing the Mind

Kenyan Ngugi wa Thiong'o's 1986 book is part memoir, part treatise, describing the storytelling traditions of his people and the ways in which the British colonial educational system attempted to eradicate Gikuyu language and culture, effectively colonizing the mind of native Kenyans. Ngugi writes: "I believe that my writing in Gikuyu . . . an African language, is part and parcel of the anti-imperialist struggles of Kenyan and African peoples."

Edward Said

Disgrace

J. M. Coetzee's 1999 novel, *Disgrace*, is set in Cape Town, South Africa, and explores the themes of racial justice, crime, revenge, and land rights in post-apartheid South Africa. Apartheid refers to the 317 laws enacted by Dr. D. F. Malan's nationalist party in the late 1940s and early 1950s. These laws legally strengthened already existing racial segregation and economic, political, and social domination by whites. The plot's action revolves around David Lurie, a divorced white university professor expelled from his school for sexual harassment. Shortly after Lurie moves to his lesbian daughter Lucy's country farm, local blacks rape her. The story concerns Lurie's response to that incident. Coetzee received his second Booker Prize for the novel.

The English Patient

Michael Ondaatje's 1992 novel, *The English Patient*, explores many of the primary themes of postcolonial discourse including the intersections between individual and national identity and how the dialogue between the two shape consciousness. The novel is set in a villa in Florence and follows the lives of a young woman and three men, all from different countries, as they revolve around the badly burned English patient who lies dying in an upstairs room. The novel was adapted into an internationally acclaimed film in 1996.

The House of the Spirits

Isabelle Allende's first novel, *The House of Spirits*, published in 1982, tells the history of Chile through female characters. As in many postcolonial novels, Allende stakes out the margins, here represented by women, to critique the center, represented as established patriarchal power. In retelling Chile's history from the position of a historically oppressed group, Allende exposes the immorality and cruelty at the heart of the colonizing authorities. In doing so, she reclaims not only the history of her country but her own personal history as well, as she refuses to play the part of victim any longer.

Midnight's Children

Salman Rushdie's 1981 Booker Award-winning novel weaves his personal history into the history of India, using a narrator, Saleem Sinai, who was born in 1947, the year of Rushdie's birth and India's independence. Rushdie employs a number of narrative devices, including Hindu story telling, Magic Realism, and a style analogous to the "Bombay talkie," a type of Indian film, to underscore how difficult it is to write history and to show the many opportunities that independence offered the country, many of which have been squandered. *Midnight's Children* secured Rushdie's reputation as a writer of international stature, but Rushdie also offended many Indians for depicting Indira Gandhi, the prime minister of India, as a tyrant. Rushdie revised the novel and apologized. His 1988 novel, *The Satanic Verses*, brought Rushdie even more trouble, as Muslim fundamentalists considered the novel blasphemous of Islam and the prophet Mohammad. The Indian government banned the book, mass protests against it sprung up around the world, and Ayatollah Khomeini, the spiritual leader of the Iranian revolution, issued a *fatwa*, a judicial decree sentencing Rushdie to death.

Outside History: Selected Poems, 1980–1990

In her 1990 poetry collection, *Outside History: Selected Poems, 1980–1990*, Eavan Boland challenges the poetic traditions of England and Ireland, suggesting that Irish women have been doubly oppressed: once by their position as a colony of England and second by their gender. Boland tackles the difficult task of rewriting history so as to give Irish women a voice and a place in the poetic traditions of her own country. Her poetry, though frequently addressing experiences that many women share, alludes to Irish poetic tradition and mythology.

Rose

Li-Young Lee's first collection of poems, *Rose*, published in 1986, provides a glimpse into the consciousness of the Chinese diaspora. Lee, whose parents emigrated from China to Indonesia and then with their family to America, was born in Jakarta. His poems, though deeply personal and full of family history, show the devastating emotional and psychological effects that forced emigration has on both families and individuals. The atmosphere of "silence" in Lee's poems illustrates the writer's own shame in his inability to speak the language of his new country.

A Small Place

In her 1988 book, *A Small Place*, Jamaica Kincaid draws on her personal experience of growing up on the British island colony of Antigua to express her contempt for the ways in which British colonialism had destroyed her country. In particular, she focuses on the British educational system and how it attempted to turn Antiguans into English. Kincaid also reserves blame for Antiguans themselves, in their willingness to adopt the worst of British culture and ignore the best. She describes the country both before and after independence, suggesting that in some ways the country has been worse off since it became self-governing.

Things Fall Apart

Chinua Achebe's 1958 novel, *Things Fall Apart*, is set in Africa at the turn of the twentieth century and explores the interaction between traditional African society and British colonialism. The protagonist, Okonkwo, a member of the Ibo tribe, struggles to understand and adjust to the changes brought by British control and Christianity. More than eight million copies of the novel have been sold worldwide, and it has been translated into more than fifty languages. *Things Fall Apart* is also regularly included on syllabi in literature, history, and philosophy classes. In 1959, Achebe was awarded the Margaret Wrong Memorial Prize for the novel. Achebe's 1987 novel, *Anthills of the Savannah*, examines the post-independence condition of a fictional West African country, showing how the legacies of colonialism continue to undermine the possibility for the country to unite.

Themes

Racism

Racial discrimination is a theme that runs throughout postcolonial discourse, as white Europeans consistently emphasized their superiority over darker-skinned people. This was most evident in South Africa, whose policy of apartheid was institutionalized in national laws. These laws included the Prohibition of Mixed Marriages Act and the Immorality Act, which prohibited sexual intercourse and marriage between whites and blacks. The Groups Areas Act limited black access into areas reserved for whites. The only blacks permitted in these areas were workers, who first had to apply for state permission. The Population Registration Act categorized Africans into racial groups, which were based upon a person's appearance, education, and manners. Perhaps the most insidious of the apartheid laws were the Bantu Authorities Act and the Abolition of Passes and Coordination of Documents Act. The former relegated all Africans to their native lands and laid the groundwork for the denationalization of black and colored Africans. The latter required all Africans to carry identity papers containing a photograph, fingerprints, and work history. Strict penalties were meted out if a person could not produce a passbook. The fiction of Nadine Gordimer and Coetzee, both white South Africans, shows how apartheid has devastated the country morally, emotionally, and economically. Coetzee's characters are often privileged whites who are forced to acknowledge the material and psychological harm that apartheid has caused black Africans. Racism is a primary theme in the writing of Walcott, Kincaid, Fanon, and Danticat, as well.

Language

In occupied countries, colonizers often controlled their subjects through imposing their language upon them and forbidding them to speak their own. Educational systems enforced this. Postcolonial writers address the issue of language in various ways. Some, like Danticat and Walcott, mix the language(s) imposed on them with their indigenous language, creating a hybrid tongue that underscores the fractured nature of the colonized mind. Others, such as Ngugi, turned away from English to write exclusively in Gikuyu. Ngugi argues that continued use of English only helps Africans to forget their own precolonial past. Yet another approach to language is Silko's who, in *Ceremony*, intersperses a conventional Anglophone narrative with Indian folk legends to create a novel that underscores how Native Americans have to create a coherent whole out of disparate ways of seeing, describing, and being in the world. Some critics worry that the postcolonial works studied in universities are chosen for their postmodern style, rather than for the ways in which they describe the real-world oppression of people from former colonies.

Identity

In their desire to reclaim a past that had been taken from them, postcolonial writers often address the question of identity, either implicitly or explicitly in their work. However, doing so often requires using the language of the colonizers, which in itself complicates the drive to become the person they thought they were or should have become. The inability to return to a past now gone forever is a consequence of the notion of hybridity. Hybridity

Media Adaptations

- British director Isaac Julien's adapted Algerian revolutionary Frantz Fanon's classic text, *Black Skin, White Mask*, into a film of the same name in 1996. It has been released by California Newsreel. The film features interviews with family members and friends, documentary footage, readings from Fanon's work, and dramatizations of crucial moments in Fanon's life.
- Michael Ondaatje's novel, *The English Patient*, was adapted into a film in 1996, directed by Anthony Minghella. It was winner of nine Oscars, including best picture.
- Director Mira Nair's film *Mississippi Masala* (1991), explores the racial tensions between immigrant Indians from Uganda and resident African-Americans in the South. Nair's film *The Perez Family* (1993), follows the lives of Cuban refugees who came to the United States in the Mariel boatlift of 1980.

refers to the admixture of practices and signs from the colonizing and colonized cultures; it is a central fact of the postcolonial experience and is evident in almost all postcolonial texts. Colonizers are as much a part of the colonized as the colonized are of the colonizers. This cross-fertilization of cultures can be positive as well as dangerous, and writers often show an ambivalent attitude towards the phenomenon.

Hybridity challenges the idea that a person or a country has any essential "uncontaminated" or unchanging identity and that the desire to reclaim such an identity is rooted in an impossible nostalgia. This idea raises issues such as whether or not a colonized people can avoid adopting colonists' behavior and attitudes. Kincaid describes this phenomenon in *A Small Place*, showing how Antiguans have become "Anglicized" in their thinking. The idea of hybridity also challenges representations of colonized people, seen in descriptions such as "black consciousness," or "Indian soul," and the notion that "they" are all the same. Totalizing descriptions like these deny the difference among colonized people, as well as reinforce the constructed differences between them and their colonizers. Danticat's Sophie, for example, struggles to understand her own identity in the welter of language and culture into which she was born and through which she moves. Her migration to New York City further complicates her understanding of who she is, as she must now also come to grips with a diasporic Haitian culture, which is itself in flux.

Style

Point of View

Point of view refers to the eyes and sensibility through which a story is told or information is presented. Postcolonial literature challenges status quo Western points of view through using narrators who represent previously silenced or oppressed people. Since much literature from colonized countries was written from the colonizers'—usually male—point of view, it's not surprising that much postcolonial literature employs narrators who themselves are doubly oppressed, being both colonized by "outsiders" and being women. Silko, Danticat, Boland, and numerous other postcolonial writers express the particular difficulties women from colonized countries face, as they battle patriarchal attitudes and institutions of their oppressors as well as from their own people.

Narration

Narration refers to how a series of events is told. The mode of narration is deeply intertwined with an author's style and subject matter. Some postcolonial novels are narrated in a relatively straightforward manner in which events are recounted chronologically. However, many postcolonial works adopt a postmodern approach to storytelling. Postmodern narration, in this sense, refers to the use of different points of view, multiple narrators, and blending of styles and genres to describe events and action. Rushdie employs a kind of postmodern narration in *Midnight's Children*, as does Danticat in *Breath, Eyes, Memory* and Silko in *Ceremony*. Critics often use "Postmodernism" to refer to literature and art produced after World War II that take literary techniques to an extreme. Heavily affected by the brutality of Nazi atrocities during the war and the specter of nuclear holocaust, much postmodern literature shows an extreme pessimism of the human condition. With its hyper self-reflexivity, its often fractured and disjointed relaying of action, and its play on language, postmodern narration makes sense for postcolonial writers, many of whom are attempting to subvert colonial representations of their world and traditions.

Setting

Setting refers to time, place, and culture in which the action of a story takes place. Features include geographic location, characters' physical and mental environments, cultural attitudes, or the historical time of the action. The setting for postcolonial literature varies from country to country, writer to writer, although a good many of the novels are set *after* the countries have declared their independence from Great Britain. Kincaid's *A Small Place*, for example, chronicles life after Antigua won the right to self-governance, and Coetzee's *Disgrace* is set in a post-apartheid South Africa, when the power relations between whites and blacks are shifting.

Movement Variations

Literary Theory

Postcolonial theorists critically study both colonial texts and texts written after colonialism. One of the primary reasons postcolonial literature has become as popular as it has is due in large part to theorists such as Said, Spivak, Fanon, Kwame Anthony Appiah, Homi Bhabha, and others, who explain the significance of the literature in relation to history,

Topics for Further Study

- In groups, list of all the countries that were colonies or territories of another country (e.g., Great Britain, Portugal, France, United States, etc.) in 1900, 1939, and today, and then note the date each achieved independence. Which territories or colonies have not yet achieved independence or have achieved only partial independence? Each group member research the independence movement(s) in one of those countries and report to the class.
- The principal overseas dependencies of the United States include the territories of Guam, the United States Virgin Islands, American Samoa, and the Commonwealths of Puerto Rico and the Northern Mariana Islands. After researching the history of United States control of these territories, argue for or against their right to independence.
- Pretend that Fidel Castro's government has been overthrown and that you have been named as a member of the committee charged with drafting a constitution for the new government. What declarations or articles will you argue should be included in the new constitution? Read the constitutions of other countries including the United States as part of your research.
- Some theorists of Postcolonialism are known for their notoriously dense and often unreadable prose. Gayatri Chakravorty Spivak is one of them. In groups, read her essay "Can the Subaltern Speak?" included in Cary Nelson and Lawrence Grossberg's *Marxism and the Interpretation of Culture* (1988), summarize it, and present its main points to your class. Discuss the differences in the main points that your group presented and those of other groups.
- The conflict of cultures is at the heart of much postcolonial literature. Think about a time when you came into contact with a culture you knew little about, and then write a short essay about that event.

politics, philosophy, and literary traditions and discuss its place in contemporary society. Many of these theorists and critics are themselves from postcolonial countries and so speak with the authority of experience. Said, for example, is Palestinian; Spivak is from Calcutta, India; Fanon is from Martinique, a French colony. In challenging how writers and others have represented colonial subjects, these theorists seek to empower themselves and the literary projects of postcolonialists in their attempts to reshape perceptions and thinking about formerly colonized people and countries. The emergence of postcolonial studies as a field of academic inquiry and the popularity of postcolonial literature in the last thirty years or so is due in no small part to these theorists. The institutionalization of postcolonial studies has also come about at the same historical moment as poststructuralist theory, which challenges fundamental assumptions as to the nature of human identity, history, language, and truth itself.

Film

As countries gained their independence from colonial powers, filmmakers sought to describe the experience of the new countries and the changes wrought by independence upon individuals and their respective states. Deepa Mehta, for example, a Canadian-based Indian director, challenges Indian traditions in films such as *Fire*, *Earth*, and *Water*, (1996–2000), which seek to de-mystify the exoticism of India for foreigners and to interrogate the politics of sexuality in pre- and postcolonial India. Another well-known Indian director, Mira Nair, gained an international reputation with her film *Salaam, Bombay*! (1988), which documents the poverty and hopelessness of Bombay street children. Since then, Nair has directed films exploring racial tensions between immigrants and minorities in the United States. In films such as *Mississippi Masala* (1991) and *The Perez Family* (1993), Nair shows the hopes and aspirations of people from postcolonial countries and what becomes of them when they encounter a different kind of oppression in the country they believed would provide them with new lives. Another Indian director, Shyam Benegal, made films depicting the feudal, colonial, and patriarchal structures undergirding Indian society. For example, his 1996 film, *Making of the Mahatma*, describes the British colonial domain in South Africa, emphasizing the formative development of Gandhi. Other directors who explicitly address postcolonial themes in their films include Farida Ben Lyazid, Ken Loach, Deepa Mehta, Ketan Mehta, Mira Nair, Peter Ormrod, Horace Ove, Satyajit Ray, Mrinal Sen, and Ousmane Sembene.

Music

When colonizers have ruled a country for long periods of time, it is inevitable that their influence would manifest itself in the art and music of the colonized peoples. The hybrid culture of colonies often integrates both native material and material of the occupying forces. Because much of this music transcends national borders and cultural boundaries, it is often referred to as "World Music." In *The Study of Ethnomusicology: Twenty-nine Issues and Concepts*, Bruno Nettl lists three motivating behaviors expressed in the music of postcolonial non-Western countries: the first is "the desire to leave traditional culture intact, survival without change"; the second is "simple incorporation of a society into the Western cultural system"; and the third is "the adoption and adaptation of . . . products of Western culture . . . with an insistence that the core of cultural values will not change greatly and does not match those of the West." Examples of postcolonial music exhibiting cultural hybridity include Aboriginal pop music groups of the 1970s such as Yothu-Yindi, which combined elements of popular music and tribal ritual songs. In *Ethnicity, Identity and Music: The Musical Construction of Place*, Martin Stokes, who writes this kind of music, shows the "restructuring of song texts by incorporating a mixture of ritual symbolism and concern with colonial hegemony." An example of a hybrid musical form that reflects the migration of peoples across national borders is Indian Ravi Shankar's blending of classical Indian music with Western sounds. Shankar became an international celebrity when he began performing with the Beatles' George Harrison in the 1960s. One album, called *Soundz of the Asian Underground*, features ambient music and hip hop songs played by Asian musicians with instruments native to their own culture.

Historical Context

Post-World War II

Britain's loss of empire in the wake of World War II is arguably the single largest defining factor in the shaping of world politics in the last fifty years. Between 1945 and 1985, Britain lost almost all of its fifty formal dependencies in Africa, the Caribbean, the Mediterranean, the Pacific, South-East Asia, and the Far East and withdrew from a number of countries in the Persian Gulf over which it exerted considerable influence. In the preceding three centuries, Britain had colonized numerous countries and lands, while competing for resources and markets with Holland, Spain, and France, each of which had its own colonies and territories. In the seventeenth century, Britain had gained control over the eastern coast of North America, eastern Canada, the Caribbean Islands, and parts of Africa, which it used to acquire slaves, and had developed markets in India. The colonization of Ireland was also undertaken in earnest during this century. After the Napoleonic Wars ended in 1815, Britain became the leading industrial power in Europe, whose world economic strength was supported by its superior military, especially its navy.

During the nineteenth century, the British Empire tottered. The abolition of slavery by Britain and its empire in the early part of the century and the emphasis on free trade created an unfavorable economic climate for Britain, and its dependencies became more and more of a burden to manage. However, Britain also viewed its imperialistic expansion as a moral responsibility, using Darwin's theories of evolution as a rationale for exerting greater control over India, Africa, and China. British writer Rudyard Kipling referred to this responsibility as "the white man's burden," meaning that it was the God-given duty of the British to civilize and Christianize people who were obviously incapable of governing themselves.

The sheer size of Britain's empire contributed to its downfall, as it simply did not have the resources—militarily, economically, or morally—to stem the rise of nationalist movements in its territories. After World War I, the size of the British Empire expanded even farther to include territories "won" from Germany and Turkey during the war, such as Egypt, for whom they became the "trustee." In 1931, Canada, Australia, New Zealand, South Africa, and the Irish Free State formed the "Commonwealth of Nations," which backed Britain during World War II. After World War II, nationalist

Compare & Contrast

- **1940s–1960s:** Numerous European colonies in Africa gain their independence including Egypt, Sudan, Tunisia, Morocco, Ghana, Guinea, Chad, Benin, Nigeria, Ivory Coast, Madagascar, Central African Republic, Mali, Niger, Senegal, Burkina Faso, Mauritania, Togo, Zaire, Somalia, Congo, Gabon, Cameroon, Sierra Leone, Burundi, Rwanda, Uganda, Kenya, Tanzania, Malawi, Zambia, and Gambia.

  Today: Although these countries have declared their political independence from European powers, many of them are still virtually economic colonies of Western powers such as the United States. The Shell Petroleum Development Company (SPDC), for example, derives almost 14 percent of its production from Nigeria, which is dependent on oil for 80 percent of government revenue. However, Nigeria's dependence on Western money for its oil has also contributed to corruption, environmental degradation, and social unrest from tribes such as the Ogoni, who claim Shell's operations are polluting their land.

- **1940s–1960s:** Numerous colonies in Asia and the Middle East gain their independence, including Yemen, Malaysia, Myanmar, India, Pakistan, Kuwait, Israel, and Jordan.

  Today: Many of these countries continue to feud over land. India and Pakistan, for example, fight over the ownership of the Kashmir region, and the Palestinian people remain locked in a bloody battle with Israel for their own state.

- **1940s–1960s:** Numerous colonies in the Caribbean, Central America, and the South Atlantic gain their independence though remain a part of the British Commonwealth, including Barbados, Guyana, Jamaica, Antigua, and Trinidad & Tobago.

  Today: Many of these countries, such as Barbados and Jamaica, have become tourist destinations for Europeans and Americans, although the majority of the native populations live in poverty.

movements succeeded in ousting European colonizers from their countries. Numerous countries won independence from Britain, including India and Pakistan (1947), Ireland (1949), Egypt (1951), Kenya (1963), and numerous others. French colonies such as Chad, Benin, Nigeria, Ivory Coast, Madagascar, Central African Republic, Mali, Niger, Senegal, Burkina Faso, Mauritania, Togo, Zaire, Somalia, Congo, Gabon, and Cameroon also declared independence in 1960, and Mozambique and Angola declared their independence from Portugal in 1975. Britain, however, is not ready to cede all of its territories, as evidenced by their battle for the Falkland Islands, a group of islands in the south Atlantic about three hundred miles east of the Argentinean coast. Although Argentina has claimed the islands since the early 1900s, Britain has occupied and administered the islands since 1833, rejecting Argentina's claims. In 1982, the two countries went to war over the Falklands, which has a total population of about 2,000 people. Britain used its superior naval power to defeat Argentina, but not before Argentina lost 655 men and Britain 236.

In the last decade, another colonial empire has crumbled, this one more rapidly than the British Empire. Former Russian colonies, once a part of the United Soviet Socialists Republic, declared their independence from Russia. In 1990, the Congress of Deputies of Russia adopted the Declaration of Independence, and in 1991, Moldavia, Azerbaijan, Ukraine, Belarus, Uzbekistan Armenia, Turkmenistan, Kazakhstan, and Tajikistan declared independence but joined the Commonwealth of Independent States, a federation created to share resources and to interact on the basis of sovereign equality. Because of the lack of translations and the heavy censorship inside the U.S.S.R., which existed for years, little academic work has been done on the literature from these emerging countries.

Critical Overview

In his 1962 book *The Wretched of the Earth*, Frantz Fanon laid the theoretical groundwork for much postcolonial theorizing to come. Fanon condemns African revolutionary programs as insufficient and argues that a new world can come into being only with a violent revolution led by the rural African peasantry. The book develops themes introduced in Fanon's first book, *Black Skin, White Mask* (1952). In this book, Fanon uses his personal experience to show how the relationship between colonized and colonizer is normalized as psychology, resulting in emotional damage to both. A French-speaking native of the French colony of Martinique, Fanon argues that language plays a central role in shaping the consciousness of the colonized people. Fanon's work anticipated studies such as Said's *Orientalism* but has been heavily criticized for its portrayal of black women.

Said's 1978 study, *Orientalism*, one of the foundational texts of postcolonial studies, critiques Western representations of the East, arguing that since the nineteenth century, Western scholars have depicted "Arab" cultures as irrational, anti-Western, primitive, and dishonest. Orientalism, Said claims, is an ideology born of the colonizers' desire to know their subjects to better control them. Said argues, "To write about the Arab Oriental world . . . is to write with the authority of a nation . . . with the unquestioning certainty of absolute truth backed by absolute force." By showing how historians routinely present their "vision" of the Orient as objective and impartial, Said demonstrates how they deceive themselves just as their writing misrepresents others. Critics agree that Said's study remains one of the most important works of postcolonial theory written.

Gayatri Chakravorty Spivak's writing has focused on the intersections of gender, ethnicity, representations of postcolonial and colonial subjects, and the place from which these representations are often made: the university. In an interview in *The Post-Colonial Critic* (1990), Spivak says that she views her job as a postcolonial critic who also teaches as twofold:

> to see how the master texts need us in the construction of their texts without acknowledging that need; and to explore the differences and similarities between texts coming from the two sides which are engaged with the same problem at the same time.

Homi Bhabha's theory and criticism on Postcolonialism investigates the ideas of hybridity and ambivalence in postcolonial discourse, especially as they contribute to constructing national and cultural identities. In his 1990 study, *Nation and Narration* (1990), Bhabha uses a mix of psychoanalysis and semiotics to explore the ways in which Third World nations and nationalities have been constructed through narrative traditions that have also positioned them as inferior to the West. In his study, *The Location of Culture* (1994), Bhabha discusses the "spaces" created by dominant social formations in the writings of Toni Morrison and Nadine Gordimer, among others.

Criticism

Chris Semansky

Semansky holds a Ph.D. in English from the State University of New York at Stony Brook, and he is an instructor of literature and writing whose essays, poems, stories, and reviews appear in publications such as College English, Mississippi Review, New York Tribune, The Oregonian, *and* American Letters & Commentary. *His books include* Death, But at a Good Price *(1991) and* Blindsided *(1998). In this essay, Semansky considers the institutionalization of postcolonial literature.*

The adoption of postcolonial literature in the English curriculum of British and American schools in the last few decades has coincided with changes in how and why literature is studied. These changes include ideas about what texts should be included in class syllabi, issues of literary taste, and the purpose(s) of studying literature.

The writing studied in literature classrooms in the United States and Great Britain is often referred to as belonging to the canon. The term derives from the Greek word "kanon" and originally denoted the list of books in the New Testament and Hebrew Bible that came to comprise the Holy Scriptures. More recently, the phrase "literary canon" has been used to denote the "major authors," critics, and historians considered to be the most important for students to read. Surveys of the great works of Western civilization, for example, traditionally would include works by Plato, Aristotle, John Milton, William Shakespeare, and so forth, in short, works by men of European descent. However, in the second half of the twentieth century, a number of events has challenged the assumptions embodied in the literary canon. These events include the Civil Rights movement in the

United States, the Women's Liberation movement, and the accelerated unraveling of the British Empire in the wake of World War II. As more and different people began to assert their own rights to explore their heritage and express their identities, critics began to expose the ideological underpinnings of the literary canon and how those underpinnings served one group of people while excluding another. Since the 1960s, a number of critics have argued for the revision, or even the abolition, of the literary canons.

In *The Empire Writes Back: Theory and Practice in Post-colonial Literatures*, Bill Ashcroft, Careth Griffiths, and Helen Tiffin point to "the development of English as a privileged academic subject in the nineteenth century," arguing that its study "has always been a densely political and cultural phenomenon . . . called into the service of a profound and embracing nationalism." Nationalism refers to a favoring of the traditions, practices, language, myths, and rituals of a group of people who believe their way of life superior to that of others. By instituting its own school system into its colonies, the British used education as a primary means of controlling colonized people. Walcott, for example, a writer of African, Dutch, and English descent, grew up in St. Lucia of the West Indies reading Milton, Spenser, Shakespeare, and other British writers. He was taught to think like a British person and to develop British tastes. His notion of what made "good" literature, then, was in large part defined by his British education. Indigenous people were "other," defined by and through their difference from the colonizers. The idea of "otherness" has helped to foster the notion that Third World countries are backward, inferior, and uncivilized. The editors of *The Norton Anthology of Theory and Criticism* summarize the insidiousness of colonial literary education as follows:

> As it inculcates Western Eurocentric values, literary education supports a kind of "cultural colonization," creating a class of colonial subjects often burdened by a double consciousness and by divided loyalties. It helps Western colonizers rule by consent rather than violence.

In many cases, however, colonized countries had no national literature of their own, no literary tradition, no concept of literature itself, and so there was no basis of comparison for colonized people, many of whom could neither read nor write. Some of these colonies had strictly oral storytelling traditions and no history of written language. The British, in their attempts to "educate" the inhabitants of their colonies, used their own language and literature as models of civilized and superior thinking and behavior.

"The British, in their attempts to 'educate' the inhabitants of their colonies, used their own language and literature as models of civilized and superior thinking and behavior."

During the independence movements of British colonies and after colonies declared their independence, natives of former colonies attempted to establish their own literary traditions. The writing produced by postcolonial natives is often a literature of resistance that integrates Western modes of writing and narrative with local traditions and ways of knowing. Walcott's plays such as *The Sea at Dauphin* (1954), for example, mixes West Indian language and customs with elements of Greek drama. And Walcott's establishment of the Little Carib Theatre Workshop, later renamed the Trinidad Theatre Workshop, was an attempt to provide native West Indian writers with a place to develop and produce plays about their own history and culture.

However, writing about one's own history and culture after centuries of colonization, for Walcott as well as for other postcolonialists, has proved a difficult, virtually impossible task. Representing the relationships between precolonial cultures and imperial cultures necessarily includes the acknowledgement of culture's hybrid nature and the futility of ever recovering a "pure" past. The idea that all cultures are representations and the result of political forces at work shows up in the postmodern forms and styles that postcolonial writers such as Walcott, Coetzee, Rushdie, and so forth have chosen to "depict" the postcolonial condition. Although the meaning of the term "postmodern" is as hotly debated as the term "postcolonial," in reference to postcolonial writing it denotes writing that mixes genres and, often, languages, integrates traditional Western forms with indigenous materials, and foregrounds how identities are social constructions

A statue of Daniel O'Connell who symbolized the fight for Irish independence in the nineteenth century

rather than essential features of people, countries, or cultures.

As style, the postmodern is most often embodied in the novels of postcolonial writers rather than, say, poetry or drama, and it is the novel to which postcolonial critics pay most attention. The novel, as a kind of writing that attempts to create and people its own world with elaborate characterizations, plots, and detailed setting, is apropos for writers motivated to reshape public as well as personal history. Coetzee's novels, for example, especially *Waiting for the Barbarians* (1982), which is set in an imaginary empire not unlike South Africa, employs postmodern strategies and devices to foreground their status as works of fiction, while at the same time suggesting a political stance towards a real place and policy, that is, South African apartheid. Postcolonial literature that overtly uses postmodern compositional strategies is not without its detractors; however, critics often claim that it can send the message that oppression and colonialism are a part of the human condition and will always be here. In his review of Coetzee's novel, Irving Howe comments on Coetzee's universalizing approach towards describing South Africa's predicament:

> That 'a heart of darkness' is present in all societies and a beast 'lurks within each one of us' may well be true. But such invocations of universal evil can deflect attention from the particular and at least partly remediable social wrongs Mr. Coetzee portrays. Not only deflect attention, but encourage readers, as they search for their inner beasts, to a mood of conservative acquiescence and social passivity.

The inclusion of postcolonial literature in English departments in the United States, Great Britain, and Australia in the last few decades has also been part of the move away from the study of literature per se and towards the study of culture broadly conceived. Some colleges and universities are even abandoning literature departments altogether and replacing them with cultural studies departments, whose courses include literature, heavy doses of theory of various stripes—literary and other—historical documents, movies, and texts not traditionally studied in literature classrooms. Some of the questions raised by the study of postcolonial literature include the following: Which writers speak best for the postcolonial nation? How does postcolonial literature ask readers to reexamine their own notions of history and "otherness?" In what language should the postcolonial writer write? Is America itself a postcolonial country, and if so, what does that say about Americans' authority to theorize about the postcolonial condition?

The shift in focus in Western schools away from the study of English and American literature and towards curricula that embrace an international worldview using a variety of texts has been for the good. Such curricula allow people whose voices have previously been stifled to speak out and allow artifacts previously ignored to be studied. This inclusion of new texts and writers can (potentially) make English departments agents of social change, rather than simply arbiters of literary taste.

Source: Chris Semansky, Critical Essay on Postcolonialism, in *Literary Movements for Students*, The Gale Group, 2003.

Arnold Krupat

In the following essay excerpt, Krupat explains that while Native American literature contains a lot of Postcolonial attributes and ideologies, it should not be classified as Postcolonial literature because Colonialism sstill exists in the Americas.

In the current climate of literary studies, it is tempting to think of contemporary Native American literatures as among the postcolonial literatures of the world. Certainly they share with other postcolonial texts the fact of having, in the words of

What Do I Study Next?

- Mark Crinson's *Empire Building: Orientalism and Victorian Architecture* (1996) examines how racial theory, as well as political and religious agendas, informed British architects and how Eastern ideas came to influence the West.
- In *The Short Century: Independence and Liberation Movements in Africa 1945–1994* (2001), Okwui Enwezor has edited a collection of writing and images, including essays, studies, speeches, manifestos, and photographs, which document the cultural and political record of Africa from 1945 to 1994 and offer a glimpse into the ideologies that shaped the continent's history and life during the period.
- Andrew Gurr's *Writers in Exile: The Identity of Home in Modern Literature* (1981) defines "exile" as a feature of West Indian, African, Australian, and New Zealand literature written in English and surveys many of the major writers from these countries.
- In 2000, Oxford University Press released *World Cinema: Critical Approaches*, edited by John Hill and Pamela Church Gibson. This collection of essays on world cinema, much of it from postcolonial countries, addresses subjects such as concepts of national cinema, East Central European cinema, Anglophone national cinemas, and African cinema.
- George Lamming's *The Pleasures of Exile* (1960) details his experiences as a West Indian in London and contains his well-known essay on Shakespeare's play, *The Tempest*, raising questions of canonicity, exile, and the relationship between the center and the margins.
- Albert Memmi's *The Colonizer and the Colonized* (1965) is an early sociological study of the destructive impact of colonialism on both colonizers and colonized.
- In *Missionaries in India* (1998), author Arun Shourie focuses on the intentional misinterpretations of Hinduism by Christian missionaries and the harm those misinterpretations have caused the country.
- Leslie Marmon Silko's novel *Almanac of the Dead* (1991) is perhaps her most controversial work. Silko addresses many issues related to American Indians, including the European conquest of them.

the authors of *The Empire Writes Back*, "emerged in their present form out of the experience of colonization and asserted themselves by foregrounding the tension with the imperial power, and by emphasizing their differences from the assumptions of the imperial Centre." Yet contemporary Native American literatures cannot quite be classed among the postcolonial literatures of the world for the simple reason that there is not yet a "post-" to the colonial status of Native Americans. Call it domestic imperialism or internal colonialism; in either case, a considerable number of Native people exist in conditions of politically sustained subalternity. I have remarked on the academic effects of this condition in the first chapter; here I note the more worldly effects of this condition: Indians experience twelve times the U.S. national rate of malnutrition, nine times the rate of alcoholism, and seven times the rate of infant mortality; as of the early 1990s, the life expectancy of reservation-based men was just over forty-four years, with reservation-based women enjoying, on average, a life-expectancy of just under forty-seven years. "Sovereignty," whatever its ultimate meaning in the complex sociopolitical situation of Native nations in the United States, remains to be both adequately theorized and practically achieved, and "independence," the great desideratum of colonized nations, is not, here, a particularly useful concept.

Arif Dirlik lists three current meanings of the term *postcolonial*. Postcolonial may intend "a

Sign in South Africa before the end of apartheid

literal description of conditions in formerly colonial societies," it may claim to offer "a description of a global condition after the period of colonialism"—what Dirlik refers to as "global capitalism," marked by the "transnationalization of production"—and it may, most commonly in the academy, claim to provide "a description of a discourse on the above-named conditions that is informed by the epistemological and psychic orientations that are products of those conditions." Is any one of these meanings useful to describe contemporary Native American literature? Dirlik's first sense of the postcolonial will not work because, as already noted, the material condition of contemporary Native "societies" is not a postcolonial one. His second sense might perhaps come a bit nearer, inasmuch as Native societies, although still in a colonial situation, nonetheless participate in the global economy of a world "after the period of colonialism." To give a fairly undramatic anecdote, in Santa Fe, Native Americans sell traditional ceramic work and jewelry (including "traditional" golf tees) across the street from where non-Native people offer the "same" wares made in Hong Kong. In something of a parallel fashion, Lakota people travel to Germany and Switzerland to promote tourism at Pine Ridge. As for the last of Dirlik's definitions, little discourse surrounding Native American literature, to the best of my knowledge, has been self-consciously aware of having been formed "by the epistemological and psychic orientations that are products" of the postcolonial. (And the "nationalist" Native critic seeks to reject any formation whatever according to these "orientations.") Perhaps, then, it may not be particularly useful to conceptualize contemporary Native American literature as postcolonial.

But even though contemporary Native American fiction is produced in a condition of ongoing colonialism, some of that fiction not only has the look of postcolonial fiction but also, as I will try to show in the second part of this chapter, performs ideological work that parallels that of postcolonial fiction elsewhere. Here, however, I want to suggest a category—the category of anti-imperial translation—for conceptualizing the tensions and differences between contemporary Native American fiction and "the imperial center." Because historically specifiable acts of translative violence marked the European colonization of the Americas from Columbus to the present, it seems to me particularly important to reappropriate the concept of translation for contemporary Native American literature. To do so is not to deny the relationship of this literature to the postcolonial literatures of the world but, rather, to attempt to specify a particular modality for that relationship.

To say that the people indigenous to the Americas entered European consciousness only by means of a variety of complex acts of translation is to think of such things as Columbus's giving the name of San Salvador to an island he *knows* is called Guanahani by the natives—and then giving to each further island he encounters, as he wrote in his journals, "a new name." Columbus also materially "translated" (*trans-latio*, "to carry across") some of the Natives he encountered, taking "six of them from here," as he remarked in another well-known passage, "in order that they may learn to speak." Columbus gave the one who was best at learning his own surname and the first name of his firstborn son, translating this otherwise anonymous person into Don Diego Colon.

Now, any people who are perceived as somehow unable to speak when they speak their own languages, are not very likely to be perceived as having a literature—especially when they do not write, a point to which we shall return. Thus, initially, the very "idea of a [Native American] literature was inherently ludicrous," as Brian Swann has noted, because Indian "languages themselves were primitive." If Indians spoke at all, they spoke very badly (and, again, they did not write). In 1851, John De Forest, in his *History of the Indians of Connecticut*, observed, "It is evident from the enormous length of many of the words, sometimes occupying a whole line, that there was something about the structure of these languages which made them cumbersome and difficult to manage."

Difficult for whom, one might ask, especially in view of the fact that De Forest himself had not achieved even minimal competence in any Native language. Further, inasmuch as these were spoken languages, not alphabetically written languages, any estimate that single words occupied the length of "a whole line" could only depend on De Forest's decision to write them that way. De Forest's sense of the "cumbersome and difficult" nature of Indian languages, as I have noted, implies that any literature the Natives might produce in these languages would also be "cumbersome and difficult." Perhaps the Natives would do better to translate themselves or be translated, to "learn to speak"—in this case, to speak English—in order to have a literature. De Forest was wrong, of course, although what most people know as Native American literature today consists of texts originally written in English.

> **"But even though contemporary Native American fiction is produced in a condition of ongoing colonialism, some of that fiction not only has the look of postcolonial fiction but also, performs ideological work that parallels that of postcolonial fiction elsewhere."**

Almost half a century after DeForest, as late as 1894, Daniel Brinton—a man who actually did a great deal to make what he called the "production" of "aboriginal authors" visible to the dominant culture—nonetheless declared, "Those peoples who are born to the modes of thought and expression enforced by some languages can never forge to the front in the struggle for supremacy; they are fatally handicapped in the race for the highest life." The winners in the "race for the highest life," therefore, would be the race with the "highest" language; and it was not the Indians but rather, as Brinton wrote, "our Aryan forefathers" who were the ones fortunate enough to be endowed "with a richly inflected speech." As Kwame Anthony Appiah explained in reference to Johann Gottfried von Herder, the *Sprachgeist*, "the 'spirit' of the language, is not merely the medium through which speakers communicate but the sacred essence of a nationality. [And] Herder himself identified the highest point of the nation's language in its poetry," in its literature. "Whoever writes about the literature of a country," as Appiah elsewhere cited Herder, "must not neglect its language." For those like the Indians with "primitive" languages, there would seem to be little hope, short of translation, for the prospects of literary achievement. Thus, by the end of the nineteenth century, the linguistic determinism expressed by Brinton—and, of course, by many others—worked against the possibility of seeing Native Americans as having an estimable literature at exactly the moment when the texts for that literature were, for the first time, being more or less accurately translated and published.

But here one must return to the other dimension of the translation issue as it affects Native American literatures. For the problem in recognizing the existence of Native literatures was not only that Natives could not speak or, when they did speak, that their languages were judged deficient or "primitive" but also that they did not write.

Here I will only quickly review what I and others have discussed elsewhere. Because *littera-ture* in its earliest uses meant the cultivation of letters (from Latin *littera*, "letter"), just as *agriculture* meant the cultivation of fields, peoples who did not inscribe alphabetic characters on the page could not, by definition, produce a literature. (They were also thought to be only minimally capable of agriculture in spite of overwhelming evidence to the contrary, but that is another story.) It was the alteration in European consciousness generally referred to as "romanticism" that changed the emphasis in constituting the category of literature from the medium of expression, writing—literature as culture preserved in letters—to the *kind* of expression preserved, literature as imaginative and affective utterance, spoken or written. It is only at this point that an oral literature can be conceived as other than a contradiction in terms and the unlettered Indians recognized as people capable of producing a "literature."

For all of this, it remains the case that an oral literature, in order to become the subject of analysis, must indeed first become an object. It must, that is, be textualized; and here we encounter a translation dilemma of another kind, one in which the "source language" itself has to be carried across—*trans-latio*—from one medium to another, involving something more than just a change of names. This translative project requires that temporal speech acts addressed to the ear be turned into visual objects in space, black marks on the page, addressed to the eye. Words that had once existed only for the tongue to pronounce now were to be entrusted to the apprehension of the eye. Mythography, in a term of Anthony Mattina's, or ethnopoetics has been devoted for many years to the problems and possibilities involved in this particular form of media translation.

Translation as a change of names—as a more or less exclusively linguistic shift from "source" to "target" language—may, historically, be traced in relation to the poles of identity and difference, as these are articulated within the disciplinary boundaries of what the West distinguishes as the domains of art and social science. Translators with attachments to the arts or humanities have rendered Native verbal expression in such a way as to make it appear attractively literary by Western standards of literariness, thereby obscuring the very different standards pertaining in various Native American cultures. Conversely, translators with attachments to the social sciences have rendered Native verbal expression in as literal a manner as possible, illuminating the differences between that expression and our own but thereby obscuring its claims to literary status. I have elaborated on these matters elsewhere, and so I will here turn from considerations of the formal implications of translation practices to their ideological implications. I want to explain what I mean by anti-imperial translation and why it seems to me that a great many texts by Native American writers, though written in English, may nonetheless be taken as types of anti-imperial translation.

I base my sense of anti-imperial translation on a well-known, indeed classic text, one that I have myself quoted on a prior occasion. The text is from Rudolph Pannwitz, who is cited in Walter Benjamin's important essay "The Task of the Translator." Pannwitz wrote, "Our translations, even the best ones, proceed from a wrong premise. They want to turn Hindi, Greek, English into German instead of turning German into Hindi, Greek, English. Our translators have far greater reverence for the usage of their own language than for the spirit of the foreign works . . . The basic error of the translator is that he preserves the state in which his own language happens to be instead of allowing his language to be powerfully affected by the foreign tongue." My use of Pannwitz was influenced by Talal Asad's paper, "The Concept of Cultural Translation in British Social Anthropology," originally presented at the School for American Research in 1984 and published in James Clifford and George Marcus's important collection *Writing Culture* in 1986. As will be apparent, I am much indebted to Asad's work.

Asad's subject, like mine, is not translation in the narrow sense but rather translation as cultural translation. The "good translator," Asad wrote, "does not immediately assume that unusual difficulty in conveying the sense of an alien discourse denotes a fault in the latter, but instead critically examines the normal state of his or her own language." Asad notes the fact that languages, if expressively equal, are nonetheless politically "unequal," those of the Third World that are typically studied by anthropologists being "weaker" in relation to Western languages (and today especially in relation to English). Asad remarks that the weaker, or colonized, languages "are more likely to submit to forcible transformation in the translation process than the other way around." Asad cites with approval Godfrey Lienhardt's essay "Modes of Thought" and quotes Lienhardt's exemplary explanation of anthropological translation: "We mediate between their habits of thought, which we have acquired with them, and those of our own society; in doing so, it is not finally some mysterious 'primitive philosophy' that we are exploring, but the further potentialities of our thought and language." This sort of translation, Asad affirms, should alter the usual relationship between the anthropological audience and the anthropological text, in that it seeks to disrupt the habitual desire of that audience to use the text as an occasion to know *about* the Other, a matter of "different *writings and readings* (meanings)" in order to instantiate the possibility that translation, as a matter "of different uses (practices)," can be a force moving us toward "*learning to live another form of life.*"

My claim is that Native American writers today are engaged in some version of the translation project along the broad lines sketched by Asad. Even though contemporary Native writers write in English and configure their texts in apparent consonance with Western or Euramerican literary forms—that is, they give us texts that look like novels, short stories, poems, and autobiographies—they do so in ways that present an "English" nonetheless "powerfully affected by the foreign tongue," not by Hindi, Greek, or German, of course, and not actually by a "foreign" language, inasmuch as the "tongue" and "tongues" in question are indigenous to America. The language they offer, in Asad's terms, derives at least in part from other forms of practice, and to comprehend it might just require, however briefly, that we attempt to imagine living other forms of life.

This is true of contemporary Native American writers in both literal and figurative ways. In the case of those for whom English is a second language (Luci Tapahonso, Ray Young Bear, Michael Kabotie, Ofelia Zepeda, and Simon Ortiz are some of the writers who come immediately to mind), it is altogether likely that their English will show traces of the structure and idioms of their "native" language, as well as a variety of linguistic habits and narrative and performative practices of traditional expressive forms in Navajo, Mesquakie, Hopi, Tohono O'odham, and Acoma. Their English, then, is indeed an English, in Pannwitz's words, "powerfully affected by the foreign tongue," a tongue (to repeat) not "foreign" at all to the Americas. Here the Native author quite literally tests "the tolerance of [English] for assuming unaccustomed forms," and an adequate commentary on the work of these writers will require of the critic if not bilingualism then at least what Dell Hymes has called some "control" of the Native language.

Most Native writers today are not, however, fluent speakers of one or another of the indigenous languages of the Americas, although their experiences with these languages are so different that it would be impossible to generalize. (E.g., Leslie Marmon Silko certainly heard a good deal of Laguna as she was growing up, just as N. Scott Momaday heard a good deal of Jemez, whereas many of the Native American writers raised in the cities did not hear indigenous languages on a very regular basis.) Yet all of them have indicated their strong sense of indebtedness or allegiance to the oral tradition. Even the mixed-blood Anishinaabe—Chippewa—writer Gerald Vizenor, someone who uses quotations from a whole range of comtemporary European theorists and whose own texts are full of ironic effects possible only to a text-based literature, has insisted on the centrality of "tribal stories" and storytelling to his writing. This is the position of every other contemporary Native American writer I can think of—all of them insist on the storytelling of the oral tradition as providing a context, as bearing on and influencing the writing of their novels, poems, stories, or autobiographies.

In view of this fact, it needs to be said that "the oral tradition," *as it is invoked by these writers*, is an "invented tradition." It can be seen, as John Tomlinson has remarked, "as a phenomenon of modernity. There is a sense in which simply recognizing a practice as 'traditional' marks it off from the routine practices of proper [*sic*] traditional societies." This is not, of course, to deny that there were and continue to be a number of oral traditions that "really" existed and continue to exist among the indigenous cultures of the Americas. Nor is it to deny that some contemporary Native American writers have considerable experience of "real" forms of oral performance. I am simply noting that "the oral tradition" as usually invoked in these contexts is a kind of catchall phrase whose function is broadly to name the source of the difference between the English of Native writers and that of Euramerican writers. This "tradition" is not based on historically and culturally specific instances.

A quick glance at some of the blurbs on the covers or book jackets of work by contemporary Indian writers makes this readily apparent. When these blurbs are written by non-Indians (and most are, for obvious reasons, written by non-Indians), reference to "the oral tradition" usually represents a loose and vague way of expressing nostalgia for some aboriginal authenticity or wisdom, a golden age of wholeness and harmony. When these blurbs are written by Native Americans—this generalization I venture more tentatively—they are (to recall the discussion I offered in the first chapter of this book) a rhetorical device, a strategic invocation of what David Murray has called the discourse of Indianness, a discourse that has currency in both the economic and the political sense in the United States. Once more, to say this is in no way to deny that the narrative modalities and practices of a range of Native oral literatures, as well as the worldviews of various Native cultures, *are* important to many of the texts constituting a contemporary Native American literature, and not merely honorifically, sentimentally, or rhetorically.

Anyone who would make the claim that a particular Native text in English should be read as an instance of cultural translation must offer a specific demonstration of how that text incorporates alternate strategies, indigenous perspectives, or language usages that, literally or figuratively, make its "English" on the page a translation in which traces of the "foreign tongue," the "Indian," can be discerned. If one then wants to claim that this translation is indeed an anti-imperial translation, it becomes necessary to show how those traces operate in tension with or in a manner resistant to an English in the interest of colonialism.

Source: Arnold Krupat, "Postcolonialism, Ideology, and Native American Literature," in *Postcolonial Theory and the United States: Race, Ethnicity, and Literature*, edited by Amritjit Singh and Peter Schmidt, University of Mississippi Press, 2000, pp. 73–94.

Sources

Achebe, Chinua, *Things Fall Apart*, William Heinemann, 1958.

Allende, Isabelle, *The House of the Spirits*, Bantam Books, 1986.

Ashcroft, Bill, Gareth Griffiths, and Helen Tiffin, eds., *The Empire Writes Back*, Routledge Kegan & Paul, 1990.

———, eds., *The Post-Colonial Studies Reader*, Routledge, 1995.

Bhabha, Homi K., *The Location of Culture*, Routledge, 1994.

———, ed., *Nation and Narration*, Routledge, 1990.

Boland, Eavan, *Outside History: Selected Poems, 1980–1990*, Norton, 1990.

Coetzee, J. M., *Disgrace*, Viking Penguin, 1999.

———, *Waiting for the Barbarians*, Penguin Books, 1982.

Fanon, Frantz, *Black Skin, White Masks*, Grove, 1967.

———, *The Wretched of the Earth*, Grove Press, 1967.

Harasym, Sarah, ed., *The Post-Colonial Critic: Interviews, Strategies, Dialogues*, Routledge, 1990, pp. 67–74.

Howe, Irving, "A Stark Political Fable of South Africa," in the *New York Times*, April 18, 1982, Sec. 7, p. 1.

Lee, Li-Young, *Rose*, BOA Editions, 1986.

Leitch, Vincent B., ed., *The Norton Anthology of Theory and Criticism*, W. W. Norton, 2001, pp. 1–28.

Nettl, Bruno, *The Study of Ethnomusicology: Twenty-Nine Issues and Concepts*, University of Illinois Press, 1983, pp. 147–50.

Ngugi wa Thiong'o, *Decolonising the Mind: The Politics of Language in African Literature*, Heinemann, 1986.

Ondaatje, Michael, *The English Patient*, Knopf, 1992.

Said, Edward, *Orientalism*, Vintage Books, 1978.

Spivak, Gyatri Chakravorty, *A Critique of Post-Colonial Reason: Toward a History of the Vanishing Present*, Harvard University Press, 1999.

Stokes, Martin, ed., *Ethnicity, Identity and Music: The Musical Construction of Place*, Oxford, 1994, p. 147.

Further Reading

Ashcroft, Bill, Gareth Griffiths, and Helen Tiffin, eds., *The Empire Writes Back*, Routledge, 1990.
This accessible study surveys new writing in cultures as diverse as India, Australia, the West Indies, Africa, and Canada and details many of the debates that animate postcolonial discourse.

———, eds., *The Post-Colonial Studies Reader*, Routledge, 1995.
This anthology provides the most comprehensive selection of texts in postcolonial theory and criticism to date, featuring ninety of the discipline's most widely read works. All the well-known theorists such as Said, Spivak, and Homi Bhaba are represented as well, and their essays have been edited for clarity and accessibility.

Fanon, Frantz, *Black Skin, White Masks*, Grove, 1967.
Fanon leans heavily on his personal experience in this book to show how his intellectual and emotional world, as well as his country, has been colonized by the French.

Said, Edward, *Orientalism*, Vintage Books, 1978.
Said's study of how the West has historically represented the Arab world ranks as one of the most important works of postcolonial theory.

Thieme, John, ed., *Post-Colonial Literatures*, Arnold, 1996.
This anthology offers writing from more than two hundred writers and is the most comprehensive selection of anglophone postcolonial writing ever published in one volume. Thieme organizes the sections according to regions including Africa, Australia, Canada, Caribbean, New Zealand and South Pacific, South Asia, South-East Asia, and Trans-Cultural Writing. Thieme also provides a useful introduction explaining his text choices and strategy of organization.

Postmodernism

Movement Origin

c. 1950

Postmodernism is the name given to the period of literary criticism that is now in full bloom. Just as the name implies, it is the period that comes after the modern period. But these are not easily separated into discrete units limited by dates as centuries or presidential terms are limited. Postmodernism came about as a reaction to the established modernist era, which itself was a reaction to the established tenets of the nineteenth century and before.

What sets Postmodernism apart from its predecessor is the reaction of its practitioners to the rational, scientific, and historical aspects of the modern age. For postmodernists this took the guise of being self-conscious, experimental, and ironic. The postmodernist is concerned with imprecision and unreliability of language and with epistemology, the study of what knowledge is.

An exact date for the establishment of Postmodernism is not easy, but it is said to have begun in the post-World War II era, roughly the 1950s. It took full flight in the 1960s in the social and political unrest in the world. In 1968 it reached its zenith with the intense student protests in the United States and France, the war for independence in Algeria, and the Soviet invasion of Czechoslovakia. The beginning of space exploration with the launch of Sputnik in 1957, culminating in the 1969 landing of men on the moon, marks a significant shift in the area of science and technology.

At the same time, Jacques Derrida presented his first paper, *Of Grammatology* (1967), outlining the principles of deconstruction. The early novels of Kurt Vonnegut, Jr. and Alain Robbe-Grillet were published; Ishmael Reed was writing his poetry. The Marxist critics, Fredric Jameson and Terry Eagleton, who saw a major shift in the social and economic world as a part of the postmodern paradigm, were beginning their creative careers. As time progressed, more and more individuals added their voices to this list: Julia Kristeva, Susan Sontag, and, in popular culture, Madonna. (In her openly sexual music and music videos she broke down the limits of sexuality and femininity. Still, while some believe that her career is a setback for feminist movement; others believe that she opened the doors to a wider acceptance of female and human sexuality.)

In a speech at Independence Hall in Philadelphia on July 4, 1994, Vaclav Havel, president of the Czech Republic, said the following:

> The distinguishing features of such transitional periods are a mixing and blending of cultures and a plurality or parallelism of intellectual and spiritual worlds. These are periods when all consistent value systems collapse, when cultures distant in time and space are discovered or rediscovered. They are periods when there is a tendency to quote, to imitate, and to amplify, rather than to state with authority or integrate. New meaning is gradually born from the encounter, or the intersection, of many different elements.
>
> This state of mind or of the human world is called postmodernism. For me, a symbol of that state is a Bedouin mounted on a camel and clad in traditional robes under which he is wearing jeans, with a transistor radio in his hands and an ad for Coca-Cola on the camel's back.

This speech outlines the essence of Postmodernism in all its forms: the mixing, the disintegration, and the instability of identities.

Representative Authors

Donald Barthelme (1931–1989)

Donald Barthelme, Jr. was born in Philadelphia, Pennsylvania, on April 7, 1931. In 1949 he enrolled at the University of Houston as a journalism major and worked on the staff of the *Daily Cougar* as an editor. After spending time in the U.S. Army he returned to Houston where he worked for several newspapers. In 1962 he went to New York where he had articles and stories published in *New Yorker* magazine. He won many honors and awards including a Guggenheim Fellowship, National Book Award, National Institute of Arts and Letters Zabel Award, Rea Short Story Award, and the Texas Institute of Arts and Letters Award. Barthelme died of throat cancer July 23, 1989, at the age of fifty-eight.

Donald Barthelme

He has been characterized as an avant-garde or postmodernist who relies more on language than plot or character. He is well known as a short story writer, novelist, editor, journalist, and teacher. Some of his publications include: *Come Back, Dr. Caligari*, 1964, *City Life*, 1970; *Sixty Stories*, 1981; and *The King*, 1990.

Jacques Derrida (1930–)

Jacques Derrida was born in El Biar, Algeria, on July 15, 1930. He earned several undergraduate and graduate degrees from the University of Paris, Sorbonne. He also did graduate study at Harvard University, from 1956 to 1957. He has taught at many of the world's finest colleges and universities: University of Paris, Sorbonne, Johns Hopkins University, Yale University, University of California at Irvine, Cornell University, and City University of New York.

His work beginning in the 1960s effected a profound change in literary criticism. In 1962 he first outlined the basic ideas that became known as deconstruction in a lengthy introduction to his 1962 French translation of German philosopher Edmund

Husserl's *Origin of Geometry*. The full strategy of deconstruction is outlined and explained in his difficult masterwork, *Of Grammatology*, published in English in 1967. It revealed the interplay of multiple meanings in the texts of present day culture and exposed the unspoken assumptions that underlie much of contemporary social thought.

Terry Eagleton (1943–)

Terence Eagleton was born on February 22, 1943, in Salford, England. He attended Trinity College, Cambridge, from which he received a bachelor of arts in 1964. He earned his Ph.D. from Jesus College, Cambridge, in 1968. He has taught at Cambridge and at Oxford. He has been a judge for poetry and literature competitions.

As one of the foremost exponents of Marxist criticism, he is concerned with the ideologies found in literature, examining the role of Marxism in discerning these ideologies. His early publications include: *Myths of Power: A Marxist Study of the Bröntes*, 1975; *Marxism and Literary Criticism*, 1976; *Criticism and Ideology: A Study in Marxist Literary Theory*, 1976, among others. His later publications include: *Literary Theory: An Introduction*, 1983; *The Function of Criticism: From the Spectator to Poststructuralism*, 1984; and *The Ideology of the Aesthetics*, 1990. His concise *Marxism and Literary Criticism*, 1976, discusses the author as producer, and the relationships between literature and history, form and content, and the writer and commitment. He is the foremost advocate of the inclusion of social and historical issues in literary criticism.

Michel Foucault (1926–1984)

Michel Foucault was born in Poitiers, France, on October 15, 1926, and received a diploma in 1952 from Ecole Normale Superieure and the Sorbonne, University of Paris. He taught philosophy and French literature at the Universities of Lille, Uppsala, Warsaw, Hamburg, Clermont-Ferrand, Sao Paulo, and the University of Tunis between the years 1960 and 1968. Foucault taught at the University of Paris, Vincennes, France, from 1968 to 1970. From 1970 until his death in 1984, he was chairman of History of Systems of Thought at College de France. The best known of his publications are *The History of Sexuality*, 1976; *The Use of Pleasure*, 1985; and *The Care of the Self*, 1987.

He used what he called the archaeological approach in his work to dig up scholarly minutia from the past and display the "archaeological" form or forms in them, which would be common to all mental activity. Later he shifted this emphasis from the archaeological to a genealogical method that sought to understand how power structures shaped and changed the boundaries of "truth." It is this understanding of the combination of power and knowledge that is his most noteworthy accomplishment.

Foucault died of a neurological disorder on June 25, 1984, in Paris, France.

Fredric Jameson (1934–)

Fredric Jameson was born on April 14, 1934, in Cleveland, Ohio. He attended Haverford College and Yale University and received a master of fine arts degree in 1956 and his Ph.D. in 1959. He taught at Harvard University, the University of California, San Diego, at Yale University, at the University of California at Santa Cruz, and at Duke University. He received many awards and fellowships including: Rotary Fellowship, Woodrow Wilson Fellowship, Fulbright Fellowship, two Guggenheim Fellowships, Humanities Institute Grant, and the William Riley Parker Prize.

Jameson is the leading exponent of Marxism in the United States. In *Postmodernism; or, the Cultural Logic of Late Capitalism* he raises concerns about the way present-day culture is constructed. His 1983 article, "Postmodernism and Consumer Society," provides basic groundwork for much of his version of Marxist criticism.

Julia Kristeva (1941–)

Julia Kristeva was born in Silven, Bulgaria, on June 24, 1941. Her formal education began in French schools in Bulgaria, where she earned her diploma at the Universite de Sofia, and ended in 1973 at the University of Paris VII, where she received her Ph.D. She has since taught at several universities and has established a private psychoanalytic practice in Paris. She has received both the Chevalier des Arts et des Lettres and the Chevalier de l'Ordre du Merite.

She is renowned as a writer, educator, linguist, psychoanalyst, and literary theorist and is also considered one of the most influential thinkers of modern France. Kristeva bases her work on two components of the linguistic operation: the semiotic, which expresses objective meaning; and the symbolic, the rhythmic and illogical aspects of meaning. What she calls "poetic language" is the intertwining of these elements. It is these same tenets that form the basis for postmodern criticism.

She has been embraced by many as a feminist writer because of her writings on social issues, but Kristeva's relationship to feminism has been one of ambivalence. Two of her most important publications are *Desire in Language, A Semiotic Approach to Literature and Art* (published in 1969, translated in 1980) and *New Maladies of the Soul* (published in 1993, translated in 1995), a collection of essays. She has also written several novels.

Toni Morrison (1931–)

Toni Morrison was born Chloe Anthony Wofford on February 18, 1931, in Lorain, Ohio, to a black working class family. She studied humanities in college, obtaining her bachelor of arts in 1953 from Howard University (a distinguished black college) and her masters degree from Cornell University in 1955. Morrison married Harold Morrison in 1958 and the couple had two sons before divorcing in 1964. Morrison has worked as an academic, an editor, a critic, and continues to give lectures.

After the publication of her first novel in 1970, Morrison's writing quickly came to the attention of critics and readers who praised her richly expressive style and ear for dialogue. She received the Pulitzer Prize in 1988 for her novel *Beloved* (1987) and won the Nobel Prize for Literature in 1993.

Morrison has written novels, plays, and nonfiction essays, including: *The Bluest Eye* (1969); *Sula* (1973); *Song of Solomon* (1977); *Tar Baby* (1981); *Dreaming Emmett* (1986, play); *Playing in the Dark: Whiteness and the Literary Imagination*, (1992); and *Book of Mean People* (2002). Morrison has also edited and/or collaborated on several volumes with other authors.

Ishmael Reed (1938–)

Ishmael Reed was born on February 22, 1938, in Chattanooga, Tennessee. He attended State University of New York at Buffalo from 1956 to 1960. Reed has written numerous novels, short stories, poetry, fiction, nonfiction, essays, literary criticism, and history, and has been accorded many honors and awards including the nomination for Pulitzer Prize in poetry in 1973 for *Conjure: Selected Poems, 1963–1970*. He has taught at many colleges and universities and at prose and poetry workshops across the United States.

His novels include: *The Free-Lance Pallbearers*, 1967; *Yellow Back Radio Broke-Down*, 1969; *Mumbo Jumbo*, 1972; *The Last Days of Louisiana Red*, 1974; *Flight to Canada*, 1976; *The Terrible Twos*, 1982; *Reckless Eyeballing*, 1986; *The Terrible Threes*, 1989; and *Japanese by Spring*, 1993.

He has written much poetry including: *catechism of d neoamerican hoodoo church*, 1970; *Conjure: Selected Poems, 1963–1970*, 1972; *Chattanooga: Poems*, 1973; *A Secretary to the Spirits*, 1977; and *New and Collected Poems*, 1988.

His poetry captures the rich texture of the novels in the combinations of language from street language to academic language, from dialects and slang to the clever use of neologisms. He includes many references to mythologies and cultures apart from his own experiences.

Kurt Vonnegut Jr. (1922–)

Kurt Vonnegut, Jr. was born in Indianapolis, Indiana, on November 11, 1922. He attended Cornell University, Carnegie Institute of Technology (now Carnegie-Mellon University), and the University of Chicago where he earned his master of fine arts degree in 1971. From 1942 to 1945 he was in the U.S. Army, Infantry, including some time as a POW (he received the Purple Heart).

He worked as editor for the *Cornell Daily Sun*, 1941 to 1942, as police reporter in 1947 for the *Chicago City News* Bureau; in the public relations department of the General Electric Co., Schenectady, NY, 1947 to 1950; and as a freelance writer beginning in 1950 to the present.

He taught at Hopefield School in Sandwich, MA, the University of Iowa Writers Workshop, Harvard University, and at the City College of the City University of New York, 1965. In 1986 he was a speaker at the hearing of the National Coalition against Censorship briefing for the attorney general's Commission on Pornography.

He has been the recipient of many honors and awards. He is the author of many novels, essays, and other writings, including plays and articles for magazines and journals. His novels include: *The Sirens of Titan*, 1959; *Mother Night*, 1961; *Cat's Cradle*, 1963; *God Bless You, Mr. Rosewater; or, Pearls before Swine*, 1965; *Slaughterhouse Five; or, The Children's Crusade*, 1969; and a collection of short stories, *Welcome to the Monkey House*, 1968. More recent novels include *Jailbird*, 1979 and *Timequake*, 1997.

His writing is filled with biting satire and irony. Many of his characters find their way into several of the novels. Kilgore Trout appears in

Breakfast of Champions, *Slaughterhouse Five*, as well as others; the Tralfamadorians show up in *Sirens of Titan* and in *Slaughterhouse Five*. He freely peppers his texts with quotes from Bartlett's *Familiar Quotations*.

Representative Works

Beloved

When Fredric Jameson said, in "Postmodernism and Consumer Society," that postmodern society has reached the end of its awareness of history, he stirred up a great controversy. Morrison's Pulitzer Prize-winning novel *Beloved* (1987) asks a similar question about the postmodern society's understanding of history.

Beloved is the story of one ex-slave's relationship with her children, herself, and the world around them. There are two considerations about the historical accuracy of the novel. The first is the use of contemporaneous accounts of slavery and the second, Morrison's imaginative recreation of the slave society. The conflict between these two arises from the concern that the version of slavery written by the ruling white class is flawed and that a fictional story is by definition unreal.

Two events in the novel raise this issue: the first is the moment Paul D sees the newspaper clipping of Sethe and remarks, "That ain't her mouth." If the news reports are not accurate, including the pictures, then the novel has relied on flawed data and it is thereby flawed.

The second incident is the scene in which Beloved lures Paul D into the shed to have sex. There is a stack of newspapers in the shed, a symbolic juxtaposition of the real and the imagined. The poststructuralist view that reality is a function of discourse is challenged in these scenes. The sources of discourse are unreliable (newspapers, photos, fictional accounts of events) and that leads to the conclusion that there is no reliable explication of "reality" present in these scenes and, by extrapolation, in the novel itself.

Cat's Cradle

Kurt Vonnegut, Jr. is one of those authors who defy easy categorization, though it might be appropriate to call him an eclectic postmodernist. But the difficulty of identifying him or his works within a trend or movement remains. If one work were representative of his philosophy, it is his 1974 book *Wampeters, Foma and Granfalloons (Opinions)*. (These concepts are found in *Cat's Cradle*.) This collection of opinion is not his best or most important, but it locates in its title the three most important aspects of his writing. Wampeters are objects around which the lives of otherwise unrelated people revolve, for example, The Holy Grail or The National Championship (in college football). Foma are harmless comforting truths such as "Prosperity is just around the corner." "There's a light at the end of the tunnel." "Everything's going to be all right!" Granfalloons are a proud and meaningless association of human beings, for example "The Veterans of Future Wars" or the "Class Colors Committee."

In many of his works he pokes fun at the quirkiness of normal life, and the grand institutions of society. He infuses his novels with a sense of humor, with the exception of *Slaughterhouse Five*, which is based on the bombing of Dresden during World War II.

Cat's Cradle is a humorous and sharp-edged novel that takes major institutions of society to task for their vapidity and shallowness: religion, the military, and science. Jonah lives in the Caribbean where the only religion tolerated is Bokononism. It is based on the teachings and songs of Bokonon, most of which are in a Caribbean dialect and sung to a calypso beat.

Jonah finds out about a corrupted production of crystals at a chemical plant that changed the way ice crystals are formed. Instead of forming ice at 32 degrees Fahrenheit (called ice-one), the process was transformed eventually creating ice-nine that freezes (crystallizes) at 130 degrees. The book tackles the problems of science gone awry, a military that saw an opportunity for a doomsday weapon, and the religion that tried to make some philosophic sense of it all.

The chief image in this novel comes from its title, a cat's cradle: a finger game played by two people with a loop of string that becomes twisted and tangled during the game. But if it is done properly, it will return to its original form and "All will be well" (a Foma!).

Conjure: Selected Poems, 1963–1970

Reed's 1972 book of poetry contains prose poems, didactic poems, and short poems offering comments on very specific incidents such as the poem "Report of the Reed Commission" which reads:

i conclude that for
the first time in
history the practical
man is the loon and the
loon the practical man

a man on the radio just
said that air pollution
is caused by jellyfish.

Not all of his poetry is this transparent and humorous. Some, for example "catechism of d neoamerican hoodoo church," explore what he sees as the oppressive nature of the American society in which he lives. His reference to "Hoodoo" (which is a variation of Voodoo) is a common theme in most of his writings. It combines aspects of conjuring, magic, and Voodoo, which he claims will help African Americans and people in the Third World rid themselves of the oppressive nature of contemporary western civilization.

The opening paragraph includes a statement confronting established value systems: "i refused to deform d works of ellison and wright." In this refusal he raises concerns about social demands and instructs others in ways to confront similar demands.

Throughout these poems he uses a kind of written language that more completely approximates the language of common people. In "catechism" stanza i, he writes: "we who hv no dreams permit us to say yr name/ all day. we are junk beneath yo feet." The look on the page may seem unusual or even wrong, but if the line is said aloud the normal sounds of everyday speech result. Another technique in the poems in *Conjure* is repeated lines, phrases, or words to emphasize the passage. These repetitions derive from an oral tradition of storytelling, learning scriptures, and hymns.

Of Grammatology

The beginnings of Deconstructionism are found in Derrida's introduction to his 1962 French translation of German philosopher Edmund Husserl's *Origin of Geometry*, and later expanded in two major works, *Of Grammatology* (1967) and *Writing and Difference* (1967). *Of Grammatology* is a difficult book that contains the basis for deconstructive analysis of language. Two of the more important issues raised in the book are: logocentrism of language and the use of binary oppositions (sets) in western culture.

Logocentrism gives precedence to the spoken word over the written word. He says that philosophies that claim that speech is a more natural form of language give speech the position of primacy. By doing so, writing is reduced to a secondary position. His argument is not that writing is not secondary but that speech is not primary, a tricky way of equalizing these two components of language without setting up another binary set.

Kurt Vonnegut, Jr.

Some may claim that writing is merely recorded speech but Derrida argues the opposite: speech is a form of unrecorded script. Here again he makes a careful argument to avoid the establishment of new hierarchies. The specific concern that he raises in this discussion is what he calls "centering," the process of giving one term (the first of a set) more importance than another.

He shows that any text, no matter what kind, can be read in ways different from what it seems to be saying, which is the central proposition in his book. Communication is an unending series of textual meanings that arise and are subverted within themselves. Then the process repeats. The result of these repeated subversions of meaning is that no text is ever stable. Any stability in a text is merely illusory.

The basis of his discussion is the signifier/signified relationship that comes from the structuralists. He raises the specter of the difficulties of interpreting the relationships between the signifier (the word) and the signified (the object). This is the problem of writing, where a written word represents a spoken word that in turn represents the object. The movement from the one to the other is the structure of the meaning, but because this movement conceals and erases itself during the very act of movement, it remains unstable. He says, "There is not a single signified that escapes, even if recaptured, the play of signifying references that constitute language." Hence, since a text has so many different meanings, it cannot have one single meaning. This is the basic conundrum of deconstruction: the very act of deconstruction is unstable and the results are indeterminate.

Overnight to Many Distant Cities

Barthelme is a noted minimalist fiction writer. In his collection *Overnight to Many Distant Cities* (1983) are several notable short stories. "Cortes and Montezuma" shows the minimalist character of Barthelme's writing style. Minimalist means using a small amount of text to create the tale. Much of this story consists of short rapid-fire sentences, some of which have only three words, giving the reader a sense of urgency. In this manner, Barthelme retells the history of the Spanish conquest of Mexico, using themes of trust and breaking trust.

Another story from the same collection, "The first thing the baby did wrong . . . ," is a humorous parable about the difficulties of living with immutable rules. A family of three has a rule that the child will be confined to its room for four hours for every page that is torn out of a book. This rule backfires because the child tears pages out at every chance it gets. Eventually, the child owed the parents eighty-eight hours. The narrator says, "If you made a rule you had to stick to it." This points out the absurdity of a society that lives by rules that are not always understood nor well thought out.

"Postmodernism and Consumer Society"

In his 1983 essay "Postmodernism and Consumer Society," Frederic Jameson explains his idea of Postmodernism, what caused it to occur, and its basic principles. He discusses what he calls pastiche and schizophrenia as they relate to "the emergent social order of late capitalism." Pastiche is the loss of personal identity, which may be the result of capitalism and bureaucracies that place no importance on the individual. Another aspect of this loss of identity lies in the possibility that there is no way for writers and artists to create new styles because "they've already been invented." The other focus of the essay, schizophrenia, is the clash of narratives resulting from the combination of the past and future into the present. Throughout this essay, and others by Jameson, he takes considerable notice of the impact of capitalism on the course of social progress and artistic expression of the time.

Desire in Language: A Semiotic Approach to Literature and Art

Julia Kristeva introduces gender politics into the postmodern discussion in *Desire in Language: A Semiotic Approach to Literature and Art.* She proposes that unconscious drives are major players in communication and language. She explains that in creating a text by writing, the author releases unconscious selves and destroys the former notion of a solid, traditional, logical self. She considers the formative possibilities of a feminine voice that can result.

Kristeva looks at this issue of the feminine voice in the context of the dissolution of binary sets discussed by Derrida. She asserts that if customary language usage privileges one sex over another, as in the male/female set, it opens up the possibility of the marginalized sex eventually being eliminated from all discussions, though, at the same time, it provides means for women to raise their concerns if they utilize their status outside the mainstream.

Themes

Deconstruction

This is the term created by Derrida that defines the basic premise of Postmodernism. It does not mean destruction, but rather it is a critique of the criteria of certainty, identity, and truth.

Derrida says that all communication is characterized by uncertainty because there is no definitive link between the signifier (a word) and the signified (the object to which the word refers). Once a text is written it ceases to have a meaning until a reader reads it. Derrida says that there is nothing but the text and that it is not possible to construe a meaning for a text using a reference to anything outside the text. The text has many internal meanings that are in conflict with themselves (called reflexivity or self-referential) and as a result there is no solid and guaranteed meaning to a text. The text is also controlled by what is not in it (referents outside the text are not a part of its meaning). The consequence of this position is that there can be no final meaning for any text, for as Derrida himself says, "texts are not to be read according to [any method] which would seek out a finished signified beneath a textual surface. Reading is transformational."

He comments on issues of identity in Western civilization that derive from the reliance on binary oppositions. These are sets that establish a hierarchy that privileges the first over the second. He calls them "violent hierarchies," and states that they give precedence (called centering) to the central term (the first) and they marginalize the remaining term. In a set "up/down" the implication is that "up" is more preferable and is better than "down." In more significant ways the "centering" in the man/woman set establishes the first as the most important and marginalizes the second. This result has important ramifications in social constructs.

The last of these three concepts that he addresses is the nature of truth. Because he doubts the ability of language to convey any absolute meaning, there results an impossibility of language to establish a "transcendental universal" or a universal truth. It is this notion that is often misunderstood as a statement of his rejection of a God. Rather it is a statement that simple languages are incapable of identifying God linguistically.

Disintegration

One of the main outgrowths of Postmodernism is the disintegration of concepts that used to be taken for granted and assumed to be stable. These include the nature of language, the idea of knowledge, and the notion of a universal truth. The application of deconstruction to the understanding of language itself results in disintegration of that very language. Even these words are not stable in the sense that they cannot convey an unalterable message. The consequence of this is that once language is destabilized the resultant knowledge that comes from that language is no longer a stable product. The end result therefore is that there can be no universal truths upon which to base an understanding or a social construct.

In literary works, authors often disrupt expected time lines or change points of view and speakers in ways that disrupt and cause disintegration in the very literature they are writing. *Gravity's Rainbow* by Thomas Pynchon is a good example of this.

In contemporary entertainment, television in particular, there has been a disintegration of the line that separates reality from fiction. Recent fictional dramas have included responses to the terrorist attacks from September 11, 2001. In other television shows from the past twenty-five years, contemporaneous events have been included in the story lines. Discussions of the political and social events of the Nixon years were a mainstay of the show *All in the Family* and during the 1992 presidential campaign there was a generous use of material from the *Murphy Brown Show* in real political conversation. In these and other situations the reality/fiction line was blurred significantly.

Media Adaptations

- *Conjure: Music for the Texts of Ishmael Reed* sets the poetry of Ishmael Reed to music. The selections are from Reed's collection of poetry published in 1972. This adaptation has received high acclaim by reviewers from *Absolute Sound* and the *Philadelphia Enquirer*.
- Morrison's *Beloved* was adapted as a film by director Jonathan Demme in 1998.

Cultural Studies

One major impact of Postmodernism on the structure of college and university courses is the introduction of multiculturalism and cultural studies programs. These are sometimes directly related to specific areas on the planet (Far Eastern studies, South American studies, or conglomerate areas like Pan-African studies) and sometimes to specific-focus groups (Gay/Lesbian studies, Women's studies, Chicano studies). Often these are not limited by political concerns and boundaries but are economically and socially organized, a major concern expressed in the writings of Jameson, Eagleton, and other Marxist critics.

Multiculturalism

Another aspect of multiculturalism is combining specific interest areas into one area of study. This aspect of Postmodernism broadens the experiences of college students through the study of literature and history of peoples from other parts of the world. Classes whose structures combine sometimes disparate elements are found in these new departments. For example, a study of prisons and prison literature might be combined with literature from Third World countries under the broad label of Literature of the Oppressed. Cultural studies may also include topics like: Arab-American Studies, or Women in European Literature.

Style

Schizophrenia

An important aspect of Postmodernism in literature and entertainment media is the relaxation of strict time lines, sometimes called discontinuous time. Often an author will construct a sequence of events that have no time relationships to each other. In literature this requires the reader to create a time line, which the author may upset later in the story. In some TV shows this is particularly important when the time line would have two things happening at the same time. Therefore, the writers show one event, then show another that happened at the same time as the first. This kind of temporal disruption is called "schizophrenia" by Jameson.

Recurring Characters

Some authors introduce a single character into several different works. Vonnegut does this with Kilgore Trout and Tralfamadorians, who appear in several of his novels.

Irony

Irony is a specialized use of language in which the opposite of the literal meaning is intended. Its former use often had the intent to provoke a change in behavior from those who were the object of the irony. But for the postmodernist the writer merely pokes fun at the object of the irony without the intention of making a social (or other kind of) change.

Authorial Intrusion

Occasionally an author will speak directly to the audience or to a character in the text in the course of a work—not as a character in the tale but as the writer. Vonnegut does this in several of his novels, including *Breakfast of Champions*.

Self-Reflexivity

Many literary works make comments about the works themselves, reflecting on the writing or the "meaning" of the work. These works are self-conscious about themselves. In some instances the work will make a comment about itself in a critical way, making a self-reflexive comment on the whole process of writing, reading, or understanding literature.

Collage

This style is characterized by an often random association of dissimilar objects without any intentional connection between them or without a specified purpose for these associations. For example, the rapid presentation of bits and pieces from old news tapes that are often used at the beginning of news programs is a collage. While it intends to introduce the news, it is not the news nor is it any hint of the news to come.

Prose Poetry

This idea seems to be a contradiction in terms but it is an effective style of writing. The passage will look like a paragraph of prose writing, but the content will be poetic in language and construction. Rather than being a literal statement, the language in this paragraph will be more figurative.

Parody and Pastiche

Oftentimes writers will take the work of another and restructure it to make a different impression on the reader than that of the original author. Some writers lift whole passages from others, verbatim, resulting in something quite different from the original writer's material.

Parody is the imitation of other styles with a critical edge. The general effect is to cast ridicule on the mannerisms or eccentricities of the original.

Pastiche is very much like parody but it is neutral, without any sense of humor. It is the imitation or a pasting together of the mannerisms of another's work, but without the satiric impulse or the humor. Jameson says that because there is no longer a "normal" language system, only pastiche is possible.

Simulacra

This is a term that comes from Plato meaning "false copy" or a debased reflection of the original that is inferior to the original. Author Jean Baudrillard claims that a simulacrum is a perfect copy that has no original. The postmodernists use this technique of copying or imitating others without reservation or hesitation. They treat it as just another process in their creative effort.

Many science fiction movies deal with simulacrum characters. In *Alien*, one of the crew members, Ash, is an android, but one of such high quality that it is only revealed when he/it is cut and the blood is a white liquid. The "replicants" from *Blade Runner* are simulacra who desire a longer life. Data from *Star Trek: The Next Generation* is a simu-

Topics for Further Study

- How have the ideas of disintegration, instability, and/or textual uncertainty (in the postmodern use of these terms) had an effect on you? Describe the issues and put into your own context a narrative describing how you perceive things to be different because of these ideas. Speculate on how things might have been different had these ideas not made an impact on you.
- Take your favorite piece of literature and deconstruct it. Show, to the best of your understanding, what the author might have meant in the text. Then show how that meaning might be quite a different thing. Use a short text for this exercise.
- Take a standard text and do a "special" reading of it. For example, examine a text from a feminist perspective, or from a Marxist perspective, or from a special point of view of your own choosing.
- Critique your favorite television program showing the postmodern features of an individual show or of a series of shows. To ensure analytical accuracy, videotape the shows you examine. Be specific in your discussion, explaining in detail how the chosen features are postmodern and how they contribute to the success (or failure) of the show or shows in question.
- Postmodernism has had an important role in the development of the MTV phenomenon. Select some music videos and describe them in terms of a postmodern aspect (social/economic influence, feminism, instability of texts regarding meaning, blurred lines between the "real" world and the "fictive" world in the video, etc.). Videos from the very early days of MTV might be compared with those now being broadcast, showing the postmodern trends in the development of videos. In your discussion be specific in the conclusions you derive from your study. Put these conclusions into theoretical terms.

lacrum character with many human traits, but one who wants to have human emotions, too.

Movement Variations

As might be expected in a relatively new philosophic movement, there are a variety of different understandings, proposals, and approaches reflecting on the particular interests of writers and contributors to that new philosophy. Postmodernism's origin in the aftermath of World War II was not a universally scripted event. By the time Derrida and others were presenting their major papers on the basics of Postmodernism, many others were already approaching these concepts in individual ways. Additionally, as time moved on and Postmodernism developed as an accepted area of discussion, the basic ideas of Postmodernism were branching off into many facets of contemporary life. Among these variations are Marxism and political studies, Poststructuralism, feminism and gender studies, and Gay/Lesbian studies.

Feminism

Feminist readings in Postmodernism were initiated as a way to consciously view and deconstruct ideas of social norms, language, sexuality, and academic theory in all fields. Feminist theorists and writers (and they were not all women, e.g., Dr. Bruce Appleby, Professor Emeritus of Southern Illinois University, is a long-standing contributor to feminist writings and theory) were concerned with the manner in which society assumed a male bias either by direct action—for example, paying women less for doing the same job; or by inaction—using the term "man" to mean all of humankind. In either case, the female segment of society had been excluded. Even the modernist penchant for binary sets for discussions, good/bad, white/black, established an unspoken hierarchy that made the first of the set more important than the second. In that way the "male/female" set defined the female half as being less important or inferior to the male half of the set. This was not acceptable to the feminist writers and to those in the subsequent feminist movement. Feminist writers and theorists attempted to separate the ideas of sex (which is biological) and gender (which is a social construct), and use those ideas as a lens through which to deconstruct language, social mores and theories, economic policies, and long-standing historical policy.

Marxism

It is not much of a stretch to move the discussion of gender discrimination into a discussion of class discrimination, which is the focus of many of the Marxist critics. While some issues are different, it is easy to see that bias based on gender is just as destructive as the elitism in a society based on class differences.

Political Marxism is a topic that engenders strong emotional opinions, especially among those who see it as a threat to Western political systems. However, the basic issues that drove Karl Marx and Friedrich Engels to formulate their theories in the nineteenth century are still valid in a discussion of literature and art and the relationship between class and the arts in a society. Marxist critics assert that the products of artistic endeavors are the results of historical forces that are themselves the results of material and/or economic conditions at the time of the creation of the art.

Art then becomes the product of those who control the economic and the intellectual production of the society. Therefore, the nature of the description of an era in human history is the product of the dominant class at the time the description is given. The present era called postmodern is so labeled by the dominant class. (It is important to note that since the present era has not yet come of age, the eventual naming of it may shift if the dominant class also shifts. What that shift may be is unknown at this time.) This concept has been reduced to the simple statement that the victor writes the story of the battle.

An enlightening example concerning this process is *The Wind Done Gone*. This novel is a retelling of the story of the American Civil War through eyes of the African-American slave in the southern United States. It tells Margaret Mitchell's story *Gone with the Wind* from another perspective. Granted this is a pair of novels, but the factual basis behind each is the history of the Civil War. For Mitchell it is history through the eyes of the white southerner; for Alice Randall it is through the eyes of the slave in that same southern society.

Poststructuralism

Poststructuralism is a term often used interchangeably with Postmodernism. While these two terms share a number of philosophic concepts, there are some differences that need to be explained. Structuralism is rooted in a theory of language that was derived from the teachings of Swiss-born linguist Ferdinand de Saussure, which were published as the *Course in General Linguistics* (in 1913 in French; in 1966 in English). These publications are a set of reconstructions of his teachings from the class notes of many of his students. As the label of the philosophy indicates, it is concerned with the underlying structures of language and meaning. The structuralists "confined the play of language within closed structures of oppositions," according to Steven Best and Douglas Kellner in their book, *Postmodern Theory: Critical Interrogations*. Saussure posited that language functions in a self-referential manner and has no "natural" relation to external reality. This movement also believes, according to Claude Levi-Strauss, that texts are universal (even if the meanings of the texts are indeterminate) and that texts are found in all activities. This is construed to include the personal life histories of individuals, which are called their "texts."

The main technique used by the structuralists in their investigations of language is the study of semiology, or the study of signs and symbols. They say that all language is arbitrary and that the culture determines the relationship between the signifier (a word) and the signified (the object). The word *book* is arbitrary and does not have any direct and irrefutable relationship to the object it is used to signify. That relationship comes from the culture alone. Additionally, the structuralist examines the underlying construct of language and is concerned with determining what is called the meta-structure, a universal structure that could be found in all language systems.

The poststructuralist responds to these investigations with the Derridean concept that there is not a universal structure and that the structures of language are indeterminate, just as the language (text) itself is. They give the signifier primacy over the signified, which opens the door to the indeterminacy of other postmodern considerations.

Historical Context

Postmodernism is an outgrowth of Modernism just as Modernism itself was an outgrowth of the Enlightenment project of the nineteenth century. In the early twentieth century, authors, composers, architects, and other intellectuals rebelled against the strictures of older forms and ways of doing things. Architects began creating more functionally oriented buildings; composers created different methods of organizing musical sounds to create new music; authors felt similarly constricted and reacted against old styles and formats of poetry and fiction. Out of this came the likes of the Bauhaus architects, Arnold Schoenberg and Anton von Webern in music, T. S. Eliot and Ezra Pound in poetry, and Virginia Woolf, Franz Kafka, and James Joyce in literature.

In the years following World War II, a new impetus in the arts and philosophy emerged that eventually resulted in Postmodernism. Writers were reluctant to fall into similar traps of conventionalization against which the modernists rebelled a generation before. They felt that the modern movement had now, through canonization, become the "old guard" and they wanted something different, more invigorating. Fiction writers like Vladimir Nabokov, Thomas Pynchon, and Kurt Vonnegut, Jr. began to experiment in their novels. Poets like Ishmael Reed wrote in new forms and created new poetic styles. Composers like John Cage experimented with new forms of and approaches to music-making, often using new sound-generating techniques. Along with this came a dissatisfaction with the old ways of looking at the issues of reality, language, knowledge, and power.

Derrida is likely the most important and controversial of the postmodern critics. His two 1967 works, *Writing and Difference*, and *Of Grammatology*, laid the groundwork for the concept known as deconstruction. Another French philosopher, Michel Foucault, presented his first major paper on the subject, *The Order of Things: An Archaeology of the Human Sciences*, in 1966. These men were followed by the Marxist critics Jameson and Eagleton, both of whom saw Postmodernism in terms of its social and economic ramifications.

Also coming out of the 1950s and the 1960s was a new approach to popular cultural arts. Among those artists who made significant impact on their art form were the Beatles, Jimi Hendrix, and The Rolling Stones. These rock groups experimented with new sounds, combinations of entertaining lyrics, and lyrics with some political or social implications. In the 1960s and early 1970s folk rock performers like Bob Dylan, Joan Baez, Judy Collins, and Pete Seeger led the way with their passionate political lyrics. In films, attitudes shifted and the role of the film changed from a more purely entertainment function to a medium with social or political emphases. These genres, including the "art film" and the sexually explicit film, reacted to the old requirement for a continuous narrative and abandoned it in favor of more disjointed and nonlinear presentations.

At the same time, television was emerging from the shadows of being "radio with pictures" to being an important medium on its own. The 1950s saw the introduction of the situation comedy, i.e., *I Love Lucy*, and the variety show *The Ed Sullivan Show*. But by the end of the 1960s these were giving way to less formal programs and moving into the beginnings of postmodern television with programs like *All in the Family* and *Laugh In*. Also at this time news became more entertaining with the introduction of the news magazine show, *60 Minutes*.

Through all of these innovations and introductions of new approaches to old idioms, there occurred a disintegration of the separation of reality and fiction. Television entertainment began to include deliberate references to current events; rock songs took on the role of political commentary; and fiction became less narrative and more obscure, less realistic and more intellectually fantastic (not to be confused with children's fantasy worlds).

The combination of the forces of suspicion, disintegration, and uncertainty led to the present postmodern world. World social situations are visited with a mouse click; economic pressures by individuals demanding specialized products have reduced the "target consumer" to ever smaller units. As Vaclav Havel has noted, seeing a Bedouin on a camel in typical Arab dress, wearing jeans beneath, listening to a CD through an ear piece and drinking a soft drink is no longer odd or unexpected. The fragmented nature of the postmodern world has created a new culturally diverse and, at the same time, culturally mixed world. Television brings war into viewer's living rooms. It shows the horror of collapsing buildings; on reality shows, it gives the consumer a window to the most intimate and tender moments in a person's life, and it reduces this to a slickly packaged product for the purpose of getting higher ratings and more profits.

Compare & Contrast

- **1920s–1930s:** The modernist philosophic paradigm can be expressed as the following: search for the truth.

  Today: The postmodernist philosophic paradigm is expressed in the following way: there is no identifiable truth.

- **1920s–1930s:** Modernists believe that the artist is not the preserver of the culture; rather the artist is the creator of culture. The art of the modernist is experimental, innovative, and formally complex. Art is a unique object and a finished work authenticated by the artist and validated by agreed-upon standards. "The Photograph never lies."

  Today: Art is repetitive and uses familiar or ready-made objects, or mechanical reproductions of objects. The artist does not believe that art or the artist occupies a special place apart from the rest of society. Art is a process, a performance, a production, using combinations of media. There are no agreed-upon standards. In the postmodern world, with digital imaging, photos and video can be altered completely or created completely, leaving the question, "What is reality?"

- **1920s–1930s:** Writers are very conscious of the act of writing and try to leave a permanent result in the reader's mind with their product. The novel is the dominant form of fiction writing. The author determines the meaning of the novel for the reader.

  Today: Postmodern writers become aware that language is not as permanent as the modernists believed and that their product is not a stable one. As Derrida claims, speech is more secure than written language because the producer of the text is present to give it immediate meaning. Since meaning is indeterminate, the meaning of a novel is unknown.

- **1920s–1930s:** Art is created to shock the audience. The cubism of Picasso and the risqué novels of Joyce are examples of these shocking creations. Once art is completed, it is a stable work of art.

  Today: Art is less shocking and more an incomplete artifact of the artist. "Performance art" is an example of this in which people 'live' in a store window or in a glass walled house revealing their everyday life to a passing public.

- **1920s–1930s:** Work in factories is for the husband; home life is for the wife who tends house and raises the children.

  Today: Men and women work at the same tasks including firefighting and construction work; however, pay scales for women are not equalized in all areas.

Critical Overview

The exact date Postmodernism began can never be known. It was first mentioned in a text by Federico de Onís in 1934. This use was not widely known and received little attention by the wider community of writers. The word was used by Arnold Toynbee in 1954 in his *Study of History, Volume 8*. But it did not move into mainstream thought and criticism until 1959 with the publication of the article "What is Modernism" by Harry Levin.

Postmodernism then took the form of a theoretical concept as a discussion point in university classrooms. These discussions were directed at the state of the development of various art forms including literature, painting, music—and particularly, how these were changing.

In literature, writers like Vonnegut and Barthelme were experimenting with new ideas of how to create their novels. Poets like Reed, Allen Ginsburg, and Lawrence Ferlinghetti were also experimenting with new poetic ideas.

Scene from the film adaptation of Beloved *written by Toni Morrison*

In painting, major shifts were occurring as painters were moving from the cubist styles into some of the less formal styles exemplified by the works of Jackson Pollack. For Pollack and others, art shifted from an intellectually driven pursuit of an intended result to a kind of art that just happened. The drip and splash paintings of Pollack show this very well. Other types of art forms to emerge included the collage and the pastiche forms of representation. In both of these the artist used items already made and combined them into a single artistic statement. The works of Andy Warhol are prime examples of these practices, including his *32 Campbell's Soup Cans* and the multiple images of Marilyn Monroe.

In music the introduction of electronically generated sounds created a shift in the course of music development. Vladimir Ussachevsky's first experiments with electronic sound seem very primitive to today's audience, but in 1951 these creations were stunningly different. They were not always welcomed, and the more mainstream composers dismissed these efforts as insignificant and unimportant. The works of John Cage are also important to this new era, including his "composition" for several radios on stage, each tuned to a different station.

Similar events happened in the course of language discussions, especially with the presentation of two works by Derrida, *Of Grammatology* and *Writing and Difference*. The combination of these two works established a new philosophic approach to the study of language and knowledge (the search for truth) called deconstruction. Basically this is an approach that reveals the instability of language and says that a stable meaning of a text is indeterminate. The author does not determine the meaning of the text because there are contradictions within the text that alter the meanings of the text in an unending cycle of text/meaning, followed by new text/meaning, and so on.

This concept and the ramifications of it have been the subject of much concern. On one end of the critical spectrum, Derrida and deconstruction have been accused of trying to destroy Western civilization. On the other end of the spectrum, he and deconstruction have been hailed as heroes by showing the difficulties of communication because of the underlying instabilities and uncertainties of language. Despite the attacks, condemnations, and praise, deconstruction has shaken the whole area of epistemology to its core. Whether the critic embraces or denies the concepts of deconstruction, he or she must begin with an acknowledgment of its existence and either build an argument on it or build an argument from a position opposing it.

In recent years the concept of Postmodernism has been widened to include discussions of social, economic, recreational, and other aspects of contemporary life. Just as deconstruction examined the relationship between language and meaning, postmodernist concepts in these areas examine the relationship between the different facets of cultural life.

Criticism

Carl Mowery

Mowery holds a Ph.D. in composition and literature from Southern Illinois University. In this essay, Mowery examines narrative techniques in postmodern fiction.

One facet of Postmodernism that sets it apart from Modernism is the attitude that postmodern authors bring to fiction. While the modernist was concerned with precision both in language and presentation, the postmodernist breaks with these established practices. Time lines are often disrupted, leaving it to the reader to determine the order of events. At other times narrative expectations are upset as the author either contradicts the narrative or intrudes deliberately into the story line.

The way an author tells a story is through a narrator. Generally the narrator is not the author but a created persona with a personality, a behavior pattern and special reasons for telling the story in the manner it is being told. For example, the narrator of the Edgar Allan Poe story "The Tell Tale Heart" desperately tries to convince the reader that he is not crazy.

These narrators fall into one of the following categories: first person narrator; third person omniscient narrator; third person limited narrator; dramatic narrator (a phenomenological narration that makes no comment on or judgments about any of the actions or scenes in the tale); and in some circumstances the stream of consciousness narration (a specialized narration in the first person through the mind and thoughts of that person). However, there are notable variations to these types. In "A Rose for Emily," Faulkner used a first person plural ("we") narrator. In this story the townspeople tell the tale.

The only contact a reader has with a tale is through "the act of its being told (or retold)" by the narrator, according to Henry McDonald in "The Narrative Act: Wittgenstein and Narratology." Therefore, the reader must have a sense of the narrator's reliability. If the narrator is lying or telling the story in a slanted fashion, the reader must then come to grips with that fact and make a judgment about the story from that vantage point. This does not mean that a story cannot be understood even if the storyteller is lying; it means that the reader must reconcile knowing about a lying narrator with the information that the narrator presents. Ludwig Wittgenstein said, "The difficulty is to realize the groundlessness of our believing." Therein lies the task of the perceptive reader: to locate and to understand the nature of the fictive world and to recognize the "truth" of that fictive world and to separate it from an unreliable presentation of it. The reader must determine the grounds for identifying that "truth."

An important aspect of the narrative presence is the structure it takes. In "The first thing the baby did wrong . . .," by Donald Barthelme, the narrator tells his story in monologue style. In the story the father describes his baby's behavior in a first person continuous narrative that describes how she is punished for tearing pages out of books. The monologue uses a familiar tone, referring to the audience as "you" to create a sense of intimacy ("She got real clever. You'd come up to her where she was playing.") and to request sympathy for the parents' dilemma with the baby's actions. As the baby seems to enjoy her punishment, the father's narrative reveals frustration and a resolve to maintain rules set by the parents. In this story the narration is a simple one drawing the audience into the family circle and asking for sympathy.

Sometimes the narrative gives the reader a sense of being a part of the story as it unfolds. In the story "Montezuma and Cortez," Barthelme uses the continuous present to tell the story. It opens: "Because Cortez lands on a day specified in the ancient writing, because he is dressed in black, because his armour is silver . . . Montezuma considers Cortez to be Quetzalcoatl." The remainder of the story maintains this use of present tense, which gives the reader a sense of immediacy and an eyewitness-to-history feeling about the tale. The reader is not told the story after the fact, but as it happens—like a live television show narrated by an announcer.

Other narrative structures include epistolary novels (novels that use a series of exchanged letters to report the story), diaries, or outline forms.

What Do I Study Next?

- Barbara Creed, the author of "From Here to Modernity: Feminism and Postmodernism" connects feminist theory with Postmodernism in her short essay in *Screen*. She compares the writing of two authors, Alice Jardine and Craig Owens, seeking a solution to the problem of the intersection of feminist and postmodern theories. Creed points out that while both authors come at this topic from different points of reference, both they and Creed agree that there is a common ground and a legitimate intersection of these theoretical philosophies. Her conclusions are that these philosophies are important, relevant, and connected but that they should not try to explain everything in a "totalizing theory."
- *Ads, Fads, and Consumer Culture: Advertising's Impact on American Character and Society* (2000), by Arthur Asa Berger, contains information that will facilitate a study of the advertising world. He examines the cross-pressures between advertisements and various social, economic, and cultural factors. His deconstruction of the now famous 1984 Macintosh TV ad is included in this text.
- *The Basic Training of Pavlo Hummel*, by David Rabe, startled the theatergoing public in 1971. This postmodern play is a story of a naïve recruit's initiation into war. It won Rabe an Obie and was hailed by the *New York Times* as "rich in humor, irony and insight." It is both brutal and hilarious, making intense critical comments on the Vietnam War and the military establishment in general. It is published along with *Sticks and Bones* by Grove Press in the 1972 volume *The Vietnam Plays*. Rabe won a Tony for his 1995 play *Hurlyburly*.
- *Gravity's Rainbow* (1973), by Thomas Pynchon, is a Pulitzer Prize–winning novel set in Europe during World War II. This novel forces readers to constantly evaluate the sense of reality constructed from page one.

The latter two are adopted by Barthelme. "Me and Miss Mandible" uses the diary format, taking the reader through the events of the story day by day. "Daumier" is in an outline form, with occasional topics indicated to tell the reader what the next section of the story will be about.

In these short story examples, the reliability of the narrator is kept at a high level. Also the author remains outside the story. But for many stories, this is not the case. Two novels that contain examples of authorial intrusions and that raise questions about the narrator's truthfulness and thereby the truth of the story itself are *The Unbearable Lightness of Being* by Milan Kundera and *The Ravishing of Lol Stein* by Marguerite Duras.

Authors often deliberately disturb the comfortable expectations of the reader. In many postmodern works the authors make direct statements to the reader, at times confronting the characters in the novel. Wendy Lesser, in her essay "The Character as Victim," wrote that among contemporary writers "the prevailing idea appears to be that authors and their characters are in direct competition." This notion is at odds with previous approaches to fiction, which keep the author out of the story. But for the postmodern writer these intrusions have become more normal. In *The Unbearable Lightness of Being*, Kundera writes, "Tomas saw her jealousy . . . as a burden . . . he would be saddled with until not long before his death." The foreshadowing shows the author's knowledge of the mortality of his own character. This phrase ends a longer passage during which Tomas has become jealous of Tereza's success as a photographer. Kundera interrupts the passage by telling the reader that Tomas will die soon. This comment seems also a kind of jealous reaction: Kundera is jealous of his own character's successes and deflates that success by telling the reader of Tomas's impending death. Lesser confirms this by stating that "the author knows too clearly and powerfully what he wants to

> "No 'truth' can happen in the tale in which the narrator does not know what is going on, the author does not know what is going on, or where the narrator of the story admits to lying."

say. Nobody else . . . has a chance to say otherwise." Nobody has the opportunity to be too successful or to be too important. Kundera will not allow it.

Kundera also makes repeated comments that are outside the context of the story line. These authorial intrusions are often comments on various aspects in the novel. For example, in chapter 16 of Part Five, he writes, "Several days later, he was struck by another thought, which I record here as an addendum to the preceding chapter." The "I" in this sentence is Kundera, who has intruded into his story, telling the reader that he will make comments about an occurrence in the previous chapter.

In this self-reflexive way Kundera refers directly to the novel itself. He writes: "And once more I see him the way he appeared to me at the very beginning of the novel." Later he comments, "In Part Three of this novel I told the tale of Sabrina." These interruptions by the author do what E. L. Doctorow claims is "the author deliberately [breaking] the mimetic spell of his text and [insisting] that the reader should not take his story to heart or believe in the existence of his characters." This act of destroying what has just been created occurs often in the works of postmodern authors.

Knowledge of the identity of the narrator assists the reader in making a connection with the story. The narrator in Barthelme's "The first thing the baby did wrong . . ." is the father, identified only as "I." But nothing further is needed. The narrator in *Lol Stein* is Jack Hold, who is reluctantly identified late in the novel. At the end of one section Duras has written: "Arm in arm they ascend the terrace steps. Tatiana introduces Peter Breugner, her husband, to Lol, and Jack Hold, a friend of theirs—the distance is covered—me." In this hesitant, circuitous way, the narrator is identified, in the third person by himself!

In Kundera's novel the narrator is never identified, leaving the reader to wonder if there is one or if the author himself is really telling the tale. But as Maureen Howard says, "Whoever the narrator may be, he's an entertaining fellow, sophisticated, professional, very European." Even though the reader does not know his identity, enough of his personality is present so his name does not matter.

Whoever the narrator is, it is imperative that the reader understands whether or not that narrator is telling the truth. Jack Hold, Duras's narrator, tells the tale of Lol but without a sense of certainty, saying things like, "I seem to remember," or "I doubt it," or "I can't say for sure." This imprecision (or indecision) leaves the reader without a sense of knowing what is really going on. Adding to the reader's uncertainty are additional phrases like: "My opinion," "I invent," and "I no longer know for sure." An additional complication to this is the fact that these imprecise statements have no effect on the narrator's attitude to story telling. He does not apologize for these lapses but ignores them after admitting them.

The most disturbing aspect of Jack Hold's narration is his admission, "I'm lying." Another passage includes the line, "I desperately want to partake of the word which emerges from the lips of Lol Stein, I want to be a part of this lie which she has forged." Further confusing the reader is the contradictory statement: "I didn't lie." In this story the narrator does not evade the issue of lying; he takes notice of it and moves ahead with the story.

In his novel, Kundera taxes the reader with the following statement: "The way he rushed into his decision seems rather odd to me. Could it perhaps conceal something else, something deeper that escaped his reasoning?" This is an admission by Kundera (the one asking the question here) that he does not know what is going on with a character of his own creation. How could a character's behavior seem odd to the author who has created that character? This asks the question: If the author does not know what is going on in the story, how can the reader expect to know? Recalling the earlier notion that Kundera confronts his own characters, in this instance the character seems to have won.

By the end of such statements the reader has no stable basis upon which to establish the veracity of the story. No "truth" can happen in the tale in which the narrator does not know what is going on, the author does not know what is going on, or where the narrator of the story admits to lying. The reader does not know what to believe. Here is the uncertainty of Wittgenstein's "groundlessness of believing." The reader does not know where to base an understanding of the fictional world the author has created.

A consequence of the self-reflexive aspects of these novels is that the reader is constantly being reminded that "it is a fiction," according to Terry Eagleton in "Estrangement and Irony." These reminders disturb the reader's ability to make the mental leap called the suspension of disbelief, which allows a reader of fiction to become immersed in the story and to care about the characters and their condition. Without this leap, the reader is more willing to dismiss both the tale and the characters.

These are just some of the manifestations of postmodernist concerns about the nature the truth in fiction. Jacques Derrida has noted that since language is unable to convey an absolute meaning, there results the impossibility for language to establish an absolute "truth." In fiction that "truth" is the creation of the author. Because postmodern authors disrupt their stories, intrude in them, and in some cases confront their own creations, there can be no "truth" in that fictional world.

Source: Carl Mowery, Critical Essay on Postmodernism, in *Literary Movements for Students*, The Gale Group, 2003.

Larry McCaffery

In the following introduction excerpt, McCaffery discusses Postmodernism's precursors and origins.

The Evolution of Postmodernism: Some Precursors and Background

As I've already suggested, there is no sharp demarcation line separating modernism and postmodernism, and the alleged differences between the two become especially difficult to pinpoint if one is examining the development of fiction in a global context and not just focusing on what has been occurring in the United States. (The impulses behind the experimentalism of, say, Latin American or Eastern European fiction are clearly different from those that motivated U.S. authors in the 1960s.) In the United States what occurred in the postmodern outburst of the 1960s seemed very radical in part because fiction in the United States during the previous 30 years had seemed, for the most part, conservative aesthetically. This is not to say that experimenting wasn't taking place in the United States at all during this period—some of the great innovators of the previous generation continued to explore new forms (Faulkner, Stein, Fitzgerald), and a few newcomers with an experimental bent appeared (Djuna Barnes, Kenneth Patchen, Nathaniel West, John Hawkes, Jack Kerouac); but for the most part, U.S. authors during this period were content to deal with the key issues of their day—the Depression, World War II, existential angst—in relatively straightforward forms. The reasons behind this formal conservatism are certainly complex, but part of its hold on writers has to do with the way the times affected many writers, especially the sense that with such big issues to be examined authors couldn't afford the luxury of innovative strategies. At any rate, for whatever reasons in the United States from the period of 1930 until 1960 we do not find the emergence of a major innovator—someone equivalent to Beckett or Borges or Alain Robbe-Grillet or Louis Ferdinand Céline—except in the person of perhaps post-modern fiction's most important precursor, Vladimir Nabokov, who labored in obscurity in this country for 25 years until the scandal of *Lolita* made him suddenly very visible indeed (though for all the wrong reasons). As a result, by the late 1950s the United States was just as ripe for an aesthetic revolution as it was for the cultural revolution that was soon to follow. The two are, of course, intimately related.

Much of the groundwork for the so-called postmodern aesthetic revolution had already been established earlier in this century in such areas as the theoretical work being done in philosophy and science; the innovations made in painting (the rejection of mimesis and fixed point perspective, the emphasis on collage, self-exploration, abstract expressionism, and so on); in theater in the works of Pirandello, Brecht, Beckett, Genet, even Thornton Wilder; the increasing prominence of photography, the cinema, and eventually television, which coopted certain alternatives for writers while opening up other areas of emphasis. And if one looks carefully enough, there were many modernist literary figures who had called for a complete overhaul of the notion of representation in fiction. It is a commonplace to note that *Tristram Shandy* is a thoroughly postmodern work in every respect but the period in which it is written, and there are dozens of other examples of authors who explored many of the same avenues of experimentalism that

"The wider social and political forces that galvanized postmodern writers and provided a sense of urgency and focus to their development were similar, in some ways, to those that provided such a great impetus to artistic innovation during the 1920s."

postmodern writers were to take: for instance, the surreal, mechanically produced constructions of Raymond Roussel; the work of Alfred Jarry, with its black humor, its obscenity, its confounding of fact, fiction, and autobiography, its general sense of play and formal outrageousness; André Gide's *The Counterfeiters*, with its self-reflexiveness and self-commentary; Franz Kafka's matter-of-fact surrealistic presentation of the self and its relationship to society (significantly, Kafka's impact on American writing was not strong until the 1950s); William Faulkner, with his multiple narrators and competing truths, and whose own voice is so insistently foregrounded throughout his fiction as to obliterate any real sense that he is transcribing anything but his own consciousness; and, looming over the entire literary landscape, is the figure of James Joyce, the Dead Father of postmodern fiction, who must be dealt with, slain, the pieces of his genius ritually eaten and digested.

The wider social and political forces that galvanized postmodern writers and provided a sense of urgency and focus to their development were similar, in some ways, to those that provided such a great impetus to artistic innovation during the 1920s. In both Cases, an international tragedy—World War I for artists in the 1920s, and Vietnam (along with a host of more diffused insanities, like the proliferation of nuclear weapons and the ongoing destruction of the environment) for postmodern American writers—created the sense that fundamental reconsiderations had to be made about the systems that govern our lives. Such systems included the political, social, and other ideological forms that had helped lead us to the position we were in, and also the artistic forms through which we could express a sense of ourselves and our relationship to the world around us. Thus, World War I was a global disaster of such unprecedented proportions, and had been produced by the very features of society that were supposed to ennoble and "civilize" us (reason, technology), that artists were forced to rethink the basic rationalistic, humanistic principles that had formed the basis of Western art since the Renaissance. One predictable response to the view that reality had become a fragmented, chaotic "Wasteland" was to turn to art as a kind of last retreat, a last source of reason, stability, and harmony. (One thinks of the magnificently ordered private systems of Joyce, Yeats, Pound, Proust, and Hemingway.) Another tactic was to develop art that turned its back on the barbarism and entropy of reality and explored instead the more abstract, rarified realm of art itself; here was a place where poets could examine language without regard to referents, where painters could explore the implications of lines, shapes, textures, and colors freed from outer correspondences. A third possibility was the development of artistic strategies that affirmed rather than denied or ignored the disorder and irrationalism around it, that joined forces with the primitive, illogical drives that Freud claimed lay within us all—the strategy of the dadaists and surrealists in painting and poetry, and of a few fiction writers as well (Anaïs Nin, Céline, Robert Desnos, Michel Leiris). Interestingly enough, all three tendencies would be evident in postmodern fiction 40 years later: the huge, intricately structured work (Pynchon, William Gaddis, Barth, Don DeLillo, Coover, Joseph McElroy, Alexander Theroux); the work that concerns only itself, its own mechanisms, the pure relationship of symbol and word (in William H. Gass, Richard Kostelanetz, Robert Pinget, Coover, Steve Katz, Barthelme); and the fractured, delirious text whose process mirrored the entropy and fragmentation outside (William S. Burroughs, Barthelme, Raymond Federman, Kathy Acker). The difference between the two periods, then, is finally one of degree—the degree to which contemporary writers have turned to these strategies, the degree to which they have moved away from realistic norms (even in elaborately ordered works), especially in the degree to which artifice, playfulness, and self-consciousness—features not so common to the innovative fictions of the 1920s—have been consistently incorporated into the fabric of postmodern fiction.

It probably seems initially peculiar that postmodernism emerged in the 1960s rather than in the years that immediately followed World War II. It may be that the war, with its Hitlers and Mussolinis, its Hiroshimas and Normandy Beaches and Dresdens, its other unthinkable horrors (the concentration camps, collective suicides, and so on), was too dreadful or overwhelming to be directly confronted. In any case, the great innovators of the 1940s and 1950s tended to be, at least at first glance, nonsocially conscious writers. Beckett, Borges, and Nabokov—the three authors from this period who were to have the most direct impact on postmodern writing—all appeared to turn their backs on the world outside in favor of a movement inward, toward the world of language, dream, and memory, to examine the nature of subjective experience, of the way words beguile, mislead, and shape our perception, of the way imagination builds its own realm out of symbols. I emphasize the word "appear" in these three cases because all three of these authors were, in fact, very much political writers in a very basic sense, for each was profoundly aware of the importance that language plays in shaping the world around us, the way power-structures use this world-building capacity of words, the way that reality and commonsense are disguised versions of ideologies that are foisted on individuals by institutions that profit from the popular acceptance of these illusions. From this perspective, the postmodern emphasis on subjectivity, language, and fiction-making is hardly as irrelevant, self-indulgent, and narcissistic as many unsympathetic critics have charged. Indeed, many of the most important postmodern works, for all their experimentalism, metafictional impulses, self-reflexiveness, playfulness, and game-playing, have much more to say about history, social issues, and politics than is generally realized.

An early postmodern event was the film 2001: A Space Odyssey, *directed by Stanley Kubrick*

Another writer very aware of the need to examine the role of language within larger contexts was George Orwell, whose *1984* remains the most famous fictional treatment of political language manipulation. *1984*, which grew out of science fiction's dystopian tradition and which was specifically influenced by Yevgeny Zamiatin's remarkable experimental novel, *We* (a "postmodern" novel published in 1920), points to another important tendency in postmodern fiction: the increasing attention being paid by serious, highly sophisticated authors to paraliterary forms such as science fiction and detective fiction—forms that proved attractive to the postmodern spirit partly because mimesis was never their guiding concern to begin with. Such genres were thus free to generate forms and conventions that were entirely different from those of traditional fiction, and that proved to be surprisingly rich and suggestive. Developments in these paraliterary forms need to be examined more thoroughly by scholars—there are fertile areas of investigation into, for example, the use of pornographical conventions by Acker, Coover, Samuel Delany, and Clarence Major (not to mention Nabokov); or the appropriation of detective novel forms by many postmodern writers (Nabokov, Stanislaw Lem, Michel Butor, Robbe Grillet, William Hjortsberg, McElroy). But the most significant evolution of a paraliterary form has been that of science fiction. Long respected in Europe and never as clearly separated from literature there as it has been in the United States (cf. the European tradition of H.G. Wells, Zamiatin, Karel Čapek, Olaf Stapledon, Orwell, Aldous Huxley, Arthur C. Clark, J.G. Ballard), SF emerged in the United States from its self-imposed "ghetto status" into a major field of creative activity during the 1960s. Although many literary critics remain suspicious of and condescending toward SF, it is obvious today that a number of the most significant postmodern innovators have been SF writers. This is certainly the case with Philip K. Dick, a writer misunderstood both inside and outside his field. Because his publishers forced him onto a treadmill of rapid-fire production, Dick's novels are always plagued by a certain amount of sloppiness, lack of verbal grace, and two-dimensional character portrayals. Nevertheless, Dick had a brilliant fictional imagination capable of inventing plots of considerable intricacy and metaphorical suggestiveness. In his best works—*The Man in the High Castle, Martian Time-Slip, Ubik, Do Androids Dream of Electric Sheep?*—he devised highly original central plot structures that deal with many of the same issues common to postmodernism: metaphysical ambiguity, the oppressive nature of political systems, entropy, the mechanization of modern life.

Similarly, other major SF figures—including Ursula LeGuin, Delany, Gene Wolfe, John Varley, Lem, Roger Zelazny—have been creating complex, ingenious fictional forms that tell us a great deal about the fantastic world around us but that do so with structures whose conventions and language differ fundamentally from that of "mundane fiction" (as Delany refers to it). Indeed, one indication of the richness and diversity of this field can be seen in the number of "mainstream" authors who have turned to SF—Doris Lessing, Anthony Burgess, Italo Calvino, Marge Piercy, Thomas Berger, Nabokov, Raymond Federman, and dozens of others.

There were, of course, other developments occurring before 1960 that would influence the direction of postmodernism. One of the most important of these has been the rapid emergence of the cinema and television as major artistic forms. It is probably no accident that postmodern experimentalists were the first generation of writers who grew up immersed in television, or that many of these writers were as saturated with the cinema as their forefathers had been with literature. The specific influences of television and the movies on postmodern fiction are diffuse, generalized, difficult to pinpoint, but obviously an awareness of the process through which a movie is presented—its rapid cutting, its use of montage and juxtaposition, its reliance on close-ups, tracking shots, and other technical devices—is likely to create some deeply rooted effects on writers when they sit down at their collective typewriters. (The process is also symbiotic: Eisenstein's theory of montage had a profound effect on an entire generation of writers, but so did Flaubert's use of montage in the famous "country-fair" scene in *Madame Bovary* affect filmmakers.) And as important as movies and television were in suggesting to writers what could be put in to their works was the example they supplied for what could be left out profitably. Not only did writers quickly realize that television and the cinema could deal with certain narrative forms more effectively than fiction (photography had similarly made certain forms of painting instantly obsolete), but a number of cinematic shorthand devices proved useful in fiction as well. Audiences trained in the conventions of the nineteenth-century novel may have required certain connections, certain details and transitions, but cinematic directors quickly discovered that many of these could be eliminated once the audience became acquainted with a different set of conventions. (Consider a typical cinematic juxtaposition of a man walking up a street and a shot of him sitting in the interior of a house—there's no need to supply the sights he saw on his walk, a view of the house approaching, the pause while knocking on the door or inserting the key, and so on.) Similarly, the pacing of television—and of television commercials, whose significance is also substantial in this regard—is directly apparent in many postmodern works (one thinks of *Slaughterhouse-Five*, *Ragtime*, of Coover's and Barthelme's short fiction, of Manuel Puig and Jonathan Baumbach). The more specific influences of individual directors cannot be discounted: Jean-Luc Godard probably had as much impact on the imaginations of writers during the 1960s as any literary figure; and in various ways, movies like *8*, *Blow Up*, *Belle de Jour*, *Repulsion*, *2001*, *Dr. Strangelove*, and a host of other innovative films, have deeply imprinted themselves in the body of postmodern fiction.

The Postmodern Awakening: 1960–1975

The early 1960s saw the publication of a number of fictional works that indicated that American fiction was heading in some very different directions than it had been during the preceding 25 years. Signaling this change in aesthetic sensibility was the appearance within a relatively short period of time (1960–1965) of a number of major works that decisively broke with the traditions of conventional realism. These key works included John Barth's *The Sot-Weed Factor* (1960) and *Giles Goat-Boy* (1966), Joseph Heller's *Catch-22* (1961), Vladimir Nabokov's *Pale Fire* (1962), Thomas Pynchon's *V.* (1963), Donald Barthelme's *Come Back, Dr. Caligari* (1964), and Robert Coover's *The Origin of the Brunists* (1965). These works were all produced by young, obviously ambitious writers (Nabokov is an exception, in terms of age). This fiction owed its unusual effects to a wide variety of sources, such as the absurdist theater (which had been flourishing in New York's Off-Broadway scene during the late 1950s), jazz and rock and roll, pop art, and other developments in the avant-garde art scene, the growing appreciation of Kafka and other experimenters (many of whom were first being translated during this period: Céline, Robbe-Grillet, and the other French New Novelists, Jean Genet, Borges, Günter Grass), the energy and hot-wired delirium of the Beats. The result was a peculiar blend of dark humor, literary parody, surrealism, byzantine plots full of improbable coincidences and outrageous action, all presented in a dazzling variety of excessive styles that constantly called attention to themselves. Postmodern fiction had arrived.

What was to characterize the direction of postmodern fiction during the rest of the decade—the push to test new forms of expression, to examine conventions and solutions critically and seek new answers, to rethink so-called natural methods of organizing perception, expose their ideological origins, and pose new systems of organization—was hardly born in an ivory-towered, academic vacuum. The art of the 1960s, including the postmodern fiction, reflected the basic ways in which the ideologies on which the U.S. order had traditionally relied, together with the cultural values by which it rules, were in deep turmoil. Fiction reflected the sense, shared by many of our most thoughtful and articulate citizens, that we had been led (and misled) into the age of nuclear nightmare, into Vietnam, into ecological apocalypse, into political oppression, and into an insane and immoral sense of values that devalued human beings by glorifying abstractions and the inanimate—all this in the name of certain labels and covert ideologies that badly needed overhauling. A natural extension of this feeling was the desire to tear down the ruling ideologies (political, sexual, moral, social, aesthetic, all of which proved to be remarkably integrated) and reveal them for what they were: arbitrary structures imposed as a result of various complex, historical, and economic forces, instated into societies as natural and commonsensical, all of which served, in one way or another, to reinforce the status quo and insure the continued world view (and hence the continued power) of those who established these ideologies. Thus, the aggressive, radicalized poetics of postmodernism was an extension of a larger sense of dissatisfaction and frustration. "Don't trust anyone over 30" was an expression commonly heard among young people in the 1960s who were fed up with the content and structure of their lives. A similar distrust of one's "elders" was equally apparent in postmodern fiction writers.

By the late 1960s and early 1970s, a new generation of writers had firmly established itself. During this period experimental fictions appeared by authors who were eventually characterized by critics as being postmodern in outlook: William Gass' *In the Heart of the Heart of the Country*, Jerzy Kosinski's *Steps*, Robert Coover's *Universal Baseball Association* and *Pricksongs and Descants*, John Fowles' *The French Lieutenant's Woman*, Peter Handke's *The Goalie's Anxiety at the Penalty Kick*, García Márquez's *One Hundred Years of Solitude*, Steve Katz's *The Exagggerations of Peter Prince*, Donald Barthelme's *City Life*, *Snow White*, and *Unspeakable Practices, Unnatural Acts*, Pynchon's *The Crying of Lot 49*, Richard Brautigan's *Trout Fishing in America*, Tom Robbins' *Another Roadside Attraction*, Raymond Federman's *Double or Nothing*, Rudolf Wurlitzer's *Nog*, Nabokov's *Ada*, and Joseph McElroy's *A Smuggler's Bible*. The point is not that these authors approached the issue of fictional innovation in a fundamentally unified fashion. Rather, quite the opposite was true: writers were busy exploring a host of innovative strategies, many of them very different in intent and effect. (One can hardly imagine, for example, two works so opposed in aesthetic orientation as, say, Federman's *Double or Nothing* and Gass' "In the Heart of the Heart of the Country.") What these experimentations did share, however, was a general sense that fiction needed to acknowledge its own artificial, constructed nature, to focus the reader's attention on how the work was being articulated rather than merely on what was happening. Distrustful of all claims to truth and hypersensitive to the view that reality and objectivity were not givens but social or linguistic constructs, postmodern writers tended to lay bare the artifice of their works, to comment on the processes involved, to refuse to create the realist illusion that the work mimics operations outside itself. In the ideology of realism or representation, it was implied that words were linked to thoughts or objects in essentially direct, incontrovertible ways. On the other hand, postmodern authors—operating in an aesthetic environment that has grown out of Saussaurian linguistics, Wittgenstein's notion of meaning-as-usage, structuralism, and deconstructive views of language—tend to manipulate words as changeable entities determined by the rules of the particular sign-system (the fiction at hand). Hardly a translucent window on to an object (the world, reality) or a mind, the language in many postmodern texts becomes "thickened," played with and shown off, and frequently becomes just another element to be manipulated by a self-conscious author.

Other conventions of the realist narrative were challenged. The notion of the unified subject living in a world of stable essences (one of the cornerstones of traditional fiction) was one such notion that was frequently mocked by postmodern authors, either by so obsessively emphasizing the schizophrenic, subjective nature of experience as to obliterate the distinction between subject and reality (as in Philip Dick or Jonathan Baumbach or Federman) or by creating characters with no definable personality or who changed from scene to scene (as with Ronald Sukenick's figures who change "like a cloud," or Ron Silliman's prose experiments in which narrator and setting disappear into the process of language selection). The commonsensical distinction between fact and fiction, author and text, also became increasingly difficult to make. "Real" authors began making increasingly common excursions into their fictional worlds (as Vonnegut did in *Breakfast of Champions* and Fowles did in *The French Lieutenant's Woman*, or as Sukenick and Federman and Katz did in nearly all their works); fragments of real events, real reportage, and news often became incorporated into works, collage-fashion, making it impossible to untangle what was being made up from what had really happened. (Here one thinks of Barthelme, Burroughs, Vonnegut, Harold Jaffe, Coover, and William Kennedy.) This tendency to break down the seam between the real and the invented, or to deny the relevance of this distinction altogether, was also evident in the writing of the New Journalists, like Tom Wolfe, Truman Capote, Norman Mailer, and Hunter Thompson. These authors, along with other writers who blurred the fact/fiction dichotomy (Robert Pirsig in *Zen and the Art of Motorcycle Maintenance*, Maxine Hong Kingston in *The Woman Warrior* and *China Men*, Peter Handke in *A Sorrow Beyond Dreams*, V. S. Naipaul in *In a Free State*, and so on), not only employed various conventions borrowed from fiction to heighten a sense of drama and plot development, but they also thrust their own subjective responses into the forefront of their works rather than making claims that their texts were objective. Likewise, the distinction between poetry and prose was also often dissolved, not just by fiction writers who emphasized poetic qualities in their prose (Gass, Barry Hannah, Stanley Elkin, Nabokov, Hawkes), but also by poets who began to explore longer forms of prose. (See Ron Silliman's discussion of this important phenomenon in this volume.) Even the familiar "look" of books—the conventions of typography, pagination, and other visual elements that actually govern the process of reading itself—was freely tampered with, in works of such visual ingenuity as Federman's *Double or Nothing*, Katz's *The Exagggerations of Peter Prince*, Gass' *Willie Masters' Lonesome Wife*, Julio Cortázar's *Ultimo Rundo*, Barthelme's *City Life*, or Butor's *Mobile*. In short, virtually all of the elements that make the reading experience what it is were being reexamined by postmodern experimenters during the 1960s. Not surprisingly, many of the experiments proved to be dead ends or were rapidly exhausted and then discarded. This seems to be the case with the New Novel experiments and with a lot of the typographical experimentation, for example. But even these innovations were useful in that they suggested avenues that writers need no longer explore.

Postmodern Criticism

As should be evident from the focus of the two critical articles dealing with postmodern criticism and from the critics I selected to be included in the individual author entry section, I have tried to emphasize critical thought that shares features of postmodern thought rather than focusing on criticism that deals with postmodern fiction. Indeed, it seems evident to me that many of the same principles and tendencies that were shaping the direction of postmodern fiction are central to the development of the most important critical schools of the past 25 years: structuralism, deconstruction, and Marxist-oriented criticism. (For a good overview of this interaction, see Charles Caramello's *Silverless Mirrors: Book, Self & Postmodern American Fiction.*) For example, the Marxist and structuralist emphasis on the constructedness of human meaning is similar to postmodern fiction's sense that reality is not given and that our way of perceiving it is hardly natural or self-evident. Terry Eagleton's fine summary of the chief tenets of structuralism in his survey of critical thought, *Literary Theory* helps clarify the interrelationship between structuralism and postmodern aesthetics very clearly. Structuralism, he notes, emphasizes that:

> Meaning was neither a private experience nor a divinely ordained occurrence: it was the product of certain shared systems of signification. The confident bourgeoise belief that the isolated individual subject was the fount and origin of all meaning took a sharp knock: language pre-dated the individual, and was

> much less his or her product than he or she was the product of it. Meaning was not "natural," a question of just looking and seeing, or something eternally settled; the way you interpreted your world was a function of the languages you had at your disposal, and there was evidently nothing immutable about these. Meaning was not something which all men and women everywhere intuitively shared, and then articulated in their various tongues and scripts; what meaning you were able to articulate depended on what script or speech you shared in the first place. There were the seeds here of a social and historical theory of meaning, whose implications were to run deep within contemporary thought. It was impossible any longer to see reality simply as something "out there," a fixed order of things which language merely reflected.

For structuralism, then, reality and our experience of reality need not necessarily be continuous—a view that is intimately connected with postmodern fiction's refusal to rely on fixed notions of reality, its emphasis on reproducing the human being's imaginative (subjective, fictional) responses to what is "out there" rather than trying to convince the readers that they are experiencing a transcription of reality unfiltered by a mediating process. Roland Barthes' early ventures into structuralist criticism produced a notion that also bears some striking relevance for what would develop in fiction during the 1960s. For example, Barthes' analysis of the healthy sign is directly applicable to what postmodern authors suggest about healthy fiction: in both cases the artifact is healthiest which draws attention to itself and to its own arbitrariness—one that makes no effort to pass itself off as natural or inevitable but that, in the very act of conveying a meaning, communicates something of its own relative, artificial status as well. Thus, very much like postmodern fiction writers, Barthes rightly perceives that one of the functions of ideologies and power-structures of all sorts is always to convert culture into nature—to make it appear that conventions, signs, and social realities are natural, innocent, commonsensical. The obvious literary analogy to this natural attitude can be found in realist fiction, which implies that it possesses the means (a natural language) to represent something else with little or no interference with what it mediates. Such a realist sign is for Barthes—and for the postmodern authors of the 1960s—essentially unhealthy, for it proceeds by denying its own status as a sign in order to create the illusion that we are perceiving reality without its intervention.

Deconstruction and poststructuralism, as developed by Derrida, Paul de Man, Barthes, and others, was essentially an attempt to topple the logic by which a particular system of thought (and behind that, a whole system of political structures and social institutions) maintains its force. By demonstrating that all meaning and knowledge could be exposed as resting on a naively representational theory of language, poststructuralism provided still another justification for postmodernism's emphasis on the free play of language, of the text-as-generating-meaning. The later Barthes (as in *The Pleasure of the Text*, 1973) suggested that only in writing (or in reading-as-writing) could the individual be freed momentarily from the tyranny of structural meaning, from ideology, from theory. As Eagleton notes, one product of this emphasis on the unnaturalness of signs was admittedly the tendency by some poststructuralists (and some fiction writers) to flee from history, to take refuge in the erotic play of writing/reading, and conveniently to evade reality and all political questions completely:

> If meaning, the signified, was a passing product of words or signifiers, always shifting and unstable, part-present and part-absent, how could there be any determinate truth or meaning at all? If reality was constructed by our discourse rather than reflected by it, how could we ever know reality itself, rather than merely knowing our own discourse? Was all talk just talk about talk? Did it make sense to claim that one interpretation of reality, history or the literary text was "better" than another?

Such questions cut to the heart of the debate that was to rage during the mid- to late 1970s about the moral responsibility of fiction—a debate most famously summarized in the series of public discussions between the late John Gardner, whose study *On Moral Fiction* sparked considerable public interest in this issue, and William Gass, whose eloquent defense of fiction's irrelevancy to conditions outside the page (in *Fiction and the Figures of Life*) became a seminal aspect of postmodern aesthetics. (The Gass-Gardner "Debate" in *Anything Can Happen*) The outline of this debate centered on Gardner's claim, echoed by a number of other critics (perhaps most effectively in Gerald Graff's *Literature Against Itself*), that postmodern experimentalism, with its willful artifice and subjectivity, its metafictional impulses and emphasis on the play of language, is fundamentally trivial, vain, self-absorbed, and narcissistic. Gass, on the other hand, took essentially the familiar art-for-art's-sake position but developed his views with considerable rigor, supporting them with theories of language and aesthetics formulated by Wittgenstein and Max Black (both of whom Gass had studied under at Cornell), Paul Valéry, and Gertrude

Stein. Words, said Gass, are the writer's chief concern, for the writer's final obligation is to build something (a world of language, with its own rules and systems of transformations), not to describe something. One senses in Gass a longing for a safe and human refuge in this world of language, a place controlled and purified, an escape from an ugly, petty reality in which history becomes a destructive monument to human greed, in which discourse has been degraded into instruments of commerce, politics, and bureaucracy. Paradoxically, then, although Gass's emphasis on fiction as an interaction of signifiers had a liberating effect on the formal concerns of postmodern authors, there was also a potentially troubling elitism about his position, with its emphasis on formal complexity and beauty, and its lack of self-irony and play. This tendency is also obvious (and troubling) when one examines the important Yale School of Critics (Geoffrey Hartman, J. Hillis Miller, de Man, and, with some reservations, Harold Bloom). These latter critics have argued, often brilliantly, that literary language—indeed, all forms of discourse constantly undermines its own meaning. But in their tendency to view all elements of reality, including social reality, as merely further texts to be deconstructed as being undecidable, there emerges the sense that one has found a means to demolish all opinions without having to adopt any of one's own. Perhaps the key factor that needs to be emphasized in this regard is that, as Derrida and Barthes, among others, have demonstrated, there is no fundamental opposition between a fiction that emphasizes its unnaturalness, its arbitrariness, that reveals (and revels in) its *différances*, and one that deals with history, politics, and social issues in a significant fashion. Indeed, by opening up a radical awareness of the sign systems by which men and women live, and by offering exemplars of freely created fictions that oppose publicly accepted ones, postmodern fiction contains the potential to rejoin the history which some claim it has abandoned. Thus, although most critics have been largely blind to the political thrust of postmodern experimentalism, it will surely soon be recognized that the fiction of Barthelme, Coover, Sukenick, Federman, Gaddis, Barth, Pynchon, DeLillo, Silliman, and other innovators of postmodernism is very much centered on political questions: questions about how ideologies are formed, the process whereby conventions are developed, the need for individuals to exercise their own imaginative and linguistic powers lest these powers be coopted by others.

Post-Postmodernism: The Evolution of Contemporary Conciousness

If a single work may be said to have provided a model for the direction of postmodern fiction of the 1970s and 1980s, it is probably García Márquez's *One Hundred Years of Solitude*, a work that admirably and brilliantly combines experimental impulses with a powerful sense of political and social reality. Indeed, Márquez's masterpiece perfectly embodies a tendency found in much of the best recent fiction—that is, it uses experimental strategies to discover new methods of reconnecting with the world outside the page, outside of language. In many ways, *One Hundred Years of Solitude* is clearly a nonrealistic novel, with its magical, surreal landscape, its dense reflexive surface, its metafictional emphasis on the nature of language and how reality is storified from one generation to the next, its labyrinthine literary references, and other features. Yet for all its experimentalism, *One Hundred Years of Solitude* also is a highly readable, coherent story, peopled with dozens of memorable characters; and it also urgently speaks to us about political, historical, and psychological realities that are central to our experience. It thus becomes an emblem of what postmodernism can be, being self-conscious about its literary heritage and about the limits of mimesis, developing its own organic form of experimentalism, yet managing to reconnect its readers with the world around them. When one examines some of the major works that have appeared since 1975—Barth's *Letters*, for example, or Gaddis' *JR*, or Salman Rushdie's *Midnight's Children*, or William Kennedy's *Ironweed* —one can see a similar synthesis at work.

This synthesis between experimentalism and more traditional literary concerns is explainable on many levels. Partly it has to do with the predictable, dialectical process that seems to govern most revolutions (aesthetical and otherwise), with the radicalism of one era being soon questioned, reexamined, and then counterattacked by more conservative attitudes. If the public spirit of rebellion, distrust, and unrest was reflected in the disruptive fictional forms of the 1960s, so, too, has the reactionary, conservative political and social atmosphere of the late 1970s and early 1980s inevitably been manifested in the literature of this period. This is not to say that experimentalism has dried up completely, but certainly it is obvious that authors today are less interested in innovation per se than they were ten or fifteen years ago—especially innovation in the direction of reflexive, nonreferential works. And, of course, the source of this shift in sensibility lies beyond the political climate alone. For one thing, the experimental fervor that seemed to sustain postmodernism for several years has been subjected to repeated counterattacks by authors and critics (one thinks of Gardner, Carver, Gore Vidal, and Graff). More significantly, we find authors simply exploring new grounds, different methods of innovation, redefining notions like realism and artifice in much the same way that, for example, photorealists did in painting. This is a familiar scenario: so-called artistic revolutions have a natural life span, and they are inevitably succeeded by a new artistic situation, with its own demands and needs, its own practitioners who do not share the enthusiasms of the previous group and who are anxious to define themselves as individuals in their own way. Thus, when we examine a number of the highly regarded writers who have emerged since 1975—authors like Ron Hansen, Ian McEwan, Frederick Barthelme, William Kennedy, Toni Morrison, Jayne Anne Phillips, Stephen Dixon, Raymond Carver, or Ann Beattie—we discover a very different aesthetic sensibility in their work than that which characterized earlier postmodern writers, a sensibility that seems interested in what I would term experimental realism. (Note that Professor Jerome Klinkowitz presents a different notion of this term in his article in this volume.) By experimental realism I mean fiction that is fundamentally realistic in its impulses but that develops innovative strategies in structure (the nonendings of Beattie, Carver, Barthelme, the absence of character and plot in Silliman), language (the poetic prose of Phillips or Maxine Hong Kingston or Marilynne Robinson, the collage-assemblage of Silliman), the use of unusual materials (as with the use of "found" materials in Beattie, the manipulations of legend and history in Hansen, Kennedy, Leslie Silko, and Kingston), and so on. Of course, some of the sense of the decline of experimentalism results from our greater familiarity with the innovative strategies that once seemed so peculiar and difficult. Because later fiction which uses these experimental strategies seems more familiar and hence less threatening, its subsequent appearance is less likely to be remarked on—it is, in fact, no longer considered to be experimental at all. To take an obvious example, it might not occur to most readers or critics to discuss John Irving's *The World According to Garp* as an experimental novel, although it obviously employs many of the same metafictional techniques—the book-within-a-book, the interweaving of fiction and reality, playful self-references to its author's previous works—that other, more radical texts were using back in the 1960s. This isn't to say that Irving's book isn't experimental or metafiction—it clearly is; it just may seem beside the point to label it as such.

Much the same point can be made about many of the best works of fiction that have appeared in the United States from 1975 to 1984. Books like Tim O'Brien's *Going After Cacciato*, Alexander Theroux's *Darconville's Cat*, John Barth's *Sabbatical*, Ann Beattie's *Falling in Place*, Kurt Vonnegut's *Jailbird*, Toni Morrison's *Song of Solomon*, William Kennedy's Albany trilogy, and John Calvin Batchelor's *The Further Adventures of Halley's Comet* (to give just a sampling) incorporated postmodern experimental strategies into their structures so smoothly that they have often been seen as being quite traditional in orientation. Naturally, more radical experimental works continue to be written, but with a few notable exceptions—most of the books published by the Fiction Collective, the remarkable prose experiments of Ron Silliman, Lyn Hejinian, Barrett Watten, and Charles Bernstein, Joseph McElroy's *Plus*, Gilbert Sorrentino's *Mulligan Stew*, Kathy Acker's "punk novels," Walter Abish's works—most of the important, vital fiction of the last decade were neither exclusively experimental in an obvious, flamboyant manner, nor representational in a traditional, realist sense. Again, this situation recapitulates what we see in the other arts, in which the advances and new directions adopted by artists of one period (say, the break with representation and fixed perspective in painting) are gradually assimilated by artists of succeeding generations until a new period of stagnation arises which subsequently produces a new revolution. Thus, like the operations that are endlessly forming and transforming the nature of reality itself (and the nature of our lives within this flux), the transformations of art will surely continue, heedless of the desires of critics for clear patterns, unassailable definitions, and useful labels.

Source: Larry McCaffery, "Introduction," in *Postmodern Fiction: A Bio-Bibliographical Guide*, edited by Larry McCaffery, Greenwood Press, 1986, pp. xiv–xxviii.

Sources

Anderson, Perry, *The Origins of Postmodernity*, Verso, 1998, pp. 4–5.

Barthelme, Donald, *Overnight to Many Distant Cities*, Penguin, 1983.

Best, Steven, and Douglas Kellner, *Postmodern Theory: Critical Interrogations*, Guilford Press, 1991, pp. 20–21.

D'Andrade, Roy, "Moral Models in Anthropology," in *Current Anthropology*, Vol. 36, No. 3, p. 402.

Derrida, Jacques, *Of Grammatology*, Johns Hopkins University Press, 1976.

Doctorow, E. L., "Four Characters Under Two Tyrannies," in *New York Times Book Review*, April 29, 1984, p. 1.

Duras, Marguerite, *The Ravishing of Lol Stein*, translated by Richard Seaver, Pantheon Books, 1966.

Eagleton, Terry, "Estrangement and Irony," in *Salmagundi*, No. 73, 1987, pp. 25–32.

Grentz, Stanley, *A Primer on Postmodernism*, William B. Eerdmans Publishing, 1996, pp. 5–6, 146.

Havel, Vaclav, "The Need for Transcendence in the Postmodern World," July 4, 1994, http://www.worldtrans.org/whole/havelspeech.html (last accessed April 25, 2002).

Howard, Maureen, "Fiction in Review," in *Yale Review*, Vol. 74, No. 2, January 1985, pp. xxi–xxxiii.

Jameson, Fredric, "The Cultural Logic of Late Capitalism," in *Postmodernism; or, The Cultural Logic of Late Capitalism*, Duke University Press, 1991.

———, "Postmodernism and Consumer Society," in *Postmodern American Fiction: A Norton Anthology*, edited by Paula Geyh, Fred G. Leebron, and Andrew Levy, W. W. Norton, 1998, pp. 656–57.

Klages, Mary, "Structuralism/Poststructuralism," at *Lecture Notes*, http://www.colorado.edu/English/ENGL2012Klages/1997derridaA.html, revised September 18, 2001 (last accessed April 25, 2002).

Kristeva, Julia, *Desire in Language: A Semiotic Approach to Literature and Art*, Columbia University Press, 1980.

Kundera, Milan, *The Unbearable Lightness of Being*, translated by Michael Henry Heim, Harper and Row, 1984.

Leffel, Jim, and Dennis McCallum, "Postmodernism and You: Religion," at the *Crossroads Project*, 1996, http://www.xenos.org/ministries/crossroads/dotrel.htm (last accessed April 25, 2002).

Lesser, Wendy, "The Character as Victim," in *Hudson Review*, Vol. XXXVII, No. 3, Autumn 1984, pp. 468–82.

Levin, Harry, "What was Modernism?" in *Refractions: Essays in Comparative Literature*, Oxford University Press, 1966, p. 292.

McDonald, Henry, "The Narrative Act: Wittgenstein and Narratology," in *Surfaces*, Vol. 4, 1994, http://www.pum.umontreal.ca/revues/surfaces/vol4/mcdonald.html (last accessed April 25, 2002).

McGowan, John, *Postmodernism and Its Critics*, Cornell University Press, 1991, p. 91.

Morrison, Toni, *Beloved*, New American Library, 1987.

Reed, Ishmael, *Conjure: Selected Poems, 1963–1970*, University of Massachusetts Press, 1972.

Rosenau, Pauline, *Postmodernism and Social Sciences: Insights, Inroads, and Intrusions*, Princeton University Press, 1992, p. 81.

Sarup, Madan, *An Introductory Guide to Post-Structuralism and Postmodernism*, 2d ed., University of Georgia Press, 1993, pp. 33, 164.

Vonnegut, Kurt, Jr., *Cat's Cradle*, Dell Publishing, 1963.

———, *Wampeters, Foma and Granfalloons: Opinions*, Dell Publishing, 1974.

Wittgenstein, Ludwig, *On Certainty*, translated by Danis Paul and G. E. M. Anscombe, HarperCollins, 1972.

Further Reading

Geyh, Paula, Fred G. Leebron, and Andrew Levy, eds., *Postmodern American Fiction: A Norton Anthology*, W. W. Norton and Company, 1997.

Postmodern American Fiction is a collection of some of the major works of literature and criticism from the postmodern era. These works are excerpted but they maintain their postmodern essence and are worthy representatives of the literature.

Grentz, Stanley J., *Primer on Postmodernism*, William B. Eerdmans Publishing, 1996.

This short text explains in simple terms some of the major aspects of Postmodernism. It is easily accessible to the interested student of postmodern thought.

Hoover, Paul, ed., *Postmodern American Poetry: A Norton Anthology*, W. W. Norton and Company, 1994.

The selections in *Postmodern American Poetry* are arranged in chronological order by the birth date of the author. There is a section of writings by many of the authors in which they explain their philosophy of writing poetry and their poetics.

Natoli, Joseph, and Linda Hutcheon, eds., *Postmodern Reader*, SUNY Press, 1993.

This is a collection of critical writings, some excerpted, by the major authors and critics in the postmodern movement. These are the original works and they do not have guides or explanations accompanying.

Science Fiction and Fantasy Literature

Movement Origin

c. 1818

Aliens, time travel, sorcerers, and dragons! The domains of Science Fiction and Fantasy literature are recognizable to many people, but it is the messages and social commentary behind these icons that has captivated readers, and more recently critics, in the past two centuries. Science Fiction and Fantasy appear from the outside to be two distinct forms of literature, and yet the two genres share some similar characteristics and roots. This paradox has inspired much debate over the past century, while the movement itself has grown into a booming publishing industry that shows no signs of slowing.

Critics and historians share widely different viewpoints about the origins of Science Fiction. Still, many have conceded that Mary Shelley's 1818 British novel *Frankenstein* was the first novel to explore the hypothetical implications of modern science. Most agree that Jules Verne's novels from his "Extraordinary Journeys" series, including *Twenty Thousand Leagues Under the Sea* and *Journey to the Center of the Earth*, helped to define the movement. Although most of the early works were published in Europe, in the first half of the twentieth century, Science Fiction and Fantasy literature exploded in the United States. This was due in large part to inexpensive, genre "pulp" magazines like *Amazing Stories*—which reprinted novels like H. G. Wells's *The Time Machine* and *The War of the Worlds*—and to more expensive magazines like *Astounding Stories*—which helped introduce influential new writers like Isaac Asimov and Robert Heinlein.

Science Fiction and Fantasy literature inspired many related movements in film, television, and art, and profoundly influenced the development of science and culture in the twentieth century. The field remains dominated by American authors, many of whom continue to use their speculative creations to comment on current realities.

Representative Authors

Isaac Asimov (1920–1992)

Isaac Asimov was born January 2, 1920, in Petrovichi, U.S.S.R. (the former Soviet Union), and moved to the United States with his parents in 1923, becoming a U.S. citizen in 1928. Asimov was a voracious reader. His love of science led to a doctorate in chemistry from Columbia University and a subsequent post as a professor of biochemistry at Boston University's School of Medicine—a position he held for much of his writing career. Although he published more than 450 fiction and nonfiction books, making him one of the most prolific writers in history, Asimov is most remembered for his Science Fiction works, which influenced many writers in America during Science Fiction's golden age. Asimov has been credited with coining the term robotics, and with creating "The Three Laws of Robotics," which make their first appearance in his early robot short stories, collected in *I, Robot*. Asimov died of heart and kidney failure on April 6, 1992, in New York City.

Ray Bradbury (1920–)

Ray Douglas Bradbury was born August 22, 1920, in Waukegan, Illinois. During the depression, Bradbury's family moved to Los Angeles to find work. Bradbury began, like many other Science Fiction authors of the golden age, publishing his fiction in the fanzine he edited. In 1941, Bradbury published his first short story, and six years later, published his first story collection. It was not until the publication of *The Martian Chronicles*, a series of interconnected short stories about the human colonization of Mars, that Bradbury achieved enough critical success to break out of Science Fiction genre magazines into the more reputed mainstream magazines—which were off-limits to most Science Fiction writers. Bradbury lives and works in Los Angeles, California.

Robert Heinlein (1907–1988)

Robert Anson Heinlein was born July 7, 1907, in Butler, Missouri. Unlike many of his contemporaries, who started writing Science Fiction in their youth, Heinlein did not enter the field until he had already worked as a naval officer and studied physics and mathematics at the University of California, Los Angeles. As one of the Science Fiction writers for genre magazines during Science Fiction's golden age, Heinlein's sophisticated writing style raised the bar on Science Fiction literature and influenced many other writers. After working as an engineer in World War II alongside fellow Science Fiction writer Isaac Asimov, Heinlein published several Science Fiction "juveniles," or young adult novels, then began a series of controversial novels, including *Stranger in a Strange Land*, his best-known work. Heinlein, considered by many to be the most influential figure in American Science Fiction, died of heart failure on May 8, 1988, in Carmel, California.

Aldous Huxley (1894–1963)

The grandson of T. H. Huxley, a noted biologist and proponent of Charles Darwin's evolutionary theory, Aldous Leonard Huxley was born July 26, 1894, in Godalming, Surrey, England. Huxley originally intended to pursue a career in medicine, but an eye disease that led to temporary blindness prevented him from doing so. Although Huxley wrote in several different fiction and nonfiction genres, his most famous work is *Brave New World*, a Science Fiction novel that draws on evolutionary theory to create a nightmarish vision of the future. Five years after the novel's publication, Huxley moved to Los Angeles, California, where he wrote more mystical works until his death on November 22, 1963, in Hollywood, California. Huxley died on the same day as his British contemporary C. S. Lewis and on the same day that United States President John F. Kennedy was assassinated.

C. S. Lewis (1898–1963)

Clive Staples Lewis, known to readers as C. S. Lewis, was born November 29, 1898, in Belfast, Ireland. An atheist as a teenager, Lewis slowly came to renew his faith in Christianity, then incorporated his beliefs into his writing. After attending Oxford University, Lewis taught English literature at Oxford for almost thirty years. During his time as a professor, Lewis, along with fellow Christian Fantasy writer J. R. R. Tolkien and others, founded the Inklings, a casual club that met to discuss the writers' works in progress. Although Lewis wrote nonfiction, Science Fiction, and Fantasy, it is his fantastical writings that made him most popular. His seven-volume children's series "The Chronicles of Narnia," a Christian allegorical Fantasy, has delighted generations of popular audiences, particularly children. Lewis died of heart failure November 22, 1963—the same day as Huxley and U.S. President Kennedy—in Oxford, England.

Mary Shelley (1797–1851)

Mary Wollstonecraft Shelley was born as Mary Wollstonecraft August 30, 1797, in London, England. The daughter of two well-known authors, William Godwin and Mary Wollstonecraft, Mary's early years were unstable. Her mother died shortly after her birth, her father remarried, and she grew up in a chaotic environment with siblings from her father's two marriages, her stepmother's previous marriage, and her mother's previous affair. When she was fifteen, Mary met and fell in love with a friend of her father's, the poet Percy Bysshe Shelley. Mary had an affair with Percy, who was already married, and the two of them fled to Europe when she was seventeen, where Mary wrote *Frankenstein, or The Modern Prometheus*, which many critics consider the first true Science Fiction work. Following the suicide of Percy's wife, Mary and Percy were married. Four years after *Frankenstein* was published, Percy Bysshe Shelley drowned. Mary Shelley lived for almost thirty years as a widow, then died of a brain tumor February 1, 1851, at the age of fifty-three, in London.

J. R. R. Tolkien (1892–1973)

John Ronald Reuel Tolkien, known to readers as J. R. R. Tolkien, was born January 3, 1892, in Bloemfontein, South Africa. When he was four years old, Tolkien's family moved to England. After attending Oxford University, Tolkien taught English language and literature first at Leeds, then at Oxford. During this time, Tolkien, along with fellow Christian Fantasy writer C. S. Lewis and others, founded the Inklings, a casual club that met to discuss the writers' works in progress. Tolkien's passion for language and literary history culminated in his creation of Middle-Earth, a mythical world, modeled on northern and ancient literatures. Middle-Earth made its debut in Tolkien's *The Hobbit*, the prelude to his trilogy "The Lord of the Rings." Because of these works, Tolkien is considered by many to be the father of modern Fantasy stories. Tolkien died of complications from an ulcer and chest infection on September 2, 1973, in Bournemouth, England.

Jules Verne (1828–1905)

Jules Verne was born February 8, 1828, in Nantes, France. At age twenty, he left for Paris, where he studied law, intending to join his father's law firm. After passing his law exam, he struggled in Paris for several years, attempting to make a living off his writing. Although one of his plays was produced in 1850, it was not until 1863, after working as both a secretary for a theater and a stockbroker, that Verne's writing attracted the attention of Jules Hetzel, the magazine publisher who printed the majority of Verne's novels in serial form. The most famous novels are those that Verne called "Extraordinary Journeys," including *Twenty Thousand Leagues under the Sea*, which helped to establish Verne's reputation as one of the two founding fathers of modern Science Fiction (along with H. G. Wells). Verne wrote up until his death on March 24, 1905, in Amiens, France.

Jules Verne

Kurt Vonnegut Jr. (1922–)

Kurt Vonnegut, Jr. was born November 11, 1922, in Indianapolis, Indiana. While serving in the United States Army in Germany during World War II, Vonnegut was captured by the Germans and kept as a prisoner of war in Dresden, Germany. There he witnessed the Allied firebombing the city on February 13, 1945, and was one of few survivors of the firestorm that killed an estimated 120,000 people. This experience earned Vonnegut a Purple Heart and, more importantly, gave him the basis for much of his fiction. Vonnegut deals with war themes in many of his early novels, but it was not until the publication of *Slaughterhouse Five: or, the Children's Crusade* that Vonnegut told the full story of his Dresden experience through his characters. Vonnegut lives and works in New York City.

H. G. Wells (1866–1946)

Herbert George Wells, known to readers as H. G. Wells, was born September 21, 1866, in Bromley, England. He won a scholarship to the Normal School of Science in London, where he studied under T. H. Huxley—the famous proponent of Darwin's theory of evolution and grandfather of noted Science Fiction writer Aldous Huxley. Although infatuated with his first-year studies with Huxley, Wells spent most of his remaining school years performing extracurricular activities like founding and editing a college magazine. It was in this magazine that he first published "The Chronic Argonauts," which was later published as *The Time Machine: An Invention*, and which details a possible outcome of human evolution. This short novel, along with many of Wells's other early novels, helped to define what he called "the scientific romance," and established Wells as one of the two founding fathers of modern Science Fiction (along with Verne). Wells died August 13, 1946, in London.

Representative Works

Brave New World

Huxley's internationally acclaimed work, *Brave New World*, first published in 1932, is a nightmarish vision of what could happen in the future if politics and technology supersedes humanity. Huxley's novel depicts a futuristic, "ideal" world where there is no sickness, disease, or war. However, to achieve this ideal, people are mass-produced in test tubes; social classes are created through genetic manipulations that predetermine a person's intelligence and body type; and unwanted emotions are suppressed with soma, a hallucinogenic drug. In this inhuman system, an outsider born of natural means is considered a savage. Critics have noted Huxley's cynicism in the work, and have examined it in context of life during the post-World War I era, when governments sought scientific and technological progress at all costs. The novel ranks with George Orwell's equally disturbing *1984* as one of the great dystopian works of Science Fiction literature.

"The Chronicles of Narnia"

"The Chronicles of Narnia," Lewis's seven-volume Fantasy series, was originally published between 1950 and 1956. The series (which followed a different order than current editions) started with *The Lion, the Witch, and the Wardrobe*, a story about four English schoolchildren who find a portal to Narnia—a parallel Fantasy world—through a wardrobe. In Narnia, they learn they are there to fulfill a prophecy. In the process, they meet fantastical creatures, battle a witch, and witness the Christlike death and resurrection of a lion named Aslan. Christian themes permeate the series. Since their publication, "The Chronicles of Narnia" have found a wide acceptance, especially among young readers. Some critics, however, do not care for the violence in the series, in which might sometimes makes right. Like the works of his contemporary and friend Tolkien, Lewis's books created a new world that inspired later writers.

Frankenstein

Shelley wrote her novel *Frankenstein, or The Modern Prometheus* when she was in her late teens. The story was her entry in a writing contest between herself; her lover, poet Percy Bysshe Shelley; the infamous poet Lord Byron; and John Polidori, who was Byron's doctor. Shelley's work, commonly referred to simply as *Frankenstein*, was published in 1818, and is widely regarded as the first true Science Fiction work for its reliance on scientific, rather than supernatural, methods. The original novel differs greatly from the screen adaptations, which focus on the horrific aspects of the tale. The story details Dr. Frankenstein's scientific experiments to galvanize a mismatched corpse into life. The unnamed monster, lacking a soul, becomes an outcast of society and goes on a vengeful killing spree, finally fleeing to the Arctic North. When Shelley first published the novel in 1818, critics treated it as just another Gothic novel and failed to recognize the depth of the work. Since then, the work has enjoyed a strong critical and popular reception.

The Hobbit

Tolkien's *The Hobbit* was first published in 1937. The story details the adventures of Bilbo, a hobbit (an imaginary creature that exists in Middle-Earth, Tolkien's mythical past world), who has a number of adventures involving other fantastical beings, including dragons, goblins, wizards, elves, and talking animals. The story also introduces a magical ring, which Bilbo finds and which features prominently in Tolkien's sequel trilogy "The Lord of the Rings." Since the publication of the four-volume series, critics and popular readers alike have been fascinated by Tolkien's imaginative tales and literary artistry. The four-volume epic influenced many later Science Fiction and Fantasy writers and also inspired a cult following.

I, Robot

Although Asimov was not the first to write about robots, he revolutionized the method of writing about them. In his early robot short stories, originally published in Science Fiction magazines in the 1940s, Asimov defined and demonstrated the Three Laws of Robotics:

> One, a robot may not injure a human being or, through inaction, allow a human being to come to harm.... Two ... a robot must obey the orders given it by human beings except where such orders would conflict with the First Law.... Three, a robot must protect its own existence as long as such protection does not conflict with the First or Second Laws.

Asimov's robot stories were collected in 1950 in one volume, *I, Robot*, which brought him widespread critical acclaim, mainly for the "Three Laws," which were accepted and used by many other Science Fiction writers. Critics praised the ethical example that Asimov set with the laws, which were so influential that many assumed they would be used as a basis for future robotics design and production.

The Martian Chronicles

The Martian Chronicles, a short story collection first published in 1950, made Bradbury famous, and was one of the first Science Fiction works to garner positive critical attention. Although many critics regard Bradbury as one of the best living Science Fiction writers, Science Fiction purists note that much of his "Science Fiction" work, including *The Martian Chronicles*—which features a Mars blatantly different than what science has revealed—is really Fantasy. The stories detail repeated efforts made by humans to colonize Mars, and feature space travel, robots, and other scientific scenarios. However, it is the emotional depth, not the scientific setting or plot, that distinguishes the work. The chilling blend of future reality and Fantasy in the story collection earned Bradbury respect from critics and popular readers alike. Unlike many of his pro-science contemporaries, Bradbury is against too much scientific and technological development at the expense of humanity, a fear that he expresses in *The Martian Chronicles*.

Isaac Asimov

Slaughterhouse Five

Vonnegut's *Slaughterhouse Five* draws on his experiences as a witness to the 1945 firebombing of the German city of Dresden. Vonnegut's main character, Billy Pilgrim, escapes the horror of these memories by traveling through time and space to visit the planet Tralfamadore. It is here that he relives the good moments in his life. Whenever he is faced with the horrors of war, Pilgrim remarks, "so it goes," a seemingly impartial phrase that resounds in the reader's mind, creating a feeling that death is inevitable. Originally published in 1969, the book was a hit with its Vietnam-era audience, who identified with the war issues the novel raised. The novel was well-received by critics, which was rare for a Science Fiction novel at the time. Although Vonnegut does not like to be called a Science Fiction writer, novels like *Slaughterhouse Five* have helped bring positive critical attention to the Science Fiction field.

Stranger in a Strange Land

Heinlein's *Stranger in a Strange Land*, first published in 1961, was Science Fiction's first bestseller. With its controversial exploration of human philosophy, religion, and sociology—as opposed to technology—it was a striking departure from his previous novels and from other Science Fiction novels. In the book, Valentine Michael Smith, a human raised by Martians, returns to Earth and experiences human culture as an outsider. With demonstrations of his paranormal powers given to him by the Martians, he becomes a messiah-like figure and inspires the establishment of a religious movement. The novel embraces the supernatural and so is perhaps Fantasy, but it caused a major upheaval in the Science Fiction world, and greatly influenced future Science Fiction writers. It was received with enthusiasm by members of the 1960s counterculture, who recognized and emulated its message of free love. It was not loved by early critics, many of whom labeled Heinlein a fascist for his radical ideas.

The Time Machine: An Invention

The first of many Science Fiction novels that would make him famous, Wells's *The Time Machine: An Invention*, commonly referred to simply as *The Time Machine*, was published in 1895. Wells drew on the evolutionary theory he had studied to tell of a future, more than 800,000 years hence, in which humans have evolved into two separate species. The attractive and ignorant Eloi, descended from humanity's upper class, become food for the working-class, ape-like Morlocks, who live underground. The time traveler who witnesses this then travels thirty million years into the future, witnessing the death of the Sun and the subsequent death of life on Earth. Critics in Wells's time regarded *The Time Machine* as a brilliant work, and later critics and popular audiences agree. Although both Wells and Jules Verne are considered fathers of modern Science Fiction, Wells and his unique literary inventions like time travel have generally been considered more influential.

Twenty Thousand Leagues under the Sea

Verne's novels in his "Extraordinary Journeys" series, particularly *Twenty Thousand Leagues under the Sea*, have delighted international audiences for more than a century. First published in 1870 in serial form in a French magazine, *Twenty Thousand Leagues under the Sea* details the adventures of Captain Nemo on the submarine *Nautilus*. Although many regard Verne as a predictor of scientific inventions, most of his futuristic ideas—like the submarine in *Twenty Thousand Leagues under the Sea*—were extrapolated either from history or from reading current scientific research. Many of Jules Verne's books, including *Twenty Thousand Leagues under the Sea*, were inaccurately translated into English from Verne's native French. Consequently many outside of the Science Fiction field regarded Verne as just a children's writer until more recent translations revealed the literary depth of his works.

Themes

Science and the Supernatural

Science Fiction often reflects the time in which it is written. So it is that in the early twentieth century, when society was still heavily focused on technological innovation through science and industry, stories were often exploratory in nature. These stories were usually dominated by natural sciences like physics and astronomy, which often manifested themselves plot devices like spaceships or evolution. These plot devices were often incorporated into tales about humanity's future or alien races on other worlds. In the more metaphysical 1960s, however, books like Heinlein's *Stranger in a Strange Land* experimented with pseudosciences (theories or practices considered to be without scientific foundation). A good example is when Heinlein's *Stranger in a Strange Land* protagonist, a human given paranormal abilities by the Martians, is first asked to demonstrate his telekinetic powers: "'Mike, will you please, without touching it, lift that ash tray a foot above the desk?' . . . The ash tray raised, floated above the desk."

Many Science Fiction purists prefer stories that employ "hard" sciences, and some maintain that pseudoscientific elements like telekinesis marks a work as Fantasy. The same is generally true of magic, which is often incorporated into Fantasy works like Tolkien's *The Hobbit*. When Gandalf, the wizard, is surprised by goblins, he uses his magical powers to defend himself: "there was a terrible flash like lightning in the cave, a smell like gunpowder, and several of them fell dead." In the imaginary realm of Fantasy, however, wizards are not the only ones with magical powers. Sometimes objects contain special powers as Bilbo discovers when he finds a mysterious ring: "It seemed that the ring he had was a magic ring: it made you invisible!" Bilbo's supernatural power to turn invisible is not only interesting, it also serves as an important plot device in the novel.

Time

Of all of the themes in Science Fiction and Fantasy, the manipulation of time has been one of the most frequently used. Most Science Fiction or

Media Adaptations

- *Brave New World* was released as an audio book in 1998. It was published by Audio Partners and read by Michael York.
- Four of the books from Lewis's "The Chronicles of Narnia" series were made into award-winning television shows by BBC Television. *The Lion, the Witch and the Wardrobe* (1988) was directed by Marilyn Fox. *Prince Caspian* (1989), *The Voyage of the "Dawn Treader"* (1989), and *The Silver Chair* (1990) were all directed by Alex Kirby. The series is also available as a boxed set.
- Director James Whale's classic, *Frankenstein*, was released as a film in 1931 by Universal Studios, and starred Colin Clive as Dr. Frankenstein and Boris Karloff as his monster. The movie is available on VHS or DVD from Universal Studios Home Video. The DVD contains many special features, including the original theatrical trailer, commentary by film historian Rudy Behlmer, production notes, a documentary (*The Frankenstein Files: How Hollywood Made a Monster*), and archival photos.
- *Frankenstein* has seen many permutations on film, including Kenneth Branagh's *Mary Shelley's Frankenstein*, released in 1994 and starring Branagh and Robert De Niro. Humorous adaptations of the Frankenstein story include Mel Brooks's *Young Frankenstein* (1974) with Gene Wilder, Peter Boyle, and Marty Feldman.
- *The Hobbit* was released as an audio book from Recorded Books in 2001, and was read by Rob Inglis. The work was also adapted as an animated film in 1978.
- *The Lord of the Rings: The Fellowship of the Ring*, the first of the "Lord of the Rings" trilogy, was made into a blockbuster hit movie and released in December 2001. It was directed by Peter Jackson and stars Elijah Wood as Frodo the hobbit. Jackson actually filmed the entire "Lord of the Rings" trilogy at once with each of the three movies scheduled to be released a year apart from each other.
- *The Martian Chronicles*, adapted as a television miniseries in 1980, was directed by Michael Anderson, and featured Roddy McDowell as Father Stone, Darren McGavin as Sam Parkhill, and Bernie Casey as Major Jeff Spender. It is available on video from USA Video.
- *Slaughterhouse Five* was released as a film in 1972 by Universal Pictures. Directed by George Roy Hill, it featured Michael Sacks as Billy Pilgrim. It is available on VHS or DVD from Image Entertainment.
- *The Time Machine*, which was released as a film in 1960 by Galaxy Films and Metro-Goldwyn-Mayer (MGM), was directed by George Pal and featured Rod Taylor as the time traveler. It is available on VHS or DVD from Warner Home Video. The DVD contains a behind-the-scenes documentary, *The Time Machine: The Journey Back*, hosted by Taylor, along with co-stars Alan Young and Whit Bissell.
- *Twenty Thousand Leagues under the Sea* was released as a silent film in 1916. It was directed by Stuart Paton and featured Allen Holubar as Captain Nemo. It is available on DVD from Image Entertainment. Walt Disney Pictures produced a movie version in 1954, starring Kirk Douglas as Ned Land and James Mason as Captain Nemo.

Fantasy stories take place in another time, either the past or the future. In some cases, as in Wells's influential novel *The Time Machine*, the protagonist travels in a machine, which physically takes him either backward or forward through time, the fourth dimension. Says the time traveler, "I am afraid I cannot convey the peculiar sensations of time travelling. They are excessively unpleasant."

Other forms of traveling through time, such as near-light-speed space travel, are more physically pleasant for the traveler. Following Albert Einstein's theory of relativity, Science Fiction writers have created a host of spaceships capable of traveling near the speed of light. Theoretically, as a ship like this approaches the speed of light, time will slow down for the ship's passengers, so that they will age less quickly than those who remain at the point where the ship started. Joe Haldeman demonstrated the potential emotional and psychological ramifications of this technology in his book *The Forever War*, in which elite soldiers retain their youth by traveling at near-light-speeds throughout the universe, chasing an elusive enemy.

In the book's conclusion, the soldier protagonist, Mandella, finally returns to his planet of origin, where he finds out that "the war ended 221 years ago." An even bigger surprise is that Mandella's lover, a fellow soldier who was separated from him by space and time during the war, left a note for him 250 years ago. However, the note includes detailed instructions on how his lover is manipulating space and time to try to meet him while they are both still alive and young.

> So I'm on a relativistic shuttle, waiting for you. All it does is go out five light years and come back . . . very fast. Every ten years I age about a month. So if you're on schedule and still alive, I'll only be twenty-eight when you get here. Hurry!

However, some Science Fiction and Fantasy writers avoid the issue of time travel altogether and choose to simply begin their stories in the future or past.

Salvation and Destruction

From the very beginning of Science Fiction, most writers have expressed one of two diametrically opposed ideas concerning the development of science and technology—it will save humanity or it will destroy it. Many of the works that have received favorable criticism or which reign as "classics" fall into the latter group. Perhaps it is because of their darker qualities that these works stand out from the others; Science Fiction has always been strongest when it issues warnings. Readers need look no further than Verne and Wells. Verne's "Extraordinary Journeys" novels tell predominantly positive tales about man's use of the machine to explore and conquer the unknown. However, it is Wells and his dark tales of scientific progress gone bad that most later Science Fiction writers claim is the stronger influence. This focus on dark, sometimes apocalyptic visions had its heyday in the years after World War II, following the advent of the atomic bomb, when the end of civilization was a distinct possibility.

One of the most chilling expressions of the global destruction idea takes place in Orson Scott Card's *Ender's Game*. Throughout the novel, a genius child trains, using military war simulation games in space. At the end of the story, after he has successfully completed a simulated mission in which he obliterates the alien enemy's home planet, both Ender and the reader learn the last battle was real. Without his knowledge, Ender has coordinated an interstellar attack on the aliens' home planet. The sense of despair in Ender, as he comes to realize how the military tricked him into launching a weapon with a destructive power exponentially greater than nuclear weapons, is almost palpable: "they were real ships that he had fought with and real ships he had destroyed. And a real world that he had blasted into oblivion." This is the dark stuff of which some of the best Science Fiction is made.

Style

Utopia and Dystopia

A utopia is a literary form that features an idealistic imaginary society. In most cases, these ideals are unattainable. The author writes about this imaginary place not because he or she hopes to achieve this ideal but because the author hopes to inspire debate about the issues expressed in the work and so bring about social change. In Science Fiction, writers have in turn commented on the unattainable quality of utopias by writing dystopias—visions of a future society that, in striving to achieve an ideal, instead becomes a nightmare. The two most famous Science Fiction examples of dystopias are Huxley's *Brave New World* and Orwell's *1984*.

In Huxley's bleak future, the dystopian society has achieved its goal of eliminating sickness, disease, and war, but in the process it has sacrificed much of what makes humanity human. People are genetically engineered to fit into a certain social class and follow a uniform way of life, and any abnormal or creative behavior is suppressed through drugs. In one of the final scenes, after a human born of natural means attempts to stage a revolt against the system, he meets with one of the world government leaders, who explains why they have sacrificed many human interests, including religion, for technological progress: "Call it the fault of civilization. God isn't compatible with machinery and scientific medicine and universal happiness. You must make your choice."

At least in Huxley's vision, the brainwashed citizens themselves are happy. Not so in *1984*. In this society, fear and paranoia are what motivate the citizens to conform to the government's demands. Politics rule, and people are wise to remember, as many posters in the society state, "Big Brother Is Watching You." The book's protagonist, Winston Smith, is unfortunate enough to attempt a revolt against Big Brother, which results in Smith's being mentally and physically destroyed by the totalitarian regime.

Description

Science Fiction by its very nature incorporates some form of scientific description in its tales. In some works, such as Asimov's *I, Robot* stories that examine the use of robots in human society, the science is meticulously explained as an integral part of the plot. Asimov writes, "Inside the thin platinum-plated 'skin' of the globe was a positronic brain, in whose delicately unstable structure were enforced calculated neuronic paths." This robot brain, like a human's, fits "snugly into the cavity in the skull of the robot." Throughout the stories, the robots' "thinking" processes feature prominently in the plot.

Other Science Fiction stories, however, incorporate minor descriptions of technologies that are not central to the story's plot. For example, in Ursula K. Le Guin's *The Left Hand of Darkness*, the human ambassador sent to the planet Gethen, which is light years away from his planet, demonstrates how he can communicate across the distance nearly instantaneously with his ansible communicator. "The principle it works on ... is analogous in some ways to gravity.... What it does ... is produce a message at any two points simultaneously." The king to whom the ambassador shows the device is not impressed and does not pay much attention to this technology. Nor do Le Guin's readers. Although the communicator is an interesting device, the real story in the book is the lack of gender bias due to unique biology that Le Guin creates for her alien society.

Setting

One of the most important choices Science Fiction and Fantasy authors make when creating stories is the setting. Because most Science Fiction and Fantasy works involve "rules" established through generations of other writers—such as Asimov's famous "Three Laws of Robotics"—the choice of a setting can introduce potential constraints. While writers sometimes bend or break those rules, deviating from them requires the formulation of a convincing and compelling alternative.

The choice of a setting is also one of the indicators of the type of tale the story is intended to be—Science Fiction or Fantasy. Although there is much debate over what distinguishes the two genres, Card, in his book *How to Write Science Fiction and Fantasy*, offers one possible definition based on his own experiences as a Science Fiction and Fantasy writer: "A rustic setting always suggests fantasy; to suggest Science Fiction, you need

Topics for Further Study

- There is no commonly accepted definition for what determines a hard science from a soft science, although many use these terms. Research some of the many sciences that Science Fiction authors have written about. Write a short report that divides your research into what you think are hard and soft sciences.
- One of the common beliefs about Science Fiction authors is that they intend to predict the future, and some works have been criticized when they have not accurately done so. Find three technologies that were correctly predicted by Science Fiction authors. Compare the fictional accounts with the real technologies, and write a paper explaining how and why each technology has had either a positive or negative impact on society.
- Many Fantasy authors begin their tales by creating a map of the imaginary world they are creating. Draw a map detailing an imaginary world of your own creation and label all of the major geographic features—mountains, forests, bodies of water, and towns. Write a three-page description of your world, describing its inhabitants, history, politics, and economics.

sheet metal and plastic. You need *rivets*." Especially since the New Wave of Science Fiction and Fantasy, which appeared in the 1960's with seminal authors such Heinlein and Harlan Ellison, a definition of Science Fiction and Fantasy by their settings is no longer so easily applied.

Movement Variations

Science fiction had a profound effect on the development of motion pictures. From almost the very beginnings of film, Science Fiction movies have pushed the envelope of special effects, starting with the first real Science Fiction film, George Méliès's, *A Trip to the Moon* in 1902.

Since then, Science Fiction films have had a hit-or-miss history, and many literary classics have been made into highly inaccurate adaptations that sacrificed plot for special effects. In 1926, Fritz Lang released his monumental *Metropolis*, a nightmarish vision of a potential future in which the city is large and impersonal and the working-class is intended to be replaced by a new race of robots.

In 1963, the British Science Fiction television series *Dr. Who* began its unprecedented, 26-season, 695-episode run. In 1966, Gene Roddenberry's *Star Trek* debuted in the United States to little fanfare. Eventually, Roddenberry's characters and ideas inspired several related television series, a host of movies, countless book tie-ins, and a widespread cultural movement of sorts. The terms Trekkie and Trekker continue to be used to refer to ardent *Star Trek* fans. The 1999 film *Galaxy Quest* is a good-natured parody of *Star Trek* fandom.

With Stanley Kubrick's 1968 critically-acclaimed adaptation of Arthur C. Clarke's *2001: A Space Odyssey*, Science Fiction films gained new respect. The release of George Lucas's original *Star Wars* trilogy in the 1970s and early 1980s helped to further revitalize the Science Fiction film and inspired widespread devotion reminiscent of the *Star Trek* phenomenon. Lucas has gone on in the early twenty-first century to create a popular trilogy prequel to the original *Star Wars* films.

In the 1980s and 1990s, several influential films were released. *Blade Runner*, a film loosely based on Philip K. Dick's novel *Do Androids Dream of Electric Sheep?*, is one of few literary adaptations to film at that time. Both the film and author acquired a cult following as a result of the film. Original Science Fiction films of note during the last two decades of the twentieth century include Steven Spielberg's blockbuster *E. T.* (re-released in an updated version in 2002), James Cameron's *Terminator* movies, and the Science Fiction comedy film series *Back to the Future*. In the early years of the twenty-first century, Science Fiction films and television shows—many of which continue to create groundbreaking new special effects—are alive and well.

Historical Context

Science Fiction has its original roots in the nineteenth century, a time when the world experienced an explosion in new inventions and an appreciation of science and scientific methods as a means of progress. With the advent of the daguerreotype (the precursor to photography) in the first half of the century, humans harnessed the power to record images quickly and accurately. This technology is further explored with the advent of motion pictures at the end of the nineteenth century.

As science and technology grew in popularity, its practitioners challenged established thought. With the publication of Charles Darwin's *On the Origins of Species* in 1859, the idea of man as a being of singular importance in the universe is shattered. With the help of geologists who date the Earth as much older than suggested by the Bible, Darwin's theories propose that humans and apes share an ancestry.

The early years of the twentieth century introduced new transportation technologies both on land in the form of gasoline-powered automobiles and in the sky in the form of airplanes. World War I introduced new weapons technologies, including tanks that are first used on battlefields in 1917. These new technologies helped fuel the ideas behind Science Fiction and Fantasy literature, which exploded in the 1920s with Hugo Gernsback's publication of several Science Fiction and Fantasy pulp magazines—named for the cheap wood pulp on which they were printed, although some used the term to indicate a lack of quality.

In 1926, American scientist Robert H. Goddard tested the world's first liquid-fuel rocket, the advent of which eventually triggered a race in the 1950s and 1960s between the United States and the Soviet Union to develop rockets for propelling weapons and space shuttles. On October 31, 1938, Orson

Compare & Contrast

- **1900s:** The Wright Brothers make their historic flight at Kitty Hawk, North Carolina, proving to the world that humans can fly.

  1940s: German-born scientist Wernher von Braun develops the V-2 rocket for Adolph Hitler, envisioning it as a means for space travel. Hitler, however, uses the rocket as a weapon during World War II, so von Braun defects to America, where he shares his knowledge with American scientists—who follow von Braun's lead and begin to apply it to space exploration.

  Today: Having experienced both extraordinary success and tragic failure, the National Aeronautics and Space Administration (NASA) continues to plan and send exploratory missions into space.

- **1900s:** Einstein proves the existence of atoms.

  1940s: The United States is the first to harness the power of the atom and demonstrates the awesome, destructive power of nuclear warfare when it drops atomic bombs on two Japanese cities, Hiroshima and Nagasaki, effectively ending World War II.

  Today: After the breakup of the former Soviet Union and the end of the Cold War, many of the nuclear weapons from the world's former superpower fall into the hands of independent terrorist groups. In 2001, after an attack on the World Trade Center in New York City that launched a war on terrorism, the American public's fear shifts to biological weapons and suicide bombings.

- **1900s:** In 1901, Italian physicist and inventor Guglielmo Marconi receives the first long-distance wireless message in Morse Code, which traveled from England to Newfoundland almost instantaneously.

  1940s: Bell Labs makes the first demonstration of its transistor, which amplifies electric current in an efficient and cheap manner. The first transistors are used in telephones.

  Today: With the advent of modern wireless technology, digital data from telephones and computers can be transmitted instantly to and from anywhere in the world by increasingly smaller devices that rely on microprocessors—computer chips that contain millions of microscopic transistors.

Welles made media and literary history by dramatizing H. G. Wells's *The War of the Worlds* on the radio. Told in the style of a newscast, hundreds of thousands of listeners mistook the story of a Martian invasion as real, and widespread panic ensued as Americans believed they were under attack.

Also in 1938, John W. Campbell, an American editor, took the reigns of the Science Fiction magazine *Astounding Stories*, which he later renamed *Astounding Science Fiction*. The magazine, which placed more emphasis on quality than other pulps, quickly distinguished itself and helped to nurture the careers of many talented, new Science Fiction writers. It effectively launched the golden age of Science Fiction, a period that lasted until a few years after the end of World War II.

When World War II began in 1939, the world experienced paper shortages that affected the publication of Science Fiction and Fantasy magazines. Publishers cut magazines that did not have strong circulations. *Astounding Stories* was one of the few that survived, and its issues, which contained stories from such heavyweights as Heinlein and Asimov, helped to define modern Science Fiction. In 1945, the United States dropped the first atomic bombs on Hiroshima and Nagasaki, two Japanese cities, effectively ending World War II.

In the 1960s and 1970s, amidst the New Wave of Science Fiction and Fantasy, a period marked by experimental writing in the field, more female Science Fiction writers began to publish under their own names. The predominantly male readership of Science Fiction works had not allowed for many works by women writers previous to this time. Those women who were published often wrote under male pseudonyms or used intentionally gender-ambiguous pen names, such as C. J. Cherryh or Leigh Brackett. The publication of Ursula K. Le Guin's *The Left Hand of Darkness* in 1969 was a direct response to the bias of the genre. In the story, a human ambassador visits a far world that has ideologically and biologically evolved to the point where gender issues are nonexistent.

The advent of the first computer, ENIAC, in 1946, had the greatest effect on modern society. Although Science Fiction writers had predicted that robots would become the most important technology in future societies, it was the computer that won out in the end. At the beginning of the twenty-first century, as new technologies—most of them based on computer technology—are introduced, Science Fiction and Fantasy writers continue to react to them in their works, reworking themes that have been used in Science Fiction since the nineteenth century.

Critical Overview

Science Fiction has always faced three problems from a critical standpoint: definition, history, and literary reputation. First, there is the two-part question of what is Science Fiction and how does it differ from Fantasy? As Frederick Andrew Lerner observes in his *Modern Science Fiction and the American Literary Community*, "the Science Fiction professionals themselves—writers, historians, and critics whose careers are closely associated with Science Fiction—have reached no consensus." Perhaps the only definition that everyone can agree on is that given by Harry Harrison in his article "The Term Defined": "The definition of science fiction is: Science fiction is."

Science Fiction is often referred to as a form of Fantasy. Critic Julius Kagarlitski maintains in his essay "Realism and Fantasy" that "all fantasy is 'scientific' in the sense that it is engendered by that type of thinking whose mission it was to determine the real natural laws of the world and to transform it." Kagarlitski also notes that "the history of fantasy is a very long one," unlike Science Fiction, which most critics agree has only been around for the last couple of centuries.

The problem of defining Science Fiction's history is steeped in controversy. Although some critics and historians claim that writings several hundreds of years old are Science Fiction, the leading argument—and the one that has seen the most acceptance—was offered by British Science Fiction author Brian Aldiss. In his book on the history of Science Fiction, *Trillion Year Spree*, Aldiss maintains that Shelley's *Frankenstein* is the first true Science Fiction work due to its reliance on scientific methods. "Frankenstein's ambitions bear fruit only when he throws away his old reference books from a pre-scientific age and gets down to some research in the laboratory," says Aldiss.

The arguments of definition and history are often laid aside, however, when it comes to discussing the literary merits of Science Fiction and Fantasy. Although some very notable authors like Wells and Verne wrote critically acclaimed Science Fiction works, it has taken a while for Science Fiction and Fantasy works to gain acceptance in the mainstream. This is due in large part to Gernsback and his publication of Science Fiction and Fantasy pulp magazines. The same magazines that helped increase popular readership in the field, also served to distance critics.

It has been through the works of specific writers like Bradbury and Vonnegut that the genre has been able to transcend its pulp image and garner the positive attention of critics. Works like *The Martian Chronicles* and particularly *Slaughterhouse Five* have also found favor with academia and are often taught in the classroom. Jack Williamson noted this trend in his 1974 article "SF in the Classroom": "From a standing start only a dozen years ago, Science Fiction has now become a popular and reasonably respectable academic subject."

This trend continues today. As for the mainstream critics, they tend to favor the types of stories they always have: the ones that transcend the genre of Science Fiction and illustrate more universal themes of humanity.

Criticism

Ryan D. Poquette

Poquette has a bachelor's degree in English and specializes in writing about literature. In the following essay, Poquette explores the similarities and differences among Science Fiction and Fantasy works, by examining three aspects of Wells's The Time Machine *and Tolkien's* The Hobbit.

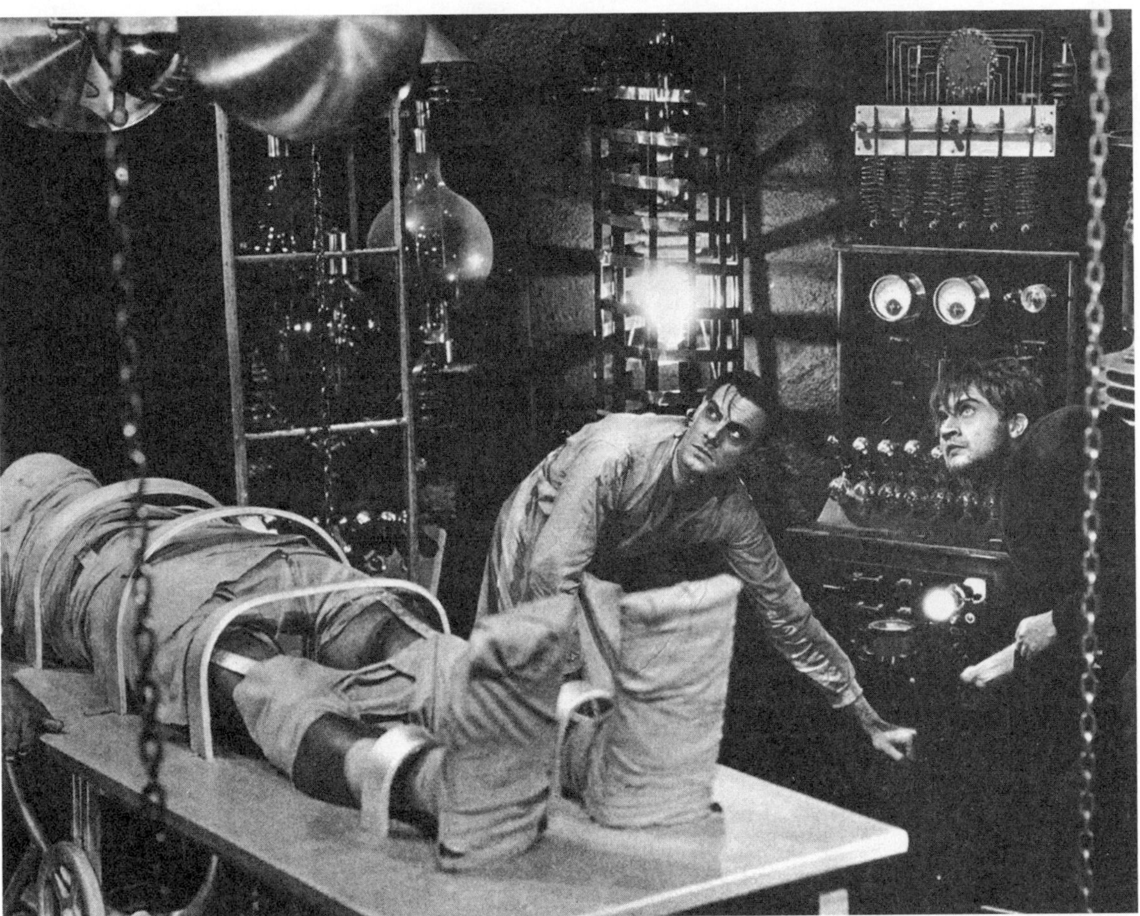

The Monster (Boris Karloff) is brought to life by Dr. Frankenstein (Colin Clive) and his assistant Fritz (Dwight Frye) in the 1931 film Frankenstein, *based on Mary Shelley's novel*

With the introduction of pulp genre magazines like *Weird Tales* and *Amazing Stories* in the 1920s, modern Science Fiction and Fantasy stories were lumped together, with no attempt to define or separate each genre. Although many critics have since tried to define each genre, no consensus has been reached, and Science Fiction and Fantasy are often referred to as one field. This is true in the popular sphere as well. Orson Scott Card (who is a Science Fiction and Fantasy writer himself) notes in his book *How to Write Science Fiction and Fantasy*, "in most bookstores, fantasy and science fiction are lumped together in the same group of shelves, alphabetized by author with no attempt to separate one from the other." However, one can make a possible distinction by examining the *specific* ways that Science Fiction and Fantasy writers use *general* ideas and techniques shared by both genres. By exploring the general similarities between Wells's *The Time Machine* and Tolkien's *The Hobbit*—two works that helped to define the modern Science Fiction and Fantasy genres, respectively—these specific differences can be identified.

The first general similarity between the two genres is in their views of science and technology. Both genres tend to take a negative view toward science and technology. In fact, much of Fantasy literature is, by its very nature, anti-technology. Fantasy authors like Tolkien often stage their tales in a rustic environment that hearkens back to a pre-industrialized past and is generally derived from a nostalgic blend of human history and mythology. In some Fantasy, however, the feelings against industrial progress are more pronounced. Take this passage from *The Hobbit*, in which Tolkien is discussing the goblins, one of many evil races in the book: "It is not unlikely that they invented some of the machines that have since troubled the world, especially the ingenious devices for killing large

What Do I Study Next?

- *Fantastic Voyages: Learning Science through Science Fiction Films* (1993), by Leroy Dubeck, Suzanne Moshier, and Judith E. Boss, uses scenes from classic and recent Science Fiction films to illustrate scientific principles of physics, astronomy, and biology, and details how the films either adhere to or violate these principles.
- Dick Jude's *Fantasy Art Masters: The Best Fantasy and SF Art Worldwide* (1999) features samples from some of the world's most acclaimed Fantasy and Science Fiction artists. The book also includes interviews with the artists, who reveal how they created some of their favorite creations and relate what it is like working in the industry.
- *Blast Off! Rockets, Robots, Ray Guns, and More from the Golden Age of Space*, by S. Mark Young, Steve Duin, and Mike Richardson, is a detailed exploration of the toys created during the 1930s through the 1950s. Published in 2001, the book examines the history of these unique collector's items, which include such memorable Science Fiction characters as Buck Rogers and Flash Gordon. It includes reprints of original advertisements, comic-strip and pulp-magazine art, and even original packaging and instructions from toys produced all over the world.
- Joseph Campbell's classic *The Hero with a Thousand Faces* (1949) attempts to discover one underlying story that unifies all of the world's mythologies through examination of the hero tales from around the world. Campbell's ideas inspired many later Science Fiction and Fantasy writers, most notably George Lucas, the creator of the *Star Wars* films.
- Richard Rickitt's *Special Effects* (2000) gives a thorough history of special effects, which are used mainly in Science Fiction, Fantasy, and horror films. Rickitt examines everything from trick photography to computer-generated effects, using examples from early films, such as George Méliès's *A Trip to the Moon* (1902), to more recent Science Fiction films, such as *The Matrix* (1999).
- Scott McCloud's *Understanding Comics* studies the history, philosophy, and mechanics of comics, which have been around for more than three thousand years and which have included notable characters from Science Fiction. Written and drawn entirely in the form of a comic strip, McCloud visually demonstrates the ideas that he discusses, drawing on scientific concepts like space, time, and motion in the process.

---

numbers of people at once." By associating this evil race with troublesome machines—a clear sign of industry—Tolkien is implying that technological progress itself is evil. It is particularly telling that Tolkien wrote this story as humanity was gearing up for World War II, during which a number of killing machines were invented. As Michael Wood notes about Tolkien's works in *New Society*:

> The enemy is science, or rather the complacency of science, the self-satisfaction of people who think they can explain everything, who have no time for myths, for forms of truth which will not fit within a narrow rationalism.

Unlike *The Hobbit*, the anti-technology view in *The Time Machine* is not apparent at first. In the beginning of the novel, the time traveler is hopeful about science and technology as he displays the model of his time machine to his assembled guests—who use scientific arguments to discuss the prospect of time travel. Says the medical man, one of the time traveler's guests, "if Time is really only a fourth dimension of Space, why is it, and why has it always been regarded as something different? And why cannot we move in Time as we move about in the other dimensions of Space?" Later, when the time traveler has returned from his journey into the future, he explains to his guests what he had hoped to find there. "I had always anticipated that the people of the year Eight Hundred and Two Thousand odd would be incredibly in front of us in knowledge, art, everything." But as the time traveler soon sees, human society has evolved from upper and lower classes into two separate species, both of which have regressed physically and mentally to the point where they have lost their humanity. The time traveler, a man from the nineteenth century, possesses more knowledge than these distant descendants, a fact that taints his view of the inevitable future.

In his history of Science Fiction, *Trillion Year Spree*, Brian Aldiss discusses the sense of despair inherent in *The Time Machine*: "Its sceptical view of the present, and its pessimistic view of the future of mankind—and of life on Earth—challenged most of the cosy ideas of progress, as well as the new imperialism, then current." Wells set the pace for many other Science Fiction writers, who imparted this dual idea of initial hope and crushing despair into their own works.

Another area in which general parallels between Fantasy and Science Fiction can be drawn is in the setting. Both Science Fiction and Fantasy works usually involve a setting that is something contrary to the writer's current reality, an "other" reality. The majority of Science Fiction works, like *The Time Machine*, take place in a future reality, which is often drastically different in either a distinctly positive or negative sense. As Aldiss notes, "Utopianism or its opposite is present in every vision of the future. There is little point in inventing a future state unless it contrasts in some way with our present one." In Wells's case, the future world his time traveler encounters is a nightmarish future Earth, where the ape-like Morlocks, the descendants of the working class who dwell underground, tend the pretty but naïve Eloi like crops. The reader, like the time traveler, is drawn to detest the Morlocks, who feed on the Eloi.

While many Science Fiction "other" realities take place in the future, Fantasy works like Tolkien's Middle-Earth are constructed as part of the mythical past. Here, Tolkien also portrays a nightmarish vision of Earth, although his is much richer than Wells's portrayal. While Morlocks served as the detested race in Wells's novel, Tolkien offers trolls, goblins, and the imaginary beast that is found in much mythology and Fantasy—the dragon. The dragon is especially nasty in *The Hobbit*. After Bilbo narrowly escapes being burned from the fire that the dragon spews from its mouth, Bilbo hides where the dragon cannot get to him or his dwarf companions. The dragon, Smaug, in a fit of rage, instead takes out his fiery anger on the nearby Lake-Town, the inhabitants of which have done nothing to the dragon. Tolkien describes Smaug's many destructive passes over the town, then gives Smaug's next thought: "Soon he would set all the shoreland woods ablaze and wither every field and pasture. Just now he was enjoying the sport of town-baiting." Fortunately for the town members, a bird carries Bilbo's news of the dragon's weakness to the town, and the dragon is slain.

A third area in which general similarities can be found between Science Fiction and Fantasy is the use of the quest, or journey, as a narrative structure. In journey stories, a protagonist travels to somewhere else, has an adventure, and is transformed. In Science Fiction, many of these stories have followed the trend set by works like Wells's *The Time Machine*, in which the traveler is a willing participant. In fact, in the time traveler's case, he travels on his journey through an invention of his own making. At the end of his first adventure through time, the time traveler has indeed changed. He has seen the bleak, far future, which saddens him, but he refuses to give up. In the end, he makes another journey, to an age not quite so far in the future, where he can try to warn people before they make the same mistakes that lead to the future he has seen. However, at the end of the book, after three years, the time traveler has still not returned, and Wells ends the book on an ambiguous note. The reader never finds out the conclusion of the time traveler's journey, or how it ultimately transforms him.

In fantastic journeys—many of which follow the ages-old storytelling form of the heroic quest—the journey's beginning, end, and outcome are clearly defined. The protagonists in Fantasy stories do not always choose to begin their journeys. In *The Hobbit*, Bilbo does not ask for his quest to rescue the treasure hoard from the dragon. At the beginning of the tale, Bilbo is happy with his quiet life in the Shire, and does not want anyone to change that. It is only with the intervention of the wizard Gandalf that Bilbo is called to go on the quest. Gandalf asks Bilbo outright to do it, but Bilbo refuses: "We are plain quiet folk and have no use for adventures. Nasty disturbing uncomfortable things! Make you late for dinner!" Gandalf leaves but, unbeknownst to Bilbo, the wizard marks Bilbo's front door to indicate that he is available as a burglar-for-hire for a group of dwarves.

After the dwarves start to arrive and Bilbo's world begins to tumble, Gandalf reveals his stunt.

"Bilbo does indeed undergo a transformation, proving himself worthy of Gandalf's prophetic praise. Unlike Wells's time traveler, the transformation is a distinctly positive one, and the book ends on a clear upbeat note."

At this point something happens that makes Bilbo change his mind about going on the journey. His "Took" side, the adventurous line of his ancestors, gets offended when the dwarves say he could not handle the adventure. As Tolkien writes about Bilbo, "He suddenly felt he would go without bed and breakfast to be thought fierce." For a hobbit, who is constantly thinking about food, this is a brave admission and is one of the first signs that Bilbo has "more in him than you guess, and a deal more than he has any idea of himself," as Gandalf puts it to the dwarves.

Throughout the quest, Bilbo slowly begins to trust his instincts and risks his life to save the dwarves from being eaten by giant spiders, imprisoned by elves, and finally, consumed by their own greed while trying to hoard the dragon's treasure. Bilbo does indeed undergo a transformation, proving himself worthy of Gandalf's prophetic praise. Unlike Wells's time traveler, the transformation is a distinctly positive one, and the book ends on a clear upbeat note.

The debate about what constitutes Science Fiction as opposed to Fantasy has been going on for more than a century. Although no consensus has been reached, many publishers label certain books as belonging to either the Science Fiction or Fantasy field, and fans generally know when they are reading one as opposed to the other.

Source: Ryan D. Poquette, Critical Essay on Science Fiction and Fantasy Literature, in *Literary Movements for Students*, The Gale Group, 2003.

Adam Roberts

In the following essay, Roberts explores feminist Science Fiction and the "images of women in science fiction."

> One of the major theoretical projects of the second wave of feminism is the investigation of gender and sexuality as social constructs. . . . The stock conventions of science fiction—time travel, alternate worlds, entropy, relativism, the search for a unified field theory—can be used metaphorically and metonymically as powerful ways of exploring the construction of 'woman'.
>
> (Sarah Lefanu . . .)

Women's science fiction, or feminist science fiction, is a more recent development than the genre as a whole, but today constitutes one of the most exciting and most vigorous aspects of the mode, in terms both of actual SF texts and of criticism. It is also, following on from the previous chapter, a development that dates primarily from the 1960s, one that has grown up in dialogue with the more male-oriented SF of the Pulps and the Golden Age. Examining some of the features of women's SF writing, then, allows us to interrogate many aspects of New Wave (the experimental, avant-garde movement in SF that started in the 1960s) and more recent developments in the mode.

After exploring various aspects of the representation of gender concerns in SF, this chapter will close with a reading of Ursula Le Guin's 1969 novel, *The Left Hand of Darkness*. But it is worth noting at the beginning how contentious Le Guin's position is within the body of female SF, as a means of pointing up that 'female SF' is not a straightforwardly or narrowly single quantity. *The Left Hand of Darkness* is one of the acknowledged classics of SF; it won, for instance, both a Hugo and a Nebula award, the two most prestigious awards in SF publishing. But much of the feminist criticism of Le Guin is rather cold, sometimes dismissive, and occasionally outright hostile. Critic Sarah Lefanu finds Le Guin's writing fatally limited, too character-based to be SF at all, and not very well realised as character studies either. Of the characters in *The Left Hand of Darkness* Lefanu asks 'how realistic are [they]? Who remembers what they look like? or what they say? Or feel?' Lefanu prefers SF writer Joanna Russ. Joanna Russ herself thought *The Left Hand of Darkness* a failure, though an honourable one. Jenny Wolmark's *Aliens and Others: Science Fiction, Feminism and Postmodernism* omits Le Guin altogether, and the critic Susan Bassnett, whilst conceding that Le Guin has been 'ex-

Ian McKellen plays Gandalf in the 2001 film adaptation The Lord of the Rings: The Fellowship of the Ring, *based on J. R. R. Tolkien's novel*

tremely popular and successful' for 'both adults and children', none the less points out in Lucie Armitt's edited collection *Where No Man Has Gone Before* that she 'has not always been treated very kindly by those critics who have actually considered her work'. There is a great deal of valuable criticism of SF from a feminist or women's writing point of view. In order to understand why as talented a writer as Le Guin has received such a poor showing in that criticism, and why her novels are so consistently judged in terms of her representation of gender, we need briefly to put her work into context.

One of the reasons why feminist criticism of SF has a radicalism that seems almost old-fashioned when compared with the subtler, more complex feminisms that characterise criticism as a whole is that women are a relatively recent arrival in the realm of SF writing itself. 'Golden Age' SF, the argument goes, was almost exclusively male; it was written by men, purchased by men or boys; its conventions were shaped by the passions and interests of adolescent males, that is to say its focus was on technology as embodied particularly by big, gleaming machines with lots of moving parts, physical prowess, war, two-dimensional male heroes, adventure and excitement. From the dawn of SF through to the end of the 1950s the female audience for SF was tiny, and those women who were interested in reading it did so with a sense of themselves as alienated or at least sidelined spectators. This is to skim swiftly over the surface of a large and complicated subject here, so a certain crudity of generalisation is inevitable; but it cannot be denied that the Golden Age readership of SF was predominantly, even overwhelmingly male; whereas the audience for SF today, particularly in America, is in the majority female. There are two things that account for this shift.

The first was the establishment, slowly at first but then, as it gained in popularity and sales, more rapidly, of a body of SF novels written by women and read in large part by women. This is something that happened particularly in the 1960s and 1970s, and there are three names associated with the success of this new mode. They are: Marion Zimmer Bradley, Andre Norton and Ursula Le Guin. Bradley has written dozens of novels set on a planet called Darkover, the chronicles of which span the world's history from a pre-technological, medievalised culture to a spacefaring technological one. Andre Norton's series of Fantasy novels set on what she calls the *Witch World* provided the first, and one of the most popular, reworkings of the Tolkien style of Fantasy Epic from a female point of view. Ursula Le Guin has not written an on-going series of novels in the SF idiom, as have these other two, but her novels have included some of the most acclaimed works in SF, not only *The Left Hand of Darkness* but also *The Dispossessed* and her Fantasy sequence *Earthsea*. For our purposes the interesting thing about all three of these writers is the way they began by writing male-centred, technological SF derived heavily from the Golden Age conventions, but as their confidence, and audience, grew, each of them shifted her perspective to female-centred studies that explored concerns more crucial to her own life. Marion Zimmer Bradley is one example of this. One of her earliest Darkover books, *Star of Danger*, has a 'Boy's Own' plot about two young lads travelling through a wilderness area of the planet, undergoing a series of adventures whilst on the run from a bandit chief. There are no major female characters in this novel, and virtually no women of any sort. More than this, the protagonist, Larry Montry from Earth, falls under the spell of the unreconstructed machismo of Darkover culture. He meets a young nobleman of that world, Kennard Dalton, after bravely fighting off a gang of toughs. Triumphing in this fight wins Larry respect. Darkovans, or at any rate male Darkovans, find it incomprehensible that people on Earth rely on the police to sort out their difficulties: on Darkover, if an individual is wronged it is that individual's duty to obtain retribution. Earth's is 'a government of laws', but, says Kennard proudly, 'ours is a government of men, because laws can't be anything but the expression of men who make them'. At no point in the novel are the masculinist prejudices of the Darkovian world challenged, or even mentioned without a sort of starry-eyed respect. But a later Darkover novel, *Stormqueen*, is more women-oriented, and marks the feminist evolution of its author's sensibilities. It is set several hundred years before the Darkover of *Star of Danger*, in an age before the technologies of space flight have reached the planet, and it is far more explicit about the perils so macho a society involves for the women who live in it. One character, about to make a sort of marriage of convenience to a powerful noble, explains to her son that 'life is not easy for a woman unprotected'. Without this unwanted marriage, the alternative would be an effective concubinage; 'for me there would be nothing but to be a drudge or a sewing woman'. As the novel progresses, the main character reveals telepathic capacities, known as *laran*, and the book explores the compensations that *laran* offers to women in a brutal and oppressive society. Bradley has talked about her shift of interests. In the introduction to *The Best of Marion Zimmer Bradley*, a collection of her short fiction published in 1985, she said her 'current enthusiasms . . . are Gay Rights and Women's Rights—I think Women's Liberation is the great event of the twentieth century, not Space Exploration. One is a great change in human consciousness; the latter is only predictable technology, and I am bored by technology'.

This emphasis on the affective, the personal, rather than the technological was also the reason for the second significant catalyst from the 1960s, one that introduced a large body of female fans to SF, fans that had previously been put off by the masculinist 'boys and their toys' posturings of Golden Age books. This catalyst was the TV series *Star Trek*. Indeed, although its importance is often underplayed, it seems clear to me that *Star Trek* brought more women to SF than all the other authors mentioned so far put together. It remains a cornerstone of female SF fandom. The success of this syndicated show in the late sixties, particularly amongst a female audience, brought hundreds of thousands of women to the genre. And this was a success based less on the technological or male-ego strands of the show, and had more to do with the way *Star Trek* represented, in the first instance, human interaction and the social dynamic as being at the heart of the SF story; and, in the second instance, and less obviously, because *Trek*, unusually for a 1960s US TV show, was interested in representing difference. The encounter with the alien is at the core of *Star Trek*, and of most SF; and questions of difference, of alien-ness and otherness, were also powerful and relevant to the female perspective on the old patriarchal world. This is why the show built up, and maintains, so large a female audience. Nor is this female audience merely a body of passive viewers; there is a vigorous and wide-ranging body of fanzines and even fan-authored novels based upon the *Star Trek* universe. As Henry Jenkins has exhaustively demonstrated, '*Star Trek* fandom is a predominantly female response to mass media texts, with the majority of fanzines edited by and written by women for a largely female readership'.

It was this issue of difference, where 'alien' becomes an encoding of 'woman', that featured prominently in the work of the 1970s new wave of radical female SF writers. This was a much more populated era of women's SF in terms of the number of women writing SF. But there are three names that crop up again and again in the criticism, so I mention them here: Octavia Butler, Marge Piercy and Joanna Russ. Russ is perhaps the most often cited. Her most famous novel, *The Female Man*, presents a four-fold perspective of women's experience of the world, including a women-only utopian realm called Whileaway. Russ is one of the most committed feminist writers and critics, and *The Female Man* has received a great deal of respectful criticism. But Gwyneth Jones is surely right when she judges this novel a relative failure compared with some others of Russ's fictions. It is set partly on the planet Whileaway where there are no men, only women, and the utopian possibilities of this world are contrasted with the trajectories of female existence on other possible worlds where women are oppressed to one degree or another. Russ has written about all-female societies elsewhere, most notably in the story 'When It Changed', but, as Jones points out, the female society in that story is 'not unreasonably idealised'. The women have the faults and strengths of 'the whole of humanity'. By the time of *The Female Man* the all-woman world 'has been got at. Its inhabitants have become female characters in a feminist science fiction, their vices and virtues bowdlerised and engineered precisely to fit the current demands of sexual politics.' Russ's novel is effectively hijacked by a feminist agenda: '*When It Changed* is feminist fiction, *The Female Man* is feminist satire'.

Of the other names mentioned, Octavia Butler, as a writer both female and black, has an especially acute perspective on issues of 'alien as other.' Her *Xenogenesis* series is examined in Chapter 4 of the present study. Marge Piercy's feminist utopia *Women on the Edge of Time* is often contrasted with *The Left Hand of Darkness* as a 'successful' version of a world without gender. Another name worth introducing at this point, although not one that seems immediately appropriate in a discussion of SF written by women, is James Tiptree Jr. Despite having the first name James, Tiptree has the distinction of having created one of the most celebrated fictional expressions of the constructions of gender, in a short story called 'The Women Men Don't See'. This tale is narrated by a man called Fenton, rather old-fashioned but basically decent, whose blindness to the actual conditions of what it means to be a woman, as opposed to his vague sense of what he *thinks* women are about, is the key point of the story. Indeed, the triumph of Tiptree's narration is the way it captures so precisely the idiom of a certain sort of male consciousness, whilst also using *only* that blinkered male point of view to delineate the women as separate characters. The story opens on a small aeroplane flying down to Mexico.

> I see her first while the Mexicana 727 is barrelling down to Cozumel Island. I came out of the can and lurch into her seat, saying 'Sorry,' at a double female blur. The second blur nods quietly. The younger one in the window seat goes on looking out. I continue down the aisle registering nothing. Zero. I would never have looked at them or thought of them again.

The plane crashes, and the narrator and the two women are forced to fend for themselves. But the story takes a striking turn when space aliens encounter them in the jungle. 'They are tall and white . . . stretching out a long white arm toward Ruth . . . the arm stretches after her. It stretches and stretches. It stretches two yards and stays hanging in the air. Small black things are wriggling from its tip. I look where their faces should be and see black hollow dishes with vertical stripes.' The narrator's response is a male one: full of terror he fires his gun at the aliens. The women are more pragmatic. They announce they are going to leave the planet with them. 'For Christ's sake, Ruth, they're *aliens*,' yells Fenton. 'I'm used to it,' Ruth replies. Ruth's point of view is that the aliens are just as men were on Earth, and that women are used to the marginal existence: 'we survive by ones or twos in the chinks of your world machine'. The aliens themselves, with their weird technology and their satellite-dish faces, seem to embody a particular, technological metaphor for maleness; just as their spaceship, a piece of technology, is no more of a 'world machine' than the machinery of patriarchy. Women's marginal role in this machine-system manages to reverse the woman-as-alien motif. From the perspective of Ruth, a space alien is not more alien than a man.

This is a story, though, celebrated for more than literary reasons. To quote Edward James:

> Robert Silverberg commented that this ['The Women Men Don't See'] was 'a profoundly feminist story told in an entirely masculine manner,' and a few pages earlier in his introduction to the collection which included this story he remarked: 'It has been suggested that Tiptree is female, a theory I find absurd, for there is to me something ineluctably masculine about Tiptree's writing.' It was not just the writing, but the lifestyle. Silverberg noted how Tiptree in a letter had admitted to having worked in a Pentagon basement during the war and to having subsequently 'batted around the jungly parts of the globe.'

> "Women who wished to become involved, as writers or readers, had to assume a certain masculine identity, to become what we might call (after Russ's novel), Female Men."

As James points out, this whole affair is especially involving to 'those interested in the difference between "masculine" and "feminine" writing (like Le Guin and Silverberg himself)', because, of course, James Tiptree Jr was a woman called Alice Sheldon, a fact which finally emerged in 1977. The embarrassment of the more chauvinist SF writers, such as Silverberg or Heinlein, at this admission was met by the delight of the more feminist critics and authors; it seemed to crystallise the ingrained sexism of assumptions governing different sorts of writing, as well as emphasising how alive this issue was. In the fiery heat of 1970s-style feminism, this was a crucial issue.

The Tiptree situation in some senses harked back to an earlier age. I have talked of the 1960s as the time when female SF really increased in popularity, yet, as Sarah Lefanu has noted, the situation was not quite as clearcut as that:

> Science fiction is popularly conceived as male territory, boys' own adventure stories with little to interest a female readership. This is true of the heyday of magazine science fiction, the 1930s and 1940s, but even then there were women writers, like C L Moore and Leigh Brackett.

The difference, she points out, is that such women more often than not 'assumed a male voice and non-gender-specific names to avoid prejudice on the part of editors and readers alike'. Women who wished to become involved, as writers or readers, had to assume a certain masculine identity, to become what we might call (after Russ's novel), Female Men. The Tiptree experiment in a sense focused exactly these prejudices, but at a more gender-aware time.

What Tiptree does, as Le Guin, Butler and Russ have also done in their various ways, is precisely to use the SF encounter with difference to focus gender concerns. An essay by Russ that was first published in the SF magazine *Vertex* in 1971 is often cited by feminist critics of SF as a classic articulation of these issues. In that essay, Russ declared that 'one would think science fiction the perfect literary mode in which to explore (and explode) our assumptions about "innate" values and "natural" social arrangements.' But whilst 'some of this has been done', Russ points out that 'speculation about the innate personality differences between men and women, about family structure, about sex, in short about gender roles, does not exist at all'. The essay is called 'The Image of Women in Science Fiction'; Russ says she chose that title rather than 'Women in Science Fiction' because 'if I had chosen the latter, there would have been very little to say. There are plenty of images of women in science fiction. There are hardly any women'. It can be argued that now, thirty years later, the situation is not quite so bleak as it was then. But there is still a sense in which the SF contact with the alien remains a powerful medium for expressing female perspectives.

Source: Adam Roberts, "Gender," in *Science Fiction*, Routledge, 2000, pp. 91–100.

Patrick Parrinder

In the following essay, Parrinder examines scientific theories and metaphors used by authors of Science Fiction.

I

A provisional and, I hope, uncontroversial definition of science fiction might run as follows: sf is a distinct kind of popular literature telling stories that arise from actual or, more usually, hypothetical new discoveries in science and technology. The science and technology must be convincing enough to invite a certain suspension of the reader's disbelief: this is how sf, as a creation of the later nineteenth century, differs from earlier fiction in which themes such as space travel and encounters with extraterrestrials were presented in a merely fantastic or satirical light. The present essay will propose a broad evolutionary model for the development of science fiction, comprising a prehistorical and at least three historical stages. The points of transition are those at which the genre can be seen to shift from one kind of discourse to another. In all science-fiction stories, scientific and technological innovation has consequential effects, causing changes at the level of the social structure, of individual experience, and in the perceived nature of reality itself. As sf has developed not only has its stock of imagined alternatives continued to multiply, but their status has changed from what I shall call the prophetic to the mythic and to the metaphorical. At present there are signs that the 'metaphorical' phase of science-fictional discourse may be breaking down, just as its predecessors did.

It is true that a periodisation of science fiction along these lines will strike some readers as being offensively schematic and dogmatic: my only excuse is that it may be a stimulus to further thought. Earlier critics to whom I am indebted, notably Darko Suvin and Mark Rose, have given their own versions of the 'philosophical history' of the genre—a philosophical history being a deliberately simplified model, or a hypothesis to be borne in mind when constructing a detailed empirical history. My model tries to foreground the relationship of sf to the physical sciences, while in the background there is a developing argument about scientific epistemology, and especially about the relationship of science to narrative discourse or, as we say, fictions.

Most early or 'proto' science fiction was the product of writers who stood at some distance from the science of their time and set out to mock, satirise, discredit, or at best to play with it. I am thinking here of Lucian, Godwin, Cyrano de Bergerac, Swift, Voltaire, Mary Shelley, and Poe. Poe comes the nearest to generic science fiction, though his imitations of scientific discourse can never be taken at face value. His cosmological essay 'Eureka' can claim to be a remarkable example of prophetic insight, since its alternately expanding and contracting universe is taken very seriously by some modern cosmologists. But 'Eureka' is also a vast leg-pull, an exercise in teasing absurdity comparable to the same author's 'Philosophy of Composition' with its satire on literary theory. In each case, Poe sets out to debunk Romantic irrationalism by showing that the mysteries of creation (whether human or divine) are susceptible of a blindingly simple, logical explanation; but the explanation collapses under its own weight, leaving both the mystical and the mechanical outlooks in ruins.

To move from proto-science fiction to the first stage of the genre itself is to move from sophisticated irony and satire to something which at first sounds very much cruder—the mode of literary prophecy. Poe gave one of his most obviously parodic stories the title 'Mellonta Tauta', Greek for 'these things are in the future', but the writers of prophetic science fiction speak of future things and mean what they say. Or rather, since it is a question of literary prophecy—that is, prophecy openly making use of fictional devices—they appear to mean it. There is, as it turns out, an intricate relationship between literary prophecy and parody or irony, which perhaps accounts for Poe's crucial influence on Jules Verne and H. G. Wells. The use of future dates in fiction will illustrate what I have in mind, since every future date is a virtual not an actual date, even though some should be taken much more seriously than others. At one extreme, Poe's character Pundita in 'Mellonta Tauta' writes her long, gossipy letter from the balloon 'Skylark' on 1 April 2848; at the other, Arthur C. Clarke sets the opening chapter of *Childhood's End* in 1975, but once that date has passed he writes a new opening chapter for the revised edition of the novel. Both editions carry Clarke's well-known prefatory statement to the effect that 'The opinions expressed in this book are not those of the author.' George Orwell's *Nineteen Eighty-Four* was made all the more ominous by its naming of a future year which rapidly became part of the political discourse of the Cold War period, even though '1984' was arrived at by reversing the last two figures of 1948 in which the novel was written; in any case, the book begins with the clocks striking 13, a manifestly satirical touch. What are we to say, then, of a date such as Wells's 802 701 AD in *The Time Machine*? Wells's story is, as he himself said in one of his letters, 'no joke', and the narrative logic just about manages to account for a date so unthinkably far in the future (provided that we do not inquire too closely). The result is prophetic science fiction, not in the sense of an accurate forecast, but of the story's power to

"The result is prophetic science fiction, not in the sense of an accurate forecast, but of the story's power to convince us of aspects of the future beyond or behind the ostensible fictional vehicle: it is, in effect, a kind of oracle."

convince us of aspects of the future beyond or behind the ostensible fictional vehicle: it is, in effect, a kind of oracle.

From Verne and Wells to Gernsback, Asimov, Clarke, Heinlein and Pohl we have a genre shaped by writers who are almost missionaries for science, and whose fiction proclaims that it has something to divulge about the future. The writers of prophetic sf are futurologists who nevertheless recognise that, in what Frederik Pohl has offered as 'Pohl's Law', 'The more complete and reliable a prediction of the future is, the less it is worth.' Characteristically, prophetic sf writers not only claim scientific authenticity for their visions but seek to promote what Wells called the 'discovery of the future' by means of essays, journalism and popular science writing as well as fiction. They celebrate and warn their readers about things to come. Taken literally and in detail, their prophecies are undoubtedly false, but then every true terrestrial prophet is also a false one. What prophetic sf writers do know about the future is that (to adapt George Orwell's comment on Wells) it is not going to be what respectable people imagine. And this implies that prophetic science fiction will be in trouble once its predictions of scientific and technological advance have started to become respectable and commonplace.

While many of Jules Verne's best-known titles speak of travel in spatial dimensions, Wells's titles often refer to travel in time, or rather to space-time. Verne's archetypal hero is Captain Nemo of the submarine *Nautilus*; Wells's is the Time Traveller. The Wellsian model of prophetic science fiction presupposes a Positivistic space-time continuum in which natural diversity is accounted for and brought under the rule of universal laws such as those of evolution and thermodynamics. Though living matter is extraordinarily plastic, the universe is a closed system of matter and energy without supernatural interference or any possibility of regeneration from outside. Space and time were bound together from the late nineteenth century onwards by the measurement of the speed of light and by the concept of the light-year. The future, like outer space, was waiting to be discovered, even though the future would be partly moulded by human choices. Within the 'classical' space-time universe which Wells called the 'Universe Rigid', the scope for human freedom of action faces severe constraints. According to Sir James Jeans, the sun is 'melting away like an ice-berg in the Gulf Stream', and humanity 'is probably destined to die of cold, while the greater part of the substance of the universe still remains too hot for life to obtain a footing. . . . [T]he end of the journey cannot be other than universal death'. Prophetic science fiction explores both the mysteries and the certainties of this scientific, material universe.

To do so it relies, above all, on the spaceship, an ethereal version of Jules Verne's submarine enabling the science fiction hero to travel across the space-time universe at just below (or, in many cases, far above) the speed of light. The spaceship as dream-vehicle gave way, in the mid-twentieth century, to the technological realities of NASA and Cape Canaveral (though sf writers have felt constrained to keep several jumps ahead of NASA's transport technology). At much the same time, a fundamental change in cosmology led to the general adoption of the expanding-universe theory according to which, far from inhabiting an entropic steady-state system, everything is perpetually getting farther away. Where Sir James Jeans in his best-selling account of *The Mysterious Universe* had been preoccupied with an apocalyptic future event, the 'Heat-Death of the Universe', physical speculation now came to centre upon a founding moment in the past, the Big Bang which initiated universal expansion. Science fiction has been deeply affected by this switch of attention from the end of everything to its beginning.

In the 1920s and the 1930s, the reaction against prophetic science fiction began in the work of 'space fantasists' like David Lindsay and C. S. Lewis. Lewis wrote that the best sf stories were not 'satiric or prophetic' but belonged to what he called 'fantastic or mythopoetic literature in general.' In the post-war decades, Lewis's view of sf gradually took precedence over Heinlein's much narrower conception of it as 'Realistic Future-Scene Fiction.' Soon science fiction began to repeat its 'prophetic' material and also to borrow quite consciously from modern fantasy (it had always had fantastic elements, of course), leading to a general shift from the prophetic to the mythopoetic mode. (At the same time, earlier science fiction had to be reinterpreted in accordance with the new paradigm, so that Bernard Bergonzi, for example, would describe Wells's science fictions as 'ironic myths.') I would count Ray Bradbury, Alfred Bester, James Blish and Walter M. Miller among the mythopoetic writers, but the earliest major sf novelist in this mode was probably Olaf Stapledon. Admittedly, his position is ambiguous. *Last and First Men* is in many ways a standard work of prophetic sf, with its chronological tables and its narrator addressing us from the far future. Stapledon's preface to *Last and First Men*, however, states that his 'attempt to see the human race in its cosmic setting' is an 'essay in myth creation', not a prophecy. His later book *Star Maker*, where the hero's journey through the space-time cosmos leads to a vision of creation imbued with post-Christian mysticism, is straightforwardly mythical. From the Sixties onwards, it became commonplace to speak of science fiction as a 'contemporary mythology', a phrase which hints at the hostility to science which is (it seems to me) latent in Stapledon's writings, as well as being explicit in Lewis. The sf critic Patricia Warrick defines myth as a 'complex of stories which a culture regards as demonstrating the inner meaning of the universe and of human life'; here the body of scientific knowledge and speculation is reduced to the level of scriptures and stories, so that 'scientism' as it is now known takes its place alongside other competing belief-systems, just as some Americans want to give creationism the same weight as evolutionism in the teaching of biology.

Where Warrick claims that the scientific model of the universe itself functions like a myth, Ursula Le Guin sees mythmaking as the special province of writers and artists. Le Guin argues on Jungian grounds that storytelling connects scientific methods and values to our collective dreams and archetypes; it is science fiction, not science itself, that deserves the title of a 'modern mythology.' In practice, once science fiction became consciously mythopoetic it began to indulge in generic self-repetition and a growing carelessness towards scientific facts. The imaginary Space Age universe crossed by magical faster-than-light spaceships and full of lifelike robots and contactable intelligent aliens has remained a staple of sf (and of the popular consciousness of science) long after it ceased to resemble a plausible scientific future. From a collection of increasingly commonplace prophecies SF had become a nostalgic theme-park of futures past.

But then in the 1960s, as Brian Aldiss claimed, 'SF discovered the Present', and the future was increasingly regarded as a metaphor for the present. Aldiss and Le Guin, among others, have frequently asserted that the genre's portrayal of the future of space travel, alternative societies and alternative life-forms is at bottom metaphorical. Much of New Wave and feminist science fiction is apparently metaphorical rather than prophetic or mythopoetic in intent. By 1970 the academic study of sf had begun, so that we can track the redefinition of science fiction as metaphor through academic theory as well as through the pronouncements of practising novelists. The philosopher Ernst Cassirer had argued that myth and metaphor were radically linked, and in a writer such as Le Guin, and in an early theorist such as Robert M. Philmus, there is a kind of slippage from myth to metaphor. On the other hand, Darko Suvin rejects talk of the artist as mythmaker and offers a fully worked-out theory of sf as a metaphorical mode: its stories, he says, are not prophecies but analogies or parables. The redefinition of science fiction as metaphor coincided with the politicisation of sf and its criticism in the Sixties and Seventies, though in my view it has served a primarily contemplative rather than an activist politics. The envisioned alternatives of metaphorical sf are fantastic and utopian possibilities, parallel worlds serving what Sarah Lefanu has called 'interrogative' rather than predictive functions. An interrogative or dialogical function is precisely what has traditionally been claimed for the literary genre of utopia. Metaphorical theory views science fiction not as an alternative to utopia (which is how the prophetic writers from Wells to Heinlein had seen it), but as one of the contemporary forms of utopian writing. This understanding of science fiction as a metaphorical mode is still dominant today, but its limitations have become increasingly evident. The metaphorical theory of the genre redefines sf as 'speculative fiction' or 'speculative fantasy', but it cannot in the long run explain why these speculations should be based on science.

II

Each of the three phases of science fiction I have outlined can be roughly correlated with a set of contemporary philosophical or metaphysical assumptions. Each set of contemporary assumptions constitutes an ideology or *Weltanschauung* exerting a gravitational pull on the fiction that comes under its influence. In this sense, prophetic science fiction belongs with Positivism and scientific materialism; science fiction as myth implies either neoChristianity or a pragmatic cultural relativism drawing on psychoanalytical and anthropological insights; while science fiction as metaphor tends to imply a post-structuralist 'conventionalism' or 'anti-foundationalism' denying or downgrading the referential aspects of fiction. In this view, statements no longer have a truth content, so that it would be absurd to judge imagined futures by their potential correspondence with any 'real' future. Prophetic sf is a propaganda device which is meaningful only in relation to the discursive present in which it arises.

Admittedly, it is tendentious to assert that theoretical defences of sf as a metaphorical mode imply a conventionalist view of reality. To do so they must argue not merely, in Le Guin's words, that 'all fiction is metaphor' but that all knowledge and description is so too. Darko Suvin's influential theory of science fiction is critical at this point, since Suvin in his best known work insists on a rigorous distinction between cognitive sf and supposedly non-cognitive fantasy. According to Suvin, not only is sf a mode of metaphor, but 'true' metaphor is by definition cognitive—so that sf's cognitive status is established with all the force of a syllogism. The theoretical defence of this assertion is to be found in Suvin's *Positions and Presuppositions in Science Fiction*, where he elaborates on the more programmatic and manifesto-like statements to be found in his earlier *Metamorphoses of Science Fiction*.

In *Positions and Presuppositions* Suvin quotes Paul Ricoeur's aphorism that 'Metaphor is to poetic language as model is to scientific language.' The equivalence is already suspiciously neat, and if poetic language and scientific language are both regarded as cognitive, then metaphor approximates to model. This is plausible to the extent that scientific theorising involves elements of metaphorisation and analogy or model-building; but Suvin describes not only scientific models but metaphors in general as 'heuristic fictions' which have a cognitive function. His intention, undoubtedly, is to turn post-structuralist scepticism inside out by arguing for the cognitive potential of all human creativity whether poetic or scientific, rational or emotional, or conceptual or non-conceptual. But in his discussion of sf as 'Metaphor, Parable and Chronotope' it is no longer clear to what extent so-called knowledge, or cognition, relies on a truth content.

Like other theorists of metaphor, Suvin relies on an apparently commonsense distinction between the properties of the 'true' or 'full-fledged' metaphor (equivalent to Cassirer's 'genuine "radical metaphor"') and low-grade or dead metaphors. This is crucial for the cognitive theory of metaphor, since all modern linguistic theorists agree on the ubiquity of metaphor. Nietzsche's assertion that in language itself there are no literal terms, only metaphors in various states of decay, has been echoed not merely by Derrida and de Man, but by a Positivist theorist such as I. A. Richards, who has described metaphor as the 'omnipresent principle of language.' If we say that all language also has a cognitive function we have, no doubt, stumbled upon a truth of sorts, but it is a truth that undermines any claim for a special cognitive status for scientific language, let alone for science fiction. Suvin's well-known view of science fiction as a literature of 'cognitive estrangement' implies a neat pyramid of discourse with ordinary language at the bottom and cognitive (scientific) thought at the apex; but the linguistic theory of metaphor leads us to view language as a seamless fabric with a repeated pattern in which theories, models, analogies, and 'ordinary' language are constantly changing places relative to one another. To say that sf, or any kind of fiction, is metaphorical is then to say nothing worth saying at all. Suvin, though well aware of this danger, has difficulty in extricating himself from it.

Fully-fledged metaphors or heuristic fictions, he argues, must fulfil the criteria of coherence, richness and novelty. Consciously or unconsciously, these three conditions seem to echo the scholastic triad of *integritas*, *consonantia* and *claritas*, proposed by St Thomas Aquinas and familiar to modern readers from Joyce's *A Portrait of the Artist as a Young Man*. For Aquinas and for Stephen Dedalus, however, these were the requirements for beauty, not for truth or cognitive value. Suvin considers and rather perfunctorily rejects a fourth criterion, that of reference to reality, on the grounds that it is already implicit in the requirements for richness and novelty. Just so did Dedalus argue that *claritas* was the same as *quidditas*, the 'whatness' of a thing. This is an economy too far, since it amounts to saying, like Keats's Grecian Urn, that 'Beauty is truth, truth beauty'. Suvin then distinguishes between metaphor as such, and narrative fictions which he regards as extended metaphors; the latter, he says, should be capable of verification or falsification, though the point is left undeveloped. Given the 'difference between brief and long writings', the criteria for distinguishing 'run-of-the-mill from optimal SF' are analogous to those for low-grade versus true metaphor. It is evident from this that Suvin no longer sees sf as a special kind of narrative exhibiting cognitive estrangement; rather, all worthwhile and, as he puts it, liberating human thought and creativity is (a) cognitive and (b) estranged. The purpose of such creativity is, to quote from a more recent essay, to 'redescribe the known world and open up new possibilities of intervening into it.' Perhaps, however, a verified or validated narrative (or metaphor, or scientific model) is no longer usefully analysed simply as an instance of metaphor. We should regard it, instead, as containing an actual or potential truth statement.

III

If sf's only distinguishing feature is that it serves 'interrogative functions' by means of its portrayal of analogical models or parallel worlds, then it is destined to disappear as a separate form, becoming in effect a subdivision of the novel of ideas. It is quite possible that the century of science fiction is over and that this form of expression born of late nineteenth-century scientific materialism has now run its course. (On the other hand, cultural history is littered with the premature obituaries of artistic forms.) The immediate cause of the genre's disappearance would be that science fiction understood as a metaphorical mode no longer has any necessary connection or concern with contemporary scientific developments.

If science fiction as metaphor is more or less played out, then it may be time to examine whether and under what conditions a return to science fiction as prophecy is possible. The genre's popular media image is still one of lurid anticipation and comic-book futurology, even though the sf community finds this embarrassingly naive and politically distasteful. Nothing is more guaranteed to excite the derision of the sf critic than the fact that Wells is still admired for predicting the tank and the atomic bomb, Clarke for the communications satellite, and Capek and Asimov for their robots. Some of the most plausibly prophetic recent science fiction is to be found in J. G. Ballard's scenarios of the end of the Space Age—but Ballard is famous, or deserves to be famous, as the one writer of his time who dared to contradict the commonplaces of respectable technocratic prophecy.

There is a trivial sense in which all scientific theories are predictive, since they assert that the regularities observed in the past will hold good in the future. But much of the most interesting scientific speculation focuses on unique (or apparently unique) events like the Big Bang, the Heat-Death of the Universe, or the course of evolution on Earth. For these events to appeal to the prophetic imagination they must have consequences in the future, and to appeal to the fictional imagination as we know it they must in principle be observable by human beings. The great advantage of the 'classical' space-time universe was the possibility of travelling around it and seeing things that had not yet happened, but even there what was directly observed would usually be a symbol or portent rather than the reality—like Wells's solar eclipse at the end of *The Time Machine*, or Clarke's Rama.

The modern counterpart to Wells's use of an eclipse to symbolise the heat-death of the sun would be a symbolic vision of the Big Bang, which is something that several writers have attempted. But where the end of the world naturally fits the prophetic mode, the beginning can perhaps best be represented as parody, as we see in Italo Calvino's marvellous short story 'All at one point' (from *Cosmicomics*). 'Naturally, we were all there', Calvino's narrator begins, 'Where else could we have been?'. What follows is an all-too-human nostalgia exercise, the loss of a primal utopia of primitive communism (written, as it happens, by an ex-Communist). Other aspects of contemporary cosmological speculation apart from the Big Bang pose an enormous challenge to direct fictional observation, even of the symbolic kind. According to string theory, for example, the universe not only contains anti-matter and black holes but has ten dimensions, six of which cannot be observed. Its fundamental building-blocks are quanta which may be conceived as either matter or energy. Meanwhile, it seems that the best chance of finding traces of extraterrestrial life is not in outer space, but in tiny fragments of meteorite on the earth's surface. Although men have been to the moon and landed a camera on Mars, and although some physicists now reckon that a time machine is theoretically possible, today's universe apparently offers no more opportunity for physical exploration than the universe of 100 years ago. We can detect more of it, but we know far more about the difficulties of actually reaching it.

Scott Bukatman in his book *Terminal Identity* argues that the Space Age has given way to an Information Age in which technology has become largely invisible, and space has been interiorised. We think of the atomic nucleus as a kind of miniature solar system, while the invention of the microchip and the spread of personal computing have led to the notions of cyberspace and of microcosmic, invisible and virtual spaces. Nevertheless, we continue to model the informational universe on the physical universe. Not only was it an sf writer who invented the term cyberspace, but science fiction and computer journalism have invested very heavily in space-time metaphors, conferring on virtual space some of the sense of challenge and adventure formerly associated with outer space (just as outer space in its time was invested with the language of geographical exploration). Hence the ubiquitous ideas of the 'net' and the 'superhighway', and Bukatman's pun on the word 'terminal', as in 'terminal identity fictions'.

John Clute has written that 'We no longer feel that we penetrate the future; futures penetrate us.' Bukatman speaks of 'our presence in the future'. The presence of the future has become a central paradox of postmodernist theory, as in Baudrillard's essay entitled 'The Year 2000 has already happened.' It is not very enlightening to describe such pronouncements as metaphorical—more significant, perhaps, is that they seem to pivot unstably between the modes of prophecy and parody. The same might be said of the literary applications of chaos theory, which is described by its proponents as a new cosmology overturning the rigid assumptions of the thermodynamic and evolutionary spacetime continuum. Scientists see chaos as driving the universe towards a more complex kind of order, but at any particular time the world of nature is theorised as being like the British weather, 'predictable in its very unpredictability.' Speculative scientific developments such as chaos theory and string theory are described by John Horgan as 'ironic science'—science which does not converge on the truth but which 'resembles literary criticism or philosophy or theology in that it offers points of view, opinions, which are, at best, "interesting", which provoke further comment.' Ironic science must necessarily find its counterpart in ironic science fiction.

If sf must respond to the aspects of contemporary knowledge that I have all too superficially touched upon, it is also affected by its now entrenched status as an established, not a new, genre with a ready-made audience and an organised body of academic interpreters. If the more successful popular sf (and above all sf cinema) now inclines to irony rather than prophecy, it also apparently has no need to prophesy, being readily available as raw material for the production of a kind of criticism and theory which itself has prophetic pretensions. If the old sf writers were also futurologists, there is little need for today's writers to double as cultural theorists, since literary critics will do the job for them. (Not only was cyberpunk instantly canonised, but if it had not existed cultural theory would surely have had to invent it, and some people have argued that cultural theory did invent it.) Popular sf no longer claims to be prophetic, but it feeds into the 'SF of theory' which does claim to speak prophetically or at least, with a parody of prophecy.

IV

In *The War of the Worlds*, H. G. Wells reminds us that 'No one would have believed' in the last years of the nineteenth century we were being watched by extraterrestrial intelligences: 'And early in the twentieth century came the great disillusionment.' Since then we have had a century full of fictions of galactic imperialism, of colonies in space, and of meetings with (and massacres of) intelligent and interestingly-gendered extraterrestrials; but no one (I suggest) can take these fictions seriously any more. If science fiction is conceived as metaphor or as myth it does not matter too much if the same old stuff goes on pouring out, but for the fact of *our* great disillusionment. And early in the twenty-first century . . . ? Not, I hope, a new war of the worlds, but perhaps a new science fiction, prophetic or parodic, keeping one step ahead of the cultural theorists, exploring both mysteries and certainties?

Source: Patrick Parrinder, "Science Fiction: Metaphor, Myth or Prophecy?" in *Science Fiction, Critical Frontiers*, edited by Karen Sayer and John Moore, St. Martin's Press, 2000, pp. 23–34.

Sources

Aldiss, Brian W., with David Wingrove, *Trillion Year Spree: The History of Science Fiction*, Atheneum, 1986, pp. 39–40, 75, 118.

Asimov, Isaac, *I, Robot*, Bantam Books, 1991, pp. 44–45, 73.

Card, Orson Scott, *Ender's Game*, Tor Books, 1977, p. 208.

———, *How to Write Science Fiction and Fantasy*, Writer's Digest Books, 1990, pp. 4, 21.

Haldeman, Joe, *The Forever War*, Avon Books, 1974, pp. 225, 229.

Harrison, Harry, "The Term Defined," in *Science Fiction: The Academic Awakening*, College English Association, 1974, p. 39.

Heinlein, Robert A., *Stranger in a Strange Land*, Ace Books, 1987, p. 115.

Huxley, Aldous, *Brave New World*, HarperPerennial, 1989, p. 240.

Kagarlitski, Julius, "Realism and Fantasy," in *SF: The Other Side of Realism*, edited by Thomas D. Clareson, Bowling Green University Popular Press, 1971, p. 29.

Le Guin, Ursula K., *The Left Hand of Darkness*, 25th Anniversary ed., Walker and Company, 1994, pp. 40–41.

Lerner, Frederick Andrew, *Modern Science Fiction and the American Literary Community*, The Scarecrow Press, Inc., 1985, pp. xiv–xvi.

Orwell, George, *1984*, Signet Classic, 1950, p. 5.

Tolkien, J. R. R., *The Hobbit*, Ballantine Books, 1965, pp. 4, 18–19, 60, 62, 85, 248.

Wells, H. G., *The Time Machine*, Bantam Books, 1991, pp. 4, 21, 29.

Williamson, Jack, "SF in the Classroom," in *Science Fiction: The Academic Awakening*, College English Association, 1974, p. 11.

Wood, Michael, "Tolkien's Fictions," in *New Society*, March 27, 1969.

Further Reading

Alkon, Paul K., *Science Fiction before 1900: Imagination Discovers Technology*, Twayne Publishers, 1994.

This book gives information on early Science Fiction works and how they were important in the beginning stages of the movement. The works are then placed in comparison with other literary works from their time period.

Asimov, Isaac, *I. Asimov: A Memoir*, Bantam Spectra, 1995.

Asimov's final collection of autobiographical essays contains many of his personal opinions and life stories. He discusses his views on such wide-ranging topics as science, society, other Science Fiction writers, and religion.

Disch, Thomas M., *The Dreams Our Stuff Is Made Of: How Science Fiction Conquered the World*, Touchstone Books, 2000.

This work contains historical information and critiques of various works and styles of Science Fiction literature. It gives an in-depth explanation of the different types of literature and gives blunt assessments of the work of the major authors from the field.

Hartwell, David G., *Age of Wonders: Exploring the World of Science Fiction*, Tor Books, 1996.

Hartwell's book is a great primer for anyone interested in learning more about Science Fiction. The book, written by a noted editor in the Science Fiction field, includes a critical overview of the field, recommended readings, and even a section on the business of Science Fiction publishing.

Roberts, Adam, and John Drakakis, *Science Fiction*, New Critical Idiom series, Routledge, 2000.

Roberts provides a great reference for Science Fiction novices, offering a brief history of the Science Fiction field, an explanation of the critical terminology, and an overview of the key concepts in Science Fiction criticism and theory.

Toffler, Alvin, *Future Shock*, Bantam Books, 1991.

Originally published in 1970, Toffler's classic book about how people either do or do not adapt to technological changes in a fast-paced, industrial society, is still relevant in today's information age.

Tolkien, J. R. R., *The Silmarillion*, Ballantine Books, 1990.

The Silmarillion is a good book for anyone interested in examining the origins of Tolkien's *The Hobbit* and "The Lord of the Rings" series. It gives background and historical information of this Fantasy world, as well as events that take place long before the beginning of Tolkien's four-volume Middle-Earth saga.

Surrealism

Movement Origin

c. 1919

The strength of the surrealist movement can be attributed in large part to one man, French poet André Breton, who helped found the movement after World War I in France. Surrealism was a reaction to Dadaism, which was itself a reaction to the "logic" that dadaists believed had caused the war. Surrealism, however, sought a more constructive way to rebel against rational thought than the more negative Dadaism. Drawing on the psychoanalytic studies of Sigmund Freud, the surrealists tried to expand the mind's potential by reconciling the apparently contradictory states of dream and reality. In a series of sometimes dangerous experiments, Breton and others attempted to put themselves in a hallucinatory state, in which they believed they could tap directly into their subconscious minds and extract pure thoughts, untainted by the conscious mind and its rational constraints. Since the surrealists prized individual revelation over conscious forms, themes varied among the poets, although many wrote about some form of love or nature.

While Breton and Phillipe Soupault wrote *The Magnetic Fields*, considered by many to be the first truly surrealist text, in 1919, it was not until 1924, when Breton published his *Manifesto of Surrealism*, that the movement was officially founded. Breton ruled the group like a dictator, and his strict adherence to surrealist principles led to many expulsions and defections from the group. Nevertheless, the surrealists, who also included Paul Eluard and Robert Desnos, flourished for the next two

decades, until the outbreak of World War II. Although the majority of the group's members were poets, some tried their hand at prose as well. Breton's novel *Nadja* was one of the most successful attempts. Surrealism inspired related movements in painting, sculpture, drama, and film, and has had a lasting influence on the creative arts as a whole.

Representative Authors

Louis Aragon (1897–1982)

Louis Aragon was born October 3, 1897, in Paris, France. As one of the leading proponents of Dadaism and Surrealism, Aragon helped Breton and others to inspire creative freedom in the arts. Like many other surrealists, Aragon's poetry was initially published in the journal *Litterature*, which Aragon helped found and edit with Breton and Soupault. However, Aragon's most famous works are his novels, including *Paris Peasant*. Aragon and the other surrealists joined the French Communist Party in 1930. Although the surrealists left the party five years later after witnessing Stalin's bloody atrocities, Aragon rejoined the party, renounced Surrealism, and produced mainly political works for several years. He attempted to write other works later in his career, but at that point, most critics only knew him for his politically oriented fictions. Aragon died December 24, 1982, in Paris.

Louis Aragon

André Breton (1896–1966)

Although he had help founding the Surrealism movement, in many ways André Breton acted alone. Born February 19, 1896, in Tinchebray, France, Breton was a medical student when he was drafted into World War I. There he served in the psychiatric wards, where he began his studies in neurology and psychology. Disillusioned by the horrors of war, Breton joined the dadaists at the war's end but left to start the surrealist movement, which he saw as a more constructive response to the war than Dadaism. He experimented avidly with automatic writing and other self-induced hypnotic and hallucinatory states attempting to reach the subconscious mind. Although he had founded and edited the journal *Litterature* with Aragon and Soupault in 1919, it was not until 1924 that he published his first of three manifestos of Surrealism. In the first manifesto, he laid out the rules that would-be surrealists should follow to tap into their subconscious. Breton was the movement's main promoter and he ran the group with a dictator-like control, expelling anyone who did not play by his rules. With his influence, surrealist painters like Dalí achieved greater recognition through exhibitions. In 1930, Breton led the surrealists in joining the French Communist Party, although they did not stay long once they saw the atrocities Stalin was committing in the name of communism. When World War II broke out, Breton was interrogated by the Nazis over his activities, at which point he moved first to the French colony of Martinique, then to the United States, where he spent most of the war years. Breton died of a heart attack on September 28, 1966, in France.

Robert Desnos (1900–1945)

Robert Desnos was born July 4, 1900, in Paris, France. He was published as a poet in his teens, but as an adult, he originally worked as a journalist before joining the surrealists in the 1920s. Of the entire group, Desnos was recognized as having the best ability to put himself in the trance required for automatic writing, a fact that Breton noted with pride in his first *Manifesto*. Desnos, like some other surrealists, pursued a flamboyant lifestyle that included sexual promiscuity and experimentation with drugs. He was also in love with a well-known singer, Yvonne George, and he wrote about her in various romantic poems. However, he is most remembered for his novel *Liberty or Love!*. Following the publication of this novel, Desnos began to pursue a more stable life. He got married, reduced his involvement with the surrealists, and even wrote his own manifesto in an attempt to win control of the surrealist movement from Breton, attempting to break Breton's formal structure. The coup failed, Desnos was expelled from the group, and he went back to his former job as a journalist. He also began writing essays, radio scripts, film critiques, and even more traditional forms of poetry, which were looked upon with disapproval by the surrealists. Desnos died of typhoid on June 8, 1945, in a concentration camp in Terezin, Czechoslovakia.

Paul Eluard (1895–1952)

Paul Eluard, the pen name of Eugène Grindel, was born December 14, 1895, in Saint-Denis, France. Eluard contracted tuberculosis as a child, and spent two years in a sanatorium, where he started writing poetry. When World War I began, Eluard joined the French military, first serving as a hospital orderly, then fighting in the trenches. After the war, Eluard met Breton and others in the dadaist movement and helped to develop Surrealism. Eluard was extremely prolific, publishing more than seventy books in his lifetime. However, it was his early volumes of poetry, including *Capital of Sorrow*, published in 1926, that helped to establish his reputation as a poet. After the Spanish Civil War broke out in 1936, Eluard's writings became more political, and by World War II, he had adopted a pro-socialist attitude. After the war, Eluard followed the lead of Aragon, denouncing Surrealism in favor of communism. His devotion to Stalin was so strong he wrote a poetic tribute to him. Because of his political affiliations, Eluard was denied a United States visa. He died November 18, 1952, in Charenton-le-Pont, France.

Phillipe Soupault (1897–1990)

Phillipe Soupault was born August 2, 1897, in Chaville, France. After serving in World War I, Soupault joined forces with Breton. Although the surrealist movement was not officially founded until 1924, in 1919, Soupault coauthored *The Magnetic Fields* with Breton, a work considered by many to be the first surrealist text. It is unfortunate that many people remember him for this achievement alone, since Soupault was one of the most active members of the group. Soupault was one of the coeditors on the journal *Litterature*. Also, while he still embodied the ideas behind Surrealism and incorporated juxtapositions of bizarre images into his work like the other surrealists, Soupault's poetry was noticeably more structured. Soupault left the group in the mid-1920s and traveled and wrote until 1938, when he moved to Tunisia. In the capital city of Tunis, he worked in radio and was outspoken against Hitler and the Nazis, which got him fired. Four years later, he was arrested in France for disseminating antifascist propaganda and was sentenced to six months in prison, where he wrote a psychological study of his fellow prisoners. Soupault died March 11, 1990, in Paris, France.

Representative Works

Capital of Sorrow

Like Aragon, Paul Eluard's greatest works were written before his writings became more political in nature. *Capital of Sorrow*, originally published in 1926, is a case in point. Although Eluard had published previous volumes of poetry, this was one of his first volumes of surrealist poetry and it helped to establish his reputation as a poet and bring attention to the surrealist movement. In *Capital of Sorrow*, Eluard focuses on two, diametrically opposed ideas—love and loneliness—and expounds on each with a passion and intensity for which he became famous. Invoking images of the individual and the universal, *Capital of Sorrow* was a key formative work in the poet's career. Of all of the French surrealists, Eluard was praised by critics as the most talented, and works like *Capital of Sorrow* have continued to receive favorable attention over the years.

Liberty or Love!

Liberty or Love!, Desnos's surrealist novel, was censured by a French court because of its graphic nature and the eroticism inherent in some passages. The novel, first published in 1927, is like other surrealist novels in that it follows a loose structure. The story details a hazy series of events in which two lovers, Corsair Sanglot and Louise Lame, drift in and out of each other's lives. Characters pop in and out of the narrative as if in a dream. The novel, which was written in very descriptive detail, was noted by critics for its dreamlike qualities. It was first translated into English in 1994, at which time it received favorable reviews.

The Magnetic Fields

The story behind the genesis of *The Magnetic Fields* is one of intense, and one could say, fanat-

André Breton, Paul Eluard, Tristan Tzara, and Benjamin Peret

ical commitment to a cause. In 1919, Breton and Soupault were performing a number of experiments, attempting to tap into their unconscious minds through techniques like automatic writing. At one point, they induced themselves into a hypnotic trance and began a writing session that lasted eight days. The output, a series of prose poems, was published initially in 1919 in their journal *Litterature*. *The Magnetic Fields*, considered by many to be the first surrealist text, was important to the movement's development.

Manifesto of Surrealism

When Breton's first *Manifesto of Surrealism* was published in 1924, it was met with opposition. The manifesto began by criticizing current forms of writing such as the novel in very abrasive and unflattering ways, so it is no wonder that it was not liked. Although the term "Surrealism" was coined by his deceased friend Guillaume Apollinaire, Breton claimed (in *Manifesto of Surrealism*) the title for his movement and offered an official definition:

> Psychic automatism in its pure state, by which one proposes to express—verbally, by means of the written word, or in any other manner—the actual functioning of thought. Dictated by thought, in the absence of any control exercised by reason, exempt from any aesthetic or moral concern.

The manifesto featured a grab bag of other items, including a list of names of the people Breton considered surrealists, an in-depth description for how to perform the method of automatic writing, and several examples illustrating what Surrealism is. Breton followed this work with two other manifestos and several other works that further defined the goals and ideals of the surrealists.

Paris Peasant

Louis Aragon's *Paris Peasant* was originally published in 1926. The surrealist novel employed two of the surrealists's favorite inspirational locations: a passageway at the Paris Opera and the Buttes-Chaumont park. *Paris Peasant* was well received, especially by critics, who praised the novel's ability to mix realistic elements of the Paris locations with the surrealist elements of Aragon's created world. Much of the critics' favorable attention stemmed from the fact that they were used to surrealists who did not base their prose or novels on real places—which were harder to produce through automatic writing—and so Aragon's novel was a welcome change. The novel also contained Aragon's own definition of Surrealism, which differed from Breton's definition in his *Manifesto of Surrealism*. Aragon emphasized (in *Manifesto of Surrealism*) the use of the image in a random and passionate way and believed that each image forced him "to revise the Universe."

Themes

Love

One of the favorite themes of the French surrealists was love, particularly the ability of love to overcome reason. One of the most striking examples of this is in a scene from Desnos's prose work *Deuil pour Deuil*. Desnos places the narrator in a desert city of uninhabited ruins along a river. "Despite our anxiousness, no one, no one at all, came to us," the narrator says. The "us" implies that somebody is with him, although later in the poem he admits that he "was always alone in reality." The narrator blindly searches for love. "Strange sicknesses, curious customs, bell-tolling love, where have you led me? In these stones I find no trace of what I seek." He cannot find the love for which he is looking and is trapped by the "curious customs" of love, which overcome his reason.

The narrator has mirage-like visions of caravans of beautiful women, whom he "waits for . . . tormented," but they turn out to be "old dust covered women," if they even exist at all. One suspects not, especially when he later sees "planes without pilots encircled with rounds of smoke." The planes land and three women get out, but at the end of the scene the women are gone, and the narrator repeats a variation of the opening lines of the scene, implying that he is in fact imprisoned in this dream world, where love is driving him mad.

The Human Body

Surrealists were noted for their descriptions of the human body, particularly the female body. Although these depictions are sometimes done graphically in a sexual manner, at other times, the surrealists describe parts of the body that are completely innocent. A good example of the latter is Breton's poem "My Wife with Her Wood-Fire Hair." In the poem, Breton starts at his wife's hair and slowly works his way down her body, through her "thoughts of heatsparks" and "eyebrows like the edge of a swallow's nest," to her "champagne shoulders" and "fingers of cut hay." Each example is a vivid picture of a particular part of his wife's anatomy, and with rare exception, each image is a unique creation that sets up a picture in the reader's mind. One can envision his wife's thoughts, for example, as literal "heatsparks" that flare with electricity around her brain.

Nature

The surrealists also incorporate nature-related images in their poetry. These generally take one of two forms: isolated images representing various aspects of nature, or larger images of nature's elements. Both types can be seen in Eluard's poem "You Rise Up." An example of the first type appears halfway through the poem when the poet writes, "You sing night hymns on the strings of the rainbow." A rainbow is a positive symbol of nature, which is consistent with the overall tone of the poem, in which Eluard sings the praises of women.

As for the second type of nature, Eluard includes three of the four elements—water, earth, and fire—elsewhere in the poem. He starts off with the two lines: "You rise up the water unfolds / You lie down the water opens." The elemental image of water often implies life, and in this case, the poet is remarking about how women are part of the process of creating life and so are one with the life-giving water, which closes and opens to accommodate the woman in the poem. This idea is reinforced in the rest of the poem first through the use of earth: "You are the earth taking root / And on which everything is built," then through fire:

> You sacrifice time
> To the eternal youth of the exact flame
> Which veils nature in reproducing it.

In the earth image, the woman takes root, providing a solid foundation from which to build humanity. In the fire image, the woman sacrifices the majority of her life to the bearing and raising of children, a cycle that repeats itself eternally. It should be noted, however, that even though this poem seems to make use of traditional contexts for images, in many cases, the word a surrealist uses does not always match its traditional meaning.

Style

Automatic Writing

In his *Manifesto of Surrealism*, Breton laid out the methods of the would-be surrealist, including a technique called automatic writing, which the surrealists used to try to obtain the most pure information, free from the bindings of rational thought. "Put yourself in as passive, or receptive, a state of mind as you can," says Breton. He advises people to "write quickly" about whatever comes into their minds, and "fast enough so that you will not re-

Topics for Further Study

- The surrealists's core philosophy involved the use of automatic writing and other methods to attempt to bypass the conscious mind and tap into the subconscious. Close your eyes and try to clear your mind of all thought, then open your eyes and write a poem, writing down the first thoughts that come into your mind. Write a report on whether or not you think you tapped into your subconscious mind.
- Communism has a complex history, involving many countries. Research three important events in the history of communism and write a short paper about these events, explaining how the events came about and what effect they had on communism and the world at large.
- The horrible casualties of World War I were due in a large part to the reliance of both sides on trenches at the Western Front. Research the origins of trench warfare, including how and when each side created their respective trenches, and what effect fighting in the trenches had on soldiers. Using this information, write a few sample journal pages from the perspective of a soldier in the trenches.
- André Breton was one of many writers and artists captured by the Germans in World War II and interrogated. Eventually he was let go and fled to the United States. Find another writer or artist who was interrogated by German forces during the war and write a one-page biography about him or her.
- Surrealism has influenced many other arts since it was founded in the 1920s, including commercial arts like advertising. Find an advertisement from the last decade you feel has a surrealist quality and write a short report explaining why.

---

member what you're writing and be tempted to reread what you have written." Breton also notes that of all of the surrealists, Desnos was the group's best practitioner, and that "Desnos *speaks surrealist* at will."

Imagery

Poets use language in their works to create different kinds of images, in a literal or figurative manner. An image can represent physical objects, emotions, metaphysical ideas, and virtually anything else that can be experienced in the real world through one or more of the five senses of sight, smell, touch, hearing, or taste. A literal image is conveyed in straight language that does not imply a hidden meaning. For example, in Paul Eluard's poem "What the Laborer Says Is Always Beside the Point," the second line reads, "A man on a bench in a street who avoids the crowd." There is nothing ambiguous about this image. As each separate part of the line is read, the image in the reader's mind becomes more concrete.

Much of surrealist poetry relies on figurative images—images conveyed by metaphors, similes, or other forms of figurative language—all of which employ ordinary words in a manner that imparts a new meaning. For example, from the same poem by Eluard:

> There are demolitions sadder than a penny
> Indescribable and yet the sun moves away from
> them singing
> While the sky dances and makes its honey.

Eluard's language has specific meanings when looked at in context. The "demolitions" caused by war are more depressing than a penny, which represents the lowest monetary value in currency, and so is almost worthless, as are these demolished buildings. While the buildings are so destroyed that they are "indescribable," their darkness does not effect the sun. The sun, a bright object that is usually given positive connotations—in this case it sings—continues to move away, or rise and set, as it always has, taking no notice of the demolished buildings. Likewise for the dancing sky (also a positive feeling), which continues to make its honey, or rain, as it always has. Eluard uses figurative language to personify—or attribute human feelings to—inanimate objects like buildings and natural objects like the sun and sky, conveying a sense of the inevitable nature of war and its ineffectiveness in the grand scheme of things.

Juxtaposition

In addition to imagery, the surrealists relied heavily on the positioning of their words to create the effects that they sought. In many cases, poets would place unrelated, often contradictory words next to each other in an attempt to achieve an image that reconciled dreams with reality. This device led to some very bizarre images. For example, in Robert Desnos's poem "Meeting," he writes:

> A very learned doctor sews the hands of the pray
> ing woman
> assuring her she will sleep.
> A very skilful cook mixes poisons in my plate
> and assures me I will laugh.

These words are obviously juxtaposed so that they contradict each other. Doctors normally heal, so if they sew somebody's hands together, that person will likely cry out in pain, not go to sleep. Likewise, if somebody is poisoned, they are not likely to laugh, they are likely to die. However, even though the lines do not make sense, they create images in the reader's mind and convey a sense of betrayal. The speaker of these lines is being ill-treated, although he or she is assured by the respected professionals that everything is going to be all right. One possible interpretation is that the speaker, like those who were asked to support World War I, is being duped by the government—the learned doctors who rely on logic—and being fed poisonous lies that the war will be over quickly and that citizens will rejoice when that happens.

Movement Variations

Surrealist Art

Surrealist painters and writers shared a number of influences, including Dadaism. However, one of the most important art influences was the early work of Giorgio de Chirico—an Italian painter who helped found a style of metaphysical painting with his famous series of unique, barren city landscapes, which he started painting in 1910. Through his use of contrasting light and shadow and his juxtaposition of objects, Chirico's paintings suggested a dark, unknown evil.

Breton supported surrealist art as well as literature. In issues of his magazine *La Révolution Surréealiste*, Breton routinely published illustrations from such artists as Max Ernst and André Masson. The biggest promotion of the surrealist artists, however, came through exhibitions. In 1925, the surrealists staged their first collective exhibition in Paris, which included work from Ernst, Masson, Joan Miró, and Man Ray, founding members of the surrealist art group. Chirico's early metaphysical work was also included. It was characteristic of surrealist art that each artist had a unique style, as each painter chose to explore the ideas of Surrealism in different, personal ways, leading to many different and exciting works. The exhibition was a success, and more soon followed.

The Surrealist Gallery, a joint venture that opened in 1926, gave many Surrealist artists a permanent exhibition space. In addition to French artists like Max Ernst, André Masson, and Joan Miró, the gallery also attracted the attention of international artists. Like the French surrealist poets, Dalí was influenced by Freud's writings. To tap into his subconscious, he induced hallucinations in himself before he began to paint. From 1929 to 1937, he created a series of dreamlike, fantastical landscapes featuring realistic objects in bizarre configurations. One of his most famous works is "The Persistence of Memory," which depicts clocks melting on tree branches in an otherwise desolate landscape. His bleak landscapes are his best-known works. After Dalí switched gears and began creating more traditional paintings in the 1930s, Breton—who expected strict adherence to surrealist ideas—expelled Dalí from his surrealist group.

Surrealist painting flourished until the outbreak of World War II. Periodic exhibitions were later seen in the 1960s and 1970s, as many of the original surrealist artists died and their work was shown in retrospectives. Surrealist art is still exhibited in the twenty-first century, and its influence continues to be seen.

Surrealist Film

The surrealist movement first expressed itself in film in the 1920s. Surrealist films embodied the concepts of its literary counterpart and featured oddly juxtaposed and often contradictory images, which were sometimes disturbing. The most famous film from this time period is *Un Chien andalou* (An Andalusian dog), released in 1928 from first-time director Luis Buñuel and painter Dalí. One of the more graphic images in the film is that of a woman slitting her eye with a razor. As English surrealist poet David Gascoyne notes in his *A Short Survey of Surrealism*, the film "caused much scandal and sensation at its first showings." The first of several surrealist films that eventually achieved widespread critical acclaim, *Un Chien andalou* continues to be viewed as a classic of surrealist film.

For the next five decades, Buñuel continued making films depicting surrealist images and worlds, culminating in the 1977 film *That Obscure Object of Desire*. The surrealist influence of Buñuel and others has survived into the twenty-first century. For example, the ideas of Surrealism were modernized in *Vanilla Sky*—director Cameron Crowe's 2001 film starring Tom Cruise as a magazine publisher who slowly loses his hold on reality and experiences a number of surrealist visions. At the end, he realizes he has been living in a self-induced, virtual reality dream.

Surrealist Drama

Although some surrealists wrote plays, their greatest influence was not through their individual works but in the movement's influence on the theatre of the absurd, a dramatic movement in the post-World-War-II 1950s and early 1960s. The theatre of the absurd, a school informally founded through the works of a number of foreign playwrights living in Paris, was a reaction against the horrors of World War II. Like the surrealists, the absurdists valued dreamlike images over logical, rational thought. Unlike the surrealists, however, who attempted to create a positive and constructive reaction to the horror, the absurdists believed that human life was meaningless and that humans were helpless creatures, having fallen into a state of absurdity. Absurdist plays mimicked this feeling, introducing unpredictable situations or contradictory images that did not seem to make sense. Some of these plays, like Samuel Beckett's *Waiting for Godot*, first produced in 1953 in France, are considered classics of world literature. Other celebrated absurdist playwrights include Eugene Ionesco, Jean Genet, Harold Pinter, and Edward Albee.

England

Just as Breton did much to promote the surrealist movement in France, English poet and novelist Gascoyne did the same in the 1930s in England. In addition to translating some of the surrealist poetry from French to English, he also wrote *A Short Survey of Surrealism* in 1935. In this book, Gascoyne analyzes the development of Surrealism, offers commentary on Breton's first and second manifestos of Surrealism, and discusses the work of other major surrealist poets.

Along with publicizing the movement through his works of history, criticism, and translations, Gascoyne's own poetry reflects the influence of the surrealists. His book of poetry titled *Man's Life Is This Meat*, published in 1936, was one of the most important surrealist works in England. However, Gascoyne was not as interested in the subconscious as Breton and others, instead focusing on more mystical elements. His poems in the late 1930s and early 1940s show his increasing interest in religion, which dominated his later poetry.

Historical Context

World War I

On June 28, 1914, Archduke Franz Ferdinand, heir to the Austro-Hungarian throne, made a fateful trip to Sarajevo, capital city of Bosnia and Herzegovina, where he and his wife were assassinated. The occupation of Bosnia and Herzegovina by Austria-Hungary led to growing unrest among people in the region who wanted to become part of Serbia once again. The assassination was staged with the help of Serbia, which also wished to reclaim Bosnia and Herzegovina.

Norman Davies notes, in *Europe: A History*, the quick consequences of the assassination, and the revelation that Serbia was involved. "Within four weeks, the gunshots of Sarajevo brought Europe's diplomatic and military restraints crashing to the ground," Davies writes. On July 28, exactly one month after the assassination, Austria-Hungary declared war on Serbia. An extensive system of preexisting alliances swiftly pulled most other European countries into the war, escalating the conflict. Eventually, Europe, parts of Asia, and the United States joined the war, aligning themselves either with the pro-Serbian Allies or with the Central powers, which supported Austria-Hungary.

When World War I began in August 1914, both sides believed that with their modern weapon technologies like hand grenades, tanks, long-range artillery, and poison gas, the war would be over quickly and with minimal casualties. Davies notes the prevailing logic that dominated people's thinking: "It was going to be over by Christmas. Conventional wisdom held that modern warfare would

Compare & Contrast

- **1910s:** Vladimir Ilyich Ulyanov, known to his supporters by the name Lenin, leads the Russian revolution, overthrowing the czar and instituting a dictatorship of the proletariat—or common people—led by himself. Over the next several years Lenin works to build the Communist Party into an organization that can effect worldwide revolution, and tries to get all separate communist parties to commit to the Soviet cause.

  Today: Many formerly communist countries, including the former Soviet Union, currently employ democratic systems of government.

- **1910s:** During World War I, in an effort to rally support at home, various countries on both sides rely on printed propaganda and other methods of psychological warfare that demonize their enemy.

  Today: After an attack on the World Trade Center in New York City and on the Pentagon in Washington, D.C., that leads to war in Afghanistan, Hollywood capitalizes on American citizens' patriotism by releasing a number of war-themed films.

- **1910s:** American poet John Masefield accompanies the United States volunteer ambulance service in France, sending many letters to his wife that record his graphic observations of the effects of war. His writings are published in *The Old Front Line* (1917) and other books.

  Today: As the United States wages war in Afghanistan, people receive up-to-the-minute updates from on-site reporters, whose video footage and commentary is transmitted to the public through radio, satellite television, and the Internet.

be more intense than in the past, but more decisive." In reality, however, the war raged for four years, leading to an estimated eight million dead and even more wounded.

One of the two main lines of fighting, the Western Front, ran through France, which experienced some of the bloodiest battles in the war. The front was defined by the extensive trench that ran along its entire length on both sides. Allied and Central soldiers occupied their respective trenches—which were often close to each other—and with a series of battles, each side attempted to drive their opponent out of his trench and force the line back, with a flurry of grenades and machine-gun fire. The results were horrific. Davies observes of the three most bloody battles, "the loss of life could be counted in tens of thousands per hour or hundreds per square yard."

For years the battle in the trenches was a virtual stalemate, and the body count rose as both sides added reinforcements to maintain the trenches. "Here was a mindless tragedy which no one had foreseen, and which no one knew how to stop," says Davies.

Dadaism and Sigmund Freud

After World War I, the dadaists tried to fight fire with fire. They believed that logic and other organized systems of thinking had created the horrors of war and responded to the war's meaningless slaughter with literature and art that was equally meaningless and created intentionally without logic. The dadaist movement, which had been founded in Switzerland in 1916 by a group of European artists and writers, spread to other areas in Europe, including France, where Breton became one of the willing converts.

As a medical student drafted to work in the psychiatric wards during the war, Breton had seen firsthand the effects of war on the human mind and wished to rebel against the logic that had caused the war. However, Breton soon became tired of the negative, meaninglessness of Dadaism, and sought a more positive and constructive means to stage his rebellion. Breton had studied the work of Sigmund Freud, the founder of psychoanalysis, and was particularly interested in Freud's theories of the unconscious mind. Drawing on Freud's studies, Breton and others formed the surrealist movement. In 1924, Breton defined the group's guiding principles in his *Manifesto of Surrealism.*

Communism and World War II

Although the surrealist movement initially began as a form of literary expression, political unrest in Europe forced many sociopolitical and cultural groups to align themselves with other groups. In 1930, Breton announced the surrealists's decision to join the French Communist Party in his second *Manifesto of Surrealism.* It was his hope that the greater Communist Party, which had its headquarters in Moscow in the Soviet Union, would adopt the surrealist way of thinking and apply it to politics, creating a totally liberated society. However, five years later, most of the surrealists left the Communist Party after witnessing the bloody acts Soviet dictator Joseph Stalin perpetrated in the name of communism.

Davies claims many of these acts were part of Stalin's political strategy: "Innocent victims were rounded up in their homes and villages; others were charged with imaginary offences of 'sabotage,' 'treason,' or 'espionage,' and tortured into confession." As part of Stalin's scare tactics, many of these victims were put on trial to discourage others from rebelling against him. Breton and others were some of the first to publicly denounce these trials.

With the outbreak of World War II in 1939, another dictator, Germany's Adolf Hitler, invaded and conquered much of Europe. When Hitler's Nazis invaded France, the surrealists broke up, and many of them fled to other European countries or overseas.

Critical Overview

Surrealism was a movement that sought to abandon all organized systems that normal literature followed, so it is tough to criticize the works as literature. Critic Mary Ann Caws notes this in the introduction to her book, *The Poetry of Dada and Surrealism*: "Dada and surrealism, which consider themselves literature's opposite, cannot be (or should not be) theorized about, exemplified, and handled at an efficient arm's length." In addition, Caws observes that Breton himself was against criticism from outsiders: "Breton firmly believed in the principle of internal criticism, and on several occasions he brilliantly demonstrated it."

To make matters more difficult, Surrealism was intended to be a movement of individual revelation for each writer. As a result, the writings were widely different in theme, style, and form, making it hard to criticize the movement as a whole. Because of this, critics have tended to follow one of two paths. Either they have commented on the ideas behind the movement itself, or they have commented on the individual surrealist writer.

The ideas behind the movement were expressed formally in Breton's *Manifesto of Surrealism.* As David Gascoyne reports in his *A Short Survey of Surrealism* in 1935, it was not well received: "It is not in the least surprising that Breton's manifesto should have aroused a considerable sensation. A great deal of animosity and blind opposition, also."

Gascoyne discusses how Breton's absolute adherence to the rigid ideals of Surrealism further alienated him personally, not just from critics, but also from members of the surrealist group, who were "unable to maintain the standards of disinterestedness and non-conformity that surrealism demands."

As for Breton's writings themselves, Balakian notes in her entry for the *Dictionary of Literary Biography* that even though he was an able poet, most people "associate him chiefly with his work, *Nadja.*" Breton's intent with this work was to undermine novels which, as he states in his *Manifesto of Surrealism*, "are nothing but so many superimposed images taken from some stock catalogue, which the author utilizes more and more whenever he chooses." Still, as Balakian observes, "instead of destroying the novel as Breton had hoped, he contributed strongly to the shaping of the antinovel as a form."

Breton's contemporaries have received a mixed bag of criticism about their works. In the case of Phillipe Soupault, one of the original and most famous surrealists—even though he was not with the group as long as others—the criticism has been very one-sided. J. H. Matthews, one of the foremost surrealist critics, notes the peculiar situation surrounding Soupault, who in 1919 was the cowriter of *The Magnetic Fields*, considered by many to be the first truly surrealist text: "[Soupault] is remembered as having written, with Breton, a book cited by many but read by few. Meanwhile,

Painting Catalan Landscape: The Hunter, *by Joan Miró, is of the surrealist style*

his other surrealist publications have not been subjected to scrutiny."

The most critically acclaimed of the surrealists, at least in poetry, was Paul Eluard. Georges Lemaitre writes in his book *From Cubism to Surrealism in French Literature* that Eluard was "certainly the most richly gifted poet of the whole surrealist group." Lemaitre points out that the themes in Eluard's poetry focus on two contradictory ideas, loneliness and love: "Love is viewed by him as a mystic center of blazing forces, a fiery nucleus of passionate vibrations, diffusing energy throughout the whole world in ardent and pulsating waves."

Lemaitre is not so praising of Desnos, in whose works, "One would search vainly . . . for the abstract metaphysical quality which characterizes most of Eluard's productions." Lemaitre goes even further, criticizing the poet's use of particularly perverse forms, which "aroused from their heavy slumber, twist and turn ignominiously, releasing in their convulsive spasms an acrid and suffocating stench."

The poetry of Aragon has also commonly been viewed as negative, due to its use of particularly violent words and its spirit of protest. These elements became especially strong when Aragon committed himself to the causes of the Communist Party.

Criticism

Ryan D. Poquette

Poquette has a bachelor's degree in English and specializes in writing about literature. In the following essay, Poquette explores Paul Eluard's use of imagery in his poem "First in the World" as an illustration of Surrealism's primary goal.

In his definitive work *Manifesto of Surrealism*, published in 1924, André Breton set the guidelines that future members of the surrealist movement would follow. Breton maintained tight control over these guidelines and promptly expelled any writer who did not observe them. Although the list of expelled members would eventually include Paul Eluard, who abandoned Surrealism for communism, Eluard was originally one of Breton's favorite writers, and one whom Breton thought exemplified the principles of Surrealism. In addition, of all the original surrealists, Eluard is the one poet praised most often by critics. For these reasons, Eluard's poetry serves as a good example of Breton's concepts. In one case in particular, the poem "First in the World," Eluard's imagery illustrates the central goal in Surrealism—the attempt to reconcile the dream world with reality.

"I believe in the future resolution of these two states, dream and reality, which are seemingly so contradictory, into a kind of absolute reality, a *surreality*, if one may so speak." With these words in his *Manifesto of Surrealism*, Breton introduced a concept built upon both the dream research of Sigmund Freud and Breton's own self-induced, hallucinatory experiments. Over the course of his manifesto, Breton defines the various tools the surrealists used to achieve this new "absolute reality," the most important of which is the surrealist image. Although Breton admits that there are "countless kinds" of these images, he places a repeated emphasis on the words themselves: "Words, groups of words *which follow one another*, manifest among themselves the greatest solidarity." In other words, the words in a surrealist poem are connected, and follow a pattern. However, the greater meaning derived from this pattern does not always resemble reality. As Frederick Brown notes in "Breton and the Surrealist Movement," these poems create "a locked, reflexive universe where language exists, to suppose the impossible, *on its own terms* . . . conveying no feeling, no experience, no image felt, experienced, or imagined outside itself."

Inside the microcosm of the poem, the images themselves define the characteristics and boundaries of the poem's world. Like a dream, these rules often differ from the natural laws of our own world. Eluard's poem "First in the World," originally published in his collection *Capital of Sorrow*, draws conspicuous attention to the surrealists' plan of merging the dream world with reality, a transformation that takes place over the course of the poem itself. In the first stanza, or group of lines, the poem describes the real, human world:

> Prisoner of the field, frenzied in agony,
> The light hides on you, see the sky:
> It closed its eyes to attack your dream,
> It closed your dress to break your chains.

The "prisoner" is the reader, the person to whom the poem is addressed. By addressing the poem directly to the reader, Eluard grabs the reader's attention and lets him or her know what he is about to discuss is of vital importance. In this case, the poet is informing his readers that they are enslaved in the real world, and he does so in a sermon-like way. Through his words, Eluard invokes images of slavery and freedom. The prisoner is "of the field," which is a common area where slaves have toiled in the past, and is "in agony," a common condition for slaves. The hiding "light" that used to be in "the sky" would in many traditional poems mean daylight or the sun, a traditional sign of goodness. However, in this surrealist poem, the meaning is skewed, and the light becomes a symbol for reality, in which the prisoner is enslaved. When viewed in this context, the slavery imagery throughout the rest of the first stanza makes sense.

In the third line the poet discusses the "dream" of his readers, which is that the ideal life can be

What Do I Study Next?

- Linda Bolton's *Art Revolutions: Surrealism* (2000) features brief text overviews of the surrealist art movement, including reproductions of famous works. The book also contains a time line and museum information.
- *The Interpretation of Dreams* (1901), Sigmund Freud's landmark book, was one of the main influences on French Surrealism. The book outlines his theory of the unconscious forces in dreams.
- *Surrealist Women: An International Anthology* (1998), edited by Penelope Rosemont and belonging to the Surrealist Revolution series, features nearly three hundred surrealist texts by ninety-six women from twenty-eight countries. The anthology, the first of its kind, also discusses the significance of women's contributions to Surrealism and gives a basic primer on the ideas behind the movement.
- *Fault Lines: Cultural Memory and Japanese Surrealism* (2001), by Miryam Sas, explores how the ideas and practices of Surrealism and other avant-garde styles of writing were transferred to Japan in the early twentieth century.

> "The dreamer still has not mastered the peculiar reason and logic of this imaginary world, which allows for the seizing of the stars themselves."

found in the real world. When reality retreats, however, it attacks this notion. Although this is a violent change for the prisoner, it is nevertheless for his or her own good, because the absence of reality redeems prisoners, by breaking the "chains."

In the absence of reality, or light, the poem and reader descend into the dream world, reality's opposite. As the second stanza shows, the characteristics of this world are strange to the prisoner:

Before the tied wheels
A fan laughs out loud.
In the treacherous nets of the grass
The roads lose their reflexion.

In this dream reality, all of the familiar hallmarks of civilization are gone. The "tied wheels" referred to in the first line of this stanza invoke the image of a car that cannot move. In the next line, the poet informs the reader that somebody or something—the word fan can mean either the device used for cooling or a person who is fond of something—is laughing, presumably at the car that is stuck. In the third line, the stuck car is revealed to be located in the "nets of the grass" that inhabit this world. This "treacherous" grass also swallows up the roads, which are now buried and so cannot reflect images or ideas.

The composite, surrealist image created by these four lines is one of nature replacing technology. In this dream world there is no place for modern technology like cars and roads—which Eluard's readers would find a comforting part of their reality. Instead the prisoner, now a dreamer, must adapt to a new set of rules and must throw out the familiarities that he or she is used to if the prisoner wants to make the most of this new world. Eluard's depiction of a disoriented dreamer who has just arrived in an imaginary world follows closely with Breton's observations about most of society, which he expressed in his *Manifesto*. Says Breton, "I have always been amazed at the way an ordinary observer lends so much more credence and attaches so much more importance to waking events than to those occurring in dreams." In Eluard's hands, the uncomfortable dreamer, like society, is yanked out of the reality of everyday life, and forced to accept the strange reality of the dream world.

After the dreamer arrives in this imaginary reality on earth, one of the four elements, the poet next summons images of another element, water:

Can't you take the waves
Whose barges are almonds
In your warm coaxing palm
Or in the ringlets of your head?

In this stanza, the poet begins to challenge his readers, taunting them with the powers they could have but currently do not possess. Unlike the poet, his readers cannot harness the sea—in which another symbol of technology, the barge, or ship, has been replaced by almonds—and coax it into their hands or their hair. Without letting go of technology and the familiar reality of the logical waking world, Eluard's readers will not be able to attain the godlike powers that the poet seems to possess. These prisoners, trapped by their familiarity with the established systems of logic and reason of the waking world, fail to see that worlds where almonds float on the sea like ships and oceans can be contained in the palm of one's hand are nevertheless valid and can be dominated. In her book *Twentieth-Century French Avant-Garde Poetry, 1907–1990*, Virginia A. La Charité observes that in Eluard's poetry, "while the image may defy reason and logic in its absurdity, it is not incomprehensible and so becomes both reasonable and logical." In other words, the images that Eluard describes create a picture in readers' minds that is definable, and so is imbued with its own sense of reason and logic.

In the next stanza, Eluard continues to taunt the reader, moving to the next largest, natural arena to demonstrate his powers, the heavens themselves:

Can't you seize the stars?
Stretched on the rack you resemble them,
In their nest of fire you dwell
And your light multiplies from them.

The dreamer still has not mastered the peculiar reason and logic of this imaginary world, which allows for the seizing of the stars themselves. Because of this, the dreamer is still a prisoner. In this stanza, Eluard says that the prisoner is being tortured on "the rack," a situation that once again implies captivity and domination. Like the stars in this world, which form a "nest of fire," the prisoner is immobile and therefore can be dominated by people like the poet, who have accepted and embraced the possibilities of this dream reality. In fact, lacking the ability to cope with this world, the reader becomes one of the stars, and the reader's reality, "the light," begins to be defined by them. In other words, over the course of four stanzas, the reader has traded a prison in the real world for one in the dream world, failing to recognize the possibilities that the latter has to offer.

With this stanza, Eluard completes the pattern he set up in the dream world. He starts out small on land, then goes to the ocean, which can be contained in the palm of his hand, then expands to include the universe itself. He does this in a dreamlike fashion, without any transition other than the spaces between the stanzas. While the imagery is rather bizarre, it still follows a general pattern, an idea that demonstrates another of Breton's observations about dreams, from his *Manifesto*: "Within the limits where they operate . . . dreams give every evidence of being continuous and show signs of organization."

In the first part of the last stanza of the poem, Eluard brings the reader back out of the dream world into reality, although it is a struggle:

> From the gagged dawn only one cry wants to rush
> out,
> A turning sun streams under the bark,
> It will be imprinted on your closed eyelids.

The waking reality, which is beginning to return, is "gagged," although it wants to "cry" out to the dreamer, and begins to slowly exert its influence, marking the dreamer's "closed eyelids." However, as Eluard notes in the final line, "Sweet one, when you sleep, night mingles with day." With this pronouncement, the poet announces to the reader that the two realities—dreams and real life—are intertwined. The "night" of the dream land will mix with the "day" of reality into one surreality. In this way, Eluard states that the ultimate goal of surrealists—to reconcile dreams and reality—has been achieved, and that by fighting it, one will only end up imprisoned, either in the real world or the dream world.

Source: Ryan D. Poquette, Critical Essay on Surrealism, in *Literary Movements for Students*, The Gale Group, 2003.

Jacqueline Chenieux-Gendron

In the following essay, Chenieux-Gendron looks at "the massive denial of prohibition" as a driving force behind Surrealism.

Three great systems of exclusion and division allow the human word to lay claim to purity: the play of prohibitions, the strongest of which is the prohibition of desire; the division between reason and madness; and the will to truth.

> We know perfectly well that we are not free to say just anything, that we cannot simply speak of anything, when we like or where we like; not just anyone, finally may speak of just anything. We have three types of prohibition, covering objects, ritual with its surrounding circumstances, the privileged or exclusive right to speak of a particular subject; these prohibitions interrelate, reinforce and complement each other, forming a complex web, continually subject to modification.

These prohibitions certainly surround the act of speech in a very powerful way. Moreover, added to them is the obligation to say *only* what is reasonable, and according to the codified modes of "non-madness." If pre-nineteenth-century Europe sometimes discerned signs of lucidity and marks of portent in the speech of the mad, this was another way of reinvesting that speech through reason, of denying its absolute *difference*. More subtly, too, as Michel Foucault shows, the very opposition between true and false defines a constraint on truth involving *power*. "Certainly, as a proposition, within a discourse, the division between true and false is neither arbitrary, nor modifiable, nor institutional, nor violent." But there *is* a will to truth, which takes different forms according to the various historical periods in the West, and which tends to exercise on other discourses, such as literature, or on other forms of expression, "a sort of pressure, a power to constrain." If we just think about the references to "verisimilitude" in Western art and literature until the naturalist period and probably beyond, we can measure its indirect force.

From the time of its foundation in France in 1919, Surrealism responded to these games of division by revolting against them. Surrealists saw these divisions with a lucidity and a violence sharpened by the postwar despair and a sense of there being no reason to go on living. After the rupture and bloodshed of World War I, in opposition to the clear conscience of Europe, which was reshaping and healing itself, the movement launched a wave of global contestation and wove a network of *other*

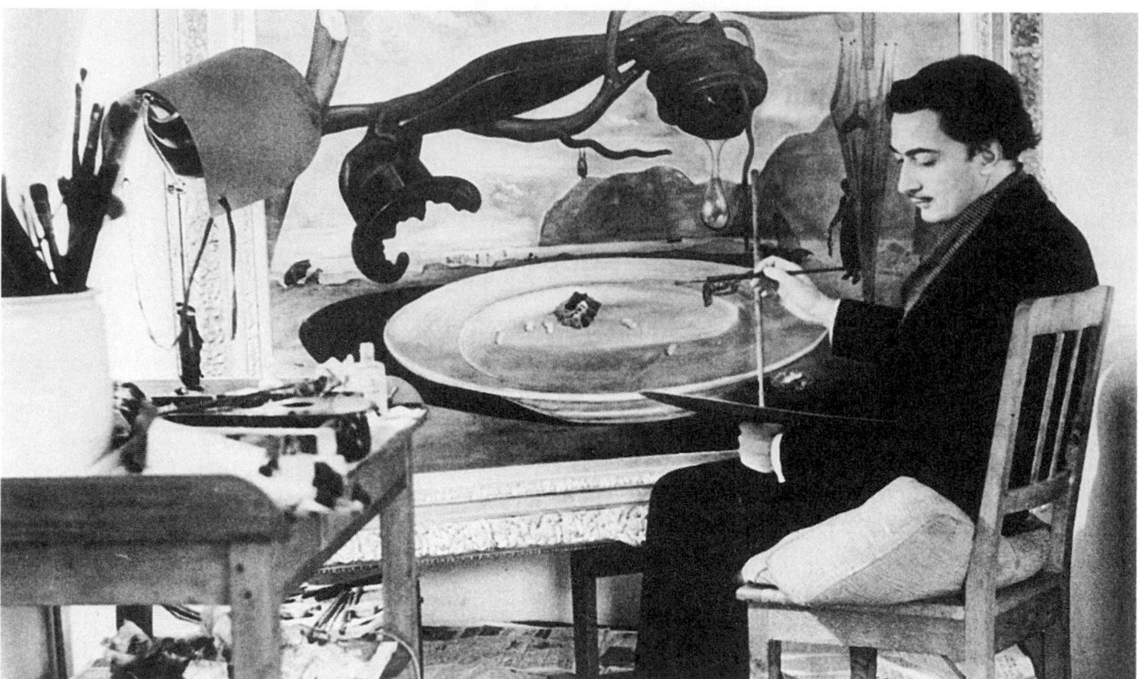

Surrealist painter Salvador Dalí

differences. In its most far-reaching projects, Surrealism claims to mingle desire with human speech, and eros with human life—not just to tell, or to describe, desire and eros. It claims to abolish the notion of incongruity or obscenity, to let the subconscious speak, and to simulate different pathologies of language. It claims to overturn the quest for the probable in art by making an astounding bet on the imagination, presented as the central power of the human mind, from which emerges a whole life-in-poetry. In this life-in-poetry the improbable, the extraordinary, the incongruous would grow in abundance; sincerity would no longer have an absolute referential value; what would be sought for its own sake would no longer be truth but living, living *otherwise* than in everyday mediocrity, living *outside* the track to which society assigns each of us.

This displacement of the system of moral and intellectual values on which centuries of Western culture were based has been and still is sometimes perceived as a perversion, or a biasing of human activity: an antihumanism.

Now that we can define it more clearly, differentiating it from other poetic movements that arose in Europe at the same time, the French Surrealist project once again makes possible and legitimizes all sorts of of behaviors and practices which are not completely *new*, but which had tended to become marginalized or encysted in the tissue of social life and poetic practice. Surrealism preaches the reversal of this tendency and the totalizing assumption of responsibility for all human behavior. Human violence had indeed been marginalized and neutralized by social life, by the norms of bourgeois capitalist society, but still rose up unpredictably and found an outlet in wars: in the example of the "just" war, as the French saw it, that was the butchery in Europe from 1914 to 1918. Surrealism proposes a recognition and a taking of responsibility for human violence in *revolt*, in every sense. It is on this very general if not symbolic level that we should understand the proclamation of Andre Breton's *Second Manifesto of Surrealism*:

> one can understand why Surrealism was not afraid to make for itself a tenet of total revolt, complete insubordination, of sabotage according to rule, and why it still expects nothing save from violence. The simplest Surrealist act consists of dashing down into the street, pistol in hand, and firing blindly, as fast as you can pull the trigger, into the crowd.

But also, and without any contradiction, Surrealism tried to channel this potential energy, until then burning away "in the open air," into an action at once inventive and concerted:

> Once again, the question here is the whole problem of the transformation of energy. To distrust, as people do out of all proportion, the practical virtue of imagination is to be willing to deprive oneself at any cost of the help of electricity, in the hope of bringing hydroelectric power back to its absurd waterfall consciousness.

Also marginalized were eroticism and the powers of love in French society of the late nineteenth and early twentieth century. Surrealism struggled constantly against the ruling hypocrisy on the double front of eroticism and the recognition of love. An article on "research into sexuality" appears in the eleventh issue of *La Révolution Surréaliste* (1928); daringly, clinically accurate for a time when Robert Desnos and Kra, his publisher, were brought into court for supposedly pornographic passages of *La liberté ou l'amour!* (1927). And there was a recognition of love's power to disturb the mind in the same issue of the review in which appear the answers to a "Questionnaire on Love," written in a tone of intense but unidealistic urgency. In the sixties, with no contradiction, Breton discounted "sex education" as a force for liberation in order to preserve love's power to disturb (Jean-Claude Silbermann, 1964, *Le surréalisme et la peinture*). Marginalized, too, were the practice of automatic writing and the use of dreams as the springboard of "inspiration"—both of which had fostered the writing of all sorts of great texts (from Horace Walpole's dream to Mallarmé's resonant obsession, "The penultimate is dead"), but neither of which had ever been explicitly advocated as a systematic exercise. In twentieth-century society, all sorts of magical behavior was veiled which the Surrealist group was to concentrate on exhibiting.

Surrealism therefore presents itself to us as a machine for *integration*—having refused the cultural divisions we have discussed, even the division between true and false, that have been the basis for language in the West since the nineteenth-century industrial and scientific revolution. This movement of integration implies a reversal in the manifestation of a function hitherto marginalized both in social life and in literary and philosophical tradition: I am referring here to the imagination. All Platonic philosophy shows the human being as a chariot guided by the intellect and carried along by the will, while imagination, the lead horse, tries to make the team run off its course. Before Surrealism, the "classical" and rationalist philosophical tradition in France, while insisting on the infinite character of will and its primary importance in defining human liberty, had thrust imagination to the side of life, of animation, of warmth, of vivacity, and thus "prepared our minds to recognize the primacy of the imagination, from the moment when life appears no longer as a secondary fact, but as a primary, primitive fact and as an indivisible energy." The meaning of the Romantic revolution (to which Surrealism is connected, from this point of view) was to give imagination a *cognitive* function.

But Romantic philosophy is a philosophy of being, in which imagination can rediscover paradise lost. The implicit philosophy of the French Surrealists, playing on the level of existence and not of essence, of beings and not of being, gives imagination a leading role: not to *re*cognize something that had previously been veiled, but to give existence to its own unprecedented forms. The power of (poetic) imagination becomes, by definition, practical. The play on words *must* become its own object (Duchamp), dreamed forms *must* be materialized in a tangible object (Breton, *Introduction au discours sur le peu de réalité*.)

But if Surrealism is a machinery for integration, it is also, in the same impulse, or perhaps from another point of view, a machinery for negating. Surrealism negates everything implied by the divisions and prohibitions on which the majority cultural structure is founded: negating ready-made "orders," denying the pertinence of codes (social, but also stylistic, linguistic, and even logical). Surrealists therefore suspect everything that organizes the sense of things, the *direction* of things, in space and in time, especially any kind of taxonomy and any presentation of evidence that has *signification* for us. Various games take shape: one consists of trying to capture the meaning of time, or of space, or of language, in the moment of their arising—in a kind of original space, with mythical evidence. The practice of automatic writing or drawing is a response to this intention: "to create a universe of words [or of forms, I should add] in which the universe of our practical and utilitarian perceptions will be completely disoriented." Is this a question of *either* refusing ready-made meanings *or* creating the conditions for the epiphany of a new meaning? What we have here is rather the two intentions at the same time, the first being the reverse side of the second. Another game (Bataille's own game, but, at one time, also André Masson's or Hans Bellmer's and the particular form eroticism takes in them) consists of negating the meaning of space and of the human body, by the introduction of all possible meanings in a dionysiac investment of space, even at the price of tearing apart and scattering the

> **"The aim—to take back the move that implicates human conduct and language in prohibitions and power structures—is turned upside down and becomes an immense confidence in 'pure' desire, in 'absolute' revolt, in the powers not of society but of the word."**

human body. The absence of "meaning" can also be seen in the practice of exhibiting as equivalent the two sides of things and of manifesting the plurality of meanings of signs: as if one had to show that "meaning" could be transparent, or that things and signs had the same value as their opposites. This is Marcel Duchamp's enterprise. For example, the *Female Fig Leaf* is the printed stamp, the "negative" of a feminine sexual organ, so that hiding the masculine organ—the role of the fig leaf in classical statuary—or exhibiting the feminine organ amounts to the same thing. In the realm of signs and letters, this is also the enterprise of Robert Desnos. And to this practice we must add the use Surrealism makes of the reverse of cultural content. I am thinking not only of Paul Eluard and Benjamin Péret's collection of updated proverbs (*152 proverbes mis au goût du jour*), but also of the reversal of the content of myths. In *Au château d'Argol*, Julien Gracq turns the myth of the Savior into a myth of the ambivalence of the mediator. Savior? Perhaps, but condemner as well.

This is a great attempt to demolish the sense of reality, stigmatized in 1947 by Jean-Paul Sartre, who put Surrealist thought in the same class as the (eternal) current of scepticism, emphasizing certain manifestations which he interprets as idealist. According to him, the Surrealists preach, particularly through automatic writing, the dissolution of the individual consciousness and also, by the symbolic annulment of "object-witnesses," the dissolution of the objectivity of the world.

But Surrealism responds to this threatening spread of idealism steadfastly with two firebreaks. One is political action, whose sparks we will see fly with some regularity in the historical part of this work; the other is the attempt, in the very heart of practical activity (ethical *or* artistic), to make *another* sense emerge, discovered by some people in and through pleasure and by others in and through the seizure of a projective desire (that is "objective chance"). Pleasure on one side, in which the body rediscovers its sense and sensibility rediscovers its comforts; on the other side, a new ethic of desire, in which time rediscovers an undeniable orientation.

Thus, the massive denial of prohibition, as it functions in Surrealism, is also a game of *displacement*. The aim—to take back the move that implicates human conduct and language in prohibitions and power structures—is turned upside down and becomes an immense confidence in "pure" desire, in "absolute" revolt, in the powers not of society but of the word. Now on the one hand this involves mythical terms ("pure" desire, "absolute" revolt), which function as the horizon of an ever-disappointing quest, or as its completely fictional premises. But more especially, in the order of speech, this voice, which the Surrealists originally gave in its full strength to *everyone* ("Secrets of the Surrealist Magical Art," in the first *Manifesto*), has been appropriated by a *few*. Is this the necessity of experimentation or the displacement of prohibitions? It is the ineluctable ambiguity of Surrealism finally to have reinforced the privileged right of the speaking subject within an already privileged group. Surrealism has reinvented, in fact, as the privileged place in which the "miracle" arises, the *group* constituted around a dominant personality. This elective constellation reproduces, with its rites of initiation, exclusion, and rehabilitation, the characteristics of a microsociety ruled by magical thinking:

> The group never presents itself here as the picture of an open community, swollen with uncontrolled contagion; on the contrary, it is rather the idea that seems to have imposed itself on Breton from the beginning: the idea of a closed, separate *order*, of an exclusive companionship, of a phalanstery which tends to be shut in by vaguely magical walls (the significant idea of a "castle" is hovering about somewhere nearby).

Membership in the group, in what Jules Monnerot calls the *Bund*, is a central condition of Surrealist life in its French definition: the place in which sensibilities are exacerbated and creativity exalted. Thus the Surrealist word sometimes becomes collective, or impersonal, and does not depend on the power of the speaking object. It replaces this power by that of Surrealism.

Is this displacement of "divisions" and cleavages a perverse effect of preaching liberation, or is it the necessary means? The Surrealist reply is obviously the latter. Moreover, it would be inaccurate to see this displacement as parallel, or the various called-for prohibitions as symmetrical. The prohibitions linked to the functioning of the group life are explicit and artificial. The prohibitions denounced by Michel Foucault, which eternalize their own everyday immediacy, are implicit and even repressed by the communal consciousness. A language and behavior that refuse the division between reason and folly, as between truth and error, in favor of imagination, analogy, and desire are words and behaviors that insert within their process an awareness of their relativity. Their intoxicating liberty and the preciosity of their discoveries are bought by an awareness of their precariousness, which is no doubt very hard to maintain without the structuring, securing interplay of *other* divisions.

The origin of new hierarchies and new differences thus lies not only in group life but in certain Surrealist "values": the search for eros, the search for political and social liberty, the search for poetry. But the functioning of these "values" is quite different from what can be seen in a morality of prohibition. It involves, by repeated transgression, reinventing a certain orientation of the world. To be exact, for Michel Leiris, we must reinvent the sacred by transgressing the taboo, "a limit in regard to which things abandon the unoriented, amorphous character of the profane and polarize themselves into left and right." And Breton, after having incriminated Judeo-Christian religion as both "blood-curdling and congealed," cannot help but subscribe to Francis Ponge's suggestion: "Perhaps the lesson we must learn is to abolish all values the instant we discover them." Value, poetic and practical, is discovered in the same moment in which it is transgressed.

We must therefore be wary of the oversimplified image of Surrealism as the breaker of prohibitions, a word on which Pierre de Massot puns when he calls his homage to Breton "Breton le septembriseur," the revolutionary: as a "pure" movement, free from any compromise with what has been repressed. But it is also too simple to see in Surrealism, as was fashionable in the criticism of the sixties, a locus for stubborn, confusional idealism, for the celebration of some sorts of vaguely conceived transgression—or, as those who are nostalgic for Dadaism believe, the proud fortress of a coercive morality whose high priest was supposedly André Breton. Some people think that the "fringe" figures and fellow travelers of Surrealism (expressions they use, as I do, in the least uncomplimentary way possible, to refer to figures like Georges Bataille and Antonin Artaud) should be relocated at the heart of the adventure of the avant-garde, lived by them in a *more* revolutionary way. Others believe that Bretonian hypocrisy must be unmasked, and authenticity tracked down amid the make-believe. Critical distance today permits us to relate the projects of some Surrealists to others without automatically establishing hierarchies and demarcating boundaries within and outside the historical group: in short, to weigh the differences with passion but without projecting preconceived schemas upon them.

Source: Jacqueline Chenieux-Gendron, "Prohibition and Meaning," in *Surrealism*, translated by Vivian Folkenflik, Columbia University Press, 1990, pp. 1–8.

Henri Peyre

In the following essay, Peyre describes the importance of the Surrealist movement for the twentieth century, calling it "one of the most far-reaching attempts at changing, not only literature and painting, but psychology, ethics, and man himself."

Surrealism is likely to occupy a very considerable place in the intellectual history of the Western world in our century. Its significance as a literary phenomenon during the years 1920–1940 is unequalled. Ever since 1940, when powerful and occasionally unfair blows were dealt it by Sartre, as trenchant a polemicist as he is subtle a dialectician, Surrealism has staged a surprising comeback. It refused to concede victory to the Existentialist movement, which was impatient to bury it along with other hollow idols of an antediluvian or pre-Sartrian age. Breton returned from his American exile, shook his lion's mane in Montmartre, rallied new disciples, excommunicated others as he explained how only the mythical and magical ambitions of the Surrealists could bring any hope of salvation to a decrepit world. The release of Desire and the triumph of Love were the new levers which could move mountains of unbelief and hatred.

Several books appeared in the aftermath of World War II telling the history of the Surrealist group, delving into the intricacies of its successive negations and assertions, assessing the results of its pictorial and poetical achievements. A Surrealist

> "... only the mythical and magical ambitions of the Surrealists could bring any hope of salvation to a decrepit world. The release of Desire and the triumph of Love were the new levers which could move mountains of unbelief and hatred."

exhibition at the Maeght Gallery in Paris in 1947 was more than a review of twenty-five years of Surrealist revolt; it brought home to many Parisians the tragic gravity which underlay most of the Surrealists' eccentricities and the bitter confirmation which their blasphemies had received from the war. Surrealism, which has received inadequate attention in this country, is one of the most far-reaching attempts at changing, not only literature and painting, but psychology, ethics, and man himself.

A span of fifteen years, *grande mortalis aevi spatium*, as Tacitus said of old, was enough to shift the emphasis from the turbulent aspect of the Surrealist movement to its deeper and lasting significance. In 1925, there were few indeed who saw in it anything more than a return to infantilism and nihilism. In 1940, its hoaxes and pranks were almost forgotten; one had to acknowledge that to Surrealism we owed one of the greatest prose writers of our age, André Breton; three or four of the purest poets—Eluard, Char and Desnos; and even an impure but occasionally brilliant one—Aragon; and several gifted painters. Surrealism was always more than a strictly literary and artistic movement; it influenced interior decoration and the film, our sensibility, our imagination, perhaps even our dreams. It left an imprint upon psychology and metaphysics; it spread to five or six European countries and to other continents. It may be that the adjective Surrealist will remain affixed to the whole era between the two World Wars as best describing its boldest ambition. It would be neither more nor less appropriate to that age than the word Symbolist as applied to the years 1880–1900.

For many a name may rightly be associated with Surrealism which never was actually on the select list of the initiates. Several of the early adepts broke away from the sanctum, or were rejected from it. Others, like Reverdy and Michaux, never actually joined the group. But posterity will disregard such fine distinctions. It calls "Romantic" men like Balzac and Michelet who never belonged to any Romantic *chapelle*, others like Delacroix who vehemently rejected the label and would have nothing to do with Balzac and Baudelaire, others still like Vigny who soon estranged themselves from the *cénacles*. In spite of their probable protests, which death will some day silence, insuring the triumph of those modest but inevitable victors, the literary historians, we may consider as Surrealists the following men: Breton, Aragon, Soupault, Péret, Hugnet, Desnos, Crevel, Artaud, Naville, Tzara, Eluard, Michaux, Reverdy, Bataille, Prévert, Césaire, Gracq, Monnerot, Leiris. The list is far from exhaustive as J. H. Matthews points out in his article printed elsewhere in this issue. Among the painters are Miró, Max Ernst, Chirico, Tanguy, Picabia, Masson, Man Ray, Magritte, Matta, Arp, etc. And, of course, Salvador Dali—*quantum mutatus ab illo*! He has, since the heroic age, become the butt of Breton's most venomous arrows and, among the faithful, has assumed the mock scrambled name of Avida Dollars. Nonetheless, the number of other talents is impressive.

Iconoclasts, in France at least, take good care to find illustrious predecessors who posthumously sponsor their audacity. One of the most considerable achievements of Surrealism was its discovery that many writers and painters of the past had been Surrealists without knowing it: Sasseta, Hieronymus Bosch, Blake, Achim von Arnim, E. A. Poe, and others. They renovated the perspective in which some of the intercessors, or exciters, of Surrealism were henceforth to be viewed. It is now impossible, and hardly desirable, to deprive Sade, Nerval, Lautréamont, Rimbaud, Jarry and Apollinaire of the new stature that Surrealism has lent them. They will eternally remain as precursors of Surrealism, as Rousseau is a forerunner of Romanticism and Baudelaire a herald of Symbolist experiments.

Among the ancestors whom they worshipped, the first place belongs to Lautréamont; for, at the beginning, the Surrealists remained strangely reticent about Rimbaud. The rehabilitation of that forgotten prose-poet is one of their durable achievements. "To that man belongs probably the chief responsibility for the present condition of poetry,"

Breton declared, implying that the condition was Surrealist, hence admirable. Maldoror, Lautréamont's hero, was hailed as "the one name flung across the centuries as an unadulterated challenge to all that on earth is stupid, base, and sickening." From him they learned a lesson of courage, finding guidance perhaps in a statement he had prophetically announced in 1869 before his mysterious disappearance at the age of twenty-four: "At this very hour, new flashes of lightning race through the intellectual atmosphere; what is wanted is only the courage to face them steadily." With Lautréamont as their *duce e signore* they descended into vertiginous pits of hell, wandered among devilish nightmares, systematically cultivated monstrous hallucinations. Jarry's bitter buffoonery took on a new meaning when the Surrealists reinterpreted it as a derision of the old bourgeois ramshackle structure which collapsed with the war of 1914. Ubu Roi was, for Breton, "an admirable creation for which I would give all the Shakespeares and the Rabelais in the world." Apollinaire's message, expressed less in his verse than in his *Cubist Painters* and in a masterly article on "Poets and the New Spirit," published three weeks after his death in *Mercure de France* (1st December 1918), was bequeathed to the Surrealists who were the first to divine its significance. The role of the artist is to become inhuman; he must look for what in art has "most energy," scorn facile charm, leap forward and assert the claims of poetry and painting to explore the world of the future, claims which are prior to those of philosophy, psychology, and science. The enigmatic Jacques Vaché is the last patron saint of Surrealism; his influence on Breton was chiefly through conversation and the strangeness of his personality. For Vaché did not condescend to write anything, except a few striking war letters to his friend; he lived with a woman to whom he never said a word, only kissing her hand in noble silence after she had poured tea; he derided literature as a vain occupation ("aiming so conscientiously in order to miss the mark") and asserted that all was vain in life. He renounced it in 1919 when, along with two young Americans, he absorbed an inordinate dose of opium.

We shall not be concerned here with the history of the Surrealist sect, with its confused political affiliations, with its painters, nor with any attempt to define the claims of the Surrealists as they would themselves view them or wish to see them defined. We would rather, with the help of a few quotations and some acquaintance with the essential Surrealist texts, endeavor to point out the deeper significance of Surrealism. Eccentricities, excesses, childish mysticism, an obsession with fortuitous coincidences in life, and sheer mediocrity in paintings, films, and poems are to be found in abundance in Surrealism; they will be forgotten. The credit side of the movement is important enough for us to disregard some ephemeral littleness and to forgive some adolescent provocations.

Every literary or philosophical movement may be said to include a negative and a positive aspect. The two are developed simultaneously, but may be envisaged separately for clarity's sake. The young men who rally under some new banner agree with relative ease on what they negate; their hunger for destruction is all-embracing. They joyfully trample under their feet the legacy of previous generations. It is harder for them to find a common ground for their positive assertions. If they have any personality, they are likely to listen to their own temperaments and to plunge into heresy if a set of positive dogmas is proposed to their literary faith.

The negative side of the Surrealist revolt was stressed by the adepts of the group with a ferocious and systematic intransigence which, in the third decade of the century, caused the hair of many a bourgeois to stand on end. Yet even then it took no exceptional clearsightedness to sense that a desperate search for a new faith lay beneath the vehement blasphemies of Breton and his friends. Their uncommon energy would not long be satisfied by mere fist-shaking. The Surrealist revolt is to be compared to the Cartesian *tabula rasa*, or brushing aside of previous confused growth in order to lay new foundations for a sounder and more ambitious structure. There always remains much logic behind any French attempt at illogic and an almost immoral passion for morals behind any Gallic denunciation of conventional ethics. The Surrealists are no exception. They are logicians and moralists primarily.

Their revolt, which appeared to be undiscriminating and universal, differed in fact from the nihilism of Dada. It concentrated on three targets which we may define as ethics and religion, the social and political realm, and literary conventions.

In the matter of religion, Breton never wavered; and extremely few, if any, of the former Surrealists ever joined the ranks of Catholic converts. There was the curious conversion to Surrealism in 1926 of the priest, Gengenbach, which provides one of the most ludicrous episodes in the movement's history. Gengenbach had previously fallen in love with an actress and consequently been unfrocked by his bishop. But the actress found him no longer attractive when he ceased to wear a cassock; the former priest, in despair, went with suicidal intentions to the lake at Gerardmer where he glanced at a Surrealist review and saw the light. This curious individual attempted to reconcile Surrealism and Christianity. He failed, ended by denouncing Breton as Lucifer, and turned again to the faith of his childhood. He is not typical, for the Surrealists' unconcern with God is even more pronounced than that of the Existentialists.

In an interview, Breton even spurned the Nietzschean phrase "the death of God" as meaningless, since "to die, one should first have existence." Yet, like many adversaries of religion, like Nietzsche himself in his tragic *Ecce Homo*, Breton is an impious rival of Christ rather than a negator. His disciple Monnerot did not err when he asserted that Surrealism aims at a total transformation such as had only been attempted by religions; and Breton liked to quote Tolstoy's words: "What truth can there be, if there is death?" A religious critic, Michel Carrouges, writing in the Dominican periodical *La Vie Intellectuelle* in November 1945, exemplifies the reactions of several latitudinarian French Catholics when he declares:

> Surrealism is no empty hoax; it is not necessarily demoniacal as is sometimes imagined; it is a great invention of the modern world still in its infancy. . . . It is perhaps the most extraordinary movement of the human spirit . . . the most terrible mental explosive in existence.

On the moral plane, too, the Surrealist pronouncements were calculated to shake our complacency; they were occasionally accompanied by determined and perverse attempts at demoralization of the youth—with lamentable success. "Morality, that weakness of the brain," a line of Rimbaud's *Season in Hell* had exclaimed. To the Surrealists, moral censorship practiced against the impulses of our unconscious had to be abolished in order that a new peace, according to Freudian therapeutics, might invade our being, and still more in order to liberate our imagination. Breton and Eluard acclaimed Sade as the prophet of the new ethical crusade. But they were soon to draw the lineaments of a new ethics, far removed front hedonist indulgence and resting on a lofty conception of desire and of love. When Breton broke with the Communists, it was clearly on moral grounds and because "moral sense was undeniably the human reality which their party trampled daily and most gleefully underfoot." Much earlier, in his volume *Les Pas perdus* (1924), that immoralist had confessed his love for all moralists, and added: "The moral question preoccupies me. . . . *La morale* is the great peacemaker. Even to attack her is to pay her a tribute. In her did I always find my most exalting inspiration."

In the field of politics, the fierceness of the Surrealist protest is best understood if one remembers that it originated during World War I. And in many ways that war shook the minds of men more powerfully than did World War II. For it burst out after a prolonged era of peace and material progress during which Europeans had become accustomed to celebrate civilization and science as undeniably beneficient. Suddenly they were faced with the glaring bankruptcy of science, of logic, of their faith in progress, of philosophy and literature which failed to protest against the great massacre and often undertook to justify it. The Surrealists were impressed by the gaping abyss which separated man's power to change the world through science and his utter inability to change himself. They became convinced that there must exist, behind what we call reality or behind the conventional layers of our minds, forces which control us. Surrealism would attempt to discover those forces and to liberate them, if they could be harnessed for man's benefit.

To the Surrealists, and especially to Breton, we are indebted for some of the most moving and intelligent denunciations of war and its glamor. The cure for the monstrous evil is to be sought in the liberation of the imagination, in fulfilling by other means the boundless needs for childhood, for joy, for risk and for play, for intense emotions, which insidiously lead men to consent to collective murder. The Russian Revolution appeared to the Surrealists, as it did to many liberals in Europe, as the great hope for a new era of justice and fraternity. Their disillusion was all the more bitter when that Revolution turned to nationalism and the worship of Stakhanovist efficiency. Their sympathies went to Trotsky, who had proved understanding toward literature and had boldly announced that "the Revolution undertakes to conquer the right of all men, not only to bread, but to poetry." "Bread and also roses," Jaurès had, before 1914, demanded for the working classes. From 1930 or thereabout, most of the Surrealists turned against Stalinist Communism and rejected a revolution deprived of idealism and "serving to improve that abominable thing, earthly comfort" (Breton). But they did not desist from their fight against any conservatism, whether it came from the right or from the left. "More than ever do I believe in the necessity of transforming the world in the direction of the rational (more exactly, of the surrational) and of justice," Breton declared in an important interview given to *Une Semaine dans le monde*. (31st July 1948).

But it is easier in France to rise in revolt against political institutions, social and ethical conventions, and, of course, against any government, than to be a literary rebel. Most liberals, from Voltaire to P. L. Courier and Anatole France, most radicals, socialists, and anarchists had always remained the most orthodox guardians of the purity of the French language and timid conservatives in matters of taste. Breton, Aragon, and Eluard have not "twisted the neck" of the French language; they have paid frequent tribute to their predecessors and have at times revived among us the shades of the Troubadours or the cadences of seventeenth century prose. But they dared attack pitilessly realism and its platitudinous dullness, eloquence always lurking behind poetical writing, above all logic which, under the guise of the detective novel, has staged an insidious offensive in the last three decades; for the detective novel is naively based upon the assumption that there is a cause or an agent for all that happens, and it banishes the inexplicable and the gratuitous from our world. Against the novel and its attraction for money-minded writers of today Surrealism restored the claims of poetry. Breton saw the novel as a prosaic game of chess with a contemptible adversary, "man, whoever he is, being only a mediocre adversary." He added scornfully, "the ambition of novelists does not reach very far."

But Surrealism did more than restore poetry. It rebelled against the very notion of culture and revealed to many moderns the strange beauty of Negro sculpture and of African and Polynesian masks. It ridiculed the concept of good taste which tends to constitute a barrier to any innovation and systematically kills the annexation of provinces of ugliness to the realm of the beautiful. The Surrealists reveled in the epic monstrosities of bad taste—"in the bad taste of our age, I endeavor to go farther than anyone else," Breton once wrote—and extracted new flowers of evil from that horrifying paradise hitherto reserved for concierges, *pompiers*, and other philistines. The last stronghold of the élite, which is its conviction that its esthetic values would survive wars, revolutions, and financial loss of caste, that good taste is the one tyrannical evidence before which men will always bow, was stormed in the Surrealist attacks.

"Only the word liberty can still produce a state of exaltation in man." This famous cry of Breton provides a key to a just appreciation of the positive achievement of Surrealism. Liberty, or rather the pursuit of a total liberation, is the keyword of its doctrinal pronouncements.

Surrealism wanted to liberate the subconscious. Its direction was thus clearly parallel to that taken earlier or at the same time by Freud, Proust, and Joyce. Unlike Proust, however, it avoided superimposing a complex structure of didactic reasoning and of refined analysis upon an attempt to capture those mysterious moments when man, escaping the inexorable flow of time, reaches the "peak of sovereignty." Unlike Freud, to whom Breton owed much, the Surrealists did not advocate bringing to the light of clear consciousness, and dissipating eventually, the strange growth of complexes in our turgid depths. Much was made, in the early stages of Surrealism, of automatic writing, uncontrolled by reason or by critical spirit, which gave itself out as spoken and written thought seized in its spontaneous immediacy. In fact, the leading Surrealists never abused that perilous device. Their verse and their prose give evidence of elaborate composition, of skillful combination of effects, of a restrained choice made among the riches of the unconscious. But their originality lay precisely in having first proceeded to a courageous clearing of all that was worn out and effete in literature, and in having made a fresh selection from a new and vast accummulation of materials hitherto unexplored. Literature tends to utilize passively only the stones already quarried, hewn and polished by robust predecessors; it must periodically spurn such tempting and neatly arranged materials and carve out its own rock. In so doing, Surrealism occasionally hit upon sparkling gems. Its will to innovate was not a mere effort after originality; it was a resolute attempt to explore a virgin expanse in or under man's mind and to dig into the hidden layers in which the civilized creature cannot dissemble or lie, as he does in his so-called " rational," or diligently controlled life.

The second ambition of Surrealism was to open up to literature the domain of dreams, and even of insanity, strangely neglected but for a few feeble trials by classical and modern writers to depict dreams of tragic characters, Hamlet's, Hermione's, or Tasso's methodical madness. In the dream, the Surrealists respected what Reverdy called "a freer and more uninhibited form of thought." They reveled in its inconsistencies, in its capricious disregard of causality, in the vividness of its images. They explored its symbolic secrets as revealing remnants of a primitive mentality only imperfectly repressed in ourselves. Not a little of the beauty of Eluard's and Char's poetry is due to its dreamlike atmosphere. Breton went farther and resumed Nerval's century-old attempt to "direct his eternal dream instead of passively submitting to it." His volume, *Les Vases communicants*, contains the most splendid description of fantastic dreams written since Nerval's record of his madness in *Aurélia*. Dreams are no longer the privilege of sleep; day-dreams are no longer mild, idyllic reveries. The realms of night and of day, sleep and wakefulness, hold a constant and fruitful interchange; the dream is respected and its luxuriance of images faithfully transcribed, while it is also interpreted and analyzed by a mystic trained in physiology and psychology. "I stand in the hall of a castle, a dark lantern in my hand, and I illuminate the sparkling armors one after the other." Thus Breton, the former medical intern, describes himself in the opening pages of his *Vases communicants*.

The twofold liberation of the subconscious and of the oneiric domain leads to a third: the unchaining of the imagination. The Surrealists are the faithful heirs of Baudelaire and Rimbaud and, beyond them, of Coleridge, Blake, Novalis, and Achim von Arnim. They have enthroned the "magical and synthetic power" as the goddess of their works; and to them, as to the English Romantics, the " renascence of wonder" became the highest achievement of the poet, recapturing the gifts of childhood in adult life.

Through an apparently spontaneous flow of images, Surrealism thaws the crust of blunted perceptions and of deductive reasoning which separates us from our deepest life and from the remnants of childhood buried in our subconscious. It maps out whole archipelagoes long submerged in a sea of dulled habit. It plunges below our intellectual vision of the world and beyond our sensory data; it seems to "see into the life of things" and to forge new and closer links between ourselves and so-called inanimate objects. The normal translation of those uncharted lands into which Blake and Rimbaud had ventured is effected through a new metaphoric langauge. One of the chief claims to greatness of Surrealist poetry lies, in our opinion, in its imagery. That poetry has replenished the threadbare stock of metaphors by which Hugo's successors and French Symbolists had long been content to live. Reverdy, a poet whom the Surrealists have always respected even though he did not join their ranks, wrote:

> An image is a pure creation of the mind... It springs from the linking of two realities more or less distant. The more unexpected and just the relations between the two realities thus linked are, the more powerful the image, the greater its emotive force and its poetical truth.

The poetry of Breton and Eluard—and even that of minor figures like Tzara and Hugnet—abounds in rare and fresh images which seem to create the object anew for our blunted senses and to allow a dreamworld to glide gently into our consciousness, first shaken, then voluptuously lulled, by the discontinuous flow of Surrealist metaphors.

The Surrealists' endeavor to bring about a total renewal of the very mainsprings of literature has nowhere proved more courageous, and more startlingly successful, than in their treatment of love.

Love between man and woman had almost disappeared from literature after 1920. It happened that the leading figures of that literary era—Proust, Gide, Cocteau, and even Montherlant and Julien Green—were only slightly interested in heterosexual relations or in the "promotion of woman," as sociologists were pleased to call it. The war had, moreover, created many causes of friction or of misunderstanding between the sexes, and the "virile fraternity," cherished by Malraux and Saint-Exupéry, appeared nobler to many former or future soldiers than any sentimental and intellectual union with women, with whom young men often felt out of tune. An affectation of brutality and of cynicism had replaced the former rhetorical delusions of romantic love. Women, by winning new rights and meeting men on an equal footing in many a profession, seemed to have waived their former privilege as inspirers of artists and of poets.

Surrealism rehabilitated woman and love poetry in our midst. It would be naive to present the Surrealists as Platonic worshippers of spiritual beauty, or as hypocritical enough to conceal eroticism behind romantic adoration. They had read Sade even more than Musset. There is more Petrarchist inspiration, in Eluard especially, than there is Platonism. Yet they have ceased to exile woman from poetry, as Rimbaud and his followers had attempted to do, or to worship and abuse her alternately as a vessel for all the treacheries of Satan, in Baudelarian fashion. Aragon's war poetry, more faithful to the Surrealist creed than his former friends were willing to acknowledge, sang the most rapturous hymns chanted to woman since the Romantics. Eluard may well rank among the three or four supreme love poets in the French language. His theme is a continuous transfiguration of woman in her body and in her mysterious and dreamy charm.

Toute tiède encore du linge annulè
Tu fermes les yeux et tu boules
Comme bouge un chant qui naît
Vaguement mais de partout

Odorante et savoureuse
Tu dépasses sans te perdre
Les frontières de ton corps

Tu as enjambé le temps
Te voici femme nouvelle
Révélée à l'infini.
(Une Longue Pensée amoureuse)

Breton's love poetry does not rise to such felicitousness of musical language, but one of his finest prose works, *L'Amour fou*, is devoted to a triumphant exaltation of love as the great constructive force. He does not indulge in any such mysticism of the flesh as do intoxicated Puritans like D. H. Lawrence and inverted woman-haters like Henry Miller. But he rarely chides men for stupidly despairing of love, for imagining, once their youth is over, that love lies behind them, in their brief adolescent years, while it is there "waiting for them, in front of them." Desire, or Eros, the old Hesiodic name of the earliest of the gods, must be emancipated and become the level which will achieve men's imaginative liberation from the mechanical forces which have made him a willing slave to tyranny and to war.

Surrealism, however, was more than an exploration of new literary realms or a rediscovery of the old theme of love. Beyond its literary or pictorial claims, it was and is a metaphysical perception of the tragic sense of human life and a desperate attempt to leap beyond the bounds usually assigned to human reason. In this respect, not only is it parallel to its jealous rival, Existentialism, but it must be linked, willy-nilly, with other significant movements of our age, whether religious (Kierkegaard) or para-religious (Kafka, Malraux, Camus), equally obsessed with the all-pervading tragedy of man's fate in a world from which man had vainly tried to banish tragedy.

The originality of the French Surrealists lies here in their sincerity. For, behind their youthful pranks and their delight in mischief and mystification, they were in truth passionately intense young men, venturing to the verge of insanity and suicide. One of their former members, Antonin Artaud, who died in 1948, spent years, as did Nerval, in an insane asylum; Eluard, always lucid and one of the most classical of poets, had to take refuge in another insane asylum and to pose as one of the deranged inmates in order to escape capture by the Germans for his activity in the French Resistance. Vaché, a precursor, had ended his life in 1919; one of the young Surrealist affiliates, Rigaut, killed himself in 1929, after writing a last message to his companions: "You are all poets and I am on the side of death." René Crevel, the gifted and promising author of a disturbing book, *Etes-vous fous?*, resorted to suicide in 1935 as "the most final of all solution." Benjamin Péret, one of the earliest inspirers of the group, denounced modern society and lived in solitude. Breton tirelessly branded as cowardice the compromise which accepts the present conditions, social and metaphysical, of our existence. In "Poetic Evidence" (in *Donner à voir*, Gallimard, 1939), a remarkable essay, Eluard declared: "Somber are the truths which appear in the work of true poets; but truths they are, and almost everything else is lies."

But Surrealist literature does not wallow in pessimism. It never consents to despair, never delights in reviling man as naturalism and even Parnassian poetry had done. It plunges into the abysses of man's unconscious only in order to emerge with reasons for living more imaginatively, more authentically. It illuminates whatever may be sordid and animal in us with the rays of poetry and of dream. After opposing an inflexible *no* to the insidious temptation to accept man's fate as it is, it attempts to carry man far above his mediocre rational self into an impetuous dash of revolt. The crucial Surrealist assertion of this kind was made in 1930 in the second Surrealist manifesto. It asked man to think outside of and beyond the principle of contradiction, to break the shackles of logic, to bring out of opposite objects and contradictory concepts a deeper unity. Hegelian and Marxist dialectics was not unknown to Breton when he wrote these lines, but he leaped beyond their technical subtleties into the purer regions of poetical faith:

> Everything leads to the belief that there exists a certain point in the mind from which life and death, the real and the imaginary, the past and the future, what is communicable and what is incommunicable, the high and the low, cease to be perceived as contradictory. Vainly would one assign to Surrealist activity another ambition than the hope to determine this point.

Again, in *Les Vases communicants*, Breton proclaimed:

> The poet of the future will surmont the depressing idea of an irreparable divorce between dream and action. He will offer the magnificent fruit of the tree with tangled roots and will persuade those who taste it that there is no bitterness in it.

There, in our opinion, lies the deeper significance of Surrealism. On one side, the movement has staged an ardent revolt against all literary conventions, and chiefly against effete images and conventional rhetoric which encumber a great mass of nineteenth century literature. It has striven toward a language deprived of eloquence and of sumptuous draperies, closely molded on reality or surreality. In this sense, Surrealism is only one aspect of the most determined attempt of French literature since Rimbaud and Mallarmé: an attempt to pierce the screen of language and to render words so transparently lucid and pure as to let objects and feelings meet us directly. Eluard, Reverdy, and Char, the supreme poets of Surrealism, have accomplished what critics like Paulhan, Blanchot, and Picon would define as the great obsession of the moderns: the creation of a literature that is nonliterary. In its form, Surrealism is thus far remote from outdated Romanticism.

In its content, however, Surrealism must be regarded as a powerful Romantic offensive. Our age fondly imagines that it has buried the illusions of the Romantics beneath its own positive preoccupations, its cynicism, its resigned acceptance of man as a creature made up of animal impulses. It has only momentarily repressed its Romanticism and is unwittingly preparing a tidal wave of Romantic revolt, which is likely to put an end to all the pseudoscientitic claims of the novel, criticism, psychology, and sociology of the last few decades. The recent evolution of Surrealism is, in this connection, prophetic. Julien Gracq, celebrated by Breton as the most brilliant new recruit of Surrealism, has revived the Romantic novel of the English pre-Romantics. Eluard's late poetry delights in sensuous litanies in praise of woman which recall the Romantic bards even more than the metaphysical poets, for irony is not among the goddesses courted by the Surrealists. Péret proclaimed Romanticism as the flint great revolutionary movement in poetry. And Breton has become the apostle of mystical union with nature as superior to any knowledge of nature:

> Scientific knowledge of nature can only be valuable if *contact* with nature through poetical, I would even say mythical, ways is re-established. (*Le Figaro*, October 1946).

Like the Romantics, the Surrealists, obsessed with frantic revolt, with the breaking of all moral and social conventions, occasionally attracted by suicide, have in truth aspired toward a total renewal of man. They have aimed at provoking first a grave intellectual and moral crisis in modern man, so as to shake him out of his complacency. Then they forced the locomotive of the human spirit off the rails of logic and reason and lured imagination to the heights where it can soar freely and meet the unknown, away from the mediocre and dull province of what is known and understood rationally. The impatience of Breton and his friends with ordinary, contented man springs from a boundless faith in the possibilities which man ignores or represses in himself. Their aim is not to create a Nietzschean superman, but to give noble and affirmative answer to the Nietzschean question echoed by M. Teste: "Of what is man capable?" "A man who has never tried to make himself equal to the gods is less than a man," said the creator of M. Teste. If he is right, the Surrealists have proved to be more than ordinary mortals. They have asserted most loudly in our century man's ability to change himself, and the extraordinary, almost magical, role that literature can play in effecting that change. To quote André Breton once more:

> Human life would not be for many of us the disappointment it is if we constantly felt ourselves capable of accomplishing acts above our strength. It seems that miracle itself can be within our reach.

Source: Henri Peyre, "The Significance of Surrealism," in *Yale French Studies*, No. 31, May 1964, pp. 23–36.

Sources

Balakian, Anna, *Dictionary of Literary Biography*, Vol. 65: *French Novelists, 1900–1930*, Gale Research, 1988. pp. 20–28.

Breton, André, *Manifestoes of Surrealism*, University of Michigan Press, 1972, pp. 7, 11, 14, 26, 29–30, 33, 38.

———, "My Wife with Her Wood-Fire Hair," in *Modern French Poets*, edited by Wallace Fowlie, Dover, 1992, p. 153.

Brown, Frederick, "Creation versus Literature: Breton and the Surrealist Movement," in *Modern French Criticism: From Proust and Valéry to Structuralism*, edited by John K. Simon, University of Chicago Press, 1972, p. 136.

Caws, Mary Ann, *The Poetry of Dada and Surrealism*, Princeton University Press, 1970, p. 5.

Davies, Norman, *Europe: A History*, Oxford University Press, 1996, pp. 877, 901, 903, 962.

Desnos, Robert, "From *Deuil pour Deuil*," in *Modern French Poets*, edited by Wallace Fowlie, Dover, 1992, pp. 202–03.

———, "Meeting," in *Modern French Poets*, edited by Wallace Fowlie, Dover, 1992, p. 207.

Eluard, Paul, "First in the World," in *Modern French Poets*, edited by Wallace Fowlie, Dover, 1992, p. 177.

———, "What the Laborer Says Is Always beside the Point," in *Modern French Poets*, edited by Wallace Fowlie, Dover, 1992, pp. 179, 181.

———, "You Rise Up," in *Modern French Poets*, edited by Wallace Fowlie, Dover, 1992, p. 183.

Gascoyne, David, *A Short Survey of Surrealism*, City Lights Books, 1982, pp. 57, 91.

La Charité, Virginia A., *Twentieth-Century French Avant-Garde Poetry, 1907–1990*, French Forum Publishers, Incorporated, 1992, p. 83.

Lemaitre, Georges, *From Cubism to Surrealism in French Literature*, Harvard University Press, 1947, pp. 212–13.

Matthews, J. H., *Surrealist Poetry in France*, Syracuse University Press, 1969, p. 17.

Further Reading

Caws, Mary Ann, ed., *Surrealist Painters and Poets*, MIT Press, 2001.

This book offers a large selection of reprinted texts from surrealist painters and poets, including some rare letters and essays that are hard to find elsewhere.

Levitt, Annette Shandler, *The Genres and Genders of Surrealism*, St. Martin's Press, 1999.

Levitt places Surrealism at the center of modernism and explores the philosophical stance of Surrealism, the creative rebellion that was more than a new way of looking at things.

Rose, Alan, *Surrealism and Communism: The Early Years*, Peter Lang Publishing, 1991.

At one point, Surrealism was linked with communism. Rose explores this link between the two ideologies and how it was established and broken.

Walz, Robin, *Pulp Surrealism: Insolent Popular Culture in Early Twentieth-Century France*, University of California Press, 2000.

Walz focuses on the little-known influences of French Surrealism, which include fantastic popular fiction, and sensationalistic journalism—part of the darker, more rebellious, side of mass culture.

Symbolism

Movement Origin

c. 1850

The symbolist movement in literature originated during the 1850s in France and lasted until about 1900. Symbolism exerted a profound influence on twentieth-century literature, bridging the transition from Realism to Modernism. Symbolism also exerted a strong influence on the arts, including theatre, painting, and music. The symbolists sought to convey very personal, irrational, and dream-like states of consciousness, relying heavily on metaphorical language to approximate, or symbolize, an eternal essence of being that, they believed, was abstracted from the scope of the five senses. These literary ideals developed as a reaction against the dominance of positivism, which emphasized rational thought, objectivity, and scientific method. Symbolism also represented a reaction against Realism and Naturalism in literature, which sought to accurately represent the external world of nature and human society through descriptions of objective reality. Stylistically, the symbolists emphasized the inherent musicality of language, developed the use of *vers libre* (free verse), and modernized the existing form of the prose poem. The symbolists were greatly influenced by the poetry of Charles Baudelaire, whose *Les fleurs du mal* (1857; *Flowers of Evil*) embodied many of their literary ideals. In addition to Baudelaire, the central figures of French Symbolism are the poets Stéphane Mallarmé, Paul Verlaine, and Arthur Rimbaud. French Symbolism affected international literature of the nineteenth and twentieth centuries, in particular, inspiring the

Russian symbolist movement, which developed in the 1880s. The literature of Germany, Great Britain, Japan, the United States, and Turkey was also influenced by Symbolism. Though poetry dominated the symbolist movement, great works of fiction and drama were also written by adherents of Symbolism.

Representative Authors

Charles Baudelaire (1821–1867)

The poetry of Charles Baudelaire was the chief inspiration for the development of Symbolism. His masterpiece, *Les fleurs du mal* (*Flowers of Evil*), and his important collection of prose poetry *Petits poèmes en prose* (1868; *Little Prose Poems*), embody the central ideals of the symbolist movement. Baudelaire was born on April 9, 1821, in Paris, France. As a young man he established himself as a popular critic of art and literature. When he first encountered the short fiction of American writer Edgar Allen Poe in 1847, Baudelaire immediately felt that Poe's literary sensibilities resonated strongly with his own. Thenceforth, he devoted much of his life to translating the works of Poe into French. Through these translations, Poe became an important influence on the later French symbolist poets. In 1848, Baudelaire participated in two major political events in France, the Revolution of 1848 and the June Days rebellion. In 1855, eighteen of his poems were published in a literary journal as a collection entitled *Flowers of Evil*. *Flowers of Evil* was eventually expanded to include over one hundred poems and published as a single volume. In the 1860s, Baudelaire began to compose the prose poems that were posthumously collected in the volume *Little Prose Poems* (later republished as *Le spleen de Paris*, or *Paris Spleen*). Baudelaire died of complications resulting from syphilis on August 31, 1867, in Paris, in financial ruin and with many of his poems still unpublished. However, the young generation of writers who developed the symbolist movement regarded him as their literary father, and Baudelaire soon came to be widely viewed as one of the greatest French poets of the nineteenth century.

Aleksandr Blok (1880–1921)

Aleksandr (Aleksandrovich) Blok is considered the greatest poet of the Russian symbolist movement. Blok's symbolist masterpiece is the epic poem, *Dvenadtsat* (1918; *The Twelve*). His literary ideals developed from a synthesis of the influences of Russian poets Aleksandr Pushkin and Vladimir Solovyov. Blok was born on November 16, 1880, in St. Petersburg, Russia, and died on August 7, 1921, in Petrograd (the postrevolutionary name given to St. Petersburg).

Maurice Maeterlinck

Joris-Karl Huysmans (1848–1907)

Joris-Karl Huysmans's *À rebours* (1884; *Against the Grain*) is considered the greatest novel to emerge from the symbolist movement. Huysmans was born Charles Marie Georges Huysmans, February 5, 1848, in Paris, France. Huysmans took up a lifelong career as a civil servant for the French government. He became associated with the naturalist school of fiction headed by the great French novelist Emile Zola. The publication of *Against the Grain*, however, signaled his break with Naturalism, as the novel embodies the ideals of the symbolist poets. His novel *Là-bas* (1891; *Down There*) is based on a real-life historical figure who was executed in 1440 for murdering children. Huysmans died of cancer May 12, 1907, in Paris.

Maurice Maeterlinck (1862–1949)

Maurice Maeterlinck was the foremost playwright of the symbolist movement and the greatest Belgian playwright of the nineteenth and twentieth centuries. Maeterlinck was born on August 29, 1862, in Ghent, Belgium. He studied law and was admitted to the bar in 1886. Maeterlinck worked as a lawyer until 1889, when he decided to devote himself to writing. In 1897, Maeterlinck went to Paris, where he met many of the leading symbolist writers of the day. He sent his first play, *La Princesse Maleine* (1890; *The Princess Maleine*), to Mallarmé, who sent it on to an important French dramatist and critic of the day. *The Princess Maleine* was an immediate success and many plays followed, including *L'Intruse* (1890; *The Intruder*) and *Les aveugles* (1890; *The Blind*). Maeterlinck's masterpiece and the greatest work of symbolist theatre, *Pelléas et Mélisande* (*Pelleas and Melisande*), was produced at the Théatre de l'Oeuvre in 1892. His book *La vie des abeilles* (*The Life of the Bee*), published in 1901, compares his observations of the behavior of bees to human society. His play *L'Oiseau bleu* (1909; *The Blue Bird*) was an international success and has been adapted several times as a children's book and a major motion picture. The phrase "the bluebird of happiness" derives from this enormously popular and enduring story. Maeterlinck won the Nobel Prize for literature in 1911. He died of a heart attack on May 6, 1949, in Nice, France.

Stéphane Mallarmé (1842–1898)

Stéphane Mallarmé was one of the founders of the symbolist movement and a major influence on nineteenth- and twentieth-century poetry. Mallarmé was profoundly influenced by the poetry of Baudelaire, from which he developed the literary ideals of Symbolism. Mallarmé was born on March 18, 1842, in Paris, France. His mother died when he was only five years old. By the time he was twenty-one, his sister and father had also died. These early experiences with death may have contributed to the deep sense of loss expressed in his later work. Mallarmé made his living as a teacher, editor, and translator while working on his poetry. His *L'Après-midi d'un faune* (1876; *The Afternoon of a Faun*) is a major work of symbolist poetry. Mallarmé also held a weekly, Tuesday-evening literary, artistic, and musical salon in his apartment in Paris. He thus was an important intellectual influence on the symbolist movement in that he devoted himself to developing and communicating the theoretical basis for Symbolism. In his poetry, Mallarmé was interested in exploring the relationship between everyday reality and an ideal world of perfection and beauty that transcends reality, what he described as the ideal flower that is absent from all bouquets. Mallarmé died September 9, 1898, in the French village of Valvins. His major works of poetry are collected in the volumes *Vers et prose* (1893) and *Poésies* (1899). His essays on literature are collected in the volume *Divagations* (1897; Wanderings).

Arthur Rimbaud (1854–1891)

Arthur Rimbaud was one of the founding poets of the symbolist movement and a major influence on modern poetry. Rimbaud was born on October 20, 1854, in Charleville, France. As a teenager he ran away from home to go to Paris on three separate occasions. During one of these ventures, he participated in the 1871 rebellion of the Paris Commune. However, disillusioned by the violent suppression of the Paris Commune, Rimbaud chose to devote his life to poetry rather than political action. Rimbaud, like Mallarmé and Verlaine, was influenced by the poetry of Baudelaire. In 1871, Rimbaud sent some of his poems to Verlaine, who was so impressed that he paid for Rimbaud to come to Paris and stay several months in his home. In Paris, Rimbaud met many important literary figures but alienated most of them with his vulgar behavior. However, Rimbaud and Verlaine (who was married at the time) developed an openly acknowledged homosexual relationship. The two men engaged in a tumultuous, passionate, intermittent love affair for several years. Rimbaud traveled with Verlaine to London and Brussels in the early 1870s, during which time Rimbaud composed the prose poetry later collected in *Les illuminations* (*Illuminations*). In 1873, the volatile nature of their relationship reached a peak when Verlaine shot Rimbaud in the wrist. Soon after this incident, Rimbaud returned to his family home in France, where he completed his volume of prose poetry, *Une saison en enfer* (1873; *A Season in Hell*). In 1875, Rimbaud saw Verlaine for the last time. He left Verlaine with the manuscript of the volume *Illuminations*, which Verlaine saw to publication in 1886. Rimbaud spent most of the remainder of his life traveling the world, largely cut off from the literary world of Paris. His period of poetry writing lasted from about age sixteen to twenty-one. In February 1891, Rimbaud returned to France for cancer treatments. He died on November 10, at the age of thirty-seven.

Paul Verlaine (1844–1896)

Paul Verlaine was one of the principal founders of the symbolist movement. Verlaine was born on March 30, 1844, in Metz, France. In 1862, he began his association with many of the literary figures of the day, including Mallarmé, Villiers de L'Isle-Adam, and Anatole France. He married in 1870, but his marriage was disrupted by the arrival of Rimbaud in 1871, with whom Verlaine carried on a passionate and tumultuous love affair over a period of years. In 1872, Verlaine abandoned his wife to travel with Rimbaud to London and Brussels and to work on his poetry. In 1873, in Brussels, Verlaine shot Rimbaud in the wrist during a quarrel and was sentenced to two years in prison. His masterpiece, the poetry volume *Romances sans parole* (*Songs without Words*), was published in 1874, while Verlaine was still in prison. His volume *Sagesse* (1880; *Wisdom*), published in 1880, has come to be regarded as one of his major works. In the early 1880s, Verlaine was recognized as a leading symbolist poet, particularly with his poem "Art poétique." His volume *Les poètes maudits* (1884; *The Accursed Poets*), includes short biographical essays on six poets, including Mallarmé and Rimbaud. In 1886, Verlaine oversaw the publication of Rimbaud's *Illuminations*. When Verlaine died of pulmonary congestion on January 8, 1896, in Paris, he was widely recognized as a major French poet of the nineteenth century and one of the founders of the symbolist movement.

The Apparition, *by Gustave Moreau, an important symbolist painter*

Representative Works

The Afternoon of a Faun

The Afternoon of a Faun, published by Mallarmé in 1876, is one of the greatest works of symbolist verse. It explores the relationship between the real world and an idealized spiritual world of perfection and beauty. It also deals with sensuality, passion, and physical sensation and how they attain significance through meditation and introspection.

Against the Grain

The novel *Against the Grain*, by Huysmans, was published in 1884 and is considered the greatest work of symbolist fiction. The story concerns a wealthy, privileged, and hypersensitive man who leaves Paris to isolate himself from human society. He does so by shutting himself in a luxurious country home where he sees no one. Even his servants are made to stay out of his sight. Huysmans is less concerned with plot than with the state of mind of his protagonist. Like the symbolist poets, Huysmans wished to explore the inner spiritual and psychological state of the individual through his writing. He employs prose that borders on the poetic, using language in experimental ways that embody symbolist ideals. With *Against the Grain*, Huysmans made a daring break from the Realism and Naturalism of his literary mentor, the famous French novelist Emile Zola. Huysmans's admiration of the symbolist poets is expressed within the story when the protagonist reads the poetry of Baudelaire, Mallarmé, and Verlaine.

Flowers of Evil

Flowers of Evil, by Baudelaire, was the primary literary inspiration for the symbolist poets, and remains one of the most celebrated works of nineteenth-century French verse. The poems embody the central ideals of Symbolism. Although Baudelaire himself was a precursor to the symbolist movement, *Flowers of Evil* is considered a major work of symbolist poetry. The first edition of 100 poems was published in 1857. A second edition in 1861 was expanded to include 126 poems. This 1861 edition is divided into six sections: "Spleen et Ideal" ("Spleen and the Ideal"), "Tableaux Parisians" ("Parisian Tableaus"), "Le Vin" ("Wine"), "Fleurs du mal" ("Flowers of Evil"), "Révolte" ("Revolt"), and "La Mort" ("Death"). In *Flowers of Evil*, Baudelaire maintains traditional formal elements of verse in poems that are highly innovative in theme and imagery. The poems address themes of original sin, beauty, love, death, and the tension between sensuality and spirituality. The subjects of the poems include the spiritual and sensual love of women, the powers of Satan, and the spiritual struggles inherent to the human condition. The section "Parisian Tableaus" was added to the 1861 edition and contains poems about the city of Paris, noted as the first modern urban poetry. *Flowers of Evil* includes Baudelaire's most famous poem, "Le Cygne" ("The Swan"), in which the memory of a swan, escaped from the zoo and stranded near the Louvre in Paris symbolizes the human plight of alienation and loss that are commonly addressed in modern literature. Other major poems in this volume include "La Chevelure" ("The Head of Hair") and "Correspondences."

Illuminations

Arthur Rimbaud's *Illuminations* is considered a masterwork of symbolist prose poetry. It consists of forty-two prose poems first composed in 1873. The collection was not published until 1886, at a time when Rimbaud was traveling the world. Paul Verlaine, to whom Rimbaud had given the manuscript, was unable to contact Rimbaud and published the volume without Rimbaud's knowledge. Rimbaud himself may never have seen this publication. In *Illuminations*, Rimbaud developed the prose poem in accordance with the symbolist aesthetic. His unique use of language, punctuation, and informal structure is extremely experimental, leaving many readers baffled about the poems' meanings and many critics at odds over how to interpret the work. Rimbaud's themes include the importance of childhood perceptions, the journey as metaphor, the spirit of rebellion, and the mysteries of nature. He frequently ends his poems with a single, powerful line that is both striking and enigmatic.

Pelleas and Melisande

Pelleas and Melisande, by Maeterlinck, is considered the greatest work of symbolist drama. This five-act play was first produced in 1893. It uses a fairytale setting and revolves around the Princess Melisande, whose passionate love for her husband's brother leads to doom and destruction. While the plot and characterization are relatively simple, the play expresses a powerful mood of longing in language notable for its musical qualities.

Songs without Words

Verlaine's *Songs without Words* was published in 1874 and is a collection of poems that captures the musicality of the French language. The volume includes twenty-one poems and is divided into four sections: "Ariettes oubliées" ("Forgotten Ariettas"), "Paysages belges" ("Belgian Landscapes"), "Birds in the Night" (titled in English in the original version), and "Arquarelles" ("Watercolors"). The tone of the poems is highly personal, expressing feelings of passion, guilt, regret, and nostalgia. These poems were written during Verlaine's travels with Rimbaud to Belgium and England and express his mixed feelings about the wife he abandoned as well as his feelings for Rimbaud. The first edition of *Songs without Words* was published while Verlaine was imprisoned after having shot Rimbaud in the wrist during a lover's quarrel. Verlaine originally dedicated the volume to Rimbaud, but the dedication was removed from the published edition because of the scandalous nature of Verlaine's relationship to Rimbaud.

The Twelve

The verse ballad *The Twelve*, by Blok, was published in 1918 and is a masterpiece of Russian symbolist poetry. It concerns twelve brutal Red Guards on a rampage during the St. Petersburg uprising of 1917 and 1918. Stylistically, *The Twelve* is celebrated for Blok's use of language that is both vernacular and musical, expressing harsh vulgarities as well as delicate moods.

Themes

The Inner Life of the Individual

The symbolist writers were concerned with expressing various elements of the internal life of the individual. They focused on subjective mental impressions, internal moods, delicate emotional states, and spiritual sentiments in reaction against the nineteenth-century focus on objective, external, concrete realities as perceived through rational scientific methods. Their use of imagery often exemplifies states of mind, the imagination, the human psyche, and dreams. Huysmans's symbolist novel *Against the Grain*, for example, concerns a man who isolates himself in a country house, avoiding contact with other people; the focus of the novel is thus on the detailed subjective perceptions of the hypersensitive protagonist within an isolated environment. Many symbolist poems, particularly those of Rimbaud, evoke the inner world of the child, capturing childhood impressions, perceptions, and flights of imagination.

The Journey

Many symbolist writers describe various journeys, voyages, or quests as metaphors for internal explorations into the inner consciousness of the individual. Baudelaire's poem "Le Voyage" ("The Voyage") describes a journey as a symbol of the quest for meaning and satisfaction in life. Rimbaud, who wrote many of his major poems while traveling with Verlaine, often focuses on symbolic journeys in his poetry, frequently describing travel as a metaphor for a quest into the imagination. For example, "Le Bateau ivre" ("The Drunken Boat"), one of Rimbaud's most famous poems, narrates a voyage by boat as a metaphor for an internal voyage into the mind of the individual. Verlaine also wrote a number of poems based on his travels with Rimbaud.

Sensual and Spiritual Love

The major symbolist poets were men, and many of their poems explore the tension in their lives between the sensual love of women and the spiritual idealization of women. These themes are addressed in the first section of Baudelaire's *Flowers of Evil*, wherein three cycles of love poetry are associated with three different women with whom Baudelaire was involved during his life. Baudelaire's poem "The Head of Hair" focuses on the sensuality of a woman's hair. The symbolist poets also strove for the realization of spiritual ideals through their love poetry. They considered beauty to be an abstract spiritual ideal that can only be hinted at through the presence of physical beauty. Mallarmé described this concept as the ideal flower that does not exist in any real bouquet. Not all symbolist poetry was inspired by heterosexual relationships. The love poetry of both Verlaine and Rimbaud was often inspired by their own homosexual relationship.

Religion and Spirituality

Symbolist literature is often preoccupied with spiritual exploration and religious questions. Symbolist writers developed religious themes in a variety of ways. Much of Baudelaire's poetry explores the Catholic concept of sin and the figure of Satan. The section of *Flowers of Evil* entitled "Revolt" focuses on Baudelaire's struggles with the allure of Satanism. Rimbaud, on the other hand, offers harsh criticism of traditional religious beliefs throughout his writing, while striving to express spiritual ideals. Verlaine, who experienced a religious awakening while in prison, wrote poetry expressing the Catholic faith in his volume *Wisdom*. Blok is noted for his verse ballad *The Twelve*, in which the exploits of a band of revolutionary rebels are described as a Christian parable.

Media Adaptations

- Maeterlinck's *Pelleas and Melisande* was adapted as an opera by Claude Debussy, with a libretto by Maeterlinck, in 1902.

Urban Life

Modern urban life is an important element and central theme of symbolist poetry that inaugurated the transition to modern literature in the twentieth century. Baudelaire, in his "Parisian Tableaus," a section of *Flowers of Evil*, wrote some of the first poetry to depict nineteenth-century urban landscapes and urban squalor. His famous poem "The Swan" expresses feelings of alienation evoked by life in the modern city.

Style

Free Verse

Free verse or *Vers libre* was developed by the symbolist poets as a form of verse liberated from the traditional formal requirements of French poetry, such as meter and rhyme. The symbolists felt the formal qualities of a poem should emerge from its content, rather than being imposed upon it by the rules of tradition. Free verse poetry thus tends to be structured according to the rhythms of everyday speech. French symbolist poets Jules Laforgue (1860–1887) and Gustave Kahn (1859–1936) were the first to develop free verse, which they began to use in the 1880s. Because of the influence of symbolist poetry, free verse came to characterize modern poetry in the twentieth century. Early English-language poets who used free verse include T. S. Eliot and Ezra Pound.

Topics for Further Study

- The symbolist movement in literature was an important influence on modern painting. The major symbolist painters were Gustave Moreau, Odilon Redon, and Puvis de Chavannes. Find art books with reproductions of symbolist paintings by these or other artists. Choose one symbolist painter and provide a brief biography of him or her, focusing on the period during which he produced the majority of his symbolist works. Discuss one painting by the artist, describing the painting in your own words. In what ways does this painting express the ideals of the symbolist movement?
- Read Mallarmé's *The Afternoon of a Faun*, then find and listen to a recording of Debussy's musical adaptation *Prelude to the Afternoon of a Faun*. Compare and contrast the poem to the prelude. In what ways are the ideals of the symbolist movement expressed through Debussy's musical composition? How are the ideals of Symbolism expressed differently in the different mediums of poetry and music?
- Maeterlinck was the foremost author of symbolist drama. Read his play *Pelleas and Melisande*. With a group of students, perform one scene from the play, then discuss as a group the scene you have performed. Describe the symbolist elements and themes of the scene. In what ways does your performance of the scene enhance your understanding of the play?
- Although the symbolist writers did not invent the prose poetry form, a number of them did develop the prose poem as a modern form of expression. For this assignment, choose *one* of the following options: a) Choose three prose poems from either Baudelaire's *Paris Spleen* or Rimbaud's *Illuminations*, and write an essay describing the major theme or themes, the poet's use of language, and the symbolist elements of the poem; or, b) Look through published volumes of prose poetry to get a sense of the form, then write five to ten of your own original prose poems.

Musicality of Language

Symbolist writers were particularly interested in bringing out the musical qualities of language. They developed works of lyrical beauty in which language was orchestrated with image to create a symphony of mood and suggestion. Verlaine and Mallarmé are particularly revered for the musical qualities of their poetry. Blok brought musicality to Russian verse in his ballad *The Twelve*. In drama, the plays of Maeterlinck are notable for the musical qualities of the dialogue.

Mood

The symbolists focused on evoking a strong sense of mood through the use of language. Moods such as longing, regret, a sense of loss, and reverie are often expressed in symbolist literature. The poets strove to evoke specific moods through the expression of subtle internal states of mind. In symbolist fiction and drama, plot is less important than the overall mood or atmosphere that is created.

The Fairy Tale

A number of symbolist writers drew from traditional folktales and fairytales in their works of poetry, fiction, and drama. Maeterlinck, for example, in his plays *The Princess Maleine* and *Pelleas and Melisande*, drew from a variety of popular folktales to create dramas set in traditional fairytale settings and featuring characters from folk literature. Rimbaud drew extensively on the fairytale in experimental narrative poems that transform this traditional genre.

Movement Variations

International Influence

The symbolist movement, though begun in France, had a profound influence on international literature of the nineteenth and twentieth centuries. Inspired by the reading of French symbolist poetry in translation, the poets of the Russian symbolist movement emerged during the 1890s. Russian Symbolism is one of the early literary movements that characterized the "Silver Age" in Russia, a period of great intellectual and literary achievement. The development of Russian symbolist literature was inspired by the writings of the Russian philosopher and poet Vladimir Solovyov (1853–1900), in conjunction with French symbolist literature. The Russian symbolist movement is dated from the 1893 publication of the essay "On the Reasons for the Decline and on the New Trends in Contemporary Russian Literature," written by Dmitry Merezhkovsky.

Russian symbolist literature developed in two waves. The first wave included the poet Valery Bryusov (1873–1924), who translated French symbolist poetry into Russian and was regarded as the leader of Russian Symbolism; the poet Zinaida Gippius (1869–1945); and the poet and novelist Fyodor Sologub. The second wave of Russian Symbolism is associated with three major literary figures: Aleksandr Blok, Vyacheslav Ivanov, and Andrey Bely. Blok, considered one of the greatest Russian poets of the twentieth century, is celebrated for his symbolist verse ballad *The Twelve*, a religious parable that takes place during the Russian Revolution. Vyacheslav Ivanov (1866–1949) is known as a symbolist poet and a major theoretical influence on Russian Symbolism. Andrey Bely (1880–1934) is best known for his symbolist novel *Petersburg*.

While other national cultures did not necessarily develop their own unique symbolist movements, the modernist literature of many nations did develop out of symbolist influence. English literature in particular was influenced by Symbolism, including the works of poet T. S. Eliot and poet and playwright W. B. Yeats, as well as novelists James Joyce and Virginia Woolf. The imagist movement in American and English poetry, developed by Ezra Pound and others, was also inspired by Symbolism. German writers, particularly poet Rainer Maria Rilke and novelist Thomas Mann, were affected by Symbolism, which also exerted influence on Japanese and Turkish literature.

Theatre

Symbolist theatre developed in France in conjunction with the works of symbolist playwrights. In 1890, Paul Fort founded the Theatre d'Art in Paris, which produced works of symbolist drama. In 1892, upon the death of Fort, Aurelien Lugne-Poe founded the Theatre de l'Oeuvre from the Theatre d'Art. Symbolist theatre was particularly influenced by the literary ideals of Mallarmé. The theatrical productions were a reaction against realist drama in staging, costumes, and performance style. The influence of symbolist painting affected the use of backdrops and stage sets to embody the symbolist ideals of recreating specific moods and internal states of mind, rather than reproducing realistic settings or scenarios. Maeterlinck is the most celebrated symbolist playwright. Other major symbolist playwrights include the French writers Auguste Villiers de L'Isle-Adam (1838–1889) and Paul Claudel (1868–1955).

Painting

Symbolist painting was as important to the development of modern art as symbolist poetry was to the development of modern literature. Symbolist painting was inspired by symbolist poetry and was a reaction against Realism and Impressionism. Symbolist painters focused on depicting the world of dream, myth, fantasy, and the imagination, and on creating visual expressions of internal moods and subjective states of mind. The most important symbolist painters were Odilon Redon (1840–1916), who was a close friend of Mallarmé; Gustave Moreau (1826–1898); and Puvis de Chavannes (1824–1898).

Music

Symbolism exerted a significant influence on musical composition of the twentieth century. Most notably, French composers Claude Debussy (1862–1918) and Maurice Ravel (1875–1937) applied symbolist ideals to their music. Like Baudelaire and other symbolist poets, Debussy was strongly influenced by the short stories of Edgar Allan Poe. Debussy's famous composition *Prelude to the Afternoon of a Faun* (1894) is based on Mallarmé's *The Afternoon of a Faun*. Debussy also adapted Maeterlinck's *Pelleas and Melisande* as an operatic composition with a libretto by Maeterlinck himself, first performed in 1902. Ravel adapted the poetry of Mallarmé to music in his 1913 vocal composition *Trois poèmes de Stephane Mallarmé* (*Three Poems by Stephane Mallarmé*).

Historical Context

Although the subject matter of symbolist poetry was focused on the individual and was generally apolitical, several of the symbolist poets themselves were involved in major political events that took place in France during the second half of the nineteenth century. These events included the Revolution of 1848, the Second Empire, the Franco-German War, and the Paris Commune.

The Revolution of 1848 in France was a uprising of citizens that resulted in the overthrow of the existing constitutional monarchy under King Luis-Philippe. The revolution consisted of three days of rioting during the month of February, in

Compare & Contrast

- **1850–1900:** France experiences several internal rebellions and major changes of government. The Second Republic, a constitutional democracy ruled by a president, lasts from the Revolution of 1848 until 1852. The Second Empire, under the rule of Emperor Napoleon III, remains relatively stable from 1852 until 1870. The Third Republic, a constitutional democracy with a president, remains relatively stable from 1871 until the German occupation of France in 1940.

  Today: The current French government, known as the Fifth Republic, is a constitutional democracy ruled by a president. The Fifth Republic was formulated in 1959 and has remained relatively stable for over forty years.

- **1850–1900:** France engages in warfare as well as alliances with several European nations. In the Crimean War of 1853 to 1856, France, in alliance with England and Turkey, is at war with Russia. In the Franco-German War of 1870 to 1871, France is invaded and defeated by Germany. In 1894 France enters a pact with Russia known as the dual alliance. According to the dual alliance, the two nations would aid one another in case of aggression by the triple alliance (1882) of Germany, Austria-Hungary, and Italy.

  Today: France—along with Germany, England, Austria, and Italy among others—is a member of the European Union, an organization of some fifteen independent European nations united by various social, political, economic, and legal interests to maintain peaceful and mutually beneficial relations with one another.

- **1850–1900:** After the Revolution of 1848, universal manhood suffrage is established in France, giving all adult males the right to vote in political elections and referenda.

  Today: Since 1945, women in France, as well as men, have been granted the right to vote.

- **1850–1900:** One of the few European nations that did *not* experience a revolution in 1848, Russia remains a vast empire ruled by an autocratic csar until the revolution of 1917. A major social reform is enacted in 1861, when the serfs in Russia, essentially peasant slaves, are emancipated and granted the right to own land.

  Today: After some seventy years of communist rule (since 1917), the U.S.S.R. is dismantled in 1991 and divided into some twelve independent nation-states, of which Russia is the largest and most powerful. The nations of the former Soviet Union remain strongly associated with one another through the formation of the Commonwealth of Independent States in 1991.

---

which the army engaged in a violent clash with a crowd of demonstrators. As a result of this public unrest, the king chose to abdicate the throne and named his nine-year-old grandson as his successor. Thus began the period of French government known as the Second Republic, which included a new constitution providing for a variety of social reforms. Four months after the formation of the Second Republic, civil unrest again erupted in Paris in a four-day-long civil war known as the June Days. The June Days were sparked when workers, supported by students and artisans, protested against government budget cuts that denied welfare to thousands of unemployed people. This rebellion ended after the army shot and killed 1,500 demonstrators and arrested 12,000 of them. The symbolist poet Baudelaire, at that time still unpublished, is known to have participated in both the February and the June uprisings of 1848.

In the first presidential election of the Second Republic, voters chose Louis-Napoleon Bonaparte, the nephew of Napoleon Bonaparte. According to the constitution of the Second Republic, no president could serve more than one four-year term. Thus, after serving several years as president, Louis-Napoleon Bonaparte, who wished to maintain his position as leader of France, staged a coup of his own government in 1851. After some seventy politicians were arrested, Napoleon presented a new constitution and formulated a new government. The citizens of France immediately responded to Napoleon's actions by staging mass protests throughout Paris and the outlying provinces. In the course of several days of demonstrations, the police and military killed hundreds of protestors and arrested some 27,000 people. Although he was not harmed or arrested, Baudelaire is known to have participated in these demonstrations. After these events, Baudelaire gave up on political activism and focused his attentions on writing. In 1852, Louis-Napoleon had himself named Emperor Napoleon III of France, beginning an era of French government known as the Second Empire.

The advent of the Franco-German War (also known as the Franco-Prussian War), brought an end to the Second Empire of France. In 1870, France declared war on Germany, after which time German troops invaded France. When war broke out, Huysmans, not yet a published author, was called to military duty. However, he almost immediately contracted dysentery and spent most of the war in various military hospitals without seeing battle. Huysmans was eventually granted sick leave from the military, and returned home to Paris. Arriving home, he found himself in a Paris besieged by Prussian forces. Huysmans diligently kept notes on his experiences of the siege that he intended to use for a later novel (a project which he continued to work on after the war but never completed).

In the Battle of Sedan, French military forces, headed by the Emperor Napoleon, were surrounded and defeated by the Germans in 1870. The French surrendered and Napoleon, along with thousands of French troops, was taken as a prisoner of war. On the home front in Paris, citizens disillusioned by the capture of Napoleon took to the streets to demand a new government. Thus, in 1870 a new government in France, known as the Third Republic, was formed without violent conflict. Early in 1871, France signed an armistice with Prussia. The Third Republic lasted until the German occupation of France during World War II.

Although the Third Republic endured until World War II, it was not without opposition. In 1871, a rebellion in France known as the Paris Commune lasted some two-and-a-half months. The Paris Commune began when a coalition of political activists in Paris, opposing a variety of Third Republic initiatives, organized an insurrection against the newly formed government. Soon, a municipal government, known as the Commune of Paris, was formed by the revolutionaries, who were known as the communards. Similar communes were formed in outlying cities, but were quickly put down by the French government. Huysmans, who held a low-level government post during and after the Franco-German war, fled with the French government to Versailles for the duration of the Paris Commune. Rimbaud, still a teenager and not yet published, ran away from home to participate in the Paris Commune. After three weeks, Rimbaud returned home, narrowly missing the bloody conflict that was to follow, when government troops violently crushed the rebellion during what became known as the "Bloody Week." The communards responded by executing hostages, among whom was the archbishop of Paris, and setting fire to major municipal buildings. Some 20,000 rebels and 750 government troops were killed during the "Bloody Week," and some 45,000 insurrectionists were arrested or deported. The defeat of the Paris Commune effectively squelched political resistance in France for years afterward. Rimbaud, disillusioned by this defeat, turned his focus from political activism to the pursuit of writing. Huysmans returned to Paris with other government officials after the insurrection was put down.

Critical Overview

Critical response to the development of Symbolism was itself an important contribution to the symbolist movement, as many of the literary critics and leading theorists of Symbolism were themselves symbolist writers. These critics contributed to the shaping, definition, and dissemination of the movement. A discussion of critical responses to Symbolism is thus also a historical narrative of the development of the movement.

If Mallarmé, Verlaine, and Rimbaud are the fathers of Symbolism, Baudelaire may be considered the grandfather. Baudelaire's first major publication was met with public controversy as well as critical acclaim. His poetry volume *Flowers of Evil*, the seminal text of the symbolist movement, was first published amidst great controversy. Of the one hundred poems in the first edition, thirteen were singled out by a government agency as violations of laws of decency and religious morality. These thirteen poems were judged in a court of law, as a

Claude Debussy adapted symbolist works as musical pieces and operas

result of which six were found illegal and extracted from the published volume. Baudelaire and his editors were also required to pay a fine. (The ban on publication of these six poems in France was not lifted until 1949.) Despite this public controversy, major critics as well as some of the most important French writers of the day, including Gustave Flaubert and Victor Hugo, offered high praise for *Flowers of Evil*, recognizing the value of Baudelaire's innovative poetry. Baudelaire himself, however, was greatly discouraged by the censorship and public notoriety of his work.

The founders of Symbolism—Mallarmé, Verlaine, and Rimbaud—developed their literary ideals against the dominance of Realism in nineteenth-century literature. The realist aesthetic in poetry was concentrated in the development of a group of writers known as the "Parnassians." The Parnassians strove to create accurate, precise, objective descriptions of external objects and events, and to resist the emotional outpouring associated with romantic poetry. Mallarmé and Verlaine were among the Parnassian poets until they broke away from these ideals to write poetry focusing on the subjective, irrational, internal states of mind of the individual that characterizes the symbolist ideal.

Before the term Symbolism was applied to this new development in French poetry, these 1880s poets were termed the "decadents," a term first applied by critics to poets Verlaine and Jules Laforgue as an insult. The poets took up the epithet with pride, however, founding the literary review *Le Decadent* (*The Decadent*) in 1886. The term Symbolism was coined in 1886 in an article by Jean Moreas that laid out the theoretical and aesthetic ideals of this literary movement. Moreas suggested that symbolist was a more apt label for these poets than decadent.

The symbolist novel developed in reaction against the realist fiction of the naturalists. The realists strove to accurately represent objective depictions of external reality in their fiction, based on close, detailed observations of the world. Emile Zola, the famous French novelist, was a leader of the naturalist movement in literature, an extension of Realism. Early in his writing career, Huysmans was associated with Zola's circle of naturalist writers. However, Huysmans became the foremost symbolist novelist when he broke away from Zola's circle and wrote *Against the Grain*, a novel that focuses almost exclusively on the internal states of mind of a hypersensitive protagonist isolated from human society. Because it so sharply broke with his own literary ideals, Zola's critical response to Huysmans's novel was predictably negative. Interestingly, although the symbolist poetry of Verlaine and Mallarmé preceded and inspired Huysmans's novel, it was Huysmans's discussion of these poets in *Against the Grain* that introduced many readers to symbolist poetry. Thus, the popularity of *Against the Grain* helped expand the readership of symbolist poetry.

Although not all of their major works were published within their lifetimes, many of the major poets of the symbolist movement were, by the time of their deaths, recognized as some of the greatest and most influential writers of the nineteenth century. Writers and literary critics throughout the twentieth century agree that the symbolist movement exerted a profound and widespread influence on modern literature. Symbolism is regarded as the bridge between nineteenth-century Realism and twentieth-century Modernism in literature. Twentieth-century literary movements such as Imagism, Surrealism, and dadaism were directly influenced by Symbolism. In the early twenty first century, Symbolism continues to be widely regarded as one of the most important influences on international literature of the previous two centuries.

Criticism

Liz Brent

Brent has a Ph.D. in American culture and works as a freelance writer. In this essay, Brent discusses the development of the modern prose poem in symbolist literature.

Symbolism and the Modern Prose Poem

One of the many lasting influences of the symbolist movement on international literature can be seen in the development of the modern prose poem during the nineteenth and twentieth centuries.

Prose poetry is written in the form of prose, yet maintains the lyrical language use, suggestive imagery, and thematic sensibilities of poetry. The formal properties of the prose poem are intended to liberate verse from traditional requirements of metrical form and line breaks. The prose poem also liberates prose from traditional requirements of story line and narrative closure. Prose poems are usually short, generally anywhere from one paragraph to several pages in length. One of the enduring literary issues raised by prose poetry is the question of how to define it as a literary form distinct from both poetry and prose. The very notion of prose poetry thus raises questions about the boundary between prose and poetry.

Although the symbolists did not invent prose poetry, they freed it from its traditional tone and themes and developed the form as a modern mode of expression. Baudelaire is credited as the inventor of the modern prose poem, producing the important volume *Little Poems in Prose* (1869; later published as *Paris Spleen*). Other important volumes of symbolist prose poetry include Rimbaud's *Illuminations* (1886) and *A Season in Hell* (1873). Mallarmé, one of the founders of Symbolism, also wrote a number of important prose poems.

The Prose Poem in the Nineteenth Century

French poets were first introduced to the prose poem, a relatively obscure genre of literature, in the mid-nineteenth century, through the French writer Louis Bertrand (1807–1841; also known as Aloysius Bertrand). Bertrand first began to publish his prose poetry in a newspaper in 1828. However, his collected volume of prose poetry *Gaspard de la Nuit* (*Gaspard of the Night*) was not published until 1842, a year after his death. With this publication, Bertrand was the first significant French writer to utilize the form of the prose poem.

The prose poems of *Gaspard of the Night* are based on Bertrand's fascination with the medieval history of the city of Dijon, France, and express a romanticized vision of the city's gothic past. Bertrand's prose poetry shows the influence of the romantic movement in literature, with which he was peripherally associated. His prose poetry, however, was entirely innovative in developing a French prose form that retains the lyrical qualities of poetry.

Baudelaire can be credited with bringing the prose poetry of Bertrand to the attention of the French literary world in 1869, when he mentioned the volume with high praise in his introduction to *Little Poems in Prose*. As Baudelaire explains in this introduction, he was first inspired to try his own hand at composing prose poetry through his reading of Bertrand's *Gaspard of the Night*. Baudelaire confesses his debt to Bertrand as his inspiration in attempting to expand the possibilities of the prose poem by applying it to expressions of life in the modern city. Baudelaire states that, while reading *Gaspard of the Night*:

> for at least the twentieth time . . . the idea came to me to try something similar, and to apply to the description of modern life, or rather *one* modern and more abstract life, the procedure [Bertrand] had applied to the depiction of ancient life, so strangely picturesque.

Baudelaire further describes his "dream" of writing in a form that combined elements of poetry and prose:

> Which of us has not, in his ambitious days, dreamed of the miracle of a poetic prose, musical without rhythm and without rhyme, supple enough and choppy enough to fit the soul's lyrical movements, the undulations of reverie, the jolts of consciousness?

Baudelaire first coined the term "prose poem" in reference to a group of his own poems published in 1861. He also describes his innovative style of prose poetry as "fables of modern life." Edward K. Kaplan, in an introduction to his 1989 volume of translations of *Little Poems in Prose*, observes that one of the modern elements of Baudelaire's fables is the fact that, unlike traditional fables that end with a clear moral prescription, they "undermine any reassuring interpretations." Kaplan further describes this modern element of moral ambiguity in Baudelaire's prose poetry:

> Dismantling all forms of complacency and idealism, the Baudelarian "prose poem" amalgamates, in a dialogically open-ended literary unit, ambiguity and judgment, kindness and cruelty, anger and generosity, reveries and analysis. There are no definitive lessons—only responses.

What Do I Study Next?

- *Axel's Castle: A Study in the Imaginative Literature of 1870–1930* (1931), by Edmund Wilson, provides an important critical discussion of the symbolist movement and its influence on such twentieth-century writers as William Butler Yeats, Paul Valéry, T. S. Eliot, Marcel Proust, James Joyce, and Gertrude Stein.
- *Six French Poets of the Nineteenth Century: Lamartine, Hugo, Baudelaire, Verlaine, Rimbaud, Mallarmé* (2000), edited by E. H. Blackmore and A. M. Blackmore, provides a bilingual edition of French symbolist poetry with an English translation on facing pages.
- *French Symbolist Poetry: An Anthology* (1980), edited by John Porter Houston and Mona Tobin Houston, provides English translations of major works of French symbolist poetry.
- *The Crisis of French Symbolism* (1990), by Laurence M. Porter, offers criticism and interpretation of the works of the major symbolist poets Mallarmé, Verlaine, Baudelaire, and Rimbaud.
- *Four French Symbolists: A Sourcebook on Pierre Puvis de Chavannes, Gustave Moreau, Odilon Redon, and Maurice Denis* (1996), by Russell T. Clement, offers a helpful guide to further sources on the major French symbolist painters.
- *Symbolist Theater: The Formation of an Avant-Garde* (1993), by Frantisek Deak, provides discussion of the development of symbolist theatre in France.
- *Models of the Universe: An Anthology of the Prose Poem* (1995), edited by Stuart Friebert and David Young, provides an introduction to prose poetry of the nineteenth and twentieth centuries from a variety of writers.
- *Debussy in Performance* (1999), edited by James R. Briscoe, includes essays on Debussy and Symbolism as well as discussion of his musical adaptations of Mallarmé's *The Afternoon of a Faun* and Maeterlinck's *Pelleas and Melisande*.
- *Debussy and His World* (2001), edited by Jane F. Fulcher, includes an essay on Debussy's participation in the Tuesday salons held by Mallarmé.
- *Paris and the Nineteenth Century* (1992), by Christopher Prendergast, provides historical analysis of nineteenth-century culture and politics in Paris, France.
- *Realism, Naturalism, and Symbolism: Modes of Thought and Expression in Europe, 1848–1914* (1968), edited by Roland N. Stromberg, offers discussion of major artistic and literary movements in Europe during the period in which the symbolist movement developed.

Baudelaire's fifty prose poems were published posthumously in the 1869 volume *Little Poems in Prose*. Although Baudelaire did not invent the prose poem, the works in this volume represent his revolutionizing impact on the genre. Baudelaire modernized prose poetry and profoundly influenced the symbolist poets, many of whose greatest works are prose poems.

The prose poems of *Little Poems in Prose* treat the subject of modern urban life in Paris, a topic Baudelaire thought to be especially suited to the form of the prose poem. Baudelaire focused on the ugliness of urban existence, but regarded his subject with hopefulness and compassion. While the poems of *Flowers of Evil*, traditional in form, express the beauty of Paris, the prose poems of *Little Poems in Prose* focus on the urban squalor and human suffering of the modern city.

Following in Baudelaire's footsteps, Rimbaud published two major volumes of prose poetry. As in Baudelaire's *Little Poems in Prose*, Rimbaud in his volume *Illuminations* explored the cityscapes of

Paris through the form of the prose poem. Unlike Baudelaire's Paris, Rimbaud's visions of the urban landscape are imbued with a sense of mystery beneath the squalid surface of modern city life. *A Season in Hell*, Rimbaud's second volume of prose poetry, represents an intensely personal delving into the poet's spiritual and artistic inner-anguish.

Prose Poetry in the Twentieth Century

During the early twentieth century many writers, influenced by the French symbolists, tried their hands at prose poetry. Following the lead of Baudelaire, Rimbaud, and Mallarmé, the later French symbolist writers Paul Valéry, Paul Fort, and Paul Claudel composed notable prose poems. Important writers outside of France, such as Franz Kafka, James Joyce, Gertrude Stein, and Sherwood Anderson, are also recognized for their outstanding prose poetry.

However, the prose poem throughout most of the twentieth century remained a relatively unpopular form among most readers and critics, as well as most writers. Thus, while the free verse poem, invented by the symbolists, became the dominant form of poetry throughout the twentieth century, the modern prose poem, also developed by the symbolists, was, until recently, relegated to a relatively obscure place in twentieth-century literature. The very form of the prose poem was not taken seriously by the majority of literary critics and many writers. As C. W. Truesdale observes in a preface to *The Party Train: A Collection of North American Prose Poetry* (1996), the prose poem "has never received its critical due despite the excitement the form has generated among poets themselves." Truesdale describes a general "critical neglect—even hostility" to the prose poem among literary critics throughout most of the twentieth century. Truesdale goes on to assert that the dominance of free verse "has forced the prose poem . . . to the sidelines, has marginalized it as a genre."

Beginning in the 1960s, however, prose poetry gained a renewed interest among writers, and small literary magazines began to publish prose poetry with increasing frequency. Influential American writers such as Allen Ginsberg and Robert Bly contributed to this renewed interest in the prose poem in the 1960s and 1970s. The volume *The Prose Poem: An International Anthology* (1976), edited by Michael Benedikt, helped to introduce English language readers to a broad range of prose poetry.

The 1980s and 1990s saw increased interest in the prose poem among English-language writers and editors of small literary journals. During these final decades of the twentieth century, a number of anthologies of prose poetry, as well as volumes of literary criticism focused on the prose poem, saw publication. In the 1990s, journals devoted entirely to prose poetry, such as *The Prose Poem: An International Journal*, sprang up to accommodate this growing interest.

"[While] the free verse poem, invented by the symbolists, became the dominant form of poetry throughout the twentieth century, the modern prose poem, also developed by the symbolists, was, until recently, relegated to a relatively obscure place in twentieth-century literature."

In the late twentieth century, a variety of terms came to designate prose poetry. Because of the brevity of the prose poem, its boundaries have also come to overlap with the emergence of a new form of very short fiction. Thus, the following terms have been applied to the prose poem form: "sudden fiction," "flash fiction," the "modern parable," the "modern fable," the "short short story," and "micro-fiction," among others.

In a 1996 essay entitled "The Poetry of Village Idiots," Charles Simic defines the prose poem as "an impossible amalgamation of lyric poetry, anecdote, fairy tale, allegory, joke, journal entry, and many other kinds of prose." However, the very definition of prose poetry remains a central topic of debate, and nearly all English-language anthologies of prose poetry during this period begin with an overview of the ongoing debate as to the question of whether or not the prose poem exists as a distinct literary form, and, if so, how it might be defined and distinguished from both poetry and prose. Nonetheless, nearly all critics and writers acknowledge the debt of modern prose poetry to the innovations of the French symbolist poets in elevating the prose poem to the status of a high art particularly suited to expressions of modern life.

Source: Liz Brent, Critical Essay on Symbolism, in *Literary Movements for Students*, The Gale Group, 2003.

Rene Wellek

In the following essay, Wellek explores the idea of Symbolism as a literary period encompassing much post-Realism Western literature, and focuses on developing an accurate system of definition for it.

The term and concept of symbolism (and symbol) is so vast a topic that it cannot even be sketched within the limits of this paper. The word goes back to ancient Greece and, there, had a complex history which has not, I suspect, been traced adequately in the only history of the term, Max Schlesinger's *Geschichte des Symbols*, published in 1912.

What I want to discuss is something much more specific: not even symbol and symbolism in literature but the term and concept of symbolism as a period in literary history. It can, I suggest, be conveniently used as a general term for the literature in all Western countries following the decline of nineteenth-century realism and naturalism and preceding the rise of the new avant-garde movements: futurism, expressionism, surrealism, existentialism, or whatever else. How has it come about? Can such a use be justified?

We must distinguish among different problems: the history of the word need not be identical with the history of the concept as we might today formulate it. We must ask, on the one hand, what the contemporaries meant by it, who called himself a "symbolist," or who wanted to be included in a movement called "symbolism," and on the other hand, what modern scholarship might decide about who is to be included and what characteristics of the period seem decisive. In speaking of "symbolism" as a period-term located in history we must also think of its situation in space. Literary terms most frequently radiate from one center but do so unevenly; they seem to stop at the frontiers of some countries or cross them and languish there or, surprisingly, flourish more vigorously on a new soil. A geography of literary terms is needed which might attempt to account for the spread and distribution of terms by examining rival terms or accidents of biography or simply the total situation of a literature.

There seems to be a widespread agreement that the literary history of the centuries since the end of the Middle Ages can be divided into five successive periods: Renaissance, baroque, classicism, romanticism, and realism. Among these terms baroque is a comparative newcomer which has not been accepted everywhere, though there seems a clear need of a name for the style that reacted against the Renaissance but preceded classicism. There is, however, far less agreement as to what term should be applied to the literature that followed the end of the dominance of realism in the 1880s and 90s. The term "modernism" and its variants, such as the German "Die Moderne," have been used but have the obvious disadvantage that they can be applied to any contemporary art. Particularly in English, the term "modern" has preserved its early meaning of a contrast to classical antiquity or is used for everything that occurred since the Middle Ages. *The Cambridge Modern History* is an obvious example. The attempts to discriminate between the "modern" period now belonging to the past and the "contemporaneous" seem forced, at least terminologically. "Modo," after all, means "now." "Modernism" used so broadly as to include all avant-garde art obscures the break between the symbolist period and all post-symbolist movements such as futurism, surrealism, existentialism, etc. In the East it is used as a catchall for everything disapproved as decadent, formalistic, and alienated: it has become a pejorative term set against the glories of socialist realism.

The older terms were appealed to at the turn of the century by many theorists and slogan writers, who either believed that these terms are applicable to all literature or consciously thought of themselves as reviving the style of an older period. Some spoke of a new "classicism," particularly in France, assuming that all good art must be classical. Croce shares this view. Those who felt a kinship with the romantic age, mainly in Germany, spoke of "Neuromantik," appealing to Friedrich Schlegel's dictum that all poetry is romantic. Realism also asserted its claim, mainly in Marxist contexts, in which all art is considered "realistic" or at least "a reflection of reality." I need only allude to Georg Lukács' recent *Aesthetik*, in which this thesis is repeated with obsessive urgency. I have counted the phrase "Widerspiegelung der Wirklichkeit" in the first volume; it appears 1,032 times. I was too lazy or bored to count it in Volume Two. All these monisms endanger meaningful schemes of literary periodization. Nor can one be satisfied with a dichotomy such as Fritz Strich's "Klassik

Loaded gun carriages during the time of the Paris Commune

und Romantik," which leads away from period concepts into a universal typology, a simple division of the world into sheep and goats. For many years I have argued the advantage of a multiple scheme of periods, since it allows a variety of criteria. The one criterion "realism" would divide all art into realistic and nonrealistic art and thus would allow only one approving adjective: "real" or some variant such as "true" or "lifelike." A multiple scheme comes much closer to the actual variety of the process of history. Period must be conceived neither as some essence which has to be intuited as a Platonic idea nor as a mere arbitrary linguistic label. It should be understood as a "regulative idea," as a system of norms, conventions, and values which can be traced in its rise, spread, and decline, in competition with preceding and following norms, conventions, and values.

"Symbolism" seems the obvious term for the dominant style which followed nineteenth-century realism. It was propounded in Edmund Wilson's *Axel's Castle* (1931) and is asumed as a matter of course in Maurice Bowra's *Heritage of Symbolism* (1943). We must beware, of course, of confusing this historical form with age-old symbolism or with the view that all art is symbolic, as language is a system of symbols. Symbolism in the sense of a use of symbols in literature is clearly omnipresent in literature of many styles, periods, and civilizations. Symbols are all-pervasive in medieval literature and even the classics of realism—Tolstoy and Flaubert, Balzac and Dickens—use symbols, often prominently. I myself am guilty of arguing for the crucial role of symbol in any definition of romanticism, and I have written at length on the long German debate from Goethe to Friedrich Theodor Vischer about the meaning of the term "symbol" and its contrast to the term "allegory."

For our purposes I want to focus on the fortunes of the concept as a term, first for a school, then as a movement, and finally as a period. The term "symbolisme" as the designation for a group of poets was first proposed by Jean Moréas, the French poet of Greek extraction. In 1885 he was disturbed by a journalistic attack on the decadents in which he was named together with Mallarmé. He protested: "the so-called decadents seek the pure Concept and the eternal Symbol in their art, before anything else." With some contempt for the mania of critics for labels, he suggested the term "Symbolistes" to replace the inappropriate "décadents." In 1886 Moréas started a review *Le Symboliste*, which perished after four issues. On September 18, 1886, he published a manifesto of "Symbolisme" in the *Figaro*. Moréas, however, soon deserted his own brainchild and founded another school he called the "école romane." On September 14, 1891, in another number of the *Figaro Moréas* blandly announced that "symbolisme" was dead. Thus "symbolisme" was an ephemeral name for a very small clique of French poets. The only name still remembered besides Moréas' is Gustave Kahn. It is easy to collect pronouncements by the main contemporary poets repudiating the term for themselves. Verlaine, in particular, was vehemently resentful of this "Allemandisme" and even wrote a little poem beginning "À bas le symbolisme mythe/ et termite."

In a way which would need detailed tracing, the term, however, caught on in the later 80s and early 90s as a blanket name for recent developments in French poetry and its anticipations. Before Moréas' manifesto, Anatole Baju, in *Décadent*, April 10, 1886, spoke of Mallarmé as "the master who was the first to formulate the symbolic doctrine." Two critics, Charles Morice, with *La Littérature de tout à l'heure* (1889) and Téodore de Wyzéwa, born in Poland, first in the essay "Le Symbolisme de M. Mallarmé" (1887), seemed to have been the main agents, though Morice spoke rather of "synthèse" than of symbol, and Wyzéwa thought that "symbol" was only a pretext and explained Mallarmé's poetry purely by its analogy to music. As early as 1894 Saint Antoine (pseudonym for Henri Mazel) prophesied that "undoubtedly, symbolism will be the label under which our period will be classed in the history of French literature."

It is still a matter of debate in French literary history when this movement came to an end. It was revived several times expressly—e.g. in 1905 around a review, *Vers et prose*. Its main critic, Robert de Souza, in a series of articles, "Où Nous en sommes" (also published separately, 1906), ridiculed the many attempts to bury symbolism as premature and proudly claimed that Gustave Kahn, Verhaeren, Vielé-Griffin, Maeterlinck, and Régnier were then as active as ever. Valéry professed so complete an allegiance to the ideals of Mallarmé that it is difficult not to think of him as a continuator of symbolism, though in 1938, on the occasion of the fiftieth anniversary of the symbolist manifesto, Valéry doubted the existence of symbolism and denied that there is a symbolist aesthetic. Marcel Proust, in the posthumously published last volume of his great series *Le Temps retrouvé* (1926), formulated an explicitly symbolist aesthetics. But his own attitude to symbolist contemporaries was often ambiguous or negative. In 1896 Proust had written an essay condemning obscurity in poetry. Proust admired Maeterlinck but disliked Péguy and Claudel. He even wrote a pastiche of Régnier, a mock-solemn description of a head cold. When *Le Temps retrouvé* (1926) was published and when a few years later (1933) Valery Larbaud proclaimed Proust a symbolist, symbolism had, at least in French poetry, definitely been replaced by surrealism.

André Barre's book on symbolism (1911) and particularly Guy Michaud's *Message poétique du symbolisme* (1947), as well as many other books of French literary scholarship, have, with the hindsight of literary historians, traced the different phases of a vast French symbolist movement: the first phase, with Baudelaire (who died in 1867) as the precursor; the second, when Verlaine and Mallarmé were at the height of their powers, before the 1886 group; the third, when the name became established; and then, in the twentieth century, what Michaud calls "Néo-symbolisme," represented by "La Jeune Parque" of Valéry and *L'Annonce faite à Marie of Claudel*, both dating from 1915. It seems a coherent and convincing conception which needs to be extended to prose writers and dramatists: to Huysmans after *A Rebours* (1884), to the early Gide, to Proust in part, and among dramatists, at least to Maeterlinck, who, with his plays *L'Intruse* and *Les Aveugles* (1890) and *Pelléas et Mélisande* (1892), assured a limited penetration of symbolism on the stage.

Knowledge of the French movement and admiration for it soon spread to the other European countries. We must, however, distinguish between reporting on French events and even admiration shown by translations, and a genuine transfer and assimilation of the French movement in another literature. This process varies considerably from country to country; and the variation needs to be explained by the different traditions which the French importation confronted.

In English, George Moore's *Confessions of a Young Man* (1888) and his *Impressions and Opinions* (1891) gave sketchy and often poorly informed accounts of Verlaine, Mallarmé, Rimbaud, and Laforgue. Mallarmé's poetry is dismissed as "aberrations of a refined mind," and symbolism is oddly defined as "saying the opposite of what you mean." The three essays on Mallarmé by Edmund Gosse, all dating from 1893, are hardly more perceptive. After the poet's death Gosse turned sharply against him. "Now that he is no longer here the truth must be said about Mallarmé. He was hardly a poet." Even Arthur Symons, whose book *The Symbolist Movement in Literature* (1899) made the decisive breakthrough for England and Ireland, was very lukewarm at first. While praising Verlaine (in *Academy*, 1891) he referred to the "brain-sick little school of *Symbolistes"* and "the noisy little school of *Décadents*," and even in later articles on Mallarmé he complained of "jargon and meaningless riddles." But then he turned around and produced the entirely favorable *Symbolist Movement*. It should not, however, be overrated as literary criticism or history. It is a rather lame impressionistic account of Nerval, Villiers de l'Isle-Adam, Rimbaud, Verlaine, Laforgue, Mallarmé, Huysmans, and Maeterlinck, with emphasis on Verlaine. There is no chapter on Baudelaire. But most importantly, the book was dedicated to W. B. Yeats, proclaiming him "the chief representative of that movement in our country." Symons had made his first trip to Paris in 1889; he had visited Mallarmé, met Huysmans and Maeterlinck, and a year later met Verlaine, who in 1893 became his guest on his ill-fated visit to London. Symons knew Yeats vaguely since 1891, but they became close friends in 1895 only after Yeats had completed his study of Blake and had elaborated his own system of symbols from other sources: occultism, Blake, and Irish folklore. The edition of Blake Yeats had prepared with Edwin Ellis in 1893 was introduced by an essay on "The Necessity of Symbolism." In 1894 Yeats visited Paris in the company of Symons and there saw a performance of Villiers de l'Isle-Adam's *Axël*. The essay "The Symbolism of Poetry" (1900) is then Yeats' first full statement of his symbolist creed. Symons' dedication to Yeats shows an awareness of symbolism as an international movement. "In Germany," he says, exaggerating greatly, "it seems to be permeating the whole of literature, its spirit is that which is deepest in Ibsen, it has absorbed the one new force in Italy, Gabriele D'Annunzio. I am told of a group of symbolists in Russian literature, there is another in Dutch literature, in Portugal it has a little school of its own under Eugenio de Castro. I even saw some faint stirrings that way in Spain."

Symons should have added the United States. Or could he in 1899? There were intelligent and sympathetic reports of the French movement very early. T. S. Perry wrote on "The Latest Literary Fashion in France" in *The Cosmopolitan* (1892), T. Child on "Literary Paris—The New Poetry" in *Harper's* (1896), and Aline Gorren on "The French Symbolists" in *Scribner's* (1893). The almost forgotten Vance Thompson, who, fresh from Paris, edited the oddly named review *M'lle New York*, wrote several perceptive essays, mainly on Mallarmé in 1895 (reprinted in *French Portraits*, 1900) which convey some accurate information on his theories and even attempt an explication of his poetry with some success. But only James Huneker became the main importer of recent French literature into the United States. In 1896 he defended the French symbolists against the slurs in Max Nordau's silly *Entartung* and began to write a long series of articles on Maeterlinck, Laforgue, and many others, not bothering to conceal his dependence on his French master, Remy de Gourmont, to whom he dedicated his book of essays *Visionaries* (1905). But the actual impact of French symbolist poetry on American writing was greatly delayed. René Taupin, in his *L'Influence du symoblisme français sur la poésie américaine* (1929), traced some echoes in forgotten American versifiers of the turn of the century, but only two Americans living then in England, Ezra Pound around 1908 and T. S. Eliot around 1914, reflect the French influence in significant poetry.

More recently and in retrospect one hears of a symbolist period in American literature: Hart Crane and Wallace Stevens are its main poets; Henry James, Faulkner, and O'Neill, in very different ways and in different stages of their career, show marked affinities with its techniques and outlook. Edmund Wilson's *Axel's Castle* (1931) was apparently the very first book which definitely conceived of symbolism as an international movement and singled out Yeats, Joyce, Eliot, Gertrude Stein, Valéry, Proust, and Thomas Mann as examples of a movement which, he believed, had come to an end at the time of his writing. Here we find the conception formulated which, very generally, is the thesis of this paper and the assumption of many historians since Wilson's sketch. Wilson's sources were the writings of Huneker, whom he admired greatly, and the instruction in French literature he received in Princeton from Christian Gauss. But the insight into the unity and continuity of the international movement and the selection of the great names was his own. We might only deplore the inclusion of Gertrude Stein. But I find it difficult to believe that Wilson's book could have had any influence outside the English-speaking world.

In the United States Wilson's reasonable and moderate plea for an international movement was soon displaced by attempts to make the whole of the American literary tradition symbolist. F. O.

> **"The symbolist conception of American literature is still prevalent today. It owes its dominance to the attempt to exalt the great American writers to myth-makers and providers of a substitute religion."**

Matthiessen's *The American Renaissance* (1941) is based on a distinction between symbol and allegory very much in the terms of the distinction introduced by Goethe.

Matthiessen's *The American Renaissance* (1941) is based on a distinction between symbol and allegory very much in the terms of the distinction introduced by Goethe. Allegory appears as inferior to symbol: Hawthorne inferior to Melville. But in Charles Feidelson's *Symbolism and American Literature* (1956) the distinction between modern symbolism and the use of symbols by romantic authors is completely obliterated. Emerson, Hawthorne, Poe, Melville, and Whitman appear as pure symbolists *avant la lettre*, and their ancestry is traced back to the Puritans, who paradoxically appear as incomplete, frustrated symbolists. It can be rightly objected that the old Puritans were sharply inimical to images and symbols and that there is a gulf between the religious conception of signs of God's Providence and the aesthetic use of symbols in the novels of Hawthorne and Melville and even in the Platonizing aesthetics of Emerson.

The symbolist conception of American literature is still prevalent today. It owes its dominance to the attempt to exalt the great American writers to myth-makers and providers of a substitute religion. James Baird, in *Ishmael* (1956), puts it unabashedly. Melville is "the supreme example of the artistic creator engaged in the act of making new symbols to replace the 'lost' symbols of Protestant Christianity." A very active trend in American criticism expanded symbolist interpretation to all types and periods of literature, imposing it on writings which have no such meaning or have to be twisted to assume it. Harry Levin rightly complained in an address, " Symbolism and Fiction" (1956), that "every hero may seem to have a thousand faces; every heroine may be a white goddess *incognita;* every fishing trip turns out to be another quest for the Holy Grail." The impact of ideas from the Cambridge anthropologists and from Carl Jung is obvious. In the study of medieval texts a renewed interest in the fourfold levels of meaning in Dante's letter to Can Grande has persuaded a whole group of American scholars, mainly under the influence of D. W. Robertson, to interpret or misinterpret Chaucer, the *Pearl* poet, and Langland in these terms. They should bear in mind that Thomas Aquinas recognized only a literal sense in a work invented by human industry and that he reserved the other three senses for Scripture. The symbolist interpretation reaches heights of ingenuity in the writing of Northrop Frye, who began with a book on Blake and, in *The Anatomy of Criticism* (1957), conceived of the whole of literature as a self-enclosed system of symbols and myths, "existing in its own universe, no longer a commentary on life or reality, but containing life and reality in a system of verbal relationships." In this grandiose conception all distinctions between periods and styles are abolished: "the literary universe is a universe in which everything is potentially identical with everything else." Hence the old distinctions between myth, symbol, and allegory disappear. One of Frye's followers, Angus Fletcher, in his book on *Allegory* (1964), exalts allegory as the central procedure of art, while Frye still holds fast to symbolism, recognizing that "the critics are often prejudiced against allegory without knowing the real reason, which is that continuous allegory prescribes the direction of his commentary, and so restricts his freedom."

The story of the spread of symbolism is very different in other countries. The effect in Italy was ostensibly rather small. Soffici's pamphlet on Rimbaud in 1911 is usually considered the beginning of the French symbolist influence, but there was an early propagandist for Mallarmé, Vittorio Pica, who was heavily dependent on French sources, particularly Téodor de Wyzéwa. His articles, in the *Gazetta letteraria* (1885–86), on the French poets do not use the term; but in 1896 he replaced "decadent" and "Byzantine" by "symbolist." D'Annunzio, who knew and used some French symbolists, would be classed as "decadent" today, and the poets around Ungaretti and Montale as "hermetic." In a recent book by Mario Luzi, *L'Idea simbolista* (1959), Pascoli, Dino Campana, and Arturo Onofri are called symbolist poets, but Luzi uses the term so widely that he begins his anthology of symbolism with Hölderlin and Novalis, Coleridge and Wordsworth, and can include Poe, Browning, Patmore, Swinburne, Hopkins, and Francis Thompson among its precursors. Still, his list of symbolist poets, French, Russian, English, German, Spanish, and Greek, is, on the whole, reasonable. Onofri was certainly strongly influenced by Mallarmé and later by Rudolf Steiner; Pascoli, however, seems to me no symbolist in his poetry, though he gave extremely symbolist interpretations of Dante. It might be wiser to think of "ermetismo" as the Italian name for symbolism: Montale and possibly Dino Campana are genuine symbolists.

While symbolism, at least as a definite school or movement, was absent in Italy, it is central in the history of Spanish poetry. The Nicaraguan poet Rubén Darío initiated it after his short stay in Paris in 1892. He wrote poems under the symbolist influence and addressed, for instance, a fervent hymn to Verlaine. The influence of French symbolist poetry changed completely the oratorical or popular style of Spanish lyrical poetry. The closeness of Guillén to Mallarmé and Valéry seems too obvious to deny, and the Uruguayan poet Julio Herrera y Reissig (1873–1909) is clearly in the symbolist tradition, often of the obscurest manner. Still, the Spanish critics favor the term "Modernismo," which is used sometimes so inclusively that it covers all modern Spanish poetry and even the so-called "generation of 1898," the prose writers Azorín, Baroja, and Unamuno, whose associations with symbolism were quite tenuous. "Symbolism" can apply only to one trend in modern Spanish literature, as the romantic popular tradition was stronger there than elsewhere. García Lorca's poetry can serve as the best known example of the peculiar Spanish synthesis of the folksy and the symbolical, the gypsy song and the myth. Still, the continuity from Darío to Jiménez, Antonio Machado, Alberti, and then to Guillén seems to me evident. Jorge Guillén in his Harvard lectures, *Language and Poetry* (1961), finds "no label convincing." "A period look," he argues, does not signify a "group style." In Spain there were, he thinks, fewer "isms" than elsewhere and the break with the past was far less abrupt. He reflects that "any name seeking to give unity to a historical period is the invention of posterity." But while eschewing the term "symbolism," he characterizes himself and his contemporaries well enough by expounding their common creed: their belief in the marriage of Idea and music—in short, their belief in the ideal of Mallarmé. Following a vague suggestion made by Remy de Gourmont, the rediscovery of Góngora by Ortega y Gasset, Gerardo Diego, Dámaso Alonso, and Alfonso Reyes around 1927 fits into the picture: they couple Góngora and Mallarmé as the two poets who in the history of all poetry have gone furthest in the search for absolute poetry, for the quintessence of the poetic.

In Germany the spread of symbolism was far less complete than Symons assumed in 1899. Stefan George had come to Paris in 1889, had visited Mallarmé and met many poets, but after his return to Germany he avoided, I assume deliberately, the term "symbolism" for himself and his circle. He translated a selection from Baudelaire (1891) and smaller samples from Mallarmé, Verlaine, and Régnier (in *Zeitgenössische Dichter*, 1905), but his own poetry does not, I think, show very close parallels to the French masters. Oddly enough, the poems of Vielé-Griffin seem to have left the most clearly discernible traces on George's own writings. As early as 1892 one of George's adherents, Carl August Klein, protested in George's periodical, *Blätter für die Kunst*, against the view of George's dependence on the French. Wagner, Nietzsche, Böcklin, and Klinger, he says, show that there is an indigenous opposition to naturalism in Germany as everywhere in the West. George himself spoke later of the French poets as his "former allies," and in Gundolf's authoritative book on George the French influence is minimized, if not completely denied. Among the theorists of the George circle Friedrich Gundolf had the strongest symbolist leanings: *Shakspeare und der deutsche Geist* (1911) and *Goethe* (1916) are based on the distinction of symbol-allegory, with symbol always the higher term. Still, the term symbolism did not catch on in Germany as a name for any specific group, though Hofmannsthal—e.g. in "Das Gespräch über Gedichte" of 1903—proclaimed the symbol the one element necessary in poetry. Later, the influence of Rimbaud—apparently largely in German translation—Iron Georg Trakl has been demonstrated with certainty. But if we examine German books on twentieth-century literature, symbolism seems rarely used. I found a section so called in Willi Duwe's *Die Dichtung des 20. Jahrhunderts* (1936) which includes Hofmannsthal, Dauthendey, Calé, Rilke, and George, while E. H. Lüth's *Literatur als Geschichte (Deutsche Dichtung von 1885 bis 1947)*, published in 1947, treats the same poets under the label "Neuromantik und Impressionismus." Later, however, we find a section, "Parasymbolismus," which deals with Musil and Broch. Hugo Friedrich, in his *Struktur der modernen Lyrik* (1956), avoids the terms and argues that the quick succession of modernist styles—dadaism, surrealism, futurism, expressionism, unanimism hermetism, and so on—creates an optical illusion which hides the fact of a direct continuity through Mallarmé, Valéry, Guillén, Ungaretti, and Eliot. The little anthology in the back of the book adds St. John Perse, Jiménez, García Lorca, Alberti, and Montale to these names. Friedrich's list seems to me the list of the main symbolist poets, even though Friedrich objects to the name. Clearly, German literary scholarship has not been converted to the term, though Wolfgang Kayser's article "Der europäische Symbolismus" (1953) had pleaded for a wide concept in which he included, in addition to the French poets, D'Annunzio, Yeats, Valéry, Proust, Virginia Woolf, and Faulkner.

In Russia we find the strongest symbolist group of poets who called themselves that. The close links with Paris at that time may help to explain this, or possibly also the strong consciousness of a tradition of symbolism in the Russian Church and in some of the Orthodox thinkers of the immediate past. Vladimir Solovëv was regarded as a precursor. In 1892 Zinaida Vengerova wrote a sympathetic account of the French symbolists for *Vestnik Evropy*, while in the following year Max Nordau's *Entartung* caused a sensation by its satirical account of recent French poetry which had repercussions on Tolstoy's *What is Art?*, as late as 1898. Bryusov emerged as the leading symbolist poet: he translated Maeterlinck's *L'Intruse* and wrote a poem "Iz Rimbaud" as early as 1892. In 1894 he published two little volumes under the title *Russkie simvolisty*. That year Bryusov wrote poems with titles such as "In the Spirit of the French Symbolists" and "In the Manner of Stéphane Mallarmé" (though these were not published till 1935) and brought out a translation of Verlaine's *Romances sans paroles*. Bryusov had later contacts with René Ghil, Mallarmé's pupil, and derived from him the idea of "instrumentation" in poetry which was to play such a great role in the theories of the Russian Formalists. In the meantime Dimitri Merezhkovsky had, in 1893, published a manifesto: *On the Causes of the Decline and the New Trends of Contemporary Russian Literature*, which recommended symbolism, though Merezhkovsky appealed to the Germans: to Goethe and the romantics rather than to the French. Merezhkovsky's pamphlet foreshadows the split in the Russian symbolist movement. The younger men, Blok and Vyacheslav Ivanov as well as Bely, distanced themselves from Bryusov and Balmont. Blok, in an early diary (1901–02), condemned Bryusov as decadent and opposed to his Parisian symbolism his own, Russian, rooted in the poetry of Tyutchev, Fet, Polonsky, and Solovëv. Vyacheslav Ivanov in 1910 shared Blok's view. The French influence seemed to him "adolescently unreasonable and, in fact, not very fertile," while his own symbolism appealed to Russian nationalism and to the general mystical tradition. Later Bely was to add occultism and Rudolf Steiner and his "anthroposophy." The group of poets who called themselves "Acmeists" (Gulmilëv, Anna Akhmatova, Osip Mandelshtam) was a direct outgrowth of symbolism. The mere fact that they appealed to the early symbolist Innokenty Annensky shows the continuity with symbolism in spite of their distaste for the occult and their emphasis on what they thought of as classical clarity. Symbolism dominates Russian poetry between about 1892 and 1914, when Futurism emerged as a slogan and the Russian Formalists attacked the whole concept of poetry as imagery.

If we glance at the other Slavic countries we are struck by the diversity of their reactions. Poland was informed early on about the French movement, and Polish poetry was influenced by the French symbolist movement, but the term "Młasoda Polska" was preferred. In Wilhelm Feldmann's *Współczesna literatura polska* (1905) contemporary poetry is discussed as "decadentism," but Wyspiański (a symbolist if ever there was one) appears under the chapter heading: "On the Heights of Romanticism." All the histories of Polish literature I have seen speak of "Modernism," "Decadentism," "Idealism," "Neo-romanticism," and occasionally call a poet such as Miriam (Zenon Przesmycki) a symbolist, but they never seem to use the term as a general name for a period in Polish literature.

In Czech literature the situation was more like that in Russia: Březina, Sova, and Hlaváček were called symbolists, and the idea of a school or at least a group of Czech symbolist poets is firmly established. The term "Moderna" (possibly because of the periodical *Moderní Revue*, founded in 1894) is definitely associated with decadentism, *fin de siècle*, a group represented by Arnošt Procházka. A hymnical, optimistic, even chiliastic poet such as Březina cannot and could not be classed with them. The great critic F. X. Šalda wrote of the "school of symbolists" as early as 1891, calling Verlaine, Villiers, and Mallarmé its masters but denied that there is a school of symbolists with dogmas, codices, and manifestoes. His very first important article, "Synthetism in the New Art" (1892), expounded the aesthetics of Morice and Hennequin for the benefit of the Czechs, then still mainly dependent on German models.

The unevenness of the penetration of both the influence of the French movement and very strikingly of the acceptance of the term raises the question whether we can account for these differences in causal terms. It sounds heretical or obscurantist in this age of scientific explanation to ascribe much to chance, to casual contacts, and to personal predilections. Why was the term so immensely successful in France, in the United States, and in Russia, less so in England and Spain, and hardly at all in Italy and Germany? In Germany there was even the tradition of the continuous debate about symbol since Goethe and Schelling; before the French movement Friedrich Theodor Vischer discussed the symbol elaborately and still the term did not catch on. One can think of all kinds of explanations: a deliberate decision by the poets to distance themselves from the French developments; or the success of the terms "Die Moderne" and "Neuromantik." Still, the very number of such explanations suggests that the variables are so great that we cannot account for these divergencies in any systematic manner.

If we, at long last, turn to the central question of what the exact content of the term is, we must obviously distinguish among the four concentric circles defining its scope. At its narrowest, "symbolism" refers to the French group which called itself "symbolist" in 1886. Its theory was rather rudimentary. These poets mainly wanted poetry to be non-rhetorical—i.e. they asked for a break with the tradition of Hugo and the *Parnassiens*. They wanted words not merely to state but to suggest; they wanted to use metaphors, allegories, and symbols not only as decorations but as organizing principles of their poems; they wanted their verse to be "musical," in practice to stop using the oratorical cadences of the French alexandrines, and in some cases to break completely with rhyme. Free verse—whose invention is usually ascribed to Gustave Kahn—was possibly the most enduring achievement which has survived all vicissitudes of style. Kahn himself in 1894 summed up the doctrine simply as "antinaturalism, antiprosaism in poetry, a search for freedom in the efforts in art, in reaction against the regimentation of the *Parnasse* and the naturalists." This sounds very meager today: freedom from restrictions has been, after all, the slogan of a great many movements in art.

It is better to think of "symbolism" in a wider sense: as the broad movement in France from Nerval and Baudelaire to Claudel and Valéry. We can restate the theories propounded and will be confronted by an enormous variety. We can characterize it more concretely and say, for example, that in symbolist poetry the image becomes "thing." The relation of tenor and vehicle in the metaphor is reversed. The utterance is divorced, we may add, from the situation: time and place, history and society, are played down. The inner world, the *durée*, in the Bergsonian sense, is represented or often merely hinted at as "it," the thing or the person hidden. One could say that the grammatical predicate has become the subject. Clearly such poetry can easily be justified by an occult view of the world. But this is not necessary: it might imply a feeling for analogy, for a web of correspondences, a rhetoric of metamorphoses in which everything reflects everything else. Hence the great role of synesthesia, which, though rooted in physiological facts and found all over the history of poetry, became at that time merely a stylistic device, a mannerism easily imitated and transmitted. This characterization could be elaborated considerably if we bear in mind that style and world view go together and only together can define the character of a period or even of a single poet.

Let me try to show, at least, how diverse and even incompatible were the theories of two such related poets as Baudelaire and Mallarmé. Baudelaire's aesthetic is mainly "romantic," not in the sense of emotionalism, nature worship, and exaltation of the ego, central in French romanticism, but rather in the English and German tradition of a glorification of creative imagination, a rhetoric of metamorphoses and universal analogy. Though there are subsidiary strands in Baudelaire's aesthetics, at his finest he grasps the role of imagination, "constructive imagination," as he calls it in a term ultimately derived from Coleridge. It gives a metaphysical meaning, "a positive relation with the infinite." Art is another cosmos which transforms and hence humanizes nature. By his creation the artist abolishes the gulf between subject and object, man and nature. Art is "to create a suggestive magic containing at one and the same time the object and the subject, the external world and the artist himself."

Mallarmé says almost the opposite in spite of some superficial resemblances and the common attachment to Poe and Wagner. Mallarmé was the first poet radically discontent with the ordinary language of communication; he attempted to construe an entirely separate language of poetry far more consistently than older cultivators of "poetic diction" such as the practitioners of *trobar clus*, or Góngora, or Mallarmé's contemporary, Gerard

Manley Hopkins. His aim of transforming language was, no doubt, in part negative: to exclude society, nature, and the person of the poet himself. But it was also positive: language was again to become "real," language was to be magic, words were to become things. But this is not, I think, sufficient reason to call Mallarmé a mystic. Even the depersonalization he requires is not mystical. Impersonality is rather objectivity, Truth. Art reaches for the Idea, which is ultimately inexpressible, because so abstract and general as to be devoid of any concrete traits. The term "flower" seems to him poetic because it suggests the "one, absent from all bouquets." Art thus can only hint and suggest, not transform as it should in Baudelaire. The "symbol" is only one device to achieve this effect. The so-called "negative" aesthetics of Mallarmé is thus nothing obscure. It had its psychological basis in a feeling of sterility, impotence, and final silence. He was a perfectionist who proposed something impossible of fulfillment: the book to end all books. "Everything on earth exists to be contained in a book." Like many poets before him, Mallarmé wants to express the mystery of the universe but feels that this mystery is not only insoluble and immensely dark but also hollow, empty, silent, Nothingness itself. There seems no need to appeal to Buddhism, Hegel, Schopenhauer, or Wagner to account for this. The atmosphere of nineteenth-century pessimism and the general Neoplatonic tradition in aesthetics suffice. Art searches for the Absolute but despairs of ever reaching it. The essence of the world is Nothingness, and the poet can only speak of this Nothingness. Art alone survives in the universe. Man's main vocation is to be an artist, a poet, who can save something from the general wreckage of time. The work or, in Mallarmé's terms, the Book is suspended over the Void, the silent godless Nothingness. Poetry is resolutely cut off from concrete reality, from the expression of the personality of the poet, from any rhetoric or emotion, and becomes only a Sign, signifying Nothing. In Baudelaire, on the other hand, poetry transforms nature, extracts flowers from evil, creates a new myth, reconciles man and nature.

But if we examine the actual verse of the symbolists of this period, we cannot be content with formulas either of creative imagination, of suggestion, or of pure or absolute poetry.

On the third wider circle of abstraction we can apply the term to the whole period on an international scale. Every such term is arbitrary, but symbolism can be defended as rooted in the concepts of the period, as distinct in meaning, and as clearly setting off the period from that preceding it: realism or naturalism. The difference from romanticism may be less certainly implied. Obviously there is a continuity with romanticism, and particularly German romanticism, also in France, as has been recently argued again by Werner Vordtriede in his *Novalis und die französischen Symbolisten* (1963). The direct contact of the French with the German romantics came late and should not be overrated. Jean Thorel, in "Les Romantiques allemandes et les symbolistes français," seems to have been the first to point out the relation. Maeterlinck's article on Novalis (1894) and his little anthology (1896) came late in the movement. But Wagner of course mediated between the symbolists and German mythology, though Mallarmé's attitude, admiring toward the music, was tinged with irony for Wagner's subject matter. Early in the century Heine, a *romantique défroqué* as he called himself, played the role of an intermediary which, to my mind, has been exaggerated in Kurt Weinberg's study, *Henri Heine: Héraut du symbolisme français* (1954). E. T. A. Hoffmann, we should not forget, was widely translated into French and could supply occult motifs, a transcendental view of music, and the theory and practice of synesthesia.

Possibly even more important were the indirect contacts through English writers: through Carlyle's chapter on symbolism in *Sartor Resartus* and his essay on Novalis; through Coleridge, from whom, through another intermediary, Mrs. Crowe, Baudelaire drew his definition of creative imagination; and through Emerson, who was translated by Edgar Quinet.

Also, French thinkers of the early nineteenth century knew the theory of symbolism at least, from the wide application to all the religions of the world made by Creuzer, whose *Symbolik* was translated into French in 1825. Pierre Leroux used the idea of "symbolic poetry" prominently in the early thirties. There was Edgar Allan Poe, who drew on Coleridge and A. W. Schlegel and seemed so closely to anticipate Baudelaire's views that Baudelaire quoted him as if he were Poe himself, sometimes dropping all quotations marks.

The enormous influence of Poe on the French demonstrates, however, most clearly the difference between romanticism and symbolism. Poe is far from being a representative of the romantic worldview or of the romantic aesthetic, in which the imagination is conceived as transforming nature.

Poe has been aptly described as an "angel in a machine": he combines a faith in technique and even technology, a distrust of inspiration, a rationalistic eighteenth-century mind with a vague occult belief in "supernal" beauty. The distrust of inspiration, an enmity to nature, is the crucial point which sets off symbolism from romanticism. Baudelaire, Mallarmé, and Valéry all share it; while Rilke, a symbolist in many of his procedures and views, appears as highly romantic in his reliance on moments of inspiration. This is why Hugo Friedrich excludes him from his book on the modern lyric and even disparages him in a harsh passage. This is why the attempt to make Mallarmé a spiritual descendant of Novalis, as Vordtriede tried, must fail. Mallarmé, one might grant, aims at transcendence, but it is an empty transcendence, while Novalis rapturously adores the unity of the mysterious universe. In short, the romantics were Rousseauists; the symbolists, beginning with Baudelaire, believe in the fall of man or, if they do not use the religious phraseology, know that man is limited and is not, as Novalis believed, the Messiah of nature. The end of the romantic period is clearly marked by the victory of positivism and scientism, which soon led to disillusionment and pessimism. Most symbolists were non-Christians and even atheists, even if they tried to find a new religion in occultism or flirted with Oriental religions. They were pessimists who need not have read Schopenhauer and Eduard von Hartmann, as Laforgue did, to succumb to the mood of decadence, *fin de siècle*, *Götterdämmerung*, or the death of God prophesied by Nietzsche.

Symbolism is also clearly set off from the new avant-garde movements after 1914: futurism, cubism, surrealism, expressionism, and so on. There the faith in language has crumbled completely, while in Mallarmé and Valéry language preserves its cognitive and even magic power: Valéry's collection of poems is rightly called *Charmes*. Orpheus is the mythological hero of the poet, charming the animals, trees, and even stones. With more recent art the view of analogy disappears: Kafka has nothing of it. Postsymbolist art is abstract and allegorical rather than symbolic. The image, in surrealism, has no beyond: it wells, at most, from the subconscious of the individual.

Finally, there is the highest abstraction, the wide largest circle: the use of "symbolism" in all literature, of all ages. But then the term, broken loose from its historical moorings, lacks concrete content and remains merely the name for a phenomenon almost universal in all art.

These reflections must lead to what only can be a recommendation, to use the third sense of our term, to call the period of European literature roughly between 1885 and 1914 "symbolism," to see it as an international movement which radiated originally from France but produced great writers and great poetry also elsewhere. In Ireland and England: Yeats and Eliot; in the United States: Wallace Stevens and Hart Crane; in Germany: George, Rilke, and Hofmannsthal; in Russia: Blok, Ivanov, and Bely; in Spain and South America: Darío, Machado, and Guillén. If we, as we should, extend the meaning of symbolism to prose, we can see it clearly in the late Henry James, in Joyce, in the later Thomas Mann, in Proust, in the early Gide and Faulkner, in D. H. Lawrence; and if we add the drama, we recognize it in the later stages of Ibsen, Strindberg, and Hauptmann, and in O'Neill. There is symbolist criticism of distinction: an aesthetics in Mallarmé and Valéry, a looser creed in Remy de Gourmont, in Eliot, and in Yeats, and a flourishing school of symbolist interpretation, particularly in the United States. Much of the French "new criticism" is frankly symbolist. Roland Barthes' new pamphlet, *Critique et vérité* (1966), pleads for a complete liberty of symbolist interpretation.

Still, we must not forget our initial reminder. A period concept can never exhaust its meaning. It is not a class concept of which the individual works are cases. It is a regulative idea: it struggles with preceding and following ideals of art. In the time under consideration the strength of the survivals was particularly great: Hauptmann's *Die Weber* was performed in the same year (1892) as *Blätter für die Kunst* began to appear; Blok's *Poems on the Beautiful Lady* were written in the same year (1901) as Gorky's *Lower Depths*. Within the same author and even within the same work of art the struggle was waged at times. Edmond Jaloux called Joyce "at the same time a realist and a symbolist." The same is true of Proust and Mann. *Ulysses* combines symbolism and naturalism, as no other book of the time, into a synthesis of grand proportion and strong tension. In Trieste Joyce lectured on two English writers and on two English writers alone: they were characteristically Defoe and Blake.

As agreement on the main periods of European literature grows, so agreement to add the period term "symbolism" to the five periods now accepted should increase. But even were a different term to be victorious (though none I can think of seems to me even remotely preferable), we should always recognize that such a term has fulfilled its function as a tool of historiography if it has made us think not only about individual works and authors but about schools, trends, and movements and their international expansion. Symbolism is at least a literary term which will help us to counteract the dependence of much literary history on periodization derived from political and social history (such as the term " Imperialism" used in Marxist literary histories, which is perfectly meaningless applied to poetry at that time). Symbolism is a term (and I am quoting the words I applied to baroque in 1945) "which prepares for synthesis, draws our minds away from the mere accumulation of observations and facts, and paves the way for a future history of literature as a fine art."

Source: Rene Wellek, "The Term and Concept of Symbolism in Literary History," in *Discriminations: Further Concepts of Criticism*, Yale University Press, 1970, pp. 90–121.

Sources

Baudelaire, Charles, *The Parisian Prowler: Le Spleen de Paris, Petits poèmes en prose*, translated by Edward K. Kaplan, University of Georgia Press, 1989, pp. 129–30.

Kaplan, Edward K., ed., Preface, in *The Parisian Prowler: Le Spleen de Paris, Petits poèmes en prose*, University of Georgia Press, 1989, pp. x–xi.

Simic, Charles, "The Poetry of Village Idiots," in *Verse*, Vol. 13, No. 1, 1996, pp. 7–8, quoted in *The Best of "The Prose Poem: An International Journal,"* edited by Peter Johnson, White Pine Press, 2000, p. 13.

Truesdale, C. W., Preface, in *The Party Train: A Collection of North American Prose Poetry*, edited by Robert Alexander, Mark Vinz, and C. W. Truesdale, New Rivers Press, 1996, p. xix.

Further Reading

Carter, A. E., *Paul Verlaine*, Twayne, 1971.

Carter provides an authoritative biography of Paul Verlaine, one of the founders of the French symbolist movement in poetry.

Eisenman, Stephen, *The Temptations of Saint Redon: Biography, Ideology, and Style in the Noirs of Odilon Redon*, University of Chicago Press, 1992.

Eisenman provides discussion of thematic and stylistic elements of the symbolist works of Odilon Redon, a major French symbolist artist.

Fowlie, Wallace, *Rimbaud and Jim Morrison: The Rebel as Poet*, Duke University Press, 1993.

Fowlie offers a comparison of the nineteenth-century French symbolist poet Rimbaud and the 1960s American rock star Jim Morrison. Fowlie asserts that both Rimbaud and Morrison expressed a similar sense of rebellion in their art and that both figures stand as modern antiheroes.

Kolakowski, Leszek, *The Alienation of Reason: A History of Positivist Thought*, Doubleday, 1968.

Kolakowski provides a historical overview of the development of positivist thinking. The symbolist movement arose in part as a reaction against the positivist ideals of rational, objective reasoning and scientific method that dominated nineteenth-century thought.

Lacambre, Geneviève, *Gustave Moreau: Magic and Symbols*, Harry N. Abrams, 1999.

Lacambre provides discussion of the life and work of Gustave Moreau, a major French symbolist painter.

Millan, Gordon, *A Throw of the Dice: The Life of Stephen Mallarmé*, Farrar Straus & Giroux, 1994.

Millan provides a biography of the French symbolist poet Mallarmé.

Peyre, Henri, *Baudelaire: A Collection of Critical Essays*, Prentice-Hall, 1962.

Peyre offers critical discussion of the poetry of Baudelaire, a major French poet often noted as the grandfather of Symbolism.

Robb, Graham, *Rimbaud*, W. W. Norton & Co., 2000.

Robb provides a biography of Rimbaud, a major French symbolist poet.

Glossary

A

Abstract: Used as a noun, the term refers to a short summary or outline of a longer work. As an adjective applied to writing or literary works, abstract refers to words or phrases that name things not knowable through the five senses. Examples of abstracts include the *Cliffs Notes* summaries of major literary works. Examples of abstract terms or concepts include "idea," "guilt" "honesty," and "loyalty."

Absurd, Theater of the: See *Theater of the Absurd*

Absurdism: See *Theater of the Absurd*

Act: A major section of a play. Acts are divided into varying numbers of shorter scenes. From ancient times to the nineteenth century plays were generally constructed of five acts, but modern works typically consist of one, two, or three acts. Examples of five-act plays include the works of Sophocles and Shakespeare, while the plays of Arthur Miller commonly have a three-act structure.

Acto: A one-act Chicano theater piece developed out of collective improvisation. *Actos* were performed by members of Luis Valdez's Teatro Campesino in California during the mid-1960s.

Aestheticism: A literary and artistic movement of the nineteenth century. Followers of the movement believed that art should not be mixed with social, political, or moral teaching. The statement "art for art's sake" is a good summary of aestheticism. The movement had its roots in France, but it gained widespread importance in England in the last half of the nineteenth century, where it helped change the Victorian practice of including moral lessons in literature. Oscar Wilde is one of the best-known "aesthetes" of the late nineteenth century.

Age of Johnson: The period in English literature between 1750 and 1798, named after the most prominent literary figure of the age, Samuel Johnson. Works written during this time are noted for their emphasis on "sensibility," or emotional quality. These works formed a transition between the rational works of the Age of Reason, or Neoclassical period, and the emphasis on individual feelings and responses of the Romantic period. Significant writers during the Age of Johnson included the novelists Ann Radcliffe and Henry Mackenzie, dramatists Richard Sheridan and Oliver Goldsmith, and poets William Collins and Thomas Gray. Also known as Age of Sensibility

Age of Reason: See *Neoclassicism*

Age of Sensibility: See *Age of Johnson*

Agrarians: A group of Southern American writers of the 1930s and 1940s who fostered an economic and cultural program for the South based on agriculture, in opposition to the industrial society of the North. The term can refer to any group that promotes the value of farm life and agricultural society. Members of the original Agrarians included

John Crowe Ransom, Allen Tate, and Robert Penn Warren.

Alexandrine Meter: See *Meter*

Allegory: A narrative technique in which characters representing things or abstract ideas are used to convey a message or teach a lesson. Allegory is typically used to teach moral, ethical, or religious lessons but is sometimes used for satiric or political purposes. Examples of allegorical works include Edmund Spenser's *The Faerie Queene* and John Bunyan's *The Pilgrim's Progress.*

Allusion: A reference to a familiar literary or historical person or event, used to make an idea more easily understood. For example, describing someone as a "Romeo" makes an allusion to William Shakespeare's famous young lover in *Romeo and Juliet.*

Amerind Literature: The writing and oral traditions of Native Americans. Native American literature was originally passed on by word of mouth, so it consisted largely of stories and events that were easily memorized. Amerind prose is often rhythmic like poetry because it was recited to the beat of a ceremonial drum. Examples of Amerind literature include the autobiographical *Black Elk Speaks,* the works of N. Scott Momaday, James Welch, and Craig Lee Strete, and the poetry of Luci Tapahonso.

Analogy: A comparison of two things made to explain something unfamiliar through its similarities to something familiar, or to prove one point based on the acceptedness of another. Similes and metaphors are types of analogies. Analogies often take the form of an extended simile, as in William Blake's aphorism: "As the caterpillar chooses the fairest leaves to lay her eggs on, so the priest lays his curse on the fairest joys."

Angry Young Men: A group of British writers of the 1950s whose work expressed bitterness and disillusionment with society. Common to their work is an anti-hero who rebels against a corrupt social order and strives for personal integrity. The term has been used to describe Kingsley Amis, John Osborne, Colin Wilson, John Wain, and others.

Antagonist: The major character in a narrative or drama who works against the hero or protagonist. An example of an evil antagonist is Richard Lovelace in Samuel Richardson's *Clarissa,* while a virtuous antagonist is Macduff in William Shakespeare's *Macbeth.*

Anthropomorphism: The presentation of animals or objects in human shape or with human characteristics. The term is derived from the Greek word for "human form." The fables of Aesop, the animated films of Walt Disney, and Richard Adams's *Watership Down* feature anthropomorphic characters.

Anti-hero: A central character in a work of literature who lacks traditional heroic qualities such as courage, physical prowess, and fortitude. Antiheros typically distrust conventional values and are unable to commit themselves to any ideals. They generally feel helpless in a world over which they have no control. Anti-heroes usually accept, and often celebrate, their positions as social outcasts. A well-known anti-hero is Yossarian in Joseph Heller's novel *Catch-22.*

Antimasque: See *Masque*

Anti-novel: A term coined by French critic Jean-Paul Sartre. It refers to any experimental work of fiction that avoids the familiar conventions of the novel. The anti-novel usually fragments and distorts the experience of its characters, forcing the reader to construct the reality of the story from a disordered narrative. The best-known anti-novelist is Alain Robbe-Grillet, author of *Le voyeur.*

Antithesis: The antithesis of something is its direct opposite. In literature, the use of antithesis as a figure of speech results in two statements that show a contrast through the balancing of two opposite ideas. Technically, it is the second portion of the statement that is defined as the "antithesis"; the first portion is the "thesis." An example of antithesis is found in the following portion of Abraham Lincoln's "Gettysburg Address"; notice the opposition between the verbs "remember" and "forget" and the phrases "what we say" and "what they did": "The world will little note nor long remember what we say here, but it can never forget what they did here."

Apocrypha: Writings tentatively attributed to an author but not proven or universally accepted to be their works. The term was originally applied to certain books of the Bible that were not considered inspired and so were not included in the "sacred canon." Geoffrey Chaucer, William Shakespeare, Thomas Kyd, Thomas Middleton, and John Marston all have apocrypha. Apocryphal books of the Bible include the Old Testament's Book of Enoch and New Testament's Gospel of Peter.

Apollonian and Dionysian: The two impulses believed to guide authors of dramatic tragedy. The

Apollonian impulse is named after Apollo, the Greek god of light and beauty and the symbol of intellectual order. The Dionysian impulse is named after Dionysus, the Greek god of wine and the symbol of the unrestrained forces of nature. The Apollonian impulse is to create a rational, harmonious world, while the Dionysian is to express the irrational forces of personality. Friedrich Nietzche uses these terms in *The Birth of Tragedy* to designate contrasting elements in Greek tragedy.

Apostrophe: A statement, question, or request addressed to an inanimate object or concept or to a nonexistent or absent person. Requests for inspiration from the muses in poetry are examples of apostrophe, as is Marc Antony's address to Caesar's corpse in William Shakespeare's *Julius Caesar*: "O, pardon me, thou bleeding piece of earth, That I am meek and gentle with these butchers!... Woe to the hand that shed this costly blood!..."

Apprenticeship Novel: See *Bildungsroman*

Archetype: The word archetype is commonly used to describe an original pattern or model from which all other things of the same kind are made. This term was introduced to literary criticism from the psychology of Carl Jung. It expresses Jung's theory that behind every person's "unconscious," or repressed memories of the past, lies the "collective unconscious" of the human race: memories of the countless typical experiences of our ancestors. These memories are said to prompt illogical associations that trigger powerful emotions in the reader. Often, the emotional process is primitive, even primordial. Archetypes are the literary images that grow out of the "collective unconscious." They appear in literature as incidents and plots that repeat basic patterns of life. They may also appear as stereotyped characters. Examples of literary archetypes include themes such as birth and death and characters such as the Earth Mother.

Argument: The argument of a work is the author's subject matter or principal idea. Examples of defined "argument" portions of works include John Milton's *Arguments* to each of the books of *Paradise Lost* and the "Argument" to Robert Herrick's *Hesperides.*

Aristotelian Criticism: Specifically, the method of evaluating and analyzing tragedy formulated by the Greek philosopher Aristotle in his *Poetics.* More generally, the term indicates any form of criticism that follows Aristotle's views. Aristotelian criticism focuses on the form and logical structure of a work, apart from its historical or social context, in contrast to "Platonic Criticism," which stresses the usefulness of art. Adherents of New Criticism including John Crowe Ransom and Cleanth Brooks utilize and value the basic ideas of Aristotelian criticism for textual analysis.

Art for Art's Sake: See *Aestheticism*

Aside: A comment made by a stage performer that is intended to be heard by the audience but supposedly not by other characters. Eugene O'Neill's *Strange Interlude* is an extended use of the aside in modern theater.

Audience: The people for whom a piece of literature is written. Authors usually write with a certain audience in mind, for example, children, members of a religious or ethnic group, or colleagues in a professional field. The term "audience" also applies to the people who gather to see or hear any performance, including plays, poetry readings, speeches, and concerts. Jane Austen's parody of the gothic novel, *Northanger Abbey,* was originally intended for (and also pokes fun at) an audience of young and avid female gothic novel readers.

Autobiography: A connected narrative in which an individual tells his or her life story. Examples include Benjamin Franklin's *Autobiography* and Henry Adams's *The Education of Henry Adams.* Compare with Biography. See also Diary and Memoirs.

Automatic Writing: Writing carried out without a preconceived plan in an effort to capture every random thought. Authors who engage in automatic writing typically do not revise their work, preferring instead to preserve the revealed truth and beauty of spontaneous expression. Automatic writing was employed by many of the Surrealist writers, notably the French poet Robert Desnos. See also Surrealism.

Avant-garde: A French term meaning "vanguard." It is used in literary criticism to describe new writing that rejects traditional approaches to literature in favor of innovations in style or content. Twentieth-century examples of the literary *avant-garde* include the Black Mountain School of poets, the Bloomsbury Group, and the Beat Movement.

B

Ballad: A short poem that tells a simple story and has a repeated refrain. Ballads were originally intended to be sung. Early ballads, known as folk ballads, were passed down through generations, so their authors are often unknown. Later ballads composed by known authors are called literary ballads. An example of an anonymous folk ballad is "Edward," which dates from the Middle Ages. Samuel Taylor Coleridge's "The Rime of the Ancient Mariner" and John Keats's "La Belle Dame sans Merci" are examples of literary ballads.

Baroque: A term used in literary criticism to describe literature that is complex or ornate in style or diction. Baroque works typically express tension, anxiety, and violent emotion. The term "Baroque Age" designates a period in Western European literature beginning in the late sixteenth century and ending about one hundred years later. Works of this period often mirror the qualities of works more generally associated with the label "baroque" and sometimes feature elaborate conceits. Examples of Baroque works include John Lyly's *Euphues: The Anatomy of Wit,* Luis de Gongora's *Soledads,* and William Shakespeare's *As You Like It.*

Baroque Age: See *Baroque*

Baroque Period: See *Baroque*

Beat Generation: See *Beat Movement*

Beat Movement: A period featuring a group of American poets and novelists of the 1950s and 1960s—including Jack Kerouac, Allen Ginsberg, Gregory Corso, William S. Burroughs, and Lawrence Ferlinghetti—who rejected established social and literary values. Using such techniques as stream of consciousness writing and jazz-influenced free verse and focusing on unusual or abnormal states of mind—generated by religious ecstasy or the use of drugs—the Beat writers aimed to create works that were unconventional in both form and subject matter. Kerouac's *On the Road* is perhaps the best-known example of a Beat Generation novel, and Ginsberg's *Howl* is a famous collection of Beat poetry.

Beats, The: See *Beat Movement*

Belles-lettres: A French term meaning "fine letters" or "beautiful writing." It is often used as a synonym for literature, typically referring to imaginative and artistic rather than scientific or expository writing. Current usage sometimes restricts the meaning to light or humorous writing and appreciative essays about literature. Lewis Carroll's *Alice in Wonderland* epitomizes the realm of *belles-lettres.*

Bildungsroman: A German word meaning "novel of development." The *bildungsroman* is a study of the maturation of a youthful character, typically brought about through a series of social or sexual encounters that lead to self-awareness. *Bildungsroman* is used interchangeably with *erziehungsroman,* a novel of initiation and education. When a *bildungsroman*is concerned with the development of an artist (as in James Joyce's *A Portrait of the Artist as a Young Man*), it is often termed a *kunstlerroman.* Well-known *bildungsromane* include J. D. Salinger's *The Catcher in the Rye,* Robert Newton Peck's *A Day No Pigs Would Die,* and S. E. Hinton's *The Outsiders.* Also known as Apprenticeship Novel, Coming of Age Novel, Erziehungsroman, or Kunstlerroman.

Biography: A connected narrative that tells a person's life story. Biographies typically aim to be objective and closely detailed. James Boswell's *The Life of Samuel Johnson,* LL.D is a famous example of the form. Compare with Autobiography and Memoirs.

Black Aesthetic Movement: A period of artistic and literary development among African Americans in the 1960s and early 1970s. This was the first major African-American artistic movement since the Harlem Renaissance and was closely paralleled by the civil rights and black power movements. The black aesthetic writers attempted to produce works of art that would be meaningful to the black masses. Key figures in black aesthetics included one of its founders, poet and playwright Amiri Baraka, formerly known as LeRoi Jones; poet and essayist Haki R. Madhubuti, formerly Don L. Lee; poet and playwright Sonia Sanchez; and dramatist Ed Bullins. Works representative of the Black Aesthetic Movement include Amiri Baraka's play *Dutchman,* a 1964 Obie award-winner; *Black Fire: An Anthology of Afro-American Writing,* edited by Baraka and playwright Larry Neal and published in 1968; and Sonia Sanchez's poetry collection *We a BaddDDD People,* published in 1970. Also known as Black Arts Movement.

Black Arts Movement: See *Black Aesthetic Movement*

Black Comedy: See *Black Humor*

Black Humor: Writing that places grotesque elements side by side with humorous ones in an attempt to shock the reader, forcing him or her to laugh at the horrifying reality of a disordered world. Joseph Heller's novel *Catch-22* is considered a superb example of the use of black humor. Other well-known authors who use black humor include Kurt Vonnegut, Edward Albee, Eugene Ionesco, and Harold Pinter. Also known as Black Comedy.

Blank Verse: Loosely, any unrhymed poetry, but more generally, unrhymed iambic pentameter verse (composed of lines of five two-syllable feet with the first syllable accented, the second unaccented). Blank verse has been used by poets since the Renaissance for its flexibility and its graceful, dignified tone. John Milton's *Paradise Lost* is in blank verse, as are most of William Shakespeare's plays.

Bloomsbury Group: A group of English writers, artists, and intellectuals who held informal artistic and philosophical discussions in Bloomsbury, a district of London, from around 1907 to the early 1930s. The Bloomsbury Group held no uniform philosophical beliefs but did commonly express an aversion to moral prudery and a desire for greater social tolerance. At various times the circle included Virginia Woolf, E. M. Forster, Clive Bell, Lytton Strachey, and John Maynard Keynes.

Bon Mot: A French term meaning "good word." A *bon mot* is a witty remark or clever observation. Charles Lamb and Oscar Wilde are celebrated for their witty *bon mots.* Two examples by Oscar Wilde stand out: (1) "All women become their mothers. That is their tragedy. No man does. That's his." (2) "A man cannot be too careful in the choice of his enemies."

Breath Verse: See *Projective Verse*

Burlesque: Any literary work that uses exaggeration to make its subject appear ridiculous, either by treating a trivial subject with profound seriousness or by treating a dignified subject frivolously. The word "burlesque" may also be used as an adjective, as in "burlesque show," to mean "striptease act." Examples of literary burlesque include the comedies of Aristophanes, Miguel de Cervantes's *Don Quixote,*, Samuel Butler's poem "Hudibras," and John Gay's play *The Beggar's Opera.*

C

Cadence: The natural rhythm of language caused by the alternation of accented and unaccented syllables. Much modern poetry—notably free verse—deliberately manipulates cadence to create complex rhythmic effects. James Macpherson's "Ossian poems" are richly cadenced, as is the poetry of the Symbolists, Walt Whitman, and Amy Lowell.

Caesura: A pause in a line of poetry, usually occurring near the middle. It typically corresponds to a break in the natural rhythm or sense of the line but is sometimes shifted to create special meanings or rhythmic effects. The opening line of Edgar Allan Poe's "The Raven" contains a caesura following "dreary": "Once upon a midnight dreary, while I pondered weak and weary...."

Canzone: A short Italian or Provencal lyric poem, commonly about love and often set to music. The *canzone* has no set form but typically contains five or six stanzas made up of seven to twenty lines of eleven syllables each. A shorter, five-to ten-line "envoy," or concluding stanza, completes the poem. Masters of the *canzone* form include Petrarch, Dante Alighieri, Torquato Tasso, and Guido Cavalcanti.

Carpe Diem: A Latin term meaning "seize the day." This is a traditional theme of poetry, especially lyrics. A *carpe diem* poem advises the reader or the person it addresses to live for today and enjoy the pleasures of the moment. Two celebrated *carpe diem* poems are Andrew Marvell's "To His Coy Mistress" and Robert Herrick's poem beginning "Gather ye rosebuds while ye may...."

Catharsis: The release or purging of unwanted emotions—specifically fear and pity—brought about by exposure to art. The term was first used by the Greek philosopher Aristotle in his *Poetics* to refer to the desired effect of tragedy on spectators. A famous example of catharsis is realized in Sophocles' *Oedipus Rex,* when Oedipus discovers that his wife, Jacosta, is his own mother and that the stranger he killed on the road was his own father.

Celtic Renaissance: A period of Irish literary and cultural history at the end of the nineteenth century. Followers of the movement aimed to create a romantic vision of Celtic myth and legend. The most significant works of the Celtic Renaissance typically present a dreamy, unreal world, usually in reaction against the reality of contemporary problems. William Butler Yeats's *The Wanderings of Oisin* is among the most significant works of the Celtic Renaissance. Also known as Celtic Twilight.

Celtic Twilight: See *Celtic Renaissance*

Character: Broadly speaking, a person in a literary work. The actions of characters are what constitute the plot of a story, novel, or poem. There are numerous types of characters, ranging from simple, stereotypical figures to intricate, multifaceted ones. In the techniques of anthropomorphism and personification, animals—and even places or things—can assume aspects of character. "Characterization" is the process by which an author creates vivid, believable characters in a work of art. This may be done in a variety of ways, including (1) direct description of the character by the narrator; (2) the direct presentation of the speech, thoughts, or actions of the character; and (3) the responses of other characters to the character. The term "character" also refers to a form originated by the ancient Greek writer Theophrastus that later became popular in the seventeenth and eighteenth centuries. It is a short essay or sketch of a person who prominently displays a specific attribute or quality, such as miserliness or ambition. Notable characters in literature include Oedipus Rex, Don Quixote de la Mancha, Macbeth, Candide, Hester Prynne, Ebenezer Scrooge, Huckleberry Finn, Jay Gatsby, Scarlett O'Hara, James Bond, and Kunta Kinte.

Characterization: See *Character*

Chorus: In ancient Greek drama, a group of actors who commented on and interpreted the unfolding action on the stage. Initially the chorus was a major component of the presentation, but over time it became less significant, with its numbers reduced and its role eventually limited to commentary between acts. By the sixteenth century the chorus—if employed at all—was typically a single person who provided a prologue and an epilogue and occasionally appeared between acts to introduce or underscore an important event. The chorus in William Shakespeare's *Henry V* functions in this way. Modern dramas rarely feature a chorus, but T. S. Eliot's *Murder in the Cathedral* and Arthur Miller's *A View from the Bridge* are notable exceptions. The Stage Manager in Thornton Wilder's *Our Town* performs a role similar to that of the chorus.

Chronicle: A record of events presented in chronological order. Although the scope and level of detail provided varies greatly among the chronicles surviving from ancient times, some, such as the *Anglo-Saxon Chronicle,* feature vivid descriptions and a lively recounting of events. During the Elizabethan Age, many dramas—appropriately called "chronicle plays"—were based on material from chronicles. Many of William Shakespeare's dramas of English history as well as Christopher Marlowe's *Edward II* are based in part on Raphael Holinshead's *Chronicles of England, Scotland, and Ireland.*

Classical: In its strictest definition in literary criticism, classicism refers to works of ancient Greek or Roman literature. The term may also be used to describe a literary work of recognized importance (a "classic") from any time period or literature that exhibits the traits of classicism. Classical authors from ancient Greek and Roman times include Juvenal and Homer. Examples of later works and authors now described as classical include French literature of the seventeenth century, Western novels of the nineteenth century, and American fiction of the mid-nineteenth century such as that written by James Fenimore Cooper and Mark Twain.

Classicism: A term used in literary criticism to describe critical doctrines that have their roots in ancient Greek and Roman literature, philosophy, and art. Works associated with classicism typically exhibit restraint on the part of the author, unity of design and purpose, clarity, simplicity, logical organization, and respect for tradition. Examples of literary classicism include Cicero's prose, the dramas of Pierre Corneille and Jean Racine, the poetry of John Dryden and Alexander Pope, and the writings of J. W. von Goethe, G. E. Lessing, and T. S. Eliot.

Climax: The turning point in a narrative, the moment when the conflict is at its most intense. Typically, the structure of stories, novels, and plays is one of rising action, in which tension builds to the climax, followed by falling action, in which tension lessens as the story moves to its conclusion. The climax in James Fenimore Cooper's *The Last of the Mohicans* occurs when Magua and his captive Cora are pursued to the edge of a cliff by Uncas. Magua kills Uncas but is subsequently killed by Hawkeye.

Colloquialism: A word, phrase, or form of pronunciation that is acceptable in casual conversation but not in formal, written communication. It is considered more acceptable than slang. An example of colloquialism can be found in Rudyard Kipling's *Barrack-room Ballads:* When 'Omer smote 'is bloomin' lyre He'd 'eard men sing by land and sea; An' what he thought 'e might require 'E went an' took—the same as me!

Colonialism: The literature of several ages reflects concerns about Colonialism in depictions of encounters with native peoples and foreign landscapes and in vague allusions to distant plantations. Rough boundaries for the literary movement of Colonialism begin c. 1875, when historians date the start of a "New Imperialism," through the waning empires of World War I and up to the beginning of World War II, around 1939. Colonialism is primarily a feature of British literature, given that the British dominated the imperial age. The literature of Colonialism is characterized by a strong sense of ambiguity: uncertainty about the morality of imperialism, about the nature of humanity, and about the continuing viability of European civilization. Colonial literature is also full of high adventure, romance, and excitement. Examples of colonial literature are Joseph Conrad's *Heart of Darkness*, Olive Schreiner's *Story of an African Farm*, E. M. Forster's *A Passage to India*, the adventure tales of H. Rider Haggard, and Isak Dinesen's memoirs, including *Out of Africa*.

Comedy: One of two major types of drama, the other being tragedy. Its aim is to amuse, and it typically ends happily. Comedy assumes many forms, such as farce and burlesque, and uses a variety of techniques, from parody to satire. In a restricted sense the term comedy refers only to dramatic presentations, but in general usage it is commonly applied to nondramatic works as well. Examples of comedies range from the plays of Aristophanes, Terrence, and Plautus, Dante Alighieri's *The Divine Comedy,* Francois Rabelais's *Pantagruel* and *Gargantua,* and some of Geoffrey Chaucer's tales and William Shakespeare's plays to Noel Coward's play *Private Lives* and James Thurber's short story "The Secret Life of Walter Mitty."

Comedy of Manners: A play about the manners and conventions of an aristocratic, highly sophisticated society. The characters are usually types rather than individualized personalities, and plot is less important than atmosphere. Such plays were an important aspect of late seventeenth-century English comedy. The comedy of manners was revived in the eighteenth century by Oliver Goldsmith and Richard Brinsley Sheridan, enjoyed a second revival in the late nineteenth century, and has endured into the twentieth century. Examples of comedies of manners include William Congreve's *The Way of the World* in the late seventeenth century, Oliver Goldsmith's *She Stoops to Conquer* and Richard Brinsley Sheridan's *The School for Scandal* in the eighteenth century, Oscar Wilde's *The Importance of Being Earnest* in the nineteenth century, and W. Somerset Maugham's *The Circle* in the twentieth century.

Comic Relief: The use of humor to lighten the mood of a serious or tragic story, especially in plays. The technique is very common in Elizabethan works, and can be an integral part of the plot or simply a brief event designed to break the tension of the scene. The Gravediggers' scene in William Shakespeare's *Hamlet* is a frequently cited example of comic relief.

Coming of Age Novel: See *Bildungsroman*

Commedia dell'arte: An Italian term meaning "the comedy of guilds" or "the comedy of professional actors." This form of dramatic comedy was popular in Italy during the sixteenth century. Actors were assigned stock roles (such as Pulcinella, the stupid servant, or Pantalone, the old merchant) and given a basic plot to follow, but all dialogue was improvised. The roles were rigidly typed and the plots were formulaic, usually revolving around young lovers who thwarted their elders and attained wealth and happiness. A rigid convention of the *commedia dell'arte* is the periodic intrusion of Harlequin, who interrupts the play with low buffoonery. Peppino de Filippo's *Metamorphoses of a Wandering Minstrel* gave modern audiences an idea of what *commedia dell'arte* may have been like. Various scenarios for *commedia dell'arte* were compiled in Petraccone's *La commedia dell'arte, storia, technica, scenari,* published in 1927.

Complaint: A lyric poem, popular in the Renaissance, in which the speaker expresses sorrow about his or her condition. Typically, the speaker's sadness is caused by an unresponsive lover, but some complaints cite other sources of unhappiness, such as poverty or fate. A commonly cited example is "A Complaint by Night of the Lover Not Beloved" by Henry Howard, Earl of Surrey. Thomas Sackville's "Complaint of Henry, Duke of Buckingham" traces the duke's unhappiness to his ruthless ambition.

Conceit: A clever and fanciful metaphor, usually expressed through elaborate and extended comparison, that presents a striking parallel between two seemingly dissimilar things—for example, elaborately comparing a beautiful woman to an object like a garden or the sun. The conceit was a popular device throughout the Elizabethan Age and Baroque Age and was the principal technique of the seventeenth-century English metaphysical poets. This usage of the word conceit is unrelated to the best-known definition of conceit as an arrogant attitude or behavior. The conceit figures prominently in the works of John Donne, Emily Dickinson, and T. S. Eliot.

Concrete: Concrete is the opposite of abstract, and refers to a thing that actually exists or a description that allows the reader to experience an object or concept with the senses. Henry David Thoreau's *Walden* contains much concrete description of nature and wildlife.

Concrete Poetry: Poetry in which visual elements play a large part in the poetic effect. Punctuation marks, letters, or words are arranged on a page to form a visual design: a cross, for example, or a bumblebee. Max Bill and Eugene Gomringer were among the early practitioners of concrete poetry; Haroldo de Campos and Augusto de Campos are among contemporary authors of concrete poetry.

Confessional Poetry: A form of poetry in which the poet reveals very personal, intimate, sometimes shocking information about himself or herself. Anne Sexton, Sylvia Plath, Robert Lowell, and John Berryman wrote poetry in the confessional vein.

Conflict: The conflict in a work of fiction is the issue to be resolved in the story. It usually occurs between two characters, the protagonist and the antagonist, or between the protagonist and society or the protagonist and himself or herself. Conflict in Theodore Dreiser's novel *Sister Carrie* comes as a result of urban society, while Jack London's short story "To Build a Fire" concerns the protagonist's battle against the cold and himself.

Connotation: The impression that a word gives beyond its defined meaning. Connotations may be universally understood or may be significant only to a certain group. Both "horse" and "steed" denote the same animal, but "steed" has a different connotation, deriving from the chivalrous or romantic narratives in which the word was once often used.

Consonance: Consonance occurs in poetry when words appearing at the ends of two or more verses have similar final consonant sounds but have final vowel sounds that differ, as with "stuff" and "off." Consonance is found in "The curfew tolls the knells of parting day" from Thomas Grey's "An Elegy Written in a Country Church Yard." Also known as Half Rhyme or Slant Rhyme.

Convention: Any widely accepted literary device, style, or form. A soliloquy, in which a character reveals to the audience his or her private thoughts, is an example of a dramatic convention.

Corrido: A Mexican ballad. Examples of *corridos* include "Muerte del afamado Bilito," "La voz de mi conciencia," "Lucio Perez," "La juida," and "Los presos."

Couplet: Two lines of poetry with the same rhyme and meter, often expressing a complete and self-contained thought. The following couplet is from Alexander Pope's "Elegy to the Memory of an Unfortunate Lady": 'Tis Use alone that sanctifies Expense, And Splendour borrows all her rays from Sense.

Crime Literature: A genre of fiction that focuses on the environment, behavior, and psychology of criminals. Prominent writers of crime novels include John Wainwright, Colin Watson, Nicolas Freeling, Ruth Rendell, Jessica Mann, Mickey Spillane, and Patricia Highsmith.

Criticism: The systematic study and evaluation of literary works, usually based on a specific method or set of principles. An important part of literary studies since ancient times, the practice of criticism has given rise to numerous theories, methods, and "schools," sometimes producing conflicting, even contradictory, interpretations of literature in general as well as of individual works. Even such basic issues as what constitutes a poem or a novel have been the subject of much criticism over the centuries. Seminal texts of literary criticism include Plato's *Republic,* Aristotle's *Poetics,* Sir Philip Sidney's *The Defence of Poesie,* John Dryden's *Of Dramatic Poesie,* and William Wordsworth's "Preface" to the second edition of his *Lyrical Ballads.* Contemporary schools of criticism include deconstruction, feminist, psychoanalytic, poststructuralist, new historicist, postcolonialist, and reader-response.

D

Dactyl: See *Foot*

Dadaism: A protest movement in art and literature founded by Tristan Tzara in 1916. Followers of the movement expressed their outrage at the destruction brought about by World War I by revolting against numerous forms of social convention. The Dadaists presented works marked by calculated madness and flamboyant nonsense. They stressed total freedom of expression, commonly through primitive displays of emotion and illogical, often senseless, poetry. The movement ended shortly after the war, when it was replaced by surrealism. Proponents of Dadaism include Andre Breton, Louis Aragon, Philippe Soupault, and Paul Eluard.

Decadent: See *Decadents*

Decadents: The followers of a nineteenth-century literary movement that had its beginnings in French aestheticism. Decadent literature displays a fascination with perverse and morbid states; a search for novelty and sensation—the "new thrill"; a preoccupation with mysticism; and a belief in the senselessness of human existence. The movement is closely associated with the doctrine Art for Art's Sake. The term "decadence" is sometimes used to denote a decline in the quality of art or literature following a period of greatness. Major French decadents are Charles Baudelaire and Arthur Rimbaud. English decadents include Oscar Wilde, Ernest Dowson, and Frank Harris.

Deconstruction: A method of literary criticism developed by Jacques Derrida and characterized by multiple conflicting interpretations of a given work. Deconstructionists consider the impact of the language of a work and suggest that the true meaning of the work is not necessarily the meaning that the author intended. Jacques Derrida's *De la grammatologie* is the seminal text on deconstructive strategies; among American practitioners of this method of criticism are Paul de Man and J. Hillis Miller.

Deduction: The process of reaching a conclusion through reasoning from general premises to a specific premise. An example of deduction is present in the following syllogism: Premise: All mammals are animals. Premise: All whales are mammals. Conclusion: Therefore, all whales are animals.

Denotation: The definition of a word, apart from the impressions or feelings it creates in the reader. The word "apartheid" denotes a political and economic policy of segregation by race, but its connotations—oppression, slavery, inequality—are numerous.

Denouement: A French word meaning "the unknotting." In literary criticism, it denotes the resolution of conflict in fiction or drama. The *denouement* follows the climax and provides an outcome to the primary plot situation as well as an explanation of secondary plot complications. The *denouement* often involves a character's recognition of his or her state of mind or moral condition. A well-known example of *denouement* is the last scene of the play *As You Like It* by William Shakespeare, in which couples are married, an evildoer repents, the identities of two disguised characters are revealed, and a ruler is restored to power. Also known as Falling Action.

Description: Descriptive writing is intended to allow a reader to picture the scene or setting in which the action of a story takes place. The form this description takes often evokes an intended emotional response—a dark, spooky graveyard will evoke fear, and a peaceful, sunny meadow will evoke calmness. An example of a descriptive story is Edgar Allan Poe's *Landor's Cottage,* which offers a detailed depiction of a New York country estate.

Detective Story: A narrative about the solution of a mystery or the identification of a criminal. The conventions of the detective story include the detective's scrupulous use of logic in solving the mystery; incompetent or ineffectual police; a suspect who appears guilty at first but is later proved innocent; and the detective's friend or confidant—often the narrator—whose slowness in interpreting clues emphasizes by contrast the detective's brilliance. Edgar Allan Poe's "Murders in the Rue Morgue" is commonly regarded as the earliest example of this type of story. With this work, Poe established many of the conventions of the detective story genre, which are still in practice. Other practitioners of this vast and extremely popular genre include Arthur Conan Doyle, Dashiell Hammett, and Agatha Christie.

Deus ex machina: A Latin term meaning "god out of a machine." In Greek drama, a god was often lowered onto the stage by a mechanism of some kind to rescue the hero or untangle the plot. By extension, the term refers to any artificial device or coincidence used to bring about a convenient and simple solution to a plot. This is a common device in melodramas and includes such fortunate circumstances as the sudden receipt of a legacy to save the family farm or a last-minute stay of execution. The *deus ex machina* invariably rewards the virtuous and punishes evildoers. Examples of *deus ex machina* include King Louis XIV in Jean-Baptiste Moliere's *Tartuffe* and Queen Victoria in *The Pirates of Penzance* by William Gilbert and Arthur Sullivan. Bertolt Brecht parodies the abuse of such devices in the conclusion of his *Threepenny Opera.*

Dialogue: In its widest sense, dialogue is simply conversation between people in a literary work; in its most restricted sense, it refers specifically to the speech of characters in a drama. As a specific literary genre, a "dialogue" is a composition in which characters debate an issue or idea. The Greek philosopher Plato frequently expounded his theories in the form of dialogues.

Diary: A personal written record of daily events and thoughts. Asprivate documents, diaries are supposedly not intended for an audience, but some, such as those of Samuel Pepys and Anais Nin, are known for their high literary quality. *The Diary of Anne Frank* is an example of a well-known diary discovered and published after the author's death. Many writers have used the diary form as a deliberate literary device, as in Nikolai Gogol's story "Diary of a Madman." Compare with Autobiography.

Diction: The selection and arrangement of words in a literary work. Either or both may vary depending on the desired effect. There are four general types of diction: "formal," used in scholarly or lofty writing; "informal," used in relaxed but educated conversation; "colloquial," used in everyday speech; and "slang," containing newly coined words and other terms not accepted in formal usage.

Didactic: A term used to describe works of literature that aim to teach some moral, religious, political, or practical lesson. Although didactic elements are often found in artistically pleasing works, the term "didactic" usually refers to literature in which the message is more important than the form. The term may also be used to criticize a work that the critic finds "overly didactic," that is, heavy-handed in its delivery of a lesson. Examples of didactic literature include John Bunyan's *Pilgrim's Progress,* Alexander Pope's *Essay on Criticism,* Jean-Jacques Rousseau's *Emile,* and Elizabeth Inchbald's *Simple Story.*

Dimeter: See *Meter*

Dionysian: See *Apollonian and Dionysian*

Discordia concours: A Latin phrase meaning "discord in harmony." The term was coined by the eighteenth-century English writer Samuel Johnson to describe "a combination of dissimilar images or discovery of occult resemblances in things apparently unlike." Johnson created the expression by reversing a phrase by the Latin poet Horace. The metaphysical poetry of John Donne, Richard Crashaw, Abraham Cowley, George Herbert, and Edward Taylor among others, contains many examples of *discordia concours.* In Donne's "A Valediction: Forbidding Mourning," the poet compares the union of himself with his lover to a draftsman's compass: If they be two, they are two so, As stiff twin compasses are two: Thy soul, the fixed foot, makes no show To move, but doth, if the other do; And though it in the center sit, Yet when the other far doth roam, It leans, and hearkens after it, And grows erect, as that comes home.

Dissonance: A combination of harsh or jarring sounds, especially in poetry. Although such combinations may be accidental, poets sometimes intentionally make them to achieve particular effects. Dissonance is also sometimes used to refer to close but not identical rhymes. When this is the case, the word functions as a synonym for consonance. Robert Browning, Gerard Manley Hopkins, and many other poets have made deliberate use of dissonance.

Doppelganger: A literary technique by which a character is duplicated (usually in the form of an alter ego, though sometimes as a ghostly counterpart) or divided into two distinct, usually opposite personalities. The use of this character device is widespread in nineteenth- and twentieth-century literature, and indicates a growing awareness among authors that the "self" is really a composite of many "selves." A well-known story containing a *doppelganger* character is Robert Louis Stevenson's *Dr. Jekyll and Mr. Hyde,* which dramatizes an internal struggle between good and evil. Also known as The Double.

Double Entendre: A corruption of a French phrase meaning "double meaning." The term is used to indicate a word or phrase that is deliberately ambiguous, especially when one of the meanings is risque or improper. An example of a *double entendre* is the Elizabethan usage of the verb "die," which refers both to death and to orgasm.

Double, The: See *Doppelganger*

Draft: Any preliminary version of a written work. An author may write dozens of drafts which are revised to form the final work, or he or she may write only one, with few or no revisions. Dorothy Parker's observation that "I can't write five words but that I change seven" humorously indicates the purpose of the draft.

Drama: In its widest sense, a drama is any work designed to be presented by actors on a stage. Similarly, "drama" denotes a broad literary genre that includes a variety of forms, from pageant and spectacle to tragedy and comedy, as well as countless types and subtypes. More commonly in modern usage, however, a drama is a work that treats serious subjects and themes but does not aim at the grandeur of tragedy. This use of the term originated with the eighteenth-century French writer Denis Diderot, who used the word *drame* to designate his plays about middle-class life; thus "drama" typically features characters of a less exalted stature than those of tragedy. Examples of classical dramas include Menander's comedy *Dyscolus* and Sophocles' tragedy *Oedipus Rex.* Contemporary dramas include Eugene O'Neill's *The Iceman Cometh,* Lillian Hellman's *Little Foxes,* and August Wilson's *Ma Rainey's Black Bottom.*

Dramatic Irony: Occurs when the audience of a play or the reader of a work of literature knows something that a character in the work itself does not know. The irony is in the contrast between the intended meaning of the statements or actions of a character and the additional information understood by the audience. A celebrated example of dramatic irony is in Act V of William Shakespeare's *Romeo and Juliet,* where two young lovers meet their end as a result of a tragic misunderstanding. Here, the audience has full knowledge that Juliet's apparent "death" is merely temporary; she will regain her senses when the mysterious "sleeping potion" she has taken wears off. But Romeo, mistaking Juliet's drug-induced trance for true death, kills himself in grief. Upon awakening, Juliet discovers Romeo's corpse and, in despair, slays herself.

Dramatic Monologue: See *Monologue*

Dramatic Poetry: Any lyric work that employs elements of drama such as dialogue, conflict, or characterization, but excluding works that are intended for stage presentation. A monologue is a form of dramatic poetry.

Dramatis Personae: The characters in a work of literature, particularly a drama. The list of characters printed before the main text of a play or in the program is the *dramatis personae.*

Dream Allegory: See *Dream Vision*

Dream Vision: A literary convention, chiefly of the Middle Ages. In a dream vision a story is presented as a literal dream of the narrator. This device was commonly used to teach moral and religious lessons. Important works of this type are *The Divine Comedy* by Dante Alighieri, *Piers Plowman* by William Langland, and *The Pilgrim's Progress* by John Bunyan. Also known as Dream Allegory.

Dystopia: An imaginary place in a work of fiction where the characters lead dehumanized, fearful lives. Jack London's *The Iron Heel,* Yevgeny Zamyatin's *My,* Aldous Huxley's *Brave New World,* George Orwell's *Nineteen Eighty-four,* and Margaret Atwood's *Handmaid's Tale* portray versions of dystopia.

E

Eclogue: In classical literature, a poem featuring rural themes and structured as a dialogue among shepherds. Eclogues often took specific poetic forms, such as elegies or love poems. Some were written as the soliloquy of a shepherd. In later centuries, "eclogue" came to refer to any poem that was in the pastoral tradition or that had a dialogue or monologue structure. A classical example of an eclogue is Virgil's *Eclogues,* also known as *Bucolics.* Giovanni Boccaccio, Edmund Spenser, Andrew Marvell, Jonathan Swift, and Louis MacNeice also wrote eclogues.

Edwardian: Describes cultural conventions identified with the period of the reign of Edward VII of England (1901-1910). Writers of the Edwardian Age typically displayed a strong reaction against the propriety and conservatism of the Victorian Age. Their work often exhibits distrust of authority in religion, politics, and art and expresses strong doubts about the soundness of conventional values. Writers of this era include George Bernard Shaw, H. G. Wells, and Joseph Conrad.

Edwardian Age: See *Edwardian*

Electra Complex: A daughter's amorous obsession with her father. The term Electra complex comes from the plays of Euripides and Sophocles entitled *Electra,* in which the character Electra drives her brother Orestes to kill their mother and her lover in revenge for the murder of their father.

Elegy: A lyric poem that laments the death of a person or the eventual death of all people. In a conventional elegy, set in a classical world, the poet and subject are spoken of as shepherds. In modern criticism, the word elegy is often used to refer to a poem that is melancholy or mournfully contemplative. John Milton's "Lycidas" and Percy Bysshe Shelley's "Adonais" are two examples of this form.

Elizabethan Age: A period of great economic growth, religious controversy, and nationalism closely associated with the reign of Elizabeth I of England (1558-1603). The Elizabethan Age is considered a part of the general renaissance—that is, the flowering of arts and literature—that took place in Europe during the fourteenth through sixteenth centuries. The era is considered the golden age of English literature. The most important dramas in English and a great deal of lyric poetry were produced during this period, and modern English criticism began around this time. The notable authors of the period—Philip Sidney, Edmund Spenser, Christopher Marlowe, William Shakespeare, Ben Jonson, Francis Bacon, and John Donne—are among the best in all of English literature.

Elizabethan Drama: English comic and tragic plays produced during the Renaissance, or more narrowly, those plays written during the last years of and few years after Queen Elizabeth's reign. William Shakespeare is considered an Elizabethan dramatist in the broader sense, although most of his work was produced during the reign of James I. Examples of Elizabethan comedies include John Lyly's *The Woman in the Moone,* Thomas Dekker's *The Roaring Girl, or, Moll Cut Purse,* and William Shakespeare's *Twelfth Night.* Examples of Elizabethan tragedies include William Shakespeare's *Antony and Cleopatra,* Thomas Kyd's *The Spanish Tragedy,* and John Webster's *The Tragedy of the Duchess of Malfi.*

Empathy: A sense of shared experience, including emotional and physical feelings, with someone or something other than oneself. Empathy is often used to describe the response of a reader to a literary character. An example of an empathic passage is William Shakespeare's description in his narrative poem *Venus and Adonis* of: the snail, whose tender horns being hit, Shrinks backward in his shelly cave with pain. Readers of Gerard Manley Hopkins's *The Windhover* may experience some of the physical sensations evoked in the description of the movement of the falcon.

English Sonnet: See *Sonnet*

Enjambment: The running over of the sense and structure of a line of verse or a couplet into the following verse or couplet. Andrew Marvell's "To His Coy Mistress" is structured as a series of enjambments, as in lines 11-12: "My vegetable love should grow/Vaster than empires and more slow."

Enlightenment, The: An eighteenth-century philosophical movement. It began in France but had a wide impact throughout Europe and America. Thinkers of the Enlightenment valued reason and believed that both the individual and society could achieve a state of perfection. Corresponding to this essentially humanist vision was a resistance to religious authority. Important figures of the Enlightenment were Denis Diderot and Voltaire in France, Edward Gibbon and David Hume in England, and Thomas Paine and Thomas Jefferson in the United States.

Epic: A long narrative poem about the adventures of a hero of great historic or legendary importance. The setting is vast and the action is often given cosmic significance through the intervention of supernatural forces such as gods, angels, or demons. Epics are typically written in a classical style of grand simplicity with elaborate metaphors and allusions that enhance the symbolic importance of a hero's adventures. Some well-known epics are Homer's *Iliad* and *Odyssey,* Virgil's *Aeneid,* and John Milton's *Paradise Lost.*

Epic Simile: See *Homeric Simile*

Epic Theater: A theory of theatrical presentation developed by twentieth-century German playwright Bertolt Brecht. Brecht created a type of drama that the audience could view with complete detachment. He used what he termed "alienation effects" to create an emotional distance between the audience and the action on stage. Among these effects are: short, self-contained scenes that keep the play from building to a cathartic climax; songs that comment on the action; and techniques of acting that prevent the actor from developing an emotional identity with his role. Besides the plays of Bertolt Brecht, other plays that utilize epic theater conventions include those of Georg Buchner, Frank Wedekind, Erwin Piscator, and Leopold Jessner.

Epigram: A saying that makes the speaker's point quickly and concisely. Samuel Taylor Coleridge wrote an epigram that neatly sums up the form: What is an Epigram? A Dwarfish whole, Its body brevity, and wit its soul.

Epilogue: A concluding statement or section of a literary work. In dramas, particularly those of the seventeenth and eighteenth centuries, the epilogue is a closing speech, often in verse, delivered by an actor at the end of a play and spoken directly to the audience. A famous epilogue is Puck's speech at the end of William Shakespeare's *A Midsummer Night's Dream.*

Epiphany: A sudden revelation of truth inspired by a seemingly trivial incident. The term was widely used by James Joyce in his critical writings, and the stories in Joyce's *Dubliners* are commonly called "epiphanies."

Episode: An incident that forms part of a story and is significantly related to it. Episodes may be either self-contained narratives or events that depend on a larger context for their sense and importance. Examples of episodes include the founding of Wilmington, Delaware in Charles Reade's *The Disinherited Heir* and the individual events comprising the picaresque novels and medieval romances.

Episodic Plot: See *Plot*

Epistolary Novel: A novel in the form of letters. The form was particularly popular in the eighteenth century. Samuel Richardson's *Pamela* is considered the first fully developed English epistolary novel.

Epitaph: An inscription on a tomb or tombstone, or a verse written on the occasion of a person's death. Epitaphs may be serious or humorous. Dorothy Parker's epitaph reads, "I told you I was sick."

Epithalamion: A song or poem written to honor and commemorate a marriage ceremony. Famous examples include Edmund Spenser's "Epithalamion" and e. e. cummings's "Epithalamion." Also spelled Epithalamium.

Epithalamium: See *Epithalamion*

Epithet: A word or phrase, often disparaging or abusive, that expresses a character trait of someone or something. "The Napoleon of crime" is an epithet applied to Professor Moriarty, arch-rival of Sherlock Holmes in Arthur Conan Doyle's series of detective stories.

Erziehungsroman: See *Bildungsroman*

Essay: A prose composition with a focused subject of discussion. The term was coined by Michel de Montaigne to describe his 1580 collection of brief, informal reflections on himself and on various topics relating to human nature. An essay can also be a long, systematic discourse.

An example of a longer essay is John Locke's *An Essay concerning Human Understanding.*

Exempla: See *Exemplum*

Exemplum: A tale with a moral message. This form of literary sermonizing flourished during the Middle Ages, when *exempla* appeared in collections known as "example-books." The works of Geoffrey Chaucer are full of *exempla.*

Existentialism: A predominantly twentieth-century philosophy concerned with the nature and perception of human existence. There are two major strains of existentialist thought: atheistic and Christian. Followers of atheistic existentialism believe that the individual is alone in a godless universe and that the basic human condition is one of suffering and loneliness. Nevertheless, because there are no fixed values, individuals can create their own characters—indeed, they can shape themselves—through the exercise of free will. The atheistic strain culminates in and is popularly associated with the works of Jean-Paul Sartre. The Christian existentialists, on the other hand, believe that only in God may people find freedom from life's anguish. The two strains hold certain beliefs in common: that existence cannot be fully understood or described through empirical effort; that anguish is a universal element of life; that individuals must bear responsibility for their actions; and that there is no common standard of behavior or perception for religious and ethical matters. Existentialist thought figures prominently in the works of such authors as Eugene Ionesco, Franz Kafka, Fyodor Dostoyevsky, Simone de Beauvoir, Samuel Beckett, and Albert Camus.

Expatriates: See *Expatriatism*

Expatriatism: The practice of leaving one's country to live for an extended period in another country. Literary expatriates include English poets Percy Bysshe Shelley and John Keats in Italy, Polish novelist Joseph Conrad in England, American writers Richard Wright, James Baldwin, Gertrude Stein, and Ernest Hemingway in France, and Trinidadian author Neil Bissondath in Canada.

Exposition: Writing intended to explain the nature of an idea, thing, or theme. Expository writing is often combined with description, narration, or argument. In dramatic writing, the exposition is the introductory material which presents the characters, setting, and tone of the play. An example of dramatic exposition occurs in many nineteenth-century drawing-room comedies in which the butler and the maid open the play with relevant talk about their master and mistress; in composition, exposition relays factual information, as in encyclopedia entries.

Expressionism: An indistinct literary term, originally used to describe an early twentieth-century school of German painting. The term applies to almost any mode of unconventional, highly subjective writing that distorts reality in some way. Advocates of Expressionism include dramatists George Kaiser, Ernst Toller, Luigi Pirandello, Federico Garcia Lorca, Eugene O'Neill, and Elmer Rice; poets George Heym, Ernst Stadler, August Stramm, Gottfried Benn, and Georg Trakl; and novelists Franz Kafka and James Joyce.

Extended Monologue: See *Monologue*

F

Fable: A prose or verse narrative intended to convey a moral. Animals or inanimate objects with human characteristics often serve as characters in fables. A famous fable is Aesop's "The Tortoise and the Hare."

Fairy Tales: Short narratives featuring mythical beings such as fairies, elves, and sprites. These tales originally belonged to the folklore of a particular nation or region, such as those collected in Germany by Jacob and Wilhelm Grimm. Two other celebrated writers of fairy tales are Hans Christian Andersen and Rudyard Kipling.

Falling Action: See *Denouement*

Fantasy: A literary form related to mythology and folklore. Fantasy literature is typically set in nonexistent realms and features supernatural beings. Notable examples of fantasy literature are *The Lord of the Rings* by J. R. R. Tolkien and the Gormenghast trilogy by Mervyn Peake.

Farce: A type of comedy characterized by broad humor, outlandish incidents, and often vulgar subject matter. Much of the "comedy" in film and television could more accurately be described as farce.

Feet: See *Foot*

Feminine Rhyme: See *Rhyme*

Femme fatale: A French phrase with the literal translation "fatal woman." A *femme fatale* is a sensuous, alluring woman who often leads men into danger or trouble. A classic example of the *femme fatale* is the nameless character in Billy Wilder's *The Seven Year Itch,* portrayed by Marilyn Monroe in the film adaptation.

Festschrift: A collection of essays written in honor of a distinguished scholar and presented to him or her to mark some special occasion. Examples of *festschriften* are *Worlds of Jewish Prayer: A Festschrift in Honour of Rabbi Zalman M. Schachter-Shalomi* and *The Organist as Scholar: Essays in Memory of Russell Saunders.*

Fiction: Any story that is the product of imagination rather than a documentation of fact. characters and events in such narratives may be based in real life but their ultimate form and configuration is a creation of the author. Geoffrey Chaucer's *The Canterbury Tales,* Laurence Sterne's *Tristram Shandy,* and Margaret Mitchell's *Gone with the Wind* are examples of fiction.

Figurative Language: A technique in writing in which the author temporarily interrupts the order, construction, or meaning of the writing for a particular effect. This interruption takes the form of one or more figures of speech such as hyperbole, irony, or simile. Figurative language is the opposite of literal language, in which every word is truthful, accurate, and free of exaggeration or embellishment. Examples of figurative language are tropes such as metaphor and rhetorical figures such as apostrophe.

Figures of Speech: Writing that differs from customary conventions for construction, meaning, order, or significance for the purpose of a special meaning or effect. There are two major types of figures of speech: rhetorical figures, which do not make changes in the meaning of the words, and tropes, which do. Types of figures of speech include simile, hyperbole, alliteration, and pun, among many others.

Fin de siecle: A French term meaning "end of the century." The term is used to denote the last decade of the nineteenth century, a transition period when writers and other artists abandoned old conventions and looked for new techniques and objectives. Two writers commonly associated with the *fin de siecle* mindset are Oscar Wilde and George Bernard Shaw.

First Person: See *Point of View*

Flashback: A device used in literature to present action that occurred before the beginning of the story. Flashbacks are often introduced as the dreams or recollections of one or more characters. Flashback techniques are often used in films, where they are typically set off by a gradual changing of one picture to another.

Foil: A character in a work of literature whose physical or psychological qualities contrast strongly with, and therefore highlight, the corresponding qualities of another character. In his Sherlock Holmes stories, Arthur Conan Doyle portrayed Dr. Watson as a man of normal habits and intelligence, making him a foil for the eccentric and wonderfully perceptive Sherlock Holmes.

Folk Ballad: See *Ballad*

Folklore: Traditions and myths preserved in a culture or group of people. Typically, these are passed on by word of mouth in various forms—such as legends, songs, and proverbs—or preserved in customs and ceremonies. This term was first used by W. J. Thoms in 1846. Sir James Frazer's *The Golden Bough* is the record of English folklore; myths about the frontier and the Old South exemplify American folklore.

Folktale: A story originating in oral tradition. Folktales fall into a variety of categories, including legends, ghost stories, fairy tales, fables, and anecdotes based on historical figures and events. Examples of folktales include Giambattista Basile's *The Pentamerone,* which contains the tales of Puss in Boots, Rapunzel, Cinderella, and Beauty and the Beast, and Joel Chandler Harris's Uncle

Remus stories, which represent transplanted African folktales and American tales about the characters Mike Fink, Johnny Appleseed, Paul Bunyan, and Pecos Bill.

Foot: The smallest unit of rhythm in a line of poetry. In English-language poetry, a foot is typically one accented syllable combined with one or two unaccented syllables. There are many different types of feet. When the accent is on the second syllable of a two syllable word (con- *tort*), the foot is an "iamb"; the reverse accentual pattern (*tor* -ture) is a "trochee." Other feet that commonly occur in poetry in English are "anapest", two unaccented syllables followed by an accented syllable as in inter-*cept*, and "dactyl", an accented syllable followed by two unaccented syllables as in *su*-i- cide.

Foreshadowing: A device used in literature to create expectation or to set up an explanation of later developments. In Charles Dickens's *Great Expectations,* the graveyard encounter at the beginning of the novel between Pip and the escaped convict Magwitch foreshadows the baleful atmosphere and events that comprise much of the narrative.

Form: The pattern or construction of a work which identifies its genre and distinguishes it from other genres. Examples of forms include the different genres, such as the lyric form or the short story form, and various patterns for poetry, such as the verse form or the stanza form.

Formalism: In literary criticism, the belief that literature should follow prescribed rules of construction, such as those that govern the sonnet form. Examples of formalism are found in the work of the New Critics and structuralists.

Fourteener Meter: See *Meter*

Free Verse: Poetry that lacks regular metrical and rhyme patterns but that tries to capture the cadences of everyday speech. The form allows a poet to exploit a variety of rhythmical effects within a single poem. Free-verse techniques have been widely used in the twentieth century by such writers as Ezra Pound, T. S. Eliot, Carl Sandburg, and William Carlos Williams. Also known as *Vers libre.*

Futurism: A flamboyant literary and artistic movement that developed in France, Italy, and Russia from 1908 through the 1920s. Futurist theater and poetry abandoned traditional literary forms. In their place, followers of the movement attempted to achieve total freedom of expression through bizarre imagery and deformed or newly invented words. The Futurists were self-consciously modern artists who attempted to incorporate the appearances and sounds of modern life into their work. Futurist writers include Filippo Tommaso Marinetti, Wyndham Lewis, Guillaume Apollinaire, Velimir Khlebnikov, and Vladimir Mayakovsky.

G

Genre: A category of literary work. In critical theory, genre may refer to both the content of a given work—tragedy, comedy, pastoral—and to its form, such as poetry, novel, or drama. This term also refers to types of popular literature, as in the genres of science fiction or the detective story.

Genteel Tradition: A term coined by critic George Santayana to describe the literary practice of certain late nineteenth-century American writers, especially New Englanders. Followers of the Genteel Tradition emphasized conventionality in social, religious, moral, and literary standards. Some of the best-known writers of the Genteel Tradition are R. H. Stoddard and Bayard Taylor.

Gilded Age: A period in American history during the 1870s characterized by political corruption and materialism. A number of important novels of social and political criticism were written during this time. Examples of Gilded Age literature include Henry Adams's *Democracy* and F. Marion Crawford's *An American Politician.*

Gothic: See *Gothicism*

Gothic Literature: See *Gothicism*

Gothic Novel: See *Gothicism*

Gothicism: In literary criticism, works characterized by a taste for the medieval or morbidly attractive. A gothic novel prominently features elements of horror, the supernatural, gloom, and violence: clanking chains, terror, charnel houses, ghosts, medieval castles, and mysteriously slamming doors. The term "gothic novel" is also applied to novels that lack elements of the traditional Gothic setting but that create a similar atmosphere of terror or dread. Mary Shelley's *Frankenstein* is perhaps the best-known English work of this kind.

Great Chain of Being: The belief that all things and creatures in nature are organized in a hierarchy from inanimate objects at the bottom to God at the top. This system of belief was popular in the seventeenth and eighteenth centuries. A summary of the concept of the great chain of being can be found in the first epistle of Alexander Pope's *An*

Essay on Man, and more recently in Arthur O. Lovejoy's *The Great Chain of Being: A Study of the History of an Idea.*

Greek Drama: Greek drama consists primarily of the surviving texts of four major playwrights from the fifth century B.C.. Three of these—Aeschylus, Sophocles, and Euripides—were tragedians. The early works focused on the good and evil that existed simultaneously in the world as well as the other contradictory forces of human nature and the outside world. All three tragic playwrights drew their material from Greek myths and legends; they each brought new developments to the art form. Examples of Greek tragedies include the *Oresteia* trilogy of Aeschylus, *Oedipus the King* by Sophocles, and the *Medea* of Euripides. Comedy most likely also developed out of the same religious rituals as tragedy. Aristophanes was the greatest writer of comedies in the early period known as Old Comedy, using biting satire in plays such as *Birds* and *Lysistrata* to ridicule prominent Athenian figures and current events. Later comedy relied less on satire and mythology and more on human relations among the Greek common people.

Grotesque: In literary criticism, the subject matter of a work or a style of expression characterized by exaggeration, deformity, freakishness, and disorder. The grotesque often includes an element of comic absurdity. Early examples of literary grotesque include Francois Rabelais's *Pantagruel* and *Gargantua* and Thomas Nashe's *The Unfortunate Traveller,* while more recent examples can be found in the works of Edgar Allan Poe, Evelyn Waugh, Eudora Welty, Flannery O'Connor, Eugene Ionesco, Gunter Grass, Thomas Mann, Mervyn Peake, and Joseph Heller, among many others.

H

Haiku: The shortest form of Japanese poetry, constructed in three lines of five, seven, and five syllables respectively. The message of a *haiku* poem usually centers on some aspect of spirituality and provokes an emotional response in the reader. Early masters of *haiku* include Basho, Buson, Kobayashi Issa, and Masaoka Shiki. English writers of *haiku* include the Imagists, notably Ezra Pound, H. D., Amy Lowell, Carl Sandburg, and William Carlos Williams. Also known as *Hokku.*

Half Rhyme: See *Consonance*

Hamartia: In tragedy, the event or act that leads to the hero's or heroine's downfall. This term is often incorrectly used as a synonym for tragic flaw. In Richard Wright's *Native Son,* the act that seals Bigger Thomas's fate is his first impulsive murder.

Harlem Renaissance: The Harlem Renaissance of the 1920s is generally considered the first significant movement of black writers and artists in the United States. During this period, new and established black writers published more fiction and poetry than ever before, the first influential black literary journals were established, and black authors and artists received their first widespread recognition and serious critical appraisal. Among the major writers associated with this period are Claude McKay, Jean Toomer, Countee Cullen, Langston Hughes, Arna Bontemps, Nella Larsen, and Zora Neale Hurston. Works representative of the Harlem Renaissance include Arna Bontemps's poems "The Return" and "Golgotha Is a Mountain," Claude McKay's novel *Home to Harlem,* Nella Larsen's novel *Passing,* Langston Hughes's poem "The Negro Speaks of Rivers," and the journals *Crisis* and *Opportunity,* both founded during this period. Also known as Negro Renaissance and New Negro Movement.

Harlequin: A stock character of the *commedia dell'arte* who occasionally interrupted the action with silly antics. Harlequin first appeared on the English stage in John Day's *The Travailes of the Three English Brothers.* The San Francisco Mime Troupe is one of the few modern groups to adapt Harlequin to the needs of contemporary satire.

Hellenism: Imitation of ancient Greek thought or styles. Also, an approach to life that focuses on the growth and development of the intellect. "Hellenism" is sometimes used to refer to the belief that reason can be applied to examine all human experience. A cogent discussion of Hellenism can be found in Matthew Arnold's *Culture and Anarchy.*

Heptameter: See *Meter*

Hero/Heroine: The principal sympathetic character (male or female) in a literary work. Heroes and heroines typically exhibit admirable traits: idealism, courage, and integrity, for example. Famous heroes and heroines include Pip in Charles Dickens's *Great Expectations,* the anonymous narrator in Ralph Ellison's *Invisible Man,* and Sethe in Toni Morrison's *Beloved.*

Heroic Couplet: A rhyming couplet written in iambic pentameter (a verse with five iambic feet). The following lines by Alexander Pope are an example: "Truth guards the Poet, sanctifies the line,/ And makes Immortal, Verse as mean as mine."

Heroic Line: The meter and length of a line of verse in epic or heroic poetry. This varies by language and time period. For example, in English poetry, the heroic line is iambic pentameter (a verse with five iambic feet); in French, the alexandrine (a verse with six iambic feet); in classical literature, dactylic hexameter (a verse with six dactylic feet).

Heroine: See *Hero/Heroine*

Hexameter: See *Meter*

Historical Criticism: The study of a work based on its impact on the world of the time period in which it was written. Examples of postmodern historical criticism can be found in the work of Michel Foucault, Haydcn White, Stephen Greenblatt, and Jonathan Goldberg.

Hokku: See *Haiku*

Holocaust: See *Holocaust Literature*

Holocaust Literature: Literature influenced by or written about the Holocaust of World War II. Such literature includes true stories of survival in concentration camps, escape, and life after the war, as well as fictional works and poetry. Representative works of Holocaust literature include Saul Bellow's *Mr. Sammler's Planet,* Anne Frank's *The Diary of a Young Girl,* Jerzy Kosinski's *The Painted Bird,* Arthur Miller's *Incident at Vichy,* Czeslaw Milosz's *Collected Poems,* William Styron's *Sophie's Choice,* and Art Spiegelman's *Maus.*

Homeric Simile: An elaborate, detailed comparison written as a simile many lines in length. An example of an epic simile from John Milton's *Paradise Lost* follows: Angel Forms, who lay entranced Thick as autumnal leaves that strow the brooks In Vallombrosa, where the Etrurian shades High over-arched embower; or scattered sedge Afloat, when with fierce winds Orion armed Hath vexed the Red-Sea coast, whose waves o'erthrew Busiris and his Memphian chivalry, While with perfidious hatred they pursued The sojourners of Goshen, who beheld From the safe shore their floating carcasses And broken chariot-wheels. Also known as Epic Simile.

Horatian Satire: See *Satire*

Humanism: A philosophy that places faith in the dignity of humankind and rejects the medieval perception of the individual as a weak, fallen creature. "Humanists" typically believe in the perfectibility of human nature and view reason and education as the means to that end. Humanist thought is represented in the works of Marsilio Ficino, Ludovico Castelvetro, Edmund Spenser, John Milton, Dean John Colet, Desiderius Erasmus, John Dryden, Alexander Pope, Matthew Arnold, and Irving Babbitt.

Humors: Mentions of the humors refer to the ancient Greek theory that a person's health and personality were determined by the balance of four basic fluids in the body: blood, phlegm, yellow bile, and black bile. A dominance of any fluid would cause extremes in behavior. An excess of blood created a sanguine person who was joyful, aggressive, and passionate; a phlegmatic person was shy, fearful, and sluggish; too much yellow bile led to a choleric temperament characterized by impatience, anger, bitterness, and stubbornness; and excessive black bile created melancholy, a state of laziness, gluttony, and lack of motivation. Literary treatment of the humors is exemplified by several characters in Ben Jonson's plays *Every Man in His Humour* and *Every Man out of His Humour.* Also spelled Humours.

Humours: See *Humors*

Hyperbole: In literary criticism, deliberate exaggeration used to achieve an effect. In William Shakespeare's *Macbeth,* Lady Macbeth hyperbolizes when she says, "All the perfumes of Arabia could not sweeten this little hand."

I

Iamb: See *Foot*

Idiom: A word construction or verbal expression closely associated with a given language. For example, in colloquial English the construction "how come" can be used instead of "why" to introduce a question. Similarly, "a piece of cake" is sometimes used to describe a task that is easily done.

Image: A concrete representation of an object or sensory experience. Typically, such a representation helps evoke the feelings associated with the object or experience itself. Images are either "literal" or "figurative." Literal images are especially concrete and involve little or no extension of the obvious meaning of the words used to express them. Figurative images do not follow the literal meaning of the words exactly. Images in literature are usually visual, but the term "image" can also refer to the representation of any sensory experience. In his poem "The Shepherd's Hour," Paul Verlaine presents the following image: "The Moon is red through horizon's fog;/ In a dancing mist the hazy meadow sleeps." The first line is broadly literal, while the second line involves turns of meaning associated with dancing and sleeping.

Imagery: The array of images in a literary work. Also, figurative language. William Butler Yeats's "The Second Coming" offers a powerful image of encroaching anarchy: Turning and turning in the widening gyre The falcon cannot hear the falconer; Things fall apart....

Imagism: An English and American poetry movement that flourished between 1908 and 1917. The Imagists used precise, clearly presented images in their works. They also used common, everyday speech and aimed for conciseness, concrete imagery, and the creation of new rhythms. Participants in the Imagist movement included Ezra Pound, H. D. (Hilda Doolittle), and Amy Lowell, among others.

In medias res: A Latin term meaning "in the middle of things." It refers to the technique of beginning a story at its midpoint and then using various flashback devices to reveal previous action. This technique originated in such epics as Virgil's *Aeneid.*

Induction: The process of reaching a conclusion by reasoning from specific premises to form a general premise. Also, an introductory portion of a work of literature, especially a play. Geoffrey Chaucer's "Prologue" to the *Canterbury Tales,* Thomas Sackville's "Induction" to *The Mirror of Magistrates,* and the opening scene in William Shakespeare's *The Taming of the Shrew* are examples of inductions to literary works.

Intentional Fallacy: The belief that judgments of a literary work based solely on an author's stated or implied intentions are false and misleading. Critics who believe in the concept of the intentional fallacy typically argue that the work itself is sufficient matter for interpretation, even though they may concede that an author's statement of purpose can be useful. Analysis of William Wordsworth's *Lyrical Ballads* based on the observations about poetry he makes in his "Preface" to the second edition of that work is an example of the intentional fallacy.

Interior Monologue: A narrative technique in which characters' thoughts are revealed in a way that appears to be uncontrolled by the author. The interior monologue typically aims to reveal the inner self of a character. It portrays emotional experiences as they occur at both a conscious and unconscious level. images are often used to represent sensations or emotions. One of the best-known interior monologues in English is the Molly Bloom section at the close of James Joyce's *Ulysses.* The interior monologue is also common in the works of Virginia Woolf.

Internal Rhyme: Rhyme that occurs within a single line of verse. An example is in the opening line of Edgar Allan Poe's "The Raven": "Once upon a midnight dreary, while I pondered weak and weary." Here, "dreary" and "weary" make an internal rhyme.

Irish Literary Renaissance: A late nineteenth- and early twentieth-century movement in Irish literature. Members of the movement aimed to reduce the influence of British culture in Ireland and create an Irish national literature. William Butler Yeats, George Moore, and Sean O'Casey are three of the best-known figures of the movement.

Irony: In literary criticism, the effect of language in which the intended meaning is the opposite of what is stated. The title of Jonathan Swift's "A Modest Proposal" is ironic because what Swift proposes in this essay is cannibalism—hardly "modest."

Italian Sonnet: See *Sonnet*

J

Jacobean Age: The period of the reign of James I of England (1603-1625). The early literature of this period reflected the worldview of the Elizabethan Age, but a darker, more cynical attitude steadily grew in the art and literature of the Jacobean Age. This was an important time for English drama and poetry. Milestones include William Shakespeare's tragedies, tragi-comedies, and sonnets; Ben Jonson's various dramas; and John Donne's metaphysical poetry.

Jargon: Language that is used or understood only by a select group of people. Jargon may refer to terminology used in a certain profession, such as computer jargon, or it may refer to any nonsensical language that is not understood by most people. Literary examples of jargon are Francois Villon's *Ballades en jargon,* which is composed in the secret language of the *coquillards,* and Anthony Burgess's *A Clockwork Orange,* narrated in the fictional characters' language of "Nadsat."

Journalism: Writing intended for publication in a newspaper or magazine, or for broadcast on a radio or television program featuring news, sports, entertainment, or other timely material. The essays and reviews written by H. L. Mencken for the *Baltimore Morning Herald* and collected in his *Prejudices* are an example of journalism. See also New Journalism.

Juvenalian Satire: See *Satire*

K

Knickerbocker Group: A somewhat indistinct group of New York writers of the first half of the nineteenth century. Members of the group were linked only by location and a common theme: New York life. Two famous members of the Knickerbocker Group were Washington Irving and William Cullen Bryant. The group's name derives from Irving's *Knickerbocker's History of New York.*

Kunstlerroman: See *Bildungsroman*

L

Lais: See *Lay*

Lay: A song or simple narrative poem. The form originated in medieval France. Early French *lais* were often based on the Celtic legends and other tales sung by Breton minstrels—thus the name of the "Breton lay." In fourteenth-century England, the term "lay" was used to describe short narratives written in imitation of the Breton lays. The most notable of these is Geoffrey Chaucer's "The Minstrel's Tale."

Leitmotiv: See *Motif*

Literal Language: An author uses literal language when he or she writes without exaggerating or embellishing the subject matter and without any tools of figurative language. To say "He ran very quickly down the street" is to use literal language, whereas to say "He ran like a hare down the street" would be using figurative language.

Literary Ballad: See *Ballad*

Literature: Literature is broadly defined as any written or spoken material, but the term most often refers to creative works. Literature includes poetry, drama, fiction, and many kinds of nonfiction writing, as well as oral, dramatic, and broadcast compositions not necessarily preserved in a written format, such as films and television programs.

Lost Generation: A term first used by Gertrude Stein to describe the post-World War I generation of American writers: men and women haunted by a sense of betrayal and emptiness brought about by the destructiveness of the war. The term is commonly applied to Hart Crane, Ernest Hemingway, F. Scott Fitzgerald, and others.

Lyric Poetry: A poem expressing the subjective feelings and personal emotions of the poet. Such poetry is melodic, since it was originally accompanied by a lyre in recitals. Most Western poetry in the twentieth century may be classified as lyrical. Examples of lyric poetry include A. E. Housman's elegy "To an Athlete Dying Young," the odes of Pindar and Horace, Thomas Gray and William Collins, the sonnets of Sir Thomas Wyatt and Sir Philip Sidney, Elizabeth Barrett Browning and Rainer Maria Rilke, and a host of other forms in the poetry of William Blake and Christina Rossetti, among many others.

M

Magic Realism: A form of literature that incorporates fantasy elements or supernatural occurrences into the narrative and accepts them as truth. Gabriel García Márquez and Laura Esquivel are two writers known for their works of magic realism.

Mannerism: Exaggerated, artificial adherence to a literary manner or style. Also, a popular style of the visual arts of late sixteenth-century Europe that was marked by elongation of the human form and by intentional spatial distortion. Literary works that are self-consciously high-toned and artistic are often said to be "mannered." Authors of such works include Henry James and Gertrude Stein.

Masculine Rhyme: See *Rhyme*

Masque: A lavish and elaborate form of entertainment, often performed in royal courts, that emphasizes song, dance, and costumery. The Renaissance form of the masque grew out of the spectacles of masked figures common in medieval England and Europe. The masque reached its peak of popularity and development in seventeenth-century England, during the reigns of James I and, especially, of Charles I. Ben Jonson, the most significant masque writer, also created the "antimasque," which incorporates elements of humor and the grotesque into the traditional masque and achieved greater dramatic quality. Masque-like interludes appear in Edmund Spenser's *The Faerie Queene* and in William Shakespeare's *The Tempest.*

One of the best-known English masques is John Milton's *Comus.*

Measure: The foot, verse, or time sequence used in a literary work, especially a poem. Measure is often used somewhat incorrectly as a synonym for meter.

Medieval Mystics: Mysticism flourished in many parts of Europe, including Germany, Italy, the Low Countries, and England, from the middle of the thirteenth century to the middle of the fifteenth. The greatest figures in Germany were Meister Eckhart, a Dominican friar of formidable intellectual gifts, and his pupils, also Dominicans, Johannes Tauler and Henry Suso. In the Low Countries, John Rusbroec developed a Trinitarian mysticism that owed much to Eckhart, despite his apparent disagreement with the earlier teacher. In Italy, the Franciscan scholar Bonaventure, St. Catherine of Siena, and St. Catherine of Genoa upheld the mystical flame, and there was also a mystical outpouring in England, associated with the names Julian of Norwich, Richard Rolle, Walter Hilton, and the anonymous author of *The Cloud of Unknowing.* Many of the continental mystics were members of the Friends of God, a movement that worked for the spiritual revival of people at a time when the worldliness of the Church, the ravages of the Black Death, and the cracks in the traditional social order created a desire in many to develop a deeper spirituality. Although some of the mystics were hermits, like Rolle, others combined their mysticism with practical concerns such as preaching, administrative duties, and caring for the poor and the sick.

Melodrama: A play in which the typical plot is a conflict between characters who personify extreme good and evil. Melodramas usually end happily and emphasize sensationalism. Other literary forms that use the same techniques are often labeled "melodramatic." The term was formerly used to describe a combination of drama and music; as such, it was synonymous with "opera." Augustin Daly's *Under the Gaslight* and Dion Boucicault's *The Octoroon, The Colleen Bawn,* and *The Poor of New York* are examples of melodramas. The most popular media for twentieth-century melodramas are motion pictures and television.

Metaphor: A figure of speech that expresses an idea through the image of another object. Metaphors suggest the essence of the first object by identifying it with certain qualities of the second object. An example is "But soft, what light through yonder window breaks?/ It is the east, and Juliet is the sun" in William Shakespeare's *Romeo and Juliet.* Here, Juliet, the first object, is identified with qualities of the second object, the sun.

Metaphysical Conceit: See *Conceit*

Metaphysical Poetry: The body of poetry produced by a group of seventeenth-century English writers called the "Metaphysical Poets." The group includes John Donne and Andrew Marvell. The Metaphysical Poets made use of everyday speech, intellectual analysis, and unique imagery. They aimed to portray the ordinary conflicts and contradictions of life. Their poems often took the form of an argument, and many of them emphasize physical and religious love as well as the fleeting nature of life. Elaborate conceits are typical in metaphysical poetry. Marvell's "To His Coy Mistress" is a well-known example of a metaphysical poem.

Metaphysical Poets: See *Metaphysical Poetry*

Meter: In literary criticism, the repetition of sound patterns that creates a rhythm in poetry. The patterns are based on the number of syllables and the presence and absence of accents. The unit of rhythm in a line is called a foot. Types of meter are classified according to the number of feet in a line. These are the standard English lines: Monometer, one foot; Dimeter, two feet; Trimeter, three feet; Tetrameter, four feet; Pentameter, five feet; Hexameter, six feet (also called the Alexandrine); Heptameter, seven feet (also called the "Fourteener" when the feet are iambic). The most common English meter is the iambic pentameter, in which each line contains ten syllables, or five iambic feet, which individually are composed of an unstressed syllable followed by an accented syllable. Both of the following lines from Alfred, Lord Tennyson's "Ulysses" are written in iambic pentameter: Made weak by time and fate, but strong in will To strive, to seek, to find, and not to yield.

Mise en scene: The costumes, scenery, and other properties of a drama. Herbert Beerbohm Tree was renowned for the elaborate *mises en scene* of his lavish Shakespearean productions at His Majesty's Theatre between 1897 and 1915.

Modernism: Modern literary practices. Also, the principles of a literary school that lasted from roughly the beginning of the twentieth century until the end of World War II. Modernism is defined by its rejection of the literary conventions of the nineteenth century and by its opposition to conventional morality, taste, traditions, and economic values. Many writers are associated with the concepts of Modernism, including Albert Camus, Marcel Proust, D. H. Lawrence, W. H. Auden, Ernest Hemingway, William Faulkner, William Butler Yeats, Thomas Mann, Tennessee Williams, Eugene O'Neill, and James Joyce.

Monologue: A composition, written or oral, by a single individual. More specifically, a speech given by a single individual in a drama or other public entertainment. It has no set length, although it is usually several or more lines long. An example of an "extended monologue"—that is, a monologue of great length and seriousness—occurs in the one-act, one-character play *The Stronger* by August Strindberg.

Monometer: See *Meter*

Mood: The prevailing emotions of a work or of the author in his or her creation of the work. The mood of a work is not always what might be expected based on its subject matter. The poem "Dover Beach" by Matthew Arnold offers examples of two different moods originating from the same experience: watching the ocean at night. The mood of the first three lines—The sea is calm tonight The tide is full, the moon lies fair Upon the straights.... is in sharp contrast to the mood of the last three lines—And we are here as on a darkling plain Swept with confused alarms of struggle and flight, Where ignorant armies clash by night.

Motif: A theme, character type, image, metaphor, or other verbal element that recurs throughout a single work of literature or occurs in a number of different works over a period of time. For example, the various manifestations of the color white in Herman Melville's *Moby Dick* is a "specific" *motif,* while the trials of star-crossed lovers is a "conventional" *motif* from the literature of all periods. Also known as *Motiv* or *Leitmotiv.*

Motiv: See *Motif*

Muckrakers: An early twentieth-century group of American writers. Typically, their works exposed the wrongdoings of big business and government in the United States. Upton Sinclair's *The Jungle* exemplifies the muckraking novel.

Muses: Nine Greek mythological goddesses, the daughters of Zeus and Mnemosyne (Memory). Each muse patronized a specific area of the liberal arts and sciences. Calliope presided over epic poetry, Clio over history, Erato over love poetry, Euterpe over music or lyric poetry, Melpomene over tragedy, Polyhymnia over hymns to the gods, Terpsichore over dance, Thalia over comedy, and Urania over astronomy. Poets and writers traditionally made appeals to the Muses for inspiration in their work. John Milton invokes the aid of a muse at the beginning of the first book of his Paradise Lost: Of Man's First disobedience, and the Fruit of the Forbidden Tree, whose mortal taste Brought Death into the World, and all our woe, With loss of Eden, till one greater Man Restore us, and regain the blissful Seat, Sing Heav'nly Muse, that on the secret top of Oreb, or of Sinai, didst inspire That Shepherd, who first taught the chosen Seed, In the Beginning how the Heav'ns and Earth Rose out of Chaos....

Mystery: See *Suspense*

Myth: An anonymous tale emerging from the traditional beliefs of a culture or social unit. Myths use supernatural explanations for natural phenomena. They may also explain cosmic issues like creation and death. Collections of myths, known as mythologies, are common to all cultures and nations, but the best-known myths belong to the Norse, Roman, and Greek mythologies. A famous myth is the story of Arachne, an arrogant young girl who challenged a goddess, Athena, to a weaving contest; when the girl won, Athena was enraged and turned Arachne into a spider, thus explaining the existence of spiders.

N

Narration: The telling of a series of events, real or invented. A narration may be either a simple narrative, in which the events are recounted chronologically, or a narrative with a plot, in which the account is given in a style reflecting the author's artistic concept of the story. Narration is sometimes used as a synonym for "storyline." The recounting of scary stories around a campfire is a form of narration.

Narrative: A verse or prose accounting of an event or sequence of events, real or invented. The term is also used as an adjective in the sense "method of narration." For example, in literary criticism, the expression "narrative technique" usually refers to the way the author structures and presents his or her story. Narratives range from the shortest accounts of events, as in Julius Caesar's remark, "I came, I saw, I conquered," to the longest historical or biographical works, as in Edward Gibbon's *The Decline and Fall of the Roman Empire,* as well as diaries, travelogues, novels, ballads, epics, short stories, and other fictional forms.

Narrative Poetry: A nondramatic poem in which the author tells a story. Such poems may be of any length or level of complexity. Epics such as *Beowulf* and ballads are forms of narrative poetry.

Narrator: The teller of a story. The narrator may be the author or a character in the story through whom the author speaks. Huckleberry Finn is the narrator of Mark Twain's *The Adventures of Huckleberry Finn.*

Naturalism: A literary movement of the late nineteenth and early twentieth centuries. The movement's major theorist, French novelist Emile Zola, envisioned a type of fiction that would examine human life with the objectivity of scientific inquiry. The Naturalists typically viewed human beings as either the products of "biological determinism," ruled by hereditary instincts and engaged in an endless struggle for survival, or as the products of "socioeconomic determinism," ruled by social and economic forces beyond their control. In their works, the Naturalists generally ignored the highest levels of society and focused on degradation: poverty, alcoholism, prostitution, insanity, and disease. Naturalism influenced authors throughout the world, including Henrik Ibsen and Thomas Hardy. In the United States, in particular, Naturalism had a profound impact. Among the authors who embraced its principles are Theodore Dreiser, Eugene O'Neill, Stephen Crane, Jack London, and Frank Norris.

Negritude: A literary movement based on the concept of a shared cultural bond on the part of black Africans, wherever they may be in the world. It traces its origins to the former French colonies of Africa and the Caribbean. Negritude poets, novelists, and essayists generally stress four points in their writings: One, black alienation from traditional African culture can lead to feelings of inferiority. Two, European colonialism and Western education should be resisted. Three, black Africans should seek to affirm and define their own identity. Four, African culture can and should be reclaimed. Many Negritude writers also claim that blacks can make unique contributions to the world, based on a heightened appreciation of nature, rhythm, and human emotions—aspects of life they say are not so highly valued in the materialistic and rationalistic West. Examples of Negritude literature include the poetry of both Senegalese Leopold Senghor in *Hosties noires* and Martiniquais Aime-Fernand Cesaire in *Return to My Native Land.*

Negro Renaissance: See *Harlem Renaissance*

Neoclassical Period: See *Neoclassicism*

Neoclassicism: In literary criticism, this term refers to the revival of the attitudes and styles of expression of classical literature. It is generally used to describe a period in European history beginning in the late seventeenth century and lasting until about 1800. In its purest form, Neoclassicism marked a return to order, proportion, restraint, logic, accuracy, and decorum. In England, where Neoclassicism perhaps was most popular, it reflected the influence of seventeenth-century French writers, especially dramatists. Neoclassical writers typically reacted against the intensity and enthusiasm of the Renaissance period. They wrote works that appealed to the intellect, using elevated language and classical literary forms such as satire and the ode. Neoclassical works were often governed by the classical goal of instruction. English neoclassicists included Alexander Pope, Jonathan Swift, Joseph Addison, Sir Richard Steele, John Gay, and Matthew Prior; French neoclassicists included Pierre Corneille and Jean-Baptiste Moliere. Also known as Age of Reason.

Neoclassicists: See *Neoclassicism*

New Criticism: A movement in literary criticism, dating from the late 1920s, that stressed close textual analysis in the interpretation of works of literature. The New Critics saw little merit in historical and biographical analysis. Rather, they aimed to examine the text alone, free from the question of how external events—biographical or otherwise—may have helped shape it. This predominantly American school was named "New Criticism" by one of its practitioners, John Crowe Ransom. Other important New Critics included Allen Tate, R. P. Blackmur, Robert Penn Warren, and Cleanth Brooks.

New Journalism: A type of writing in which the journalist presents factual information in a form usually used in fiction. New journalism emphasizes description, narration, and character development to bring readers closer to the human element of the story, and is often used in personality profiles and in-depth feature articles. It is not compatible with "straight" or "hard" newswriting, which is generally composed in a brief, fact-based style. Hunter S. Thompson, Gay Talese, Thomas Wolfe, Joan Didion, and John McPhee are well-known New Journalists. See also Journalism.

New Journalists: See *New Journalism*

New Negro Movement: See *Harlem Renaissance*

Noble Savage: The idea that primitive man is noble and good but becomes evil and corrupted as he becomes civilized. The concept of the noble savage originated in the Renaissance period but is more closely identified with such later writers as Jean-Jacques Rousseau and Aphra Behn. First described in John Dryden's play *The Conquest of Granada,* the noble savage is portrayed by the various Native Americans in James Fenimore Cooper's "Leatherstocking Tales," by Queequeg, Daggoo, and Tashtego in Herman Melville's *Moby Dick,* and by John the Savage in Aldous Huxley's *Brave New World.*

Novel: A long fictional narrative written in prose, which developed from the novella and other early forms of narrative. A novel is usually organized under a plot or theme with a focus on character development and action. The novel emerged as a fully evolved literary form in the mid-eighteenth century in Samuel Richardson's *Pamela; or, Virtue Rewarded.* Compare with Fiction, Narrative, and Novella.

Novella: An Italian term meaning "story." This term has been especially used to describe fourteenth-century Italian tales, but it also refers to modern short novels. The tales comprising Giovanni Boccaccio's *Decameron* are examples of the novella. Modern novellas include Leo Tolstoy's *The Death of Ivan Ilich,* Fyodor Dostoyevsky's *Notes from the Underground,* Joseph Conrad's *Heart of Darkness,* and Henry James's "The Aspern Papers." Compare with Novel. See also Tale.

Novel of Ideas: A novel in which the examination of intellectual issues and concepts takes precedence over characterization or a traditional storyline. Examples of novels of ideas include Aldous Huxley's *Crome Yellow, Point Counter Point,* and *After Many a Summer.*

Novel of Manners: A novel that examines the customs and mores of a cultural group. The novels of Jane Austen and Edith Wharton are widely considered novels of manners. Compare with Comedy of Manners.

O

Objective Correlative: An outward set of objects, a situation, or a chain of events corresponding to an inward experience and evoking this experience in the reader. The term frequently appears in modern criticism in discussions of authors' intended effects on the emotional responses of readers. This term was originally used by T. S. Eliot in his 1919 essay "Hamlet."

Objectivity: A quality in writing characterized by the absence of the author's opinion or feeling about the subject matter. Objectivity is an important factor in criticism. The novels of Henry James and, to a certain extent, the poems of John Larkin demonstrate objectivity, and it is central to John Keats's concept of "negative capability." Critical and journalistic writing usually are or attempt to be objective.

Occasional Verse: poetry written on the occasion of a significant historical or personal event. *Vers de societe* is sometimes called occasional verse although it is of a less serious nature. Famous examples of occasional verse include Andrew Marvell's "Horatian Ode upon Cromwell's Return from England," Walt Whitman's "When Lilacs Last in the Dooryard Bloom'd"—written upon the death of Abraham Lincoln—and Edmund Spenser's commemoration of his wedding, "Epithalamion."

Octave: A poem or stanza composed of eight lines. The term octave most often represents the first eight lines of a Petrarchan sonnet. An example of an octave is taken from a translation of a Petrarchan sonnet by Sir Thomas Wyatt: The pillar perisht is whereto I leant, The strongest stay of mine unquiet mind; The like of it no man again can find, From East to West Still seeking though he went. To mind unhap! for hap away hath rent Of all my joy the very bark and rind; And I, alas, by chance am thus assigned Daily to mourn till death do it relent.

Ode: Name given to an extended lyric poem characterized by exalted emotion and dignified style. An ode usually concerns a single, serious theme. Most odes, but not all, are addressed to an object or individual. Odes are distinguished from other lyric poetic forms by their complex rhythmic and stanzaic patterns. An example of this form is John Keats's "Ode to a Nightingale."

Oedipus Complex: A son's amorous obsession with his mother. The phrase is derived from the story of the ancient Theban hero Oedipus, who unknowingly killed his father and married his mother. Literary occurrences of the Oedipus complex include Andre Gide's *Oedipe* and Jean Cocteau's *La Machine infernale,* as well as the most famous, Sophocles' *Oedipus Rex.*

Omniscience: See *Point of View*

Onomatopoeia: The use of words whose sounds express or suggest their meaning. In its simplest sense, onomatopoeia may be represented by words that mimic the sounds they denote such as "hiss" or "meow." At a more subtle level, the pattern and rhythm of sounds and rhymes of a line or poem may be onomatopoeic. A celebrated example of onomatopoeia is the repetition of the word "bells" in Edgar Allan Poe's poem "The Bells."

Opera: A type of stage performance, usually a drama, in which the dialogue is sung. Classic examples of opera include Giuseppi Verdi's *La traviata,* Giacomo Puccini's *La Boheme,* and Richard Wagner's *Tristan und Isolde.* Major twentieth-century contributors to the form include Richard Strauss and Alban Berg.

Operetta: A usually romantic comic opera. John Gay's *The Beggar's Opera,* Richard Sheridan's *The Duenna,* and numerous works by William Gilbert and Arthur Sullivan are examples of operettas.

Oral Tradition: See *Oral Transmission*

Oral Transmission: A process by which songs, ballads, folklore, and other material are transmitted by word of mouth. The tradition of oral transmission predates the written record systems of literate society. Oral transmission preserves material sometimes over generations, although often with variations. Memory plays a large part in the recitation and preservation of orally transmitted material. Breton lays, French *fabliaux,* national epics (including the Anglo-Saxon *Beowulf,* the Spanish *El Cid,* and the Finnish *Kalevala*), Native American myths and legends, and African folktales told by plantation slaves are examples of orally transmitted literature.

Oration: Formal speaking intended to motivate the listeners to some action or feeling. Such public speaking was much more common before the development of timely printed communication such as newspapers. Famous examples of oration include Abraham Lincoln's "Gettysburg Address" and Dr. Martin Luther King Jr.'s "I Have a Dream" speech.

Ottava Rima: An eight-line stanza of poetry composed in iambic pentameter (a five-foot line in which each foot consists of an unaccented syllable followed by an accented syllable), following the abababcc rhyme scheme. This form has been prominently used by such important English writers as Lord Byron, Henry Wadsworth Longfellow, and W. B. Yeats.

Oxymoron: A phrase combining two contradictory terms. Oxymorons may be intentional or unintentional. The following speech from William Shakespeare's *Romeo and Juliet* uses several oxymorons: Why, then, O brawling love! O loving hate! O anything, of nothing first create! O heavy lightness! serious vanity! Mis-shapen chaos of well-seeming forms! Feather of lead, bright smoke, cold fire, sick health! This love feel I, that feel no love in this.

P

Pantheism: The idea that all things are both a manifestation or revelation of God and a part of God at the same time. Pantheism was a common attitude in the early societies of Egypt, India, and Greece—the term derives from the Greek *pan* meaning "all" and *theos* meaning "deity." It later became a significant part of the Christian faith. William Wordsworth and Ralph Waldo Emerson are among the many writers who have expressed the pantheistic attitude in their works.

Parable: A story intended to teach a moral lesson or answer an ethical question. In the West, the best examples of parables are those of Jesus Christ in the New Testament, notably "The Prodigal Son," but parables also are used in Sufism, rabbinic literature, Hasidism, and Zen Buddhism.

Paradox: A statement that appears illogical or contradictory at first, but may actually point to an underlying truth. "Less is more" is an example of a paradox. Literary examples include Francis Bacon's statement, "The most corrected copies are commonly the least correct," and "All animals are equal, but some animals are more equal than others" from George Orwell's *Animal Farm.*

Parallelism: A method of comparison of two ideas in which each is developed in the same grammatical structure. Ralph Waldo Emerson's "Civilization" contains this example of parallelism: Raphael paints wisdom; Handel sings it, Phidias carves it, Shakespeare writes it, Wren builds it, Columbus sails it, Luther preaches it, Washington arms it, Watt mechanizes it.

Parnassianism: A mid nineteenth-century movement in French literature. Followers of the movement stressed adherence to well-defined artistic forms as a reaction against the often chaotic expression of the artist's ego that dominated the work of the Romantics. The Parnassians also rejected the moral, ethical, and social themes exhibited in the works of French Romantics such as Victor Hugo. The aesthetic doctrines of the Parnassians strongly influenced the later symbolist and decadent movements. Members of the Parnassian school include Leconte de Lisle, Sully Prudhomme, Albert Glatigny, Francois Coppee, and Theodore de Banville.

Parody: In literary criticism, this term refers to an imitation of a serious literary work or the signature style of a particular author in a ridiculous manner. A typical parody adopts the style of the original and applies it to an inappropriate subject for humorous effect. Parody is a form of satire and could be considered the literary equivalent of a caricature or cartoon. Henry Fielding's *Shamela* is a parody of Samuel Richardson's *Pamela.*

Pastoral: A term derived from the Latin word "pastor," meaning shepherd. A pastoral is a literary composition on a rural theme. The conventions of the pastoral were originated by the third-century Greek poet Theocritus, who wrote about the experiences, love affairs, and pastimes of Sicilian shepherds. In a pastoral, characters and language of a courtly nature are often placed in a simple setting. The term pastoral is also used to classify dramas, elegies, and lyrics that exhibit the use of country settings and shepherd characters. Percy Bysshe Shelley's "Adonais" and John Milton's "Lycidas" are two famous examples of pastorals.

Pastorela: The Spanish name for the shepherds play, a folk drama reenacted during the Christmas season. Examples of *pastorelas* include Gomez Manrique's *Representacion del nacimiento* and the dramas of Lucas Fernandez and Juan del Encina.

Pathetic Fallacy: A term coined by English critic John Ruskin to identify writing that falsely endows nonhuman things with human intentions and feelings, such as "angry clouds" and "sad trees." The pathetic fallacy is a required convention in the classical poetic form of the pastoral elegy, and it is used in the modern poetry of T. S. Eliot, Ezra Pound, and the Imagists. Also known as Poetic Fallacy.

Pelado: Literally the "skinned one" or shirtless one, he was the stock underdog, sharp-witted picaresque character of Mexican vaudeville and tent shows. The *pelado* is found in such works as Don Catarino's *Los effectos de la crisis* and *Regreso a mi tierra.*

Pen Name: See *Pseudonym*

Pentameter: See *Meter*

Persona: A Latin term meaning "mask." *Personae* are the characters in a fictional work of literature. The *persona* generally functions as a mask through which the author tells a story in a voice other than his or her own. A *persona* is usually either a character in a story who acts as a narrator or an "implied author," a voice created by the author to act as the narrator for himself or herself. *Personae* include the narrator of Geoffrey Chaucer's *Canterbury Tales* and Marlow in Joseph Conrad's *Heart of Darkness.*

Personae: See *Persona*

Personal Point of View: See *Point of View*

Personification: A figure of speech that gives human qualities to abstract ideas, animals, and inanimate objects. William Shakespeare used personification in *Romeo and Juliet* in the lines "Arise, fair sun, and kill the envious moon,/ Who is already sick and pale with grief." Here, the moon is portrayed as being envious, sick, and pale with grief—all markedly human qualities. Also known as *Prosopopoeia.*

Petrarchan Sonnet: See *Sonnet*

Phenomenology: A method of literary criticism based on the belief that things have no existence outside of human consciousness or awareness. Proponents of this theory believe that art is a process that takes place in the mind of the observer as he or she contemplates an object rather than a quality of the object itself. Among phenomenological critics are Edmund Husserl, George Poulet, Marcel Raymond, and Roman Ingarden.

Picaresque Novel: Episodic fiction depicting the adventures of a roguish central character ("picaro" is Spanish for "rogue"). The picaresque hero is commonly a low-born but clever individual who wanders into and out of various affairs of love, danger, and farcical intrigue. These involvements may take place at all social levels and typically present a humorous and wide-ranging satire of a given society. Prominent examples of the picaresque novel are *Don Quixote* by Miguel de Cervantes, *Tom Jones* by Henry Fielding, and *Moll Flanders* by Daniel Defoe.

Plagiarism: Claiming another person's written material as one's own. Plagiarism can take the form of direct, word-for-word copying or the theft of the substance or idea of the work. A student who copies an encyclopedia entry and turns it in as a report for school is guilty of plagiarism.

Platonic Criticism: A form of criticism that stresses an artistic work's usefulness as an agent of social engineering rather than any quality or value of the work itself. Platonic criticism takes as its starting point the ancient Greek philosopher Plato's comments on art in his *Republic.*

Platonism: The embracing of the doctrines of the philosopher Plato, popular among the poets of the Renaissance and the Romantic period. Platonism is more flexible than Aristotelian Criticism and places more emphasis on the supernatural and unknown aspects of life. Platonism is expressed in the love poetry of the Renaissance, the fourth book of Baldassare Castiglione's *The Book of the Courtier,* and the poetry of William Blake, William Wordsworth, Percy Bysshe Shelley, Friedrich Holderlin, William Butler Yeats, and Wallace Stevens.

Play: See *Drama*

Plot: In literary criticism, this term refers to the pattern of events in a narrative or drama. In its simplest sense, the plot guides the author in composing the work and helps the reader follow the work. Typically, plots exhibit causality and unity and have a beginning, a middle, and an end. Sometimes, however, a plot may consist of a series of disconnected events, in which case it is known as an "episodic plot." In his *Aspects of the Novel,* E. M. Forster distinguishes between a story, defined as a "narrative of events arranged in their time-sequence," and plot, which organizes the events to a "sense of causality." This definition closely mirrors Aristotle's discussion of plot in his *Poetics.*

Poem: In its broadest sense, a composition utilizing rhyme, meter, concrete detail, and expressive language to create a literary experience with emotional and aesthetic appeal. Typical poems include sonnets, odes, elegies, *haiku,* ballads, and free verse.

Poet: An author who writes poetry or verse. The term is also used to refer to an artist or writer who has an exceptional gift for expression, imagination, and energy in the making of art in any form. Well-known poets include Horace, Basho, Sir Philip Sidney, Sir Edmund Spenser, John Donne, Andrew Marvell, Alexander Pope, Jonathan Swift, George Gordon, Lord Byron, John Keats, Christina Rossetti, W. H. Auden, Stevie Smith, and Sylvia Plath.

Poetic Fallacy: See *Pathetic Fallacy*

Poetic Justice: An outcome in a literary work, not necessarily a poem, in which the good are rewarded and the evil are punished, especially in ways that particularly fit their virtues or crimes. For example, a murderer may himself be murdered, or a thief will find himself penniless.

Poetic License: Distortions of fact and literary convention made by a writer—not always a poet—for the sake of the effect gained. Poetic license is closely related to the concept of "artistic freedom." An author exercises poetic license by saying that a pile of money "reaches as high as a mountain" when the pile is actually only a foot or two high.

Poetics: This term has two closely related meanings. It denotes (1) an aesthetic theory in literary criticism about the essence of poetry or (2) rules prescribing the proper methods, content, style, or diction of poetry. The term poetics may also refer to theories about literature in general, not just poetry.

Poetry: In its broadest sense, writing that aims to present ideas and evoke an emotional experience in the reader through the use of meter, imagery, connotative and concrete words, and a carefully constructed structure based on rhythmic patterns. Poetry typically relies on words and expressions that have several layers of meaning. It also makes use of the effects of regular rhythm on the ear and may make a strong appeal to the senses through the use of imagery. Edgar Allan Poe's "Annabel Lee" and Walt Whitman's *Leaves of Grass* are famous examples of poetry.

Point of View: The narrative perspective from which a literary work is presented to the reader. There are four traditional points of view. The "third person omniscient" gives the reader a "godlike" perspective, unrestricted by time or place, from which to see actions and look into the minds of characters. This allows the author to comment openly on characters and events in the work. The "third person" point of view presents the events of the story from outside of any single character's perception, much like the omniscient point of view, but the reader must understand the action as it takes place and without any special insight into characters' minds or motivations. The "first person" or "personal" point of view relates events as they are perceived by a single character. The main character "tells" the story and may offer opinions about the action and characters which differ from those of the author. Much less common than omniscient, third person, and first person is the "second person" point of view, wherein the author tells the story as if it is happening to the reader. James Thurber employs the omniscient point of view in his short story "The Secret Life of Walter Mitty." Ernest Hemingway's "A Clean, Well-Lighted Place" is a short story told from the third person point of view. Mark Twain's novel *Huck Finn* is presented from the first person viewpoint. Jay McInerney's *Bright Lights,*

Big City is an example of a novel which uses the second person point of view.

Polemic: A work in which the author takes a stand on a controversial subject, such as abortion or religion. Such works are often extremely argumentative or provocative. Classic examples of polemics include John Milton's *Aeropagitica* and Thomas Paine's *The American Crisis.*

Pornography: Writing intended to provoke feelings of lust in the reader. Such works are often condemned by critics and teachers, but those which can be shown to have literary value are viewed less harshly. Literary works that have been described as pornographic include Ovid's *The Art of Love,* Margaret of Angouleme's *Heptameron,* John Cleland's *Memoirs of a Woman of Pleasure; or, the Life of Fanny Hill,* the anonymous *My Secret Life,* D. H. Lawrence's *Lady Chatterley's Lover,* and Vladimir Nabokov's *Lolita.*

Post-Aesthetic Movement: An artistic response made by African Americans to the black aesthetic movement of the 1960s and early '70s. Writers since that time have adopted a somewhat different tone in their work, with less emphasis placed on the disparity between black and white in the United States. In the words of post-aesthetic authors such as Toni Morrison, John Edgar Wideman, and Kristin Hunter, African Americans are portrayed as looking inward for answers to their own questions, rather than always looking to the outside world. Two well-known examples of works produced as part of the post-aesthetic movement are the Pulitzer Prize-winning novels *The Color Purple* by Alice Walker and *Beloved* by Toni Morrison.

Postcolonialism: The term "Postcolonialism" refers broadly to the ways in which race, ethnicity, culture, and human identity itself are represented in the modern era, after many colonized countries gained their independence. However, some critics use the term to refer to *all* culture and cultural products influenced by imperialism from the moment of colonization until today. Postcolonial literature seeks to describe the interactions between European nations and the peoples they colonized. By the middle of the twentieth century, the vast majority of the world was under the control of European countries. At one time, Great Britain, for example, ruled almost 50 percent of the world. During the twentieth century, countries such as India, Jamaica, Nigeria, Senegal, Sri Lanka, Canada, and Australia won independence from their European colonizers. Examples of Postcolonial writings include Edward Said's *Orientalism*, Salman Rushdie's *Midnight's Children*, Chinua Achebe's *Things Fall Apart*, Michael Ondaatje's *The English Patient*, Frantz Fanon's *The Wretched of the Earth*, Jamaica Kincaid's *A Small Place*, Isabelle Allende's *The House of the Spirits*, J. M. Coetzee's *Waiting for the Barbarians* and *Disgrace*, Derek Walcott's *Omeros*, and Eavan Boland's *Outside History: Selected Poems, 1980–1990.*

Postmodernism: Writing from the 1960s forward characterized by experimentation and continuing to apply some of the fundamentals of modernism, which included existentialism and alienation. Postmodernists have gone a step further in the rejection of tradition begun with the modernists by also rejecting traditional forms, preferring the anti-novel over the novel and the anti-hero over the hero. Postmodern writers include Alain Robbe-Grillet, Thomas Pynchon, Margaret Drabble, John Fowles, Adolfo Bioy-Casares, and Gabriel Garcia Marquez.

Pre-Raphaelites: A circle of writers and artists in mid nineteenth-century England. Valuing the pre-Renaissance artistic qualities of religious symbolism, lavish pictorialism, and natural sensuousness, the Pre-Raphaelites cultivated a sense of mystery and melancholy that influenced later writers associated with the Symbolist and Decadent movements. The major members of the group include Dante Gabriel Rossetti, Christina Rossetti, Algernon Swinburne, and Walter Pater.

Primitivism: The belief that primitive peoples were nobler and less flawed than civilized peoples because they had not been subjected to the tainting influence of society. Examples of literature espousing primitivism include Aphra Behn's *Oroonoko: Or, The History of the Royal Slave,* Jean-Jacques Rousseau's *Julie ou la Nouvelle Heloise,* Oliver Goldsmith's *The Deserted Village,* the poems of Robert Burns, Herman Melville's stories *Typee, Omoo,* and *Mardi,* many poems of William Butler Yeats and Robert Frost, and William Golding's novel *Lord of the Flies.*

Projective Verse: A form of free verse in which the poet's breathing pattern determines the lines of the poem. Poets who advocate projective verse are against all formal structures in writing, including meter and form. Besides its creators, Robert Creeley, Robert Duncan, and Charles Olson, two other well-known projective verse poets are Denise Levertov and LeRoi Jones (Amiri Baraka). Also known as Breath Verse.

Prologue: An introductory section of a literary work. It often contains information establishing the situation of the characters or presents information about the setting, time period, or action. In drama, the prologue is spoken by a chorus or by one of the principal characters. In the "General Prologue" of *The Canterbury Tales,* Geoffrey Chaucer describes the main characters and establishes the setting and purpose of the work.

Prose: A literary medium that attempts to mirror the language of everyday speech. It is distinguished from poetry by its use of unmetered, unrhymed language consisting of logically related sentences. Prose is usually grouped into paragraphs that form a cohesive whole such as an essay or a novel. Recognized masters of English prose writing include Sir Thomas Malory, William Caxton, Raphael Holinshed, Joseph Addison, Mark Twain, and Ernest Hemingway.

Prosopopoeia: See *Personification*

Protagonist: The central character of a story who serves as a focus for its themes and incidents and as the principal rationale for its development. The protagonist is sometimes referred to in discussions of modern literature as the hero or anti-hero. Well-known protagonists are Hamlet in William Shakespeare's *Hamlet* and Jay Gatsby in F. Scott Fitzgerald's *The Great Gatsby.*

Protest Fiction: Protest fiction has as its primary purpose the protesting of some social injustice, such as racism or discrimination. One example of protest fiction is a series of five novels by Chester Himes, beginning in 1945 with *If He Hollers Let Him Go* and ending in 1955 with *The Primitive.* These works depict the destructive effects of race and gender stereotyping in the context of interracial relationships. Another African American author whose works often revolve around themes of social protest is John Oliver Killens. James Baldwin's essay "Everybody's Protest Novel" generated controversy by attacking the authors of protest fiction.

Proverb: A brief, sage saying that expresses a truth about life in a striking manner. "They are not all cooks who carry long knives" is an example of a proverb.

Pseudonym: A name assumed by a writer, most often intended to prevent his or her identification as the author of a work. Two or more authors may work together under one pseudonym, or an author may use a different name for each genre he or she publishes in. Some publishing companies maintain "house pseudonyms," under which any number of authors may write installations in a series. Some authors also choose a pseudonym over their real names the way an actor may use a stage name. Examples of pseudonyms (with the author's real name in parentheses) include Voltaire (Francois-Marie Arouet), Novalis (Friedrich von Hardenberg), Currer Bell (Charlotte Bronte), Ellis Bell (Emily Bronte), George Eliot (Maryann Evans), Honorio Bustos Donmecq (Adolfo Bioy-Casares and Jorge Luis Borges), and Richard Bachman (Stephen King).

Pun: A play on words that have similar sounds but different meanings. A serious example of the pun is from John Donne's "A Hymne to God the Father": Sweare by thyself, that at my death thy sonne Shall shine as he shines now, and hereto fore; And, having done that, Thou haste done; I fear no more.

Pure Poetry: poetry written without instructional intent or moral purpose that aims only to please a reader by its imagery or musical flow. The term pure poetry is used as the antonym of the term "didacticism." The poetry of Edgar Allan Poe, Stephane Mallarme, Paul Verlaine, Paul Valery, Juan Ramoz Jimenez, and Jorge Guillen offer examples of pure poetry.

Q

Quatrain: A four-line stanza of a poem or an entire poem consisting of four lines. The following quatrain is from Robert Herrick's "To Live Merrily, and to Trust to Good Verses": Round, round, the root do's run; And being ravisht thus, Come, I will drink a Tun To my *Propertius.*

R

Raisonneur: A character in a drama who functions as a spokesperson for the dramatist's views. The *raisonneur* typically observes the play without becoming central to its action. *Raisonneurs* were very common in plays of the nineteenth century.

Realism: A nineteenth-century European literary movement that sought to portray familiar characters, situations, and settings in a realistic manner. This was done primarily by using an objective narrative point of view and through the buildup of accurate detail. The standard for success of any realistic work depends on how faithfully it transfers common experience into fictional forms. The realistic method may be altered or extended, as in stream of consciousness writing, to record highly subjective experience. Seminal authors in the tradition of Realism include Honore de Balzac, Gustave Flaubert, and Henry James.

Refrain: A phrase repeated at intervals throughout a poem. A refrain may appear at the end of each stanza or at less regular intervals. It may be altered slightly at each appearance. Some refrains are nonsense expressions—as with "Nevermore" in Edgar Allan Poe's "The Raven"—that seem to take on a different significance with each use.

Renaissance: The period in European history that marked the end of the Middle Ages. It began in Italy in the late fourteenth century. In broad terms, it is usually seen as spanning the fourteenth, fifteenth, and sixteenth centuries, although it did not reach Great Britain, for example, until the 1480s or so. The Renaissance saw an awakening in almost every sphere of human activity, especially science, philosophy, and the arts. The period is best defined by the emergence of a general philosophy that emphasized the importance of the intellect, the individual, and world affairs. It contrasts strongly with the medieval worldview, characterized by the dominant concerns of faith, the social collective, and spiritual salvation. Prominent writers during the Renaissance include Niccolo Machiavelli and Baldassare Castiglione in Italy, Miguel de Cervantes and Lope de Vega in Spain, Jean Froissart and Francois Rabelais in France, Sir Thomas More and Sir Philip Sidney in England, and Desiderius Erasmus in Holland.

Renaissance Literature: See *Renaissance*

Repartee: Conversation featuring snappy retorts and witticisms. Masters of *repartee* include Sydney Smith, Charles Lamb, and Oscar Wilde. An example is recorded in the meeting of "Beau" Nash and John Wesley: Nash said, "I never make way for a fool," to which Wesley responded, "Don't you? I always do," and stepped aside.

Resolution: The portion of a story following the climax, in which the conflict is resolved. The resolution of Jane Austen's *Northanger Abbey* is neatly summed up in the following sentence: "Henry and Catherine were married, the bells rang and every body smiled."

Restoration: See *Restoration Age*

Restoration Age: A period in English literature beginning with the crowning of Charles II in 1660 and running to about 1700. The era, which was characterized by a reaction against Puritanism, was the first great age of the comedy of manners. The finest literature of the era is typically witty and urbane, and often lewd. Prominent Restoration Age writers include William Congreve, Samuel Pepys, John Dryden, and John Milton.

Revenge Tragedy: A dramatic form popular during the Elizabethan Age, in which the protagonist, directed by the ghost of his murdered father or son, inflicts retaliation upon a powerful villain. Notable features of the revenge tragedy include violence, bizarre criminal acts, intrigue, insanity, a hesitant protagonist, and the use of soliloquy. Thomas Kyd's *Spanish Tragedy* is the first example of revenge tragedy in English, and William Shakespeare's *Hamlet* is perhaps the best. Extreme examples of revenge tragedy, such as John Webster's *The Duchess of Malfi,* are labeled "tragedies of blood." Also known as Tragedy of Blood.

Revista: The Spanish term for a vaudeville musical revue. Examples of *revistas* include Antonio Guzman Aguilera's *Mexico para los mexicanos,* Daniel Vanegas's *Maldito jazz,* and Don Catarino's *Whiskey, morfina y marihuana* and *El desterrado.*

Rhetoric: In literary criticism, this term denotes the art of ethical persuasion. In its strictest sense, rhetoric adheres to various principles developed since classical times for arranging facts and ideas in a clear, persuasive, appealing manner. The term is also used to refer to effective prose in general and theories of or methods for composing effective prose. Classical examples of rhetorics include *The Rhetoric of Aristotle,* Quintillian's *Institutio Oratoria,* and Cicero's *Ad Herennium.*

Rhetorical Question: A question intended to provoke thought, but not an expressed answer, in the reader. It is most commonly used in oratory and other persuasive genres. The following lines from Thomas Gray's "Elegy Written in a Country Churchyard" ask rhetorical questions: Can storied urn or animated bust Back to its mansion call the fleeting breath? Can Honour's voice provoke the silent dust, Or Flattery soothe the dull cold ear of Death?

Rhyme: When used as a noun in literary criticism, this term generally refers to a poem in which words sound identical or very similar and appear in parallel positions in two or more lines. Rhymes are classified into different types according to where they fall in a line or stanza or according to the degree of similarity they exhibit in their spellings and sounds. Some major types of rhyme are "masculine" rhyme, "feminine" rhyme, and "triple" rhyme. In a masculine rhyme, the rhyming sound falls in a single accented syllable, as with "heat" and "eat." Feminine rhyme is a rhyme of two syllables, one stressed and one unstressed, as with "merry" and "tarry." Triple rhyme matches the sound of the accented syllable and the two unaccented syllables that follow: "narrative" and "declarative." Robert Browning alternates feminine and masculine rhymes in his "Soliloquy of the Spanish Cloister": Gr-r-r—there go, my heart's abhorrence! Water your damned flower-pots, do! If hate killed men, Brother Lawrence, God's blood, would not mine kill you! What? Your myrtle-bush wants trimming? Oh, that rose has prior claims—Needs its leaden vase filled brimming? Hell dry you up with flames! Triple rhymes can be found in Thomas Hood's "Bridge of Sighs," George Gordon Byron's satirical verse, and Ogden Nash's comic poems.

Rhyme Royal: A stanza of seven lines composed in iambic pentameter and rhymed *ababbcc.* The name is said to be a tribute to King James I of Scotland, who made much use of the form in his poetry. Examples of rhyme royal include Geoffrey Chaucer's *The Parlement of Foules,* William Shakespeare's *The Rape of Lucrece,* William Morris's *The Early Paradise,* and John Masefield's *The Widow in the Bye Street.*

Rhyme Scheme: See *Rhyme*

Rhythm: A regular pattern of sound, time intervals, or events occurring in writing, most often and most discernably in poetry. Regular, reliable rhythm is known to be soothing to humans, while interrupted, unpredictable, or rapidly changing rhythm is disturbing. These effects are known to authors, who use them to produce a desired reaction in the reader. An example of a form of irregular rhythm is sprung rhythm poetry; quantitative verse, on the other hand, is very regular in its rhythm.

Rising Action: The part of a drama where the plot becomes increasingly complicated. Rising action leads up to the climax, or turning point, of a drama. The final "chase scene" of an action film is generally the rising action which culminates in the film's climax.

Rococo: A style of European architecture that flourished in the eighteenth century, especially in France. The most notable features of *rococo* are its extensive use of ornamentation and its themes of lightness, gaiety, and intimacy. In literary criticism, the term is often used disparagingly to refer to a decadent or over-ornamental style. Alexander Pope's "The Rape of the Lock" is an example of literary *rococo.*

Roman a clef: A French phrase meaning "novel with a key." It refers to a narrative in which real persons are portrayed under fictitious names. Jack Kerouac, for example, portrayed various real-life beat generation figures under fictitious names in his *On the Road.*

Romance: A broad term, usually denoting a narrative with exotic, exaggerated, often idealized characters, scenes, and themes. Nathaniel Hawthorne called his *The House of the Seven Gables* and *The Marble Faun* romances in order to distinguish them from clearly realistic works.

Romantic Age: See *Romanticism*

Romanticism: This term has two widely accepted meanings. In historical criticism, it refers to a European intellectual and artistic movement of the late eighteenth and early nineteenth centuries that sought greater freedom of personal expression than that allowed by the strict rules of literary form and logic of the eighteenth-century neoclassicists. The Romantics preferred emotional and imaginative expression to rational analysis. They considered the individual to be at the center of all experience and so placed him or her at the center of their art. The Romantics believed that the creative imagination reveals nobler truths—unique feelings and attitudes—than those that could be discovered by logic or by scientific examination. Both the natural world and the state of childhood were important sources for revelations of "eternal truths." "Romanticism" is also used as a general term to refer to a type of sensibility found in all periods of literary history and usually considered to be in opposition to the principles of classicism. In this sense, Romanticism signifies any work or philosophy in which the exotic or dreamlike figure strongly, or that is devoted to individualistic expression, self-analysis, or a pursuit of a higher realm of knowledge than can be discovered by human reason. Prominent Romantics include Jean-Jacques Rousseau, William Wordsworth, John Keats, Lord Byron, and Johann Wolfgang von Goethe.

Romantics: See *Romanticism*

Russian Symbolism: A Russian poetic movement, derived from French symbolism, that flourished between 1894 and 1910. While some Russian Symbolists continued in the French tradition, stressing aestheticism and the importance of suggestion above didactic intent, others saw their craft as a form of mystical worship, and themselves as mediators between the supernatural and the mundane. Russian symbolists include Aleksandr Blok, Vyacheslav Ivanovich Ivanov, Fyodor Sologub, Andrey Bely, Nikolay Gumilyov, and Vladimir Sergeyevich Solovyov.

S

Satire: A work that uses ridicule, humor, and wit to criticize and provoke change in human nature and institutions. There are two major types of satire: "formal" or "direct" satire speaks directly to the reader or to a character in the work; "indirect" satire relies upon the ridiculous behavior of its characters to make its point. Formal satire is further divided into two manners: the "Horatian," which ridicules gently, and the "Juvenalian," which derides its subjects harshly and bitterly. Voltaire's novella *Candide* is an indirect satire. Jonathan Swift's essay "A Modest Proposal" is a Juvenalian satire.

Scansion: The analysis or "scanning" of a poem to determine its meter and often its rhyme scheme. The most common system of scansion uses accents (slanted lines drawn above syllables) to show stressed syllables, breves (curved lines drawn above syllables) to show unstressed syllables, and vertical lines to separate each foot. In the first line of John Keats's *Endymion,* "A thing of beauty is a joy forever:" the word "thing," the first syllable of "beauty," the word "joy," and the second syllable of "forever" are stressed, while the words "A" and "of," the second syllable of "beauty," the word "a," and the first and third syllables of "forever" are unstressed. In the second line: "Its loveliness increases; it will never" a pair of vertical lines separate the foot ending with "increases" and the one beginning with "it."

Scene: A subdivision of an act of a drama, consisting of continuous action taking place at a single time and in a single location. The beginnings and endings of scenes may be indicated by clearing the stage of actors and props or by the entrances and exits of important characters. The first act of William Shakespeare's *Winter's Tale* is comprised of two scenes.

Science Fiction: A type of narrative about or based upon real or imagined scientific theories and technology. Science fiction is often peopled with alien creatures and set on other planets or in different dimensions. Karel Capek's *R.U.R.* is a major work of science fiction.

Science Fiction and Fantasy Literature: See *Science Fiction* and *Fantasy*

Second Person: See *Point of View*

Semiotics: The study of how literary forms and conventions affect the meaning of language. Semioticians include Ferdinand de Saussure, Charles Sanders Pierce, Claude Levi-Strauss, Jacques Lacan, Michel Foucault, Jacques Derrida, Roland Barthes, and Julia Kristeva.

Sestet: Any six-line poem or stanza. Examples of the sestet include the last six lines of the Petrarchan sonnet form, the stanza form of Robert Burns's "A Poet's Welcome to his love-begotten Daughter," and the sestina form in W. H. Auden's "Paysage Moralise."

Setting: The time, place, and culture in which the action of a narrative takes place. The elements of setting may include geographic location, characters' physical and mental environments, prevailing cultural attitudes, or the historical time in which the action takes place. Examples of settings include the romanticized Scotland in Sir Walter Scott's "Waverley" novels, the French provincial setting in Gustave Flaubert's *Madame Bovary,* the fictional Wessex country of Thomas Hardy's novels, and the small towns of southern Ontario in Alice Munro's short stories.

Shakespearean Sonnet: See *Sonnet*

Short Story: A fictional prose narrative shorter and more focused than a novella. The short story usually deals with a single episode and often a single character. The "tone," the author's attitude toward his or her subject and audience, is uniform throughout. The short story frequently also lacks *denouement*, ending instead at its climax. Well-known short stories include Ernest Hemingway's "Hills Like White Elephants," Katherine Mansfield's "The Fly," Jorge Luis Borge's "Tlon, Uqbar,Orbis Tertius," Eudora Welty's "Death of a Travelling Salesman," Yukio Mishima's "Three Million Men," and Milan Kundera's "The Hitchhiking Game." Compare with Novel and Novella.

Signifying Monkey: A popular trickster figure in black folklore, with hundreds of tales about this character documented since the 19th century. Henry Louis Gates Jr. examines the history of the signifying monkey in *The Signifying Monkey: Towards a Theory of Afro-American Literary Criticism,* published in 1988.

Simile: A comparison, usually using "like" or "as", of two essentially dissimilar things, as in "coffee as cold as ice" or "He sounded like a broken record." The title of Ernest Hemingway's "Hills Like White Elephants" contains a simile.

Slang: A type of informal verbal communication that is generally unacceptable for formal writing. Slang words and phrases are often colorful exaggerations used to emphasize the speaker's point; they may also be shortened versions of an often-used word or phrase. Examples of American slang from the 1990s include "yuppie" (an acronym for Young Urban Professional), "awesome" (for "excellent"), wired (for "nervous" or "excited"), and "chill out" (for relax).

Slant Rhyme: See *Consonance*

Slave Narrative: Autobiographical accounts of American slave life as told by escaped slaves. These works first appeared during the abolition movement of the 1830s through the 1850s. Olaudah Equiano's *The Interesting Narrative of Olaudah Equiano, or Gustavus Vassa, The African* and Harriet Ann Jacobs's *Incidents in the Life of a Slave Girl* are examples of the slave narrative.

Social Realism: See *Socialist Realism*

Socialist Realism: The Socialist Realism school of literary theory was proposed by Maxim Gorky and established as a dogma by the first Soviet Congress of Writers. It demanded adherence to a communist worldview in works of literature. Its doctrines required an objective viewpoint comprehensible to the working classes and themes of social struggle featuring strong proletarian heroes. A successful work of socialist realism is Nikolay Ostrovsky's *Kak zakalyalas stal* (*How the Steel Was Tempered*). Also known as Social Realism.

Soliloquy: A monologue in a drama used to give the audience information and to develop the speaker's character. It is typically a projection of the speaker's innermost thoughts. Usually delivered while the speaker is alone on stage, a soliloquy is intended to present an illusion of unspoken reflection. A celebrated soliloquy is Hamlet's "To be or not to be" speech in William Shakespeare's *Hamlet.*

Sonnet: A fourteen-line poem, usually composed in iambic pentameter, employing one of several rhyme schemes. There are three major types of sonnets, upon which all other variations of the form are based: the "Petrarchan" or "Italian" sonnet, the "Shakespearean" or "English" sonnet, and the "Spenserian" sonnet. A Petrarchan sonnet consists of an octave rhymed *abbaabba* and a "sestet" rhymed either *cdecde, cdccdc,* or *cdedce.* The octave poses a question or problem, relates a narrative, or puts forth a proposition; the sestet presents a solution to the problem, comments upon the narrative, or applies the proposition put forth in the octave. The Shakespearean sonnet is divided into three quatrains and a couplet rhymed *abab cdcd efef gg.* The couplet provides an epigrammatic comment on the narrative or problem put forth in the quatrains. The Spenserian sonnet uses three quatrains and a couplet like the Shakespearean, but links their three rhyme schemes in this way: *abab bcbc cdcd ee.* The Spenserian sonnet develops its theme in two parts like the Petrarchan, its final six lines resolving a problem, analyzing a narrative, or applying a proposition put forth in its first eight lines. Examples of sonnets can be found in Petrarch's *Canzoniere,* Edmund Spenser's *Amoretti,* Elizabeth Barrett Browning's *Sonnets from the Portuguese,* Rainer Maria Rilke's *Sonnets to Orpheus,* and Adrienne Rich's poem "The Insusceptibles."

Spenserian Sonnet: See *Sonnet*

Spenserian Stanza: A nine-line stanza having eight verses in iambic pentameter, its ninth verse in iambic hexameter, and the rhyme scheme ababbcbcc. This stanza form was first used by Edmund Spenser in his allegorical poem *The Faerie Queene.*

Spondee: In poetry meter, a foot consisting of two long or stressed syllables occurring together. This form is quite rare in English verse, and is usually composed of two monosyllabic words. The first foot in the following line from Robert Burns's "Green Grow the Rashes" is an example of a spondee: Green grow the rashes, O

Sprung Rhythm: Versification using a specific number of accented syllables per line but disregarding the number of unaccented syllables that fall in each line, producing an irregular rhythm in the poem. Gerard Manley Hopkins, who coined the term "sprung rhythm," is the most notable practitioner of this technique.

Stanza: A subdivision of a poem consisting of lines grouped together, often in recurring patterns of rhyme, line length, and meter. Stanzas may also serve as units of thought in a poem much like paragraphs in prose. Examples of stanza forms include the quatrain, *terza rima, ottava rima,* Spenserian, and the so-called *In Memoriam* stanza from Alfred, Lord Tennyson's poem by that title. The following is an example of the latter form: Love is and was my lord and king, And in his presence I attend To hear the tidings of my friend, Which every hour his couriers bring.

Stereotype: A stereotype was originally the name for a duplication made during the printing process; this led to its modern definition as a person or thing that is (or is assumed to be) the same as all others of its type. Common stereotypical characters include the absent-minded professor, the nagging wife, the troublemaking teenager, and the kind-hearted grandmother.

Stream of Consciousness: A narrative technique for rendering the inward experience of a character. This technique is designed to give the impression of an ever-changing series of thoughts, emotions, images, and memories in the spontaneous and seemingly illogical order that they occur in life. The textbook example of stream of consciousness is the last section of James Joyce's *Ulysses.*

Structuralism: A twentieth-century movement in literary criticism that examines how literary texts arrive at their meanings, rather than the meanings themselves. There are two major types of structuralist analysis: one examines the way patterns of linguistic structures unify a specific text and emphasize certain elements of that text, and the other interprets the way literary forms and conventions affect the meaning of language itself. Prominent structuralists include Michel Foucault, Roman Jakobson, and Roland Barthes.

Structure: The form taken by a piece of literature. The structure may be made obvious for ease of understanding, as in nonfiction works, or may obscured for artistic purposes, as in some poetry or seemingly "unstructured" prose. Examples of common literary structures include the plot of a narrative, the acts and scenes of a drama, and such poetic forms as the Shakespearean sonnet and the Pindaric ode.

Sturm und Drang: A German term meaning "storm and stress." It refers to a German literary movement of the 1770s and 1780s that reacted against the order and rationalism of the enlightenment, focusing instead on the intense experience of extraordinary individuals. Highly romantic, works of this movement, such as Johann Wolfgang von Goethe's *Gotz von Berlichingen,* are typified by realism, rebelliousness, and intense emotionalism.

Style: A writer's distinctive manner of arranging words to suit his or her ideas and purpose in writing. The unique imprint of the author's personality upon his or her writing, style is the product of an author's way of arranging ideas and his or her use of diction, different sentence structures, rhythm, figures of speech, rhetorical principles, and other elements of composition. Styles may be classified according to period (Metaphysical, Augustan, Georgian), individual authors (Chaucerian, Miltonic, Jamesian), level (grand, middle, low, plain), or language (scientific, expository, poetic, journalistic).

Subject: The person, event, or theme at the center of a work of literature. A work may have one or more subjects of each type, with shorter works tending to have fewer and longer works tending to have more. The subjects of James Baldwin's novel *Go Tell It on the Mountain* include the themes of father-son relationships, religious conversion, black life, and sexuality. The subjects of Anne Frank's *Diary of a Young Girl* include Anne and her family members as well as World War II, the Holocaust, and the themes of war, isolation, injustice, and racism.

Subjectivity: Writing that expresses the author's personal feelings about his subject, and which may or may not include factual information about the subject. Subjectivity is demonstrated in James Joyce's *Portrait of the Artist as a Young Man,* Samuel Butler's *The Way of All Flesh,* and Thomas Wolfe's *Look Homeward, Angel.*

Subplot: A secondary story in a narrative. A subplot may serve as a motivating or complicating force for the main plot of the work, or it may provide emphasis for, or relief from, the main plot. The conflict between the Capulets and the Montagues in William Shakespeare's *Romeo and Juliet* is an example of a subplot.

Surrealism: A term introduced to criticism by Guillaume Apollinaire and later adopted by Andre Breton. It refers to a French literary and artistic movement founded in the 1920s. The Surrealists sought to express unconscious thoughts and feelings in their works. The best-known technique used for achieving this aim was automatic writing—transcriptions of spontaneous outpourings from the unconscious. The Surrealists proposed to unify the contrary levels of conscious and unconscious, dream and reality, objectivity and subjectivity into a new level of "super-realism." Surrealism can be found in the poetry of Paul Eluard, Pierre Reverdy, and Louis Aragon, among others.

Suspense: A literary device in which the author maintains the audience's attention through the buildup of events, the outcome of which will soon be revealed. Suspense in William Shakespeare's *Hamlet* is sustained throughout by the question of whether or not the Prince will achieve what he has been instructed to do and of what he intends to do.

Syllogism: A method of presenting a logical argument. In its most basic form, the syllogism consists of a major premise, a minor premise, and a conclusion. An example of a syllogism is: Major premise: When it snows, the streets get wet. Minor premise: It is snowing. Conclusion: The streets are wet.

Symbol: Something that suggests or stands for something else without losing its original identity. In literature, symbols combine their literal meaning with the suggestion of an abstract concept. Literary symbols are of two types: those that carry complex associations of meaning no matter what their contexts, and those that derive their suggestive meaning from their functions in specific literary works. Examples of symbols are sunshine suggesting happiness, rain suggesting sorrow, and storm clouds suggesting despair.

Symbolism: This term has two widely accepted meanings. In historical criticism, it denotes an early modernist literary movement initiated in France during the nineteenth century that reacted against the prevailing standards of realism. Writers in this movement aimed to evoke, indirectly and symbolically, an order of being beyond the material world of the five senses. Poetic expression of personal emotion figured strongly in the movement, typically by means of a private set of symbols uniquely identifiable with the individual poet. The principal aim of the Symbolists was to express in words the highly complex feelings that grew out of everyday contact with the world. In a broader sense, the term "symbolism" refers to the use of one object to represent another. Early members of the Symbolist movement included the French authors Charles Baudelaire and Arthur Rimbaud; William Butler Yeats, James Joyce, and T. S. Eliot were influenced as the movement moved to Ireland, England, and the United States. Examples of the concept of symbolism include a flag that stands for a nation or movement, or an empty cupboard used to suggest hopelessness, poverty, and despair.

Symbolist: See *Symbolism*

Symbolist Movement: See *Symbolism*

Sympathetic Fallacy: See *Affective Fallacy*

T

Tale: A story told by a narrator with a simple plot and little character development. Tales are usually relatively short and often carry a simple message. Examples of tales can be found in the work of Rudyard Kipling, Somerset Maugham, Saki, Anton Chekhov, Guy de Maupassant, and Armistead Maupin.

Tall Tale: A humorous tale told in a straightforward, credible tone but relating absolutely impossible events or feats of the characters. Such tales were commonly told of frontier adventures during the settlement of the west in the United States. Tall tales have been spun around such legendary heroes as Mike Fink, Paul Bunyan, Davy Crockett, Johnny Appleseed, and Captain Stormalong as well as the real-life William F. Cody and Annie Oakley. Literary use of tall tales can be found in Washington Irving's *History of New York,* Mark Twain's *Life on the Mississippi,* and in the German R. F. Raspe's *Baron Munchausen's Narratives of His Marvellous Travels and Campaigns in Russia.*

Tanka: A form of Japanese poetry similar to *haiku.* A *tanka* is five lines long, with the lines containing five, seven, five, seven, and seven syllables respectively. Skilled *tanka* authors include Ishikawa Takuboku, Masaoka Shiki, Amy Lowell, and Adelaide Crapsey.

Teatro Grottesco: See *Theater of the Grotesque*

Terza Rima: A three-line stanza form in poetry in which the rhymes are made on the last word of each line in the following manner: the first and third lines of the first stanza, then the second line of the first stanza and the first and third lines of the second stanza, and so on with the middle line of any stanza rhyming with the first and third lines of the following stanza. An example of *terza rima* is Percy Bysshe Shelley's "The Triumph of Love": As in that trance of wondrous thought I lay This was the tenour of my waking dream. Methought I sate beside a public way Thick strewn with summer dust, and a great stream Of people there was hurrying to and fro Numerous as gnats upon the evening gleam,...

Tetrameter: See *Meter*

Textual Criticism: A branch of literary criticism that seeks to establish the authoritative text of a literary work. Textual critics typically compare all known manuscripts or printings of a single work in order to assess the meanings of differences and revisions. This procedure allows them to arrive at a definitive version that (supposedly) corresponds to the author's original intention. Textual criticism was applied during the Renaissance to salvage the classical texts of Greece and Rome, and modern works have been studied, for instance, to undo deliberate correction or censorship, as in the case of novels by Stephen Crane and Theodore Dreiser.

Theater of Cruelty: Term used to denote a group of theatrical techniques designed to eliminate the psychological and emotional distance between actors and audience. This concept, introduced in the 1930s in France, was intended to inspire a more intense theatrical experience than conventional theater allowed. The "cruelty" of this dramatic theory signified not sadism but heightened actor/audience involvement in the dramatic event. The theater of cruelty was theorized by Antonin Artaud in his *Le Theatre et son double* (*The Theatre and Its Double*), and also appears in the work of Jerzy Grotowski, Jean Genet, Jean Vilar, and Arthur Adamov, among others.

Theater of the Absurd: A post-World War II dramatic trend characterized by radical theatrical innovations. In works influenced by the Theater of the absurd, nontraditional, sometimes grotesque characterizations, plots, and stage sets reveal a meaningless universe in which human values are irrelevant. Existentialist themes of estrangement, absurdity, and futility link many of the works of this movement. The principal writers of the Theater of the Absurd are Samuel Beckett, Eugene Ionesco, Jean Genet, and Harold Pinter.

Theater of the Grotesque: An Italian theatrical movement characterized by plays written around the ironic and macabre aspects of daily life in the World War I era. Theater of the Grotesque was named after the play *The Mask and the Face* by Luigi Chiarelli, which was described as "a grotesque in three acts." The movement influenced the work of Italian dramatist Luigi Pirandello, author of *Right You Are, If You Think You Are.* Also known as *Teatro Grottesco.*

Theme: The main point of a work of literature. The term is used interchangeably with thesis. The theme of William Shakespeare's *Othello*—jealousy—is a common one.

Thesis: A thesis is both an essay and the point argued in the essay. Thesis novels and thesis plays share the quality of containing a thesis which is supported through the action of the story. A master's thesis and a doctoral dissertation are two theses required of graduate students.

Thesis Novel: See *Thesis*

Thesis Play: See *Thesis*

Third Person: See *Point of View*

Three Unities: See *Unities*

Tone: The author's attitude toward his or her audience may be deduced from the tone of the work. A formal tone may create distance or convey politeness, while an informal tone may encourage a friendly, intimate, or intrusive feeling in the reader. The author's attitude toward his or her subject matter may also be deduced from the tone of the words he or she uses in discussing it. The tone of John F. Kennedy's speech which included the appeal to "ask not what your country can do for you" was intended to instill feelings of camaraderie and national pride in listeners.

Tragedy: A drama in prose or poetry about a noble, courageous hero of excellent character who, because of some tragic character flaw or *hamartia*, brings ruin upon him- or herself. Tragedy treats its subjects in a dignified and serious manner, using poetic language to help evoke pity and fear and bring about catharsis, a purging of these emotions. The tragic form was practiced extensively by the ancient Greeks. In the Middle Ages, when classical works were virtually unknown, tragedy came to denote any works about the fall of persons from exalted to low conditions due to any reason: fate, vice, weakness, etc. According to the classical definition of tragedy, such works present the "pathetic"—that which evokes pity—rather than the tragic. The classical form of tragedy was revived in the sixteenth century; it flourished especially on the Elizabethan stage. In modern times, dramatists have attempted to adapt the form to the needs of modern society by drawing their heroes from the ranks of ordinary men and women and defining the nobility of these heroes in terms of spirit rather than exalted social standing. The greatest classical example of tragedy is Sophocles' *Oedipus Rex.* The "pathetic" derivation is exemplified in "The Monk's Tale" in Geoffrey Chaucer's *Canterbury Tales.* Notable works produced during the sixteenth century revival include William Shakespeare's *Hamlet, Othello,* and *King Lear.* Modern dramatists working in the tragic tradition include Henrik Ibsen, Arthur Miller, and Eugene O'Neill.

Tragedy of Blood: See *Revenge Tragedy*

Tragic Flaw: In a tragedy, the quality within the hero or heroine which leads to his or her downfall. Examples of the tragic flaw include Othello's jealousy and Hamlet's indecisiveness, although most great tragedies defy such simple interpretation.

Transcendentalism: An American philosophical and religious movement, based in New England from around 1835 until the Civil War. Transcendentalism was a form of American romanticism that had its roots abroad in the works of Thomas Carlyle, Samuel Coleridge, and Johann Wolfgang von Goethe. The Transcendentalists stressed the importance of intuition and subjective experience in communication with God. They rejected religious dogma and texts in favor of mysticism and scientific naturalism. They pursued truths that lie beyond the "colorless" realms perceived by reason and the senses and were active social reformers in public education, women's rights, and the abolition of slavery. Prominent members of the group include Ralph Waldo Emerson and Henry David Thoreau.

Trickster: A character or figure common in Native American and African literature who uses his ingenuity to defeat enemies and escape difficult situations. Tricksters are most often animals, such as the spider, hare, or coyote, although they may take the form of humans as well. Examples of trickster tales include Thomas King's *A Coyote Columbus Story,* Ashley F. Bryan's *The Dancing Granny* and Ishmael Reed's *The Last Days of Louisiana Red.*

Trimeter: See *Meter*

Triple Rhyme: See *Rhyme*

Trochee: See *Foot*

U

Understatement: See *Irony*

Unities: Strict rules of dramatic structure, formulated by Italian and French critics of the Renaissance and based loosely on the principles of drama discussed by Aristotle in his *Poetics.* Foremost among these rules were the three unities of action, time, and place that compelled a dramatist to: (1) construct a single plot with a beginning, middle, and end that details the causal relationships of action and character; (2) restrict the action to the events of a single day; and (3) limit the scene to a single place or city. The unities were observed faithfully by continental European writers until the Romantic Age, but they were never regularly observed in English drama. Modern dramatists are typically more concerned with a unity of impression or emotional effect than with any of the classical unities. The unities are observed in Pierre Corneille's tragedy *Polyeuctes* and Jean-Baptiste Racine's *Phedre.* Also known as Three Unities.

Urban Realism: A branch of realist writing that attempts to accurately reflect the often harsh facts of modern urban existence. Some works by Stephen Crane, Theodore Dreiser, Charles Dickens, Fyodor Dostoyevsky, Emile Zola, Abraham Cahan, and Henry Fuller feature urban realism. Modern examples include Claude Brown's *Manchild in the Promised Land* and Ron Milner's *What the Wine Sellers Buy.*

Utopia: A fictional perfect place, such as "paradise" or "heaven." Early literary utopias were included in Plato's *Republic* and Sir Thomas More's *Utopia,* while more modern utopias can be found in Samuel Butler's *Erewhon,* Theodor Herzka's *A Visit to Freeland,* and H. G. Wells' *A Modern Utopia.*

Utopian: See *Utopia*

Utopianism: See *Utopia*

V

Verisimilitude: Literally, the appearance of truth. In literary criticism, the term refers to aspects of a work of literature that seem true to the reader. Verisimilitude is achieved in the work of Honore de Balzac, Gustave Flaubert, and Henry James, among other late nineteenth-century realist writers.

Vers de societe: See *Occasional Verse*

Vers libre: See *Free Verse*

Verse: A line of metered language, a line of a poem, or any work written in verse. The following line of verse is from the epic poem *Don Juan* by Lord Byron: "My way is to begin with the beginning."

Versification: The writing of verse. Versification may also refer to the meter, rhyme, and other mechanical components of a poem. Composition of a "Roses are red, violets are blue" poem to suit an occasion is a common form of versification practiced by students.

Victorian: Refers broadly to the reign of Queen Victoria of England (1837-1901) and to anything with qualities typical of that era. For example, the qualities of smug narrowmindedness, bourgeois materialism, faith in social progress, and priggish morality are often considered Victorian. This stereotype is contradicted by such dramatic intellectual developments as the theories of Charles Darwin, Karl Marx, and Sigmund Freud (which stirred strong debates in England) and the critical attitudes of serious Victorian writers like Charles Dickens and George Eliot. In literature, the Victorian Period was the great age of the English novel, and the latter part of the era saw the rise of movements such as decadence and symbolism. Works of Victorian literature include the poetry of Robert Browning and Alfred, Lord Tennyson, the criticism of Matthew Arnold and John Ruskin, and the novels of Emily Bronte, William Makepeace Thackeray, and Thomas Hardy. Also known as Victorian Age and Victorian Period.

Victorian Age: See *Victorian*

Victorian Period: See *Victorian*

W

Weltanschauung: A German term referring to a person's worldview or philosophy. Examples of *weltanschauung* include Thomas Hardy's view of the human being as the victim of fate, destiny, or impersonal forces and circumstances, and the disillusioned and laconic cynicism expressed by such poets of the 1930s as W. H. Auden, Sir Stephen Spender, and Sir William Empson.

Weltschmerz: A German term meaning "world pain." It describes a sense of anguish about the nature of existence, usually associated with a melancholy, pessimistic attitude. *Weltschmerz* was expressed in England by George Gordon, Lord Byron in his *Manfred* and *Childe Harold's Pilgrimage,* in France by Viscount de Chateaubriand, Alfred de Vigny, and Alfred de Musset, in Russia by Aleksandr Pushkin and Mikhail Lermontov, in Poland by Juliusz Slowacki, and in America by Nathaniel Hawthorne.

Z

Zarzuela: A type of Spanish operetta. Writers of *zarzuelas* include Lope de Vega and Pedro Calderon.

Zeitgeist: A German term meaning "spirit of the time." It refers to the moral and intellectual trends of a given era. Examples of *zeitgeist* include the preoccupation with the more morbid aspects of dying and death in some Jacobean literature, especially in the works of dramatists Cyril Tourneur and John Webster, and the decadence of the French Symbolists.

Cumulative Author/Title Index

C

D

E

F

G

H

I

J

K

L

S

T

U

V

W

Z

Nationality/Ethnicity Index

Flemish

French

German

Greek

Guatemalan

Hispanic

Indian

Indonesian

Irish

Italian

Jamaican

Jewish

Martinican

Mexican

Moroccan

Polish

Roman

Romanian

Russian

Scottish

South African

Spanish

Sri Lankan

St. Lucian

Swedish

Swiss

West Indian

Subject/Theme Index

E

F

G

H

I

J

K

L

M

Subject/Theme Index

O

P

R

S

T

U

W